The
International Critical Commentary

on the Holy Scriptures of the Old and
New Testaments

UNDER THE EDITORSHIP OF

The Rev. CHARLES AUGUSTUS BRIGGS, D.D.

*Sometime Professor of Theological Encyclopædia and Symbolics
Union Theological Seminary, New York*

AND

The Rev. SAMUEL ROLLES DRIVER, D.D.

Regius Professor of Hebrew, Oxford

The Rev. ALFRED PLUMMER, M.A., D.D.

Late Master of University College, Durham

THE BOOKS OF EZRA–NEHEMIAH

THE INTERNATIONAL CRITICAL COMMENTARY

A

CRITICAL AND EXEGETICAL COMMENTARY

ON

THE BOOKS OF EZRA AND NEHEMIAH

BY

LORING W. BATTEN, Ph.D., S.T.D.

PROFESSOR OF THE LITERATURE AND INTERPRETATION OF THE OLD TESTAMENT,
GENERAL THEOLOGICAL SEMINARY, NEW YORK

NEW YORK
CHARLES SCRIBNER'S SONS
1913

TO

MY CHIEF AND MY FRIEND

WILFORD LASH ROBBINS

DEAN OF THE

GENERAL THEOLOGICAL SEMINARY

PREFACE.

ONE of the editors of the International Critical Commentary, the Rev. Professor Charles A. Briggs, D.D., D.Litt., died while this volume was going through the press. I was fortunate in having the benefit of his editorial supervision of the manuscript and of a part of the proof. So the work was well under way when the message came that he was too ill to read proof any longer and that I must assume full responsibility. I have done my best that his illness should result in no loss to this work.

In the death of Dr. Briggs, American Biblical scholarship has lost one of its ablest and most widely known representatives. He was called upon to suffer much for his convictions, and he did suffer bravely. Nor did he suffer in vain. He had the satisfaction of justification in the end; for the views which aroused so much opposition have met with general acceptance. Dr. Briggs was really conservative; he formed his opinions slowly and deliberately; but once they were formed, he would yield them only to new evidence. I am glad to have this opportunity to express my appreciation of the character and attainments of Dr. Briggs and the great privilege I have enjoyed in frequent friendly association with him.

The preparation of this volume has occupied my available time for several years. I should have despaired of finishing what proved to be a far bigger task than I ever anticipated save for my return, two years ago, to the professorial office so that my summers were really free for work. The task proved unexpectedly big, for I discovered early in my studies that Ezra–Nehemiah bristled with hard problems which had not really been solved. Many have ignored them altogether; others have reached conclusions without adequately recognising

vii

and weighing all the available evidence.   There was, therefore, a great deal of pioneer work to be done, and I have laboured perseveringly in the hope of making some contribution to our scanty knowledge of the important Persian period of Jewish history and to our understanding of Biblical books which have suffered from neglect.

Nevertheless, I confess that I am heavily indebted to scholars who have laboured in this field, even to some from whose conclusions I dissent.   The references show at least a list of liabilities. But there is another debt, and a larger one, which cannot be exhibited in references, and which I desire to put on record here, and that is the obligation to the three teachers under whom it was my privilege to study years ago, and who awakened in me an absorbing interest in the study of the Old Testament.   In the order of my acquaintance with them, the three are: Professor David G. Lyon, of Harvard University; the Rev. Dr. John P. Peters, formerly professor in the Philadelphia Divinity School; and the late Dr. William R. Harper, president of the University of Chicago.

LORING W. BATTEN.

The General Theological Seminary,
New York, *June* 28, 1913.

CONTENTS.

X   **CONTENTS**

ABBREVIATIONS.

I. TEXTS AND VERSIONS.

ARV. = American Revised Version.

AV. = Authorised Version.

BD. = Baer and Delitzsch, Hebrew text.

Chr. = The Chronicler, author of Ch.-Ezr.-Ne.

E. = Memoirs of Ezra.

Esd. = The Greek text known as 1 Esdras.

Esd.$^{B, A \text{ or } L}$ = The Vatican, Alexandrian, or Lucian text of the same. The letters standing alone refer to the same texts.

3 Esd. = The Latin text of 1 Esdras.

EV^s. = English Versions.

𝕲 = Greek Septuagint Version. In Ezr.-Ne. this always means 2 Esdras as distinguished from 1 Esdras.

𝕲^A = The Alexandrine text.

𝕲^B = Vatican text of Swete.

𝕲^N = The Sinaitic text.

𝕲^L = The Lucian text; ed. Lagarde.

𝕳 = Hebrew consonantal text.

𝕵 = Latin Version of Jerome.

J = Judaic sources of the Hexateuch.

Kt. = K^{e}thib, the Hebrew text as written.

MT. = The Massoretic pointed text.

N. = Memoirs of Nehemiah.

NT. = The New Testament.

OT. = The Old Testament.

P = The priestly sources of the Hexateuch.

Qr. = Q^{e}rê, the Hebrew text as read.

R. = The Redactor, or editor.

RV. = The Revised Version.

RV.^{m} = The margin of the Revised Version.

𝖁 = The Vulgate Version.

Vrss. = Versions, usually ancient.

xi

II. BOOKS OF THE OLD AND NEW TESTAMENTS.

Am.	= Amos.	Je.	= Jeremiah.
Apocr.	= Apocrypha, Apocryphal.	Jn.	= John.
		Jo.	= Joel.
		Jos.	= Joshua.
1, 2 Ch.	= 1, 2 Chronicles.	Ju.	= Judges.
Dn.	= Daniel.	1, 2 K.	= 1, 2 Kings.
Dt.	= Deuteronomy.	Lv.	= Leviticus.
Est.	= Esther.	1, 2 Mac.	= 1, 2 Maccabees.
Ex.	= Exodus.	Mal.	= Malachi.
Ez.	= Ezekiel.		
Ezr.	= Ezra.	Na.	= Nahum.
		Ne.	= Nehemiah.
Gn.	= Genesis.	Nu.	= Numbers.
Hg.	= Haggai.	Ps.	= Psalms.
		1, 2 S.	= 1, 2 Samuel.
Is.	= early parts of Isaiah.		
Is.²	= exilic parts of Isaiah.	Zc.	= Zechariah.
Is.³	= postexilic parts of Isaiah.	Zp.	= Zephaniah.

III. AUTHORS AND WRITINGS.

BDB.	= Hebrew and English Lexicon of the OT., edited by F. Brown, S. R. Driver, C. A. Briggs.	Dr.Intr	= Introduction to Literature of OT.
		Du.	= B. Duhm.
		EB.	= Encyclopædia Biblica.
Berth.	= Bertholet, *Esra u. Nehemia.*	ES.	= Ezra Studies (Torrey).
		Ew.	= H. Ewald.
B.-Rys.	= Bertheau-Ryssel, *Esra, Neh. u. Esther.*	Ges.ᴮ	= Gesenius, Heb. Lex. ed. Buhl.
Br.ᴾˢ	= Psalms, ICC.		
Bud.	= K. Budde.	Ges.⁵	= his Heb. Gram. ed. Kautzsch.
Che.	= T. K. Cheyne.		
Curt.	= Curtis, Chron. ICC.	ICC.	= International Critical Commentary.
DB.	= Hastings' *Dictionary of the Bible.*	JBL.	= Journal of Biblical Literature.
De.	= Friederic Delitzsch.		

Jer.	= Jerome.
Jos.	= Fl. Josephus.
Kost.	= Kosters, *Wiederher-stellung.*
Kue.	= A. Kuenen.
Lag.	= P. de Lagarde.
Mar.	= Marti, Bib-Aram. Gram.
Mey.	= Meyer, *Entstehung.*
PSBA.	= Proc. Soc. Bib. Arch.
Ryle	= Ezr.–Neh. Camb. Bible.
RS.	= W. Robertson Smith.
Sachau	= *Aram. Pap. u. Ost. aus Elephantine.*

Seis.	= Seisenberger, *Esd. Neh. u. Est.*
Sieg.	= Siegfried, *Esr., Neh. u. Est.*
Sm.	= R. Smend.
Sta.	= B. Stade, *Bib. Theol. des A. T.*
Str.	= Strack, *Gram. d Bibl.-Aram.*
We.	= J. Wellhausen.
ZAW.	= *Zeitschrift f. alttest. Wissenschaft.*
ZMG.	= *Z. d. deutsch. Morgenländ. Gesellschaft.*
ZPV.	= *Z. d. deutsch. Pal. Vereins.*

IV. GENERAL, ESPECIALLY GRAMMATICAL.

abr.	= abbreviation.
acc.	= accusative.
acc. cog.	= cognate acc.
acc. to	= according to.
act.	= active.
adj.	= adjective.
adv.	= adverb.
α.λ.	= ἀπαξ λεγόμενον, word or phrase used once.
app.	= apposition.
Ar.	= Arabic.
Aram.	= Aramaic.
art.	= article.
As.	= Assyrian.
Bab.	= Babylon, Babylonian.
Benj.	= Benjamin, Benjamite.
B. Aram.	= Biblical Aramaic.
c.	= *circa*, about; also *cum*, with.

c.	= chapter, chapters.
chron.	= chronological.
cod., codd.	= codex, codices.
cf.	= *confer*, compare.
cog.	= cognate.
comm.	= commentary, commentaries.
conj.	= conjunction.
consec.	= consecutive.
cstr.	= construct.
del.	= *dele*, strike out.
Deut.	= Deuteronomic.
dittog.	= dittography.
dub.	= dubious, doubtful.
dup.	= duplicate.
elsw.	= elsewhere.
emph.	= emphasis, emphatic.
esp.	= especially.
equiv.	= equivalent.

et al.	= and others, esp. associates.		obj.	= object.
			op. cit.	= work quoted.
et pass.	= *et passim*, and here and there.		opp.	= opposite, as opposed to or contrasted with.
exc.	= except.			
exil.	= exilic.		p.	= person.
			pap.	= papyrus.
f.	= feminine.		parall.	= parallel with.
fig.	= figurative.		part.	= particle.
fpl.	= feminine plural.		pass.	= passive.
freq.	= frequentative.		Pers.	= Persia, Persian.
fs.	= feminine singular.		pf.	= perfect.
			Pi.	= Piel of verb.
gent.	= gentilic.		pl.	= plural.
gl.	= gloss, glossator.		postex.	= postexilic.
Gk.	= Greek.		pr.	= priest, priests.
			pred.	= predicate.
Heb.	= Hebrew.		pre-ex.	= pre-exilic.
Hiph.	= Hiphil of verb.		prep.	= preposition.
Hithp.	= Hithpael of verb.		prob.	= probable, probably.
			pron.	= pronoun.
ib.	= *ibidem*, in the same place.		ptc.	= participle.
			Pu.	= Pual of verb.
i. e.	= *id est*, that is.			
impf.	= imperfect.		qu.	= question.
imv.	= imperative.		*q. v.*	= *quod vide.*
inf.	= infinitive.			
intr.	= introduction.		rd.	= read.
			rel.	= relative.
Jerus.	= Jerusalem.			
juss.	= jussive.		Sam.	= Samaria, Samaritans.
			sf.	= suffix, suffixes.
l.	= line.		sg.	= singular.
Lev.	= Levite, Levites.		*sq.*	= followed by.
lit.	= literal, literally.		st.	= *status*, state, stative.
			subj.	= subject.
m.	= masculine.		subst.	= substantive.
mng.	= meaning.		*s. v.*	= *sub voce.*
mpl.	= masculine plural.		syl.	= syllable.
ms.	= masculine singular.		syn.	= synonymous.
n.	= noun.		t.	= times (following a number).
n. p.	= proper name.			
n. pr. loc.	= proper noun of place.		tr.	= transfer.
Neth.	= Nethinim.			
Niph.	= Niphal of verb.			

trans.	= transitive.	*v.*	= *vide*, see.
txt. err.	= textual error.	vb.	= verb.
		v. i.	= *vide infra*, see below.
v., vv.	= verse, verses.	*v. s.*	= *vide supra*, see above.

V. OTHER SIGNS.

† prefixed indicates all passages cited.

‖ parallel, of words or clauses chiefly synonymous.

= equivalent, equals.

+ plus denotes that other passages might be cited.

″ = sign of abbreviation in Hebrew words.

VI. NAMES RECURRING FREQUENTLY.

Art.	= Artaxerxes I Longimanus.	Neh.	= Nehemiah.
		Sanb.	= Sanballat.
Art. II.	= Artaxerxes II Mnemon.	Shes.	= Sheshbazzar.
Cy.	= Cyrus.	To.	= Tobiah.
Dar.	= Darius I.	Zer.	= Zerubbabel.
Jes.	= Jeshua or Joshua.		

VII. REMARKS.

Biblical passages are cited according to the verses of the Hebrew text.

Numerals raised above the line (1) after numerals designating chapters indicate verses (Gn. 6³); (2) after proper names refer to sections of grammars or pages of books (Ges.⁵⁴²).

INTRODUCTION.

§ 1. THE ORIGINAL FORM OF THE BOOKS.

The books of Ezr. and Ne. were originally one, and ought really to be so combined now. The evidence of this is over-whelming. Two points suffice for a demonstration: (1) The story of Ezr. is partly in one book, Ezr. 7–10, and partly in the other, Ne. 7^{70}–8^{12}.* In 1 Esd. these two parts are united in a single book. (2) At the end of each book of the OT. there are certain Massoretic notes, giving the number of verses, the middle point in the volume or roll, etc. There are no such notes at the end of Ezr., and those at the end of Ne. cover both books, showing that the two constituted a single work when those notes were made.†

It is also generally agreed that Ezr.–Ne. originally was a part of the book of Ch., so that the whole work was a com-prehensive history of the Jews from Adam down to the end of the Persian period.

It is true that in the Heb. Bible our books precede Ch., though the right order is found in ᵹ. The order in the Heb. canon is naturally illogical, and is prob. due to the fact that Ezr.–Ne. was accepted as canonical before Ch. The fact is that Ch. was under a great deal of suspicion. It was a book parall. the earlier histories long es-tablished as authorities, and differing from them so much that the presence of the new work created difficulties. Ezr.–Ne., on the other hand, contained the only account of the important Pers. period. A part of the large work of Ch. was, therefore, severed from the rest, and naturally just that part dealing with the otherwise unknown period, and of which there was no dup., and this part was accepted. Later the rest of the work found its place at the very end of the canon.

The order in ᵹ really does not contravene this conclusion, for the Gk. translators made a new arrangement of the canon on a literary basis,

*The grounds for this limitation are given below in the treatment of the history under the reign of Art. II.

† See further my art. "Ezr.-Ne.," in *DB.* i,²¹ᵃᵇ.

1

putting all the historical books together. When the transposition was made on this basis, Ch. was put before Ezr.–Ne. from chron. considerations.

When the disjuncture was made, there appears to have been an accident, for the severed parts overlap, Ezr. 1^{1-3a} being identical with 2 Ch. $36^{22\ f.}$. The latter ends in the middle of a sentence "and let him go up," and in the middle of Cy.'s decree. The simplest explanation of the strange fact is that a copyist who was working on the book of Ch. had as his exemplar one of the older editions containing the whole original Ch.–Ezr.–Ne. He got beyond the point of division before he noted his mistake, and this slip has been perpetuated down to the present day. Howorth explains differently (PSBA. 1901,[2]).

It is indisputable that Ch. and Ezr.–Ne. come from the same hand. There is no book in the OT. which has more marked peculiarities than Ch. These cover both literary features, favourite words and expressions, peculiar style, etc. (for a list of which, see Curt.[7]), and also historical features, for the Chr. had his own way of looking at the history, and his theory colours his work so markedly that it is often quite valueless to the student of history. There is scarcely one of these peculiarities that is not found also in Ezr.–Ne. Evidence of the original unity is furnished from Esd., which contains two whole c. of Ch. (2 Ch. 35, 36) and then goes on directly to Ezra, without the duplication found in Heb. Further evidence is given by Curt. *Intr.* § [2].

§ 2. THE DATE.

It is difficult to deal satisfactorily with this problem, for Ezr.–Ne. is a composite work and contains sources from different periods. If the decree of Cyrus in Ezr. 1 is original, this is the earliest portion and belongs to 538 B.C. Ezr. 4^{7-24a} is made up chiefly of two letters which belong to the reign of Artaxerxes, and before his 20th year, therefore is dated somewhere in the period 464–444 B.C. But the letters are imbedded in a narrative, and it is impossible to say when the compilation of the letters was made, except that it was before the Chronicler's time. The Memoirs of Nehemiah were apparently written soon after his second administration, certainly not later than the end of the reign of Artaxerxes, 424 B.C. As for the date of the whole work, Ch.–Ezr.–Ne., it is unnecessary to duplicate the excellent work of Curtis (*v. Intr.* § [3]). Certainly our books go down to the Greek age, and it is quite impossible to place the work earlier than 300 B.C. We can with a good deal of confidence name the third century B.C. as the time of the Chronicler, but cannot be more exact.

§ 3. THE CONTENTS OF THE BOOKS.

Ezra 1. The return of exiles under Sheshbazzar bringing the sacred vessels of the temple and having permission to rebuild the temple.

2^{1-69}. A list of residents of the province of Judah.

2^{70}–4^3. The Hebrew story of the rebuilding of the temple under the leadership of Zerubbabel and Jeshua.

4^{4-6}. A fragment, descriptive of the opposition of the Gentile neighbours of the Jews.

4^{7-24a} (Aram.). The complaint to Artaxerxes and his order to stop the building operations.

4^{24b}–6^{18} (Aram.). The Aramaic version of the history of the rebuilding of the temple; parallel to 2^{70}–4^3.

6^{19-22}. The keeping of the Passover.

7–10. The principal part of Ezra's history, containing the letter of Artaxerxes 7^{12-26} (Aram.), a description of the gathering of his caravan, the discovery of the marriages with foreigners, and the dissolution of these marriages.

Nehemiah 1, 2. Nehemiah learns of the sad plight of Jerusalem, obtains leave of absence from Artaxerxes, goes up to Jerusalem with a caravan, makes an inspection of the walls, and appeals successfully to the people to start the restoration of the walls.

3^{1-32}. A list of the forces engaged in the rebuilding of the walls and the portion restored by each body.

3^{33}–4^{17} (EV^s. 4^{1-23}). The efforts of Sanballat, Tobiah, and others to prevent the restoration of the walls.

5. The distress of the impoverished Jews and Nehemiah's measures for their relief.

6^1–7^5. Further efforts of Sanballat and his associates to wreck Nehemiah's projects; the completion of the walls, and the care for the protection of the city.

7^{6-72}. A duplicate of Ezr. 2^{1-69}.

8^{1-12}. Resumption of the history of Ezra, describing the promulgation of the law.

8^{13-18}. The observance of the Feast of Booths.

9. The prayer of the Levites.

10^{1-28}. A list of names on a sealed record.

10^{29-40}. Measures taken to maintain a pure race and to support the worship of the temple.

11. The drafting of a population for Jerusalem, a list of those who dwelt in the holy city, and a record of the towns of Judah and Benjamin. A sequel to 7^5.

12^{1-26}. Lists of priests and Levites of the various parts of the Persian period.

12^{27-43}. The dedication of the walls.

12^{44-47}. Provision for the support of the temple officers.

13. The reforms instituted in Nehemiah's second administration.

§ 4. THE CHRONOLOGICAL ORDER.

The material has come down to us in an order that is often very puzzling. As the result of successive editings, the material is very badly arranged. For the most part, however, it is possible to restore the sections to a proper chronological sequence.

With a single exception Ezr. $1-4^{24a}$ is in its true order. C. 1 belongs to the time of Cy.; $2^{70}-4^3$ to the reign of Dar.; 4^{4-6} to Xerxes, and 4^{7-24a} to Art.; 2^{1-69} is one of the late passages in the books, at least as late as Ezr. To the reign of Art. belongs also all of the Ne. narrative, viz., Ne. $1-7^5$, exc. c. 3^{1-32}, which is late, 11 12^{27-43} and 13. There is left in the book of Ezr. three sections, $4^{24b}-6^{18}$ 6^{19-22} and $7-10$. $4^{24b}-6^{18}$ belongs to the time of Dar. and should directly follow $2^{70}-4^3$, the Heb. version of the same story, the.place it practically has in Esd., where it follows 4^5. It is a story apparently late in its origin and not of very great value. Torrey holds that 4^7-6^{18} was incorporated bodily by the Chr. (ES.[161]), and that the temple was chiefly in mind in the complaint of the Sam. But his reasoning is not convincing (v. 4^{24}). The two passages 4^{7-24a} and $4^{24b}-6^{18}$ really have little in common. The latter passage was removed from its proper position because the former was wrongly interpreted. It was a comparatively late addition, for its insertion worked havoc with some of the earlier material. An editor had the Heb. story of the rebuilding of the temple (2^{70}–4^3), followed by the correspondence with Art. about the rebuilding of the city; the Aram. story differed somewhat from the Heb.; the editor incorporated this version and made it the basis of his history. He then proceeded to modify the Heb. story to make it an unsuccessful attempt at rebuilding the temple, and found in 4^{7-24a} a cause of failure. The original sequence was, therefore, 1 2^{70}–4^3 4^{24b}–6^{18} 4^{4-24a}. Where 6^{19-22} belongs, it is hard to say. By its subject it connects with another fragment (Ne. 8^{13-18}), or it may be very early (v. comm.). 7–10 belongs to a period after Neh.

Another possibility cannot be ignored. We note that Ezr. 1 belongs to the time of Cy., 2^{70}–4^3 to that of Dar., 4^{4-6} to that of Xerxes,* and 4^{7-24a} to that of Art. The last-named passage leads right up to the work of Neh., which is also in the time of Art. Now between Ezr. 4^{24a} and Ne. 1 we have, first, the story of Ezra (7–10), which should follow Neh.'s story; second (4^{24b}–6^{18}), a late and practically valueless document; and third (6^{19-22}), also prob. late. It is, therefore, perfectly possible that the original order was 1 2^{70}–4^{24a}, Ne. The Aram. version of the temple-building story should have been put in directly after 4^3, as it practically is in Jos. But the compiler failed to see that the Aram. was but a dup., and thus the mischief was wrought.

In Ne. it is easy to follow a correct order, as shown in the notes on the sections, so far as his own work is concerned. The order is 1 2 3^{33}–7^5 11 12^{27-43} 3^{1-32} 5 13 and 10, which is a sequel to c. 13. There follows the story of Ezra's administration (Ezr. 7–10, Ne. 8^{1-12}). The rest of the material cannot be dated, and must be grouped by subjects. The chron. order of the whole, so far as it can be determined, is as follows:

(a) Ezr. 1; (b) Ezr. 2^{70}–4^3 4^{24b}–6^{18}; (c) Ezr. 4^{4-6} 4^{7-24a} Ne. 1 2 3^{33}–4^{17} 6^1–7^5 11 12^{27-43} 3^{1-32} 5 13 10 12^{44-47}; (d) Ezr. 7–10 Ne. 8^{1-12} Ezr. 6^{19-22} Ne. 8^{13-18}; (e) Ne. 9 12^{1-26} 7^{6-72} = Ezr. 2^{1-69}, and perhaps Ne. 11^{3-35}.

That under (a) belongs to the reign of Cy., (b) to Dar., (c) to Art. (exc. 4^{4-6}), (d) to Art. II, and (e) is uncertain, but prob. is to be dated in the same reign as (d), as it is either a part of Ezra's work or a natural consequence of what he had done. Ne. 9, however, as shown in the notes, bears evidences of the Gk. period, and may be one of the latest sections in the books.

In reading a historical book it is desirable to have the material in proper chronological order. To rearrange the whole of Ezr.–Ne. would be needlessly confusing; but it is deemed best in a few particulars to undo the mischief of R. Therefore in

* At least that is certain of 4^6, and that suffices.

the commentary I have joined Ezr. 7–10 to Ne. 8–10, and placed the whole after Ne. 13; and Ezr. 4^{4-24a} is transposed to follow Ezr. 6. The advantages are manifest: the two temple-building stories are brought together; the brief passage belonging to the time of Xerxes has its proper place; the Aramaic letters (Ezr. 4^{7-24a}) come just before Ne. 1, to which they are an introduction; the whole story of Nehemiah's work comes in proper sequence; and Ezra's history is combined and placed where it probably belongs chronologically.

§ 5. THE TWO EDITIONS OF EZRA–NEHEMIAH.

Ezr.–Ne. is peculiar in that it has come down to us in two recensions, which at certain points differ from each other quite radically. It is true that something of the same condition is found in other OT. books. In S. there is a long section in Hebrew which was not originally in 𝔊 (1 S. 17^{12-31} 17^{55}–18^5). There is a vast difference also between the Greek texts and the Hebrew in the books of Je. and Dn. In the case of Ezr.–Ne., however, the so-called 𝔊 follows MT. very closely, but the so-called Apocryphal book of Esd. constitutes really a different edition of Ezr.–Ne.

> In the Apocr. there are additional sections to some of the OT. books; thus, the Rest of Est.; Baruch is an addition to Je.; the Song of the Three Holy Children, the history of Susanna, and Bel and the Dragon are additions to Dn. But in all these there is nothing corresponding to any part of 𝔐; the passages are additions pure and simple and found only in Gk. Esd., on the other hand, is merely a variant edition of a part of Ch.–Ezr.–Ne. For the most part, it is a faithful translation of 𝔐, but with addition and subtraction and rearrangement. This book is of such vital importance to our work that a fuller discussion is essential, and it is well worthy of a section by itself.

§ 6. 1 ESDRAS.

In Greek this edition of the history, as the title Esd.[A] shows, has the priority; the Greek translation of the whole of Ezr.–Ne. is known as 2 Esd. or Esd.[B] In Lagarde's edition of Codex Lucianus this order is reversed, an evidence of an effort, manifested on every page of this nevertheless valuable text, to conform to the MT. more closely than other Greek texts. But the evidence is overwhelmingly in favour of the priority of Esd., and the explanation can only be, as I infer to be Torrey's conclusion too, that this edition was preferred. Indeed, Sir Henry Howorth has argued (of whose work more anon), that Esd. is the original Septuagint text, and that our Hebrew edition is really the Apocryphal book.

The subjoined table will show the contents of this edition in comparison with MT.

ESD.		MT.
c. I	=	2 Ch. 35, 36.
2^{1-15}	=	Ezr. 1
2^{16-30}	=	" 4^{7-24}
3^{1}–5^{6}	=	not in MT.
5^{7-73}	=	Ezr. 2^{1}–4^{5}
6, 7	=	" 5, 6
8^{1}–9^{36}	=	" 7–10
9^{37-55}	=	Ne. 7^{72}–8^{12}

It will be noted that there is one long addition (3^{1}–5^{6}). This is the only element in the book which acc. to other usage can be called Apocr., for the Apocr. comprises the books or sections of books which were known only in a Gk. original. This addition contains the story of the Three Youths, or Guardsmen of Dar. At the time of a great feast, the Three Guardsmen competed in a test of wisdom, to determine which was strongest, wine, the king, or women. The third contestant, who was the victor, is identified with Zer. in what is usually regarded as a gl. (4^{13}), easily suggested by 5^{6}, acc. to which Zer. spoke wise sentences before Dar. This statement may account for the placing of this whole story as a prelude to the mission of Zer. By some rather mysterious process not made clear in the text, probably because of an addition here from a moral interest, Zer. switches off to prove that truth is stronger than either wine, kings, or women. Down to this point (4^{32}), the story is a sort of a joke, and might belong to court jesters, but at the close the story is given a serious turn.

At 4^{42} we reach a new section, doubtless originally quite independent of the preceding. Torrey has sufficiently demonstrated this point (ES.[25 ff.]). Now we come to an important passage, fully discussed in the intr. to Ezr. 3, in which Zer. obtains a grant from the king, collects a company, and goes up from Pers. to Jerus. to rebuild the temple.

To revert to the table, we note that Esd. contains two c. of Ch., all of Ezr. exc. a single v. (4^{6}), but only a very small section of Ne. There is not a word about Neh.'s great work, nor is there anything of Ne. 8¹ᵃ⁻¹⁰, which are almost universally, but incorrectly, as I shall try to show later, regarded as a part of the Ezra story.

The rearrangement appears at two points. First, the Art. letters, Ezr. 4⁷⁻²⁴ = Esd. 2¹⁶⁻³⁰, are placed immediately after the story of Shes.'s return, and so between the reigns of Cy. and Dar., whence Jos. substituted Cambyses for Art. in the letters, so that following this text as he did, his chronology is consistent. Second, a part of the Ezra story is removed from its familiar place in the middle of Ne. and joined directly to the part of Ezra's story contained in the book called by his name; i. e., Ne. 7⁷²⁻8¹² follows Ezr. 7–10.

The latter of these variant arrangements undoubtedly preserves the original order. If one could maintain that Ezra went to Jerus. in the 7th year of Art., a date shown later to be impossible, it would still be out of the question for Ezra to begin publishing the law at least fifteen years later. Even if Ezra and Neh. were contemporaries, no historian would have severed the Ezra story by the insertion of a part of the Ne. narrative without adequate reason, and there is no reason at all here.

But it is shown elsw. that the place of the Art. letters (Ezr. 4⁷⁻²⁴ᵃ) in the Esd. text is not original. Indeed, their situation is more inconsistent in this text than in 𝔐, for to say nothing of the putting of Art. before Dar., we have in this edition an account of the stopping of the building of the temple before that work had been begun. In this edition the passage stands as a bald interpolation. It has neither ancestry nor posterity, so that one may wonder whether it was an original part of the Esd. text at all. It may have been put in by a later hand because it was in the Heb. The striking result would be that the original Esd. edition of the history knows of no interference with the Jews in their efforts to rebuild the temple.

There is reason to believe that when this Art. correspondence was placed directly after the reign of Cy., the name of the king was changed to Cambyses, and that it so stood in the Esd. text in the time of Jos., for that historian would not have been likely to change the name of a king, and that here he actually followed his source. If that is the case there are some interesting considerations to be noted. The author of Esd. was pretty well informed, and may easily have rebelled against placing an event of the reign of Art. before the building of the temple. This writer knew that the temple was built in the time of Dar. He knew that Art. did not precede Dar. Therefore he transposed the passage and substituted the name Cambyses for Art.

In MT. the name of Xerxes also appears before that of Dar. (Ezr. 4⁶), but this name is not found in Esd. anywhere. In other words, Esd. knows of but one king between Cy. and Dar., and the author must have known that that was Cambyses. We might then infer that he was right, and follow many scholars in thus changing the name of the king. But it is apparent that the contents of the passage are inconsistent with its position, for it would give us an account of the interruption of the temple-building before the foundations were laid. While the position of the passage would fit the reign of Cambyses, its contents are inconsistent with that date.

To return to the addition, one part of it (3^{1}–4^{41}), as Torrey has shown (ES.^{45}), has nothing to do with Heb. history, but the rest (4^{42}–5^{6}) is, or at least contains, what we absolutely need as an explanation of the events described in Ezr. 3. To jump from Ezr. 1 to Ezr. 3 involves a wild flight, and in our text nothing intervenes but a list of names, which certainly does not seem to make a historical connection. Incidentally we have here a possible explanation of the insertion of the list of Ezr. 2. There was certainly a historical section between Ezr. 1 and 3. The Chr. or some later editor cut out the passage because it spoiled his theory of the delay in building the temple. The gap was supplied in MT. by the insertion of the strange list (2^{1-69}). Later this list was put into the Esd. text, and as it is joined closely to Ezr. 3 it was separated from Ezr. 1, for it could not join at both ends in a text which preserved the lost material which was original between the two c. What this material was is fully stated in the intr. to Ezr. 3. Its great importance lies in the fact that it fixes the history related in Ezr. 2^{70}–4^{3} as belonging to the reign of Dar. It is hard for me to understand how so accomplished a scholar as Torrey can insist that the events narrated here belong to the reign of Cy. It is no more reasonable to substitute Cy. for Dar. in this text than for Jos. to substitute Cambyses for Art. in his account of the letters in 4^{7-24a}. The appeal is made to Esd. 5^{71} = Ezr. 4^{3}, where the Jews say they will build the temple as King Cy. commanded them (so Thackeray, DB. art. " 1 Esd."). But surely there is no reason why Zer. in the time of Dar. should not appeal to the earlier decree of Cy. The edicts of Cy. were not invalidated by his death.

Sir Henry Howorth has written many interesting articles about this book.* One of the points upon which he is most insistent is that Esd. is the original 𝕲, while the Gk. 2 Esd., usually known as 𝕲, is really Theodotion's translation. Much credit is due to this accomplished scholar for his persistent efforts to bring Esd. into the prominence it deserves. And yet I agree with Torrey that his main contention is of little value. His fundamental mistake is the underlying theory that there was an authoritative and standard Gk. translation of the OT. comparable to the AV. in English, a sort of official *textus receptus*. The fact is that 1 and 2 Esd. are quite independent translations of Semitic originals, but they are renderings of different editions. 1 Esd. had one Semitic text of which it is a free and idiomatic version; 2 Esd. is a slavishly literal rendering of our present MT.

* *Academy*, 1893, *Proceedings of the Society of Biblical Archæology*, 1901-2.

It follows from this indisputable fact that Esd. is of vastly greater value to the OT. student than 𝔊 and all the other Vrss. which depend upon it. Sir Henry's point is well taken in this respect. Few scholars have availed themselves of the treasures hidden away in this storehouse. As Howorth suggests, there has been too much of a tendency to make a fetish of MT. Even scholars are not dissociated entirely from the theory once held as essential to orthodoxy that the words and even the pointing of MT. are inspired. This comm. will show ample use of this important text by whose aid alone some of the grave problems have been solved.

An interesting question about Esd. concerns its original form. Many scholars maintain that it is complete as it stands. Others, like Howorth and Torrey, insist that it is a fragment from the middle of the complete Ch.–Ezr.–Ne. The question is not of vital importance here, yet some consideration is necessary. In favour of the latter view, it is noted that Esd. ends with one word of Ne. 8¹³, καὶ ἐπισυνήχθησαν = נאספו. Torrey believes that the surviving fragment came from a Gk. not a Semitic MS., as Ne. 8¹³ begins וביום השני (ES.³⁶). In Cod.ᴸ this v. is completed, and I am convinced that we have here one of the many attempts to bring Esd. into conformity with MT. In other words, Esd. really ends the Ezra story with Ne. 8¹², and in my opinion that text never contained any more about Ezra.

This conclusion is supported by the testimony of Jos. It is contended by Howorth and Torrey that Jos. uses Ne. 8¹³ ᶠᶠ·. This does not seem to me to be the case. He does, indeed, refer to the Feast of Booths, but only as a note of time; for he makes it the occasion of the assembly in the 7th month at which the law was read as described in Ne. 8¹⁻¹² = Esd. 9³⁷⁻⁵⁵ (*Ant.* xi, 5, 5). There is not a reference to anything related in Ne. 9, 10. Jos. knew nothing of any event in the story of Ezr. after the reading of the law.

If Esd. is but a fragment of Ch.–Ezr.–Ne., it must have contained an account of Neh.'s work. Jos. deals with Neh. rather summarily (*Ant.* xi, 5, 6–8), whom, as well as Ezra, he places in the reign of Xerxes. His treatment is most full in that which corresponds to Ne. 1, 2, though in this there are rather more than the usual number of glaring inaccuracies. He has a considerable account of the trouble Neh. encountered from the enemy, a summary of Ne. 4, 6. He then proceeds with a brief account of the dedication of the walls as in Ne. 12²⁷⁻⁴³, and then takes up the peopling of the city as in Ne. 7¹⁻⁵ᵃ 11¹ ᶠ·, and finally he describes the provisions for the pr. and Lev. (Ne. 13¹⁰⁻¹²).* Now the amazing fact is that Jos. shows a knowledge of every part of N. exc. c. 5, and that he uses nothing else from the book of Ne. save 8¹⁻¹², a part of Ezra's story. It is clear, therefore, that if Esd. ever went

---

* This statement differs somewhat from Torrey's (ES.¹²), but is, I believe, as accurate a determination as can be made with confidence.

any further than it does now, the lost contents comprised N. and
nothing else whatever. Jos. never could have picked out this story
from our present text. In his treatment of the book of Ezr. he does
not quote the lists of names, but he refers to them, showing that they
were in the text he used, but in the use of the book of Ne. there is no
hint of a list of names anywhere, not even of the wall-builders.

In what form the memoirs were to which Jos. had access it is impossible to say. These could hardly have survived as a separate production in his time; yet they were originally published in that form;
and what we have includes all that Jos. knew. It is not unlikely that
he used the same text for the whole Pers. period, and certainly he had
these records in Gk.; therefore we may with a certain degree of probability conclude that Esd. originally contained the unadulterated N.
In that case the fragmentary hypothesis is the only tenable one.

One other point, though, it is commonly known, needs mention. In
his account of the return and the rebuilding of the temple, related in
Ezr. 1–6, Jos. follows Esd., not MT. He puts $4^{7\,\text{ff.}}$ after c. 1, and he
incorporates the story of the Three Guardsmen. But he unmistakably
puts the events described in 3^1–4^5 in the reign of Dar., making 3^{6-13} an
actual completion of the temple (*Ant.* xi, 4, 2; see further under the
reign of Dar.). He is quite consistent, making 5, 6 a sort of sequel to
the preceding story, omitting entirely 4^{24b}–5^1. His date for 3^1–4^5 is
the only possible one to be derived from Esd., and his use of 3^{6-13} =
Esd. 5^{53-65} shows that he had a better text than most of those which
have come down to us.

It is sometimes stated that Jos. goes beyond Esd. and shows a knowledge of 2 Esd. ⑹ (*e. g.,* *DB.* i,[759]). At the end of Shes.'s story, he
does say that 42,462 came up at that time, as in Ezr. 2, but he uses
this list fully where it stands in Esd. He gives an intr. to the Art.
letters which is based on Ezr. 4^{1-5}, but he uses that material again,
and these are probably but patches. Jos. sometimes follows his sources
so loosely that such usage hardly serves as an argument. The exception is about enough to prove the rule. Jos. certainly does not make
any use of our canonical Ezr.–Ne.

Reference has been made to the numerous changes in Esd. to bring
this edition into nearer agreement with MT. It is manifest that many
of these changes have been made since the time of Jos., for in several
important points he bears witness to another text than that which
has come down to us. This is esp. the case in Ezr. 3^{6-13}. It is also
probable that Cambyses was in the text of Esd. which Jos. used
instead of Art. The cause of this revising is determinable to a high
degree of probability. In the first place, it is well known that the
tendency to correct the Gk. version on the basis of the Heb. is discoverable in every book of the OT. But there is a special reason why
that correcting process should be marked in this particular book. For

this work existed in two quite different Vrss., and these were struggling for supremacy the one against the other. In the time of Jos. it is clear that Esd. was preferred among the Jews; for Jos. was in bad repute with his brethren because of his pro-Romanism, and he was politic enough to use the most popular sources for his history.

Three centuries later this edition had lost caste. Jerome's attitude shows that plainly. He would not translate the story of the Three Youths. He insists that the proper discourses of Ezr. and Ne. are contained in a single volume, and that whatever is not contained in them is to be rejected (pref. to Ezr.). Confessedly he formed this opinion from his Heb. teachers, so that in his day—the preface was written A.D. 394—Esd. had lost its former popularity. The advocates of this edition would not see it sink into disuse without a serious effort to save it. The chief count against it was its departure from the received text. Then began a process of editing to remove these departures as far as possible. In many of the texts the original is pretty well erased. But in Cod.^{L} the changes were often made simply by adding a translation of MT. to the original Esd., so that it is still possible in places to recover the primitive text.

The Vrss. available for the textual criticism of Ezr.–Ne. are the same as those for Ch., a full and scholarly discussion of which is given by Curtis, *Intr.* §[8], and need not be repeated here. The Vrss. really serve little purpose, with the single exception of Esd., which has been fully treated above, and of which but a few more words are necessary from the point of view of textual criticism.

It has been shown that Esd. is a translation of a Semitic text. Torrey has given pretty convincing evidence that the story of the Three Guardsmen is from an Aram. original (ES.[20 ff.]). It has long been suspected that Esd. 5^{1-6} is from a Heb. source, and that is doubtless correct. But it is equally plain that Esd. is not a translation of the present MT. No translator would take such liberties as we find in that version. Those who rendered the Scriptures into Gk. were moved, as all other translators, to give a faithful version of the text before them, which they desired to make accessible to people who knew only the Gk. tongue. The conclusion is inevitable that there were two editions of this book in Semitic, of which the one finally adopted in the Heb. canon is the longer and the worse. On these two editions, see further ES.[11 ff.]

The most complete presentation of the apparatus for the textual criticism of our books is presented in ES, c. 4. Torrey greatly prefers

Cod.^A to ^B, and urges great caution in the use of ^L. The caution is wise, and yet some of the most important aids to the correction of the text are hidden in that version.

§ 7. THE SEMITIC TEXT.

In places the text of Ezr.–Ne. is very well preserved. In N. especially there is as a rule very little trouble once the interpolations are recognised. But on the whole MT. is in decidedly bad shape. At times the confusion is so great that the work of the critic is most difficult. In some places there is a wholesale corruption of the text in the interest of the historical theory of the editor.

The great majority of writers have accepted MT. and have simply tried to make out of it the best they could. There is no reason, however, for confining ourselves to one text in a case in which we have good support for another and a better reading. In places the result is most surprising and important. Many of the critical theories of both the older and newer writers are dependent on the corrupt MT. A reconstruction of these theories is only possible in the light of a thorough-going criticism of the text. This needs to go much further than Guthe's in Haupt's *SBOT*. I myself worked for years on the supposition that there was an early and fruitless effort to rebuild the temple. But the discovery of the true text of Ezr. 3 compelled a radical change of opinion.

The discovery of these corruptions, and in many places the recovery of the true text, has another important consequence. It proves beyond a doubt that there are original sources where previously a passage has been assigned wholly to Chr. If a text has been corrupted to make it suit a purpose, it is obvious that the text in its original form is not the work of R. In that way it is demonstrated that there are Hebrew sources in these books, and so the contributions of the Chronicler are correspondingly diminished.

§ 8.   THE SOURCES.

In the book of Ch. we find many sections of S. and K. inserted almost verbatim.   There is a claim further that the compiler used many other sources (see Curt. *Intr.*[21 ff.]).   It is true that some scholars, as Torrey, deny that these sources were genuine, insisting that the Chronicler pretends to quote to add plausibility to his history (ES. c. 7).   Our books were originally a part of the book of Ch., and we should expect the same method to have been pursued.   And our expectations are realised, for it is possible to pick out some of the sources, even though we have no parallels for control as we have in S. and K.   There is not, unfortunately, much agreement among scholars as to the limits of some of these sources.   There is nothing then left for me but to give my conclusions, which are, however, based on many years' study of these books.   The results will be seen to be decidedly conservative.

(1)   *The Memoirs of Nehemiah* = N.

Beginning with a source about the presence of which there is no difference of opinion, there is certainly incorporated in the book which bears his name some personal memoirs of Nehemiah.   These are all written in the first person, and the narrative is terse and vivid.   The memoirs were written for the most part soon after the close of his first administration (*v.* 5[14]), and as a historical source rank among the very best in OT. Nehemiah knew how to accomplish results, even in the face of the gravest difficulties, and he also knew how to tell what he had done without waste of words.   In some places N. has somewhat the character of a diary or journal.   The brief prayers and imprecations scattered through the document make the impression of a narrative originally written for the author's eye alone.

The agreement of scholars ceases, however, the moment we attempt to determine the limits of the memoirs.   There is a minimum about which all are agreed, but the moment we step beyond that boundary contention arises.

The vast majority of modern scholars set rather large limits to these memoirs. Berth. Sieg. Ryle, and Dr. practically agree that N. covers Ne. 1–7 12$^{27-43}$ 13$^{4-31}$. Berth. and Sieg. exc. 12$^{27-30.\ 33-36}$, but Sieg. adds 11$^{1\,f.}$ and Dr. adds 13$^{1-4}$. Torrey, on the other extreme, finds N. only in 1^1–2^7 2^{9b-20} 4^1–6^{15}. All agree that 7$^{6-72}$ was not written by Neh., but the scholars who include this in N. suppose, wrongly I believe, that it was incorporated in N. by Neh.

It seems certain that 3$^{1-32}$ is not from N. It has none of the characteristics of that document, but is very like other lists in our books, and it is quite out of place where it stands, interrupting the narrative sadly (v. notes on Ne. 3). I have shown in the notes reasons which are sufficient to reject 2^{7-9a}. I can see no satisfactory evidence against 3$^{33-38}$ 6$^{16-19}$ 7^{1-5a} 13^{6-31a} exc. v. ^{22}. The last passage is not only written in the first p., but also has numerous characteristics of N. On the other hand, I have no hesitation in rejecting 1^{5-11a}, the major portion of Neh.'s prayer, which is too close to a type to be composed by Neh. (v. notes), one point in which I go beyond Torrey, who only goes so far as to assume editorial revision. I believe it a piece of editorial composition. In the passage describing the dedication of the walls (12$^{27-43}$), there are unmistakable traces of N., e. g., in $^{31\,f.\ 38.\ 40b}$, but a story like this was too tempting to the Chr., and he has so embellished it with interpolations to bring pr., Lev., music, and sacrifices into prominent place that Neh.'s own simple, straightforward story is buried beyond hope of recovery. Torrey notes that 2^{19b} 3$^{33\,ff.}$ 4$^{1\,ff.}$ repeat one another rather awkwardly, an awkwardness much increased by the elimination of 3$^{1-32}$ (ES.^{226}). That is quite true, and yet I doubt if any of the passages exc. possibly 3$^{33-35}$ can be legitimately questioned. The portions which are from N. are, therefore, 1$^{1-4}$ 1^{11b}–2^7 2^{9b-20} 3^{33}–7^{5a} 13$^{6-31}$.

(2) *The Memoirs of Ezra* = E.

It has been the practically unanimous opinion of Biblical scholars that another important and trustworthy source is found in E. This, it is claimed, includes Ezr. 7^{27}–8^{34} 9$^{1-15}$; such, at all events, are the conclusion of such competent scholars as Driver, Ryle, Cornill, Kosters, Siegfried, and Bertholet.

Before discussing the matter further, it is necessary to reduce the space of the memoirs somewhat. First, we must eliminate 8$^{1-14}$, the list of the heads of the fathers who went up with Ezra. There is nothing to suggest E. in the whole passage save the "with me" עִמִּי in v. ¹. The v. is disjointed and shows an editor's hands, for "from Bab." is connected with "went up," and we may infer that "with me" was inserted from 7²⁸, or else that we should read by a very slight change "with him." The passage is out of place here, as it gives a list of his company before Ezra makes his inspection (v. ¹⁵). It would come better after 7¹⁰, as 7¹⁻¹⁰ summarises the whole story and commits other sins of anticipation. Yet it must be noted that the list is peculiar in the designation "males," and in the silence about the temple officers so liberally supplied in 7⁷. The explanation about the Neth. in 8²⁰ is suspicious; indeed, the whole v. is prob. an addition by the Chr. The same hand prob. produced vv. ²⁶ ᶠ. ³⁰. ³³. ³⁵, for reasons given in the notes. Also 9¹¹ᵇ⁻¹² are to be excluded, so that for E. we have 7²⁷ ᶠ. 8¹⁵⁻¹⁹. ²¹⁻²⁵. ²⁸ ᶠ. ³¹ ᶠ. ³⁶ 9¹⁻¹¹ᵃ. ¹³⁻¹⁵, though 8³⁶ is dub.

Now if these are genuine memoirs there can be no doubt of their historical value. But Torrey has for years maintained that the Ezra memoirs are a myth, insisting that the whole Ezra story is composed by the Chr., and in fact the character of Ezra was created by him, so that Ezr. 7-10 and Ne. 7⁷⁰-10 are fiction pure and simple (ES.²³⁸⁻²⁴⁸; cf. Comp. ¹⁴ ᶠᶠ. ⁵⁷ ᶠᶠ.). A part of this radical opinion will be examined later. Here we are concerned with the memoirs only. Torrey's conclusion rests essentially on linguistic material. He gives a list of some thirty words from the parts which are assigned to E. and which he declares to be characteristic of the Chr. (cf. Comp.¹⁶ ᶠᶠ.). He goes so far as to declare deliberately, as the "result of a good deal of hard study," that "there is no portion of the whole work of Ch.-Ezr.-Ne. in which the Chr.'s literary peculiarities are more strongly marked, more abundant, more evenly and continuously distributed, and more easily recognisable than in the Heb. narrative of Ezr. 7-10 and Ne. 8-10" (ES.²⁴¹).

The use of the first p. is easily explained by Torrey on the ground that the Chr. employed it in deliberate imitation of N. He cites other cases in which there is transition from the first p. to the third. Torrey has overlooked, so far as I recall, what might be a strong argument in support of his contention, viz., that in some places certain Vrss. have the third p. where MT. has the first, e. g., 8³¹ ᶠ. in Esd.ᴮ, 9¹⁻⁵ in Esd.ᴸ.

But we note that the first p. occurs in Esd. where N. is not found, and where it may never have existed. The Ezra story may have been once published quite independently of that of Neh. Then again it is inconceivable that the Chr. should have written by far the major part of the Ezra story in the third p., and then employed the first in such a limited part. That is esp. the case as these passages in the first p. are precisely those which raise no suspicion on the ground of credibility.

But the most decisive argument is the relation of the various parts of the narrative to each other. It is incredible that Ezr. 7-10 was all written by the same person, the Chr. or any one else whatsoever. In 7¹⁰ Ezra's whole company arrives in Jerus., and the members of the company are enumerated in 8¹⁻¹⁴, while in 7²⁸ and its direct sequel, 8¹⁵, Ezra is beginning to gather a caravan at Ahava. Then, in the letter of Art., Ezra is clothed with enormous powers, but in the actual record of his deeds he never once calls upon any authority but the law. The difference in this respect between Ezra and Neh. is very marked. Neh. acts as governor and uses his authority, but Ezra can only appeal to the people to obey the law. Surely a single author would have aimed at greater consistency.

It has been conceded by several scholars, esp. since the publication of Torrey's *Composition* (1896), that E. has been worked over a great deal, and that the numerous marks of the Chr. which Torrey has pointed out are due to his revision. But Torrey in his later work (ES. 1910) asserts that the Chr. does not revise his material, that he either incorporates bodily or composes entirely. Torrey cites as an instance the parallel N. which he says the Chr. has practically not revised.

My own studies constrain me to dissent from this contention. As a matter of fact, I am persuaded that the Chr. revised his material pretty freely whenever it suited his purpose to do so. I may cite as an impressive instance his change from Yahweh to Satan as the tempter of David (1 Ch. 21¹ = 2 S. 24¹). (See further evidence in Curt. *Intr*.⁹⁻¹⁴, ¹⁹). But the testimony of our own books is decisive. The Chr. has liberally revised Ezr. 3 to make it square with his theory of the deferred building of the temple. In fact, his hand is visible almost everywhere.

It is true, however, that N. has been tampered with comparatively little. But that fact is eloquent in its description of the Chr.'s method. The building of the wall was of so little interest that in one recension the whole story may have been omitted. But when the Chr. came to Neh.'s story of the dedication of the walls, he was in a field in which he was perfectly at home, and on a subject in which he had a profound interest. He revised the story, which certainly existed in N. until there are only dim traces of the original, while the work of his own hand is to be seen all through.

Now Torrey is right in asserting that Ezra was the Chr.'s hero. The editor found the work of a kindred spirit in E. That document presented material with which he was familiar and on which he had very pronounced opinions. But Ezra lived more than a century before the Chr. In the meanwhile, many changes had taken place. The Chr. was almost forced to bring Ezra's work down to date, as he does David's. He could hardly use such a source without revision. Otherwise there would have been a historical development in religion, and such a phenomenon was abhorrent to him. Therefore, Torrey's list does not seem to me at all decisive, even if we grant its validity, as we must in part.

As a matter of fact, the Chr. has revised even N. considerably. He puts a suitable prayer in the cup-bearer's mouth (1^{5-11a}); he furnishes the leader with letters which he seemed to think Neh. had overlooked (2^{7-9a}; but $v.$ notes); he provided a systematic account of the method of building the wall, and as Neh. had afforded nothing to work on he had to make it himself, unless, indeed, he found it ready from some other hand, just as he elaborates Ezra's work; by the twist of a sentence he changes the purpose of Neh.'s assembly and makes him discover a then non-existent record of names (7^{5}); and finally in c. 13, where Neh. approaches closely to the editor's own field, the Chr.'s hand has crept in so conspicuously that Torrey gives him the credit of the whole.

There is one more argument for the existence of E., which is entirely subjective, and yet which is of very great force to one who feels it. Every time I study Ezr. 7–10, I feel afresh the fact that two voices speak in the various sections. The whole story as told in E. seems so simple and natural and unaffected, and so lacking in the pomposity which attaches to Ezra where the Chr. uses a free hand, that it bespeaks its own genuineness. The very details of the gathering at Ahava are just the things the Chr. would never think of composing, as we may see from the summary way in which he actually deals with the journey (7^{1-10}), in which he is careful to present abundant names and dates, but no personal history at all.

Torrey's arguments have failed to convince those who have been diligent students of the story of Ezra, and with all regard to his undoubted scholarship and industry, I find myself among the number who must still take the Ezra story seriously.

(3) *The Aramaic Documents.*

There are three sections of the book of Ezr. which are written in Aramaic: (1) The correspondence with Artaxerxes, 4^{7-24a}. (2) The history of the rebuilding of the temple, Ezr. 4^{24b}–6^{18}. (3) The edict of Artaxerxes authorising Ezra's mission, 7^{12-26}. As 6^{19-22} is a late insertion and 7^{1-10} is the Chronicler's introduction to Ezr., we have practically a long continuous section in Aramaic, 4^{7}–7^{26}. It may be, therefore, that before the Chronicler there was an Aramaic history of this period, which he used to a limited extent. If there was such a source, it must have consisted mainly of official documents with a minimum of introduction and comment.

The first two of these pieces are alike in one respect, that while the bulk of the material consists of the letters, there are introductory and other notes also written in Aramaic. In the case of the third, however, there is nothing in Aramaic save the letter, the brief introduction (7^{11}) being written in Hebrew. The Chronicler, therefore, does not get his material for (1) and (2) at first hand. Before his time the letters had been published with the various notes before and after the epistles. The third he may have quoted at first hand; at all events, if there ever had been any notes on the letter, the Chronicler left them out entirely.

Mey. is the stoutest modern defender of these Aram. documents (*Ent.*[8-71]). He emends the text of Ezr. 4^7, reading "the despatch was written in Pers. and translated into Aram.," so that originally there was here one of the polylingual inscriptions which abounded in the Pers. empire. This argument would be stronger if there were nothing but the letters. As a matter of fact, there are the compiler's comments. Mey. would hardly contend that these, too, were written in Pers. and translated into Aram. Besides it is shown in the notes that Mey.'s interpretation of 4^7 is more than doubtful. Mey. claims to find a considerable list of Pers. words in the documents, and thus reinforces his belief in Pers. originals and in the authenticity of the letters. But it does not seem possible to group the documents and formulate a single conclusion which will cover them all. They must be treated separately.

(1) There can be no doubt that the Chr. incorporated the Art. correspondence in 4^{7-24a} and did not compose it, for he misunderstood its tenor. Further, there is no good reason whatever to question its genuineness. It describes just the conditions necessary to explain Neh.'s work, as I have shown in the intr. to the passage, where also Kost.'s arguments against its authenticity are examined in detail. Further, the charge of a tendency to exalt the Jews, and to exult over the Sam. (ES.[154]), certainly does not apply here, for in this source the Sam. triumph over the Jews, and leave Jerus. in the worst state it had known since 586, a state which nearly broke Neh.'s heart when he heard of it.

(2) I have myself repeatedly called this the Aram. version of the temple-building story. In reality, it is better described as the correspondence with Dar. about the rebuilding of the temple. There is

very little in the whole narrative except the story of what the Sam. rulers did when they heard of the operation at Jerus. and the Pers. king's action on their report.   But the Chr. certainly was not the author of the piece.   The prominence of the prophets in $5^{1\,f.}$, which Mey., with strange obtuseness, assigns to the Chr., could never have come from his hand.   He makes the pr. prominent even in building the walls, Ne. 3, while the temple-construction is supported chiefly by the prophets. Even Torrey, who regards the source as worthless historically, admits that it is quoted by the Chr.

It is a favourite theory of modern scholars that this document has been freely edited, and that there is an original and authentic substratum.   Torrey really jeers at this conclusion, saying of a quotation from Dr.[Intr]: "The documents are not genuine, but in substance are thoroughly trustworthy" (ES.[144]).   Now, as a matter of fact, the text of this document has been liberally edited and is decidedly corrupt in some places, as I have shown in the notes.   It can hardly be supposed that a Jewish R. would modify such material without a certain tendency creeping in.   And the fact that he modified his material shows that he had something to modify.

The bare outline of the narrative is as follows: Under the inspiration of the prophets the Jews begin the rebuilding of the temple in the 2d year of Dar.   Tattenai, the governor of the Syrian province, and others go to Jerus. to see what authority the Jews had for building a temple and who were the leaders in the movement.   They report to Dar. by letter the claim of the authority of Cy., and ask for instructions.   Dar. orders a search of the archives and finds the original decree of Cy., which is quoted, not in Dar.'s letter, but in the narrative portion.   The king confirms the decree of his predecessor and orders his officials not to interfere.

Now in all this there is no note of improbability.   The Jews in Elephantine could not rebuild their temple without authority of the Pers. officials, and surely Tattenai would have been remiss had he taken no steps under the circumstances.   The temple was certainly rebuilt in the reign of Dar., and that task could hardly have been accomplished without his knowledge and sanction.

The most serious difficulty is the inconsistency with the story in Esd. $4^{62\,f.}$ that Zer. came to Jerus. in the reign of Dar. carrying with him permission to rebuild the temple, and the silence of Hg. and Zc. about interference from any source whatever.   There is further the statement in Ezr. 4^{1-3} that the Sam. desired to aid the Jews in building, and there is in that story no note of any opposition.   We are compelled to choose between two contradictory stories, and I have no hesitation in accepting the Heb. story as correct.

The fact is that this story is inconsistent with itself.   In 5^2 the temple is *begun* under Zer., but in 5^{16} the building has been going on ever since the time of Shes. in the 1st year of Cy. and was still incomplete. Now this last passage is the basis of the Chr.'s construction of all his material of the period, Ezr. 1–6. In accord with this theory he makes c. 3 but a futile beginning of the work, and by leaving out dates would make it appear that Zer.'s work was done in the time of Cy. It is very likely, as Torrey contends, that he regarded this Dar. as Dar. II (423–404), and so the time spent on building the temple was a very long one indeed, certainly more than a century. The Chr., in other words, had a very misleading source here, but he fell into the trap, and made a mess of his good material accordingly.

Kost. has tried to solve the problem of the contradictory statements by assuming that there are, in fact, two original stories which have been woven together and worked over by the Chr. or an earlier compiler. This dissection leaves in one part, A, 5^{1-10} 6^{6-15} (exc. ^{14b}, which with $^{16-18}$ he ascribes to the Chr.), and in the other, B, 5^{11-17} $6^{1.\ 3-5}$ (*Wied.*$^{22\ ff.}$). But the grave difficulties of this piece cannot be solved in this way. There are no linguistic or other marks to support such an arbitrary analysis. The fact is that the whole piece is Jewish to the core. Tattenai and his fellows, in their letter to the Pers. king, really plead the cause of the Jews, and Dar. goes even beyond Cy. in his generosity toward the temple.

Torrey holds now that 4^7–6^{15} was incorporated bodily by the Chr., though he formerly held that 4^{24} was the Chr.'s connecting link (ES.$^{159\ f.}$; *cf. Comp.*$^{7\ ff.}$). I am unable to follow Torrey in his change of opinion. Had one author written the whole piece, he would hardly have been entirely silent in two whole c. about the important letters in 4^{7-24}, and Tattenai could hardly have been ignorant of Art.'s decree. Doubtless "Artaxerxes" was inserted in 6^{14} to make the two pieces go better together.

And yet the piece in its original form was doubtless a sincere attempt of some devout Jew, living very long after the event, to describe the manner in which the temple was rebuilt. He was doubtless ignorant of other sources, and could hardly have been familiar with official documents or he would not have put such a pathetic Jewish plea as 5^{6-17} into the letter of a Pers. official. The passage is eloquent of the tribulations of the poor Jews, and doubtless the writer expressed some true sentiments, however ill-informed he was of the history.

(3) Concerning Art.'s grant to Ezr. 7^{12-26} little need be said. In the notes on the passage, I have shown that the letter as a whole is apparently incompatible with Ezra's work so far as we know it. We are forced to conclude that if Ezra had any authority from Art. it must have been what is contained in the first part of the letter (vv. $^{12-20}$), and the rest is an amplification by one who exaggerated Ezra's mission more than even the Chr. did.

But there is no sufficient reason to doubt that the Chr. really found it as a source. The fact that he composed an intr. in Heb. (7¹¹) confirms that opinion. Moreover, the Chr. would not have composed a letter giving Ezra powers which even the Chr. himself never permits him to use.

An effort has been made to fix the date of the composition of these Aram. documents from the language. Torrey has given considerable attention to this matter (ES.¹⁶¹⁻¹⁶⁶), and reaches a very positive opinion. He asserts that the Aram. of Dn. is exactly the same as that of our documents, and Dn. is assigned to the Gk. period. The whole of these sources are placed in the second and third centuries B.C. from linguistic considerations. This result is confirmed by the discovery of the Aram. papyri in Egypt, which belong to the fifth century B.C. An examination of some of these papyri is made, and the conclusion reached that their language is much earlier than that of the documents in Ezr.

Other scholars have held different opinions. Sachau, in his earliest work, *Drei. Aram. Pap.* 1907, asserted that the Aram. of the papyri was identical with that of the Biblical documents, and he has said nothing to the contrary in his latest and largest contribution, *Aram. Pap. u. Ost.* 1911. Sayce and Cowley maintained essentially the same position. My own somewhat meagre examination of the papyri makes me feel that their language and expressions are very like the B. Aram.

Torrey has pointed out some clear differences in usage, but he may have drawn too big a conclusion from his premises. The papyri were never copied, but are preserved in their original form, while our documents were copied hundreds of times, and are found in living books. It would be almost inevitable, therefore, that a certain modernisation would result. The archaic relative זי, *e. g.*, would easily become the common די. Then again we must admit that the language of people of the same blood, but living long apart, tends to differ. Lowell showed that many Americanisms were simply survivals of the language of Shakespeare. The Jews in Elephantine were doubtless the successors of those who migrated to that land soon after the fall of Jerus., 586 B.C. The Jews who wrote these stories had prob. come from Bab., certainly not from Egypt. The two bodies of Jews had lived apart for more than a century before these documents could have been written. There seems no adequate grounds for denying that these records may belong to the fifth century, even if it is to be confessed that there is little evidence to support that date. Then again it is shown in the critical notes that many peculiar words are common to the two sources and are used in precisely the same way.

(4) *The Hebrew Sources.*

It is held by some modern scholars that all of our books, save the parts enumerated above, viz., N., E., and the Aramaic documents, were composed by the Chronicler. That contention cannot be maintained unless we adopt the old device, worked so liberally in the criticism of the Pentateuch, and fall back on a Chronicler, Chronicler[1], Chronicler[2], and so on as far as necessary. An adequate textual criticism makes impossible the verdict that the Chronicler wrote all of these books, outside of the sources previously considered.

It is agreed, however, that the Chr. is the compiler of the books in their present form. He could not then be the author of Ezr. 2^{70}–4^3, for, as shown in detail in the notes, this piece has been subjected to such sweeping revision that its original purport is quite lost. The Chr. did the rewriting to make the stubborn piece fit his theory of the history, and therefore he had before him an original Heb. story of the rebuilding of the temple by Zer. and Jes., which harmonises perfectly with the information we have in Hg. and Zc.

It seems further necessary to analyse Ezr. 1. Every time I read the chapter I feel strongly that it is not all from the same hand. A part of it is smooth and simple, esp. when correction is made in the text, and a part of it rough and disjointed. The part which I venture to assign to a Heb. source, used by the Chr., is vv. $^{1-4.\ 7\ f.\ 11b}$. These vv. make a complete and consistent story in themselves, and the other vv. have all the earmarks of the embellishments which the Chr. loved to interject into his narrative.

Whether the Chr. is the author of the Ezra story in Ezr. 10, Ne. 8 is difficult to determine. It is possible that he had some memoirs which he rewrote. It is certainly possible that he composed the whole, esp. as the Ezra story so far as we know ends with Ne. $8^{12\ or\ 18}$.

In Ne. 10, which, contrary to the usual opinion, has nothing whatever to do with Ezra, we have a piece quite out of place, and for that reason it was prob. in existence before the Chr. He would hardly have composed a passage so out of harmony with its setting; but in his method of editing and compiling he might easily have used it as he did because he wanted to make it tell a different story from what it does. An agreement of the people to do certain specific things is ridiculous after the law had been given and the people were sworn to obey it. Personal agreements have nothing to do with a code like that in the Pentateuch.

(5) *The Lists.*

There is little left but the lists of names. These occupy a
liberal space; Ezr. 2 (= Ne. 7^{6-72}) 8^{1-14} 10^{18-43} Ne. 3^{1-32} 10^{2-28}
11^{4-36} 12^{1-26} are practically nothing else. These lists are by
many scholars confidently attributed to the Chronicler. Now,
that the Chronicler was fond of such lists is beyond a doubt.
The way he sets forth the history down to David (1 Ch. 1–9)
is sufficient evidence. He was an expert in genealogies. But
it does not follow that he composed all the lists.

> Lists of names were common in the postex. period, and now we have
> long lists of Jewish names from Egypt (Sachau, *Tafeln*,[17-20]). It is hard
> to believe that any one person composed all of these lists, for while there
> are striking resemblances, there are also many differences; note esp.
> the peculiar use of " males " in the list of Ezra's company (Ezr. 8^{1-14}).
> It is, at all events, highly prob. that the Chr. merely incorporated
> lists which he found to his hand.
>
> The real work of the Chr. in these books consists, therefore, of edit-
> ing and compiling. There is not a great deal which can be proved
> to come from his pen; and yet there is very little that he has not
> retouched acc. to his own ideas. The work of compilation was badly
> done, but fortunately there is enough guidance for the revision of the
> Chr.'s blundering work and for bringing the various parts into their
> right relations.

§ 9. THE SAMARITAN OPPOSITION.

The restoration of Jerusalem was greatly hindered by the
interference of other peoples who were living as neighbours to
the Jews. And yet the real extent and character of this opposition has been greatly misunderstood, owing largely to the
confusion of the text wrought by the compiler. The fact is
that save in one brief and obscure passage (Ezr. 4^{4-6}) there is
no hint of an attempt of any one to place obstacles in the way
of the Jews until the time of Artaxerxes.

> The corrupt passage in Ezr. 3^3, when properly corrected (*v.* notes),
> shows an entirely friendly disposition on the part of the Jews' neigh-
> bours. In Ezr. 4^{1-3} the Sam., so far from desiring to impede the build-

ing of the temple, sincerely offer their aid in the work. Even if we accept Ezr. 5 f., there is still no opposition. Tattenai and his associates betray no hostility and accept the statement of the leaders that they had authority from Cy. and did not attempt to secure a cessation of the building operations, but distinctly allowed them to continue (5⁴), while their report and inquiry went to the Pers. court.

There is, indeed, the perplexing passage Ezr. 4⁴⁻⁶ which I have placed in the time of Xerxes, but it is too obscure and uncertain to throw much light on our problem. At most it is a very vague and general statement about some opposition from foreigners. Vv. ⁴· ⁵ might be from the Chr.'s hand, but that would leave v. ⁶ in rather a sorry state, for it is inconceivable that the Chr. should have written that much and no more about the reign of Xerxes.

When we come to the reign of Art. there is plenty of material to show that this hostility was very marked. The sources of our information are two, and both unquestionably authentic: the Art. correspondence (Ezr. 4⁷⁻²⁴ᵃ) and N. The complainants against the Jews in the former document were certainly the Sam. They describe themselves as the colonists whom Asnappar—certainly some Assyrian king—had brought to Sam. The hostility of these people is apparent. They came to Jerus. on no mission of friendliness or inquiry, but, on the contrary, point out to the king that the accomplishment of the Jews' purpose spells disaster to the Pers. dominions in the west. Their intense opposition was due to the fact that the Jews in their time were engaged in the building of the walls, the same cause that provoked the fierce enmity toward Neh.

While the Jews were engaged in restoring the temple, there was no trouble with their neighbours, but the moment they attack the walls, opposition breaks out. Naturally, for the building of the temple had no political significance. The Pers. officials kept their hands off as long as the Jews were dealing with purely religious institutions. But a city enclosed by a wall created another situation, for a walled city could cause any amount of trouble to the officers of the satrapy of which it was a part.

This consideration confirms the interpretation of this passage (Ezr. 4⁷ ᶠ.). Torrey puts a strange construction on the complaint, alleging that Rehum et al. mention the building of the city rather than the temple in order to reinforce their plea for interference, the complainants thus making a false report of the actual conditions. As there is otherwise not a shred of evidence of any opposition to the building of the temple, and as the Sam. used every possible effort to prevent the building of the walls, the right interpretation of this passage is fixed beyond reasonable doubt.

Neh.'s story of the building of the walls is contained in Ne. 2¹⁰⁻²⁸ 3¹¹⁻4¹⁷ 6¹⁻7¹ᵃ. As a matter of fact, these sections, comprising almost all of

N. save the story of his leave of absence and his reforms, have as their true subject the efforts of the enemy to stop Neh.'s operations.

Three men stand out as the leaders of this opposition, Sanb. the Horonite, To. the Ammonite slave, and Geshem (or Gashmu) the Arabian. In every case exc. 6¹², where To. is prob. a gl., Sanb. stands first, and while in some sections Geshem is not named (2¹⁰ 4¹), and in another To. fails (6²), Sanb. always occurs, twice alone (3³³ 6⁵). It is worth our while to try to discover who this arch-enemy of Neh. was.

Torrey thinks we have a choice between two, one of whom is named by Jos. as the governor of Sam. at the time of the Sam. schism (*Ant.* xi, 8) about 335 B.C. If Neh.'s date were the reign of Art. II, 404–358 B.C., then in 384, when Neh. would come to Jerus. fifty years before, Sanb. might have been a young man, provided he was sufficiently aged at the time in which Jos. places him. But this date for Neh. is out of the question, and as we have the person in exactly the period required we need waste no time in vague possibilities.

In Pap. 1 from Elephantine, l.²⁹, we find "Delaiah and Shelemaiah the sons of Sanb. the governor of Sam." The correspondents assert that they had sent a letter to these men, detailing all the information contained in the letter to Bagohi about the temple in Jeb. Sachau believes that Sanb. was still living, though Buhl asserts that he was certainly dead (*Aram. Pap.*⁴ᶠ·). Sachau's argument is convincing, although the point is immaterial. It suffices to assume, however, that Sanb. was an old man, and that his sons had succeeded him, or were the real administrators of the governorship. As this was in 407 B.C., thirty-seven years earlier, 444 B.C., the date of Neh., Sanb. would have been about thirty-five, in the very prime of life. This is undoubtedly the enemy of Neh.

As his sons both bear Jewish names, Sachau argues that Sanb., in spite of his Bab. name, was a Hebrew. With this position Torrey is agreed, but deems it probable that the name is Heb. as well as the man (ES.¹⁶⁸· ³³⁰).

Neh. never calls him the governor of Sam., but still that office is quite consistent with other statements in the memoirs. Sanb. appears supported by the "army of Sam." (Ne. 3³⁴), which Torrey regards as a note by the Chr. (ES.²²⁶), but he admits that Sanb. comes forth with an army in a suitable place (4²). The rendezvous proposed by Sanb. in the plain of Ono (6²) was, roughly, midway between Jerus. and Sam. It is quite impossible, were Sanb. a private citizen, that he should act with such a high hand toward a governor of Judah, an appointee of the Pers. king. Neh., however, never gives him other designation than "the Horonite," explained by Torrey as marking his contempt. Winckler, followed cautiously by Berth., connects the appellative with Horonaim (Is. 15⁵) in Moab, and makes Sanb. a Horonite sheik. The Elephantine letters dispose of that contention, and we must connect the term with Beth-horon, a town on the border of Sam. (Jos. 16³· ⁵; *cf*. Montgomery, *Samaritans*,⁵⁸), of which place Sanb. might be a native and still governor of Sam. In what respect the appellative contained a note of contempt in Neh.'s time is not known.

The letter shows that the Jewish colonists in Elephantine looked upon the sons of Sanb. as friends who would be likely to assist their plea for the rebuilding of the temple in their garrison. This could not have been very long after Neh.'s second administration, and may seem to raise a doubt about the above identification. As a matter of fact, our sources show that, violently as Sanb. and others struggled against the rebuilding of the walls, and consequently against Neh. as the leader of that great work, there were friendly relations maintained by these foes with some prominent persons in Jerus. Jehohanan, the high priest in 407, or one of his brothers, had married a daughter of Sanb. (Ne. 13²⁸); correspondence was conducted between To. and the nobles of Judah (6¹⁷); and these were allied to him by marriage and agreements; Sanb. was able to hire a prophet to mislead the governor (6¹²). Neh.'s troubles were, in fact, greatly augmented by the disaffection of some of the leaders in Jerus. Again the Jewish colonists in Jeb show that they are not very well informed about affairs in the world outside, and they may have been ignorant of Sanb.'s intrigues against their fellow-Israelite. Finally, Sanb.'s sons, with their good Heb. names, may not have shared their father's hostility, esp. at a time when the wall had long been an accomplished fact.

To account for this hostility there is no need to go back to the repulse of the Sam.'s offer to aid in building the temple (Ezr. 4¹⁻³), still less to the later bitter feud between the Sam. and the Jews. As Montgomery has pointed out in his able work on the Sam. (⁵⁹), the opposition was political, not religious. In the time of Neh. the relations of the Sam. toward the Jews was exactly what the relations of the northern kingdom, the predecessors of the Sam., had always been to the kingdom of Judah. The exile, with the colonising and the return, had not materially altered the conditions. The Sam. and Jews could no more be one people than Ephraim and Judah could long be one state. As shown above, the rival people picked no quarrel with their southern neighbours as long as they were using their efforts to build up their ecclesiastical institutions. The temple would not interfere with the political supremacy of the north. But the building of the walls was another matter. Once let Jerus. be made impregnable again, as it had been in the days of old, and the balance of power would be almost certain to move from the north to the south. The Sam. would have been blind, indeed, had they not seen the significance of the movement, and foolish, indeed, if they had not used every possible means to prevent it.

Their first attempt succeeded. They frightened the weak Art. and

cowed the Jews who under some unknown inspiration and leadership
had started the work. Their second attempt failed, and the cause of
their failure was the presence of a personality against whom their
utmost struggles were in vain.

§ 10. THE DATE OF EZRA'S MISSION.

It has been assumed in the preceding pages that Ezra belongs
to a later period than Nehemiah. That conclusion seems to
me inevitable. It is true that the editor of the books thought
otherwise. His placing of Ezr. 7–10 before Ne. 1 shows that
the Artaxerxes who authorised Ezra's administration was, in
his view, the same as the Artaxerxes who appointed Nehemiah
to be governor of Judah, and his placing of the promulgation
of the law by Ezra (Ne. 8$^{1-12}$) in the midst of Nehemiah's rule
shows his belief that they were contemporaries. Further to
support his view, he has introduced Nehemiah in the story of
the reading of the law (Ne. 8^9). He also drags Ezra's name
into the story of the dedication of the walls (Ne. 12^{36}), but it is
a manifest gloss. In spite of the dissimilarity of their work,
these two leaders could not be contemporaries.

For Art. would scarcely send two men to Judah at the same time,
both clothed with similar powers. It would be strange, were Ezra such
a prominent figure in Jerus., that there is no genuine reference to him
in Neh.'s story. Neh. in his second administration was the first to
discover mixed marriages and to apply a sharp remedy. Such a condition would not arise naturally after the wholesale dissolution as described in Ezr. 9 f. Neh.'s reforms, as narrated in c. 13, would be
strange after Ezra, but are very natural before his time. It is inconceivable that the Lev. should be driven to work in the fields directly
after Ezra's mission, or even possibly while it lasted. The measures
Neh. took for the support of the temple show that his action could not
have been preceded by the rule of a scribe-priest with ample authority
to enforce the law. Moreover, the Jerus. of Neh.'s time was a desolation, without walls or houses or people (7^4). Ezra's whole career
is spent in the holy city, and there appears to have been plenty of
houses and people in his time.

There is the evidence of Esd. which connects Ne. 7^{72}–8^{12} directly
with Ezr. 10, thus bringing the Ezra story together. There is nothing
about Neh.'s work in this the earliest edition of our books. Jos. has a
section dealing with Neh.'s administration (*Ant.* xi, 5, 6–8). Before

he takes up the story of Neh. he describes the death of Ezra at an advanced age (*ib.* § 5). Jos. follows Esd. as his authority, so that the testimony is emphatic on this negative point—that Ezra and Neh. were not contemporaries. Further Jos. says that both Ezra and Neh. flourished in the reign of Xerxes (485–464), and he relates that the death of Joakim the high pr. took place at about the same time as that of Ezra. Now Joakim was the son of Jes. (Ne. 12¹⁰), and he might have ruled in the time of Xerxes, but he could hardly survive till the reign of Art. As Jos. followed his sources pretty closely, it is perfectly possible that the date of Ezra in the original text of Esd. was the reign of Xerxes, and that Art. is one of the many modifications in that text based on MT. As the version of Esd. lost favour largely owing to Jer.'s great influence (*cf.* ES.¹³), there was an evident effort to recover its lost prestige by eliminating its variations from MT. Such a date for Ezra is not impossible, esp. when the scope of his mission is properly limited. He must be separated from Neh. by a considerable space of time.

Such evidence as we have in our sources, however, points to the conclusion that Ezra followed Neh. To that evidence we now turn.

In Ezra's prayer he refers to God's grace as manifested before his time, and among other evidences cites "the giving of a wall [in Judah and] in Jerus." (Ezr. 9⁹). As shown in the notes, the reference can only be to the wall built by Neh. We are told that Ezra went into the chamber of Jehohanan the son of Eliashib to spend the night (Ezr. 10⁶). The succession of high pr. in Ne. 12²² shows that Jehohanan is identical with Jonathan (12¹¹) and that he was the grandson of Eliashib (so Sta. *Gesch.* ii,¹⁵³). Now as Eliashib was a contemporary of Neh., Ezra is two generations later, or exactly where he belongs, in the reign of Art. II. Neh.'s administration began in 444, and Ezra's in 397 or later. Finally in Ne. 12²⁶ we have the order " Neh. the governor and Ezra the pr., the scribe," and these are not contemporaries, but belong to successive periods. It does not help, therefore, to correct the text of Ezr. 7⁷, as proposed by We. (*Gesch.*¹⁶⁹,ⁿ), reading 27th instead of 7th. Indeed, that would make matters worse, for as Neh. was governor of Judah from the 20th to the 32d years of Art., we should then have Ezra coming up in the very midst of Neh.'s rule. It is certainly simpler to suppose that the reference is to Art. II.

These considerations fix the date of Neh. as that of the reign of Art. I (Longimanus), 464–424. Torrey insists that "the tradition represented by the Aram. document and the Chr." places Neh.'s work in the reign of Art. II (Mnemon), 404–358 B.C., and says that we have no means of determining which Art. was the benefactor of Neh. (*Comp.*⁶⁵, ES.³³⁵). This conclusion comes from taking Chr.'s arrangement too seriously. Ezra could hardly have been later than Art. II, and I have shown that he followed Neh. Moreover, Neh. must have been familiar with Pers. history. He could hardly have held high place at the court without knowing the succession of the Pers. kings. If his benefactor had been preceded shortly before by a king of the same name, he would in all probability have taken pains to specify the later Art., as Jos. does, τοῦ ἄλλου Ἀρταξέρχου (*Ant.* Ed. Niese, iii,[60 f.], quoted by Sachau,[7]).

This date has received strong confirmation from the Eleph. pap. Jehohanan was high pr. at Jerus. in 407 B.C. As he was the grandson of Eliashib, a contemporary of Neh. (*v. s.*), Neh. must have preceded this time. This argument has been elaborated by Sachau ([7 f.]). Another notice from the same letter supports the conclusion. Sanb.'s sons were prominent men in Sam. at the date given above, 407 B.C. As this person is to be identified with Neh.'s persistent foe, Sanb., if still living, must have been a fairly old man, so that his prime of life would exactly coincide with the date of Neh. Arnold has added confirmation of this date from the presence of a Hananijah, as a high Pers. official in Egypt, and who was probably the same as Hanani, the brother of Neh. (JBL. 1912,[30]).

Taking all the evidence there is no longer room for the slightest doubt that the protector of Neh. was Art. Longimanus. In his later work Torrey now admits the probability of this date, but he will go no further (ES.[140. 226. 335]).

§ 11. THE HISTORY OF THE PERSIAN PERIOD.

Outside of some prophetic passages and Psalms, which cannot always be positively dated, our books contain all the information we have about the historical events of the important Persian period, 538–332 B.C., and so slightly more than two centuries. If every word of Ezr.–Ne. were authentic, our knowledge would be meagre, for we have practically nothing until we reach the reign of Darius I, 521–485, and but a brief note, which yields little information, from the reign of the famous Xerxes, 485–464. From the completion of the temple, about 515 B.C., until the advent of Nehemiah, 444 B.C., there is a long period, nearly three-quarters of a century, about the history of which we have but slight knowledge.

A characteristic of our books is that they give us information about a very few specific events, each of which occupies but a short time, and then a great gap is left. Thus Ezr. 3–6 (exc. 4[4-24]) contains the story of the rebuilding of the temple, Ne. 1–6 the story of the building of the walls, Ezr. 7-10 the dissolution of mixed marriages. And there is no attempt to tell what happened in the intervals.

Since Kost.'s arraignment, however, there has been a tendency to discredit a large part of the scanty material contained in our books, so that for some scholars the Pers. period is essentially a blank. Those who hold this position regret the state of affairs. Thus Torrey says finely: "We are in the direst need of information as to the history of the Jews in the Pers. period, and every scrap of material that promises help ought to be treasured and put to use. But no extremity of need can outweigh the obligation to follow the evidence" (ES.[157]). With this statement every one will heartily agree. It is far better to have no knowledge of the period than false knowledge. It is necessary to be on one's guard lest the wish should be father to the thought. But it is equally necessary to be on one's guard in another direction, and after years of studying these books, I am convinced that some students have used insufficient caution. Some portions of these books must be rejected as historical sources, but in the process of rejection it is easy to throw away the good with the bad. I am convinced that some of the poverty of information which Torrey laments is due to an indiscriminate criticism in which authentic sources have gone by the board.

The method is a very simple one. A passage shows certain notes of the Chr.; it is immediately ascribed to him as a whole; it is a fundamental principle that the Chr. never wrote history correctly, but is really a novelist, and all his work is worthless. As N., pruned to the last degree, is all that escaped his hand, barring some late and romantic Aram. documents, pretty nearly all of our sources are cast aside. The case does not seem to me so desperate by any means. Much of the material frequently labelled Chr. was not his composition, and even when it is there is no reason to distrust it on that ground alone. The Chr. could, indeed, make sad havoc of history, when a favourite theory was to be supported, as that all the temple ritual goes back to David; but in the Pers. period there is much in regard to which he had no theory that would control his writing of history.

The Chr.'s theory of the history of the period may be stated briefly thus. He puts all the events described in Ezr. 1-4⁵ in the reign of Cy. The statement in 4⁵ that the builders were frustrated " all the days of Cy., king of Persia, even until the reign of Dar., king of Persia," proves that conclusively. That he supposed Art. to have reigned between Cy. and Dar. is the only possible construction to be placed on the position of the Art. letters in 4⁷⁻²⁴. The Chr. then held that Cy. allowed the Jews to go from Bab. and that the large company described in 2¹⁻⁶⁹ actually returned to Judah as a result. He held that they built the altar and started to build the temple, but their efforts were checked by the opposition of the neighbouring foreigners, and finally stopped by the decree of Art. The building was resumed under the urging of the prophets Hg. and Zc. in the 2d year of Dar., and by this king's approval carried on to completion in that king's 6th year.

Now the above is often accepted as the actual course of events, as they are described in Ezr. 1–6. As a matter of fact, the sources are not consistent with any such theory. The Chr. did, indeed, modify his sources, but he was an indifferent editor, and did not eliminate all the traces of a vastly different story. His theory would require the once widely accepted identification of Shes. with Zer., an identification flatly contradicted in the Aram. document, where Zer. built the temple of which Shes. had laid the foundations long before (5^{16}). Moreover, it is Zer., not Shes., who comes up from captivity (2^2), and it is he who made the abortive attempt to rebuild the temple (3$^{2-13}$), and it was he whose work was interfered with by the foreigners (4$^{1-3}$). Moreover, the passage in 4$^{7-24}$ has nothing to do with the building of the temple.

Again, the Chr. makes Ezra come to Jerus. in the 7th year of the same Art. in the 20th year of whose reign Neh. appeared in Judah, and the latter came while the former was in the midst of his labours. Here again the sources used by the Chr. do not bear out his theory, as shown in § 10.

It is possible to reconstruct the history on the basis of the sources used by the Chr., for, as indicated above, all the traces of the true course of events were not obliterated by his sometimes extensive revision. In parts this work has been done by others, though in some respects incompletely. But there does not exist to my knowledge any satisfactory reconstruction of the period covered by Ezr. 1–6, and this is the part in which my results show the greatest divergence from the conclusions of other students.

The history can best be considered under four periods, indicated by the reigns of the Persian kings.

(1) *The Reign of Cyrus*—559–529 B.C.

There is a wide departure at the outset from current opinion in the limitations set for the material bearing on this reign (for further demonstration, *v. i.* on the reign of Darius). As a matter of fact, all that our books tell us about this period is contained in Ezr. 1. Stripped of the Chronicler's embellishments, vv. $^{5.\ 6.\ 9-11\,a}$, which really furnish no historical information, we learn from vv. $^{1-4.\ 7\ f.\ 11b}$, that in the 1st year of Cyrus's rule in Babylonia he issued a decree* authorising the Jewish exiles to return to Jerusalem and rebuild their temple. He restored the sacred vessels which Nebuchadrezzar had taken from the temple, giving them to Sheshbazzar, the prince of Judah, by whom, in company with a caravan of returning exiles, they were carried to Jerusalem.

In this section we come to the crux of the historical problem. One of the most startling of the results of Kost.'s criticism was his assertion that there was no return of the Jews from the Bab. exile until the time of Ezra. The only arguments necessary to consider here are two, the fact that the temple was first begun under Dar., and the silence of Hg. and Zc. (*Wied.*[14 ff.]). Kost. makes a fundamental mistake from his misinterpretation of Ezr. 3. He begins with evidence from the prophets just named that the temple was begun in the time of Dar. As Ezr. 3[8-13] is held to assert that the building was started under Cy., this passage is unhistorical. Then he proceeds to demolish Ezr. 3[1-7], and c. 1 goes down in the ruin. Now we shall return to this point later, but here it suffices to repeat the conclusion demonstrated later, that Ezr. 3 describes events in the reign of Dar., not of Cy.

Then Kost. argues that if more than 40,000 exiles had returned in the time of Cy., as stated in Ezr. 2, Hg. and Zc. must have contained some reference to this stupendous movement, which was but a few years before their time. In the first place, Ezr. 2 does not profess to give a list of those who returned with Shes. in the reign of Cy., but of those who came up with Zer. and others in the time of Dar. It is only in Ne. 7[5] that this record is designated as a list of those "who came up at first," presumably with Shes., and therefore this prefatory note contradicts the statements in the list itself. Kost. seems never to have noted the evidence of Esd., in which text it is sufficiently plain that Ezr. 2 is an interpolation, and really belongs to a late period, and where the date of Dar. is fixed by the place in which the list is interpolated. We have absolutely no hint even as to the number who came up from Bab. with either Shes. or Zer. The whole number of both companies may have comprised but a few hundred persons.

In view of these considerations, the silence of the two prophets of the period is unimportant. If a few hundred people had come from exile, their presence would not be the matter of supreme moment. The prophets were concerned with the task of arousing the people to restore the temple, not with the birthplace of their audiences. There

* We may note the wise caution of Kue., and realise that even the rejection of the authenticity of either form of Cy.'s decree (Ezr. 1[2-4] 6[3-5]) does not prove that there was no return of the Jews at this time (*Abh.*[215]).

is a tradition going back to Dorotheus, Epiphanius, and others that Hg. was born in Bab. (*Hg.* in ICC.[27]). Mitchell assumes that Zc. came from Bab., with his father Iddo (*op. cit.*[83], and see note on Ne. 11[24]). If these prophets were themselves returned exiles, it is natural that they should not refer to the return of others. The fact is that these prophets really tell a somewhat different story from that extracted by Kost.

That story is found the moment we search for the occasion of these prophetic utterances. Why was it that just in this 2d year of Dar. these prophets were led to appeal to the people to build the house of Yahweh? The temple had already been in ruins for nearly seventy years. On Kost.'s theory the work of rebuilding might just as well have started earlier. There must have been some movement at this particular period which made the prophets feel that the moment for action had come.

The prophecies are full of the idea of a new era. Yahweh says: "I am returned to Jerus. with mercies" (Zc. 1[16]). A revival of prosperity is to mark the new era. The advent of Zer. as the governor of Judah best explains the new conditions which led the prophets to perceive the God-given opportunity. This person bulks large in the utterances of both prophets. He was a capable man, he had authority to act, and he was quick to respond to the inspiration of the men of God. Without a return from exile it is hard to find any impulse to start this movement.

Without presupposing the return of most of those who resided in Jerus., it is difficult to explain the plea of the people that the time had not yet come for Yahweh's house to be built (Hg. 1[2]). On what ground should people say that who had lived undisturbed in Judah all their lives? If the leading figures had returned recently from Bab., their objection could be well sustained. Even David did not feel the incongruity of Yahweh's dwelling in curtains until he himself had erected his own house. These men from a foreign country could naturally plead that they needed time for the establishment of their own affairs before undertaking such a stupendous task as the erection of the temple.

According to 1 Ch. 3[16 ff.] both Shes. and Zer. were descendants of Jeconiah or Jehoiachin, who was taken to Bab. as prisoner, Shes. (= Shenazzur) being his son, and Zer. his grandnephew or his grandson. Both of these men have Bab. names and, therefore, both were in all probability born in Bab.

The return of exiles in the time of Cy. is certainly not improbable in itself. By the help of some of the people of the land, disaffected Bab., and possibly foreign colonists, Cy. made short work of Nabonidus and effected an easy conquest of his empire. His own realms then extended from northern India to the border of Egypt (*KAT.*[113]). Cy.

was a Zoroastrian, and the seeming devotion to Marduk in his inscription was contributed for political effect (Jastrow, *Relig. Ar. and Bab.*[45]). The policy by which he proposed to rule these vast new dominions is clearly shown in his own words. On the cylinder inscription he wrote: "The cities across the Tigris whose sites had been established from former times, the gods who live within them, I returned to their places and caused them to dwell in a perpetual habitation. All of their inhabitants I collected and restored to their dwelling places, and the gods of Sumer and Akkad whom Nabonidus, to the anger of the lord of the gods, had brought into Bab. at the command of Marduk the great lord, in peace in their own shrines I made them dwell, in the habitation dear to their heart. May all the gods whom I brought into their own cities daily before Bel and Nebo pray for a long life for me, may they speak a gracious word for me" (Prince's translation in *Mene Mene Tekel Upharsin*, 1893). In l.[26] there is a passage which Prince renders: "I caused their troubles to cease," but which Sayce translates: "I delivered their prisoners" (*H. C. M.*[506]). Rogers renders: "I cleared out their ruins" (*Cun. Par.*[382]).

This passage leaves no reason for doubt that (1) any foreign people colonised in Bab. could easily have gained permission to return to their own land; (2) that any such people could have obtained authority to rebuild any sanctuaries destroyed by the Bab.; and (3) that any sacred objects plundered from the captured people, and resting as trophies in the temple at Bab., would have been freely given back by Cy. Hammurabi similarly orders the return of certain Elamite goddesses to the shrines from which they had been taken (Clay, *Light from Babel,*[160]). The Elephantine documents present remarkable evidence of the favour of the Pers. kings toward the Jews. In the letter to Bagohi the writers says that when Cambyses came into Egypt the temples of the Egyptian gods were all torn down, but that to the temple of Jaho no damage was done. If, therefore, the events narrated in Ezr. 1 are not historical, the passage was certainly written by one well acquainted with the policy of Cy., and he took great pains to avoid a single note of improbability (*v.* Barton, *Semitic Origins,* [154. 310]).

Long before Cy. approached the empire of Nabonidus, but after his conquests foreshadowed the fall of Bab. (Rogers, *Cun. Par.*[377]), a Heb. prophet arose among the Jewish exiles. The whole burden of his message is the release from captivity and the restoration of Jerus. He discerned clearly the character and policy of Cy., and exalts him as the divinely appointed deliverer of the people of Yahweh (Is. 44[24]– 45[7]). His glowing utterances continue until the conqueror enters Bab., at which time he pours out his fervent appeal: "Go ye forth from Bab., flee ye from the Chaldeans; with a voice of singing declare ye, tell this, utter it even to the end of the earth: say ye, Yahweh has redeemed his servant Jacob" (*ib.* 48[20]). This fine prophecy is too well known to need any elaboration. Long ago I showed that we could follow the prophet through the period of Cy.'s approach to the actual return to Jerus. (*The Hist. Movement Traceable in Is.* 40–66, in *And. Rev.* Aug. 1888). It is true that some scholars, apparently possessed with a zeal to bring all the OT. writings down to later and later dates, have removed this prophecy to a period subsequent to the reign of Cy. (*e. g.*, Kent, in *Makers and Teachers of Judaism,*[91 f.]). One of Kent's arguments is that the prophet is concerned primarily with Jerus. This does not seem to me true of c. 40–48, but if it were, it is only necessary to say that on this ground one could prove that Ez. spoke in Jerus., for the holy city was the constant centre of his interest. Without any prejudice against a late date as such, the transfer seems to me to take the prophecy away from the only good historical background that was ever found for it. It may be suspected that the prophecy was pushed out of its true place because of the grave doubts entertained about the favour shown to the Jews by Cy. Kost., however, in his work admits the high expectations of Is.[2], but contents himself with saying that his hopes were never realised.

Other prophets expressed their confidence in the return from exile and the restoration of Jerus. One of the most beautiful sections of Je. (30–33), belonging to the time when the hopes of Judah were all centred in the future, the present period being one of disaster, show the prophet's confidence that the overthrow of the state was temporary; we note, esp. 32[36-44], where the restoration of the state is associated with a return from exile. A large section of Ez. (40–48), the product of the prophet's older years, and worked out among the exiles in southern Bab., is a new constitution for the revived state. Prophets in all ages have visions that are never realised, but at all events it may be confidently said that there was nothing to prevent the fulfilment of these prophetic hopes.

The literature of the exile is abundant, and naturally sounds many notes. But there is one strain running through it with singular persistency, a lamentation over the necessity of a sojourn in a foreign land and a longing for the turning again of the captivity. It is impossible to read such a touching lyric as Ps. 137 without the conviction that there were Jews in Bab. who would not stay there a single day once the road to Jerus. were free. If there was no return of Jews in the time of Cy., that fact is one of the most stubbornly inexplicable of all the events in Heb. history.

Yet Kost. has done a real service in forcing the students of the Bible to take a truer view of postex. Israel. The men who restored Jerus. were not wholly nor even chiefly those who had been born on a foreign soil. The depopulation of Judah by Nebuchadrezzar was no more complete than that of Sam. by Sargon. Thousands of the leading citizens had been carried away in the two great deportations of 597 and 586 B.C.   But more thousands were left, enough to form a sort of state under Gedaliah (Je. 40–44);   and even after the large migration to Egypt, described in the c. cited, the foundation of the colony at Elephantine, from which in recent days such interesting information has come to light, Jews were still abundant in every part of Judah exc. the ancient capital.   The people who came in from the Judean towns to help Neh. build the walls, and doubtless the same class who were the chief helpers of Zer. and Jes. in building the temple, were mainly those who had been born and reared on the soil of the God of their fathers.

The real problem of this period is the apparent paucity of numbers of the returned exiles.   If the Chr. conceived Ezr. 2 to be a list of those who returned in response to Cy.'s decree, he shows that he was awake to the actual possibilities.   Yet there would be a natural reluctance to leave Bab. after so many years' sojourn there.   The Jews have always been good emigrants and are alive to business opportunities.   Bab. was a more prosperous country than Judah, and the commercial chances greater there.   In our day the lack of zeal to go back to Palestine halts the Zionistic movement.   People who had established themselves securely would naturally be loath to tear up the roots and start all over again in an impoverished land and to build again on the ruins of a city long lying in a state of desolation.

The real need of Judah was not an increase of people, but competent and aggressive leadership.   The best people had been carried into exile; witness among other things the prophecy of the good and bad figs (Je. 24).   From the land of exile must come those who would arouse the sluggish spirits of the native Judeans.   Sheshbazzar, Zerubbabel, and Jeshua, Nehemiah and Ezra, and probably Haggai and Zechariah, were the products of Jewish blood and Babylonian enterprise, and their presence in Jerusalem counted for more than 40,000 ordinary men who may, indeed, have returned from exile, but in the course of the two centuries of Persian rule, not in one great company.

(2) *The Reign of Darius I Hystaspis—*521–485 *B.C.*

What Sheshbazzar and the small body of Jews who came up with him did, we do not know.   In the Chronicler's use of his sources, he has destroyed any information that he may have

had. There is a late tradition that Sheshbazzar began the temple (Ezr. 5[16]), but that statement is inconsistent with other good evidence and must be discredited. It is not difficult to conjecture the conditions though. Even later it required great efforts to induce the people to undertake the stupendous task of setting up a sanctuary worthy to stand on the site of the splendid edifice erected by Solomon. Sheshbazzar may have sincerely striven to carry out the mandate of Cyrus, who was concerned to have every native god in his new dominions properly housed, and if he had been so fortunate as to have more than 40,000 who had come to Judah inspired by the same high purpose, and especially a royal grant of all the funds necessary, as magnanimously accorded by a late but badly informed Aramaic writer (Ezr. 6[4]), his task would have been easy. Alas, Sheshbazzar came back with royal blood in his veins, but with few people and with no other resources for the great work than a few temple vessels, and with such meagre funds as the Jewish exiles had seen fit to contribute. The people who did come with him were not the rich—they are never the first to emigrate—but the poor, and they would necessarily be compelled to devote their attention to the pressing problem of keeping the wolf from the door.

In the time of Darius conditions were changed. There was a new governor in Judah, there was a high priest sure to be dominated by a zeal for the temple; above all, there were at least two active prophets, and very likely there was a considerable company of returned exiles. The apathy of the native-born population could now be removed, and the great work could be undertaken with every prospect of success.

It is expedient at this point to gather up the evidence that Ezr. 3[1]–4[3] belongs to the reign of Dar., and not to that of Cy., a point at which my study has led me to diverge from the current opinion.

In the first place, the witness of Jos. is clear beyond a question. Referring to the procuring of lumber from the Sidonians (Ezr. 3[7]), he says "that was what Cy. had commanded at first, and what was now done at the command of Dar." (*Ant.* xi, 4, 1). He speaks of the work beginning in the 2d year of the coming of Zer. and his company to Jerus., and adds that it was finished sooner than any one would have expected. He then tells the story of the disappointment of the older people (Ezr. 3^{12}), but this was after the completion of the building. In the account of the interview with the Sam. (Ezr. 4^{1-2}), he makes Zer. and the others say they had been appointed to build that temple at first by Cy. and now by Dar. (*Ant.* xi, 4, 3). In other words, Jos. gives a clear and consistent account of the actual history of the period and the only one that meets all the conditions.

Now, as well known, and shown above in § 6, Jos. follows Esd., not MT. It is clear that he put the only possible construction upon his source. It must be remembered, too, that Jos. had that text before the extensive modification to conform to MT. Those who insist that Esd. 5^{47-71} (= Ezr. $3^1–4^3$) is dated in the reign of Cy. in that version seem to me to be led astray by a theory. Under any circumstances we must judge by the large indications and not by a single doubtful phrase. The arrangement of the material in Esd. leaves no doubt about the editor's position. In that version the reign of Cy. is separated from the reign of Dar. by the presence of the Art. letters (Esd. 2^{16-30} = Ezr. 4^{7-23}). This passage ends with the statement that "the building of the temple in Jerus. ceased until the second year of the reign of Dar., king of the Pers.," showing conclusively the idea that the events described in the letter belonged to the period between Cy. and Dar. Then immediately we come to the story of the Three Guardsmen, with its sequel in the expedition of Zer. (Esd. $3^1–5^6$), which is certainly dated in the reign of Dar., and that is followed by a list of those who came up with Zer. and other leaders (5^{7-43} = Ezr. 2^{1-67}); and then the story of the rebuilding of the altar and of the temple (5^{44-71} = Ezr. $3^1–4^3$). Those who insist that in Esd. the last-named passage is put in the reign of Cy. are required to assume that the compiler goes back to Cy. after taking up in turn the reigns of Art. and Dar. The appeal to 5^{71} ff. is really vain, for the passage closes with the words, "they were hindered from building for two years until the reign of Dar." This is mere patchwork to connect with the dup. account which follows, but even so, two years will never carry us back from Dar. to Cy., for their reigns are separated, not by that of Art., as this text has it, but by the seven years of the reign of Cambyses.

Even the Heb. text, in spite of all its editing to make it tell a different story, lends itself but poorly to the theory that $3^1–4^3$ belongs to the reign of Cy. Zer. and Jes. were unquestionably the temple-builders, and they belong to the reign of Dar. Now Ezr. 2, on the face of it, has no word about Cy. or Shes., but purports to be a list of those who came up with Zer. *et al.* The only date in the whole passage, other than of the month, is " in the second year of their coming to Jerus." (3^8), and to assume that that means Shes.'s return is purely gratuitous and plainly contradictory to Ezr. 2^2. Then in the whole passage there is not a word about any halt in the building of the temple, for I have shown in the notes on the passage that Ezr. 4^{4-6} is from a different source, and has nothing to do with 4¹⁻³. The Sam. show no purpose of interfering in this passage any more than they do in Hg. and Zc., where any serious interruption is excluded.

Fortunately we have a final witness whose testimony is decisive. No one can rd. Ezr. 3⁸⁻¹¹ without recognising the deep corruption. It has been my good fortune to recover the original on the basis of Esd., by which it is made unmistakable that we have here an account of the building of the temple, and not merely an abortive attempt that was soon halted (v. comm.).

It is plain, therefore, that our material for the reign of Dar. is Ezr. 2⁷⁰⁻4³ 4²⁴ᵇ⁻6¹⁸, to which must be added the important fragment found in Esd. 4⁴²⁻5⁶, and it is possible now to give a clear account of the events as they actually happened, without being trammelled by the theory of the Chr.

The first step was the restoration of the altar on its ancient site (Ezr. 3¹⁻⁶), even this small undertaking being accomplished by the aid of friendly foreigners, perhaps Samaritans (v. corrected text of Ezr. 3³).

Now Kost. rejects this passage, and makes merry over the notion that the Jews had offered no sacrifices from 586 to 520 (Wied.¹³), apparently one of the chief grounds for its rejection. But the passage implies only that the altar had never been restored. Kost. seems to think that sacrifices had never been offered upon any other altar. He evidently forgot the ancient shrines scattered all over the land, which Josiah had tried so hard to wipe out, but which persisted none the less.

The erection of the altar by the temple site in Jerusalem, the resumption of the regular sacrifices there, the observance of one of the great festivals, all tended to kindle the enthusiasm of the people whose fathers had worshipped at Jerusalem. But all this was terribly incomplete without a suitable sanctuary, making possible the residence and work of the priesthood, and soon the people were ready to respond to the prophet's call, and the foundations of the new temple were laid on the 24th day of the 9th month of the 2d year of Darius, 520 B.C. (Hg. 1¹ 2¹⁸).

The Jews had accepted the aid of foreigners in the setting up of the altar, and now the Samaritans proffer assistance in the larger task of rebuilding the temple (Ezr. 4¹⁻³). But they couple their request with a claim to be essentially the same people and to have the same religion. Had their aid been accepted, it would have carried with it a sort of recognition of this claim. Now there was doubtless a good deal of looseness in the religious practices of even the Judeans, who were inclined to mingle pretty freely with their foreign neighbours, certainly to the extent of intermarriage, and it is difficult to go much further without complete amalgamation. Jeshua the high priest may have been especially anxious to see the temple restored as an effective move toward the preservation of a pure religion and consequently a pure blood. He could hardly look with favour upon as mixed a population as the Samaritans certainly were, and doubtless it was largely owing to his influence that the offer was declined.

It is stated in Ezr. 6¹⁵ that the temple was completed in the 6th year of Dar., 516 B.C., that is, this building was put up in four years. Even allowing, as we must on the best of evidence, for the comparative meanness of this building (Ezr. 3¹² Hg. 2³), considering the force and resources of the people, this is a surprisingly short time. Now Solomon had no lack of either men or money, and yet it required seven years to put up his temple (1 K. 6³⁷ ᶠ·). As I have shown, the Aram. account of the rebuilding of the temple in Ezr. 5–6 is not very trustworthy. At several points it is certainly wrong, and yet this single statement is all that we have to support that date. Ezr. 6¹⁶⁻¹⁹ is quite generally regarded as the work of the Chr. The mention of Art. in 6¹⁴ is certainly his doing. He is very fond of specific dates, and 6¹⁵ has probably no other basis than his own opinion as to the length of time required. We have no trustworthy knowledge then, and it is safe to assume that it took considerably more than four years to put up the temple.

This is all the information we have from the reign of Dar. The long story in Esd. 3–5⁶ is inserted because it prepares the way for the description of the building of the temple. The restoration of this building was the great achievement of the reign of Dar. and of the governorship of Zer., and we do not know what else happened in the long period.

(3) *The Reign of Artaxerxes I Longimanus—464-424 B.C.*

This is the golden age of the period of the restoration. The greatest achievements of the Persian period fall in this reign. We have here a fuller story than for any other part of the two

centuries of the Persian dominion of Judah. And yet the
whole reduces itself to pretty much one single subject, the
enclosing of the city of Jerusalem with walls.

There is a wide gap in the history before this event. The temple
had been finished certainly before 500 B.C. For more than fifty years
after that the records are silent, save for the obscure Ezr. 4⁴⁻⁶, which
creates more darkness than light. During the closing years of the
reign of Dar. the Jews would not be able to go much further than they
had. They were a poor people, and the erection of the temple must
have drained their resources, so that a period of recuperation was
necessary.

The inactivity during the reign of Xerxes must be due in part to the
exhaustion of the people, and in part to his unfriendliness toward the
Jews. The fact that at the beginning of his reign, Bishlam, Mithredates, and Tabeel, apparently Pers. officials, lodged an accusation with
this king against "the inhabitants of Judah and Jerus." (Ezr. 4⁶), would
tend to prevent Xerxes from doing anything in their favour. The
book of Est. has its setting in this period, and it tells a wonderful story
of the prominence which certain Jews attained at the court of Xerxes.
But to say nothing of the romantic character of the story, the scene
is laid in the Pers. capital, and even Mordecai in his exalted station
never does anything to serve the interests of his brethren in Judah.
Moreover, the book reveals an inveterate hostility to the Jews on the
part of the Pers. officials. It may be, if my surmise is right regarding
Ezr. 4⁴⁻⁶, that the completion of the temple and the re-establishment
of the cult in Jerus. had provoked the hostility of the foreign peoples
in the province, and that enmity would be a decided check upon any
further achievements.

But the condition described in the vv. named above creates an urgent
demand for the great enterprise of the Pers. period. The vv. certainly
connect better with the building of the walls than with the building of
the temple. In ancient times a city without walls was no city at all.
A handful of people could walk into Jerus., with its few houses and
sparse population, and do what they listed with temple, pr., and people. Jerus. could not possibly maintain its place, or advance to a position worthy of its temple, and of its being the religious centre of the
Jewish world, unless it was enclosed with walls.

In the early part of the reign of Art. a new and large caravan of
exiles had come back to Jerus. (Ezr. 4¹²), and, seeing the situation of
affairs, immediately set to work to build the walls. The fact that it is
primarily these returned exiles who are found at work on the walls,
for Rehum *et al.* name no others, shows that there must have been a
large body. That conclusion is confirmed by the disastrous conse-

quences which the complainants fear should the walls be completed.
The fact that Rehum *et al.* took the matter seriously indicates plainly
that there must have been a large number at work. We may contrast
their attitude to the sneers of Sanb. and To. at the notion that the
feeble Jews under Neh. could rebuild the walls (Ne. $3^{33 \text{ f.}}$ EV. $4^{2 \text{ f.}}$).

Rehum, Shimshai, and others at once write a letter to Art., relating
their discovery of the operations at Jerus., and warning the king that
once the walls are up his peaceful rule of the Judean province will
be at an end. The authors of the letter show exactly the same hostility to the Jews that we find in $4^{4 \text{ f.}}$. They are no mere investigators
like Tattenai *et al.*, but have a definite purpose to keep down the Jews,
so that they will continue easy prey. They were all the more alarmed
as they perceived the large size of the company of workmen who were
evidently preparing to make Jerus. their permanent abode. Perhaps
just because of the large numbers found in the city, they were constrained to appeal to the Pers. king rather than attempt to act for
themselves.

Art. indorsed the charge, finding on the historical records confirmation as to the rebellious character of the people, and ordered the work
to come to an end. Backed by this royal edict, and in view of the possible opposition of the large number of Jews, supported by a considerable armed force (*v.* on 4^{23}), the complainants go to Jerus. and exceed
at least the letter of their instruction by destroying the work already
completed. And judging from the ample force of workmen and the
considerable time which had elapsed, the major portion of the work
may have been finished, so that it could easily be said of their depre-
dations: "The walls of the city are breached and its gates burned with
fire" (Ne. 1^3). For if Neh. completed the walls in fifty-two days, as
said in Ne. 6^{15}, there could have been little left to build after work
which may have continued for a much longer time than fifty-two days.
The destruction of the work already done was necessary. It would
have been vain merely to serve an injunction on the Jews, as that
would leave open the possibility of completing the walls secretly.

Soon after this, certainly within twenty years, Neh. comes to Jerus.
with an appointment as governor of Judah, and with permission to
build the city of his fathers' sepulchres (Ne. 2^5). His commission
seems to have been purposely left somewhat vague; it is quite certain
that he said nothing specifically about the city walls.

Neh. is thoroughly familiar with the abortive attempt to build the walls
which had been made a few years before, and in his own plans provides
against the causes of failure. In the first place, he carefully screens
his main purpose until the time for action has come. At the first
appearance of the enemy, they only know that he has come "to seek
good for the sons of Israel" (2^{10}). In the second place, he makes no
move until he has completed his arrangements so that the work can be

done quickly. If another appeal is made to Art., by the time a reply comes no force that can be collected in Sam. will be able to undo his undertaking. Very likely the remainder of the earlier unsuccessful enterprise facilitated his work, for there may have been some sections undisturbed or but partly demolished by Rehum and his army.

In the third place, he came to Jerus. backed by an armed guard, so that a force mustered from the peoples of the lands would not be a serious menace at any time. Ezra was content to take his caravan across the desert without military escort, trusting in the protection of the Most High (Ezr. $8^{21 f.}$); but Neh. did not trust the gracious influence of his God upon the enemies of his people, and was glad to be supplied with a guard (2^9), which, it is safe to assume, was as large as he could possibly secure. Apart from that he seems to have carried from Pers., or secured elsw., a liberal supply of weapons, so that at the proper moment he could convert his whole force of workmen into a well-equipped army (4^{8-17}).

In the fourth place, contrary to the Chr.'s idea as revealed in c. 3, Neh. did not attempt to erect the gates until the last stone was laid in the walls (6^2 7^1). The wooden gates of the city, acc. to c. 3 ten in number, were the most vulnerable parts of its defences. An enemy might easily slip up at night with a torch and undo in a moment the labour of days. The gates were of little use, save as a check, exc. as they were guarded by troops, a guard established by Neh. as soon as the gates were in place ($7^{2 ff.}$). While the people were at work on the walls, the guarding of all the gates would be impossible, and so that part of the work was deferred until the last, so that it would never be possible to say of his work " that its gates had been burned with fire."

These considerations are sufficient to show why Nehemiah succeeded where others had failed, and that in spite of the fact that from the moment he set foot in Jerusalem until the last gate was built, locked, and guarded, the enemies of his people had been persistent, numerous, active, and resourceful. Despite all their efforts, by scorn, cajolery, open war, secret intrigue, and black treachery, they failed, because they were overmatched in the struggle by their great opponent, Nehemiah the son of Hachaliah.

The only other achievement of Neh.'s first period as governor of Judah, barring the measures to procure a population for Jerus. ($11^{1 f.}$), was the relief of the distress of the poor people who had been ground down by their richer and more powerful neighbours (c. 5). The pas-

sage is of great importance in the light it throws upon the social conditions of Judah in the period 444–432 B.C., and for the welcome addition to our knowledge of the character of Neh. He was not for an
instant deaf to the cries of distress, and he was generous in his own
contributions for their relief. He constantly used his personal funds
to redeem his brethren who had been sold into slavery. If Neh.
was a eunuch, as is quite possible, he had probably entered the service of the Pers. king as a poor slave, and in the later days of his power
and wealth did not forget his early suffering, and was keenly sympathetic toward others in like situation. Further, he served without
salary. He knew that the people were poor; he had learned that his
predecessors, who may have been Pers. since the time of Zer., had
borne hardly upon the people by their exactions.

It is usually said that Nehemiah's second administration began in 432 B.C. That statement is incorrect. Nehemiah says
plainly that he was governor of Judah for twelve years, from the
20th to the 32d year of Artaxerxes (5^{14}), and that in the latter
year he returned to the king (13^6), so that 432 was the end of
his first administration.

All the evidence we have for the date of the second period is the
scrap in $13^{6 \text{ f.}}$, "and at the end of days I asked [leave of absence] from
the king and I came to Jerus." But the text is much at fault, as the
notes show, and in his memoirs there is no hint about the time when
he returned to Jerus. But it must have been later than 432; for in his
absence several grievous wrongs had developed: To. had been given
a residence in one of the temple chambers (13^{1-9}); the Lev. had been
compelled to give up their ministrations in the sanctuary and scatter
into the country to earn a living (13^{9-14}); a general disregard of the
Sabbath had grown up, so that work in the fields and traffic at Jerus.
went on unquestioned and unhindered (13^{15-22}); marriages had been
contracted with the Philistines, and the speech was becoming corrupt
(13^{23-27}); one of the members of the high pr.'s family had married
the daughter of Sanb. the Horonite (13^{28-30}). All these things presuppose that Neh.'s absence from Jerus. was a protracted one. That
is most probable from other considerations. Neh. never lost the
favour of the king, and it is doubtful whether Art. would have permitted another immediate absence. Indeed, it seems clear that Neh.'s
second visit to Jerus. was occasioned, like the first, by unfavourable
reports of conditions in the holy city. The brief way in which he
describes the big wrongs and the summary methods by which he sets
them right, all point to his coming to Judah with a definite purpose
in his mind. It is probable that Neh. secured his second leave of ab-

sence by relating to the king the evil conditions about which he had
heard and his desire to remedy them.

But if we lack a *terminus a quo* we are more fortunate in the recent
discovery of data which provide a reliable *terminus ad quem*. For the
letter from the Jewish garrison at Elephantine was addressed "to
Bagohi the governor of Judah" (בגוהי פחת יהודה), the very same title
which Neh. applies to himself (5[14]). The date of this letter is 407 B.C.,
and therefore Neh.'s rule came to an end before that. Bagohi was
ruler in the time of Dar. II, 423–404, and prob. by his appointment. Now Art., the patron of Neh., died in 424 B.C. As Neh.'s
second appointment must have come from him, at least the beginning
of the second administration must have preceded that date. An interval of five or six years must have separated the two administrations,
and therefore the second leave must fall very near the end of the
period of Art. The material we have indicates that the second administration was very short; prob. it came to an abrupt end by the
death of the king. Certainly the events described in 13[6-31] fall between
432 and 424 B.C., and most likely close to the latter date.

The historicity of the second administration of Neh. depends upon
the conclusion reached above that 13[6-31] is a genuine part of N., though
in a less pure form than c. 1–6. Those who, like Torrey, assign c. 13
to the Chr. must needs begin and end Neh.'s mission with the building of the walls. Torrey's chief point against the passage, outside of
the language, is that the Neh. here "is simply Ezra (*i. e.*, the Chr.),
under another name" (ES.[248]). There is, indeed, enough resemblance
to lend colour to such a view. But the differences are too marked to
make it tenable. The basis for the objection to foreign marriages is
very far removed from that in Ezr. 9 *f.* To suppose one person to be
the author of both passages seems to me impossible. Then the animus against To. and Sanb. is certainly characteristic of Neh. Again,
the methods by which wrong conditions are set right are absolutely
at variance with all that we know of Ezra. Ezra does, indeed, pluck
out hair, but from his own head (Ezr. 9[3]); Neh. also plucks out hair,
but from the head of the wrong-doers (13[25]). It is impossible to think
of Ezra saying to the traders: "if you do it again, I will lay my hand
upon you" (13[21]). If the Chr. wrote this passage with Ezra in his mind,
I should say that he made Ezra act throughout in a manner perfectly
characteristic of Neh.

Further, it is inconceivable that the Chr. should abruptly have changed
to the first p. in v. [6]. He had been travelling along very well in the
third so far. If he lent colour to the story by the adoption of the first
p., why did he not employ it throughout and thus make the whole
narrative probable? Surely the Chr. did not intend to leave Ne. 8–13[5]
open to suspicion, and then suddenly put the closing section in such a
form that we must accept it alone as genuine. He must have con-

sidered his own writing just as good as Neh.'s. Moreover, why should
the Chr. invent such a pitiably incomplete story of a second administration?

It is apparent that the section of N. found in 13⁶⁻³¹ was not a separate composition, but a part of the story found in 1–6. And yet a
section is lacking, for 13⁶ presupposes information which we do not
possess, *i. e.*, the occasion of Neh.'s return to Jerus.; 13¹⁻⁵ suggests
what the material was like. Just as Neh. had heard of the bad condition of the people and of the walls (1³), that report being the occasion
of his first visit, so now there had been brought to him reports of other
evil conditions which stir him to make a second appeal to the king
and a second journey to Jerus. Unfortunately the memoirs have been
condensed in some respects—a passage must have fallen out between
vv. ⁶ ᵃⁿᵈ ⁷—and expanded in others, as best accorded with the editor's views.

(4) *The Reign of Artaxerxes II Mnemon*—404–358 B.C.

We have seen good reason to place the mission of Ezra after
that of Nehemiah (*v. s.* § 10), but the grounds for fixing the
date more closely are very slender. We have apparently no
authority save that of the Chronicler for the name of any Persian king in connection with Ezra, and whatever may be said in
his favour as a historian, he certainly is not to be trusted on
questions of chronology. Ezra himself alludes to his royal
benefactor simply as " the king," and Artaxerxes is only mentioned in the Chronicler's introduction, Ezr. 7¹· ⁷, and in the
Aramaic document. The latter is certainly not authentic in
its present form, and may be wholly an invention. At the
same time 7²⁷ requires some antecedent, and there may have
been in the genuine E. the original decree, of which we have
only an amazing elaboration. Certainly we dare not follow
Kosters and give Ezra's date as 398 B.C., for "the 7th year"
is entirely untrustworthy. And yet the conclusions reached
above as to the interval between the two leaders would suggest that Ezra's work was done in the first quarter of the fourth
century.

For the history of Ezra we have two sources, his own memoirs,
7²⁷ ᶠ· 8¹⁵⁻¹⁹· ²¹⁻²⁵· ²⁸ ᶠ· ²¹ ᶠ·᷎ ³⁶ 9¹⁻¹¹ᵃ· ¹³⁻¹⁵; and the rest of Ezr. 7–10, and Ne.
8¹⁻¹² ᵒʳ ¹⁸, partly if not wholly due to the Chr.

We turn first to sure ground in E. As said above, 7²⁷ shows that we are forced to begin *in medias res*. E. must have contained some account of the favour of the king, a parallel to Ne. 2¹⁻⁹. The outburst of praise is due to the fact that the Pers. king had given Ezra permission to go up to Jerus. at the head of a caravan. That is exactly what we have in the beginning of the decree, 7¹³, and therefore we cannot deny the possibility that there is a germ of an original element here, of which element more anon.

Ezra's story is very unlike Neh.'s. He loves graphic details, and spends much of his space on such points as the gathering and composition of his company, the measures taken for a safe journey, the custody of the treasures intrusted to him—that is all that we find in the authentic portions of c. 8. Upon his arrival in Jerus. we have information in E. merely of the report of the mixed marriages, of his distress over these tidings, and of his prayer—for that is all there is in c. 9.

How much dependence is to be placed on the rest of the story about Ezra is certainly open to question. We have, at all events, a note to guide us, even though it is somewhat indefinite. In praising God for the favour of the king, he states what that favour consists in, viz., "to glorify the house of God which is in Jerus." (7²⁷). The word "glorify" is found elsw. only in Is. 55⁵ 60⁷· ⁹· ¹³ and is used there of the temple twice; it is, indeed, somewhat vague, and yet these words must provide the key to Ezra's mission. It is consistent with this key that when Ezra inspected his company at Ahava and found neither pr. nor sons of Levi (*v.* on 8¹⁵), he kept his caravan in camp until he had brought from Casiphia a sufficient number of "ministers for the house of God" (8¹⁷). Another leading subject in this part of E. is the proper safeguarding of the large treasures which Ezra had collected for the temple. In other words, all of E. in c. 8 supports absolutely the conclusion that Ezra's whole mission was designed to carry out the king's purpose "to glorify the house of God which is in Jerus."

Now if we examine the Aram. document containing the decree, we find a part of it in harmony with this key. The pr. and Lev. were expressly authorised to return with Ezra; he was directed to take to Jerus. the offerings made by the king and his officers and by others (presumably Jews), which had been given for the purpose of glorifying the house of God; and was given instructions to use these funds for the purchase of supplies required for the temple ritual. Therefore this part of the decree 7¹²⁻²⁰, barring a few obvious amplifications, is perfectly consistent with the main purpose of Ezra, and if it is not original, but a production of the Chr., then this strange historian for once composed a work more than usually in harmony with its setting. If this part of the decree is authentic, then of course the date of Ezra is fixed in the reign of an Art., and that could only be Art. II.

The rest of the story of Ezra must be judged by its consistency with

this central theme. Now the Lev., whom Ezra was at such pains to
bring with him, are employed in other ways than in the ministrations
at the temple, and therefore the passage Ne. 7^{70}–8^{12} is open to grave
suspicion, while the later portions of that c., the account of the Feast
of Booths (8^{13-18}) is in better state.

It may seem that Ezr. 9, which is mostly from E., would have to be
rejected on these grounds. But a closer inspection establishes a good
connection. When Ezra learned that a large number of people, including pr. and Lev., had intermarried with foreigners, he could see
that his plan to glorify the house of God would be hopeless. To maintain the temple ritual with proper dignity requires a people of pure
blood, for the amalgamating people will result in an amalgamating
religion. This intermarriage must be checked before any glorifying
of the temple is possible. The sequel to Ezra's lament (Ezr. 10) is
not from his hand, but in the main it tells a true story. There are
striking features which suggest another pen than the Chr.'s. Surely
something must have happened after Ezra's prayer, and there is no
improbability in the divorce story in its main features.

If Ezra had anything to do with the establishment of the law—and
our sources for this event are really scanty and poor—this part of his
work could have come about only as the conditions he discovered constrained him to turn aside from his main purpose. Sta. emphasises
the fact that according to our sources Ezra was the possessor of the
law, not its author (*Gesch.* ii,$^{140, n. 2}$). When he learned of the mixed
marriages and had taken appropriate measures to break them up, he
might well have felt that the people must conform to the law in all
respects before there was any hope of making the temple worship the
central interest in Jewish life and religion. But it must be remembered that at most Ezra's connection with the law was slight and
incidental. Our idea of Ezra's part in the law must depend largely
upon our opinion of the credibility of the decree (7^{12} ff.).

The c. dealing with the reading of the law (Ne. 8) has caused much
discussion, chiefly as to its proper place. Kost. is confident that
it must follow Ne. 10. He argues that in c. 8 a new law is introduced, and the only new law must be the pr. code. He analyses
c. 9, 10 and finds no reference to this code. In this way he thinks he
finds a suitable place for the troublesome list, 7^{6-72}, for after Ne. 9, 10
the people felt the need of organisation, and a list was made of those
in the newly organised community. As he deems the list closely
bound with c. 8, he places the whole section, 7^{6}–8^{18}, as the direct sequel
to Ne. 9, 10 (*Wied.*$^{73-87}$).

Torrey with equal confidence places this section, 7^{70}–8^{18}, between
Ezr. 8 and 9. He gives the following reasons for the transposition
(ES.^{252} ff.): (1) To quote his own words: "here is a clear and consist-
ent story, the only clear and consistent story dealing with Ezra that

has ever been told by any one." (2) "The dates given in such pro-
fusion throughout the narrative are now all intelligible for the first
time." (3) He sees an incongruity between c. 8 and the c. following,
finding nothing to account for the sackcloth and ashes in 9¹, but deem-
ing Ezr. 10, which he thinks lacks a conclusion, good grounds for the
mourning. (4) "Ezra makes his journey to Jerus. in order to teach
and administer the law, but it is not until 13 years after his arrival
that he first presents it to the people." (5) Another point on which
much stress is laid is that in the present arrangement the divorce of
the foreign wives (Ezr. 9 f.) was effected according to the law, and that
before the law was made known.

Formidable as the array of arguments is, it is not convincing. I
make a few comments. (1) It is not possible to make any clear and
consistent story out of Ezr. 7–10 and Ne. 8–10, for the latter c., outside of c. 8, never contain Ezra's name, and there is no reason for connecting them with Ezra at all. If the Chr. had written them as a part
of his Ezra story, Ezra being his great hero—a point emphasised by
Torrey—he would not have omitted his name in that long passage.
(2) Many of the dates are too indefinite to enable us to make a chron.
sequence that is convincing. (3) Ezr. 9 is certainly not very closely
connected with Ezr. 8. But after c. 8 we must advance to some report
of the first thing Ezra did after establishing himself in Jerus. There
is no reason why he should have done one thing more than another.
As for the grounds for the sackcloth and ashes of Ne. 9¹, it seems to
be a poor sequel to Ezr. 10⁴⁴. After the compliance with Ezra's plea
and the putting away of the foreign wives in accordance with the
law, it would be more natural to expect a period of rejoicing, such as
we have in Ne. 8⁹⁻¹², than a scene of humiliation as described in Ne.
9. It would be vain to comply with the law, if the result were only
sackcloth and ashes. (4) In E. the law is never mentioned, but his
appeal is general to the commandments of God (Ezr. 9¹⁰· ¹⁴). As shown
above in his own description of the purpose of his mission, the establishment of the law has but a dub. place. (5) This point is not well
taken. The Hebrews were always averse to foreign marriages. Abraham makes his servant swear that he would get a wife for Isaac from
his own people (Gn. 24 J); Samson's parents are disturbed at the
plea of the hero for a Philistine wife (Ju. 14³); and finally the prohibition of foreign marriages is in "the little book of the covenant" and in
Dt. only (Ex. 34¹⁶ Dt. 7³), pre-ex. laws. Since there was a temple of
Jaho in Jeb., contrary to the Deut. law, Sachau argues that this law
could not exist in 407 B.C. Others have given a different interpretation
of the surprising fact. But in any case there is no doubt of the pre-ex.
ban upon marriage with foreigners. It is really absurd to suppose
that the Jews must wait upon Ezra's reading of the law to learn that
such marriages were forbidden.

It is necessary now to consider Torrey's radical theory that Ezra is wholly a creation of the Chronicler; in other words, that Ezra is not a historical personage, but a character of fiction.

Torrey's arguments are based largely upon the language of the Chr., which he deems esp. abundant in the Ezra story. Again, he urges that Ezra "was a man precisely like the Chr. himself: interested very noticeably in the Lev., and esp. the class of singers; deeply concerned at all times with the details of the cult and with the ecclesiastical organisation in Jerus.; armed with lists of names giving the genealogy and official standing of those who constituted the true church: with his heart set on teaching and enforcing the neglected law of Moses throughout the land; and—most important of all— zealous for the exclusion of the 'people of the land,' the condemnation of mixed marriages, and the preservation of the pure blood of Israel! There is not a garment in all Ezra's wardrobe that does not fit the Chr. exactly" (ES.²⁴²).

A large part of this description does not fit the Ezra we know in the memoirs, e. g., there is not a single reference to singers in E.; there is not a word about the law; there is no genealogical or other list of names. The criticism is decidedly indiscriminate.

Further, no person would contend that in all the period from 400 down to his own time, the Chr. was the only person interested supremely in the matters enumerated in the passage quoted above. Ezra was a kindred spirit to the Chr.—and there must have been many such before the Chr.'s time—and the Chr. by his revisions and additions has doubtless made Ezra more kindred to himself than he really was.

Another reason urged by Torrey is the silence of Sirach (*Comp.*⁶¹ᶠ·). Sirach writing apparently *c.* 180 B.C., composed a long passage (c. 44–50) in praise of the great men of the Jewish nation. Of those in our period, Zer. and his associate Jes., and Neh. are accorded brief mention (49¹¹⁻¹³), but Ezra's name is not found. This seems to me the weightiest of Torrey's arguments. It is certain that Ezra did not have the place in the Jewish church in the time of Sirach that the Chr. would have liked. But it is certain that there was never an edition of the book of Ch. (including Ezr.–Ne.) which did not contain the story of Ezra, though there may have been an edition silent about Neh. The book of Ch. may be pretty late, but it is not as late as Sirach. To give no other reason here, the author of the hymn had these records for Zer. Jes. and Neh., and therefore he must have had them for Ezra. Why he made no mention of Ezra's name, it is impossible to learn. He left out other names, e. g., Shes., and he omitted Ezra for some good reason, possibly because he was not in as deep sympathy with the ruthless proceedings described in Ezr. 10 as the Chr. was.

If Sirach was silent, other writers made up for the defect by the exaltation of the priest-scribe. In several prophetic lists, *e. g.*, Iræn. *Ag. Her.* l. xxx. 11, Ezra appears in the list of prophets in place of Mal. (*v.* Nestle, *ZAW.* 1907,[115]).

§ 12. CHAPTER AND VERSE DIVISIONS.

It is unfortunate that in several books of the OT. the EV^s. follow 𝔐 and in places have a different arrangement of chapters from those in MT. It is necessary in a critical commentary to follow the original text. Fortunately there is but one section in Ne. where the confusion exists, and there is none in Ezr. The appended table will serve as an adequate guide. The English division is really the better, as it conforms to subject matter.

MT.	Eng.	MT.	Eng.	MT.	Eng.
III, 33	IV, 1	3	9	11	17
34	2	4	10	12	18
35	3	5	11	13	19
36	4	6	12	14	20
37	5	7	13	15	21
38	6	8	14	16	22
IV, 1	7	9	15	17	23
2	8	10	16		

The only other variation is in Ne. 10, where MT. 10^1 = Eng. 9^{38}, 10^2 = 10^1, etc., the number of the vv. in EV^s. throughout the c. being one less than that of MT.

§ 13. LITERATURE.

As there is a comprehensive bibliography in Curt. covering much the same ground, for the most part only special works on Ezr.–Ne. are named here.

Commentaries.

Rabbi Saadiah, *Ezr. and Neh.* ed. by H. J. Mathews, 1882. E. Bertheau, *Die Bücher, Esra, Nech. u. Ester,* 2d ed. by V. Ryssel, 1887. S. Oettli u. J. Meinhold, *Die Gesch. Hagiographen,* 1889. H. E. Ryle, *Ezr. and Neh.* in Camb. Bib. 1893. W. F. Adeney, *Ezr.–Neh.–Est.* Exp. Bible, 1893. H. Guthe and L. W. Batten, *Ezr. and Neh.* in *SBOT.* 1901. M. Seisenberger, *Die Bücher Esd., Neh. u. Est.* in

Kurzgef. wissensch. Com. z. d. H. S. des A. T. 1901. D. C. Siegfried,
Esr., Neh. u. Est. in *Handkom. des A. T.* 1901. A. Bertholet, *Die
Bücher Esr. u. Neh.* in *Kurzer Handkom. des A. T.* 1902. G. Hölscher,
H. S. A. T. 1910.

Monographs.

Kleinert, *On the Origin, Elements and Antiquity of the Books of Ezr.
and Neh.* 1832. R. Smend, *Die Listen d. Bücher Esr. u. Neh.* 1881.
A. H. Sayce, *Int. to Ezr. Neh. and Est.* 1885. J. Imbert, *Le Temple
Reconstruit par Zorob.* 1889. G. Rawlinson, *Ezr. and Neh.* (*Men of the
Bible*), 1890. P. H. Hunter, *After the Exile*, 1890. A. van Hoonacker,
Neh. et Esd. 1890; *Zorob. et le Second Temple*, 1892; *Nouvelles Études sur
la Restaur. Juive,* 1896. W. H. Kosters, *Die Wiederherstellung Israels
in der persischen Period* (from the Dutch *Herstel van Israel in het.
Perzische Tijdoak*), by A. Basedow, 1895. E. Meyer, *Die Entstehung
des Judenthums*, 1896. Bertholet, *Die Stellung der Israeliten u. d.
Juden z. d. Fremden*, 1896. E. Sellin, *Serubbabel*, 1898; *Studien z.
Entstehungsgeschichte der jüd. Gemeinde*, 1901. T. K. Cheyne, *Jewish
Religious Life After the Exile*, 1898. J. Geissler, *Die liter. Beziehungen
der Esra Memoiren*, 1899. Rosenzweig, *Einl. in d. Bücher Esr. u.
Neh.* J. Nikel, *Die Wiederherstellung d. jüd. Gemeinwesens nach d.
babyl. Exil*, 1900. C. Holzhey, *Die Bücher Ezr. u. Neh.* 1902. S.
Gelbhaus, *Esra u. seine reformatorischen Bestrebungen*, 1903. J. Fischer,
Die Chron. Frage in d. Büchern Esr.-Neh. 1903. J. Theis, *Gesch. u.
literarkritik Fragen in Esr.* 1-6 (in Nikel's *Alttest. Abhandl.* 11, 5),
1910. C. C. Torrey, *Comp. and Hist. Value of Ezr.-Neh.* (*Beihefte zur
ZAW.*), 1896; *Ezra Studies*, 1910. *Apparatus for Text. Crit. of Chr.-
Ezr.-Neh.* (Harper Studies).

Articles.

H. Winckler, "Die Zeit der Herstellung Judas"; "Nehemias Reform."
Alt. Forsch. II, ii, 1; "Die Zeit v. Ezras Ankunft in Jerus." *ib.* II, ii,
2; "Die doppelte Darstellung in Ezr.-Neh." *ib.* II, iii, 2. E. Schrader,
"Die Dauer d. zweiten Tempelbaues," *Stud. u. Krit.* 1867. E. Nestle,
"Marginalien u. Materilien,"[23-31], 1893; *Real-Ency.*[3] V. J. Wellhau-
sen, "Die Rückkehr d. Juden a. d. Babyl. Exil," *G. G. N.* 1895.
T. F. Wright, "Nehemiah's Night Ride," JBL. 1896; "The Stairs
of the City of David," *ib.* 1897. C. C. Torrey, "Old Testament
Notes," JBL. 1897. W. J. Moulton, "Über die Überlieferung u. d.
text-krit. Werth des dritten Esrabuchs," *ZAW.* 1899,[209-258], 1900,[1-34].
Fraenkel, "Zum Buch Ezra," *ZAW.* 1899. T. K. Cheyne, "From
Isaiah to Ezra," *AJT.* 1901; "The Times of Neh. and Ezra," *Bib.
World*, 1899. H. Howorth, *PSBA.* 1901, 1902. H. G. Mitchell, "The
Wall of Jerus. Acc. to the Book of Neh." JBL. 1903. L. W. Batten,

"Ezr.–Neh."; "Ezr."; "Neh." Hast. *DB.* Kosters, "Ezr.–Neh." *EB.*
J. V. Prášek, "Kambyses u. d. Überlieferung d. Altertums"; "Zur Chronologie des Kyros," *Forsch. z. Ges. d. Alt.* L. W. Batten, "Israel of the Post-exilic Period," *Hom. Rev.* April, 1913.

General.

A. Kuenen, *Gesammelte Abhandlungen,*[212-251], 1894. B. Stade, *Bibl. Theologie des A.T.*[311-356], 1905. Addis, *Ezra and the Issue of the Law, Documents of the Hexateuch*, II,[189 ff.] Robertson, *Poetry and Religion of the Psalms*, c. 5. Marquart, *Fundamente israel. u. jüd. Geschichte*, 1896. C. F. Kent, *Israel's Hist. and Biog. Narratives,*[339-364], 1910.

Biblical Aramaic.

Powell, *The Supposed Hebraisms in Biblical Aramaic*, 1907. S. Baer, *Chaldaismi Biblici Adumbratio*, in the Baer-Delitzsch ed. of MT. vol. Dn.–Ezr.–Ne.[xiii-lx]. H. L. Strack, *Grammatik des B. Aram.*[4], 1905. K. Marti, *Kurzgef. Gram. der B.-Aram. Sprache*, 1896. E. Kautzsch, *Grammatik des B. Aram.* 1884. Sachau, *Aramäische Papyri und Ostraka aus Elephantine*, 1911. C. R. Brown, *An Aramaic Method*, 1884. Schulthess, *Miscellen zum Bibl. Aram. ZAW.* 1902,[162 ff.]

Some Important Dates.

B.C.
559–521 Cyrus.
521–485 Darius I Hystaspis.
520 Rebuilding of the temple.
485–464 Xerxes.
464–424 Artaxerxes I Longimanus.
444–432 Nehemiah governor of Judah.
424–404 Darius II Nothus.
404–359 Artaxerxes II Mnemon.
Mission of Ezra.

A COMMENTARY ON EZRA-NEHEMIAH.

EZR. I = ESD. 2¹⁻¹⁴. THE END OF THE BABYLONIAN EXILE.

Bab. was conquered by Cy. in 539 B.C. In that country he found many colonies of foreigners who had been brought there as prisoners of war in accordance with the As. and Bab. policy of transplanting conquered peoples. Cy. reversed this policy, and allowed all such peoples to return to their homes. In the city of Bab. Cy. found also many sacred images and other objects from foreign temples, brought there as trophies, or by Nabonidus for protection (*cf.* Is. 46¹ ᶠ·). The new king directed all these images to be taken back to their native shrines. This policy was designed to effect the pacification of the peoples he conquered. Indeed, he appeared in Bab. as a redeemer rather than a conqueror. In accordance with this general programme we have the statement that a special decree was issued in favour of the Jews (*v. Intr.* § ¹¹· ¹). Vv. ¹⁻⁴· ⁷ ᶠ· ¹¹ᵇ are from a Heb. source, the rest by the Chr. (*Intr.* § ⁸· ⁴).

1-4. The decree of Cyrus.—In the first year of his reign in Babylon we are told that Cyrus set forth an edict, allowing all captive Jews to return to Jerusalem, directing them to rebuild the house of their God, and enjoining their Jewish neighbours who remained behind to strengthen their hands with gifts to be used for the temple, and probably ordering the restoration to the returning pilgrims of the sacred vessels which had been taken from the temple in 586.

1. *And in the first year of Cyrus*]. Cyrus had ascended the throne in 559 B.C. His first year is put here twenty years later, either because the Chronicler only knew of Cyrus as ruler of Babylonia, or because the previous years of his reign are deemed unimportant in connection with Jewish history. Cyrus entered Babylon in the late autumn of 539 B.C., and this decree may, therefore, fall in the year 538. Cyrus, like his successor Darius, was a descendant of Achæmenes and was, therefore, an Aryan and a Zoroastrian. However much of a monotheist he may have been in Ansan, he was very liberal in his attitude toward the gods of other peoples.—*King of Persia*]. The great Persian empire did not reach its full height of power until the time of Darius, and this title, therefore, has been regarded as a mark of the Chronicler's hand. This contention is invalid, for in the inscription of Nabonidus, 546 B.C., the same title is employed.—*To fulfil the word of Yahweh*]. Here we have a conception of history which abounds in the Gospels, especially in Matthew. The idea of the evangelist is that the acts of Jesus are determined by the predictions which have been made long before. The true conception from the Hebrew point of view is that God controlled both the messages of the prophets and the actions of kings, and therefore the king is led to fulfil the prediction. In the pre-exilic period the apologetic appeal is based on the works of God; in our period this new element is introduced. The exiled Jews are aroused to a new faith in God because things happen as the prophets have foretold. This idea is brought out prominently in Is. 48, a passage belonging to this very time. "The restoration was the last special proof and sign that God was a factor in the life of the Hebrew people under the old dispensation" (Simon, *Bible as Theocratic Literature*,[69]).—*From the mouth of Jeremiah*]. In 2 Ch. 36[22] we have "*by* the mouth," but without any difference of meaning. *By* places the emphasis on the prophet as a mere instrument of God.

In 2 Ch. 36[21] there is a reference to the fulfilment of another Jeremian prophecy that the exile would last seventy years (Je. 29[10]; *v.* Curt.). This passage is sometimes loosely interpreted as referring to the same thing; but that is incorrect. The prediction refers to the moving of Cy. to issue his decree in favour of the Jews. Je. contains no passage referring to such an event, but the required prophecy is found in Is.[2] (*v.* 41[2 f. 25] 44[28] 45[1]). This prophet ascribes Cy.'s victories to Yahweh, using language very similar to Cy.'s own, only that in the latter Marduk is the moving spirit (*cf.* Cy.'s Inscription, Rogers, *Cun. Paral*,[380]). In Is. Cy. is called Yahweh's shepherd, having responsible care of his people, and even by the Messianic title "his anointed." This prophet certainly had great expectations from Cy., and he watches his conquering career with keen anticipations of good for his own people. Jos. regards Is. as the prophet who influenced Cy., saying that Cy. rd.

the book written by Is. one hundred and forty years before the temple
was destroyed (*Antiq.* xi, 1, 2). "Je.," therefore, is either a txt. err.,
or else this anonymous prophecy (Is. 40–66) was attributed to that
prophet instead of to Is. (*v.* Duhm, *Jer.*ix). Berth. and Ryle refer
the passage to Je., but wrongly. If a txt. err., it is an early one, for
it is reproduced in all the Vrss. Prob. it is explained from the reference to Je. properly in the preceding v. of Ch., this name being
repeated instead of the correct one.

Yahweh moved the spirit]. (See v. ⁵.) This expression shows
the more refined theological ideas of the later times. The
prophet makes Yahweh address Cyrus directly. Now we find
a spirit in man which may be influenced to action by Yahweh,
and henceforward that is the method by which God's will
is accomplished among men. *Cf.* Nehemiah's expression "my
God had put in my heart" = moved my spirit (Ne. 2¹²).—*And
he issued a proclamation*], literally, *caused a voice to go through.*
The words suggest a herald rather than a written document,
and the heraldic method is not improbable here, though the
words might refer to a decree, especially if it were read by the
heralds.—*In his whole kingdom*]. The empire of Cyrus embraced regions where there were no Jews. The Hebrews were
apparently settled in districts and were pretty well localised.
The writer seems to have ignored any realm of Cyrus except his
latest conquest. The edict would naturally be sent only to the
Jewish colonies in Babylonia.—*And also in writing*]. These
words imply that the proclamation was oral, and are intended
to show that the Chronicler had a written source for his version
of the edict.—*Saying*], better *as follows.* The literal translation mars the Scriptures sadly, recurring hundreds of times, and
proving a stumbling-block in reading aloud.—**2.** *All the kingdoms of the world*]. With the conquest of Babylon, all its de-
pendencies fell to Cyrus, and his became a vast empire, extending from Elam on the east to the Mediterranean on the west.
This did not cover all the countries of the world, but the exaggeration is more natural for Cyrus than for a Jewish writer, for
on the cylinder inscription he calls himself "the king of the four
quarters of the earth," *i. e.*, of the whole world.—*Has Yahweh*

given me]. Here we have the reflection of the prophetic utterance in Is. 45¹ ᶠᶠ·. In his own inscription Cyrus attributes his conquest of Babylon to Marduk, its chief deity. But he may have become acquainted with the prophecies above referred to, and then in an edict to the Jews given their God credit for his victories. Such credit would please the Jews, as the aid of Marduk was certainly claimed to placate the Babylonians. —*The God of heaven*] is an expression not found in pre-exilic writings. The common terms are God of Israel, of hosts, or of our fathers.* Nehemiah, however, regularly uses the expression (1⁴ ᶠ· 2⁴· ²⁰). In a magic bowl from Babylonia of about 500 B.C. "Lord of heaven and earth" occurs.† The term "God of heaven" is found in the Eleph. pap. Marti regards the expression as the equivalent of the "high God," or "God of the height," in Mi. 6⁶ and thinks it portrays the transcendence of God (*Dodekapropheton*,²⁹²). The expression was never common among the Hebrews. Stade explains it as an adaptation to the religious terms of the governing peoples (*BT*.³²⁵).

To build a house for him in Jerusalem]. In Is. 44²⁸ we have a prediction that Cyrus would direct the rebuilding of Jerusalem and of the temple. If Cyrus had been made familiar with this prophecy, as Josephus says, he might easily see in it the commission to which he here refers. The Chronicler knew that the temple was not built by Cyrus or in his lifetime; it is, therefore, difficult to see why he should have invented a statement contrary to fact. The truth is that the Chronicler tried to make it appear that the temple was begun under Cyrus, and was compelled to misconstrue his material in justification of his theory.—A Jewish writer would not have deemed it necessary to say *Jerusalem which is in Judah* unless he were endeavouring to give colour to an imitation decree, a device in which the Jews were not expert. It appears from the terms of the edict that the interest of Cyrus was not in the freedom of the Jews, but in the building of the temple to the God to whom he here as-

---

* It is a curious fact, mention of which has not been observed by the present writer, that in Ch. "God of Israel" is used with great regularity up to II 7¹¹, and after that almost invariably "God of (our) fathers."

† J. A. Montgomery, *Mus. Jour. U. P.* Dec. 1910.

cribes his wonderful victories. The release of the captives was
incidental to the main purpose.—**3.** In MT. this verse is corrupt, so that the sense has been changed.—*Among you*] indicates
that the edict is addressed to the whole people of Cyrus's realm;
but the edict primarily concerns *all his* (Yahweh's) *people*. As
the text stands, the edict enjoins all Jews to return to Jerusalem
to build the temple; whereas in v. ⁵ it is stated that those only
went up whose heart was stirred by Yahweh. With hints found
in the Vrss. it is possible to reconstruct the text, obtaining a
terse and lucid statement which might well be a part of a royal
decree. The restored text gives: *whoever wills of all the people
of Yahweh the God of Israel, he is the God who dwells in Jerusalem,
now let him go up to Jerusalem and build the house of Yahweh
his God.*

> The statement that Yahweh is the God who dwells in Jerus. is nat-
> ural in this text. Cy. found many gods in Bab. who had been brought
> there from other places, and whose devotees were distressed by their
> removal. He sent all these gods back to their ancient shrines. To
> him Yahweh seemed much like the other deities. Further, according
> to this text, Cy. did not command all Jews to return; but he permitted
> those to go back who desired, and thus the decree is in harmony with
> the statement of v. ⁵. The amended text shows clearly that Cy.'s main
> object was the rebuilding of the temple.

4. The next subject in the decree is the provision of funds for
building the temple. The implication of the text is that the
Babylonian neighbours of the returning Jews were called upon
for contributions. *All that survive* covers the whole body of
Jews in Babylonia, and as they are to be *supported* by *the men
of his place* these can be no other than the Babylonians. Cyrus
did all in his power to placate the conquered peoples, and he
was too politic to demand from them subscriptions to build a
temple for the despised Jews. If we accept this text we are
forced to admit a powerful Jewish colouring. With the help of
Esdras we are enabled to reconstruct the passage (v. ᵃ) thus:
and all that dwell in the places, let them support him. This naturally means that the Jews, who dwell in the districts from
which certain exiles are departing, shall send by their hands

gifts for the temple. The wealthiest people would be most likely to remain for commercial reasons, and they are the ones able to contribute most.—*With silver and gold, goods and cattle, besides the free-will offerings for the house of God*] implies donations for the caravan of pilgrims as well as for the temple. We might well wonder whether Cyrus would be concerned about the people. The last clause is different in Esd., *and with other things added by vows for the temple of the Lord*, implying that all the gifts were for the temple. *Goods and cattle* is probably a gloss.—*Which is in Jerusalem*] is the translation of 𝔊, but Esd. has *who*, requiring *God* as antecedent instead of *house*. It is not possible to differentiate in Hebrew. The rendering *which* tends to discredit the decree, as Cyrus would not order a temple built and in the next sentence imply that it was already built. The rendering of Esd. harmonises best with the expression in v. ³, *he is the God who is in Jerusalem.*

> *The edict of Cyrus.*—There is another version of this edict in 6²⁻⁵, claiming to be a copy of an original found at Ecbatana. The two Vrss. differ materially. In the Aram. version there is nothing about Yahweh's aid in Cy.'s conquests, the permission to return to Jerus., or the contributions; but plans are prescribed for the new temple, the cost is to be borne by the royal treasury, and the return of the sacred vessels is expressly enjoined.
>
> Both Vrss. profess to be original, but one or both must be wrong. Few defend the Heb. version, though Dr., Ryle, *et al.* accept the substance, admitting a marked Jewish colouring. Mey. accepts the Aram. as authentic, and deems the Heb. a product of the Chr. It is difficult to understand why the Chr. should incorporate an authentic edict, and then himself compose one so at variance with his source, though he might easily insert two different forms which he found in the documents he used. Mey. starts with the hypothesis that all the letters and edicts in Ezr. are Aram. Vrss. of the Pers. originals (*v. i.* on 4⁷). This position has been widely accepted, apparently without much critical sifting. Torrey has shown its weakness (ES.¹⁴⁴ ᶠᶠ·); indeed, it seems to rest on little more foundation than bare assumption. We are, therefore, really driven to purely internal evidence. From this point of view the Aram. edict does not commend itself. For Cy. would not be chiefly concerned with the dimensions of the temple, and the figures given are altogether improbable. Nor would he be likely to order the expenses paid out of the royal treasury. Certainly the best evidence we have, in Hg. and Zc., indicates that the cost was borne

by the Jews themselves. Indeed, the long delay was accounted for on
the ground of the people's inability in material things (Hg. 1² ᶠ·).   '

In the Heb. edict, on the other hand, there is no note of improbability, save in the matter of Bab. contributors, and here the Chr. apparently retouched the passage to suit himself (v. s.). The original
very likely enjoined the Jews who remained in Bab. to send contributions by those who returned. Yet few scholars have any good to say
of this version. Sieg. remarks that it shows itself to be a forgery, since
it is given in the Heb. tongue, and since it is dominated by Jewish religious ideas. Against this it may be remarked that the Chr. would
scarcely incorporate the Pers. or Bab. original. Moreover, since the
edict was for the benefit of the Jews, it may have been originally issued
in Heb. As to the Jewish conceptions, they do not seem to be any
more marked than we should expect. To pacify the Bab., Cy. writes
in his inscription with pronounced Bab. religious ideas; why should he
not do the same thing for the Jews?

It is difficult to think that the Chr. composed the edict at all. Save
in v. ⁴ it does not seem to have any of his peculiar characteristics. If
he had invented it, he certainly would have followed his Aram. source
in c. 6, to which he could have had no earthly objection. To be consistent with his policy Cy. must have allowed the Jews to return and
to rebuild their temple and to take back any treasures which had been
taken from it. Nikel notes that "'may his God be with him' has a
genuine Bab. tinge" (PB.⁵⁷). The Chr. would not have said " he is the
God who is in Jerus.," nor would he have explained that Jerus. was in
Judah; and he never calls Yahweh " the God of heaven." It is very
doubtful if he would have exalted Cy. as this document does. On
the whole, then, there seems to be ample reason for asserting that Cy.
did give the Jews permission to return and to rebuild the temple. The
emended text which I have proposed confirms the belief that we may
have an authentic document here. It is true that Hg. and Zc. make
no reference to this decree, and it would have served their purpose
well; but they were speaking a score of years later, and were concerned more with the will of God than with the will of a dead king.

1. The conj. ו, with which the book begins, is explained by the
original connection of Ezr. with Ch. (Berth. Sieg.). But Ex. Lv.
Nu. Jos. Ju. 1 and 2 S. 1 and 2 K. Ruth, Est. 2 Ch. and Ne. (disregarding the title) also begin with ו. It seems to be the rule to begin a Heb. narrative with the conj.—שנת] st. cstr. before a prep. (cf.
Ges.§ ¹³⁰).—כורש] Pers. *Kūruš*, Bab. *Kuraš*, whence Rawlinson would
point כּוּרֶשׁ.—We must rd. לְכַלּוֹת] since דברי is the obj. The mng. *to
fulfil a prediction* is not found elsw., but the context requires that sense
here; *cf.* 2 Ch. 36²¹, where למלאות has the same mng.—מפי] 2 Ch. 36²²
has בפי, preferred by Guthe, Torrey, *et al.* Esd. ἐν στόματι, but 𝔊
supports MT. Both forms are common, but מפי is better when utter-

ance is implied (so Ryle).—העיר רוח], only in late writers, v. ⁵, Hg.
1¹⁴ 1 Ch. 5²⁶ 2 Ch. 21¹⁶; but vb. alone has same mng. in Is. 41². ²⁵ 45¹³,
all referring to Cy., and influencing our author (*cf.* Mar. *Jes.* on 41²).
—ויעבר-קול] lit. *he caused a voice to pass over*, an oral proclamation,
Ex. 36⁶ (P); *cf.* "he caused a trumpet to pass over," *i. e.*, to be blown,
Lv. 25⁹. That is the sense here as we note from the added *and also
in writing.* In 2 Ch. 30⁵ the term is used where runners carry letters
from Hezekiah.—במכתב] would mean here *in a written form*, as 𝔊ᴸ
(in 2 Ch. 36²²) ἐν λόγοις γραφῆς, but this sense is not found elsw.
As the words are unnecessary and as לאמר goes back to the proclamation we suspect a gl.

2. ממלכות נתן לי] Obj. first for emph. Ges.§ ¹⁴² ᶠ. Esd. ἐμὲ ἀνέδειξεν
βασιλέα, 3 Esd. *me constituit regem*, RV. "hath made me king," better
proclaimed me king. After Esd. 1³⁴. ³⁷ = 2 Ch. 36¹. ⁴ this expression
would represent המליכני, lacking כל and נתן. The mng. is not the same,
as this text would be based on a phophecy, and MT. on the result
of a conquest. Esd. shows a text more closely associated with the
prophecies in Is.².—יהוה אלהי השמים] Esd. κύριος [+ ὁ θεὸςᴸ, κύριοςᴬ]
τοῦ Ἰσραήλ κύριος ὁ ὕψιστος. This suggests אלהי מרום as in Mi. 6⁶.
Guthe follows this text, but it may well be a Jewish amplification—
והוא]. The use of the pron. emphasises the fact of Yahweh's directing
Cy. to build the house.—פקד עלי] usually means *to bring upon*, or *visit
upon*, *i. e.*, punishment; there are, however, several passages, mostly
late, in which the sense required here is found, *i. e.*, *assigned to me.*
Esd. renders ἐσήμηνέν μοι, *he has given me a sign*, prob. by the word
of his prophet, showing again a closer dependence upon Is.²; ἐσήμηνεν,
however, usually represents הרוע, *shout*. In Is. 44²⁸ Cy. is called רעי,
and in view of the close relationship of that passage to our text, it is
tempting to propose here הרעיני, *he has made me shepherd.*

3. This v. is obscure and difficult. בכם barely admits of interpretation. The sf. in עמו and אלהיו refer, one to Yahweh and the other to
מי, a dub. construction; the phrase *may his God be with him* is in an
awkward place; the Chr. has יהוה for יהי; the last clause is superfluous
where it stands; and *which is in Judah* is tautologous after v. ². Turning to the Vrss. we find in modern editions of 𝔊 that the first clause is
an interrogative, *Who is there among you of all his people?* For יהי 𝔊 has
καὶ ἔσται; ויעל is ἀναβήσεταιᴮᴬ, ἀναβήτωᴸ. 𝔊ᴮ ends with לירושלם. ᴬ
lacks יהוה after בית. 𝔊ᴸ adds μετ' αὐτοῦ at end of v. In Esd. we find
ὑμῶν for בכם instead of ἐν ὑμῖν as 𝔊. אלהיו appears as κύριος αὐτοῦ in
ᴮ, showing an original יהוה; in ᴬ κύριος is repeated; in ᴸ we have
κύριος without the pron. following. The last clause is rendered οὗτὸς
ὁ κύριος ὁ κατασκηνώσας ἐν Ἰερουσαλήμ. This clause is lacking in ᴸ,
but most of it appears earlier in the v. ᴸ is quite divergent in the
first part thus: τίς οὖν ἐστιν ὑμῶν ἐκ τοῦ ἔθνους αὐτοῦ ὃς προθυμεῖται
τοῦ πορευθῆναι; ἔστω ὁ κύριος μετ' αὐτοῦ ὁ κατασκηνώσας ἐν Ἱερου-

σαλήμ, καὶ ἀναβὰς κ. τ. λ. Here we note a part. οὖν (BA εἰ . . . οὖν), really necessary to the sense, and the verbs προθυμεῖται and κατασ-κηνώσας, which are not in Heb. 3 Esd. has also a peculiar and brief text, viz., *si quis est ex genere vestro, Dominus ipsius ascendat cum eo in Jerus.* *Among you* is lacking, but there is a faint reflection in the *your* people instead of *his.* The superfluous *which is in Judah* fails here as in Esd.B, which appears in L only as an adj. τὴν Ἰουδαίαν. The commentators mostly ignore the difficulty, though Berth. after Guthe favours restoration of προθυμεῖται as making the permit less general, and regards the last clause as "an intentional imitation of the style of the foreign king." Guthe regards the last words as a gl., noting their change of place in Esd.L. He wrongly says in 𝔊L also, for 𝔊L has the clause in same place as MT. with μετ' αὐτοῦ added. For προθυμεῖται τοῦ πορευθῆναι Guthe proposes המתנדב ללכת (or יתנדב), and προθυμεῦται invariably represents התנדב; but unless one disregards MT. altogether, it is impossible to extract this word. We have not far to go, however, to find a word closer to the text, for בחר suits the sense, and might easily be corrupted to בכם. עמו is obviously impossible, but the moment we make the necessary changes of יהי to יהוה, it follows that we must rd. עַמֵּי, or possibly עַם. In the first case we have only the common change of י to ו; in the latter ו was attached to the vb. when יהוה was changed to יהי (*v.* 𝔊, cited above), and was moved back to the n. If the pl. was original the mng. was practically *tribes* or *clans.* Perhaps there was enough discord among the Bab. Jews to make Cy. think that many peoples worshipped Yahweh. Then to get a suitable text we must presume that two lines were transposed: rd. *people of Y. the G. of Is., he is the God who dwells in Jerus.*, a change supported by Esd.L. This clause then bears no marks of a gl., nor of an attempt to imitate Cy., but is a necessary definition to be exact in an edict. אשר is corrected after Esd. to השכן. אשר ביהודה is prob. an accidental repetition from the preceding v.; it is certainly unnecessary here. אלהיו fits admirably after בית יהוה. The whole v. then I would restore thus: מי לכן בחר מכל־עם יהוה אלהי .ישראל הוא האלהים השכן בירושלם ועל לירושלם ויבן את־בית יהוה אלהיו

It is granted that this result requires considerable changes, but the Vrss. show that correction is necessary. As frequently happens in these books, L preserves some original features, which, as usual, are obscured by corrections to conform to MT., corrections fortunately mostly by addition, so that the original may still be picked out.—
4. This v. is not much clearer. The involvement is so great that translation is almost impossible. Moreover, the Vrss. again show departures which can hardly be due to the freedom of a translator, and the Gk. renderings elsw. in these books show close fidelity to their original. 𝔊 proper shows mostly the surviving MT. But Esd.L has some good material. That text has καὶ ὅσοι κατὰ τόπους οἰκοῦσι

βοηθείτωσαν αὐτῷ προθυμείσθωσαν τῷ κυρίῳ ἐν τῷ τόπῳ αὐτοῦ ἐν χρυσίῳ κ. τ. λ. 3 Esd. *quotquot ergo circa loca habitant adjuvent eos qui sunt in loco ipso.* We note that the perplexing נשאר is lacking and that גר becomes the leading vb.; in this respect BA agree. אנשי is lacking while מקומו has a new connection. A new vb. is introduced. This may represent וְכָל־הַנָּרִים בְּמְקוֹמִית יְנַשְׂאֻהוּ וְיִתְנַדְּבִי לִיהוה בְּמְקוֹמִו. This is a vast improvement over MT. and shows an earlier and better text. It is prob. not original, but is more primitive than MT. In the list of gifts 𝕲L has δώρων for הנדבה, τοῦ ἑκουσίουBA. וברכוש = ἐν δόσε-σιν μεθ' ἵππων καὶ κτηνῶν in Esd., so 3 Esd. This would, perhaps, be ברכוש עס־רכש ובהמה. Guthe corrects רכוש to רכש, but ignores δόσεσιν. עס־הנדבה is in 𝕲L μετὰ δώρων = עַס־נְדָרִים, and more fully in Esd. σὺν τοῖς ἄλλοις τοῖς κατ' εὐχὰς προστεθειμένοις. This is found in 3 Esd. too, and may be a priestly amplification, though it more likely shows a different text. אשר is rendered in 𝕲 with האלהים as antecedent, but in Esd. with בית. With the emendations proposed above, based on Esd., the edict as a whole runs thus: *All the kingdoms of the world has Yahweh the God of heaven given me, and he has charged me to build him a house in Jerus. which is in Judah: therefore whoever wills of all the people of Yahweh the God of Israel, he is the God whose abode is in Jerus., now let him go up and build the house of Yahweh his God. And all that dwell in the places let them support him, and make free-will offerings to Yahweh, with silver and gold and with the free-will offerings for the house of God who is in Jerus.*

If the above be the original form, many of the objections urged against the edict are removed, although the emendations were not made with that end in view. Esd.L certainly had no such purpose. It appears that the decree was not issued to the whole Bab. nation, but only to the Jews. Cy. would hardly proclaim to the Bab. that his conquests were due to Yahweh and thus contradict his inscription. But he might have said this to the Jews. Moreover, the Jewish element in Bab. fifty years after the fall of Jerus. must have been comparatively insignificant. There would be no use of a national proclamation to authorise their release.

[הנשאר] might easily mean *those who are left behind, i. e.,* in Bab. (*cf.* Ex. 10²⁶ Nu. 11²⁶); but it means also *those who survive, a remnant,* being equivalent to שארית (*cf.* Ne. 1² ᶠ·).—[גר] always refers to a temporary rather than a permanent residence and shows that the Jews regarded their stay in exile as transient.—[ינשאהו] from *lift* or *carry* the mng. *support* or *assist* is naturally derived, a sense found also in 8³⁶ Est. 9³ 1 K. 9¹¹.—[רכוש] is a very comprehensive term covering personal property of any kind, including cattle. It is rather a general term for an edict. What it is intended to comprise here it is impossible to say. The word occurs only in P and other late sources, and is prob. a loan-word from Bab. *rukušu.* It occurs curiously 5 t. in Gn. 14, the story of Abraham's campaign against the kings of the East.

5-11. Gifts for the temple.—The decree having been issued, the next step is to put it into effect, and this is immediately undertaken. The people prepare to depart; contributions are secured; and the sacred vessels, of which the temple had been plundered a half century before, are returned by Cyrus.

In a part of this passage at least the Chr.'s hand is manifest. The vv. which come from his hand, [5. 6. 9-11a], really add nothing in the way of historical information.

5. *And arose to go up*]. קוּם is often used as here in a sense like *prepared*. Three classes are mentioned, the chiefs, the priests, and the Levites, the last two being separate classes as in P, no longer identical as in Dt.—*The heads of the fathers*], *i. e.*, the chiefs of the clans, an expression occurring frequently in P and the Chronicler (BDB.). *Fathers* in these passages has the sense of family or clan. It is an abbreviation of "house of the fathers," which naturally means family.—*Of Judah and Benjamin*]. These two tribes are named as the elements out of which postexilic Israel is composed (*cf.* 4^1 Ne. 11^4). In other books we find the same combination (1 K. 12^{23} 1 Ch. 12^{16} 2 Ch. 11^{12}). In the last-named passage we have the definite statement that Benjamin as well as Judah adhered to Rehoboam after the revolt of the northern tribes. The boundary between the two kingdoms was never very sharply defined, and as Jerusalem was on the Benjamite border, it would be natural that this tribe should for the most part cast in its fortunes with the south. There were, therefore, Benjamites as well as Judeans in Babylonia.—*All whose spirit God stirred up*]. This is interpreted in exactly opposite senses. B.-Rys. finds a fourth class of Jews, as if it read "and all others whose spirit God stirred up." But that implies that the leaders alone went of their own accord, and others only as they were moved of God. The Chronicler shows in c. 2 that his primary interest is in the leaders, lay and ecclesiastical. It is, therefore, better to construe the clause as a case of apposition limiting the preceding, so that the sense is that not all the chiefs, priests, and Levites left Babylonia, but only those whom God moved to go up to build the temple (so Sieg.). In v. ¹ it was *Yahweh* who stirred the spirit of Cyrus; here *God* moves the people. The former name may be due to the influence of Is.²; the latter is the Chronicler's usual term. The Chronicler says "house of Yahweh," but that is a technical term.*

6. *And all their neighbors*], equivalent to *the men of his place* in v.⁴, and referring to the Jews whose spirit was not moved to go to Jerusalem. The use of *all* indicates that every neighbour of the returning exiles made an offering for the temple. —*Strengthened their hands*], literally, *put strength in their hands*, is a common expression in Hebrew for "encourage," Ju. 9²⁴ Is. 35³ Ezr. 6²² Ne. 2¹⁸ 6⁹. There is no other case where it refers to material support, and yet that would be the most natural meaning. The list of gifts should be exactly the same as in v. ⁴. Here we have *vessels* of silver, *choice things*, a new element, and a different expression for the free-will offerings. We have seen evidence of textual errors in v. ⁴ and there may be more of it here. *Vessels*, which is not found in v. ⁴, is certainly an error creeping in from v. ⁷.—**7.** *Now King Cyrus had brought out*]. The unusual order, subject preceding verb, brings out the fact of an attendant circumstance rather than a chronological sequence. The delivery of the temple vessels did not necessarily follow the gathering of a caravan and the collection of subscriptions, but may have been coincident with the issue of the decree. Indeed, in the Aramaic version (6⁵) the surrender of these vessels was a part of Cyrus's original order.—*Vessels*]. כלי means *vessels* or *implements*. The list shows that both are meant here. English has no single word to cover both suitably, though *utensils* approximates the requirement. Nebuchadrezzar had plundered the temple each time he captured Jerusalem, in 598 B.C. (2 K. 24¹³) and 586 B.C. (*ib.* 25¹³ ʰ·).—*And placed them in the house of his God*], as trophies of victory and as tokens of the superiority of his god. Similarly the ark had been placed in the temple of Dagon (1 S. 5²). The temple in Jerusalem probably had such treasures from the shrines of conquered

---

* G. A. Smith notes that in Ch.-Ezr.-Ne. "Sion" is not found, but the phrase "house of God which is in Jerus." occurs often to describe the temple site (*Jer.* i,¹⁵⁰).

nations. "The things which David his father had dedicated" (2 Ch. 5¹), which were put in the temple by Solomon, were doubtless booty from David's wars. In Esd. we have *in his house of idols*, showing the narrower Jewish conception of the Babylonian temple.—**8.** *By the hand of Mithredath the treasurer*]. Mithredath, or, as it is better known in the Greek form, Mithredates, is a Persian name. In the time of Xerxes there was a Persian officer of Syria bearing this name (4⁷). He must have been the treasurer of the temple, since he is intrusted with the disposition of the property of the sanctuary.—*And he counted them*]. The subject must be "Mithredath," though a strict construction would require "Cyrus." The verb has a pregnant sense, the full meaning being, *he counted them as he delivered them* to Sheshbazzar.

> Shes. has often been identified with Zer. The motive was largely apologetic, and yet there is this textual evidence, that in the Aram. document (5¹⁴⁻¹⁶) Shes. is said to have laid the foundation of the temple, whereas in later parts of this book as well as in Hg. and Zc., Zer. is the temple-builder. Again, it may be urged that Shes. disappears completely after c. 1, and in c. 3 Zer. appears as leader without any intr. On the other hand, the Aram. document describes the work of Zer. and speaks of Shes. as an earlier leader, as he undoubtedly was. The fact is that there is a gap between c. 1 and c. 3. Indeed, the history in these books is not continuous, but fragmentary, as evidenced by the fact that there is no hint about the death of any of the leaders, nor even of the close of their rule.

9 f. According to our text the list of utensils comprises 30 *golden vessels*, 1,000 *silver vessels*, 29 *censers*, 30 *golden bowls*, 410 *silver bowls*, 1,000 *other utensils*, 2,499 in all, a surprisingly large number, yet in v. ¹¹ the total is given as 5,400, the sort of discrepancy commonly found in such lists.

> In Esd. we find a larger total, 5,469, and the itemised figures agree with this, the only consistent text, and therefore accepted by Nikel. But the agreement of the total with the separate items may be artificial. There is a list of articles taken from the temple in 586 B.C. (2 K. 25¹⁴ ᶠ·), but no numbers are given. Some of the words used here do not occur elsw., and it is difficult to identify the objects confidently. Doubtless the Solomonic temple contained many votive offerings of gold and silver which were of little use.

11. *The whole Sheshbazzar took up*]. He was not only the receiver of the temple treasures, but the leader of an expedition, known as the *golah*, which went from Babylon to Jerusalem. —*Golah* properly means *exile*, but it has also a figurative sense, *a company of exiles*, and that is the meaning here. It is used constantly in these books as a national name (Kue. *Abh.*[219 f.]), and that use is responsible for the erroneous idea that the post-exilic community was made up entirely of those who had come from Babylonia.

The c. ends abruptly and the story is incomplete. Torrey professes to have restored the missing section (ES.[25 ff.]). As a matter of fact, the recovered material serves far better as an intr. to c. 3, and is fully discussed in that connection. Pretty nearly all the stories in these books end abruptly.

5. ראשי האבות] is a technical term occurring often in P and Ch. The full but less frequent form (see Dn. on Ex. 6[14. 25]) is ר׳ בית הא״, *heads of the fathers' house*, and therefore chiefs of clans.—לכל] The prep. is explained by Haupt as an emph. part. like the Ar. and Bab. use (Johns Hopkins circulars, XIII, No. 114, Ges.[§ 143]). Such a foreign influence is unlikely in Ch. and a nearer explanation is possible since the writer may have been influenced by the ל with יהודה. Torrey explains in sense of "namely," calling it a characteristic of Ch. (ES.[121, n. 1]). The clause is rel., אשר being omitted as it frequently is (*cf. Dav. Syn.* § 144 r 5).—**6.** סביבתים] properly means *surrounding places*, but in both m. and f. there are cases where *surrounding people* is the true sense, m. Ps. 76[12] 89[8] Je. 48[17. 39]; f., Ps. 44[14] Ez. 16[57] 28[24] Dn. 9[16].—בידיהם] the only case where a prep. is used in this phrase, though Lv. 25[35] is very similar, but this is the sole instance where material support is meant. Torrey regards it as a mere copyist's error.—בכלי כסף] cannot be right; *vessels* would be appropriate below in connection with the temple, and this list must originally have agreed exactly with that in v. 4. Esd. reads ἐν πᾶσιν ἐν ἀργυρίῳ = בכל בכסף, putting כל in app. with the rest of v. This text is accepted by Guthe, Kittel, *et al.* The mng. would then be: *supported them with everything* [named in the above decree, viz.] *with silver*, etc.—ברכוש] Esd. 2[8] ἵπποις = רכֶשׁ.—ובמגדנות] Esd.[BA] καὶ εὐχαῖς ὡς πλείσταις πολλῶν ὧν ὁ νοῦς ἠγέρθη, Esd.[L] εὐχαῖς πλ. ὧν ἠγέρθη ὁ νοῦς εὐθύς. לבר has been rd. as לֵבָב not לְרֹב as Guthe suggests. Torrey calls Guthe's change indispensable (ES.[122, n. o]). The passage is pretty corrupt, but the sense of this text is good, *with the numerous votive offerings of many whose heart was stirred.*—**7.** יהוצי[א]] 𝕲 ἔλαβεν, Esd. μετήγαγεν[B] μετήνεγκε[AL], both texts testifying to a different word from יהוציא.—Guthe and Kittel suggest הסיר on basis of Esd.

Torrey with greater probability proposes הביא.—8. Before על־יד] 𝕲ᴸ
has ἔδωκεν, Esd. παρέδωκεν, and Sieg. accordingly adds ויתנם. In
8²⁶˙ ³³ we have שקל על־יד, a better expression, but our text may be interpreted as a pregnant expression, and 𝕲 may be only an effort at
clearness. The equiv. of על־יד occurs in Tell-Amarna Tablet No. 72.
ביד has same sense in Gn. 32¹⁷.—הגזבר] 𝕲 did not understand the word
and transliterates as a n. p., Τασβαρηνοῦᴮ Γαρβαρηνοῦᴬ, γανζαβραίουᴸ;
Esd. τῷ ἑαυτοῦ γαζοφύλακι. 𝕲 is apparently influenced by Bab. form
ganzabaru (Peiser, *ZAW*. xvii,³⁴⁷). The word occurs elsw. only in B.
Aram. 7²¹; it is originally Pers., though occurring also in Bab. (see
Mey. *Ent.*²⁴, and other references in Ges.).

9. אגרטלי] occurs only in this v. The mng. and derivation are both
unknown (*v.* Sta. *Heb. G.* § ²⁴³˙ ⁸). 𝕲 has ψυκτῆρεςᴬᴸ, a word not elsw.
found in 𝕲. The mng. *winecoolers*, or *cool places*, is impossible here.
Esd. reads σπονδεῖα. This is 𝕲's word for קשׂות, Ex. 25²⁹ 37¹⁶ Nu. 4⁷ 1 Ch.
28¹⁷, which means some vessel for holding liquid, and in those cases
was made of gold; *flagon* may therefore be the right mng. Torrey derives אגרטלי from Gk. κρατηρ, bowl.—מחלפים] α. λ. The mng. usually
given here is *knives*, based on derivation from חלף, but חלף does not
have the assumed mng. of *bore* (*v.* Moore's *Ju.* on 5²⁶), and the primary
office of a knife is to cut not to bore. In the Talmud חליפות means
knives. Esd. has θυίσκαι ἀργυραῖ, *silver pans*. Θυίσκη is the regular Gk.
rendering of כף, which is in the list of vessels carried from the temple
in 586 (2 K. 25¹⁴), and elsw. of temple vessels. Torrey proposes מלקחים
"snuffers."—**10.** כפור] elsw. only in 1 Ch. 28¹⁷, but 6 t. in this v. and
Ezr. 8²⁷; the mng. is plainly *bowl*.—משנים] RV. *of a second sort* is impossible, since no other silver bowls are mentioned. Guthe leaves a
blank in his text, but Esd. confirms the suspicion that the word is a
corrupted numeral. Esd. has 2,410 (3,410ᴬ). These silver bowls would
naturally be very numerous, and therefore אֲלָפִים should prob. be substituted. Torrey reads אלפים שנים, but there is no other case of the
dual אַלְפַּיִם with a numeral.—**11.** ל־ל] like As. *lu—lu = both—and* (*v.*
Ges.§ ¹⁴³ ᵉ).—הגולה . . . הכל] Esd. ἀνηνέχθη δὲ ὑπὸ Σαμανασσάρου ἅμα
τοῖς ἐκ τῆς αἰχμαλωσίας. So Guthe emends in part to העולים מחשבי.
The mng. is the same, but Esd.'s expression is better, *these were carried
from Bab. to Jerus. by Shes. together with those from the captivity.* Esd.ᴸ
has a different reading of whole v.: τὰ δὲ πάντα σκεύη χρυσᾶ καὶ ἀργυρᾶ
ἐκομίσθη ὑπὸ κ. τ. λ. There is no total number mentioned, and so a
little more emph. is laid on the transportation. This puts us on the
track of what the original text of Esd. must have been, since ᴮᴬ begins τὰ δὲ πάντα σκεύη ἐκομίσθη and then adds gold and silver and a
number. Having done this another vb. must be introduced, as ανηνέχθη.
Esd. then originally had merely *all the vessels were carried from Bab.
to Jerus. by Shes. and those from the captivity.*

Shes. 1⁸˙ ¹¹ 5¹⁴˙ ¹⁶ᵇ †. The Heb. form of the name is always the same

שֵׁשְׁבַּצַּר. But the Vrss. show great diversity. 𝔅 has *Sassabasar* in Ezr., and *Salmanasarus* in Esd. 𝔊 has these forms: (1) Βαγασαρ[B] 5[14], (2) Σαρβαγαρ[B] 5[16], (3) Σαβανασαρ[B] 1[8] (B lacks the name in 1[11]), (4) Σαβασαρης[L] always in Ezr., (5) Σαβανασσαρος[B] Esd. 6[17], (6) Σασαβαλασσαρος[L] always in Esd., (7) Σασαβασσαρος[A] always in Ezr., (8) Σαναμασσαρος[B] Esd. 2[11], (9) Σαμανασσαρος[B] Esd. 2[14], (10) Σαναβασσαρος[B] Esd. 6[19] [A] always in Esd.

It is clear that (1) and (2) are the same, *sar* being in one case initial, in the other final; and that (8) and (9) are the same, the μ and ν being transposed. In fact, the forms (3), (8), (9), (10) are easily reducible to one, and that should prob. be Σαναβασσαρος. It will be noted also that [AL]𝔅. have only two forms, one in Ezr., the other in Esd. By transposition of letters these texts agree with the Heb. in Ezr., *i. e.*, *Sassabasar*, but they disagree in Esd. It is generally held that the name is Bab., and may be *Samaš-bil-uzur* or *Sin-bal-uzur* (*v.* Selbie, *DB.* art. "Shes." *KAT.*[3, 286]). The question is therefore one of reading σας as *Shemesh*, or σαν for *Sin*. It is difficult to identify *Sin-bal-uzur* with שׁשׁבצר, therefore the former would be preferable; but if Shes. is the same person as Shenazzar, then the latter is better, and both Heb. names are a corruption of סִנְבַּצַּר, represented in several forms of Gk. of which No. 10 is the most original.

Shes. has been regarded as a Jew, as a Pers., as identical with Zer., with Shenazzar, and as an independent personage. Schroeder held that he was a Pers. officer, sent to secure the safety of the caravan (*cf.* B.-Rys. Kue. *Abh.*[219]). He was almost certainly a Jew. Bab. names were often given to Jewish children in Bab. (*cf.* Clay, *Light fr. Babel*,[403], Daiches, *Jews in Bab.*). Cy. would not have sent a Pers. in charge of the sacred vessels, for his policy was to pacify, not to irritate. The Chr. would not call a foreigner "prince of Judah," a distinctive Heb. title often applied to kings.

The identification with Zer. rests on his having credit for laying the foundations of the temple (5[16]), a task really performed by Zer. (Zc. 4[9]); on the title "governor" (5[14]), which really belonged to Zer.; and on his appointment by Cy. Zer. is called "governor of Judah" only in Hg. 1[1. 14] 2[2. 21]. Cy. prob. appointed Shes. as governor because he was already a Judean prince, and therefore his rule would please the Jews.

With far better reason Shes. is identified with Shenazzar (1 Ch. 3[18]), a son of the captive king Jehoiachin, and the uncle of Zer. (Mey. *ZAW.* xviii,[342], Winckler, *KAT.*[3, 288]). In that case he must have been about sixty years of age in 539, and by 520 would naturally have given place to his nephew. Both rulers would therefore hold office by virtue of their royal descent (Torrey rejects this identification, ES.[138]). נשיא is a general term, one who is exalted, and therefore applicable to any high officer. It is used rarely before Ez. The term is applied

to Solomon (1 K. 11³⁴), to Zedekiah (Ez. 7²⁷), to a future Davidic king
(*ib.* 34²⁴ *et pass.*), and to foreign princes (*ib.* 26¹⁶; Smith, *Jer.* i,³⁸⁷,
BDB.). The Chr. applies the term to tribal chiefs. The most that
we can infer from its use is that Shes. was the natural chief of Judah.
It is difficult to think of any one holding such a place who was not of
the house of David. The statement of the release of Jehoiachin in
561 by Evil-Merodach and his restoration to the royal state becomes
significant in this connection (*cf.* Mey. *Ent.*⁷⁸ ᶠ·).

Winckler maintains that Shes. continued his rule through the reign
of Cambyses (529–522), and that the opposition of the foreigners in
Ezr. 4⁴⁻⁶ was directed against him, as he regards Cambyses, not Xerxes,
as the right name of the king (*KAT.*³· ²⁸⁵ ᶠᶠ·). Kue. holds that he is
the *Tirshatha* of Ezr. 2⁶³, and that he was superior in authority to
Zer. and Jes. (*Abh.*²²⁰). The fact is that Shes. appears without intr.
and disappears without notice. Our sources contain no account of
his work other than the bare mention here, for Ezr. 5¹⁶ is certainly
unhistorical.

EZR. 2¹⁻⁶⁹ = NE. 7⁶⁻⁷¹. THE CENSUS OF RETURNED EXILES.

The passage falls into the following divisions: (1) A census
of the people of Israel, vv. ¹⁻⁵⁸ = Ne.⁶⁻⁶⁰ = Esd. 5⁷⁻³⁵. (2) A
list of laity who could not show their stock, and of priests who
could not prove their official status, vv. ⁵⁹⁻⁶³ = Ne.⁶¹⁻⁶⁵ = Esd.
5³⁶⁻⁴⁰. (3) The total figures of the census and the number of
slaves and animals, vv. ⁶⁴⁻⁶⁷ = Ne.⁶⁶⁻⁶⁹ = Esd. 5⁴¹ ᶠ·. (4) A list
of contributions, vv. ⁶⁸ ᶠ· = Ne.⁷⁰ ᶠ· = Esd. 5⁴³⁻⁴⁵.

There are really but three separate parts to the passage, for (1) and
(3) belong together, and the other two sections are independent. The
figures in (3) seem to be the totals of those catalogued in (1). In (2)
there is a figure given for the laity, which is prob. a gl., as there is no
figure for the suspended pr. (4) is the only section which in part is
duplicated in Esd.. for Esd. does not contain Ne. 7⁶⁻⁷¹. It is the part
which has been most liberally edited to make it a suitable preface in
the one place to the temple-building, in the other to the assembly for
reading the law. The passage seems to be more original in Ne., though
Ezr.⁶⁸ seems to be an original part of the temple-building story, and
this was probably amplified from Ne.

Acc. to Ne. 7⁵ this list is a record of "those who came up at the first,"
and it is assumed that this means the company of Shes. But "at the
first" is very vague, since Neh. wrote a hundred years later than Shes.

Neh. proposed to secure an enrolment with a view to securing residents
for the newly fortified Jerus. In the note on 7^5 it is shown that the
text is in error here; so Sm. (*Listen*) and many others. Manifestly a
record of a caravan a century before his time would have been of no
use for his purpose. Therefore the passage cannot be original in that
place, but Kue. regards the list as older than Ne. (*Abh.*[215]). Then the
narrative runs right on into the time of Ezra (8^1). It is evident that
the Chr. uses the list as a record of those who came with Zer. and Jes., a
disposition still clearer in the text of Esd.; indeed, in that version no
other connection is possible. But such an accounting for this list is
untenable. For (1) when we compare with other companies, the numbers are suspiciously large. (2) The place-names suggest a time when
the people were already settled in Judah (*cf.* Ne. 11^{25} ff.). (3) The
term "sons of the province" in v. 1 presupposes a time when Syria was
a regularly instituted satrapy of the Pers. empire. (4) The suspension
of pr. from the holy office (v. [62]) could scarcely precede the building
of the temple. (5) It is prob. that Neh. or Ezra ordered this suspension (v. [65]). (6) The interpolated v. [68] shows that the original was
later than the building of the temple. (7) The term "all the congregation" (v. [64]), a term inappropriate to a caravan, suggests a census of
the whole nation. (*v.* further We. *Isr. Jud. Ges.*[155]). If we accept Torrey's view of Esd. 4^{47}–5^6 (*v.* Intr. to c. 3), it is plain that further criticism is necessary; Esd. 5^4 begins "and these are the names of the
men who went up," but the only names found are those of Jes. and
Zer.; 5^7 virtually repeats the statement, showing that while the Esd.
text originally had a list, this is not the original list, but a substitute
prob. from a later Heb. source. Moreover, Ezr. 3^1 (or 2^{68}) seems to me
to join directly to Esd. 5^6, though Torrey sees no difficulty in the present arrangement.

It is easy to dismiss the matter as a mere invention of the Chr., Torrey saying that it was "deliberately repeated by him (to add as much
as possible to its importance)" (ES.[135]). Against this view, see Berth.[8].
The mere catalogue of names does, indeed, seem like the Chr.; but
many others cared for genealogies besides the oft-abused Chr. and there
are integral parts of the c. which are not due to his pen. There are
some positive results which may be deemed reasonable. Ne. certainly
contained a list of those who took up residence in the newly walled
city, bare of inhabitants (Ne. 11). Esd. shows clearly that it originally
had a list of those who came up with Zer. Lists are required, therefore, in both places.

There are many lists of names in these books, but the one before us
is the most comprehensive of all. The largest of all the caravans of
returning exiles may have been that which came with Zer. But on
the face of it this list is a record of those who came up with a number of
different leaders (v. 2). It appears to be an attempt to gather a com-

prehensive list of all who had come to Judah from the time of Zer. to
the time of Ezra. Indeed, what may be the original title of the list,
"the number of the men of the people of Israel" (v. ²ᵇ) would suggest
that the list is a census of all the Israelites in Judah, for Mey.'s interpretation of the term *Israel* as meaning those who came back from
captivity is exceedingly doubtful (*Ent.*¹⁸⁵, ⁿ. ²). The leaders are grouped
together, and so are the chief men who composed the various caravans.
It was probably made up in the time of Ezra, and may have stood as a
part of the Ezra documents. Certainly the unrelated passage, No. 2,
above, fits his age. The earliest notice of any attempt to make a line
of cleavage between Israel and its neighbours was in Neh.'s second
administration (Ne. 12²³ ᶠᶠ·). There is no indication of a concern about
the purity of the priesthood before Ezra's time. The whole list may,
therefore, stand in its true place in connection with Ne. 8, in spite of
the evidence of Esd. to the contrary.

Now it was the theory of the Chr. that postex. Israel was made up
exclusively of those who had returned from captivity. He therefore
must have a large number of returning exiles at the beginning, certainly before the building of the temple, at which task none but pure
Israelites must have a hand (Ezr. 4¹⁻³). Therefore he takes the largest
list found in any of his documents and substitutes it for the brief list
of those who had come up with Zer. When he interjected the reading
of the law into the history of Neh., he took the whole document Ne.
7ᵃ–8¹². By changing the purpose of Neh.'s assembly 7⁵ᵃ, and adding
7⁵ᵇ, he secured a suitable connection.

What value the list may have is hard to say. There was an interest
in such records in the postex. period, prob. growing out of the effort
to separate Israel from "the peoples of the lands." From that point
of view the section vv. ⁵⁹⁻⁶³ may be quite appropriate in its place.
Allowing for corruption this may be an authentic census of Israel in
the latter part of the Pers. period.

The numbers in the lists.—The numbers vary greatly in the two Vrss.
In the list of laity Ezr. and Ne. differ in half the cases, and there is
not a single figure in which all the texts agree. On the other hand,
there is but little variation in the lists of temple officers, pr. Lev. etc.,
suggesting a later text for that part. There is virtual agreement in
the grand total, 42,360, but we could scarcely hold with Seis. that the
agreement proves the figure to be correct. That total is far in excess
of the sum of the various figures scattered through the lists and from
which it presumably is derived. This has been explained by Guthe as
due to the loss of a number of individual data; but it is easier to suppose errors in the numbers than loss from the lists of such large numbers
as would be necessary to make the totals agree. Mey. supposes that
the numbers were not originally written in alphabetic characters, but
in cipher like the Phœnician (*Ent.*¹³⁶). The variation is a good illus-

tration of the extent of textual corruption in the OT., though it is
likely that numbers have suffered more than words. It is a curious
fact that if we take the maximum number in each case, and add the
3,005 in Esd. 5^{12} (B), we get a total of 43,761, not far from the correct
figure. But no conclusion can safely be drawn from this fact, as there
may have been an attempt to make the text consistent.

The variations in the names is explained by Seis. as due to three
reasons: (1) Jews who had enrolled to return with Zer. changed their
minds and remained behind, while others may have joined the caravan on the way; (2) many may have died on account of hardships of
the journey; (3) and minors may have been enrolled in one list and not
in another (Esd.–Ne.–E. *in loc.*). These reasons presuppose a fidelity
in the records which is scarcely borne out by the evidence. The
variations are not greater than in other cases of deuterographs, and
are to be explained as txt. err., sometimes made intentionally, more
often accidentally. The real interest is in the numbers, not in the
names, for names of living individuals are few. The people are grouped
by clans, towns, offices, and the importance lies in the number of
each group. Sm. calls attention to the fact that in this list the laity
stand first, while in other lists the temple officers take precedence
(*Listen*,[26]). He is in error to a degree, for in the strikingly similar
list in Ne. 11 = 1 Ch. 9, the laity are named first. Sm. explains the
precedence of the laity as due to the fact that in the first century after
the return the laity had the upper hand. He notes the invariable
naming of Zer. before Jer., and the absence of the high pr. in N. and E.

1–2[a] = Ne. 7[6–7a] Esd. 5[7f]. The introduction to the list.

—**1.** *And these are the sons of the province who came up from the
captivity of the golah*] shows a double limitation, the census
covering residents of the Persian province of Judah, but who
had been in Babylon. *Sons of the province* points to a period
when the country was well settled. The terms suggest an
effort to procure a list of Judeans who had come from the exile,
in distinction from those who had always lived in Judah. There
is no indication of a list of a caravan.—*Each to his city*] shows
that the pilgrims were already scattered over the country.—
2. *Who came with*]. There follow eleven names, twelve in Ne.,
usually regarded as a body of elders having supreme authority
at the time (Sta. *Gesch.* ii,[106]; Kue. *Abh.*[220]; Sm. *Listen*,[17]). It
is claimed that hints of such an official body are found in 5[5]
6[7, 14]. It is more likely that these men were the leaders of the

various caravans of returning exiles which kept coming to Judah throughout the Persian period (*v.* crit. n. on 2^b). *Nehemiah* would then be the well-known wall-builder.

1. בני המרינה] *cf.* Ps. 149^2, "sons of Zion," Ez. 23^{15}, "sons of Babylon," though text is dub. מרינה is applied in Est. 38 t. to the Pers. province, and it might here mean the district in Bab. whence the exiles had come. But in Ne. 1^3 it certainly means Judah, and it has the same mng. here.—ושבי הגולה] is redundant and is found only in parall., Ne. 7^6; elsw. שבי alone is used in the same sense. In the earlier books שבי means "prisoners," but in Ch.–Ezr.–Ne. it has the abstract sense. In 8^{35} we have "the captivity the sons of the exile"; בני הגולה may be a gl., or בני may have dropped out of our text.—לבבל] lacking in Ne. but found in all texts of Esd. The omission in Ne. was prob. accidental on account of the preceding בבל. The error is early, as the Vrss. testify. The word means Babylonia, the country, not Babylon, the city.—וליהורה] as Ne.^{6} is the more correct form.—**2.** אשר באו]. Ne.^{7} הבאים a difference shown also in 𝔊. Esd., however, has οἱ ἐλθόντες, supporting Ne. ^{B} lacks the expression in Ne. Ezr. has 11 names, Ne. 12, Esd.^{L} 13, Μαιφαρ being added; 𝔊^B in Ne. has 14, adding Ἔσρα and Μασφαρ. Ezra's name properly belongs in the list; the latter may be a repetition of מספר.—ישוע] is regarded as a late form of יהושע, יהו becoming יו and יו becoming יֵ (*v.* Gray,^{156}). In the contemporary Hg. and Zc. this name appears as יהושע, from which it would appear that the shortened name was later than this period and may be due to the influence of 𝔊, which usually renders: Ἰησοῦς = ישוע.—שריה] Ne.^{7} עזריה. Esd. 5^8 Ζαραίος^B Σαραίος^L. Since Ἀραίος^B is an evident error for Σαραίας^{AL}, the Vrss. offer no real help. Both are common names. Seraiah was the name of Ezra's father. He might be the one intended here. In that case we should infer that Ezra came up with his father.—רעליה] Ne. רעמיה. Ῥεέλμα^A (in Ne.) gives slight support to Ezr. Neither name occurs elsw. After this Ne. has a name נחמני which E. lacks. The name is supported by Esd. Ἐνήνιος and even in Ezr. Νεμάνι^L. This person is not mentioned elsw.—מרדכי. This can scarcely refer to Est.'s kinsman, and the name does not occur otherwise.—מספר] Ne. מספרת. The Vrss. support their texts exc. that Esd. (Ἀσφαράσος) suggests the latter form, and this is accepted by Guthe. Marquart suggests *Aspadat*, a Pers. name (*SBOT.*^{69}). Neither name occurs elsw.—בגוי] 𝔊 Βαγουα, Βαγουαι^A, Βαγουαι^L, Βατουσι, Βατοει^B. The name may have been בִּגְוַיָה, but that form does not help in its explanation. Halévy reads: אבי־גוי, rejected by Gray (*Pr. N.*^{22}), and really without any support.—רחום] Ne. נחום Esd.^{B} Ῥοειμος, Ναουμ^L. The former is a well-known name in the postex. period, the latter does not occur elsw.

2ᵇ-35 = Ne. 7⁷ᵇ⁻³⁸ Esd. 5⁹⁻²³. The list of the laity.—
These are enumerated under two classes: (1) under the head
of the clan, the people being designated as *sons of Parosh*, etc.;
(2) under the name of the town in which they lived, these
being designated as *men of Bethlehem*, etc. Wherever these
designations are confused a textual error may be regarded as
responsible. There is less of such confusion in Ne. than in Ezr.

We note that we have: (1) a long list of personal names, ³⁻²⁰ or ³⁻¹⁹
if the *Gibeon* of Ne. is the correct reading; (2) a considerable list of
place-names, ²⁰ (or ¹⁹)⁻²⁹; (3) a short list of personal names, ³⁰⁻³²; (4)
place-names, ³³ ᶠ·; (5) and a single personal name, ³⁵. There are two
cases where the order in Ne. differs from that in Ezr., vv. ¹⁷· ¹⁹. It
is very prob. that in its original form all the personal names stood first,
with the place-names following, and Guthe has so arranged them in
his text. Otherwise we should have to explain the list as a growth,
names being added at the end and so causing the disarrangement in
the order.

Esd. here shows wide divergence from MT. Esd.ᴸ agrees throughout with MT. so far as the names are concerned, but ᴮᴬ lacks Hashum,
v. ¹⁹, Gibbar, v. ²⁰, Ai, v. ²⁸, Nebo, v. ²⁹, the other Elam, v. ³¹, and
Harim, v. ³². On the other hand, ᴮᴬ contain the following names
not found in MT. v. ¹⁵ Κειλὰν καὶ Ἀζητάς (קעילה ועזקה) Ἀζάρου (עֻזֻּר)
Ne. 10¹⁸) v. ¹⁶, Ἀννείς (Ἀννίαςᴬ), (חֲנַנְיָה Ne. 10²⁴), Ἀρόμ (חרים v. ³²);
v. ¹⁷, Βαιτηροῦς; v. ²⁰, οἱ χαδιάσαι καὶ Ἀμμίδιοι. It will appear, therefore, that Esd. follows Heb. in vv. ¹⁻¹⁶· ²¹⁻²⁸ᵃ· ³³⁻³⁵, but in the rest leaves
out some names and introduces others, and curiously the number lacking and the number added, counting combined names, is the same (six).
Four of the six added names stand between Ater of Hezekiah and Besai
(after v. ¹⁶), while four of the lacking Heb. names are virtually continuous. This is the place where Ezr. and Ne. have a different order. Following Guthe's identifications we get easily a new and prob. place-name,
the men of Keilah and Azekah sixty-seven, and two new clan-names,
Azzur and *Hananiah*. Βαιτηροῦς is certainly a place-name; Guthe
reads בֵּיתֵר and substitutes this for Gibbar, v. ²⁰; but Esd. has the incredible number, 3,005, while Gibbar has but 95. A more prob. explanation is found in 1 Ch. 2⁵¹ חרף אבי בית־גדר. The first word is a name
in Ne. (= Jorah v. ¹⁸). The meaningless Gibbar may be a corruption of Beth-Giddar, which in Ne. becomes the well-known but
unsuitable Gibeon. Beth-Giddar is in Judah and would be a proper
locality to connect with Bethlehem; in fact, these two places are
connected in 1. Ch. 2⁵¹. Each name is preceded by בני or אנשי. Here
again there is considerable diversity in use. In Ezr. we find *sons* exc.

before Netophah, Anathoth, Michmas, Bethel, and Ai; but in 𝔊 before
the last three only.   In Ne. we find *men* before the names Bethlehem
to Nebo, with which 𝔊 agrees exc. in having "men" before *the other
Elam*, and ^{LA} having "sons" before Bethlehem, Netophah, Anathoth,
and Azmaweth, these places not occurring in ^{B}.   Esd.^{BA} agree with
Ne., since οἱ ἐκ = אנשי, but ^{L} has "sons" exc. in two places, with
Michmash and with Bethel and Ai, and here we find ἄνδρες, a word
not occurring in ^{BA}.   It is safe to conclude that it was intended to use
"sons" before personal names, and "men" before place-names, but
that there was doubt about some of the names.   The system in Ne.
is nearly correct, "sons" being used for "men" before some place-
names at the end on account of the disarrangement of the list.   It
will appear below (on the place-names) that there are some doubtful
cases.

   The personal names.—There are 24 such names, though Jes. and Joab
are not given as heads of clans, and Senaah is very uncertain.   There
are other groups of personal names in our books: (1) Ezra's company
of returning exiles (Ezr. 8); (2) the list of those who divorced their
foreign wives (Ezr. 10); (3) the builders of the wall (Ne. 3); and (4)
those who subscribed to the covenant (Ne. 10).   List (1) contains the
clan-names, and then the individuals belonging to the clan.   Of the
12 clans there are but 2, Shekaniah^{5} and Shelomith^{10}, which are not
found in our list.   But in list (4), a record of clan-names only, less than
half are found in our list.   There are but 2 clans found in all the
lists, Parosh and Pahath-Moab, and these have the largest numbers
attached; 4 are found in three lists, while but 1, Arah, occurs only in
one list.   Reference should here be made to the valuable tables in
Sm.'s *Die Listen*, and to the glossary at the end of Berth.'s comm.

   The place-names.—Of the 20 place-names in MT., 14 are well known,
being found in pre-ex. records (or 15 if we include Gibeon as in Ne.).
Of the others, *Azmaweth* is dub., for it may be a personal name.   *Lod*,
Hadid, and *Ono* are place-names in Ne. 11$^{34 \text{ f.}}$ and located in Benj.
Hadid does not occur elsw.   Ono and Lod are named as Benj. towns
in 1 Ch. 8^{12}, and the same Ono may be intended in Ne. 6^{2}.   In regard
to *Nebo* there is much doubt.   We know a mountain and city of that
name in Moab, but that situation is unsuitable.   We find the "sons
of Nebo" in Ezr. 10^{43} among those divorced, but, contrary to BDB.,
it is a personal name.   We note further that in Ezr. "men of" (v. ^{28})
changes to "sons" at this point, after which we have personal names.
Therefore *Nebo* may be a personal name here.   Otherwise we may
regard the text as slightly in error and identify with Nob, a Benj. city
(Is. 10^{32} Ne. 11^{33}).   There are thus several names concerning which
we cannot positively determine whether they are personal or geographical.   These are *Magbish, Harim, Senaah, Azmaweth*, and *Nebo*.

   In Ne. 11$^{25-35}$ there is an important geographical list of the places in

Judah and Benj. inhabited at the time that record was made. We find
there 17 Judean towns, not one of which is found in our lists. On the
other hand, there are 15 Benj. places, and of these 10 are in this list,
and of these 9 are continuous. As our list is later than that in Ne.,
it would appear that the localities on the north of Jerus. remained
stationary, while those on the south changed almost completely with
the course of time. The Judean towns of our list are all near Jerus.;
some of them in Ne. 11 are more remote; it would appear, therefore,
that the pilgrims for the most part settled near Jerus., or else that the
census taken did not cover much ground. There are several place-names
in the list of temple-builders (Ne. 3), and, strange to say, Jericho is the
only name that is common, though Keilah is found in Ne. 3 in agreement with Esd.

Mey. explains the separation of these people designated by towns
from those indicated by clans on the theory that these are the poor
people (*Ent.*¹⁵²), who were not reckoned by families. The conclusion
seems to me fanciful. In other lists the people are grouped by towns
to distinguish them from the Jerusalemites (*v.* esp. Ne. 11); the same
course is followed here.

2ᵇ. *The number of the men of the people of Israel*] is a heading
for the lists which follow. The word *number* expresses the idea
shown in most of the table that the interest is not in the names,
but in the figures. Except in the case of some of the temple
officers, the names of living individuals are not given.—**3.** *The
sons of Parosh*] meaning the members of the clan of which Parosh
was the head. It was a large body, having 2,172 individuals.
The clan appears often in Ezr.–Ne. 8³ 10²⁵ Ne. 3²⁵ 10¹⁵.—**5.**
The sons of Arah, 775], Ne. 652.—**6.** The scheme of the list
fails here, MT. reading, *the sons of Pahath-Moab: of the sons of
Jeshua, Joab, 2,812*]. Ne.¹¹ reads *Jeshua and Joab.* The text
is corrupt, as the departure from the mechanical system of the
list shows (*v, i.*).—**7.** *Elam* is well known as the country over
which Cyrus ruled. The name recurs in v. ³¹ with the distinguishing adjective *other;* otherwise the verses are the same.
This is a case of accidental repetition, and "other" was added
to cover up the error.—*Zattu*] 10²⁷ Ne. 10¹⁵; 945 Ne. 845.—**9.**
Zakkai] only here, but he may be the same as *Zabbai* Ne. 3²⁰
(so Qr.).—**10.** *Bani*] Ne.¹⁵ *Binnui.* Both forms recur; indeed,
there are numerous forms from the root בנה. 642 Ne. 648.—
12. *Asgad*] 8¹² Ne. 10¹⁶ explained by Gray as containing the

name of the deity *Gad—Gad is mighty.* He regards the
name as proof of the worship of this deity during the exile
(*Pr. N.*[145]). But these chiefs may have lived long before the
exile, as the list deals with their posterity. *Gad* may, therefore,
be David's prophet (1 S. 22[5]), or the tribe across the Jordan,
representatives of which may have been in the postexilic community.—**14.** *Bigvai*] is also the name of one of the leaders,
v. ²; also 8⁶ Ne. 10¹⁷.—**16.** *The sons of Ater of Hezekiah*] cf. Ne.
10¹⁸, where *Hezekiah* follows *Ater* as a separate name. It is
possible that Ater was a descendant of King Hezekiah.—**18.**
Jorah] Ne.²⁴ *Hariph.*—**20.** *Gibbar*] Ne.²⁵ *Gibeon*, a place-name.
Probably the correct form is *Beth-Giddar* (*v. s.*).—**22.** *Netophah*] the home of two of David's heroes (2 S. 23²⁸). Identified
with *Beit Nettif* at the entrance to the vale of Elah (*DB.*). Ne.
groups the Bethlehemites and Netophites together with 188
for the two; the figures in Ezr. are 123 and 56, 179 in all.—
23. *Anathoth*] was but three miles from Jerusalem, and was
Jeremiah's home.—**24.** *Azmaweth*] Ne.²⁸ *Beth-Azmaweth*, a form
found nowhere else. *Azmaweth* is a personal name (2 S. 12³¹
1 Ch. 11³³ 12³), and a place-name in Ne. 12²⁹, the home of the
singers near Jerusalem. As it is among the place-names, this
town may be meant.—**29.** *The sons of Nebo*] Ne.³³ *the men of
the other Nebo.* The only known Nebo is the Reubenite town
in Moab (Nu. 32³˙ ³⁸). From Ne. we infer that there was another place of this name.—**30.** *Magbish*] lacking in Ne., and
not mentioned elsewhere.—**32.** *Harim*] means *consecrated* and
is a good priestly name.—**35.** *Senaah*] is the name of a wall-
builder (Ne. 3³) and is probably personal (*v. i.*).

2^b. מספר אנשי עם ישראל] 𝕲^B ἀνδρῶν ἀριθμὸς [+ λαοῦ^A] Ἰσραήλ, an
evident transposition, as ^{L} has ἀριθμὸς αν. In Ne. 𝕲 has Μασφάρ
ἄνδρες υἱοῦ Ἰσραήλ, Μαιφάρ ἄνδρες λαοῦ Ἰσραήλ^L. Esd. 5^{36} has a
different text τῶν προηγουμένων αὐτῶν, ἀριθμὸς τῶν ἀπὸ τοῦ ἔθνους
καὶ οἱ προηγούμενοι αὐτῶν. Here we have an equiv. of ראשיהם accepted
by Guthe as a suitable ending of the list of the leaders of returning
caravans, and a slightly different heading for the following census.
It would be in Heb. מספר מעם [or מגוי] וראשיהם and is less awkward
than MT. 3 Esd. has a still different text, *Emonia unus de principi-
bus eorum. Et numerus a gentilibus eorum ex præpositis eorum.* Seis.

holds that Israel is used advisedly rather than Judah, for the twelve leaders indicate representatives of all the tribes. There may have been men from the ten tribes in the later Judean province, but certainly the use of the name Israel does not even suggest such a conclusion. The Heb. phrase would make a good title for the list which follows, indicating a census of the whole nation, such as was taken in David's time (2 S. 24). It is the Chr.'s theory that these all returned from captivity.—**5.** חמשה ושבעים] units preceding tens shows txt. err. Rd. as Ne.[10] חמשים ושנים.—**6.** פחת מואב] 8[4] 10[30] Ne. 3[11] 10[15]. 𝔊[B] has Φαλαβ-μωάβ, Esd.[B] Φθαλειμωάβ, but otherwise Φααθμωάβ as 𝔥. The lexicons derive from פחת, *a pit = pit of Moab;* but *governor of Moab* is preferable (B.-Rys. Ryle), an interpretation supported by a dup. in [L]: Φααθ ἡγουμένου Μωαβ. The name is strange for a Heb. family. Seis. supposes it was borne by a Moabite family which had wandered into Judah as Ruth did. Ryle supposes the family to have been rulers of part of Moab, and the official has displaced the family name. B.-Rys. explained as a Judean ruler in Moab and held that פחת was a late substitution for an older word of the same meaning. He cites 1 Ch. 4[22], where we find בעלו למואב. The name might have been בעל-מואב, and the change made to get rid of the offensive *Baal*, as Ish-baal was changed to Ish-bosheth. Ew. held that the name belonged to a governor of Moab appointed by the Chaldeans, and who had later returned to Jerus. (*Hist.* v,[86]), a view from which Sm. dissents. All that we can say surely is that an official title has become a common clan-name.

ישוע יואב] It is held that Jes. was the head of one branch of his family and Joab the head of a smaller branch. In that case we should have the genealogy of Joab traced back through Jes. to an earlier Pahath-Moab. But Ne. reads Jes. *and* Joab; so 𝔊[A] and Esd., a rendering adopted by Guthe. There is no other case in the personal names where clans are grouped together or where genealogical information is added. The most prob. explanation is that a number has dropped out after Pahath-Moab, that Jes. has crept in by accident, and "the sons of Joab" is an independent clan. Otherwise we must regard *of the sons of Jes.: Joab* as a gl.—**10.** בני] 𝔊, Βανού, Βανουι, Βανει, Βαναια, Βαναιου. Perhaps both Ezr. and Ne. (בנוי) are corrupt. We might get בָּנוּי "built," or בָּנָיָה "Yahweh has built," comparable to the Bab. Bâniia. Names from this root are very common (*v.* forms in Ne. 10[14] 11[15] 1 Ch. 2[25]).—**11.** בבי] is found in Bab. as Bîbâ.—**16.** There is a + in Esd.[BA] 5[15], *the sons of Azer, of Hezekiah, the sons of Keilan and Azetas,* 67; *the sons of Azaru,* 432; *the sons of Anneis,* 101; *the sons of Arom.* Twice a number is wanting, and once both "sons of" and a number fail.—**18.** יורה] Ne. חריף 𝔊[L] has Ιωρης in Ezr. and Ne., but Esd.[L] reads Ωραι, Esd.[BA] Αρσειφουρειθ, showing both names in a corrupt form. יורה has rather the better support.—**20.** גבר] may be an error for גבעון, as Ne. Esd.[L] has Γαβαων, and Gibbar is not found

elsw. Gibeon is north of Jerus. The list begins with southern places
and later gives those in the north; therefore, if Gibeon is right the v. is
misplaced.—**21.** In Ne. $\mathfrak{G}^B$ lacks Bethlehem, Netophah, and Anathoth.
—**24.** עַזְמוּת] is the correct pointing, as all the varied forms of $\mathfrak{G}$ end
in μωθ.—**26.** Esd. has + οἱ χαδιάσαι καὶ Ἀμμίδιοι (422).—**27.** מכמס]
so Ne., but מכמש is the form in 1 S. 13² ff. Is. 10²⁸ Ne. 11³¹.

29. ונבו] + אחר in Ne., a form supported by ᴮ alone, the other Gk.
texts following Ezr. Guthe holds that *the sons of Nebo* must be a clan,
comparing Ne. 10²⁰. The *other Nebo* of Ne. means another clan of the
same name. As the number 52 is the same in both texts, Guthe's
contention is dub.—**30-32.** *Magbish, Elam,* and *Harim* are usually
treated as place-names (Sieg. Seis. B.-Rys.). The evidence points to
personal names. *Magbish*, lacking in Ne., but supported by $\mathfrak{G}$, does
not occur elsw., but as all the other places are well known, an unheard-
of place would hardly be named here. There is a personal name מגפיעש
in Ne. 10²¹ which might be the same. We know of no Judean town
named *Elam*, still less can we find two of that name. *Harim* recurs
pass. v. ³⁹ 10²¹· ³¹ Ne. 3¹¹ 7³⁵· ⁴² 10⁶· ²⁸ 12¹⁵, and always is a person.
Ḥa-ri-im-ma-' is a personal name on the contract tablets (Clay, *Murashu Sons,* x,⁵⁰).—**35.** סנאה] Ne. 3³ is deemed a place-name by many.
The number in this group is 3,630, 3,930 in Ne., about one-twelfth of
the whole. This big number could not belong to an unknown place,
nor to an otherwise unknown clan. The number may, of course, be
wrong, esp. as $\mathfrak{G}^B$ in Ne. has 930. In 1 Ch. 9⁷ there is בן־הסנאה a
Benj., the same person as בן־הסנוה in Ne. 11⁹ (*v.* Benz. and Curt. on
1 Ch. 9⁷). The art. is found in Ne. J. D. Michaelis explained as "the
sons of the unloved wife" (שנואה). Mey. notes (Is. 60¹⁵) Jerus. shall
be no longer "abandoned and hated," but a pride and joy. He holds
that "abandoned and hated" covers these people, so that the name
indicates neither a place nor a person, but a class, men without property,
servants, and the like. But if Is. is cited, "the sons of the hated"
would be a national name, covering all of despised Israel. In our lists
personal or place names are required throughout. The pointing is
attested by all Gk. texts. A personal name must be meant, and the
same name is to be assumed in 1 Ch. 9⁷ Ne. 11⁹. Guthe notes that in
the Mishna סנאה is a Benj. clan.

36-58. = Ne.³⁹⁻⁶⁰ Esd. 5²⁴⁻³⁵. The temple officers.—These
are arranged in six groups: (1) Priests. (2) Levites. (3) Singers.
(4) Porters. (5) Nethinim. (6) Sons of Solomon's servants.

(1) *The priests,* vv. ³⁶⁻³⁹ Ne.³⁷⁻⁴² Esd.²⁴ ᶠ·.—The number of pr. is large,
4,289, almost exactly one-tenth of the whole list, but as only four clans
are named, we have an average of over a thousand to each clan. It is
very likely that pr. would be interested above all others in the rebuild-

ing of the temple, as that would be a necessary step in their restoration to office. Nevertheless, it would be difficult to conceive of such a vast number returning at one time; and still more difficult to comprehend the delay in the rebuilding of the temple if more than 4,000 pr. were on the ground from the first.

It is noteworthy that in the list of pr. Ezr. and Ne. agree in both names and numbers, and even 𝕲 offers no important variation. It is natural to infer from this harmony that the list belongs to a late date, a conclusion supported by the absence of any mention of these pr. in Jos. There are large lists of pr.' names found in other parts of our books (Ne. 10¹ ff. 11¹⁰ ff. 12¹ ff.). The heads of the priestly houses here are the same as those in the list of divorced pr. (Ezr. 10¹⁸ ff.), exc. that here we have " the sons of Jedaiah of the house of Jes." and in the other " the sons of Jes. the son of Jozadak"; and in the latter list Harim precedes Pashhur. Among the pr. who had taken foreign wives were all the families named in our list, and no others. There were four other priestly clans which came up with Ezra (8² f.): the sons of *Phinehas, Ithamar, David,* and *Shecheniah.* These would naturally not have foreign wives, being fresh arrivals, while those in our list must have been for some time in Judah. In Ne. 12¹ ff. we have the Chr.'s list of the priestly chiefs who came up with Zer. and Jes. and there we find 22, not one being identical with our list. It is worthy of note that Esd.ᴮ gives a total of 2,588 pr. as against 4,289 of MT. The large numbers and the few names may be due to the necessary grouping in large divisions, because pr. were, indeed, very plentiful when the list was made. Yet the number seems to be exaggerated. Smith considers the 1,500 of the pseudo-Aristeas the maximum for any period (*Jer.* i,³⁶¹ f.).

We. notes that the first priestly clan appears to be composed of the descendants of Jes., the contemporary of Zer., and that the list, therefore, belongs to a much later period than that of Cy. or Dar. (*GGN.* 1895,¹¹⁷); but Mey. questions, I think wrongly, the conclusion and the identification (*Ent.*¹⁶⁹).

Jedaiah] recurs in the other lists of priests, and also in 1 Ch. 9¹⁰ 24⁷; in the last passage a priest of the second class. 𝕲 shows a great variety of forms, but the Hebrew pointing is correct.—*Of the house of Jeshua*] means that the family of Jedaiah is traceable to an earlier Jeshua.—**37.** *Immer*] recurs in the lists and in 1 Ch. 9¹² 24⁷. There was a priest of this name in Jeremiah's time (Je. 20¹). The name has accidentally dropped from 𝕲ᴮ in Ne. 7⁴⁰.—**38.** *Passhur*] is the name of the priest who was the son of Immer and who put Jeremiah in the stocks (Je.

20).—**39.** *Harim*] was found among the laity, v. [32]; as the name means "consecrated," it is peculiarly appropriate for a priest. Mey. suggests that there might be lay elements in a priestly clan (*Ent.*[170]), but we must not make too much out of a name.

36. Esd.^{L} begins "the sons of pr.," but this is an error. ^{BA} contain an additional name, and a slightly different construction: *the sons of Jeddon of the son of Jesus, for the sons of Sanabeis*, 872 (A Anaseib, by metathesis). This does not afford much help. It is barely possible that Esd.'s name is Sanb. and the omission from the lists would be due to hatred of Neh.'s bitter opponent. ᵹ suggests another name: 'Ιεουδά^B, 'Ιεδδουα^{AL}, *i. e., Jaddua* (Ne. 12$^{11.\ 22}$), who was high pr. in the time of Alexander the Great (*v.* Mey.[169]). But Jaddua and Jedaiah are not necessarily the same, for ᵹ makes sad havoc of Heb. names. The question arises whether this Jes. is the high pr. and the companion of Zer. If so, We.'s contention is correct, that we are here far removed from the time in which Jes. lived (quoted by Mey. *op. cit.*). But Mey. says that that identification is by no means certain, since there was also a Levitical family named Jes. We. is probably right though, for there would be no reason for adding Jes.'s name unless it were well known. It is not unlikely that we should correct the text here on the basis of Ezr. 10^{18} $^{ff.}$ Among those divorced were four priestly families, the sons of Jes. of Immer, of Harim, and of Passhur; the best result would be obtained by regarding ידעיה לבית as an explanatory gl.

(2) *The Levites*, v. [40] Ne.[43] Esd.[26]—Two facts engage our attention in connection with this list, the small number of the Lev. and their separation into a distinct class from the pr. The paucity of this class in the restoration is usually explained on the ground of the unwillingness of the degraded Lev. to accept the humbler duties to which they were consigned in the postex. period. But there is not a hint of this feeling in our sources. When Ezra's company assembled at the river Ahava and a muster was taken, it was learned that there was not a Lev. in the whole assembly. By a diligent search through the country Ezra secured 38 Lev. (8$^{18\ f.}$). It appears that the trouble was due to the fact that in this period there were not many Lev. apart from the priestly order. It seems clear that from the small numbers and from the character of the v., which is very broken, that we have here but a fragment of the original list of Lev.

This is the first instance in our books where pr. and Lev. are reckoned as distinct classes. It is not difficult, however, with the material at hand to trace the course of events which led to this distinction. In the early days Lev. like pr. and prophet indicated an office rather than a tribe. There were plenty of pr. who were not Lev., but there were

prob. no Lev. who were not pr. By the seventh century, as the book
of Dt. shows, the non-Levitical pr. had disappeared or had been received into the order, for pr. and Lev. are syn. When Josiah central-
ised the cult at Jerus. the pr. of the local shrines either came to Jerus.
and acted in a subordinate capacity or were left without occupation
and support. Ez. knows the identification, but he declares that only
the sons of Zadok, who are nevertheless Lev., shall serve in the priesthood (40⁴⁶ 44¹⁵); all other Lev. are to do the humble offices at the
sanctuary, tending the doors, butchering the sacrifices, and doing such
other menial services as are required. At the end the Lev. are spoken
of as a separate class (48¹² ᶠ·).

It is apparent that now the Lev. is no longer a pr. in his own right.
The priesthood had once embraced many who were not Lev., now the
Lev. embrace many who are not pr. It would surely happen during
the exile that these deposed Lev. would enter the secular life (*cf.* Ne.
13¹⁰), with the result that when the exile was over but few of this order
survived. In P this distinction is treated as if it had always existed,
it being said that Moses gave the tribe of Levi unto Aaron that they
might minister to the priesthood (Nu. 3⁶). Their duties in the later
days were manifold and various; they killed the sacrificial animals;
they served as doorkeepers and singers; they did duty as scribes (2
Ch. 34¹³) and as teachers (*ib.* 35³ Ne. 8⁷· ⁹); they went about begging
money for the temple (2 Ch. 24⁵ ᶠᶠ·).

40. MT. runs: *the sons of Jes. and Kadmiel: of the sons of Hodaviah*].
It would appear from this that there was but one Levitical guild, whose
two branches, Jes. and Kadmiel, are represented in the return. But
in 3⁹ there are apparently three independent guilds, Jes. Kadmiel,
Judah (= Hodaviah). Among the Lev. sealed we find Jes. Kadmiel,
and Hodiah (Hodaviah); in Ne. 9⁵, another list of eight Lev. "who
went up with Zer.," we find Jes. Kadmiel, and Judah; while in Ne.
12²⁴ Jes. is given as the son of Kadmiel. (We have also Jes. the son of
Azaniah, Ne. 10⁹). In other lists we find of these three only Jes. and
Kadmiel (Ne. 9⁴· ⁵) or Jes. and Hodiah (Ne. 8⁷). It is evident that
there is much confusion in the lists of Lev., but it is prob. that our
text should read: *the sons of Jes. Kadmiel, Bani, and Hodaviah*, so that
this record names four small Levitical guilds. 3 Esd. has an extraordinary text: *Levitæ filii Jesu in Caduhel et Baneis, et Serebias et Edias
septuaginta quattuor; omnis numerus a duodecimo anno: triginta millia
quadrigenti sexaginta duo, filii et filiæ et uxores: omnis computatis: quadraginta millia ducenti quadraginta duo.* No lack of Lev. acc. to this
source.

(3) *The singers*, v. ⁴¹ Ne. 7⁴⁴ Esd. 5²⁷.—These are treated as
a distinct class like the Levites. There may have been such

a body in the pre-exilic age (*OTJC.*^{219}). Their office would naturally be that of choristers in the temple service, and they played their own accompaniment (1 Ch. 15^{16}); they were appointed by the king for service in the temple and received regular pay (Ne. 11^{22} $^{f.}$); their dwellings were in the environs of Jerusalem (*ib.* 12^{29}); Nehemiah found them scattered in the fields on account of non-support (*ib.* 13^{10}).—*The sons of Asaph*] the only name, indicating but a single guild. To Asaph are ascribed a group of Psalms, 50, 73–83, and he may have been the head of a choir in the Persian period (*cf.* Br.$^{\text{Ps, lxvif.}}$).

(4) *The porters,* v. ^{42} Ne. 7^{45} Esd. 5^{28}.—*Sons of*]. Wanting in Ne. and unnecessary. The porters or doorkeepers are usually mentioned with the singers, though their functions were different. They must have been found wherever there was a sanctuary; Samuel was virtually the porter of the temple at Shiloh (1 S. 3^{15}). According to Ne. 12^{25} they were the guardians of the storehouses of the gates, but this must have been a special function.

There are six names as heads of the guilds of porters.—*Shallum*] is a name given to many Hebrews. It is interesting to note that Maaseiah the son of Shallum was a keeper of the threshold in Jeremiah's time (Je. 35^4). There were three such officers, and all were put to death at the fall of Jerusalem (*ib.* 52^{24} $^{ff.}$).—*Ater*] occurs also as the head of a lay clan, v. ^{16}. We know nothing further about him.—*Akkub*] is named among the Levites who interpreted the law (Ne. 8^7).—*Hatita* and *Shobai*] are not mentioned elsewhere.—*The whole*] *i. e.,* the sum of all the guilds of porters is 139 (Ne. 138). From the words in Ps. 84^{11}, "I had rather be a doorkeeper in the house of my God than to dwell in the tents of wickedness," the office must have been rather a humble one. Br. gives quite a different rendering (Ps. *in loc.*).

Singers and porters are mentioned many times in Ezr.–Ne. and in Ch., but rarely elsw. (singers not at all, and porters not in the sense of temple officers). The attempt has been made to show that in Ezr.–Ne. they are sharply differentiated from the Lev., while in Ch. they belong to that class (*v.* Baudissin, *DB.* iv.,$^{92\,b}$). Torrey, on the other hand, holds that there is no such distinction (*Comp.*[22 f]). In most of the cases where they are named in Ezr.–Ne. they are distinguished from the Lev. as a class (Ezr. 2[20] 7[7] Ne. 10[29. 40] 13[5], the porters usually named first). But in Ne. 12[27] the Lev. were brought to Jerus. to sing at the dedication of the wall, though it is apparently said in 12[42] that the singers performed this office. In 13[10] the singers and Lev. are classed together as doing the same work and sharing the same hard fate. In 1 Ch. 9[33] certain singers are called heads of Lev. clans, and they are called the brethren of the Lev. *ib.* 15[16]. On the other hand, the singers and porters are distinguished from the Lev. in 2 Ch. 35[15] as sharply as in any place in Ezr.–Ne. The mention of these classes in our books is due chiefly to the Chr., and he knows nothing of a development in religion. In the pre-ex. temple, little as we know about its rites, we may be sure there were porters and prob. singers. But guilds like these would not be preserved intact during the exile. The origin of these classes must date from the second temple, and such functions as they performed would naturally fall to the Lev. The Chr. knows certain famous names belonging to these guilds, and he uses them wherever the occasion demands. In Ezr. 3[10] Ne. 11[22] the Lev. are identified with the sons of Asaph. Singing and playing were certainly functions of the Lev. This list does not pretend to give the name of a singer of this period nor do we find such a list in our sources. The Lev. are frequently named also as doorkeepers (Ne. 12[25] 13[22] 1 Ch. 9[26] 2 Ch. 8[14] 23[4] 34[9. 13]).

41. המשררים] Esd.[L] υἱοὶ Ασαφ οἱ ᾠδοί. 3 Esd. *filii sacredotum qui psallebant in templo,* an explanatory gl.—**42.** בני] *del.* as Ne., though 𝔊[L] in Ne. supports text of Ezr. 𝔊[B] is correct enough, υἱοὶ τῶν πυλῶν, reading השערים, *gates,* instead of gatekeepers; this may be the original Ezr. text. Esd.[BA] reads differently from MT., viz., *the porters,* 400; *those of Ishmael, the sons of Lakoubatos,* 1,000; *the sons of Tobeis, all* 139. The total has been made to agree with Heb. without reference to the other figures.

In other lists of porters, Ne. 11[19] has Akkub and Talmon; Ne. 12[25] Meshullam (= Shallum), Talmon, and Akkub; 1 Ch. 9[17] Shallum, Akkub, Talmon, and Ahiman, Shallum being designated as the chief. Ahiman is apparently a misreading of אחיהם, *their brothers,* so that we have but three constant names, Shallum, Talmon, and Akkub. Therefore Ater, Hatita, and Shobai are prob. later than the Chr.—הכל] wanting in Ne., but supported by Gk. texts of Ezr.

(5) *The Nethinim,* vv. [43-54] Ne. 7[46-56] Esd. 5[29-32].—Noteworthy is the unusually long list of this class. There are 35 names in Ezr., Ne. having 3 less. But Esd. has a longer list, 38 names in [B], 39 in [A]; [L] agrees with MT. On this ground Guthe adds 5 names to the list, making 40 in all. They are all given as

heads of clans, and we should expect a large number of individuals. There were, however, but 392 of the Nethinim and sons of Solomon's servants combined, separate numbers not being given. It is evident that these clans or guilds were very small, averaging about nine persons each. The Nethinim were subordinate temple officers, performing the humblest functions at the sanctuary.

The name Neth. occurs but once elsw. than Ezr.–Ne. (1 Ch. 9^2), but many times in our books, Ezr. 2$^{43.\ 58.\ 70}$ 7$^{7.\ 24}$ 8$^{17.\ 20}$ (bis) Ne. 3$^{26.\ 31}$ 7$^{46.\ 60.\ 73}$ 10^{29} 11$^{3.\ 21}$ (bis). Torrey holds that all these passages are from the Chr. Of most of them that statement is true; when we find an institution like this traced back to David (Ezr. 8^{20}), it is good evidence of the hand of the Chr. But the reference to the house of the Neth. in Ne. 3^{31} is earlier than the Chr. and attests the existence of this body before his time. This house was prob. occupied by those who were on duty at the temple, the rest living in Ophel (Ne. 3^{26} 11^{21}). The site of the house opposite the water gate has been supposed to connect them with the drawers of water (Jos. 9^{21}) (Ryle, DB.), but that is fanciful. Acc. to Ezr. 8^{20} they were given for the service of the Lev. They are generally regarded as temple slaves (Schürer, Jewish People, ii,$^{1.\ 273}$, BT.^{312}). They are called ἱερόδουλοι by Jos. (Antiq. xi, 5, 1 and Esd.^{BA}). Kue. holds that they were mere foreigners held as slaves and finds a reference to them in Zc. 14^{21}, "and in that day there shall no more be a Canaanite in the house of Yahweh" (Einl. ii,^{400}). Mitchell supposes Canaanite to mean "trader" (Zc. ICC., so Mar. Dodekapr.).

It is held that they were descendants of prisoners of war, as the Gibeonites were made hewers of wood and drawers of water (Jos. 9^{21}), and support for this contention is found in the presence of foreign names in the list (Berth. OTJC.^{359}). This view is scarcely tenable; for this term is applied to the Lev. in Esd. 1^3, since ἱερόδουλοι standing there for the Lev. is given to the Neth. in 5^{29}. If they were foreign slaves we should scarcely have such a painstaking record of the names of their clans. They are usually named in connection with the other classes of temple officers, pr. Lev. singers, and porters; with pr. and Lev. alone in 1 Ch. 9^2, or with pr. Lev. and sons of Solomon's servants (Ne. 11^3). The leaders of this body were Siha and Gishpa (Ne. 11^{21}), showing some sort of organisation. The identification of the Neth. with the Lev. as in Esd., along with the constant connection above mentioned, makes it highly probable that they were a branch of the Levitical body, which gradually disappeared in the later religious development. This view is supported by Nu. 3^9, where it is said that the Lev. were given to the pr. It is prob. that Nu. 3^9 has the name

of the Neth. The text stands now נחונים נתונים המה לו‎, rendered in RV.
"they are wholly given to him" (Aaron), a rendering accepted by Gray
(*Nu.*). The repetition recurs in Nu. 8[16], but written defectively (נתונים‎).
We should, perhaps, rd. נתונים נחונים‎ "as Neth. are they given to him."
Nu. 18[6] should then be rendered: "to you they are a gift, Yahweh's
Neth., to do the work at the tent of meeting."

An extraordinary thing about this list is the large number of names
which are not found elsw. Of the 35 there are only 9 which recur. One
of these, Siha, may be disregarded, as its repetition is in the same connection; two others are names of foreign kings, Rezin and Sisera; a
fourth is otherwise found only of one of the sons of Solomon, Giddel;
a fifth is corrupt, Meunim. Virtually we have a long list of peculiar
names. It is highly prob. that this list was not made up by the Chr., for
he uses the same names over and over again. Another peculiarity of
the list is the considerable number with the ending א—, of which there
are 14 (reading אסנא‎, v. [50], and taking Ne.'s forms). This apparently is
due to an Aram. influence. Many of the names are explicable as Heb.,
but the list seems to have been written by one whose tongue was Aram.

Che. has a characteristic interpretation: like Nathan, Nathanel,
Nethanim is a disguise of Ethani. Ethan the Ezrahite was a Jewish
Jerachmeelite, since *bene Neahol* (1 K. 4[31] 5[11]) = *bene Jerachmeel* (*AJT.*
1901,[438]). Similarly he holds that for the sons of Solomon's servants
(v. [55]) we should rd. בְּנֵי עֶרֶב שַׁלְמָה‎] "the people of Salmaean Arabia."

Still the foreign element in the names is a serious difficulty. The fact
is we have very little information about this class of officers. The
designation in 3 Esd. *sacerdotes servientes in templo* would indicate that
the Neth. were considered a branch of the pr.

43. *Siha*] was one of the leaders of the Nethinim (Ne. 11[21]).
It is singular that the name of the other leader, Gispah, is not
found in this list.—**46.** *Hanan*] occurs in 1 Ch. 11[43] as a warrior
of David's time. The sons of Hanan (Bab. *Xananâ*) had a
chamber in the temple in Jeremiah's day (Je. 35[4]), and they may
have performed similar functions to the later Nethinim. The
name is also Levitical (Ne. 8[7] 10[11] 13[3]).—**47.** *Giddel*] recurs as
one of the servants of Solomon (v. [56]).—*Reaiah*] also in 1 Ch.
4[2] (a Judahite) 5[5] (a Reubenite).—**48.** *Rezin*] is found elsewhere only as the name of the king of Aram, who joined Pekah
against Ahaz (Is. 7[1]).—**49.** *Uzza*] was the name of the man who
was slain in moving the ark (2 S. 6[6]).—*Pareah*] ("lame") is
found in 1 Ch. 4[12] and in Ne. 3[6] as the father of Joiada, one of
the wall-builders.—**50.** *Meunim*] is a gentilic noun (1 Ch. 4[41]

2 Ch. 20¹ 26⁷), a people in Arabia (Benz. *Chr. KAT.*[3, 140 ff.]) of whom it is held that these Nethinim are descendants; from this conclusion Taylor argues that the Nethinim were foreign slaves (*DB.*). But the names in this list are personal, and there can scarcely be two exceptions in the middle of the list. It is probable that a personal name is disguised under this form, but it is not possible to tell what it is. In Esd. we find *Manei* and *Maani,* but little dependence can be placed on its testimony. —*Nephisim*] is interpreted by Taylor (*DB.* iii,[519a]) as "representatives of the race mentioned in Gn. 25¹⁵"; in this passage *Naphis* (נפיש) is given as a descendant of Ishmael (so 1 Ch. 1³¹), but apparently a different people is meant in 1 Ch. 5¹⁵. There is no other mention of this people, and it is scarcely likely that their descendants would turn up in the postexilic period among a Levitical order. Moreover, a personal name is required here. —**53.** *Barkos*] is unusually well attested by 𝕲. There is a Babylonian name which closely corresponds, *Barqûsu.*—*Sisera*] also well attested by 𝕲 (though [B] lacks it in Ezr. and [L] in Ne.), was the name of the king whose defeat is celebrated in the song of Deborah. On the name, see Moore, *Ju.* 4², and *PAOS.* xix,[160]; Moore holds that Sisera was a Hittite.

43. הנתינים]. We find the word without the article (Ezr. 8²⁰), and in Nu. if my emendation is correct (*v. s.*). In one place we find the regular participial form נתונים (Kt. Ezr. 8¹⁷), but the text is corrupt; 𝕲 bears abundant testimony to the Heb. form, and it is therefore to be regarded as a n. formation from the root נתן. The idea of giving a person to the temple service is at least as old as Samuel; in Hannah's vow she says: "I will give him to Yahweh all the days of his life." Samuel may therefore be regarded as one of the Neth.—ציחה] Ne. צחא but 11²¹ as Ezr. 𝕲 Σουθια[B], Σουαα[A], Σουδδαει[L]; Ne. Σηα[BA], Σουλαι[L]; Esd. Hσαυ[BA], Σουδαει[L]. 𝕲 suggests that the first syl. should be יצ; it is hard to tell about the rest.—חשופא] Ne. חשפא 𝕲[B] in Ne. Ασφα, but [A] in Ne. and Esd. has Ασειφα (חשיפא), but Ezr. is supported by 𝕲 Ασουφε.—**44.** קרס] Ne. קירס 𝕲[L] always Κορες = regular ptc. קורס, [B] has Καδης (Ezr.) Κειρα (Ne.) Κηρας (Esd.); [A] has Κηραος (Ezr.).—סיעהא] Ne. סיעא 𝕲[L] Ιωστου, Ιωστα (Esd.), [B] Σωηλ (Ezr.), Ασουια[B], Σιαια[A], Ιασουια[א] (Ne.), Σουα, Σουσα[A] (Esd.). 𝕲 therefore gives little support to either Heb. form.— **45.** לבנה] Ne. לבנא 𝕲[L] Λοβνα. Other Gk. forms attest MT. Prob. Ne. is right, with its Aramaised ending.—חגבה] Ne. חגבא; latter prob.

right.—עקוב] lacking in Ne., but found in Gk. exc. ᴮ and Esd.ᴸ. The name is suspicious in the list, because of its recurrence elsw. (*cf.* v. ⁴²).— **46.** חגב] also lacking in Ne., though found in 𝕲 (exc. ᴮ); it is prob. a repetition of חגבא v. ⁴⁵.—שמלי] Ne. שלמי 𝕲ᴮ (Ezr.) Σαμααν; otherwise 𝕲 supports Ne. Berth. cites שלמי as evidence of the foreign origin of the Neth. In NH the name שַׁלְמַי occurs (BDB.), corresponding to 𝕲 Σελαμει. Esd. 5²⁹ adds two names, Ουτα, Κηταβ, so 𝕲ᴬᴺ in Ne.⁴⁸. —**47.** גרל] Esd. Κουα, Κεθουαᴬ; otherwise 𝕳 is attested, though in Ne. the form Γαδηλ occurs in ᴮᴸ.—**48.** נקודא] *cf.* Bab. *Niqûdu.*—**49.** בסי] Βασερᴸ, Βεσσερ (Esd.); otherwise 𝕲 attests MT.—**50.** אסנה] lacking in Ne. but supported by 𝕲ᴮᴬᴺ, Ασενναᴸ. Perhaps we should write אסנא, "thorn bush" (*cf.* BDB.).—נפיסים] Qr. נפוסים, Ne. נפושסים] Qr. נפישסים. The form in Ne. is explained as a mixture of two variants; it is certainly a corrupt form, but the corruption is older than 𝕲, where we have Νεφωσασειᴮᴬ, Νεφωσαειμᴬ. 𝕲ᴮ in Ezr. has Ναφεισων (נכיסן), or perhaps since μ and ν final are often confused (נסיסם), which under the influence of מעונים has been pointed as a pl.; Esd. has Ναφεισει. It is not possible to tell what the original name was.—**52.** בצלות] Ne.⁵⁴ Kt. בצלית. There is much variation in 𝕲, but most of the forms show that they rd. the last syl. לית.—חרשא] 𝕲 offers great variety: Ezr. Αρησαᴮᴬ, Αβασαᴸ; Ne. Αδασα(ν) (ר being rd. as ד); Esd. Δεδδαᴮ, Μεεδδαᴬ, Βαασαᴸ.—ברקוס] a south Ar. name (Euting), *cf.* Bab. *Barḳusu.* The second element is regarded as the Edomite deity *Kos* (*KAT.*⁴⁷², *Murashu Sons*, ix,²⁷, Gray, *Pr. N.*⁶⁸). Hilprecht and Clay explain the first syl. as the deity *Bir*, but Gray with greater probability suggests *bar*, "son."

(6) The sons of Solomon's servants, vv. ⁵⁵⁻⁵⁸ Ne. 7⁵⁷⁻⁶⁰ Esd. 5³³⁻³⁵. —This body is named elsewhere only in the corresponding passage in Ne. and in Ne. 11³. There is no other light on this class, and we have no sure indication of their origin or functions. As they are grouped so closely with the Nethinim, but one number being given for the two classes, it is probable that their office was much the same.

There is no sufficient reason for Torrey's statement that this body is a subdivision of the Neth. (*Comp.*⁴⁰); it would be more analogous to regard them as a subdivision of the Lev. They are grouped with the pr. Lev. and Neth. in Ne. 11³ as dwelling in their own cities. The Bible throws no further light on them. Torrey regards the name as evidence of the Chr.'s habit of tracing temple institutions back to the great kings who established the temple ritual (*op. cit.*). Baudissin notes that Solomon put the surviving Canaanites to forced service (1 K. 9²⁰ ᶠ·) and presumes this postex. body to be a survival from that time (*DB.*

iv,^{74b}). Taylor also regards them as foreigners like the Neth., and for
the same reason, viz., the presence of foreign names. All that we can
say with any great degree of probability is that the "servants of Solomon" was an unimportant body of temple servants which grew up
in the period of the second temple and then soon disappeared as a
separate class. It is to be noted that the Neth. are often mentioned
without them, and there is no ground for holding, as Taylor does,
that in such cases they are included with the Neth. It is, however,
prob. that they are mentioned in the Aram. section (Ez. 7^{24}), where
after pr. Lev. singers, porters, and Neth. there is added "servants
of the house of God." That may be another name for the servants
of Solomon and would further define their office. There are but ten
names in the list, and there is but one name found elsw. (Shephatiah),
and there is the same tendency to Aram. terminations that was noted
in the case of the Neth.

55. עבדי שלמה]. The Gk. translators were as much perplexed about
this title as their modern followers. ^{B} gives here a partial transliteration, Αβδησελ; in v. ^{58} Ασεδησελμα, but ^{A} has Αβδησελμα: in this case
the whole thing was taken as a n. p., for the translators did not see the
name Solomon. This agrees with Peshito, which eliminates the office
entirely. In other cases 𝕲 gives δούλων Σαλωμων, or παίδων Σ. (^{BA} in
Esd. 5$^{33. 35}$).—סטי] Ne. סוטי 𝕲 offers every variety of vocalisation Σατει
(^{B} in Ezr.) = סָטֵי, Σουτει (^{BA} in Ne.) = סוּטִי, and Σωται (^{A} in Ezr. and ^{L}
always). The name is lacking in Esd.^{BA}.—הספרת] Ne. ספרת. 𝕲 sup-
ports Ezr., for though ^{BAℵ} agree with Ne. in that passage, ^{L} has Ασοφερεθ,
and a similar form is found in Ezr. and Esd. in all texts.—פרודא] Ne.
פרידא supported by 𝕲 in Ne. 𝕲 Φαδουρα in Ezr. and ^{L} in each case
= פרורא. On the basis of this evidence any one of the three forms is
possible: Perudah, Pereidah, or Pedurah.—**56.** יעלה] Ne. יעלא. In Ezr.
we find Ιεηλα^{B}, Ιελα^{A}, Ιεδλαα^{L}; in Ne. Ιελη^{B}, Ιεαηλ^{Aℵ}, Ιεδαλαα^{L}; in
Esd. Ιεηλει^{B}, Ιεηλι^{A}, Ιεδλαα^{L}. It is difficult to see what name could
have been at the bottom of all these variants.—גרל] occurs elsw. only
among the Neth., v. ^{47}. 𝕲^{L} has Σαδδαι, Esd.^{BA} Ισδαηλ. As the recurrence of a single name is doubtful, prob. MT. has lost the original
name which might have been סרי.

57. שפטיה] ("Yahweh judges") is a good Heb. name, and well attested by 𝕲, though in Esd. we find Σαφυει^{B}, Σαφυθι^{A}. The name
occurs as one of David's sons (2 S. 3^{4}); one of the enemies of Jer. (Je.
38^{1}); one of the lay chiefs, v.^{4}; and of various other persons, 1 Ch.
9^{8} 12^{5} 27^{16} 2 Ch. 21^{2} Ezr. 8^{8} Ne. 11^{4}. On account of the familiarity of
this name, it is suspicious in this list.—פכרת הצבים] (Ne. הצביים) "the
binder of the gazelles" (BDB.). In spite of the peculiarity of the name
and its anomalous character in this list, the Gk. texts afford no real help.
Esd.^{BA} 5^{34} has eight additional names at this point, each preceded by
υἱοί: Σαρωθει, Μεισαιας, Γας, Αδδους, Σουβας, Αφερρα, Βαρωδεις, Σαφαν.

These names were scarcely invented by a translator, but where he got
them it is not possible to say.—אמי׳] Ne. אמון. 𝔊 supports Ezr.; ᴸ has
Αμεει in every case; ᴮᴬ Ημει (Ezr.) Ημειμ (Esd.). Perhaps the original
was אמי, changed in Ne. to the more familiar אמון.—**58.** 𝔊ᴮ in Ezr.
and Esd. has 372 instead of 392. ᴸ agrees with Heb.

59-63. = Ne. 7⁶¹⁻⁶⁶ Esd. 5³⁶⁻⁴⁰. A supplementary list of those whose genealogy could not be accurately traced.

There is first a list of the laity, v. ⁶⁰, an appendix to vv. ³⁻³⁵; then of
pr., v. ⁶¹, an appendix to vv. ³⁶⁻³⁹. As these pr. were unable to find a
record of their genealogy, they were deprived of the emoluments of their
office by order of the governor until a pr. should arise for the Urim and
Thummim, that is, with the oracular apparatus and power.

59. *Now these are those who went up from Tel-Meleh*, etc.]. It
is assumed that the places are in Babylonia, but not one of
them occurs elsewhere, and two are quite suspicious, *Kerub* and
Immer. It is likely from the inability of these people to trace
their connections, that they were from small places in Babylonia, and our ignorance of the names, therefore, should not im-
pugn their accuracy.—*The house of their fathers and their stock
whether they were of Israel*]. The first words would imply that
a very exact genealogy was required, but the following qualifying expression shows that the purpose was simply to determine
the question of nationality. Meyer infers that these men had
the position of proselytes (*Ent.*¹⁶⁰). They may have come from
the mixed marriages which figure in the history of the period
(Ezr. 9 *f*. Ne. 13). Smend recalls the nomadic Rechabites who
had come into Jerusalem at the time of the siege (Je. 35), and
thinks that these people may have lived in a distant part of
Babylonia (*Listen*,²¹). *Stock* or *seed* is used very frequently of
descendants, rarely as here of ancestors. "Seed of Abraham"
is often used in a national sense, being equivalent to Israel
(Ps. 105⁶); and *seed* alone is apparently used with the same
meaning in Est. 10³. That would give a good sense here, so
that we might render *their genealogy and their race*.—**60.** Since
the heads of the clans are given, *Delaiah*, *Tobiah*, and *Nekodah*,
the question must have been whether these chiefs were Israelites
or not. Delaiah is a well-established Hebrew name ("Yahweh

has drawn"), and was borne by a priest of David's time (1 Ch. 24^{18}), by one of the princes before whom Jeremiah was tried (Je. 36^{12}), and by a descendant of Zerubbabel (1 Ch. 3^{24}; *cf.* Ne. 6^{10}). The same may be said of Tobiah ("Yahweh is good"), though it was the name of one of Nehemiah's enemies, and he was an Ammonite. *Nekodah* is found elsewhere only among the Nethinim, v. ^{48}. Ne. has 642 instead of 652 in Ezr.; 𝕲 agrees with Ezr. —**61. And of the sons of the priests**]. With Ne. omit *the sons of*. Though Ezr. has some support, it is a faulty construction, and doubtless the error of a scribe. The names of three priests are given as belonging to this class, but the number is not given in any text. *Habaiah* does not occur elsewhere. *Hakkos* occurs in Ne. 3$^{4.\ 21}$, as grandfather of one of the wall-builders. Bertholet notes that this clan is deemed legitimate in Ne. 3$^{4.\ 21}$, whence he argues for the priority of this list (*Es. Neh.*^{8}). Meyer identifies Hakkos with a guild of Ezra's time (Ezr. 8^{33}, *Ent.*^{170}). Without the article (*Kos*) it is given as the name of a Judean (1 Ch. 4^{8}). Barzillai is the name of a well-known Gileadite, mentioned further on in this verse, who was the benefactor of David when he fled from Absolom (2 S. 17^{27} *et pass.*).

A Barzillai is also mentioned in 2 S. 21^{8} as the father of Michal's husband, but there are so many errors in the v. that this name may be wrong. The name is Aram. (*v.* Smith, Bud. on 2 S. 17^{27}). This Barzillai, head of a priestly guild, had taken the name because he had married into the family of the famous Gileadite. Perhaps the name had been used first as what we call a nickname. It was given in mature life after the man was married. Seis. suggests that this daughter was an heiress and that the name was taken to secure the fortune. But he offers no proof to support the theory that the name must go with the fortune. *Daughters*, like *sons*, means the descendants of Barzillai. As Barzillai's son went to David's court, the family became an important one, and such a tradition as we have here might long have persisted. It surely is not the Chr.'s invention. The importance of the family is further shown by the husband's taking his name from its founder. The number of these pr. is not given; Jos., not satisfied to acknowledge the defect, says there were about 525 (*Ant.* xi, 3, 10).

62. *These sought their register among those that were reckoned by genealogy, but they were not found*]. So ARV. But this is taking liberty with the text in an effort to get sense; even so, the result at the end is not satisfactory. BDB. renders: "*These sought their writing*, namely, *the enrolled*," i. e., "their genealogical record." But the text requires a slight correction and then we get good sense: *These searched for their record, but their enrolment was not found.—And they were barred* (literally, *desecrated*) *from the priesthood*], because they could find no record showing priestly descent. This is evidently a different matter from the question of nationality (v. [59]), for there is no question of race, but only of official standing. In his usual way of confusing things, the Chronicler has brought together here quite unrelated matters, which probably belong to entirely different periods, though both incidents seem to be authentic.—**63**. *And the governor said*] (or perhaps "his Excellency"). The case was settled by a decree of the civil ruler, not by a high priest. Who the governor was we do not know; it is generally assumed to be Sheshbazzar,* but this thing happened long after Sheshbazzar's time. If the name had been known to the writer of the underlying original it would surely have been given here. Esd. 5[40] supplies the name Nehemiah, perhaps because this unusual word for governor is elsewhere applied to him (Ne. 8[9] 10[2]); but Nehemiah seems to have concerned himself very little with the affairs of the priesthood. The conjecture of the Greek writer warns us that the identification is far from assured.—*Unto them*] cannot be right, unless we regard the construction as a loose one, changing to the indirect discourse; we should expect, *ye shall not eat*, instead of *that they should not eat*. But 𝕲 supports the text as it is, and it may pass.—*From the holy of holies*]. But "holy of holies" means the inner part of the temple in the earlier literature, though in P and Ez. it applies also to sacrificial food. Gray has shown that "holy" and "holy of holies" are used rather indifferently (*Nu.*[222]). Esd. 5[40] has *from the holy things*. That is preferred by Kittel.—*Until a priest stood for Urim and Thummim*]. The meaning is clearly that the unrecorded priests must refrain from exercising their functions until there should be one qualified to give a divinely

---

* *E. g.*, Kue. *Abh.*[228], Mey. *Ent.*[194]; but Zer. B.-Rys.

guided decision.   The decision was to come from a priest using the Urim and Thummim.

In 1 Mac. 4^{46} a question about the stones of a defiled altar was postponed "until the advent of a prophet to give an answer concerning them."   The matter is not one of relative time, for both methods of divination were used, that is, by prophetic oracles and by pr.   There was this difference, that the prophet always gave a reply supposed to be by direct divine enlightenment, while the pr. determined the question by some instrument as the ephod, or by Urim and Thummim.   The last method is obscure, but apparently some way of casting the sacred lot is meant.   One might naturally ask why this could not be done now, since pr. abounded.   Mey. explains this difficulty by supposing that the art of casting the lot had been lost in the postex. community, and would be restored only by the advent of the Messianic rule (*Ent.*^{194}, so Smith on 1 S. 14^{41}).   But such divination would be required during the exile as well as at other times, and it would be more natural to suppose that the Urim and Thummim, mng. some peculiar priestly apparatus, had been lost, prob. in the destruction of the temple.   It must be confessed, however, that a strict construction of the words rather favours Mey.'s view, since the desideratum is "a pr. for the Urim and Thummim"; otherwise we should expect "until Urim and Thummim appear for the pr."   It is possible that the loss was due to the absence of Lev. or their deterioration.   From Dt. 33^8 it would appear that this method of divination was practised by the Lev., and with the disesteem of this guild the art may have been lost, at least so far as this early period in Judah is concerned.

Berth. says the fact that there was no pr. capable of using this method of divination, but that it was expected that one might arise, points to the earliest stage in the new community where there was prob. no high pr. (so Sm. *Listen*,^{18}).   The sacred lot was used, he says, in later times (*cf.* Jos. *Ant.* iii, 8, 9, Sirach 36^3).

There is an elaborate treatment of Urim and Thummim in *AJSL.* 16$^{193 \text{ ff.}}$ by Muss-Arnolt.   He identifies the divination by the ephod with that of the Urim and Thummim, and connects with the Bab. "tablets of destiny" and explains the words as derived from the Bab. *u'uru*, "command," and *tummu*, "oracle."   If a signification is to be invented, it would be well to seek something more appropriate, such as "favourable" and "unfavourable."   On the use *v. i.*

59. חל] is As., "hill of ruins," and applied to mounds which are sites of ancient cities.   As part of n. p. in OT. only in *Tel-Abib* (Ez. 3^{15}), a place in Bab.—כרוב] is the name of a spiritual being, common in pl., cherubim.   As a n. pr. loc. it is dub.   Esd. joins with the word following: χαρααθαλαν^B, χερουβιδαν^L.   It might be a metathesis for כבר (Ez. 1^1), identified by Hilprecht as a canal near Nippur, *Kabaru*

(*Murashu Sons*, ix,[76]).—ארין] Ne. ארין 𝕲 Hδαν favours Ezr., though in Ne.
B has Hρων.—אמר] Ne. ואמר is a common priestly name, but improb.
as a Bab. n. pr. loc.—*Kerub, Addan* and *Immer*] have been explained as
n. p., the preceding n. pr. loc. being marked by the prefixed *tel*, which
is not found with these three; but the n. p. are given in vv. [60 f.], and
could not belong here unless text is disarranged. Esd. 5[36] yields better results than MT.: *their leaders were Charathalan and Allar.* Guthe
emends on this basis, thus: *from Tel-Meleh and from Tel-Harsha : Kerub-
Addan and Immer were their leaders.* Ἡγούμενος αὐτῶν (Esd.) = ראשם,
and this could easily be corrupted to הרשא. 3 Esd. shows same text:
principes eorum. This reading suggests that the people described in
vv. [59-63] constituted an independent caravan.—**60.** 𝕲[B] has a fourth
name, Βουα. Esd.[BA] has but two names, Ασαν, Βαεναν.

61. Esd.[BA] 5[38] has an explanatory + *these laid claim to the priesthood, and did not obtain it.*—חֲבַיָה] Ne. חֲבָיָה a reading adopted by Baer
but not by Kittel. 𝕲 gives various forms, among which are Αβ(ε)ια
(אL in Ne.) and ΟββειαB, ΟββιαA (in Esd.) and ΩδουιαL (in Ezr. and
Esd.). The variants make Heb. suspicious, but do not afford material
for a restoration.—הקוץ] is unusually well attested in 𝕲, the only significant variation being Αχβως (Esd.B), but there is doubt about the
pointing, as we find Αχ(κ)ους in Ezr. and in Ne.L (*i. e.*, הקוץ).—ברזלי]
Esd. 5[38] reads *Jaddous* (Jaddua) *who took to wife Augia of the daughters
of Phaezeldaius and he was called by his name*, an evident confusion of a
simple passage. The interesting point is the name of the wife. What
havoc is made of names by metathesis is shown by B: Ζαρβελθει in
the first occurrence, but Βερζελλαει in the second.—שמס]. With Guthe
rd. שמו as antecedent is Barzillai.—**62.** Some correction of the text
is required. *Those who are enrolled by genealogy* cannot be in app.
with *their register*, and in fact there is no grammatical construction
at all. 𝕲 offers great variety; BA transliterates οἱ μεθωεσείμ; L οἱ
γενεαλογοῦντες (so in Ne.); Ne.[BA] has *their writing of the caravan*
(or company). Esd. 5[39] renders ἐν τῷ καταλογισμῷ: Esd. yields: *the
genealogical writing of these being sought in the register, and not being
found, they were restrained from their office.* This makes good sense, but
it shows merely a free handling of the same text. By a slight transposition we can restore the text, putting the inf. before the ptc., and reading sg. as Ne.: ולא התיחשם נמצא, *these searched for their record, but their
enrolment was not found.* The ptc. המתיחשים does not occur elsw., and
inf. is used regularly in late Heb. mng. genealogy or enrolment (Ne.
7[5] 1 Ch. 4[33] 5[7] 7[5] *et pass.*). We then have a suitable subj. for *found.*
The rendering "they [the pr.] were not found" does not give the right
idea, for the mng. is that the pedigrees could not be found.—ויגאלו]
means *defile* (ARV.[m] "polluted from the priesthood"). But v. [63],
which is a further statement about the case of these pr., shows that
they were simply barred from service until a pr. arose with authority

to adjudicate the matter. Further we find the term used in Mal. 1⁷· ¹² (only other use of Pu.) where the defiling is not actual. There was no formal deposition or desecration from office, but only a suspension.

63. התרשתא] is found elsw. in Ne. 7⁶⁵· ⁶⁹ 8⁹ 10², in the last two passages prob. interpolated. 𝕲 takes it as a n. p. ᾿Αθερσαα, ᾿Ασερσαθα, but Esd. 5⁴⁰ Ναιμιας καὶ Ατθαριας^B, Νεεμιας ὁ καὶ Αταρασθας^L. The word is Pers., *Taršata*, but the exact definition is not clear. Moss regards it as referring to a royal commissioner (*DB.* iv,⁷⁷⁹ ᵇ). Mey. holds that it is not the name of an office like governor, but rather a title, "his Excellency" (*Ent.*¹⁹⁴) or "his Reverence," as Moss suggests. —אשר] is here used as a simple conj. The word is little more than a mark of relation as inverted commas are a mark of a quotation; this is a common usage, the word being translatable by many different English conjs.—ויאכלו] Esd. 5⁴⁰ μετέχειν "share in." This text also renders last part of v. *a high priest [priest^B] clothed with the manifestation and the truth.*—כהן] Ne.⁶⁵ הכהן a reading preferred by Kittel, but Esd. supports Ezr. *Urim* and *Thummim* are found here only without the art. The words are usually (Ex. 28³⁰ Lv. 8⁸ Dt. 33⁸), but not always (1 S. 28⁶ Nu. 27²¹) joined. The best explanation of the usage is found in the restored text of 1 S. 14⁴¹, "and Saul said unto Yahweh the God of Israel, why dost thou not answer thy servant to-day: if this guilt be on me or on Jonathan my son, O Yahweh the God of Israel, give Urim, but if this guilt be on thy people Israel give Thummim." Urim and Thummim would then be two objects drawn out of some place by the pr., one mng. "yes" and the other "no." The usage was apparently early, and was quite unknown exc. historically in the postex. age (*cf.* Bud. on 1 S. 14⁴¹, *DB.* and BDB., where other references are given).

64–67 = Ne. 7⁶⁶⁻⁶⁸ Esd. 5⁴¹⁻⁴³. The total figures of the census.

—It appears that the Judeans had a large number of slaves, male and female, besides 736 horses, 245 mules, 435 camels, and 6,120 asses.

64. *All the company together* (literally, *as one*)]. The word קהל means *community, the sacred congregation,* or *company.* It refers to an organised body and suggests a date later than Cyrus. The total is 42,360 or 42,308 (𝕲^B in Ne.). Esd. 5⁴¹ contains a limiting clause, reading: *The whole Israel from ten years and upward besides slaves and women* (^L): *from twelve years besides male and female slaves* (^BA). The latter is the better text, and accepted by Guthe, for if slaves and women had been mentioned we should have expected to find a further statement about women as well as about slaves. **65.** *And they had* 245 (200 in Ezr.) *singers and songstresses*]. These are not the temple singers, for they have been already enumerated in v. [41], and women were excluded from the temple service.

Therefore the reading שרות "songstresses" of the temple in Am. 8[3], though adopted by We., is scarcely possible. The form משררות occurs only here, and the m. without the art. occurs elsw. only in 2 Ch. 20[21]. All the 𝕲 texts have the words, and therefore such an emendation as "bulls and cows" has no support.

The true explanation is not far to seek. In 2 S. 19[35], where curiously Barzillai is the speaker, there is named among the pleasures of the court "the voice of singers and songstresses." In Eccl. 2[8] we have the same singers and songstresses mentioned among the various pleasures which Koheleth had sought. They were men and women employed by kings and nobles for entertainment. *And they had*, is lacking in Esd. and may be a gloss added here to serve as a connecting link. Siegfried argues that the number should be 245, as Ne. 7[67], so Zillessen, *ZAW*. 1904,[143]. **67.** *Four hundred and thirty-five camels*] seems a large number for a company as poor as these exiles were. 𝕲[B] in Ne. mentions 2,700 asses and omits the other animals altogether. The best MSS. of MT. lack the horses and mules of our text (*v*. Kittel and Berth.). The text has been changed to agree with Ezr.

64. כאחד]. In early Heb. כאיש אחד is used to express joint action, *e. g.*, "all the people rose as one man" (Ju. 20[8]). The text shows a late usage. The mng. required here is "combined," which in early Heb. would be יחדו. The word is unnecessary and is stricken out by Guthe. —**65.** משררים ומשררות]. As these words are followed directly by the list of animals, it has been proposed to rd. שורים ופרות "bulls and cows." This is rejected by Halévy on the ground that these animals could not live in the journey across the desert (*JA*. Nov.–Dec. 1899,[533]). We should prob. rd. as 2 S. 18[36] 2 Ch. 35[24] Eccl. 2[8] שרים ושרות as the same class of professional singers is meant. The writer has mistaken the word to mean *temple singers* and modified it accordingly. Fischer argues for the early date of the list from the mention of these classes, for he says they would soon be scattered after the return so that a census would be impossible (*Chr. Fragen*,[15]).—**67.** חמריהם] must be

′ rd. as we have *their horses*, etc., so 𝕲ᴮᴬ in Ezr., 𝕲ᴸ in both. 𝕲ᴮ in
Ne. mentions no other animals than the asses.—רבוא] "myriad," "ten
thousand," is common in postex. Heb., but is not found earlier; for
Kt. רבו (Hos. 8¹²) is better rd. as Qr. רְבִּי though Harper accepts former
(ICC.).—גמליהם] is preferable to גמלים of Ne.

This last part of the list (vv. ⁵⁹⁻⁶³) offers peculiar difficulty to the
interpreter. If we supposed the list to be early, we should be puzzled
to know how this company of pilgrims got more than 7,000 slaves, 245
singers for entertainment, and a large number of animals. The knowledge we have of this period all suggests a people few in number and poor
in worldly goods. In Neh.'s time there were a few slaves, but these
were Hebrews reduced to that condition by poverty. Neh. struggled
hard against the system by which the poor were sold into slavery.
After his rule ended, the system may have had a free hand, so that by
Ezra's time there may have been 7,000 slaves in the Judean province.

On the other hand, there is some reason for believing the list itself
to be composite, a growth resulting from additions. The priestly part
esp. bears traces of lateness in the close agreement of all the texts.

68 f. = Ne. 7⁶⁸⁻⁷¹ Esd. 5⁴³ᶠ·. A list of contributions.—As
shown below, in Ne. the gifts come from the governor, the chiefs,
and the people. Ne. says nothing about the temple, but only
says the gifts are for the workers. Here the temple is the object for which the contributions are made.—**68.** *When they came
to the house of Yahweh, which is in Jerusalem*]. These words
imply that the temple was already built, and would require us
to date the passage later than 515. But the following expression, *to set it upon its site*] implies just the contrary. We must
regard the words as a later gloss. As we find first "house of
Yahweh," then "house of God," we may suspect different hands
in the gloss.—*They made free-will offerings for the house of God*].
The purpose is plainly indicated by what follows, *to set it upon
its site, i. e.,* to rebuild it where it was, on the spot where Yahweh had in ancient time placed his name.—**69.** *They gave according to their ability*]. Even if we took the figures of the returned literally (v. ⁶⁴), the ability of these people would not
explain the vast total of perhaps a half-million dollars (*v.* Mey.
*Ent.*¹⁹⁴ ᶠᶠ·). All the information drawn from the best sources
shows that the restored community was poor.—*To the treasury
of the work*], intended here to refer to the treasury of the build-

ing fund.—*Priests' tunics*]. The tunic was a long garment, something like a wrapper. It was worn by men and women.

The same word is used for Joseph's famous coat (Gn. 37³), and for the robe of office which Is. declared Shebna would be required to take off (Is. 22²¹). On this garment, *v. DB.* i,⁶²⁴, Benz. *Arch.*⁹⁸ ᶠ·, Now. *Arch.* i,¹²¹· ¹⁹³. The pr.'s tunic was made of linen (Lv. 16⁴) and was embroidered (Ex. 28⁴). In shape it was like that worn by laymen. In Zc. 3³ we have a picture of Jes. clothed in soiled garments, interpreted usually in a fig. sense (*e. g.*, by Mar. and G. A. Smith); but Ew. referred the vision to the investiture of the pr. in new robes which had just come from Bab. Modern interpreters have scarcely improved on Ew. In the postex. period pr.' garments would naturally be scarce and therefore suitable for gifts.

68. [התנדבו] Esd. 5⁴³ εὔξαντο = התנדרו though the Hithp. of נדר is not found. Our preference for one or the other will depend upon our conception of the purpose of the gifts, whether for the rebuilding of the temple (Ezr.) or the maintenance of the service after the temple was built (Ne.).—[אוצר] means *treasure*, אוצר בית Ne. 10³⁹, *treasury*, but בית is often omitted as here.—**69.** [המלאכה]. Mey. holds that this word means here *worship* (*Gottesdienst*) (*Ent.*¹⁸⁴· ¹⁹⁵). The word applies to many kinds of work, but the term is always general. In 1 K 5³⁰ it is the work of temple-building, and that sense is meant by the Chr. here; in 2 Ch. 29³⁴ the work is killing animals preparatory to sacrifice; in Ne. it is used many times of the wall-building. When it means religious work it is usually qualified as "service of the house of our God" (Ne. 10³⁴). The passages esp. cited by Mey. are Ne. 2¹⁶ 13¹⁰, but in both cases the idea is "engaged in business," secular employment. The importance of the question lies in the fact that Mey. contends that this passage precedes the building of the temple. The character of the gifts shows that Mey. is right in one respect, though he is wrong in another. The pr.' garments and the bowls (Ne. 7⁶⁹) would serve for the worship, not for the rebuilding. These gifts show that the passage followed the rebuilding of the temple, though R. has made it seem otherwise in Ezr. —[דרכמונים] 𝕲 μναῖ^B δραχμας^AL. The authorities are divided, some connecting with Pers. *daric*, others with Gk. *drachma*, itself of foreign origin (*v.* BDB. *DB.* iii,⁴²¹). Sm. says that if this term is meant, the word must have been introduced later; but he is influenced by his belief that the list is really early (*Listen*,¹⁸).—[מנים]. This is a Heb. weight used often in OT. The value in silver is *c.* $30. If we take the *drachma* instead of the *daric*, the total sum given, according to Ezr., is about $300,000; or taking the *daric*, about $450,000. The figures show the hand of the Chr., whose fondness for large numbers is apparent in all his work.—[כתנת] 𝕲 μεχωνώθ Ne.^B χοθωνώθ^AN, χοθωνοί Ezr.^B χιτω-

νας^A. ᴸ always has στόλάς, which is also found in Esd. The word
means *tunic*. It is here not a vestment to be worn only at religious
exercises, but the garment worn all the time.

68 f. Ezr. and Ne. differ widely, Ne. having a much fuller text, as
may be seen from the following parallels (including Esd.):

NE. *Some of the heads of the fathers gave for the work. The Tirshatha*
EZR.
ESD.

NE. *gave to the treasury: gold, 1,000 darics, 50 bowls, 530 pr.'*
EZR.
ESD.

NE. *tunics.   And some of the heads of the fathers*
EZR.   *And some of the heads of the fathers, when they came to the*
ESD.   *And some of the leaders according to their family, when*
              they came to the

NE.
EZR. *house of Yahweh, which is in Jerus. gave free-will offerings for*
ESD. *temple of God,   which is in Jerus. made a vow*

NE.
EZR. *the house of God, to set it upon its site.   According to their ability*
ESD.   *to set the house upon its site, according to their*
                        ability

NE.   *gave (𝕲^B ἔθηκαν, placed) to the treasury of the work (𝕲^B*
        τοῦ ἔτους, yearly) : gold, 20,000 darics, and
EZR. *they gave to the treasury of the work : gold, 61,000 darics, and*
ESD. *and to give to the holy treasury of the work : gold, 1,000 minæ, and*

NE. *silver, 2,200 minæ.   And what the rest*
EZR. *silver, 5,000 minæ, and 100 pr.' tunics.*
ESD. *silver, 5,000 minæ, and 100 pr.' tunics.*

NE. *of the people gave was : gold, 20,000 darics, and silver, 2,000 minæ*
EZR.
ESD.

NE. *(𝕲^{BA} lacks the passage so agreeing with Ezr.), and 67 pr.' tunics.*
EZR.
ESD.

The longer text is very systematic: the gifts come from three sources,
the governor, the chief, and the people, while in Ezr. they are all credited to the chiefs. The table makes this clear:

		GOLD	SILVER	ROBES	BOWLS
Ne.	Governor	1,000		[5]30*	50
				(𝕲 30 𝕲ᴸ 33)	
	Chiefs	20,000	2,200		
	People	20,000	2,000	67	
	Total	41,000	4,200	97	
				(100 in 𝕲ᴸ)	
Ezr.		61,000	5,000	100	
Esd.		1,000	5,000	100	

Nowhere in this section do we find so great a discrepancy. Ne. contains two statements which are lacking in Ezr.: (1) 30 of the pr.' garments were given by the Tirshatha and the others by "the rest of the people," and (2) the chiefs and the people each gave 20,000 darics of gold. In Ezr. these contributions were expressly given for the re-building of the temple, which in Esd. was the result of a vow made after their arrival in Jerus., a statement irreconcilable with Hg. Ne. has not a word about the rebuilding of the temple, saying simply that the offerings were "for the work," and that they were paid into a treasury. Each text conforms to its setting, as Ezr. precedes the temple-building while in Ne. we are getting close to the promulgation of the law by Ezra.

Ne. bears unmistakable signs of a composite origin, for we have the unusual ומקצת ראשי האבות (Dn. 1² being the only parallel) in one place, v. ⁶⁹, and ומראשי האבות as Ezr. in another, v. ⁷⁰; in v. ⁶⁹ we have *they gave for the work*, in v. ⁷⁰ *they gave to the treasury of the work*, and again *he gave to the treasury*, v. ⁶⁹. We find שתי רבות, v. ⁷⁰, directly followed by שתי רבוא, v. ⁷¹. We notice further that the passage is very disjointed. The first statement, "some of the heads of the fathers gave for the work," v. ⁶⁹, is suspended without any conclusion, but it is repeated in v. ⁷⁰ with a suitable continuation.

In Ezr. we find the clause about the purpose of the contributions pushed in between the subj. and the vb.: "and some of the heads of the fathers [when they came to the house of Yahweh which is in Jerus. made free-will offerings for the house of God to place it upon its site according to their ability] gave to the treasury of the work." In Ne. the subj. and vb. are directly joined, as they must be; therefore we may pronounce positively that the bracketed passage is an interpola-tion, inserted by the Chr. to make the statement agree with its context, and a part of the preparation for the rebuilding of the temple. The whole c. is therefore unquestionably later than the time of Zer.

The text of Ne. has manifestly been edited to conform to Ezr., and yet it bears traces of greater originality. Mey. prefers it as it stands,

* 𝕲 has 30, and as the 500 follows the 30 in the text, it is an obvious error.

an evidence of the insufficiency of the text criticism upon which conclusions have been drawn (*Ent.*¹⁹⁴ ᶠ·). It is difficult to think that an
editor would have systematically distributed the gifts among the three
classes, the governor, the chiefs, and the rest of the people. If we
eliminate the part that is common and two prob. glosses we get a surprisingly good text: *and some of the heads of the fathers gave for the work*
[*the Tirshatha gave into the treasury*] *1,000 gold darics, 50 bowls,* [5]30
*pr.' tunics. And the rest of the people gave 20,000 gold darics, 2,000 sil-
ver minæ, and 67 pr.' tunics.* When the passage from Ezr. was pushed
in, the clause bracketed was added of necessity. 𝕲 evidently has some
clew to the mystery when it rd. "to Neh." The figures are, of course,
too large, but we cannot rely upon the text, and they are doubtless
greatly exaggerated.

The character of the gifts and the work indicate a date later than
515. The time of Ezra is, on the whole, most suitable. Under his
rule gifts for the temple would be sought diligently, and from the greatness of his influence prob. large sums would be obtained.

EZR. 2⁷⁰–4³. THE HEBREW STORY OF THE REBUILDING OF THE TEMPLE.

A section recovered.—In MT. the period of Cy. and Shes. ends with
c. 1; for c. 2 is mostly a mere table of names, and has nothing to do
with that period; while c. 3 brings us to the time of Zer. and Dar.
Moreover, c. 3 begins *in medias res,* "when the 7th month approached."
In the original story some year must have been indicated. Then Zer.,
the builder of the temple, appears as leader without a word of intr.
In Esd. we have quite a different story. There is a long narrative,
3–5⁶, to which there is nothing correspondent in MT. Here we have
the tale of the Three Youths, contesting in wisdom before Dar., the
victory of one who proves to be Zer., the promise of King Dar. to give
him whatever he asks, the reminder of his vow to restore the vessels
and to rebuild the city, and a liberal permit from the king to undertake these things, with a brief list of those who availed themselves of
this privilege.

Torrey has made the brilliant suggestion that we have imbedded in
this story, a fragment of the Chr.'s original narrative (ES.²⁵ ᶠᶠ· ¹¹⁵ ᶠᶠ·).
Torrey believes that the story of the Three Youths ends at 4⁴², that
4⁴³⁻⁴⁷ᵃ· ⁵⁷⁻⁶¹ are interpolations, so that the recovered narrative consists
of 4⁴⁷ᵇ⁻⁵⁶ 4⁶²–5⁶. Torrey has painstakingly retranslated the passage
into Heb. and appended an English translation. But this acute scholar
has by no means let the text stand, for he transfers the narrative bodily
from the reign of Dar. to that of Cy., so that the passage becomes the

sequel to c. 1 and the hero is Shes., though Zer. is named in 5⁴. This
event is placed in the 2d year of Cy., and so in 3¹ we are dealing with
the 7th month of that year.

There are two difficulties in accepting this date. In our text, esp.
in the better version of Esd., there is a statement that Shes. and a company went from Bab. to Jerus., taking the temple vessels with them.
This whole passage would be a mere amplification of that statement.
A more serious difficulty is found in the fact, as shown in intr., that
c. 3 does belong to the time of Dar. I believe, therefore, that Torrey's
main premise is correct and that we have here a genuine section of the
OT.; but it has nothing to do with c. 1, though it is a necessary intr.
to c. 3. In some way Zer., who is here given Davidic lineage, had won
the favour of Dar., and so received authority to carry out the decree of
Cy., which according to Esd. 4⁴³ he had already vowed to do. The
date given is exactly what we need, agreeing with 4²⁴.

A suitable intr. of so conspicuous a figure as Zer. is too valuable to
ignore. Therefore it seems wise to give a part of the Esd. story, following in a measure Torrey's translation (ES.¹³³ ᶠ·)

C. 4. (47) Then King Dar.⁽¹⁾ arose and wrote⁽²⁾ letters for him to all
the satraps and governors and captains and deputies to the effect that
they should help along him and all with him who were going up to build
Jerus.⁽³⁾ (48) And Dar.⁽⁴⁾ wrote letters to all the governors in the
province Beyond the River and to those in Lebanon to bring cedar
timbers from Lebanon to Jerus. so that they might build the city with
them.⁽⁵⁾ (49) And he wrote concerning freedom for all Jews who
went up from his kingdom to Judah, that no ruler, deputy, governor,
or satrap should enter their doors, (50) and that all the country which
they possessed should be free from tribute; and that the Edomites⁽⁶⁾
should give up the villages which they had wrested from the Judeans.
(51) And for the building of the temple twenty talents of silver⁽⁷⁾ should
be paid annually until it was built; (52) and for offering daily upon the
altar whole burnt sacrifices, as they had commandment to offer them,
other ten talents annually. (53) And freedom should be given to all
who had come from Bab. to build the city and to their children and to
all the pr. . . . (57) And Dar.⁽⁸⁾ sent away all the vessels which Cy. had
brought out from Bab.; and everything which Cy. had said should be
done, he commanded to be done, and to be sent to Jerus. (58) And
when the youth came out [from the royal presence] he lifted his face
to heaven in the direction of Jerus. and praised the king of heaven. . . .
(61) And Zer. took the letters and⁽⁹⁾ went out and came to Bab. and
told everything to his brethren. (62) And they praised the God of
their fathers, because he had given them release and relief (63) to go
up and build Jerus. and the temple that is called by his name. And
for some days they kept a feast with musical instruments, drums,
and cymbals, and all their brethren danced⁽¹⁰⁾ and rejoiced. **C. 5.** (1)

Afterward heads of the fathers by tribes were chosen to go up, with their wives and sons and daughters and their men-servants and maid-servants and their cattle. (2) And Dar. sent with them a thousand⁽¹¹⁾ horsemen to bring them safely to Jerus. (3) And they made⁽¹²⁾ . . . for them to go up with them. (4) And these are the names of the men who went up acc. to their families by tribes by their divisions; (5) the pr., the sons of Phineas the sons of Aaron, Jes. the son of Josedek the son of Saraios. Then arose⁽¹³⁾ Zer. the son of Shealtiel of the house of David, of the family of Phares, of the tribe of Judah, (6) who spoke wise words to Dar. the king of Pers. in the 2d year of his reign, in the month Nisan the 1st month.

Notes. 1. Torrey substitutes Cy. for Dar. to agree with his theory of the chronology; but the evidence in favour of the text seems to me convincing.

2. "Arose and wrote" is a good evidence of a Heb. or Aram. original. It is true that a Jew might use the Hebraism, even if composing in Gk.

3. The document bears evidence of a composite character, as we find references here to building the city as well as the temple. The temple rather than the city is meant in v. ⁴⁸, as that was the purpose of the cedar timbers (*cf.* 3⁷).

4. The name is found in ᴸ here and in v. ⁵⁷, and is correct.

5. After 3 Esd. *cum eis.* The antecedent is cedar timbers. The whole construction is improved by this slight correction.

6. ᴮ has Chaldeans, but all other texts Edomites. This is the earliest mention of the Edomite aggression upon Judah, and may be the occasion of some of the many fierce prophecies against this people.

7. "Of silver" is found only in ᴸ, but it is prob. right; at all events silver is more prob. than gold.

8. See note 5.

9. The name is found only in ᴸ, but is right.

10. The text is sadly confused, and I have attempted to restore order out of chaos by transposing a clause from 5² ᶠ˙. Torrey tries to straighten the matter out by a smaller transposition and rendering: "and all their brethren, playing upon musical instruments, drums, and cymbals, sent them on their way as they went up," that is, the Jews who remained played music as the caravan proceeded on its way. This rendering seems to me to require some straining of the text.

11. This number is doubtless an exaggeration, though some escort would be prob. Neh. had such a guard (2⁹), and Ezra implies that his dispensing with an escort was unusual (8²²).

12. I do not understand this passage. It seems clear that some-thing is omitted from the text, as I think it is a direct sequel to the provision of the guard.

13. Seeing ויקם in the meaningless name Ιωαχειμ seems to me one of Torrey's most brilliant suggestions.

Vv. ⁴⁻⁶ presents a serious puzzle. The passage begins with an intr. to a list of names such as begins in v. ⁷, but the only names which occur here are those of the leaders Jes. and Zer. The passage as a whole is senseless as it stands, note esp. v. ⁵ᵃ after v. ⁴. If we place Torrey's discovered ויקם before Jes. we have an amplified parall. Ezr. 3². It certainly improves the text greatly to substitute this clause for the briefer statement in Ezr. 3²ᵃ, then v. ⁴. ⁵ᵃ serves as a heading for the genealogical list which follows. The added information about Zer. fits into the building story admirably. Moreover, the account of the migration in vv. ¹⁻³ paves the way for the statement of the settlement in the province in Ezr. 2⁷⁰, cf. Ezr. 3².

The dates in the section 2⁷⁰–4³ are somewhat hard to reconcile. In the first place, "seventh" month in 3¹ is an error which got into our text from the excerpted passage from Ne. The reconstructed text of 3² fixes the 1st month of the 2d year of Dar. as the date of building the altar, and so of the assembly described in 3¹. In the same year in the 6th month, as the text should be (cf. on 3⁸⁻¹⁰), the foundation of the temple was laid. We thus have a consistent scheme, although the events described by this passage cover a much larger period than the text suggests. The date is recorded for the beginning but not for the ending.

2⁷⁰ Ne. 7⁷² = Esd. 5⁴⁵. The settlement of the returned exiles in Judah.

—We require the help of Esd. to get good sense out of this verse, which by the omission or substitution of one or two words is sadly confused. The original was: *And the priests and the Levites and the singers and the porters and some of the people were living in Jerusalem and all Israel [were living] in their villages.* The passage then becomes of great value in bearing witness to the conditions before the building of the temple. The temple officers naturally clung to the holy city, while all Israel (in contrast with the temple officers) sought a refuge and a livelihood in the towns of the province, for Jerusalem was a desolation and offered no means of procuring a living.

3¹⁻⁶ᵃ = Esd. 5⁴⁶⁻⁵³. The building of the altar.

—1. *When the seventh month was come*]. This is the original date in Ne., but this assembly is fixed in the first month. The year is the second of Darius (Hg. 1^{15}), not of the return under Cyrus.— *The sons of Israel were in cities*]. These words have no place here. Esd. has a fitting connection rendering, *the sons of Israel being each occupied in his own affairs*, meaning that when the assembly was called all the people were scattered over the country working for their bread. The words are probably accidentally repeated from the preceding verse.—*The people*]. Read with Ne. *all the people;—as one man*]. This may mean all together, or as Esd. *with one accord*, for a common purpose;— *unto Jerusalem*]. Ne. has a fuller text, *unto the broad place which is before the water gate*, to which 𝕲^L prefixes *Jerusalem*. Esd. brings the assembly to the temple: *unto the broad place of the first porch towards the east.* (The simpler text of Ezr. is preferable here.) But the temple was not yet built.

> At this point the deuterograph ends, each narrative now going its own way, Ezr. to the temple-building, and Ne. to the reading of the law.

2. *Joshua*] (or Jeshua) is named the high priest, or the great priest. It is the same person mentioned in 2^2, and he was a prominent figure in the temple-building and the restoration of the cult.

> He is the first high priest in the list going down to the time of Alexander the Great (Ne. 12^{10} ff.). Jes. is named first here, but in 2^2 3^8 4^3 5^2 Ne. 12^1 and throughout Hg., Zer. stands first. It is interesting to note that in Hg. Zer. is evidently the more important of the two (*v.* esp. 2$^{21-23}$), while in Zc. he is only mentioned in 4$^{6-10}$ as the builder of the temple. Zer. is never given a title in Zc., while Hg. four times calls him "the governor of Judah." Zc. again never names his father, as Hg. does, though Zc. calls Jes. the son of Jehozadak. Jes. here comes before us for the first time in action. We know nothing about his forebears except the name of his father. He joined Zer. in a company returning from Bab. (2^2 Ne. 12^1), and it may have been the second large company. At all events, it was later than the return under Shes.

And his brethren the priests]. Joshua is here put as one of the priests, while the contemporary Haggai calls him high priest. The Chronicler has not exalted the priesthood as much as we

should expect according to those who credit that worthy with
the production of the larger part of these books.—*And they
built the altar*].* So David built the altar on the temple mountain long before the temple was erected (2 S. 24^{25}). The purpose for which the altar was built is *to offer sacrifices upon it*].
The altar could be built in a very short time, and so the religious exercises could begin without waiting for the temple, which
it would take long to build.—*The law of Moses*] probably refers
only to Dt. here, not to the priest code, nor to the complete
Pentateuch. Dt. was attributed to Moses, and it makes abundant provision for the one altar and the sacrifices upon it.—
Man of God] is a term applied to Moses, Dt. 33^1 Jos. 14^6 1 Ch.
23^{14} 2 Ch. 30^{16}; to an angel, Ju. 13^6; to Samuel, 1 S. 9^6; to Elijah,
1 K. 17^{18}; to Elisha, 2 K. 4^7; to David, 2 Ch. 8^{14} Ne. 12$^{24.\ 36}$;
it is therefore a prophetic title. In the NT. it is applied to
Timothy, the disciple of Paul, 1 Tim. 6^{11} 2 Tim. 3^{17}.

3. This v. has been a sore puzzle to the interpreters. Sense cannot
be extorted from the text as it stands. ARV. renders "and they set
the altar upon its base; for fear was upon them because of the peoples
of the countries, and they offered burnt-offerings thereon unto Jeho-
vah, even burnt-offerings morning and evening." But in the critical
part the Heb. runs, *for in fear against them from the peoples of the lands.*
Much stress is laid upon the longer text in Esd. 5^{50}: *And certain men
gathered unto them out of the other nations of the land, and they erected
the altar upon its own place, because all the nations of the land were at
enmity with them, and oppressed them; and they offered sacrifices according to the time, and burnt-offerings to the Lord both morning and evening*
(RV.). Various reconstructions of the text have been made on the
basis of this evidence, but it really confuses matters worse than ever;
for the hostile peoples here become the altar-builders; and "the peoples
of the land" is unnecessarily repeated. Moreover, while the statements are amplified, there is nothing new exc. the hostile assembling
of the enemy. Torrey tried a modification and rendered his emended
text: "And some of the peoples of the land gathered themselves together against them; and when they perceived that they were come
with hostile purpose, they withstood them, and built the altar in its
place," etc. (*Comp.* ^{13}). The point is, therefore, that the returned Israelites succeeded in building the altar in spite of the hostility of their

---

* Jos. quotes Hecataeus's statement that the altar was 20 cubits square and 10 cubits high
(Smith, *Jer.* ii,^{208}).

neighbours. This emendation I formerly accepted (*SBOT*.⁶⁰); but it
does not touch the real difficulties, which are two: (1) The altar was
already built, v. ²; no one has attempted to explain the repetition of the
altar-building; the words are slightly different in Heb., it is true, ויכינו
for ויבנו, but the meaning is exactly the same.   (2) There is great difficulty in bringing in at this point the terror of the neighbours.   In
c. 4 these people come with a sincere and friendly proposition to join
the Jews in rebuilding the temple.   So forcible is this objection that
following Ew. various attempts have been made to show that the
passage means that these other peoples were in fear of the Jews, or of
their God.   To say nothing of the impossibility of extracting this
mng. from any text whatever, the Jews were scarcely in a position to
inspire much terror among the neighbouring peoples.

There is one text of Esd. (Cod.ᴮ) which curiously has either been
overlooked or misunderstood.   And this text is on the whole the best
Gk. version we have.   Correcting this text on the basis of the corresponding passage of the same version in Ezr. and making other slight
modifications, we get this striking result: *for there were gathered unto
them some from other nations of the land; and they were well disposed
towards the altar, and they aided them, and they offered sacrifices at the
proper season and burnt-offerings to Yahweh morning and evening.*   Zc.'s
vision (8²³) was based on past history.   The other peoples in Palestine came forward and helped the feeble Jews in the rebuilding of the
altar, and thus we can understand their coming forward at a later
period (c. 4) to render similar assistance in the rebuilding of the temple.   As thus understood the fatal objections to our present text and
all the reconstructions are removed, and we have a most welcome
light on the early relation of the Jews to their neighbours.   One result
of the right understanding of the passage is indubitable evidence that
we have here a good historical source.   The Chr. has worked over the
material until its sense was lost.   But the evidence is important as
showing that he had something to go on in this part of his story.   On
the oft-recurring "peoples of the land," *v.* on 4⁴.

4. *And they kept the Feast of Booths*].   "Booths" is better
than "tabernacles" of our versions.   The latter term comes from
𝔊 through 𝔙, *tabernaculum*, which means *tent*.   The booth was
made of branches from the trees (Lv. 23⁴⁰).

This feast was of Canaanite origin, as it was observed by the Shech-
emites (Ju. 9²⁷).   In the earliest law, the code of the covenant, it is called
the feast of the harvest, and it is to be kept at the end of the year (Ex.
23¹⁶).   Dt. prescribes seven days for the festival, but leaves the date
as in the earlier code, making the important addition that the festival

was to be kept at Jerus. In P we find the date fixed as the 15th day
of the 7th month, the time is lengthened to eight days, and the whole
character of the festival is changed. The joyful harvest feast becomes
a solemn assembly for the offering of sacrifices to Yahweh (Lv. 23³⁴⁻⁴⁴
Nu. 29¹²⁻⁴⁰).

As it is written]. Esd. adds *in the law*. The rest of the verse,
as Esd. shows, consists mostly of the Chronicler's amplification of
a simple statement to make it harmonise with the feast as it
was observed in his own time. There is no ground for the contention that the festival was kept in accordance with P (Chap-
man, *DB.* iv,⁶⁶⁹ ᵃ). The original said no more than that sacrifices were offered according to the custom (not "ordinance,"
as RV.). Sacrifices were offered at this feast in pre-exilic days
(1 K. 8² 12³²).—*As the duty of every day required;* literally*, the requirement of each day in its day*]. This is a gloss to make this
celebration agree with Nu. 29¹²⁻⁴⁰, where detailed offerings are
prescribed for each of the eight days. The Chronicler, however, happily overlooked the fact that the text he worked over
so carefully had not stated that the feast was observed on the
15th day, and there is nothing to guarantee that it was kept in
the 7th month. Kosters regards the whole verse as an interpolation (*Wied.*³⁰). **5.** *And afterwards the continual burnt-offering*].
This rule is first found in P (Ex. 29³⁸ ᶠᶠ·). Two yearling lambs
were offered, one in the morning, the other at evening. It
is the sacrifice called in v. ³ *the offerings of the morning and
evening*, and like that is due to the Chronicler.—*And for the
new moons*] *i. e.*, offerings for the feasts of the New Moon. This
was an ancient festival, as we know from its observance by
the prophets (*cf.* 1 S. 20⁵ 2 K. 4²³). On that day no business
was transacted (Am. 8⁵). In the law it finds place only in P,
where there are abundant regulations (Ex. 40². ¹⁷ Nu. 10¹⁰ 28¹¹⁻¹⁵
29⁶).—*And for all the holy seasons of Yahweh*]. The list of these
is given in Lv. 23, Sabbath, Passover, Weeks, Trumpets, Atone-
ment, Booths. The Sabbath and the New Moon were early
festivals (2 K. 4²³ Am. 8⁵). To these are added "the sacred
seasons" in Is. 1¹⁴ as the general name for feasts other than New
Moon and Sabbath. The passage, therefore, is in harmony

with pre-exilic usage. **5ᵇ–6.** *And of every one that willingly
offered a free-will offering unto Yahweh.* In 𐤄 this passage is
without antecedent or consequent. As it stands we should
have to translate *and for every one*, etc., a manifest absurdity.
We get good sense by connecting with the following verse as
in Esd., *And every one who made a vow to Yahweh, from the new
moon of the first month, he began to offer sacrifices to God.* Vows
had been made by the people, as for a safe journey back to
Judah, for a prosperous year, but there had been no opportunity to pay these vows until the altar was set up. Now it was
possible to discharge these obligations. That is, we have here
underneath the confusion of the Chronicler a clear trace of the
re-establishment of the religious life of the community, though
on rather simple lines.

The events described cover a period of several months, from the
7th month of one year to the early part of the year following. As
v. ⁶ stands in Heb. it is a restrospective statement. The people began
the routine of the regular offerings on the 1st day of the 7th month.
As that statement requires us to suppose that the assembly gathered,
the altar was rebuilt, and offerings made all on one day, it is manifest
that the chron. scheme is impracticable.

70. A comparison of the three texts is enlightening here:

NE. *And the pr. and the Lev.*
EZR. *And the pr. and the Lev. and some of the people*
ESD. *And the pr. and the Lev. and some of the people*

NE. *and the porters and the singers and some of the*
EZR. *and the singers and the porters*
ESD. *were living in Jerus. and in the country, but the*

NE. *people and the Neth. and all Israel were living*
EZR.   *and the Neth.*
ESD. *singers and the porters and all Israel in*

NE. *in their cities*
EZR. *in their cities, and all Israel in their cities*
ESD. *their villages.*

The Heb. texts are both impossible. Sense could be secured by
omitting ומן־העם, but then the statement would be pointless, as all the
people would abide in the same place. If we turn to Esd. and perceive that καὶ τῇ χώρᾳ is a gl., prob. inserted from 𐤄 בעריהם (3 Esd. has
region in both places), we get excellent sense and the very statement

necessary, as this v. goes back to Esd. 5¹⁻⁶, and describes the first step after reaching Judah. The pr. the Lev. and a few of the people settled in Jerus.; the singers and the porters and the rest of Israel turned to the more promising life in and around the country villages. But it is not necessary to depart so far from MT. In Ne. v. ⁷² we note that בעריהם is not repeated. If we substitute the necessary בירושלם for והנתנים we have a good text, and exc. for the transposition of singers and porters exactly what we have in Esd.

III. 1. ויגע] is used nowhere else of the coming of time; but as the Hiph. has this meaning we should prob. point וַיַּע as Is. 6⁷.—בעריכ] Ne. בעריהם, so 𝕲 ἐν πόλεσιν αὐτῶν. The phrase "the sons of Israel were in their villages" is of peculiar difficulty here, as the passage is undoubtedly connected closely with 2⁷⁰ and the repetition is awkward. We might connect 2⁷⁰ closely with Esd. 5¹⁻⁶ and presuppose a full break in a paragraph, or supply a word, *the sons of Israel being still in their villages*, i. e., up to the 7th month the people had not come to Jerus. Esd., however, offers an alternative; in that text (5⁴⁶) we find καὶ ὄντων τῶν υἱῶν Ἰσραὴλ ἑκάστου ἐν τοῖς ἰδίοις. So 3 Esd., *cumque essent filii Israel unusquisque in suis rebus, the sons of Israel each being occupied with his own affairs*, i. e., with the gaining of a livelihood. This gives a satisfactory sense, and we must either adopt this reading, or suppose the clause to be an accidental repetition from 2⁷⁰. As the subj. of "gathered" is expressed, and as this clause really breaks the connection of the 7th month and the assembling of the people, the latter is preferable. In a MS. of 𝕲 (in Ne.) the coming of the 7th month follows the statement that the sons of Israel were in their cities. —**2.** ויקם] is sg., but following vb. is pl. The first vb. is sg. on account of close connection with ישוע.—זרבבל] is a Bab. name (*v.* my note in *Poly. Bib. Ezr.-Neh.*⁶⁸). Some, indeed, make it Heb. זְרֻעֶבֶל, "begotten in Bab." But it is now generally explained as *ziru Babili*, "seed of Bab." (Mey. *Ent.*⁷, Sieg. on 2²). In our sources and in Hg. he is called the son of Shealtiel, but in 1 Ch. 3¹⁹, son of Pedaiah the grandson of King Jehoiakim. But Pedaiah had several brothers, among whom we find Shenazar (= Shes., *v. s.* on 1⁸) and Shealtiel, the latter being Zer.'s uncle. Either the Chr. has confused the names, or Zer. was brought up by his uncle and thus became known as his son.—שאלתיאל]. In Hg. 1¹². ¹⁴ 2² שלי. 𝕲 Σαλαθιηλ ("I have asked of God").—ואחיו] is difficult; 𝕲ᴮ lacks part of the v., *i. e., the pr. and Zer. the son of Shealtiel and his brethren*, but a copyist has jumped over the words on account of the repeated ἀδελφοί. The word can only be used here in a general sense of the laity. In our books it has much the same mng. as Aram. כנות "associates," men of the same class.—תורת] meant in the earlier literature the oral word of Yahweh, esp. by the mouth of the prophet; it is there almost equiv. to teaching; here it has the later sense of the written law.

3. Rarely have we so much to choose from in determining a text, both from ancient Vrss. and from modern conjecture. All agree that MT. is impossible and there agreement ends. The basis of most efforts at restoration is Esd.ᴸ (5⁵⁰), here rendered into Heb. for easy comparison with MT.

ויקבצו עליהם מעמי הארץ ויכינו המזבח על מכונתו כי באימה עליהם וֹם־] כל־עמי

הארץ ויתחזקו ויעלו עליו] זבחים במועדו ועלות ליהוה ועלות] לבקר ולערב.

The underlined and the bracketed parts represent MT.; it appears thus that Esd. contains all of MT. with one significant additional clause at the beginning. This is virtually the text accepted by Guthe, but instead of clearing up the difficulty it only adds to the confusion. Torrey worked on somewhat freer lines, with this result, so far as it differs from the above: ויבינו כי באיבה עליהם ויתחזקו ויכינו (*Comp.*¹²). Torrey is obliged to translate his text with much freedom. Haupt says forcibly that on this reconstruction we should rd. כי באו באיבה עליהם (*SBOT*.⁶⁰). Various slight modifications have been proposed. Ryle omits prep. מ before עמי and so gets: "for the people of the countries were a terror to them." Van Hoonacker regards בימה as an Aram. word: "they established the altar upon its bases; for a *bamah* was found above, erected by the care of the peoples of the land" (*Restaur.*¹⁴⁴). In justification he says: "The cult had not been suppressed, but the altar where it had been celebrated was a sacrilegious altar." Zillessen proposed כי אימת אלהים בעמי הארץ (*ZAW*. 1904,¹⁴⁴), but this lacks any textual support.

The attempts to reconstruct the text on the basis of Esd. all work on the easier text of ᴸ. When we turn to ᴮ we note some significant variations. That text runs: καὶ ἐπισυνήχθησαν αὐτοῖς ἐκ τῶν ἄλλων ἐθνῶν τῆς γῆς καὶ κατωρθώθησαν ἐπὶ τὸ θυσιαστήριον ἐπὶ τοῦ τόπου αὐτῶν· ὅτι ἐν ἔχθρᾳ ἦσαν αὐτοῖς κατίσχυσαν αὐτοὺς πάντα τὰ ἔθνη τὰ ἐπὶ τῆς γῆς· καὶ ἀνέφερον θυσίας κατὰ τὸν καιρὸν καὶ ὁλοκαυτώματα κυρίῳ τὸ πρωινὸν καὶ τὸ δειλινόν. This should be rendered somewhat differently from the prevalent translations, thus: *And there were gathered to them some from all the other peoples of the land, and they were favorably disposed towards the altar [upon its place, for they were at enmity with them] so that all the peoples which were in the country helped them and they offered sacrifices according to the season, and burnt-offerings to Yahweh morning and evening.* At the start αὐτοῖς represents עליהם in the sense of אליהם, so that the gathering is friendly not hostile (*cf.* Esd. 9⁵). From this text we cannot extort "they erected the altar on its base." The vb. κατωρθώθησαν represents ישר in Mi. 7² Ps. 119¹²⁸ Pr. 2⁷· ⁹ 14¹¹, and followed by ἐπί must be rendered as above. Χατίσχυσαν might mean *overpowered*, but followed by acc. we find it standing for עזר in 1 Ch. 15²⁶ 2 Ch. 14¹⁰. Putting into Heb. the parts not in brackets we have: ויקבצו אליהם מעמי הארץ האחרים ויישרו אל המזבח ויעזרום כל עמי הארץ

ויעלו זבחים כעת ועלות ליהוה לבקר ולערב.

To demonstrate in the usual way how this grew out of our present text by slight changes here and there is beyond the critic's art; but to show how this statement was reduced to the confusion we now have is not so hard. The idea that the altar was built with the aid of the peoples in Palestine was intolerable to the people who had drunk deeply of the spirit of Ezra. By a few strokes of the pen that friendly aid has been changed to a fear. The text of Esd. has been corrected from MT. by putting in the new parts, but where they make no sense. ᴸ has worked over the passage and made it intelligible but entirely wrong. It is possible to put the substance of the passage in still closer conformity to MT.: כי באו המה עליהם מעמי הארצות ויישרו אל־המזבח ויעזרום ויעלו. We might go a little further in our reconstruction, reading Kt. ויעל (supported by 𝔊ᴮᴬ). Connecting then with v. ² we get this clear sense: *And Jes. . . . got ready and they built the altar of the God of Israel to offer burnt-offerings upon it . . . for there were gathered unto them some of the peoples of the lands, and they were well disposed towards the altar, and they helped them, and he [Jes.] offered upon it,* etc. Comparing emended text (1) with MT. (2) we have:

⁽¹⁾ כי באו המה עליהם מעמי הארצות ויישר המזבח עליהם   ויעל עליו עלות ליהוה.

⁽²⁾ כי באימה   עליהם מעמי הארצות ויכינו המזבח על מכונתו ויעל עליו עלות ליהוה.

This reconstruction is as near to the original as practicable to preserve the sense. The changes are not very great after the clauses are transposed. The rest of v., "offerings morning and evening," is a later gl.; for the original writer would not have repeated עלות. Moreover, this passage describes the first offering made upon the newly erected altar, whereas our text betrays the later point of view in bringing in the regular establishment. The daily offering is described in v. ⁴.

4. וְעֹלֹת]. So we should rd. with all texts of 𝔊; Esd. lacks במספר and דבר יום ביומו. ᴸ further lacks יום ביום, having only עלת במשפט. Since "offerings" lacks a governing vb. it may be that the whole clause was lacking in the original text. At all events, the clumsy hand of the Chr. is apparent in the glosses.—**5.** עֹלֹת]. With 𝔊 rd. pl. as in v. ⁴.—לשבתות] a word added in Esd. 5⁵¹. The Chr. is fond of combining sabbaths, new moons, and holy seasons (1 Ch. 23³¹ 2 Ch. 2³ 8¹³ 31³ Ne. 10³⁴, so Ez. 45¹⁷).—יהוה] is lacking in 𝔊ᴮᴬ. It is better to om. the redundant המקרשים. Elsw. we find מועדי יהוה, Lv. 23 (4 t.) 2 Ch. 2³, or מועדים alone. —תמיד] is added by the Chr. to bring the passage up to date. The intr. of this word has made the passage quite ungrammatical, requiring the addition of "offerings" as in RV. As so often happens, Esd. preserves both the original and the substitution.—ולכל המתנרב נרבה] Esd. 5⁵² καὶ ὅσοι εὔξαντο εὐχήν = וכל־הנרר נדר a far better text.—מיום אחר לחרש— χαὶ ὅσοι εὔξαντο εὐχήν = וכל־הנרר נדר a far better text.—מיום אחר לחרש— מחרשי [השביעי] Esd. ἀπὸ τῆς νουμηνίας τοῦ πρώτου μηνός (ᴬᴸ ἐβδόμου) = לחרש האחר, a correction by the Chr. to agree with the idea of v. ¹ that all these things happened in the 7th month. But as he has here the 1st day of that month, his chronology is impossible.

6ᵇ–4³ is a pretty complete parallel to the Aram. story of the rebuilding of the temple, c. 5, 6. We have in both places the actual building,
the appearance of the neighbouring peoples, and the dedication. The
greatest divergence is in connection with the foreigners, for in one case
the neighbours came with an offer of assistance, while in the other they
came for investigation. There is a striking parallel in the fact that in
both cases the Jews appealed to the edict of Cy. (4³ 5¹³). The reconstructed text shows that the original was a true parallel. But the Chr.
made sad havoc of his sources. He had a conviction, which may have
been based on a tradition explaining the long delay in the restoration
of the temple, that the interference of the enemy was effective for several years, and he has modified the sources accordingly. But such
effective interference is unknown both in the contemporary prophets
Hg. and Zc., and in the Aram. account, for 5¹⁶ is surely a gl. by the Chr.,
since it would be strange for interference to begin after the work had
gone on for fifteen years, and according to 5² *they began to build the
house of God.*

As the Chr.'s editing is so conspicuous throughout, it is evident that
before his time there was a Heb. account of the rebuilding of the temple. The Chr. could not be author and editor too, esp. since the editor changed the whole significance of the story. The recognition of
the original character of the passage disposes of Kost.'s assertion that
vv. ⁸⁻¹³ are unhistorical.

6ᵇ–10ᵃ. The temple is rebuilt.—6ᵇ. *Now the temple of
Yahweh was not yet begun*]. This begins a new section, yet
EVˢ. separate from preceding only by a colon. The awkward
paraphrase in our Vrss.—"the foundation of the temple of Je-
hovah was not yet laid"—is unnecessary. The words describe
the condition at the time indicated in vv. ¹⁻⁶ᵃ, and they lead us
to expect another step, and we are not disappointed.—**7.** *And
they paid money to the quarrymen and stonecutters*]. 𝔊ᴸ reads,
he paid, i. e., Zerubbabel. The workmen named here are not
masons and carpenters as EVˢ., but the two classes of stone-
workers: those who did the wood-work are named further on.
These were men working in the quarries near the temple site,
perhaps in the ruin-heaps of the old temple, and were paid
wages.—*And food and drink and oil to the Sidonians and to the
Tyrians*]. These were not paid in cash, but in subsistence. According to 2 Ch. 2⁹ Solomon agreed to give to the Phœnician carpenters who prepared the timber for the first temple wheat, bar-

ley, wine, and oil; but in 1 K. 5^{25} only wheat and oil are named.
The present builders are following the *modus operandi* of their
famous predecessor, or this account is coloured by the Chronicler's version of the early event.   The Phœnicians were famous
for dressing timber (1 K. 5^{25}).—*To bring cedar timbers from the
Lebanon unto the sea at Joppa*].   This follows closely the Chronicler's story also (2 Ch. 2^{15}).   In 1 K. 5^{23} the place where the
timbers were delivered is not mentioned.   *Joppa* is on the coast
north-west of Jerusalem and is the natural port of entry.   The
Phœnicians were to bring the timbers down the coast, the Jews
naturally being inexpert in that kind of service.   Hg. probably
refers to Lebanon in 1^{8} (Mitchell, *in loc.*).   Marti thinks reference to the hills of Judah (*Dodekapr.*).—*According to the permit of Cyrus, king of Persia, in their favor*].   Happily para-
phrased in 𝔈: "as Cyrus . . . had directed them."   This would
naturally imply that the grant of Cyrus referred to the securing
of timber from the Lebanon, and royal sanction would be necessary, as that range was now under the control of Persia.

> In the decree of 1$^{2-4}$ nothing is said of timber, but in 6^{4} this material
> is named, though only in connection with the specifications for build-
> ing.   Therefore we are driven to a freer interpretation: Cy. authorised
> the construction of the temple, and that warrant carries with it by
> implication the right to procure the materials wherever they may be
> found.   The implication is that we are still in the reign of Cy., though
> the words will permit a later date.   The phrase may be a note by the
> Chr. to support his theory that these events fell in the reign of Cy.   But
> it is permissible to suppose that the terms of Cy.'s decree would hold
> in the time of Dar.   Another possibility is that the Chr. substituted
> Cy. for Dar. for the latter gave such a decree (*cf.* Esd. 4^{48} and note at
> beginning of this c.).   Therefore we need not be disturbed by the state-
> ment that Cy. had not authority to give such a permit because Cam-
> byses was the first to control the west country (Justi, *Gesch. Iran.*^{424}).

8–10^{a}. The text in part is scarcely intelligible; it runs (8)
*And in the 2d year of their coming to the house of God at
Jerusalem, in the 2d month, Zerubbabel the son of Shealtiel and
Jeshua the son of Jozadak and the rest of their brethren, the priests
and the Levites, and all who had come from the captivity to Jerusa-
lem began—and they appointed the Levites from twenty years old*

and upward to superintend the work of the house of Yahweh. (9)
*And Jeshua, his sons and his brethren, Kadmiel and his sons the
sons of Judah, stood up with one accord to superintend the workmen at the house of God, the sons of Henadad, their sons and their
brethren the Levites.* (10) *And the builders began the temple of
Yahweh.* In this text we notice a sentence that is never finished, v. ⁸; Zerubbabel *et al.* began something, but we are not
told what they began, or what the result was. We have two
distinct statements about superintendence, in one place of the
Levites, in the other of Jeshua. Finally we learn that the builders began or laid the foundations of the temple, but it goes no
further. Esd. shows duplication after MT., but it contains
three clear statements: (1) Zerubbabel *et al.* laid the foundation of the temple in the 2d year of the return (or of Darius);
(2) Jeshua and other Levites served as superintendents of the
building (or as chief workmen); (3) the temple of Yahweh was
building at this time, not merely the foundations, but the
structure. So in 4¹ the Samaritans heard that the Jews were
building a temple. Torrey sees that Esd. has the true reading
(*Comp.*⁵⁵), but he does not apparently recognise its full significance.

The passage may be reconstructed with the help of Esd. so
that it tells a surprising and clear story of the work on the temple, advanced to completion, or certainly beyond anything suggested in MT. The revised text, which in its essential features
is justified in the notes, is rendered thus: *And in the 2d year
of Darius, in the 6th month, Zerubbabel the son of Shealtiel
and Jeshua the son of Jozadak and their brethren, and the priests,
the Levites, and all (others) who had come in from the captivity
to Jerusalem began and laid the foundation of the house of God.
On the 1st day of the 2d month of the 2d year of their coming
to Judah and Jerusalem, then they appointed the Levites of twenty
years and upward for the work on the house of Yahweh; then arose
Jeshua and Bani and Ahijah and Kadmiel, the sons of Hodaviah
and the sons of Henadad their sons and their brothers, all the Levites doing the work on the house of God, and the builders were
erecting the temple of Yahweh.*

Unto the house of God in v. ⁸ is a gl. of the Chr. showing his tendency
to anachronism; the sequence to their coming is "to Jerus." The important date, the 2d year of Dar., is found in Esd.ᴸ and is doubtless
correct. Virtually all interpreters have explained this note of time
as being the 2d year of the return under Shes., 538 B.C. But neither
Zer. nor Jes. was in that party, and it is certain that the temple was
not begun at that time. We have here further the important fact
indirectly disclosed that there was a large migration to Judah in the
1st year of the reign of Dar., a fact inferred from Esd. 5¹⁻⁶. The dates
are given with the particularity characteristic of the time, as in Hg.,
first by the king's reign, and then by the sojourn in Jerus. That two
dates were in the original is suggested by the separation of the year
and month by several intervening words. The later law of P made
thirty years (instead of the twenty years in text) the age for the Lev.
to begin their holy service (Nu. 4³· ²³· ³⁰· ³⁵, but twenty-five years in
8²⁴). The Chr. has both thirty years (1 Ch. 23³) and twenty (*ib.* v. ²⁴).
The passage may be due to the Chr.'s efforts to make history conform
to law. In regard to Jes. and Bani, no reconstruction of the hopeless
confusion inspires much confidence. But as "their sons and their
brethren" (v. ⁹), are comprehensive, we may suspect that in the bewildering mass of sons and brothers preceding we have corrupted proper
names.

Erecting is a contribution from Esd., but in spite of its significance
it has generally been ignored by commentators. Yet it might have
been inferred from the fact that those who had seen the old temple
were disappointed at the new one, v. ¹². If nothing had been done
but laying the foundation, such a comparison with the Solomonic temple would have been impossible. It is true that the celebration (v. ¹¹)
might have come after the foundations were laid, at least arguing from
the modern ceremonious laying of corner-stones; but it would surely
be more suitable at a time when the temple was well under way. The
"builders" are identified with the Phœnicians (Berth. *et al.*), but that
can scarcely be the case, for these were designated to prepare the ma-
terials in the mountains, while the Jews themselves, or the hired workmen named in v. ⁷, did the building. The term is comprehensive, and
covers all who were engaged in the big task.

A vexing problem is the work of the Lev. The term מלאכה does mean
"worship" (*v.* on 2⁶⁹), and Mey. seems to insist that it has that sense
throughout. But his contention ignores the use of the term in Hg. 1¹⁴,
"they did the work on the house of Yahweh," where "work" certainly
refers to the building operations. If the meaning "worship" were in-
sisted on, we should have to regard a large part of this passage as an
addition by the Chr., who strove hard enough to make it fit his theory.
There is no good reason though to doubt that the pr. and the Lev. did
much of the building. Certain classes of skilled labourers were en-

gaged in cutting timber and stones (v. ⁷). But there was a vast amount
of labour which pr. could do as well as laymen. In Ne. 3, pr. took a
conspicuous part in the rebuilding of the wall. But there the Chr. has
tried to obscure the correct meaning (*v. i.* 3¹); and he has presumably
done the same thing here.

6ᵇ. היכל]. As. *ekallu,* "palace" or "temple," prob. from Accadian
e-gal, "big house." In Heb. it means "palace" or, oftener, "temple."
As a rule, it stands alone for "temple," and is equiv. to בית יהוה, which
𝕲 reads here οἶκος κυρίου. Subj. precedes vb. to mark a circumstantial
clause (*Har. Syn.* § ⁴⁵).—יסר] means "lay a foundation" in 1 K 5³¹, but
"repair" or "restore" in 2 Ch. 24²¹ Is. 44²⁸. The latter is completely
parall. our passage: "saying to Jerus., thou shalt be rebuilt, and to the
temple (reading as Kt. ולהיכל) thou shalt be restored." Laying the
foundation as EVˢ. is not the idea of our passage; "begun" is the
right sense, and that use is found, *e. g.,* in Hg. 2¹⁸ Zc. 4⁹ 8⁹. Esd. renders ᾠκοδόμητο, "built."—**7.** חצבים] means *hewers.* It signifies "stone-
cutter" in 1 Ch. 22², but that is a loose use. We find as obj. "copper"
Dt. 8⁹, "cisterns" Dt. 6¹¹ Ne. 9²⁵, "sepulchre" Is. 22¹⁶, "wine-fat" Is.
5². In 1 K. 5²⁹ (EV. 5¹⁵) חצב בהר = "digging stone in the mountain";
so here the proper mng. is "quarrymen."—חרשים] = cutters of wood,
metal, or stone, generally with a genitive to define exactly. In 1
Ch. 22¹⁵ there is חרשי אבן ועץ, "cutters of stone and timber." The
proper mng. here is not "carpenters," since those are named later, but
"stonecutters," those who dressed the quarried stone.—שמו] Esd.ᴮ 5⁵⁵
χάρα = שמחה, which might stand for *whatever they pleased to ask.* 𝖧
cum gaudio. Esd. 5⁵⁵ adds after Lebanon *to transport it by rafts,* a
reflection of the older story, 1 K. 5²³.—ים] Esd. λιμένα and so *to the
harbor of Joppa.*—רשיון] α. λ. 𝕲ᴮᴬ ἐπιχώρησιν, γνώμηςᴸ (decree), Esd.
τὸ πρόσταγμα τὸ γραφέν, "the written order." 𝖧 *decretum quod scriptum
erat.* This may represent רשׁום בכתב (*cf.* Dn. 10²¹). The mng. of רשיון
"permit" is established by the Vrss., the context and by the cog.
languages.

8–10ᵃ. The textual problem in this passage is one of the most difficult in even this perplexing book. We note first that לנצח, a favourite
word of the Chr., is lacking in 𝕲ᴮ v. ⁸ and in 𝕲ᴮᴬ v. ⁹; as it is wanting in
Esd.ᴮᴬ, it may safely be discarded from the original. כאחד v. ⁹ is not
found in 𝕲ᴮᴬ and also should be omitted. But these minor details do
not relieve the passage of its almost hopeless confusion. The Chr.
might think that the establishment of Levitical duties was important
enough for all the preliminary notice in v. ⁸, but Zer. may have deemed
the temple-building as a more vital matter. Esd. does make the work
on the temple the prominent subj.; and his suggestion must be followed to extract order out of this chaos. The proposed text contains
all that we have in Heb., but in a different order and with some addi-

tions and variations. Any reconstruction must aim at good sense, and
make the passage a connecting link between v. ⁷ and c. 4. Combining
the two texts where necessary, the following is proposed: ובשנה השנית
לדריוש בחדש הששי החלו זרבבל בן־שאלתיאל וישוע בן־יוצרק ואחיהם הלוים
וכל־הבאים מהשבי לירושלם ויסדו את־בית־האלהים ביום אחד לחדש השני לשנה השנית
לבואם ליהודה ולירושלם ויעמידו את־הלוים מבן עשרים שנה ומעלה על־מלאכת בית־
יהוה ויעמר ישוע ובני ואחיה וקדמיאל בני הודוה ובני הנרד בניהם ואחיהם כל־הלוים
עשי המלאכת בבית האלהים ויבנו הבנים את־היכל יהוה.

’Επι Δαρείου is from Esd.ᴸ 5⁵⁶. This year agrees with Hg. 1¹.—[הששי]
both MT. and 𝔊 in all texts rd. השני. I have ventured to substitute
"sixth" from Hg. 1¹. It is not unlikely that the original author of
this piece took his whole date from Hg., where we have: "in the 2d
year of Dar. the king, in the 6th month, on the 1st day of the month."
—[החלו] a peculiar and impossible use of this vb. in MT., for it requires
another dependent upon it. Esd. supplies the necessary sequence. A
somewhat similar use is found in 2 Ch. 20²² and Dt. 2²⁴: "begin, possess." So here they began and laid the foundation, i. e., laid the foundation as the first step.—Esd.ᴮᴬ 5⁵⁶ has a longer list of Levitical workmen, adding to those in Heb. οἱ υἱοὶ ’Ιησοῦ ’Ημαδαβούν, unless this
stands for בני הנרד, which I suspect to be the case. There is also Εἰλι-
αδουν (= אלידון, "El judges"). It seems quite necessary to convert
בניו ואחיו into n. p., for the final "their sons and their brothers" refers
comprehensively to all the names in the list.—[בני] occurs frequently in
the Levitical lists.—The double date is explicable on the ground that
we have two stages of the work. In the 6th month of the 2d year of
Dar. the work of rebuilding began by laying the foundations. In the
6th month, the work not progressing fast enough, the pr. and Lev. were
set to the task.

To go back to our reconstructed text once more, it will be noted
that the main difference between MT. and Esd. is the clause ויסדו את־
בית האלהים. But MT. has ביח־ה׳ in v. ⁸, where it does not belong,
and it has ויסרו v. ¹⁰, where ויבנו is required by the connection and by
the Esd. text. I suspect that the required word is concealed in הבנים,
where οἱ οἰκοδόμοι of Esd. may be a correction. MT. first suffered
from dropping out a clause bodily, easily explained on account of the
repeated date, then the text was further modified to make what was
left as reasonable as possible.

Even in this reconstruction there is evidence of the Chr.'s amplification. Hg. addressed the temple-builders as Zer. Jes. and "all the people of the land," exactly what we have here, though we have a great
deal more. To reduce it to the Chr.'s source is a mere matter of conjecture, but the following is a fairly safe hazard: "And in the 2d year
of Dar. in the 6th month, Zer. the son of Shealtiel and Jes. the son of
Jozadak, and all who had come to Jerus. from the captivity began and
laid the foundations of the house of God. And in the 1st day of the

2d month of their coming to Jerus. they put the Lev. from twenty years and upward at the work of the house of God. And they were building the temple of Yahweh."

The one point assured is that in this passage we have a description of the laying of the foundations and the partial completion of the building. Jos. says specifically that the celebration described in 10ᵇ⁻13 occurred when "the temple was finished" (*Ant.* xi, 4, 2).

10ᵇ-13. The celebration.—This passage originally contained an account of the dedication of the temple.—**10ᵇ.** Not they "set the priests" (EVˢ.), but *the priests stood.* Nor is it right to render "in their apparel," though supported by BDB. and Ges.ᴮ, meaning *in their vestments,* but *furnished with trumpets.* The trumpet or clarion is the straight trumpet (Br. *Ps.*ˡˣˣᵛⁱⁱⁱ) in distinction from the crooked ram's horn. It is described as "a long, straight, slender metal tube with flaring end" (BDB. Benz. *Arch.*²⁷⁷, *DB.* iii,⁴⁶², where there is a cut from the arch of Titus). This was particularly the instrument of the priest (Ne. 10⁸) and was used to call an assembly (Ne. 10²), to sound an alarm (2 Ch. 13¹². ¹⁴), and to celebrate any joyful occasion (1 Ch. 16⁶).—*The Levites the sons of Asaph*]. In 2⁴¹ the sons of Asaph are singers. The reference is to that part of the order of Levites whose office was to furnish music. Not all Levites were sons of Asaph, but that term includes the musical class. The use of this expression probably shows a different source from 2⁴¹.—*With cymbals*]. This is parallel with the preceding clause, a word being understood, *i. e.*, the Levites furnished with cymbals. Cymbals only in Ch.-Ezr.-Ne. and 2 S. 6⁵ Ps. 150⁵, but in the Ps. a different Hebrew word is used. According to 1 Ch. 15¹⁹ cymbals were made of brass. The cymbals were for the Levites or sons of Asaph as distinctly as the trumpet was for the priests. They are often coupled with psalteries and harps, and are used to accompany the singers. They seemed to have been esteemed for the loud noise they made (1 Ch. 15¹⁹).—*After the order of David* (literally, *by the hands of David*)]. This is a characteristic note of the Chronicler. He naturally ascribes the Levitical use of musical instruments to David (2 Ch. 29²⁵ ᶠ·).—**11.** *And they answered in their praise*]. That is, they sang responsively. The words which follow are not, however, the praise song which was sung, but only the refrain which served as the response; therefore we might render: *they praised with the response.* It is difficult to think that a refrain which was so great a favourite with the Chronicler was quoted here in a mutilated form, therefore we should almost certainly read:

> Give thanks to Yahweh, for he is good;
> For his mercy is for everlasting.

This chorus is found in Ps. 106¹ 136¹ 1 Ch. 16³⁴ 2 Ch. 5¹³ 7³.— *Towards Israel*] would then have to be regarded as a gloss added by one who did not see the poetical quotation and who deemed it necessary to point the application. In any case the connection is awkward. Esd. felt the difficulty and rendered freely: *for his goodness and glory are eternal towards all Israel.—Now all the people shouted with a great shout*]. The unusual order, the subject preceding the verb, marks a concomitant circumstance. While the priests were blowing the trumpets and the Levites were playing the cymbals and singing, the mass of the people broke out with triumphant cries.—*Because the house of Yahweh was begun*]. Better with Esd. *because the house of Yahweh was building.* The Jews were not wont to celebrate the beginning of a building operation, but its completion.

> Acc. to the text we have judged to be the most original (*v. s.*), the foundation had been laid some time before, and at this period the building was well under way. No great stress can be laid upon the event, however, for the hand of the Chr. is conspicuous, and he was a far better idealist than historian. It may be that Esd. preserves a note of an original story when it says, *all the people blew the trumpets and shouted.* The whole population participated, making the demonstration more democratic than MT. suggests.

12. *Many of the priests and Levites*]. Esd. here as in other places omits the conjunction and thus preserves the deuteronomic expression *the priests the Levites.* This is an important reading, and it is quite possible that the sharp distinction between priest and Levite belongs to a later period than the early post-exilic, and was put back into this period by the Chronicler. —*The elders*] in our text is in explanatory opposition with *heads*

of clans, but in 𝕲^L it is separated by a conjunction and thus
made a separate class. That is an error, for the elders are not
here an official body, but the old people of all classes.—*Who
had seen the former house*], that is, the temple of Solomon which
had been destroyed by the Babylonians in 587.

RV. continues, "when the foundation of this house was laid before
their eyes"; but this is a desperate expedient to extract sense from an
unintelligible text. The Heb. will not yield that mng. by any possible
straining. The words "when its foundations were laid" refer not to
the new temple, but to the temple of Solomon! Manifestly no one living could have survived from Solomon's time, and the text is impossible.
The next clause is no better: *now the house in their eyes* has no connection fore or aft. Hg. 2³ throws important light on the passage both
for interpretation and date: "Who is there surviving among you that
saw this house in its former splendor? And what do you see it now?
Is it not of small account in your eyes?" The prophet saw that some
of the old people by making the invidious comparison were discouraging
the builders (*cf.* Halévy, *Rev. Sem.* xv,²⁹⁹). These words were spoken
by Hg. when the work on the temple was well under way. Kost. holds
that the Chr. excerpted the passage from the prophet, changing terms
to suit himself (*Wied.*¹⁷). Esd. has a somewhat confused text, but
it easily yields an intelligible mng.: *Some of the pr. et al., having seen
the former house, came to this building with crying and great weeping.*
The idea is the same: the wailing was due to the comparative insignifi-
cance of the temple that was now erecting. But that rendering presupposes a different text. Possibly the corruption was due to the
misconception about the chronology. It might serve to make a slight
change in the pointing and render: *the old people who had seen the
former house in its place, this was the house in their eyes.* "This" refers
to the old temple, and the mng. would be that in their conception
that building was the proper temple, and the new and insignificant
structure a cause for weeping rather than rejoicing. But the corruption is prob. deeper. In v.ᵇ our text yields no sense, it runs lit.,
many with a shout with joy to raise the voice. RV., "many shouted
aloud for joy," is paraphrastic and unmindful of original text. The n.
"shout" must be changed to a vb., as RV. in fact does. In contrast
to the old people who were weeping, many (others) shouted joyfully,
in order to make a noise so as to drown out the weeping.

13. *But the people could not distinguish the sound of the joyful
shouting from the sound of weeping*]. *Of the people* follows in the
text, but after 𝕲^B it should be omitted; otherwise "people"

would be used in this v. three times and in each case referring
to a different group. The passage means that the efforts of
the younger element were not successful in smothering the
weeping of the old people. Esd. 5⁶² reads: *so that the people
could not hear the sound of the trumpets on account of the weeping
of the people.* That makes very good sense and paves the way
for the following clause, *therefore* (not *for*) *the multitude trumpeted loudly so that it was heard afar*], *i. e.*, they redoubled their
efforts to silence the wailers, so that the noise was heard at a
great distance. On the whole, the celebration was decidedly
unique. The priests blew the trumpets, the Levites played the
cymbals and sang; the old people wept and the younger ones
shouted joyfully and trumpeted loudly, so that the noise of the
tumult of sounds carried to a great distance.

10ᵇ. Following 𝕲 we should rd. ויעמדו, a reading found in some Heb.
MSS., as it is better to take pr. *et al.* as subj. rather than obj.—מלבשים
בחצצרות] is to be rendered "equipped with clarions." לבש does mean
put on clothing, but it is an easy transition to "furnish" or "equip."
Esd.ᴮᴬ has μετὰ μουσικῶν καὶ σαλπίγγων, 3 Esd. *habentes stolas cum
tubis.*—במצלתיים] lacking in 𝕲ᴮ. Esd. has ἔχοντες τὰ κύμβαλα. This
word is used only in Ch.-Ezr.-Ne. Another form is צלצלים (2 S. 6⁵
Ps. 150⁵). It is scarcely correct to say that one form is earlier than
the other (BDB.), as the evidence is too scanty.—ידי] Esd. 5⁵⁷ reads
εὐλογοῦντες (להודות) and connects על with דויד, *praising according to
David the king of Israel*, unless, indeed, they rd. ידי as a vb. in Qal with
a sense assigned only to the Hiph.—**11.** ויענו] Esd. ἐφώνησαν, 3 Esd. *et
cantabant canticun Domino.*—כי טוב"] Esd. 5⁵⁸ ὅτι ἡ χρηστότης αὐτοῦ
καὶ ἡ δόξα; also παντὶ Ἰσραήλ = לכל-ישראל. The passage is plainly a
corruption of a favourite refrain found in Ps. 106¹ 136¹ 1 Ch. 16³⁴ 2 Ch.
5¹³ 7³, *i. e.*, וכל-העם.—הודו ליהוה כי-טוב כי לעולם חסדו]. The subj. precedes
vb. to mark the circumstantial clause.—הריעו] 𝕲ᴮ ἐσήμαινον, ᴸ ἠλάλαξαν,
Esd. ἐσάλπισαν καὶ ἐβόησαν, 3 Esd. *tuba cecinerunt et proclamerunt.*—הרועה]
𝕲 φωνήν or φωνῆᴸ = קול.—הוסר] 𝕲ᴮᴬ θεμελιώσει = הוּסַד. But Esd. has
ἐγέρσει = הקים, 3 Esd. *in suscitatione.*—**12.** ביסדו זה הבית] Sieg. explains
the sf. as anticipatory of הבית, very dub. Ges.§ 126 regards זה הב' as
a txt. err. for הבית הזה. Van Hoonacker dismisses the clause as an
Aramaism (*Zorob.*¹⁰⁴). On the basis of Esd., Guthe adjudges הבית a
gl. to which Haupt adds זה (*SBOT. in loc.*). But οἰκοδομήν in Esd.
may stand for בית. The word surely wanting in Esd. is בעיניהם. It is
prob. that Esd. understood יסד here, as in previous cases, as having the
sense of בנה. The rest of the passage also is quite different in Esd., καὶ

πολλοὶ διὰ σαλπίγγων καὶ χαρὰ μεγάλη τῇ φωνῇ, 3 Esd., *et multi cum tubis et gaudio magno.* The obscurity of the texts is very great. There is a certain similarity in MT. to Hg. 2³ and also to Esd. We may, however, extract possible sense by disregarding accents, omitting the sf., and treating זה as an enclitic: *when this house was building before their eyes.*

Yet that result is not entirely satisfactory. What we should expect is something like: "because the house now was mean in their eyes, they wept with a loud voice." It may be quite surely said that בעיניהם indicates that there preceded some words describing how the new building appeared to those who compared it with the old. No present text suggests a suitable word. By substituting כמעט in the sense of Ps. 10²⁰ for ביסדו we get the required sense as indicated above, but the emendation is purely conjectural. Another possibility is to let the text stand with a slight change of pointing, בְּיסֹדוּ, taking the n. in the sense of "base" or "place," and referring to the temple of Solomon. We should expect על rather than ב, it is true, but some demands will fail in this passage. We may compare Hg. 2³, הבית הזה בכבודו הראשון, "this house in its former glory." ביסדו may be an error for בכברו due to the Chr.'s insistence that the temple was not advanced beyond the foundations at this period. Hg. has כאין before בעיניכם. We should get good sense, therefore, by reading *who saw the former house in its glory, now the house was as nothing in their eyes.*—רבים] 𝕲ᴮᴬ ὄχλος, other texts, πολλοί.—[בתרועה] 𝕲ᴮᴬ ἐν σημασίᾳ, 𝕲ᴸ ἐν ἀλαλαγμῷ. Esd. διὰ (μετὰᴸ) σαλπίγγων. But a vb. is required here. Heb. syntax has been freely manufactured to explain corrupt texts, but the strain is too great here. We should rd. מריעים as in v. ¹³. Following Esd. many would rd. ובשמחה, but that is due to a misunderstanding. The mng. is that in contrast to the loud wailing many others raised a cry of joy.—להרים קול]. The Gk. translators were puzzled by this expression. In ᴮᴬ we find τοῦ ὑψῶσαι ᾠδήν, τοῦ ὑψοῦν τὴν φωνήνᴸ, Esd. μεγάλη τῇ φωνῇ. The inf. clause expresses purpose, and is not to be treated adverbially as RV. "aloud." —13. העם²] is lacking in 𝕲ᴮ and does not belong here (so Guthe). Esd. here offers a quite different text: ὥστε τὸν λαὸν μὴ ἀκούειν τῶν σαλπίγγων [τὴν φωνήνᴸ] διὰ τοῦ κλαυθμὸν τοῦ λαοῦ. It is doubtful if this is any improvement.—כי] must be taken in the sense of "therefore," and העם³ thus means the same ones that could not separate the joyful cries from the wailing. Esd. shows a different text: ὁ γὰρ ὄχλος ἦν ὁ σαλπίζων μεγάλως ὥστε μακρόθεν ἀκούεσθαι. 𝕲ᴮᴬ lacks תרועה and represents בקול הגדול (φωνῇ μεγάλῃ), placing קול in a different connection from Heb.

4¹⁻³ = Esd. 5⁶³⁻⁶⁸. The rejection of the Samaritans' offer.

—The Samaritans heard of the building operations, and they

came to Jerusalem with an offer of assistance on the ground
that they were also worshippers of Yahweh. The offer was
flatly rejected by Zerubbabel and the chiefs.

This passage has nothing to do with vv. ⁴⁻⁶ with which it is invariably
connected. The two sections show that broad difference in style which
precludes common authorship. In one place the hostile party is called
"enemies of Judah and Benjamin" (v. ¹), in another, "the people of
the land" (v. ⁴); the Jews are called "sons of the golah" in v. ¹, but
"people of Judah" in v. ⁴. The prevalent use of participles in vv. ⁴ ᶠ·
betrays a different hand. In vv. ⁴⁻⁶ we find "building," but there is
no indication that the building of the temple is meant. There is nothing in c. 5 or in Hg. or Zc. to indicate any serious stoppage of the building operations. The opposition of the nations is, in Briggs's opinion,
well brought out in Ps. 4.

The passage is obviously out of place. The proposal of the Sam.
would naturally be made as soon as the temple was begun. It is
tempting to transpose this section to follow 3⁹. The connection would
then be all that can be desired. Vv. ⁸ ᶠ· describes the laying of the foundations and the start of the structure. At this point the proposal of
the Sam. would come in most appropriately. Then the statement
"and the builders built the temple of Yahweh" (v. ¹⁰) has its proper
place, while vv. ¹⁰ᵇ⁻¹³ finds its best explanation as the dedication of the
completed temple. The passage may have been transposed to suit the
Chr.'s theory that the temple was only begun at this time, or to bring
together in c. 4–6 all the stories of the interference of the foreigners.

1. *The enemies*] are shown by their own statement in v. ² to
be the Samaritans.—*The sons of the golah*] or *the captivity* indicates the writer's theory that the temple was rebuilt by those
who had come back from Babylonia.—*Were building the temple*]. The Chronicler evidently overlooked those words, since
he has doctored the text of c. 3 to exclude any work on the
temple save laying the foundations. The words presuppose
some progress on the structure itself. Esd. contains an elaborate statement connecting this passage more closely with 3¹³:
*and the enemies of the tribe of Judah and Benjamin hearing,
came to ascertain what the sound of the trumpets [meant], and they
perceived that those from the captivity were building the temple of
the Lord, the God of Israel.* If those enemies lived in Samaria,
the noise made by the trumpets must have been loud indeed.

But the Samaritans may have spread during the exile into the bounds of the later Judean province. The Hebrew is better, for the offer seems to have been deliberate, not on the spur of the moment, as the Esd. text implies.

2. *Zerubbabel*] add *and to Jeshua and the rest* as in v.³, a reading supported by several texts, and required by the sense, since the offer was rejected by the same ones to whom it was made. Associated with Zerubbabel and Jeshua, the prince and the priest in the government, were chiefs of clans, making a sort of informal assembly.—*We will build with you*] or *let us build with you*. Possibly these were the same people that had assisted at the erection of the altar (*v.* 3³).—*For we seek your God as ye do*] RV. According to early usage "seek" would mean to make inquiries of God by prophets or oracles. In Ch. it is used in what Driver calls a weakened sense (*Intr.*⁵³⁶), seeking God in any religious way. Esd. renders "obey." These people acknowledge their foreign characters by saying "*your* God." —*To him we have offered sacrifices*] MT. reads: *We have not offered sacrifices*. The purpose of the corruption is to show that the foreigners had obeyed the law and had not dared to sacrifice, contrary to the law in any other place than Jerusalem. That would add strength to their plea, but it was hardly the truth. *Since the time of Esarhaddon*], referring to the story of their transportation from other Assyrian provinces to take the place of the deported people of the northern kingdom. They were led to seek Yahweh, because they were beset by wild beasts, in which they saw a punishment for their neglect of the local deity. They were taught the cult of Yahweh by an Israelitish priest who was sent back from exile for that purpose (*v.* 2 K. $17^{24 \text{ ff.}}$).

Esarhaddon was king of Assyria 681–668 B.C., and was the son of the famous Sennacherib and grandson of Sargon who captured Sam. in 722 B.C. The deportation of these particular people may have been delayed. According to 2 K. 17, Shalmanezer transported the colonists to Sam., and Jos. has that name here. In 4⁹ Asnappar is supposed to be Assurbanipal, and Mey. would so rd. here. Torrey thinks the Chr. deliberately put the wrong name here to make the heathen origin of the Sam. more apparent (ES.¹⁶⁹). We know almost nothing about conditions in Sam. after 722, and must draw conclusions cautiously (*v.* further, Smith, *OTH.*[230], Mar. *Jes.*[74], GAS. *Jer.* ii,[185]).

3. *For you and for us*]. "And for us" is wanting in Esd., and its omission gives force to the contrasting assertion, *we alone will build.—As King Cyrus commanded us*] referring to the edict in 1^{2-4} (*cf.* 3^7). The impetus for the building operations is here derived from the royal order. It is possible to interpret the statement as the ground of the Jews' refusal of the Samaritan offer, King Cyrus ordered us (not you) to build this temple. The reason commonly urged is that the Jews would have no dealings with this mixed race, being solicitous for a pure people and a pure religion. Such a consideration would have had more force with Ezra than with Zerubbabel. The motive was probably political. The old feelings against the people of the north would be intensified by the addition of foreign elements. (See Rogers, *Hist. Bab. and Assy.* ii,[159].)

1. צרי] 𝕲 οἱ θλίβοντες, Esd. 5^{68} οἱ ἐχθροί. Esd. adds τῆς φυλῆς (מטה). —היכל] 𝕲 οἶκον, Esd. ναον. Esd. adds ἤλθοσαν ἐπιγνῶσαι τίς ἡ φωνὴ τῶν σαλπίγγων, mng. that the attention to the temple was attracted by the noise of the trumpets.—הגולה] 𝕲 ἀποικίας = המדינה as 2^1. Esd. οἱ ἐκ τῆς αἰχμαλωσίας = משבי also in 2^1.—**2.** זרבבל]. We should add ואל־ישוע in harmony with v.[3], as Esd. and 𝕲[L].—לאלהיכם] 𝕲[B] τῷ θεῷ ἡμῶν, 𝕲[L] ἐν τῷ θεῷ ὑμῶν. MT. is right though; ל is found in this connection only in Ch.—ולא] as Qr. and all Vrss. we must rd. ולו.—אסרחרן] elsw. only 2 K. 19^{37} (= Is. 37^{38}). As. *Ašur-aḫ-iddina.* Most of the Gk. texts make sad havoc of this name; thus we find Ασβακαφαθ Esd.[B], Ναχορδαν[L]. ᴬ preserves correct form Ασαραδδων. —**3.** שאר] is lacking in Esd. both here and in v.[2] (it is best omitted); 𝕲[L] has a curious dup. in v.[2]: *Zer. and Jes. and the rest of the chiefs and to the chiefs of the clans.*—ולנו] is lacking in Esd.[B].—יחד] 𝕲 ἐπὶ τὸ αὐτό. Esd. μόνοι = לבד, a better reading, since יחד means *together* and would rather imply the acceptance of the offer. But see BDB., *s. v.*—אלהי ישראל] 𝕲[BA] τῷ θεῷ ἡμῶν, Esd. τῷ κυρίῳ τοῦ Ἰσραήλ.

4^{24b}–6^{18}. THE ARAMAIC ACCOUNT OF THE REBUILDING OF THE TEMPLE.

In its present form this story cannot be authentic. We find in the letter to Dar. some incorrect information, esp. the statement that Shes. had begun the work. But as shown in the notes the text in that part of the letter is very corrupt. I have been able to restore a suitable intr. to the letter of Dar. (*v.* 5⁶ ᶠ·); but there is more lacking still. For Dar.'s orders are based upon the decree of Cy., to which there is no reference in the letter. The decree of Cy. is practically quoted in the letter to Dar., whereas its place should be in his reply. The decree in 6³⁻⁵ has been amplified by a later hand, and a similar elaboration is found in the letter of Dar., esp. vv. ⁹ ᶠ· The story of the dedication (vv. ¹⁴⁻¹⁸) also excites suspicion in part.

It seems plain that the underlying theory of this document is that the temple had been begun by Shes. and that the building had continued for many years. There may have been some interruption, as 4²⁴ indicates, and with which 5¹⁶ is not inconsistent, esp. if the cessation had only lasted for two years, as is stated in Esd. 5⁷³. This narrative is therefore the basis for the Chr.'s arrangement of his material in c. 1–6. He found this story, and not only used it, but made it the framework for his whole structure. Whether the text was freely amplified by him or whether that had already been done by another hand, it is not easy to determine. He was not the only Jew holding strong views about the temple and priesthood.

The corresponding Heb. story knows nothing of an appeal to Dar., and yet it does not exclude it; for there is nothing to indicate what the Sam. did when their offer was rejected. This account, on the other hand, contains no hint of the tendered aid of the Sam.

The narrative in brief is as follows: Under the influence of the prophets Hg. and Zc., Zer. and Jes. in the 2d year of Dar. begin the construction of the temple. At once the Pers. officers Tattenai and Shethar appear on the scene (4²⁴ᵇ–5⁶). These officers write a letter to King Dar., relating their discovery of the Jews' building operations, the claim of the latter to authority from Cy., and asking for instructions (5⁶⁻¹⁷). A search is made by order of Dar., and the original decree of Cy. is discovered (6¹⁻⁵). Dar. thereupon replies to Tattenai *et al.*, upholding the decree of Cy. and bestowing liberal gifts upon the Jews (6⁶⁻¹²). The temple is then finished in the 6th year of Dar., and dedicated with a festival accompanied by appropriate sacrifices (6¹³⁻¹⁸).

It appears from the above outline that here, as in 4⁷⁻²⁴ᵃ, we have chiefly some correspondence with the Pers. court. But the proportion of narrative is very much greater than in 4⁷ ᶠᶠ·, as the letters occupy but half of the passage. There is a striking parallel between the two documents. In both cases the Jews are engaged in building, the Pers. officials write a report of the operations to the Pers. king, and the king sends an answer, though in one case the answer orders the building stopped, and in the other allows it to go on with liberal support. But in 4⁷⁻²⁴ᵃ the attitude of the Pers. officials is hostile, while in this section it is neutral. In 4⁷ ᶠᶠ· the complainants put their own construction upon the actions of the Jews, while in 4²⁴ ᶠᶠ· the Jews are invited to plead their cause, and their plea is forwarded to the Pers. court.

4²⁴ᵇ–5⁵ = Esd. 5⁷⁰–6⁶. The temple is begun.

The text is in bad condition, esp. in the latter part of the section; we find a question without an answer, and an answer without a question. The letter to Dar. which follows, however, supplies the material that is lacking here.

24ᵇ. *And the cessation was until the second year of the reign of Darius the king of Persia*]. Esd. 5⁷⁰ has the more specific statement, *and they were restrained from the building two years until the reign of Darius.* It is possible that some attempt had been made to begin earlier, or it may be that these words are but an editorial attempt to connect c. 5 with the correspondence with Artaxerxes.—**1.** Here we may confidently follow the text of Esd.: *In the second year of the reign of Darius.* This date appears to be original, and it may be that it has been carried back from this place to 4²⁴ᵇ.—*Prophesied Haggai the prophet and Zechariah the son of Iddo the prophet*]. The text shows a dependence upon Hg. This prophet's father is never named, but he is called habitually "Haggai the prophet" (Hg. 1¹· ¹² 2¹· ¹⁰). According to Zc. 1¹ Zechariah was the grandson of Iddo, an instance of the untrustworthiness of our genealogies.—*In the name of the God of Israel unto them*]. ARV. inserts "prophesied they," but has a marginal alternative, "which was upon them." Torrey renders "which was over them." So 3 Esd., *super eos.* "In the name of the God of Israel" certainly is connected with "prophesy," either as it stands at the beginning of the verse, in which case "unto them" is an error (it is not found in 𝔅), or else we must supply the verb as ARV. By a slight change we might get "their God" for "unto them" (*cf.* Hg. 1¹⁴ "the house of Yahweh of hosts their God").

2. Zerubbabel comes before Jeshua here as Hg. 1¹, and contrary to 3² where Jeshua precedes.—*And began to build the house of God*]. This statement makes it difficult to suppose that there had preceded any attempt to rebuild the temple. Torrey says that it is a characteristic redundant use of the Aramaic word

"begin" (ES.¹⁸⁹).   In Esd. 3¹⁶ he renders the same Greek word
"proceeded."   Still it would be extremely difficult to make the
passage mean "resumed building."—*Which is in Jerusalem*].
Cf. 1⁴ 4²⁴.—*And with them were the prophets of God helping
them*].   It is generally assumed that Haggai and Zechariah are
meant; but they were named in v. ¹ of which this is not neces-
arily a mere duplication.   "Helping" may refer to material
assistance, and the prophets are probably the members of the
prophetic guilds which continued in post-exilic times (*v.* my
Heb. Prop. c. 4).   We note the prophetic tone in this story and
the lack of prominence for the priests as in c. 3.   The prophets
may have shared in the actual manual labour.

3. *At that time came unto them*].   Work must have progressed
for some time before the Persian officials could hear of it and
appear on the scene.   Tattenai or, as found in contract tablets,
Uštani, *v. i.*, *the satrap of the province beyond the River*] (Syria)
the exact title found in the contract tablets, except that there
we learn that Uštani was ruler of Babylonia as well as Syria.
—*Shethar-bozenai*].   The real name was probably Shethar, as
Est. 1¹⁴, and *bozenai* is the unknown or corrupted title of his
office.   Perhaps Shethar was the scribe, like Shimshai (4⁸).   It
is the custom in these documents to give both the name and
the title of the writers.—*Thus they said to them*] *i. e.*, thus they
inquired of them.—*Who gave you an order to build this house*]
implying that the rebuilding of the temple could not be
permitted without proper authorisation.   That undoubtedly
was a fact.   There is a good illustration in the Eleph. pap.
The Jewish colony there had had a temple, but it had been
destroyed by their enemies; they wished to rebuild it, and so
sent a long letter to Bagohi, governor of Judah, asking the
necessary permission.   This letter is dated the 17th year of
Darius Nothus (408 B.C.), that is, a little more than a century
later than our period.—*And to finish this wall*] is almost certainly wrong; but it is not so easy to say what is surely right.
The meaning of the word translated "wall" is not known.   It
may be that "foundation" is right (*v. i.*).   The word is found
in *Eleph. Pap.* i,¹¹, but the meaning is doubtful save that it

refers to some part of the temple, and to something made of wood, as it was burnt. Sachau proposes here "establishment" (*Pap. u. Ost.*[14]).

> In. vv. [1-3] the text of Esd. is usually close to MT. But in vv. [4f.] the departure becomes very considerable. The peculiar rendering throws little light on the text, which here has suffered severely apparently by the compiler's omissions.

4. *Then we said to them as follows*]. But what they said is lacking. In Esd. the difficulty is relieved, for this phrase is wanting. In 𝕲 we find a slight change, *then they* [*the Persians*] *said these things to them* [*the Jews*], *i. e.*, inquired further. But that gives us two questions suitably introduced, while there is no answer to either one. ARV. cuts the knot by turning the second question into the missing answer to the first, though unhappily the reply has no relation whatever to the question. RV. and AV. more wisely render the text as it stands, though it does not make sense. But not to know is sometimes better than to know wrongly. In the letter which Tattenai sent to Darius we find the missing answer of the Jews (vv. [11-16]), and it is a good answer, for here is related the history of the attempts at temple-building, which it is declared had been authorised by Cyrus. It may be that on account of the length of the reply, and to avoid repetition, the Chronicler left out the long answer here. —*What are the names of the men who are building this building*]. The answer would naturally be Zerubbabel and Jeshua. The only name found in the letter, however, is Sheshbazzar, vv. [14. 16.] —**5.** *And the eye of their God was upon the elders of the Jews*]. *Elders* is used for the leaders, the men called so often "heads of the fathers" (*cf.* 1[5]). In 𝕲 we find *captivity of Judah*, also found in Esd., and giving a more suitable sense, for the divine favour was not limited to the leaders, but was extended to the whole people. If "elders" is right the meaning is that the reply to Tattenai had been so happily framed that he had no excuse for present interference. Esd. has a different text, *and they had favour, there being an overseeing of the captivity from the Lord, the elders of the Judeans.*—*And they did not restrain*

them] i. e., from continuing the building.—*Until a report should
go to Darius, and then they would return an answer concerning
this*]. We have clear evidence of confusion. The last part is
plainly an indirect reproduction of the verdict of the Persian
officials. We must assume something like this: *then they [the
Persians] said to them [the Jews]* that they would not restrain them
until a report should go to Darius, and then they would give them
a reply about this.* This would be a reply to the assertion of
the Jews that they were building the temple under the express
sanction of Cyrus, a sanction assumed by all parties to hold
good. The real question, therefore, referred to Darius was
whether there was any authorisation by Cyrus. The Jews
evidently had not at hand a copy of the important document.

1. ἐν δέ τῷ δευτέρῳ ἔτει τῆς Δαρείου βασιλείας is the reading of
Esd., and is correct, for v. ¹ᵃ is taken almost bodily from Hg. 1¹ "in
the 2d year of Dar. [prophesied] Hg. the prophet," etc. The date, the
silence in regard to Hg.'s father, and the repetition of the prophetic
title are sure marks of the source. The clause is much like 4²⁴.—נביאיה]
𝕲 προφητείαν, but Esd. προφῆται (so 𝕲 in v. ²); rd. נְבִיָּה in both cases.
—אלה] + κυρίου 𝕲ᴬ Esd.—עליהון] 𝕲 Esd. ἐπ' αὐτούς. In spite of this
support the word has no connection. It may have been originally *their
God.—2. שרין*] is explained as Pa. from שרא, used often with mng.
"loosen." 𝕲 Esd. render ἤρξαντο.—סעד] only here in B. Aram., but it
is a good Heb. word mng. "support." Aid by taking part in the work
is the sense here.—3. בה־זמנא] 𝕲 ἐν αὐτῷ τῷ καιρῷ (χρόνῳ Esd.); lit.,
in it, the time, i. e., at that time. On the construction v. Kautzsch, § ⁸⁸.
זמן is by some derived from old Pers. *zrvan* (Str.), but Zimmern traces
it to As., *simanu* (*KAT.⁶⁵⁰*). The word occurs in late Heb. (Eccl. 3¹
Est. 9²⁷·³¹).—אתה] v. Kautzsch, § ⁴⁷.—תתני] 𝕲 Θανανοιᴮ, Θαθθαναιᴬ, Ταν-
θαναιοςᴸ, Esd. Σισιννης, so Jos. Andreas says, "surely a Pers. name
which has not been correctly transmitted." Mey. sees the correct form
in Esd., and connects it with *Thishinaja* (*Ent.³²*). Meissner finds in
contract tablets of the 1st and 3d years of Dar., *Uš-ta-an-ni pihat
Babili u ebir nari,* "Uštani the satrap of Bab. and beyond the River,"
the very title and place of our text. He holds that we have here the
same person and should correct our text and rd. ושתני (*ZAW.* 1897,¹⁹¹ ᶠ·,
so *KAT.³·²⁹³*). This is a very prob. identification. There is no sufficient reason for making this officer a Pers.; he may just as well have

---

*This may be what was originally in the puzzling clause in 4ᵃ, *then we said to them as
follows*, a clause accidentally transposed, and then changed in form.

been a Bab., Aramean, or Sam.—פחת] 𝕲 ἔπαρχος^{BA} and Esd. στρατηγός^L.
—שתר בוזני] 𝕲 Σαθαρβουζανα^{BA}, Θαρβουζαναιος^L (first syl. lacking), Σαθ-
ραβουζανης Esd. Mey. accepts last form; *buzanes*, he says, is Pers.
barzanes, and *shethar* might be Pers. *citra*, but as a divine name is required, he corrects the text to מתרבוזני = Μιθραβουζανης. In this he
follows Andreas, who gives Iranian form *Mithrabauzana*, "Mithra is the
rescuer." Scheftelowitz connects with old Iran. *Ṧethrabuzana*. Winckler
finds the word an official title (*MVAG*. 1897,^{281 f.}). There is a Pers.
officer named שתר in Esd. 1¹⁴, and as the text offers two words the
conjecture is good that שתר was the name and בוזי the title of his
office. Mey. thinks he was subordinate to Uštani; he was a royal
secretary like Shimshai (4⁸).—אשרנא] v. ⁹ 𝕲 χορηγίαν; στέγην Esd. It is
a word of obscure origin and mng.; various Pers. and As. derivations
have been proposed (*v.* Ges.^B, BDB.). The various meanings proposed
are "wall" (Mar. from As.), "sanctuary" (Haupt, As. *ašru*), "palace"
(Marquart, Pers.), "breach" (Scheftelowitz, Pers.). It seems pretty
clear that it is the same word (one or the other being a corrupt form)
as אשיא 4¹² 5¹⁶ 6³, the similarity of vocalisation being pointed out long
ago by Kautzsch, § ⁶². In all cases the reference is to an initial stage in
rebuilding either walls or edifice, something finished before the rest is
begun. In v. ¹⁶ Shes. put in the foundation as the first step (similarly
6³). In all these cases "foundation" makes the best sense, and may
be provisionally adopted. Contrary to Berth. "sanctuary" does not
seem to me to make good sense. It is admitted that the query, "who
issued a decree to you to build this house and to finish this foundation?"
reverses the natural order. At present there is no satisfactory solution.
I suspect that the clause was added here by an editor to force a sort
of agreement with 4¹².—**4.** אמרנא] 𝕲 εἴποσαν^B, εἴπον^{AL}. Evidently the
incomplete and disordered text was before the translators, and they,
like EV^S. made the best out of it they could. Esd. lacks v. ^a and thus
connects the two questions as they may well be.—בנינא] 𝕲 πόλιν, Esd.
ταῦτα.—**5.** עין] 𝕲 ὀφθαλμοί, Esd. χάριν = Heb. חן and prob. right text,
corrupted here by similarity of sound. חן does not occur in B. Aram.,
but the vb. חנן is found. עין also appears in Esd. as ἐπισκόπης.—אלההם]
Hebraism, Mar. corrects to אלההון; apparently in Esd. as ἔσχοσαν; Heb.
אליהם "unto them."—שבי] 𝕲 αιχμάλωσιν. 𝕲 rd. the Heb. word שְׁבִי.
It is Pe. ptc. used as subst. (v. ⁹ 6^{7. 8. 14} †), "elders" (Mar. § ^{83b}). Esd.
has a dup. adding πρεσβύτεροι.—טעמא] is here used in the sense of
"report," which Tattenai will send to Dar.—יהך] on the form see
Mar. § ^{62 a}. 𝕲 has prob. a free rendering, ἀπενέχθη, Esd. ἀποσημανθῆναι.
—נשתונא] 𝕲^{BA} persist in the rendering φορολόγω, διάταγμα^L. "Letter"
is certainly unsuitable here; it is something which Tattenai *et al.* will
bring back to the Jews after they hear from Dar., therefore "decision"
or "order," as 𝕲^L, really "answer." ℍ has a different text, *but the eye
of their God was made over the elders of the Jews, and they were not able to*

*restrain them. And it sufficed that the matter should be referred to Dar.,
and they would give adequate proof against that accusation, i. e.,* that they
were building without authority.

6–17 = Esd. 6⁷⁻²². The report to Darius.—Vv. ⁶· ⁷ᵃ (to
Darius) is introductory by R.—**6.** *A copy*] or perhaps translation, *v.* on 4¹¹. The letter purports to be quoted exactly.
His companions, because Tattenai is chief (*v.* Mey.³²). The
Apharsachites, v. 4⁹. Torrey explains the word as equivalent
to *eparchs*, Esd. similarly has "leaders" or "rulers."—**7.** *They
sent a report to him and therein was written like this*] is redundant,
and lacking in Esd. together with the preceding *unto Darius the
king.*—*To Darius the king, all peace*]; the beginning of the letter.
There is a textual error; for reconstruction *v. i.*—**8.** *To Judah
the province*]. Esd. adds, *and to the city of Jerusalem; we discovered in the city of Jerusalem.* "Province" refers to one of
the districts of the Syrian satrapy, as in 2¹.—*To the house of
the great God*]. A strange statement for the Persian officials.
Berth. compares Cyrus's calling Marduk "the great lord," but
Cyrus thought he had conquered Babylon by Marduk's aid.
—*And it is building of great stones*]. The text is literally, *stone
of rolling, i. e.,* "too big to carry"; but on basis of 𝔊 we should
probably substitute *hewn* or *splendid* (costly) (*v. i.*). Esd. has
a suggestive variant: *the elders of the Jews that are of the captivity are building a great new house for the Lord of hewn and splendid stones.*—*And timbers are being set in the walls*]. So the passage is understood by Meyer (*Ent.*⁴¹) *et al.*, but Sieg. insists that
it means *wainscotting* placed on the walls as described in 1 K.
6¹⁵. Berth. thinks that "wainscotting" would suggest a progress in building too advanced for this stage. The Aramaic
word means *tree* or *wood* and might be used of "beams" or
"boards." The older view "timbers" is preferable, for the
wainscotting would scarcely be worth reporting to the king.
The report aims to show that considerable progress has already
been made, and that the work is pushed forward rapidly.—
And it prospers in their hands] is redundant, and may be the
Chronicler's amplification. Esd. has an addition, *and it is being
completed with all glory and diligence.*—*Then we asked these elders,*

thus we said to them] is surely not original. The second clause
was apparently added from v.⁴; it is quite superfluous here.
In its place Esd. has simply *saying*. The question is word for
word that of v.³. "These elders" has no antecedent in Aramaic text, but Esd. supplies it in v.⁸.

10. The second question is repeated indirectly: *and also we
asked of them their names*]. Esd. amplifies: "we asked them for
the register (ὀνοματογραφίαν) of the principal men."—*To inform thee and to write for thee the names of the men who are their
chiefs*], so we must read as 𝕲 and Esd., changing the finite verb
to the infinitive. It is to be noted that the letter contains in
great detail the Jews' answer to the first question, but there
is no mention of the names which are said to have been written. Evidently we have not the whole of the letter, but only
that part which is material from the Jewish point of view.—
11. *And in this manner they answered us*]. The answer of the
Jews is recited at great length, continuing through v.¹⁶; it is
apologetic in tone and is such a review of the history as the
Jews were fond of making, containing a good deal of moralising; it might be the actual words spoken to Tattenai, but
much of it would be quite immaterial to Darius, and would
scarcely find a place in this letter unless the writers were kindly
disposed toward the Jewish project. Now it is generally assumed that Tattenai *et al.* betrayed a hostile purpose, but that
spirit can only be discovered by reading into this story the ideas
of its parallel 4⁷ ᶠᶠ·. In the whole story there is not the slightest
note of hostility, but on the contrary the zeal with which Darius's orders were executed (6¹³) reveals a friendly purpose.—
God of heaven and earth] is unusual. Esd. offers a more appropriate phrase, *the Lord who created the heavens and the earth* (*cf.*
Gn. 14¹⁹·²², where 𝕲 has same words).—*The great king of Israel*]
is, of course, Solomon; for another reading *v.* crit. note.—**12.**
Cf. 2 Ch. 36¹⁶ ᶠ·. *King of Babylon the Chaldean*] is not very probable. Esd. has *king of Babylon, king of the Chaldeans*, the last
title added by the Chronicler from 2 Ch. 36¹⁷ = Esd. 1⁵³.—
And this house he destroyed]. Esd. *and they pulling down the
house burned it.* That agrees with the earlier history in

which it is said that the house was burned with fire (2 K.
25⁹ 2 Ch. 36¹⁹ = Esd. 1⁵⁶).—**13.** Here the story reaches Ezr.
1. Nothing is said about the permission to return from exile;
but that was unnecessary, that not being the point at issue.—
In the first year of Cyrus king of Babylon], exactly what we have
in 1¹ except that Babylon takes the place of Persia. Esd. gives
more correctly *in the first year that Cyrus ruled over the country
of Babylon.* The *decree* may be that in 1²⁻⁴ or that in 6³⁻⁵. In
the second there is nothing about permission to return from
Babylon, but had the decree contained that, it would not be
necessary to quote it here.—**14.** In regard to these vessels
cf. 1⁷ ᶠᶠ· 6⁵ 2 K. 25¹³ ᶠᶠ·.—*Sheshbazzar whom he had appointed
governor*]. In 1⁸ Sheshbazzar was called "prince of Judah," a
title due to his Davidic descent; here only do we find notice of
his appointment as governor by Cyrus. The title (*pihat*) is the
same given to Zerubbabel in Hg. 1¹. It is the title of Tattenai
also.—**15.** In this verse we reach serious difficulty: *And he
said to him these vessels take up, go, deposit them,* but it continues *in the temple which is in Jerusalem,* and then in direct
contradiction, *and the house of God shall be built upon its place.*
𝕲ᴮᴬ solves apparently by omission (*v.* crit. note) but that is
more easy than effective; Esd. has our text, so the confusion is
very old.

One may consult the comm. without getting much assistance. Ryle,
Sieg. Berth. and Seis. have not a syl. on the passage. B.-Rys. offers
this easy explanation: "Because this [the temple] is still destroyed it
is added, and the house of God shall be built at its place . . . the sentence subjoined by ו afterward explains the command to replace the
vessels in the temple in this way; I speak of a temple, that is to say,
the house of God or the temple shall be rebuilt." Exactness of statement is surely unnecessary for one who has that kind of an interpreter. In the first place, that expression "temple which is in Jerus.,"
recurring frequently in our sources, is a mark of a late and careless
hand, prob. the Chr. Again in this letter "house" or "house of God"
is used for the temple at Jerus. 8 t., for in v. ¹⁴ the Gk. preserves the
true reading, while "temple" (היכלא) is used for the sanctuary of Nebuchadrezzar at Bab. It is prob., therefore, that "temple" is a later
interpolation, the original reading being "store the vessels in Jerus."
Cy. would not be apt to specify the place where they were to be put,

and if he did he would not specify a place that did not exist. Another solution may be that the last clause is a later addition, esp. as the decree authorising the rebuilding of the temple has already been cited (v. 13). It is, indeed, perfectly possible that the letter ended with v. 13 and that vv. 14-16 were appended by a later writer who felt that important information contained in 18 ff. had been neglected. These vv. have really nothing to do with the question at issue, which was not the title to the temple vessels nor the disposition of them, but only the authority to rebuild the temple.

16. *Then the said Sheshbazzar came and laid the foundation of the house of God which is in Jerusalem, and from that time until the present it has been building and is not finished*]. It would be difficult to get more misstatements into a short space. In a contemporary record it is said positively that "the hands of Zerubbabel laid the foundations of this house" (Zc. 4⁹, *cf.* Ezr. 3⁸⋅ ¹⁰). The only correct statement in the passage is that the temple was still unfinished.—**17.** *And now*, to come to the heart of the matter, *if it seem good to the king*], a polite expression, which curiously Esd. lacks here, but has it in 2¹⁸ (Ezr. 4¹⁵) in the complaint to Artaxerxes, where it is not found in MT.— *Let search be made in the royal treasures*], but correctly in 6¹ *in the library*, so Esd. reads here *in the royal libraries*. The library is located in Babylon, though the record was actually found at Ecbatana (6²). It is possible that these Jews, associating Cyrus with Babylon, expected the edict concerning the Babylonian exiles to be filed there. The object of the search is clearly stated, to find whether such a decree as the Jews claimed had ever been issued by Cyrus. It was a question of veracity merely. The Jews had made a statement, and the task was to ascertain whether the official records confirmed it.—*And the pleasure of the king in this matter let him send unto us*]. This implies that the king might or might not ratify the decree of Cyrus if it were found. In the rendering in Esd. this implication is weakened: *and if it is found that the house of the Lord in Jerusalem stands with the approval of Cyrus the king, and it seems good to our lord the king, let him signify unto us thereof.* This is probably the right idea, for Darius would be likely to honour an edict of Cyrus.

6 f. The text is in evident disorder here, as in 4⁷⁻¹¹. Acc. to MT. the letter begins with לדריוש (v. ⁷). But in that case the letter does not contain the names of the complainants, the names being only in the intr. They are unnecessary there, since they have been given already in v. ³, but are required in the letter itself as in the reply (6⁶). Esd. has ἀντίγραφον ἐπιστολῆς ἧς ἔγραψεν Δαρείῳ καὶ ἀπέστειλαν. Σισίνης ὁ ἔπαρχος Συρίας καὶ Φοινίκης καὶ Σαθραβουζάνης καὶ οἱ συνέταιροι οἱ ἐν Συρίᾳ καὶ Φοινίκῃ ἡγεμόνες Βασιλεῖ Δαρείῳ χαίρειν πάντα γνωστὰ κ.τ.λ. MT. has פרשגן אגרתא תתני פחת עבר־נהרה ושתר בוזני וכנותה אפרסכיא די בעבר נהרה על־דריוש מלכא פתגמא שלחו עלוהי וכדנה כתיב בגוה לדריוש מלכא שלמא כלא ידיע. Esd. was plainly taken from this text, as shown by the underlined words. Ἔγραψεν has no corresponding word until we reach כתב. Ἡγεμόνες represents correctly אפרסכיא, cf. κρίται for דיניא in precisely similar connection in 4⁹. In 6⁶ = Esd. 6²⁶ we find τοῖς ἀποτεταγμένοις ... ἡγεμόσιν. Ἀπέστειλαν represents שלחו not שלח. The translation of the plus in Aram. text runs: *unto Dar. the king they sent an answer unto him and therein was written as follows:* "Unto the king" and "unto him" show a redundancy as 4¹¹. The *pahath* could hardly send an answer (the proper mng. of פתגמא here as in v. ¹¹) to the king. Disregarding for the moment the על made necessary by a false connection, restoring the original place of שלח, and correcting a sf., we may render: *Dar. the king sent an answer unto them and therein was written as follows.* Now when we turn to 6⁶ we have an order of Dar. without the necessary words of intr. The superfluous sentence here makes a very suitable intr., and we may confidently restore them to their proper place, reading עדין for על. Esd. has an intr., but not a very suitable one. V. on 6⁶.

The text here, therefore, originally stood as follows: פרשגן אגרתא (intr.) די שלחו על־דריוש (the letter) תתני פחת עבר נהרה ושתר בוזני וכנותה אפרסכיא די בעבר־נהרה לדריוש מלכא שלמא אדין. Then to 6⁶ we should transpose די בעבר־נהרה לדריוש מלכא שלמא דריוש מלכא פתגמא שלח עלוה וכדנה כתיב בגוה.

6. פרשגן] 𝔊ᴮᴬ διασάφησις, a word occurring only in 7¹¹, and Gn. 40⁸, for Heb. פתרון, "interpretation"; so here 𝔊 understands "translation"; cf. on 4¹¹, the original being in some other language, perhaps Bab.—**7.** פתגמא] 𝔊 ῥῆσινᴮᴬ, ῥῆμαᴸ (so ᴮᴬ in v. ¹¹).—שלמא כלא] 𝔊 with exact literalness εἰρήνη πᾶσα, Esd. with greater freedom χαίρειν (שלמא) and connects כלא (πάντα) with v. ⁸, πάντα γνωστὰ ἔστω.—8.—[ליהוד מדינתא 𝔊 Ἰουδαίαν χώραν, Esd. χώραν τῆς Ἰουδαίας, Esd. has a + καὶ Ἱερουσαλὴμ τὴν πόλιν κατελάβομεν τῆς αἰχμαλωσίας τοὺς πρεσβυτέρους τῶν Ἰουδαίων ἐν Ἱερουσαλὴμ τῇ πόλει, showing a שבי rd. in two ways as in v. ⁵.—רבא] is attributive of אלהא, but Esd. (οἶκον τῷ κυρίῳ μέγαν καινόν) connects with בית, a more natural statement from foreigners.—גלל] 6⁴ †, equivalent to the Heb. word and mng. "rolling." But 𝔊 has ἐκλεκτοῖς (יקר in Ez. 27²²), Esd. ξυστῶν πολυτελῶν = Heb. אבן גזית

יקר. In view of the forced mng. which must be given to גלל we must accept the testimony of the Gk. and rd. either "hewn stones" or "splendid stones"; the latter is best supported, the former makes the best sense. Otherwise we might correct on basis of אבנים גדלות, but גדול does not occur in B. Aram.—כתלא] Dn. 5⁵, Kautzsch,⁹⁴ᵉ, Mar. § ⁷⁹, cf. Heb. כתל, As. *kutallu*. 𝕲 τοίχοις, Esd. οἴκοις ᴮ, τοίχοις ᴬᴸ. B's reading is a blunder.—אספרנא] 𝕲 ἐπιδέξιον ᴮᴬ, ἀσφαλῶς ᴸ, Esd. ἐπὶ σπουδῆς. It is a word of frequent occurrence (6⁸· ¹²· ¹³ 7¹⁷· ²¹· ²⁶) and connected with עבד exc. in two cases (6⁸ 7¹⁷). Andreas derives from Iranian *uspuru*, late Pers. *ispari*, "completed." So the mng. assigned is "carefully," "thoroughly." Mey. cites a stamp mark on the lion from Abydos, where he holds אספרן has the mng. "precise" or "accurate" (*Ent.*¹⁰· ²⁴ ᶠ·). The best sense here would be as 𝕲 "skilfully" or Esd. "rapidly."—מצלח] 𝕲 εὐοδοῦται ᴮᴬ, κατευθύνει ᴸ, εὐοδούμενον Esd.—**9.** למבניה] in v. ³ לבנא; this is the only place where the repeated question differs from the original in v. ³. We should rd. here לבנא, or prob. in both cases למבנא as in v. ², which is the normal form (Mar. § ⁶⁴, Str., § ²³ ¹).—**10.** ונכתוב] is difficult, the construction changing from inf. to impf. with די. 𝕲 has ὥστε γράψαι [σοι ᴬ], apparently a correction; Esd. καὶ γράψαι σοί, and that is prob. the original form.—שם] 𝕲 ὀνόματα, so Guthe reads שימהת.—בראשיהם] is usually regarded as a Hebraism, but Torrey shows that it is good Aram. (ES.¹⁹¹).—**11.** מקדמת דנא] 𝕲 πρὸ τούτου, taking מ' as prep., Esd. ἔμπροσθεν.—רב] Esd. μεγάλου καὶ ἐσχυροῦ.—ושכללה] 𝕲 κατηρτίσατο αὐτὸν αὐτοῖς, suggesting that the original rd.: *and a great king built it for Israel and completed it for them.* Thus we should better understand לישראל.—**12.** הרגזו] † but cf. Heb. רגז, 𝕲 παρώργισαν, Esd. παραπίκραντες ἥμαρτον.—כסדיא] om. 𝕲ᴮ. Χαλδαίου ᴬᴸ, Esd. βασιλέως τῶν Χαλδαίων, after which we might emend מלך כדריא.—**13.** די בבל] lacking in 𝕲ᴮᴬ. The difficulty of calling Cy. king of Bab. in this connection is obviated in ᴸ τοῦ βασιλεύσαντος (καὶ) τῶν βαβυλωνίων, and in Esd. β. χώρας Βαβ. The better sense suggests that Esd. has the original text. The vb. מלך is not found in B. Aram., but it might well be. We should thus understand the repetition of Cy.—**14.** הנפק]. On the form, unassimilated, see Mar. § ⁵⁸.—להיכלא] 𝕲ᴮᴬ rightly ναόν (so Esd.), since in this letter it means the Bab. temple.—שמה די פחת שמה] can scarcely be right; 𝕲 θησαυροφύλακι [τῷ ἐπὶ τοῦ θησαυροῦ] bracketed part not in ᴸ. This may be a confusion of the offices of Mithredath and Shes. (1⁸). Esd. has Ζοροβαβὲλ καὶ Σαβανασσάρῳ τῷ ἐπάρχῳ, an evidently harmonistic note. שמה may be an accidental anticipation of שמה (so Str.) and its omission seems necessary.—**15.** אלה] 𝕲 πάντα ᴮᴬ, ταῦτα ᴸ. אלה is Heb., the Aram. being אלן and Mar. § ⁴⁴ so reads.—אזל] v. Mar. § ⁶⁰, Baer, BD.⁵⁹.—אחת] is Haph. imv. from נחת Mar. § ⁵⁸, Kautzsch, § ¹⁵. On the peculiar combination of three imperatives, v. Kautzsch, § ⁷⁴. Maqqeph joins the words to show close connection, "go, place," expressing but a single

idea.—אתרא] is used in same sense as Heb. מכונה (3³). The word occurs
in *Eleph. Pap.* in same connection, "on the place where it had stood
before" (Sachau,²⁹).—**16.** יהב] is not to be explained as a Hebraism;
it is used in Palestinian Aram. in the sense of "lay" and that is required here (Schueltens, *ZAW.* 1902,¹⁶²).—שלם] 𝔊 ἐτελέσθη, Esd. ἔλαβεν
συτέλειαν; it is Pe. pass. ptc.—**17.** בית גנויא] 𝔊ᴸ γαζοφυλακίοις, Esd.
βιβλιοφυλακίοις; both represent בית by φυλακίοις, one having "treasury"
as MT., the other "library." But *v.* 6¹. Prob. Esd. represents an interpretation, the annals being preserved in the royal treasury, a general
storehouse. תמה and די בבל, *videtur delendum esse* (Str.³), *cf.* 6¹, but
as the edict was found at Ecbatana, בבבל in 6¹ must be stricken out.
In this *v.* it is better to om. תמה which is lacking in 𝔊ᴮᴬ, and which
may have got here from 6¹. 𝔊ᴮᴬ, however, has a larger variant, running: τοῦ βασιλέως βαβυλῶνος; Esd. correctly ἐν τοῖς βασιλικοῖς βιβλιοφυλακίοις τοῦ κυρίου (Κυρου) [βασιλέως dup.] τοῖς ἐν βαβυλῶνι.—אתי =
Heb. אִי, 𝔊 ὅπως γνῷς.

**6¹⁻⁵ = Esd. 6²³⁻²⁵. The decree of Cyrus is found at Ec-
batana.—1.** *Made a decree*] is unnecessarily formal here; the
reference is scarcely to a public proclamation, therefore *gave an
order* is better.—*In the library* (literally, *house of books*) *where
the treasures were stored in Babylon*]. This is fuller than *house
of treasures* of 5¹⁷. Probably the former passage should be corrected to agree with this (so Torrey). We should infer that the
library or book-room was a part of a larger treasury. *In Babylonia* is either an addition, or was probably an error, for *in
Ecbatana* as v.². A Jewish writer may have meant Babylonia
to include Persia.—**2.** *And there was found in Achmetha*] *i. e.*,
Ecbatana, the capital of Media and the summer residence of
the Persian kings; it was captured by Cyrus in 550 B.C. It has
been identified by Jackson with modern Hamadam (*Persia
Past and Present*,¹⁵²).—*In the castle which is in the province of
Media*]. The exact spot where the record was found is described; it appears that the library was a part of the treasury
and that a part of the royal residence.—*A certain roll, and thus
it was written therein*]. "Roll" apparently shows a Hebrew
colouring, for there can be little doubt that these records were
all made on the now familiar clay tablets.—*Memorandum*] is
interpreted rightly by Mey. as a sort of title to the document
which follows.—**3.** The record of Cyrus is now quoted: *In*

the first year of King Cyrus]. It is quite unlikely that Cyrus would call 539 (or 538) his 1st year. It would be all right if put as Esd. 2[17] (Heb. 5[13]), *in the first year that Cyrus was king of Babylonia.* R. may have changed the year to agree with 1[1]. —*The place of sacrificing sacrifices*] may be construed as in apposition with "house of God." The following clause is unintelligible: "let the foundations thereof be strongly laid," as ARV. cannot be made out of the text, and has poor support in the Vrss. Esd. combines with the preceding clause and renders: *house of the Lord where they continually offer sacrifices by fire.* This is the simplest and only intelligible text.—*Its height sixty cubits and its breadth sixty cubits*]. But its length is not mentioned. It is certain that we have an omission here. The obscure and corrupt clause must have given the length of the building, for Cyrus would not have given two dimensions and left out the third. The dimensions of Solomon's temple were: 60 cubits in length, 20 in breadth, and 30 in height (1 K. 6[2]). So that the new temple was six times as big as the old one. These figures are wrong, for the new temple was much smaller than the old one (3[12] Hg. 2[3]).—**4.** *Three layers of hewn stone and one layer of timber*] continuing the description of the building specifications. "One" is the correct reading, though the text has "new"; "new" is in ARV. and without even a marginal alternative; RV.[m] is correct. It is difficult to understand this method of building. According to 1 K. 6[36] 7[12] Solomon built the inner court of the temple and the outer court of his palace with three courses of hewn stone and one course of cedar beams. Delitzsch supposed that the rows or layers were vertical, but that has little to commend it, and it fails to explain an unintelligible method of building. The similarity to 1 K. 6[36] would suggest that the statement is due to R. rather than to Cyrus.—*The outlay shall be given from the house of the king*]. Esd. *Cyrus the king.* In v. [8] we have "from the property of the king," and that more appropriate expression should be read here. As the temple was not begun in the time of Cyrus, this grant was naturally inoperative.—**5.** This verse begins exactly like 5[14] and it agrees in substance with 5[14b. 15], but not in words.

It appears that both passages were originally the same, but now
both are in part corrupt. But one is supposed to be a statement of the Jews in 520 B.C., and the other a copy of a decree
of Cyrus in 538. The identity of language shows that both
passages are not authentic. One may be original and the other
made up from it.

V. ⁵ᵇ is even more corrupt than 5¹⁵. It is true that 5¹⁴ ᶠ· casts the
decree partly into narrative form, while this purports to quote directly.
My own belief is that both passages are late interpolations to make
the decree agree with 1⁸ ᶠᶠ·, and that they represent a growth. They
are quite unnecessary and really drag in an extraneous element into
the question at issue, which was not the title to temple vessels, but the
building of the temple. It is instructive to compare the decree of
Cy. with the quoted statement of the Jews in 5¹³⁻¹⁵.

בשנת חדה לכורש מלכא די בבל כורש מלכא שם טעם 5¹³
בשנת חדה לכורש מלכא   כורש מלכא שם טעם 6³

בית אלהא דנא   לבנא (5¹⁴) ואף מאניא די 5¹³
בית אלהא בירושלם ביתא יתבנא (6⁵) ואף מאני 6³

בית אלהא די דהבה וכספא די נבוכדנצר הנפק מן־היכלא 5¹⁴
בית אלהא די דהבא וכספא די נבוכדנצר הנפק מן־היכלא 6⁵

די בירושלם והיבל המו להיכלא די בבל ויהיבו ... 5¹⁴ אחת המו
די בירושלם והיבל   לבבל יהתיבון ויהך 6⁵

בהיכלא די בירושלם ובית אלהא יתבנא על־אתרה 5¹⁵
להיכלא די־בירושלם לאתרה ותחת בבית אלהא 6⁵

In each version there is an omission of a practically complete section.
In one case the lacking passage is Cy. *the king brought them out from the
temple of Bab. to Shes. by name, whom he had appointed governor, and he
said to him, take these vessels, go place.* By omitting this the sense is not
impaired, but rather improved. In the other passage the lacking section has the dub. phrase *where sacrifices are offered,* etc., the statement about the dimensions of the temple, and about payment from the
royal funds. The decree loses nothing by this omission.

That the passages are dependent is made clear by the most cursory
inspection. The report made by Tattenai and the decree of Cy. afterward discovered at Ecbatana could not have accidentally agreed to
such an extent as we find here. The differences even in words are very
few. The extra clause in 5¹⁴ די להיכלא is possibly added on the basis of

1⁷; יהיבו and יתחיבון are only accidental variations. The final clause in
6⁵ is absolutely unintelligible, and its resemblance to the clear statement of 5¹⁵ is so close that the former is manifestly a corruption of the
latter. The awkward ותחת curiously has a parallel in 5¹⁵, where it corresponds to ויהך.

Rendering the passage now and making certain selections we have:
*In the first year of Cy. the king of Bab., Cy. the king made a decree that
the house of God should be built, and that the vessels of the house of God,
both gold and silver, which Nebuchadnezzar carried away from the temple
in Jerus. and brought to Bab. should be restored to the temple in Jerus.;
and the house of God shall be built upon its site.* The last clause is superfluous. It might originally have been "let therefore the house of God
be built upon its site." Or this clause may be the comment of the
complainants, "and (now) the house of God is building upon its site."

This is prob. all that was in the original decree. It is certainly sufficient that Cy. should have authorised the building of the temple and
the restoration of the sacred vessels. In 1²⁻⁴ there is no mention of the
vessels, but the statement that they were returned (1⁷ᶠ·) indicates that
they may well have been covered by the decree. The added material
in 6⁴, to the effect that support was to come from the king, has its
parallel in 1⁴, where the aid was to come from the Jews, and it may
have crept in from 6⁸. But the comparison certainly increases our
distrust of the Jewish *apologia* in 5¹¹ᵇ⁻¹⁶. We are constrained to pronounce against the authenticity of that passage.

1. בית ספריא] 𝕲 βιβλιοθήκαις, Esd. as in 5¹⁷ βιβλιοφυλακίοις. Esd.ᴬ
has βασιλικιοις βιβ.—**2.** אחמתא] old Pers. *Haugmatana*, Bab. *Agmatanu*.
𝕲 om. ᴮ, Αμαθαᴬ, Εκβατανοιςᴸᴱˢᵈ.—בבירתא] † 𝕲ᴮᴬ has a dup. ἐν πόλει
ἐν τῇ βάρει, Esd.ᴸ βάρει only. Βάρις is found in Jos. Ἐν πόλει is a gl.,
explaining a word unknown to all the Gk. translators. The corresponding Heb. בירה occurs many times in late Heb., esp. in Est., *cf.*
Ne. 1¹ 2⁸ 7². It is from As. *birtu*, the common word for "fortress" or
"citadel" (Mar.⁵⁶). It here means the castle in which the king lives.
—במדי מדינתא] lacking 𝕲ᴮᴬ and rejected by Berth.—מגלה] is pure Heb.
and only here in B. Aram. 𝕲 has κεφαλίς, which represents מגלה in
Ez. 2⁹ 3¹·²³ Ps. 40⁷. As it is followed by μία, and so = c. 1, it can
only be a marginal reference to the other decree of Cy. in Ezr. 1.—
דכרונה] can scarcely be different from דכרן, 4¹⁵; 𝕲 ὑπόμνημα.—**3.** בית
אלהא] after 𝕲 περὶ οἴκου we should prefix ל. 𝕲ᴮ shows a dup., adding ἱεροῦ. Or we may follow Esd. and om. ביתא. 𝕲ᴮ lacks ביתא יתבנא,
so that the decree concerned only sacrifices and vessels, and not the
rebuilding.—אתר] is suspended in air as completely as ביתא. 𝕲 has
τόπου connected apparently with περὶ understood.—אשי] 𝕲ᴮᴬ ἔπαρμα,
which does not occur elsw. in 𝕲, but in Aq. Th. Sym. in Job 20⁶ =
שיא α. λ.—מסובלין] † 𝕲 ἔθηκενᴮᴬ, τιθήτωᴸ. The sense of Heb. סבל will

not fit; the traditional "raised" has no authority. 𝕲 scarcely makes sense, "and let the foundation be laid," but ᴸ adds, *a foundation of a cubit*. Haupt suggests that אשיהי = Heb. אשה, "fire offering," and *cf.* As. *zabalu*, so "and bring in his fire offerings." He compares Esd. ὅπου ἐπιθύουσιν διὰ πυρὸς ἐνδελεχοῦς, *where they continually offer sacrifices by fire;* but those who quote this overlook the fact that it is the only mention of the sacrifices in Esd., that is, this text lacks דִּבְחִין. ואשיהי = διὰ πυρός, מסובלין = ἐνδελεχοῦς = Heb. תָּמִיד. The corruption seems quite hopeless, the Vrss. having as much difficulty and reaching as many conclusions as modern scholars.—פתיה–שתין] lacking in 𝕲ᴮ Esd.ᴮᴬ; ᴸ has ἕξ (שתין). It is most prob. that the original passage gave the missing dimension of the temple. I venture to make the conjecture that the original text was וארכה אמין מאה עשרים רומה. 4.—נרבכין] is generally derived from the As. *nadbaku*, which means "mountain slope," but Zimmern says this remains questionable (Mar.⁷¹, Mey.⁴⁶). The mng. "course" is quite certain; 𝕲 δόμοι.—גלל] lacking in 𝕲ᴮ, κρα- ταιόιᴬᴸ, *v.* on 5⁸.—אע] Esd. adds ἐγχωρίου, which represents אזרח in Ex. 12⁴⁹ Lv. 18²⁶ 24²² Nu. 15²⁹; in Ps. 37³⁵ אזרח רענן, "a native tree"; hence here native wood to distinguish it from the wood brought from Lebanon. The native and cheaper wood would serve to build into the walls.—חדת] † 𝕲, εἰςᴮᴬ, καινῶν ἕναᴸᴱˢᵈ·, a dup. reading both חדת, "new," and חד "one." The latter is correct.—נפקתא] *v.* ⁸ † from root נפק, *cf.* 5¹⁴, "what is brought out," "outlay." 𝕲 δαπάνη, which oc- curs only in Apocr.—בית] but in v. ⁸ more appropriately נכסי.—5. [מאני but in 5¹⁴ מאניא די.—היכלא] rd. with 𝕲 ביתא, as in 5¹⁴.—אלהא . . . והיבל]. To this point our text follows 5¹⁴ verbatim except as noted above. Here we have a summarising of 5¹⁴ ᵇ⁻¹⁵. 𝕲ᴮ has only ἐπὶ τόπου ἐτέθη ἐν οἴκῳ τοῦ θεοῦ, *i. e.*, it lacks all but לאתרה ותחת בבית אלהא. ᴬᴸ follows MT., but with manifest corruptions. Esd.ᴮᴬ supports a shorter text: ἀπο- κατασταθῆναι εἰς τὸν οἶκον τὸν ἐν Ιερ, οὗ ἦν κείμενα and adds a dup. reading, ὅπως τεθῇ ἐκεῖ; ᴸ has only the double reading at the end. Mar. suggests a restoration thus: ויהתיבון להיכלא די בירושלם ויהחתון לאתרהון בבית אלהא; but this source used היכל only of the temple of Bab.— לאתרה] is surely connected with על-אתרה as 5¹⁴; it is impossible here. Indeed, the passage is hopelessly corrupt.

6–12 = Esd. 6²⁷⁻³⁴. The reply of Darius.—6. As shown

above on 5⁶ the introduction to Darius's letter has been trans- posed. (Torrey notes a lacuna between vv. ⁵ ᵃⁿᵈ ⁶, ES.¹⁵⁹). This section should begin: *Then Darius the king sent an answer unto him, and therein was written as follows.—Be ye far from thence*] is not a striking command. Esd. *keep away from the place* is stronger.—7. *Let the work of this house of God alone*], forbidding any kind of interference. Esd. names Zerubbabel here as "the servant of the Lord and governor of Judah." 3 Esd. lacks the whole verse.—**8.** The king further commands that the decree of Cyrus be executed by providing the money for the building operations out of the royal tribute collected in the Syrian province. That we have no evidence of any such help for the Jews does not disprove the authenticity of this order; for it was one thing for the king to give such an order, but quite another matter to get the satrap of a distant province to carry it out. In Esd., however, the satrap is enjoined to help in the work of rebuilding, but the payments out of the tribute are only for sacrificial purposes.—**9.** *And whatever is necessary*]. There follows in apposition the list of articles to be furnished: young bullocks, rams, and sheep for burnt-offerings to the God of heaven (*v.* on 1², where this expression occurs in a Persian decree), and wheat, salt, wine, and oil as required by the priest. The latter list provides for the *minchah*, or meal-offering, which was made of fine flour, moistened with oil and salted (Lv. 2¹⁻¹³). Wine was required for the daily drink-offering (Ex. 29⁴⁰).—*Day by day without fail*] implies that this provision was for the daily offering, and while we might suspect that the Persian officials would not be concerned about such details, still it is possible that this is a reflection of a Jewish priestly influence at the Persian court.—**10.** *That they may offer pleasing sacrifices*]. "Sacrifices of sweet savor" (ARV.) is scarcely justifiable, an error as old as 𝔊. The root idea is "rest," therefore "pleasing" or perhaps "propitiating."—*And pray for the life of the king and of his sons*]. This explains the motive of the grant for sacrifices. The sacrifice would be pleasing to God and incline him favourably toward the offerer. The Persian king was not averse to the good offices of other gods than his own. This expression is surely a sign of the Persian point of view. Sachau compares this with "the sons of the royal house" in *Eleph. Pap.*¹⁰.

11. *Any man that alters this command*]; "frustrate" (BDB.) is scarcely justifiable; the idea is not to punish the one who interferes with the execution of the decree, but the one who would venture to change its terms. Berth. interprets in the sense of "transgress" or "violate." The punishment will be twofold; the culprit will be impaled on a beam or stake pulled from his own house, and the house will be made a ruin. The impalement was a Semitic method of execution, and, as Sieg. says, to be distinguished from the Roman crucifixion. Sieg. claims that impalement existed among the Hebrews, citing Nu. 25⁴ 2 S. 21⁶⁻⁹. BDB. says correctly that the method of execution was uncertain. Herod. testifies to the custom among the Assyrians (iii,¹⁵⁹). The words may be rendered, "let him be lifted up and stuck upon it" (the beam). The punishment has quite a different turn in Esd. 6³¹, *let a beam be pulled from his own house, and let him be hung thereon, and his property shall become the king's.* That has a more modern and less Oriental note.—**12.** This verse has been generally discredited. Esd. has the original text, if we may judge by inherent fitness, thus: *and the Lord, whose name is called there, shall annihilate all kings and the nation who stretches forth his hand to hinder or to harm that house of the Lord which is in Jerusalem.* The writer has in mind the petty neighbours of Judah, who had shown marked hostility to the Jews, and who are now warned that Yahweh himself shall do them harm if they bar the progress of the temple. As the king had sought the favour of Yahweh for his own house (v. ¹⁰), so he naturally invokes his displeasure upon all who interfere with the restoration of his cult.

6. חתני] 𝕲ᴮᴬ has δώσετε, forgetting the n. p.—וכנותהון]. The sf. should be second p.—וחיקין הוו] 𝕲 μακράν ὄντεςᴮᴬ, μ. ἀπέχετεᴸ, Esd. ἀπέχεσθαι.—מן־תמה] 𝕲 ἐκεῖθεν, Esd. τοῦ τόπου = מן־אתר.—7. פחת יהודא] is lacking in 𝕲ᴮ, Mar. om. also, οἱ ἀφηγούμενοι τ. Ἰουδᴬ. Esd. ἔπαρχον τ. Ιουδ. prefixing τὸν παῖδα κυρίου Ζοροβαβέλ.—לשבי] with 𝕲 Esd. we must om. ל, since שבי as well as פחת is subj. of יבנון. Esd. has a + after טעם: ὁλοσχερῶς οἰκοδομῆσαι καὶ ἀτενίσαι.—8. שבי] Esd. 6²⁸ αἰχμαλωσίας = שְׁבִי, a word not found in B. Aram.—אלך] lacking in 𝕲ᴮᴬ, a text approved by Mar. Esd. has μέχρι = עד. למבנא, Esd. ἐπιτελεσθῆναι, so "until the house of God is finished."—נכס] 7²⁶ †. The word occurs in late Heb. and the mng. is clearly established as "property."—אספרנא]. V. on 5⁸.—9. חשחן] pl. of חשחה †, 𝕲ᴮᴬ ὑστέρημα, 𝕲ᴸ δέον.—בני תורין] (Heb. שורים) means "young bullocks." This is associated with Lv. 4³⁻¹⁴ פר בן בקר. But בני is lacking in 𝕲ᴸ and in Esd., also in v. ¹⁷ 7¹⁷, and may have been introduced here under the influence of Lv. 𝕲 has three render-

ings of חורין: βοῶνᵇᴬ, μόσχουςᴸ, ταύρουςᴱˢᵈ·. Μόσχους may represent בני.
—[רי לא שלו GᵇᴬBᴬ ὃ ἐὰν αἰτήσωσιν, reading שאל, and being a repetition
of "כמאמר כ. Gᴸ has apparently a dup., the above preceded by ἀπα-
ραλλάκτως, a word found elsw. only in Est. 3¹³ (Apocr.), but which
may represent our text, since "unchangeably" would be a suitable rendering.—10. [להון Mar. § ⁶⁵ᵃ.—[ביחותין (Dn. 2⁴⁶ †) is a Hebraism, occurring in J (Gn. 8²¹) and very often in P; G εὐωδίας gives a wrong
sense.—[מצלין Mar. § ⁷⁴ᶜ. In As. ṣaltu is used in sense of "entreat," but
not to pray to a deity, Zim. KAT.³· ⁶¹⁰· ⁸).—[חיי Gᴸ σωτηρίας, ζωήνᴮᴬ.
The former may represent a theological interpretation.—11. [נסח here
only in B. Aram., but it is a common Semitic word and occurs 4 t. in
B. Heb.—[קיף † here only in B. Aram. Pe. pass. ptc. The word occurs
twice in late B. Heb.—[מחא]. The mng. usually given, "smite," is
scarcely appropriate here. BDB. gives two ideas, one of impalement
(v. s. זקף) and the other nail. The latter would imply crucifixion,
whereas the mng. is *impalement*. Gᴮᴬ πληγήσεται gives the true
sense. Gᴸ has παγήσεται, which has the mng. *impale*.—[נולו G τὸ
κατ᾽ ἐμεᴮᴬ, εἰς διαρπαγήνᴸ. Dn. 2⁵ 3²⁹ †. Jensen compares As. nawalu,
"ruin" (BDB.). The mng. given "dunghill" is not appropriate, though
that sense is found in Targum; "ruin" is better in every case. Gᴸ·
"plunder" would give good sense, but it is dub. whether that mng.
is permissible.—[על-דנה] lacking in G, but found in Esd.; "besides" or
"in addition to" is better than "on this account," since the latter
would apply to both parts of the punishment.—12ᵃ is regarded as
spurious by virtually all modern scholars; Sta. Gesch. ii,¹²², Kost.²⁹,
Sieg. Mey.⁵¹. Mey.'s argument is typical: "It is quite impossible
that Dar. in an official document should call in question the continuance of the Pers. sovereignty and speak of kings and peoples who in
the future might make his orders inoperative." Berth. defends the
passage, but does not go far enough. Mar. rejects להשניה as gl. with
reference to Antiochus Epiphanes; but the Gk. Vrss. all show that some
word belongs here, though not this one. Esd. here offers a simpler and
better text: ὁ κύριος, οὗ τὸ ὄνομα αὐτοῦ ἐπικέκληται ἐκεῖ, ἀφανίσαι πάντα
βασιλέα καὶ ἔθνος ὃς ἐκτενεῖ χεῖρα αὐτοῦ κωλῦσαι ἢ κακοποιῆσαι τὸν οἶκον
κυρίου ἐκεῖνον τὸν ἐν Ἱερουσαλήμ. The Deut. phrase is more accurately
given than in MT. Dt. more than P appears in the programme of
the restoration.

13-18 = Esd. 7¹⁻⁹. The temple is finished and dedicated.

Tattenai and his fellows respected the decree of Dar.; the work on
the temple was pushed forward and finished in the 6th year of Dar.
(515 B.C.). A service of dedication was held; many sacrifices were
offered; the pr. and Lev. were assigned their tasks according to the
book of Moses.

13. Our text gives but a general and rough statement, that Tattenai *et al. because Darius the king had sent acted accordingly with all care*]; but in Esd. this is much amplified, *following closely the commands of King Darius they with all care presided over the holy works laboring with the elders of the Jews and temple officers.* This is very unlike MT., but it agrees with the Esd. version of the Darius letter (*cf.* v. ⁸). The passage is hard to explain as a later addition, since the Jews would not be likely to invent the notion that hostile foreigners presided over the rebuilding of the temple, especially as they had rejected the offered assistance of the Samaritans (4¹⁻³).—**14.** *And the elders of the Jews built successfully because of the prophesying of Haggai and Zechariah*] *cf.* 5¹. The reference here is to the problem at home; all outward difficulties had been overcome by the decree of Darius confirming that of Cyrus; but the books of the prophets named above show that the Jews themselves were not very eager to engage in public works; they were aroused to their duty and kept at it by the inspiriting oracles of these prophets, without whom the command of God and the edicts of kings would have been alike ineffective. The mention of Artaxerxes is a gloss, as he belongs to a later period. As we have the singular, *king* of Persia, Darius or Cyrus may also be a gloss.—**15.** *And they continued that house until the third day of the month Adar*]. The verb means, literally, *brought out*, or *continued until it was finished.* Esd. reads 23d day. *Adar* only elsewhere in Est. (8¹) is a loanword from the Babylonian. It is the 12th month, February–March. Our text runs, *which is the sixth year of the reign of Darius the king*]. We must read *of the sixth year of King Darius*, as we find in Esd., or more probably an original Hebrew year was first given, which was synchronised with the Persian reign. The temple was finished, according to the text, in the spring of 515 B.C.

16. *The sons of Israel*] in apposition with which stands, *the priests and the Levites and the rest of the sons of captivity*]. That is, these three classes constituted the postexilic community.— *Made a dedication of the house of God with joy*]. Upon the completion of the work there was a joyful service of dedication.

Esd. gives quite a different reading, *the sons of Israel and the priests and the Levites and the rest of those from the captivity who had joined them did in accordance with those things in the book of Moses*. This is interesting from the implication that many who had returned from exile had taken no part in the rebuilding of the temple, a statement in itself highly probable. The reference to the requirements of the book of Moses is explained by the sacrifices made at the dedication.—**17.** The numbers of the animals sacrificed, 100 bullocks, 200 rams, 400 lambs, and 12 he-goats, are small compared to those offered by Solomon at the dedication of the first temple, 1 K. 8⁵· ⁶³, and are not unsuitable, in spite of Sieg.'s doubt, to the poorer conditions of the new community.—*For all Israel according to the number of the tribes of Israel*]. "Those returned deemed themselves the representatives of all Israel" (Sieg.). They may have taken to heart their brethren scattered over the world and made the offerings in their behalf.—**18.** *And they established the priests in their divisions and the Levites in their classes*]. According to 2 Ch. 35⁵ the priests were established in divisions in Josiah's time. The ordering of the priests and Levites is described minutely in 1 Ch. 23–26, each class or division being on duty for a week at a time. For the condition in NT. times *v.* Lu. 1⁵· ⁸ ᶠ·.—*For the service of God who is in Jerusalem*]. 𝕲ᴸ shows a later conception, reading, *for the service of the holy things of the house of God*. Esd. reads, *and the priests and the Levites stood in full vestments, according to their tribes (or classes) for the works of the Lord*.—*According to the writing of the book of Moses*] *i. e.*, as written in the book of Moses. *V.* Nu. 3, 8. Esd. adds, *and the gatekeepers at each gate*, but that suggests a period after Nehemiah had built the walls.

13. V. ᵇ in Esd. is as follows: κατακολουθήσαντες τοῖς ὑπὸ τοῦ βασιλέως Δαρείου προσταγεῖσιν ἐπιεστάτουν τῶν ἱερῶν ἔργων ἐπιμελέστερον συνεργοῦντες τοῖς πρεσβυτέροις τῶν Ἰουδαίων καὶ ἱεροστάταις. ·This gives a clear sense which is wanting in MT.—**14.** מצלחין] for which 𝕲 has οἱ Λευεῖται ᴮᴬ, κατηύθυνον ᴸ, Esd. εὔοδα ἐγίνετο τὰ ἱερὰ ἔργα. The word is to be taken adverbially with בנין, *they built successfully*.—נביאה and בר־עדו] are wanting in Esd. V. ᵇ is regarded as a gl. by many (Mar. Sieg. Mey. *et al.*). With Berth. we must excise the name of Art., which

finds a place here on account of 4⁷⁻²³, though the name is supported by all the Gk. Vrss. Sieg. urges against the passage the combining of a command of God and of the Pers. kings. But in Esd. we find different words used: διὰ προστάγματος τοῦ κυρίου—μετὰ τῆς γνώμης τ. Κύρου κ. τ. λ., *by the command of Yahweh and with the permission of Cy.* That part of the text seems unobjectionable. בנין, בנו] are both lacking in Esd., and Berth. may be right in changing the latter to "prophets." Otherwise it is to be combined with שכללו, *they finished building.*— **15.** שיציא] or Qr. שיצי. Kautzsch,⁶⁹ prefers a pl. form שיצין, adopted by Mar. on basis of 𝕲 𝕳. Kautzsch interprets as a pass. from אתא, but De. regards it as Shafel from Bab. *aṣu,* and that fits better. The usual rendering, "complete," will not serve here unless we dispose of the following עד, which is well attested. We cannot say "they finished the house until the 3d of Adar"; that is no better in Aram. than in English. But from the root *aṣu* we get "they brought out or continued the work until," etc.—יום תלהה] Esd. τρίτης καὶ εἰκάδος. It is impossible to tell which text is right, though Sieg. follows Guthe in preferring the latter. Jos. (*Ant.* xi, 4, 7) agrees with Esd.—דּי הוא"] is certainly wrong. Esd. has τοῦ ἕκτου ἔτους βασιλέως Δαρείου. Mey. (*Ent.*⁵⁴) supposes some words to have fallen out, and suggests, "that is (the 12th month) of the 6th year of Dar." explanatory of the Bab. term *Adar.* It is more prob. that a year was first given acc. to a Jewish calendar and that this date was dropped accidentally. 𝕲ᴸ tries to help along by an addition of ἕως, thus: ὅς ἐστιν ἕως ἔτους.—**17.** הורין] 𝕲 μόσχους, but Esd. correctly ταύρους.—אמרין] 𝕲 ἀμνούς, Esd. with better Gk. ἄρνας.—צפירי עזין] 𝕲 χιμάρους αἰγῶν, Esd. χιμάρους. The same redundancy is found in late Heb. Dn. 8⁵⁻⁸ 2 Ch. 29²¹, but *cf.* 8³⁵. In Lv. 9³ the he-goat is a sin-offering.—שבטי] Esd.ᴮᴬ φυλάρχων.—**18.** עבירת] which referred to the building in 5³ here indicates the temple cult. —אלהא] 𝕲ᴸ ἁγίων οἴκου τοῦ θεοῦ.—ספר] 𝕲ᴸ βιβλίῳ νόμου. Esd. adds: καὶ οἱ θυρωροὶ ἐφ' ἑκάστου πυλῶνος, 3 Esd. *et ostearii per singulas januas.* This passage is important, for it indicates that the Aram. narrative has broken off abruptly. The story evidently went on to describe the installation of other officials of the temple. Torrey regards the words as the work of the Chr. Esd. prob. lacked from חנכת v. ¹⁶ to בירושלם v. ¹⁸, as shown by the repeated ἐν τῷ Μωσέως βίβλῳ, and by the suspiciously close agreement with MT.

EZR. 6¹⁹⁻²² = ESD. 7¹⁰⁻¹⁵. THE OBSERVANCE OF THE PASSOVER.

This passage has suffered like many other parts of these books from a mutilation of the text. The purpose of the mutilation is plain. The passage was attached by the Chr. to the temple-building story, and then was modified to make it conform to its new position and to the ideas

of the editor. To comprehend what we have to deal with, we must
have the original text so far as it can be recovered; and therefore a
translation of the reconstructed text is given here. The justification
for the changes will be found in the critical notes. In this passage the
Heb. language is employed.

(19) *And the sons of Israel kept the passover on the fourteenth
day of the first month. (20) Now the priests and the sons of the
captivity were not cleansed, but the Levites to a man were all of them
clean, and they [the Levites] sacrificed the passover for all the sons
of the captivity, and for their brethren the priests [and for them-
selves]. (21) And the sons of Israel, all that had separated themselves from the uncleanness of the nations of the earth, and those
who had returned unto them from the captivity to seek Yahweh ate
the passover. (22) And they kept the feast of unleavened bread
seven days, rejoicing before Yahweh, because he had turned the
purpose of the king of Assyria unto them to strengthen their hands
for the worship of Yahweh the God of Israel.*

A company of exiles had recently arrived in Judah through
the favour of one known only as "king of Assyria." The
Israelites already in Judah celebrated the Passover at its regular
time, and so far as their condition permitted the recent arrivals
participated. The passage shows an amalgamating process between the Jews returning from exile and those who were native
in Judah. There is not a word about the temple or its building.

It is usually assumed that the Chr. wrote the passage as a fitting conclusion to the temple-building story. Torrey notes that the temple
was finished in the 12th month, Adar, v. [15], and that the Chr., with his
usual exactness in dates, fills in the next month with the keeping of the
Passover. The Chr. has an elaborate description of the celebration of
the Passover in 2 Ch. 35[1-19]. Many phrases are identical in the two
passages. But in our passage we rd. that the Lv. slew the Passover
for the others, v. [20], while in 2 Ch. 35[14] the phrase is "prepared." Indeed, the points of identity are mostly in stock phrases, which any
writer would use. The Chr. cannot be the author of this piece, for he
would not mutilate his own work to the extent we find here. Those
who attribute the fragment to the Chr. do so on the basis of the corrupt text.

There is not sufficient evidence to determine the date of the piece, but
such indications as we have suggest that it belongs to the early period.

It may well belong to the time of Cy., or to the period when Zer. and
his company first arrived in Jerus. C. 3 describes various festivals
that were kept, and this may have been among them. It is separated
only by the long Aram. insertion 4^7–6^{18} and may originally have stood
after 4^3, or even in the early part of c. 3.

19. The day for this feast is fixed in Ex. 12^6.—*The sons of
the captivity*] is an error for *the sons of Israel.* These two classes
are named in this passage in contrast. The sons of Israel are
those who had always remained in Judah, and the sons of
the *golah* are those who returned from Babylonia.—**20.** This
verse in MT. runs thus: *For the priests and Levites had cleansed
themselves, to a man they were all clean, and they slew the passover
for all the sons of the captivity and for their brethren the priests and
for themselves*]. "For themselves" can only refer to the Levites. The expression is cumbersome, but it has the support of
all texts. Nevertheless it may be a gloss. The idea is clear
that the clean Levites sacrificed the Passover on behalf of the
two classes stated in v.^{a} to be unclean. As the Passover was
kept in memory of the return from the captivity in Egypt, the
festival would be highly significant for those who had just returned from the exile in Babylonia.—**21.** This verse also requires correction as above. "The sons of Israel" is further
defined. During the exile the Jews in Judah had probably
mingled freely with the surrounding peoples, called in our books
"the people of the land." Now with the return of some exiles,
there was an earnest revival of Yahweh worship, in the interest
of which some of the Israelites dissociated themselves from the
loose ways of their neighbours.—**22.** The Feast of Unleavened
Bread was virtually a part of the Passover, continuing for
seven days thereafter (Ex. 12^{15}). Instead of *with joy for Yahweh made them rejoice*] it is better to read with Esd. *rejoicing
before Yahweh.—He turned the heart*] (or *counsel* as Esd.) refers
to some especial act of favour shown to the Israelites.—*King
of Assyria*] is strange here. We should expect "king of Persia."

B.-Rys. notes that in Judith 2^1 Nebuchadrezzar is called king of the
Assyrians (the same confusion is found in 2 K. 23^{29}); as the kings of
Pers. ruled over the old As. domain, the title might be used by a Pers.

king (so Berth.). In Ne. 13⁶ Art. is called king of Bab. As the text
is supported by all Vrss. we may assume that the phrase was in the
original text. It is usually assumed that Dar. is meant, *e. g.*, Sieg.,
but, save the position of the passage assigned by the Chr., there is no
evidence to support that identification. There seems to be room to
doubt whether such a mistake would have been made as this by any
postex. writer. However ignorant the Jews may have been of contemporary history, they knew that As. had long been defunct and that
Pers. was the real power of this time. As the reference is to one who
had conferred favours upon the people as a whole, we naturally suppose the king of Pers. to be meant. Yet it may be that it was really
a satrap in the old As. domains who was called by courtesy king of
Assyria.

To strengthen their hands] in 1⁶ refers to material support,
and that sense would be admissible here. Were our text correct that meaning would be required. As a matter of fact,
the last clause originally read *for the worship of Yahweh the God
of Israel*]. The favour of the Assyrian king then consisted of
the privilege of keeping the Passover, for which very little
expenditure was necessary. The king's grace may refer to a
gift of lambs, which were slain at the feast, or to the privilege
conferred upon the sons of the *golah* in allowing them to return to Judah. In the latter case the king would naturally be
Cyrus.—*For the work of the house of God*] is badly supported by
the Vrss., and is inconsistent with the tenor of the passage,
which is concerned with the keeping of festivals, *i. e.*, the worship at the temple, not with its building.

19. ויעשו] 𝕲 ἐποίησαν, but Esd. uses a more technical word, ἠγάγο-
σαν^BA ἤγαγον^L.—בני הגולה] is suspicious, for the Passover was slain for
the sons of the *golah* (v. ²⁰). Esd. has οἱ υἱοὶ Ἰσραὴλ τῶν ἐκ τῆς αἰχμαλωσίας, 𝕳 *filii Israel transmigrationis*, 3 Esd. *filii Israel cum his qui
erant ex captivitate*, *i. e.*, *the sons of Israel together with those who had
come from the captivity*. Now Esd. cannot be rendered "the sons of
Israel that came from captivity," as RV.; the τῶν forbids that, for
the text is defective; the Latin is good. 3 Esd. shows two distinct
classes, the sons of Israel and the sons of the *golah*, and these two
classes are kept distinct in this whole passage. Now the original
reading must have been "sons of Israel" and the rest is a correction
from MT. As so often happens Esd. has preserved the original text
with a dup. derived from Heb.—20ᵃ. Esd. has a striking text, ὅτε

ἡγνίσθησαν οἱ ἱερεῖς καὶ οἱ Λευεῖται ἅμα καὶ πάντες οἱ υἱοὶ τῆς αἰχμαλωσίας ὅτι [ουκ^L] ἡγνίσθησαν ὅτι οἱ Λευεῖται ἅμα πάντες ἡγνίσθησαν, 3
Esd. *quando sanctificati sunt sacerdotes et Levitae. Omnes filii captivitatis
non sunt simul sanctificati, quia Levitae omnes simul sanctificati sunt.*
The reading ὅτι in ^{BA} is senseless, and ^L supported by 3 Esd. is correct.
Some parties were clean and others not. Now the subj. of וישחטו can
only be the Lev. We can get good sense for a part of the v., *i. e., but
the Lev. to a man were all of them clean, and they sacrificed the passover
for all the sons of the golah, for their brethren the pr. and for themselves.*
In this part Esd. and MT. agree. The preceding part is meaningless
as it stands in both texts. Esd. shows corrections from the Heb. in
the repeated clause οἱ Λ. ἅμα καὶ πάντες. Omitting that and putting
the remainder back into Heb., we have a good text: כי לא הטהרו הכהנים
ובני הגולה. It may be that we should go further. When the Chr. dropped the negative to get rid of the intolerable implication of the passage, he may have inserted "pr."; in that case the Esd. text is correct from οἱ υἱοί, the preceding being added from MT. The antithesis
is then between the sons of Israel, v. ¹⁹, and the sons of *golah*, v. ²⁰.—
21 is unintelligible; there is no obj. for ויאכלו; "sons of Israel" and
"sons of the *golah*" are identified; there is a third class otherwise unknown in this section "and all who had separated," etc., and there
is no antecedent for the pron. in אלהם. 𝕲 has an obj., τὸ πάσχα, in place
of השבים, but ἀπὸ τῆς ἀποικεσίας is disconnected (οἱ ἐξελθόντες ἀπό^L).
𝕲 has εἰς ἀκαθαρσίας for מטמאת. Esd. follows MT. exc. that it has
πάντες for וכל and lacks אלהם and אלהי ישראל. Sense may be obtained
by transposition so as to rd. ויאכלו הפסח בני ישראל כל הנבדל . . . הארץ
והשבים מהגולה. It is better with Esd. to drop אלהי ישראל . . . אלהם.—
22. In 𝕲^B יהוה is lacking; in 𝕲^A it is found here and with הסב. Esd·
has τὴν βουλήν for עצת=לב, and lacks בית האלהים or rather has κυρίου
instead.—יהוה . . . [בשמחה] appears in Esd. as ἔναντι κυρίου^L, εὐφραιόμενοι
ἔναντι κυρίου^{BA}. "House of God" was added by the Chr. when he
attached the passage to the temple story. Esd. gives better sense, for
Yahweh made them rejoice and turned is awkward. We should rd.
therefore שמחים לפני יהוה כי הסב עצת מלך אשור . . . במלאכת יהוה אלהי ישראל.

EZR. 4⁴⁻⁶. THE COMPLAINT TO XERXES.

This is a fragment describing an event in the reign of Xerxes (485-
464), and the only passage we have from his period. It is given different connections in MT. and Esd. In the latter the name of Xerxes
does not occur; in fact, the only part of v. ⁶ preserved in that text is
against the inhabitants of Judah and Jerus., and that is imbedded in the
letter to Art. The section is usually divided, vv. ⁴ ᶠ· being connected
with vv. ¹⁻³ and v. ⁶ made a section all by itself. It has been shown
above that this passage did not come from the same hand as vv. ¹⁻³, and

vv. ⁴ ᶠ· give a suitable setting for v. ⁶. As the text stands the arrangement in Esd. is the only logical one, for the dates of Cy. and Dar. in v. ⁵ᵇ lead up to 5¹. It is clear that these dates are later glosses. The connection of "all the days of Cy." shows that it is interpolated. As it stands it is connected with "hiring counsellors," but manifestly the enemy would not be engaged in hiring counsellors during a whole reign—to ignore the intervening period of Cambyses. As the editor supposed the events narrated in 3¹–4⁵ to have happened in the time of Cy., it would be natural for him to add this date. "Unto the reign of Dar." is easily explained as a duplication from 4²⁴, which v. is substantially a repetition of the passage before us. It must be remembered that in the original text preserved in Esd., 4⁵ was directly followed by 4²⁴.

The troubling of the Jews referred to here of course really took place in the reign of Dar., since the complaint was lodged with Xerxes in the beginning of his reign. The key to the situation lies in the word "build," v. ⁴. That could not refer to the building of the temple, for we have three accounts of that performance (3¹–4³ 5 ƒ., Hg. and Zc.), in no one of which is there a hint of even an attempt to check the building. Even with the poor and few people for the task, the work was apparently done in a shorter time than Solomon took with all of his resources. The building could only refer then to the building of houses in Jerus. or of the walls or both. Now houses in the city and walls around it would naturally be the next step after the erection of the temple; for the temple standing alone would be subject to raids for plunder and desecration. Ne. shows that any preceding attempts to put up either houses or walls had failed. The complaint accomplished its purpose.

As Dar. was favourably disposed toward the Jews, there would be no use in appealing to him. Consequently the enemies had to fall back upon themselves, and do what they could to impede the progress of those Jews who were bravely struggling to restore Zion. A new king always raises new hopes. When Xerxes succeeded to the throne, there might be a chance of turning him against the rising people of Palestine. The advent of a new king was a favourite time for the rebellion of subject peoples. The freshly crowned monarch must be on the alert for uprisings, and he would naturally be suspicious. Upon the accession of Xerxes, therefore, the counsellors, Bishlam, Mithredates, and Tabeel, who had been employed by the enemy, wrote their charges against the Jews.

What they wrote and what the result of their letter was we do not know, for that part of the narrative has been lost. We may, however, draw a pretty safe inference. In our books we have stories which show the favourable attitude of Pers. kings toward the Jews; Cy. Dar. Art. and Art. II, each one in his way, furthered the desires of these people. We have nothing from the long reign of Xerxes. Before him a good beginning had been made, but after his time the situation described in Ne. 1 *f*. indicates that all the work of the Jews had been undone, save in the fact that the temple had not been destroyed. It is evident then that Xerxes showed no favour to the Jews, and that their hostile neighbours had a free hand to work their own will.

The term "people of Judah" in v. 4 would not naturally be applied to a body of exiles who had just returned. The words imply a people settled for some time in the land, and hence a later date than that of Cy. is necessary.

It has, indeed, been proposed by many to change the name Xerxes to Cambyses (*e. g.*, *KAT*.³, ²⁸⁸), but that is an attempt to support a chron. system in the present arrangement of our books which on all grounds is impossible. Even if this name were disposed of, we still have the passage vv. ⁷⁻²³, and would have to dispose of Art. as well as Xerxes.

4. *The people of the land*] occurs in the contemporary prophets, in Zc. 7⁵ as a term for the laity, in Hg. 2⁴ as equivalent to the rest of the people named in 2², *i. e.*, all others than Jeshua and Zerubbabel. In our books this term occurs nowhere else, and as Esd. reads "peoples," the text must be corrected accordingly.

We have this expression "peoples of the land" in 10². ¹¹ Ne. 9²⁴ 10³¹. ³² and "peoples of the lands" in 3³ 9¹. ². ¹¹ Ne. 9²⁴. ³⁰ 10²⁹. In Ezr. 10². ¹¹ Ne. 10³¹ "peoples of the land" describes the peoples from which the foreign wives had come; there the mng. is manifestly the non-Israelite nations dwelling in Judah or its immediate neighbourhood. "Peoples of the lands" has the same sense in Ezr. 9¹. ². ¹¹, "peoples of these abominations" (9¹⁴) being used synonymously, but the emph. here is on the difference of religion rather than of race. In Ne. 9³⁰ the term refers to the As. and Bab., therefore the foreign people distant from Judah. In Ne. 10³² it is rendered "traders" in BDB., but the real mng. is country people as distinguished from those in Jerus. In Ne. 9²⁴ the word for *peoples* has an unusual form (עַמְמֵי), but as in Zc. 7⁵, it means the people as distinguished from the king; the reference, however, is to foreigners. These are all the cases in our books, and it is apparent therefore that the phrase refers to foreigners, and while originally "peoples of the land" was distinguished from the others as mng. foreigners near by, the distinction is lost as the texts stand. The reference here is very prob. to the Sam.

Were weakening the hands]. *Cf.* "their hands will drop from the work" (on the walls), Ne. 6⁹. The phrase usually means *to discourage*, but literally it would be *making the hands drop*, and so stopping whatever the people of Judah were doing. In view of the following clause, "disheartening" is the better sense.—*Troubling them in building*]. The history of the efforts of the foreigners to stop Nehemiah's work is the best commentary on the passage. The meaning is that the people of the land interfered with the Jews, putting every possible obstacle in their way. There may have been actual assaults made upon them as well. What the people of Judah were building is not stated, but it must have been either the city walls or houses (*v. s.*). Esd. has a somewhat different account: *The nations of the land, lying down upon* (or *sending a message to*) *those in Judea and besieging them, prevented the building*. This hostility is still more emphasised in 3 Esd., where an ambush is described (*v. i.*).—**5.** *Hiring counsellors against them*]. Cf. Ne. $6^{12\,f.}$, "counsellors of the king," $7^{28}\,8^{25}$, but here BDB. gives the meaning "agents." The counsellors were not employed for advice, but to represent them in their complaint to Xerxes. To make an appeal like this effective, it would have to be supported by names that would carry weight with the king. It is certain that the agents were Bishlam, Mithredates, and Tabeel (*v. on* $^{7\cdot23}$), and they may have been Persian officers, to whose report Xerxes would give heed, and who knew how to draw up a suitable document.—*To defeat their purpose*]. Their purpose was the rebuilding of the city. It would appear that in spite of the efforts of the enemy the work had continued, though with diminished success. Despairing of completely stopping the progress by their own efforts, they now prepare to secure a restraining decree from the Persian king.—*All the days of Cyrus*] is a harmonising gloss added here when this passage was placed in a false connection (*v. s.*); similarly *until the reign of Darius* is carried back from v. ^{24}. The Esd. text shows plainly how this was done.—**6.** *In the reign of Xerxes*], the only mention of this king in our books, but he is named often in Est.—*In the beginning of his reign*], that is, immediately upon his accession (485 B.C.), when an accusation of rebellion would be most effective.—*Wrote*] in our text has no subject. The implied sub-

ject is "the people of the land" in v. ⁴, but to say nothing of
the distance and change of construction, a multitude could not
well be the author of a letter. Proper textual criticism shows
that Bishlam, Mithredates, and Tabeel should be transposed
from v. ⁷ to serve as the subject of this verb.—*Accusation*], in
Esd. *letter*, and probably that is correct; for the Hebrew verb
"write" is not used with a figurative subject. "Accusation"
would mean a letter containing an accusation.

The abrupt end is what we may expect in any fragmentary piece the
original form of which has been lost by editing to fit a new situation.
That abruptness of termination is, however, a characteristic of our
books.

4. עם הארץ] Esd. τάδε ἔθνη τῆς γῆς, 3 Esd. *gentes terrae*, rd. עמי as in
other places.—מרפים ידי] only case of Pi. in this connection. Qal is
used several times with יד as subj., *e. g.*, 2 S. 4¹, where we have also בהל.
Esd. gives us ἐπικοιμώμενα^BA (*incumbentes*, 3 Esd.) = ליד, Dt. 21²³ =
שכב, 1 K. 3¹⁹, hardly a suitable sense here; ἐπικοινωνοῦντα^L occurs
only in Sirach 26⁶ 4 Mac. 4³. This gives quite a different sense, *sent
a communication to those in Judah*, possibly ordering them to stop the
work.—מבלהים] *trouble*, Qr. מבהלים, *frighten*. ᵍ ἐνεπόδιζον (= הלם in Ju.
5²²) supports Kt. Esd. has πολιορκοῦντες εἶργον. The first word often
represents לחם, and this text apparently rd. נלחמים. Εἶργον stands for
some vb. concealed in אותם. As Esd. has ἀπεκώλυσαν for "prevent"
in 5⁷⁰ and 2³¹, it appears that we have two sources woven together
here. 3 Esd. has a further elaboration, *et levantes opus ædificationis
et insidias et populos adducentes prohibebant eos ædificare*, "and impair
the work of building and bringing an ambush and peoples prevented
them from building." This is very like Neh.'s troubles.—5. סכרים †]
an error in sibilants; the correct form is שכרים. The text of Esd. is
radically different in this v.: καὶ βουλὰς καὶ δημαγωγοῦντες (δημαγω-
γίας^AL) καὶ συστάσεις (ἐπισυστάσεις^L) ποιούμενοι ἀπεκώλυσαν τοῦ ἀποτε-
λεσθῆναι τὴν οἰκοδομὴν (τοῦ οἰκοδομῆσαι καὶ ἐπιτελεσθῆναι τὴν οἰκοδομὴν^L)
πάντα τὸν χρόνον τῆς ζωῆς τοῦ βασιλέως Κύρου. There is added καὶ εἴρχ-
θησαν τῆς οἰκοδομῆς ἔτη δύο ἕως τῆς Δαρείου βασιλείας, but that is a
translation of v. ²⁴, so that the clause "until the reign of Dar." of
MT. is lacking in Esd., and correctly, for it has nothing to do with
this section. The above contains more than we have in MT., but it
appears to be chiefly the work of R., who wanted to emphasise the
good ground for the cessation of the work on the temple. Yet he did
not venture to insert any word that necessarily refers to the temple.
The difference from MT. is so great that the text can hardly be a

translation at all. Indeed, in the whole passage (⁴⁻⁶) Esd. shows that the material has been worked over perhaps by several hands. The passage may be translated, *and using plans and demagoguery and tumults they prevented the building from completion all the days that Cy. lived.* The following clause, *they hindered the building for two years*, is a dup. —**6.** שטנה] does not occur elsw. 𝕲ᴮ lacks the word, ᴬ has ἐπιστολήν, while ᴸ has a dup., ἐπισ. καὶ ἐναντίωσιν. Other forms of the root are common.

EZR. 4⁷⁻²⁴ᵃ = ESD. 2¹⁶⁻³⁰. THE ARTAXERXES LETTERS.

The material in this passage covers two letters, that of Rehum, Shimshai, and their associates to Artaxerxes, and that of the king in reply; an introduction to each letter; and a description of the execution of the king's decree. The section has been the subject of much discussion, for it presents difficulties to an unusual degree. Some of these will be considered here.

(1) Contrary to the general impression, the whole passage exc. ⁷ᵇ is in Aram. It is usually said that v. ⁷ is the Heb. intr. to the Aram. letters, a conclusion due in part to an inadequate criticism of the text. As a matter of fact, we find that v. ⁷ᵃ is a part of the warp and woof of the intr. to the first letter, an intr. mixed all through vv. ⁷⁻¹⁰, and which I have fortunately been able to disentangle (*v. i.*). The v. can be rd. as Aram. as well as Heb. The word כנותו is, in fact, an Aram. word, and the passage can only be forced into Heb. by assuming a loan-word. The mistake was originally made by the Massorites, and has been perpetuated ever since. V. ⁷ᵇ is Heb., but at most it is an editor's note; and it is certainly out of place. It has never been understood, but it clearly has nothing to do with the interpretation of the passage which follows. It may be only some copyists' notes (*v. i.*). (2) The letters are placed in different chron. situations in the two editions which have come down to us. In MT. the passage stands between the Heb. and Aram. stories of the temple-building, that is, *in* the reign of Dar., an obvious absurdity. In Esd. the passage comes directly after Ezr. 1, between the reigns of Cy. and Dar. This position was not that of the original text of Esd., but was due to a later editor. In the Esd. text of vv. ⁷⁻²⁴ there are two references to the building of the temple, both in the letter of complaint, neither being in the Aram. text (Esd. 2¹⁷· ²⁰ = Ezr. 4¹²· ¹⁴). Now those references to the temple must have been added to the text after it was placed in the position it has in MT. In the Esd. text the beginning of the building operations of the temple follows this passage (*i. e.*, 5⁴⁷ ᶠᶠ·). The references to the temple-building are therefore impossible in an earlier section. If these references

had been in the original text, they surely would not have been over-looked by the Chr., who believed that this passage explained the delay in building the temple. The section must have been transposed in the Esd. text in an attempt to get rid of the obvious absurdity of placing the Art. letters in the midst of the reign of Dar. That would be all the more necessary, since the Esd. text makes it clear that 3^{1}-4^{3} of MT. do belong to the time of Dar., a fact disguised in MT. by the aid of numerous textual changes.

It seems possible to go a step further and attempt to account for the fact that there are no references to the temple in the Aram. version of the letter. At all events, a simple explanation may be proposed. In the original text of Ezr.-Ne. this passage stood where it belongs, immediately preceding Ne. 1. The passage was transposed in Esd., which has nothing of Neh.'s work at all, and was edited to fit its new place. Then in MT. it was also separated from its context by the insertion of c. 5-10, but without the textual changes. Later, to get rid of the problem of chronology, it was again pushed back in the Esd. text by an editor who was certainly, and perhaps pardonably, ignorant of the true order of succession of the Pers. kings.

(3) The passage is dated in the time of Art., presumably Art. I (464-424). This date is inconsistent with the position of the passage in either text. Therefore many scholars have supposed that the name of the king is wrong, and that we should substitute Cambyses for Art. Cambyses reigned 529-522, between the reigns of Cy. and Dar. That substitution would make the Esd. text chronologically consistent. But we have seen that the position of the passage in that version was not original, and consequently the gain is nothing. The substitution does not help out the version in MT.; for here we have the sequence of kings, Cy. Dar. Xerxes, Art. Dar. (4$^{5\,ff.}$), thus placing Art. too early. If Cambyses is assumed, he becomes as much too late in this scheme as Art. is too early. With better success we might substitute the name Xerxes. We could then interpret v. ^{6} as a Heb. beginning of the matter in vv. $^{7-24a}$. The chron. sequence is then not so bad, for while c. 5 f. does belong to the reign of Dar., we might suppose that the Aram. account of the temple-building story had been added to this Aram. section without regard to chron. order. Then it is a singular fact that in the book of Est. the Pers. king Xerxes appears in 𝔊 as Art.; if the same mistake had been made here, the error in 𝔊 might have crept back into the Aram. Finally that substitution would rid us of the serious difficulty that Art. authorised Neh. to do the very thing forbid-den in this edict (v. Intr.).

Alluring as this hypothesis is, it is certainly unnecessary. After all, it scarcely relieves us of any real difficulties, for as the passage is in the wrong place, to remove it one reign further along is no strain. Fur-ther, the change, as shown below, creates a difficulty of its own.

In its original form the letter to the Pers. king charges that the Jews are rebuilding the walls of Jerus., and erecting houses in it. That much we may gather in spite of the corrupt and obscure text. There is not a word about the temple; indeed, it is excluded; for the complainants urge that if the Jews finish their undertaking, the city will be in a position to rebel against the king of Pers. The restoration of the temple as the basis of that charge would be ridiculous. Further, the most trustworthy source we have for the history of this period demands just such events as are described here. Neh. learns with surprise and chagrin that Jerus. is lying waste, its walls are thrown down, and its gates burned (Ne. 1³ 2³). To suppose that Neh. refers to the destruction in 587, nearly a century and a half before his time, is absurd. The reference can only be understood of some recent calamity. Neh.'s audience with Art. was in the 20th year of his reign. Therefore the events narrated as occurring "in the days of Art." may have come at any time in the first twenty years of his reign. But if we transfer the letters to Xerxes, they must be put in the beginning of his reign (4⁶), i. e., 485, or forty years before Neh., and therefore presenting too long an interval between the calamity and the report brought to Neh.

There is then the difficulty of supposing that Art. retracted his own words in giving Neh. permission to rebuild the walls. In the Aram. form of the letter, there is the saving clause "until a decree is issued by me." Esd. lacks the passage, but that might easily be due to its unfitness, as the letter was understood. If words are to be pressed overhard, as is apt to be the case in dealing with Pers. laws, that clause would have to be omitted, or the temple could never have been built, for Art., in spite of 6¹⁴, never issued a decree in favour of building the temple.

We cannot rd. the story in Ne. 1–2⁶ without seeing that Neh. realised that he had a delicate and difficult problem. If he knew of the king's letter, vv. 17 ff., and had just heard how ruthlessly the decree to stop the work had been carried out, we can well understand his fear and perplexity. Finally, it is by no means inconceivable that a weak monarch like Art. could be induced to do almost anything by a court favourite.

By placing the section just before Neh. we get an exceedingly good connection. In the early part of the reign of Art., perhaps under the inspiration of the patriot Neh., a large body of exiles had gone up to Jerus., possibly the very company confused with Ezra's. They had the purpose, so near the heart of Neh., of rebuilding Jerus., and began to execute the project. The jealous Sam., rebuffed by the Jews years before, realise the danger to their supremacy, and write a letter to the king. Neh. being at court, knows of the complaint and the tenor of the king's reply. After the Sam. forces had made havoc of the Jews' work, some of the disheartened colonists returned to Pers., and are brought straight to the royal cup-bearer. He learns now that the enemy had taken advantage of the edict and had gone far beyond its terms in their passion for destruction.

With this situation clearly in mind, we can comprehend the patriot's disappointment and sorrow. We can further understand the secrecy with which he surrounds his own enterprise, and the constant conflicts with the very people who had succeeded once before in breaking down the walls of Jerus.

(4) The authenticity of the letters has been assumed in the above discussion. Any other theory seems to me untenable. The text is in places very bad, esp. in the intr. and in the complaint, v. [12], due doubtless to tampering with the text to make it fit a false position. But the main purport of the letters can be ascertained beyond a doubt, and if this passage were lacking we should be obliged to assume, in order to understand Neh., just such an occurrence as is here described. The passage cannot be attributed to the Chr. on any conditions; for he could not have composed a passage which he so egregiously misunderstood, and which is so hopelessly inappropriate for the purpose for which he would have invented it. Whatever his faults, and they were many, he was not as stupid as that. Had the Chr. composed the passage, he would almost certainly have written all in Heb. save the letters themselves, as is the case in the story of Ezra, whereas the whole document is in Aram. Moreover, the passage does contain more than the letters themselves, and I cannot understand Torrey's declaration that the "Aram. source contains *nothing but* these suspicious documents" (ES.[142]).

Kost. was the first to deny the historicity of the passage, admitting that if it were authentic it would refer to Ezra's *golah* and overthrow his theory that Ezra is later than Neh. The points raised by Kost. (*Wied.*[54 ff.]), with some comments thereon, follow:

(1) The colonising by Asnappar (Assurbanipal) is improbable. But it is by no means certain that Asnappar is to be identified with Assurbanipal (*v. i.*). (2) There is a suspicious similarity between this correspondence and that of c. 5 f. The agreement is rather fanciful and is mostly in unimportant matters. Both complaints are in Aram., are aimed at the Jews, and are addressed to a Pers. king. But in the important matters there is great divergence. One contains a grave charge and urges action; the other is an inquiry, and the correspondents await orders. In one the complaint is heeded and drastic measures ordered; in the other the Jews are upheld. (3) The phrase "in the book of thy father's memoirs," v. [15], could not apply to Bab. inscriptions. This argument ignores simple textual criticism, the Esd. text reading "in the library of thy fathers," in which Bab. inscriptions may well have been stored. (4) "The mighty kings" of v. [20] admits of no satisfactory explanation, since the history of David and Solomon

would not be recorded in Bab. annals. But the phrase could apply just as well to later kings like Hezekiah, who held a Bab. vassal as a prisoner and who bulks large in the inscriptions of Sennacherib. (5) The phrase "until a command is given by me," v. ²¹, shows a knowledge of Art.'s later consent to Neh. Here again we may note that Esd. lacks the passage, and Kost. is certainly wrong in his assumption that Art. orders the destruction of the walls. Further, we may well question Kost.'s inference. The king might easily issue a conditional decree. As he merely orders the work to stop, it is natural to assume that some further investigation was intended. (6) The impression made by Ne. 1–7⁵ is that Neh. was engaged in an entirely new work, and that a story of a previous attempt to rebuild the walls is inconsistent. The fact is that Neh. was urged to his task by learning that the walls had been thrown down and the gates burned. (7) The mocking attitude of Sanb. and To. is inexplicable if the walls had previously been carried close to completion. It seems to me that if the Sam. had recently destroyed what the Jews had built, they would have sufficient ground to jeer at any one else who attempted to resume the work. The fact that they trust to their own devices, and do not appeal to the king, indicates that they regarded their task as easy. (8) Ne. 2¹⁻⁸ is silent about an existing order to destroy the walls, Neh. does not ask for a reversal of a previous decree, and the king only considers the loss of a faithful servant. Strictly speaking, there had been no order to destroy the walls. Neh. would not be likely to provoke opposition by reminding the king of his former action.

Kost. then gives his ideas as to the origin of the passage. As the first *golah* in the time of Cy. had attempted to rebuild the temple, and were hindered by the Sam., so the walls must have been attempted before the 20th year of Art. Therefore the Chr. makes the *golah* attack the walls after the completion of the temple. It would be difficult to frame a weaker hypothesis. The *golah* under Cy. did not attempt to rebuild the temple and there was no hindrance from the Sam. The Chr. had no idea that this passage dealt with the walls of the city. He incorporates the passage on the theory that the letters referred to the building of the temple. It is easy to agree with Torrey that "Kost.'s methods were not thoroughly scientific, and his conclusions, in the main, were of little value" (ES.¹⁴³).

7–11. The occasion of the letter to Artaxerxes and its beginning.—7. *In the days of Artaxerxes*]. The writer evidently had no exact knowledge of the date or he would have been more specific.—*The rest of their associates*] suggesting an official body which joined in the complaint whose word would add

weight to the charge. The word rendered "associates" occurs in the Eleph. pap., where the meaning is determinable. In I, l.[1] we find "Jedaniah and his associates, the priests who are in Jeb." The word is used like "brother" in Hebrew to indicate those in the same official class. Sachau limits the meaning needlessly to those who joined in the letter, but the word covers all the priests in Jeb.—*And the writing of the letter was written in Aramaic*]. "Character" added by RV. is wrong, for the reference is to the language, not to the script.—*And translated into Aramaic*]. But as it has already been said that the letter was written in Aramaic, the statement that it was translated into Aramaic is manifestly impossible. Marquart proposed "Persian," the letter being translated into the native speech of the king, and so being a bilingual document. Mey. substitutes Persian for the first Aramaic, and omitting the redundant "writing" gets "the dispatch was written in Persian and translated into Aramaic." Berth. regards the second Aramaic as a gloss; it is lacking in 𝔊. The phrase is a copyist's note, and is not of much importance (*v. i.*).—*Rehum*] is a good Hebrew name, and occurs frequently in Ezr.–Ne. (*v. on* 2[2]).—*Commander*] is better than "chancellor," RV. Arnold proposes "master of the decrees" (JBL. 1912,[24]). Rehum then would be the chief officer.—*Shimshai the scribe*] vv. [9. 17. 23] †. The name usually is traced to Iranian (BDB.), but it might easily be Hebrew. The accusers of the Jews in this case, though holding presumably Persian offices in Syria, may themselves have been of Hebrew stock. In that case they certainly would not have written in Persian. The words are a gloss due to the confusion of the text. —*As follows*] but the letter does not begin till v. [11b].—**9.** *Dinaites*] or "judges" according to 𝔊[L], so Hoffmann, Mar.—*Apharsath-chites*] also interpreted as "generals" (BDB.).—*Tarpelites*] or an official title *tabellarii* (Jensen): it has also been interpreted as Iranian and equal to the frequently used term "beyond the River" (Syria).—*Apharsites*]. Marquart renders "secretaries." —*Archevites*] the people of Erech (Mey. *Ent.*[40]), a city in Babylonia.—*Babylonians*] only occurrence of the gentilic form in OT.—*Shushanchites*] the people of Susa, the Elamite capital.

—*Dehavites*]. Following 𝕲ᴮ now generally interpreted as "that is," a rendering requiring a slight emendation. We should then have "the Susians, that is, the Elamites," people of the country over which Cyrus had first ruled.—*And the rest of the peoples*]. In spite of the above rather lengthy list, there were other nationalities involved in the hostility toward the Jews.— *Whom the great and famous Asnappar had taken captive*]. That is, all these peoples had been brought to Samaria from other places, referring to the story in 2 K. 17. Asnappar is usually identified with Assurbanipal, apparently because it is more like his name than any other. 𝕲ᴸ offers Shalmaneser who began the siege of Samaria. As the name is corrupt, as the resemblance to Assurbanipal is not very close, and as there is no evidence of his colonising Samaria, we might conjecture Sargon, who conquered Samaria in 722 or Esarhaddon as v. ².—*In the city of Samaria*]. Better with 𝕲 *in the cities of Samaria*, since all these peoples would scarcely reside in one city.—*And the rest beyond the River*] *i. e.*, other peoples of the country west of the Euphrates. The term "beyond the River" is used in this period for all the country from the Euphrates to Egypt.—*And so forth*]. Usually interpreted as equivalent to "and others," and so "too tedious to mention." But Torrey (JBL. 1897) has shown that it means "and now," the preface to the real matter of the letter. The word is misplaced in our text, being repeated from the end of v. ¹¹.—**11.** *This is a copy of the letter which they sent unto him*] obviously an editorial note, and should stand between the narrative and the beginning of the letter proper, as shown below in the reconstructed text.—*Thy servants*]. The names have been transposed, and are wanting here, so that as the text stands the complaint was anonymous.

It would be difficult to find a more corrupt text than vv. ⁷⁻¹¹. At first sight the case seems quite hopeless, for while there can be but a single letter, there are two sets of complainants, and there are three different introductions. The whole is so confused in MT. that we seem balked at every point. We may easily assume that preceding the letter proper there was a simple and straightforward intr., stating the time of writing, the complainants, the accused, and the person with whom the complaint is lodged. The text of Esd. is simple and straightforward, but a careful examination shows that even that does not have the original text. It does, however, afford a basis for reconstruction.

The letter proper begins at v. ^{11b} with the complainants, *thy servants, the men of Abar-Naharah*. Plainly we lack something here, viz., the addressee and the names of the accusers. Esd. has a part of the necessary material beginning, *to King Art. lord*. Then after οἱ παῖδές σου we have Ῥάθυμος ὁ (Torrey rightly supplies γράφων) τὰ προσπίπτοντα καὶ Σαμέλλιος ὁ γραμματεὺς καὶ οἱ ἐπίλοιποι τῆς βουλῆς αὐτῶν καὶ (κρι-ται^{L}) οἱ ἐν κοίλῃ Συρίᾳ καὶ Φοινίκῃ. And in v. ^{17} we find in the address of the king's reply an additional clause, οἰκοῦσιν ἐν Σαμαρείᾳ. Combining this material we see that the beginning of the letter then must have been: לארתחששתא מלכא אדון עבריך רחום בעל־טעם ושמשי ספרא ושאר כנותהון די יתיבין בקריה די שמרין ושאר עבר־נהרה. If now we turn to MT. here reprinted for easy inspection, we find all this, as will appear by noting the words with a single underline: (8) רחום בעל־טעם ושמשי ספרא כתבו אגרא חדה על־ירושלם לארתחששתא מלכא כנמא: (9) אדון רחום בעל־טעם ושמשי ספרא ושאר כנותהון דיניא . . . : (10) ושאר אמיא די הגלי אסנפר רבא ויקירא והותב המו בקריה די שמרין ושאר עבר־נהרה וכענת: (11) דנה פרשגן אגרתא די שלחו עלוהי על ארתחששתא מלכא עבריך אנש עבר־נהרה וכענת. It is a support to our reconstruction to note that ^{L} has κρίται, 3 Esd. *judices* just where דיניא occurs in v. ^{9}; *v. i.* in note on text. Κυρίῳ, which is always found in Esd. with Art., is a rendering of אדון reading אָדוֹן. והותב המו of MT. shows a modified construction to fit the connection as the text stands. It is to be noted that we find this beginning of the letter in two sections of our present text separated by the clause "and the rest of the peoples whom the just and noble Asnappar took captive," and this intervening portion is plainly an explanation of "their companions," or "their counsel," as Esd. has it. Thus we are able to put together the passages which are required as the first part of the letter proper.

If now we take the sections of the text preceding and following our extracted passages and preface the date from v. ^{7}, we get this surprising result: *And in the days of Art. Rehum the reporter* (or *commander*) *and Shimshai the scribe wrote a letter against Jerus.*, (11) *and this is a copy of the letter which they sent to him to Art. the king*, from a source indicated above by double underlining. From this it appears that we have now also a simple and straightforward intr. to the letter. If we compare this result with the text of Esd., we find: (1) Instead of "against Jerus.," "against [those dwelling in Judah and] Jerus.," showing an addition (within brackets), and that exactly what we find in v. ^{6} in the letter to Xerxes, no other note of which is found in Esd. (2) The complainants are (Βήλεμος καὶ Μιθραδάτης καὶ Ταβέλλιος καὶ) Ῥάθυμος καὶ Βεέλτεθ-μος καὶ Σαμέλλιος ὁ γραμματεὺς (καὶ οἱ λοιποὶ οἱ τούτοις συντασσόμενοι) οἰκοῦντες δὲ ἐν Σαμαρείᾳ καὶ τοῖς ἄλλοις τόποις. Now the additions here (within parentheses) are taken from v. [7], adding three names, and having וישאר כנותו, which belongs to the intr., and besides is Aram., not Heb. The last clause, *dwelling in Samaria and the other places*, belongs to the letter itself, for even Esd. lacks it in its proper place. To this we might make a further addition from v. [7] and so get as the original: *And in the days of Art. Rehum the reporter and Shimshai the scribe and the rest of their companions wrote a letter against Jerus. to Art. the king of Pers.* This may as easily be all Aram. as partly one language and partly the other. In v. [7] we have left the three names, Bishlam, Mith-redates, and Tabeel. These names have no place in the letter to Art. For as they stand first here they would certainly be named in the reply; but they do not recur at all. Now we have noted that כתבו in v. [6] lacks a subj. The three names are manifestly the accusers of v. [6]. Bishlam, Mithredates, and Tabeel were the hired agents of v. [5]. Considering the vast amount of transposition which has taken place, the tr. of those names is not singular (so Torrey, ES.[178], Mey. *Ent.*[17]).

V. [7b] is lacking in Esd. and is easily explained as a marginal note, or an explanation by the Chr. in a text with which havoc was already made. Its place would be more appropriate after v. [11a]. We have still to account for the passage, vv. 9[b]–10[a], *i. e.*, the list of names and the explanatory note *and the rest of the peoples whom the great and noble Asnappar took captive.* This clause seems to be a late gl., describing the origin of the Sam. and showing marked hostility to them. The last part may easily be taken from v. [2]. The absence of the whole passage in Esd. shows that it was prob. later than that translation; for there would be no motive for its omission.

Further כנמא in v. [8], to which there is nothing corresponding in Esd., was added after the dislocation was made. And finally אנש עבר-נהרה וכענת is a repetition due to the misplacing of עבריך. אנש is a mistake for שאר. וכענת is the beginning of the letter and could not occur twice. "To Art. the king of Pers." is superfluous, rendered necessary only after the dislocation was made to explain the preceding "to him." Mey. notes the use of על before Art., used in the sense of "unto," but that is good Aram. usage (*cf.* vv. [17. 18]). The confusion is not so great as appears from the difficulty of reconstruction. The principal changes necessary are but two: the tr. of the three names from v. [7] to v. [6], and the tr. of [11a] to [8b].

V. [6] did not appear at all in the text used by Esd., or else the translator omitted it because he saw that it was an unintelligible scrap. Torrey holds that "v. [6], or at all events v. [6b], is *exactly reproduced*" (ES.[179]; italics mine). But his reasons are not convincing. He is obliged to assume that Art. was substituted for Xerxes, whereas Esd. begins exactly as v. [7], showing in κατέγαψεν (though [L] has the correction κατέγραψαν) כתב of v. [7], not כתבו of v. [6]. This is followed by αὐτῷ = עלוהי of v. [11]. שטנו Torrey finds in ἐπιστολήν and cites 𝕮[L]; but

𝕲ᴸ has ἐπιστολὴν καὶ ἐναντίωσιν, an obvious and characteristic dup.
Since "letter" appears three times in the section, vv. ⁷· ⁸· ¹¹, it is strange
to suppose that this well-informed translator misconceived the mng.
of so easy a word as שׁנוה. Esd. has ὑπογεγραμμένην before ἐπιστολήν,
which Torrey regards as representing כנמא; but to get an unnecessary
adj. the translator would hardly jump from v. ⁶ to v. ⁸; moreover, כנמא
is, I think, a late interpolation. The words stand at the end of the
passage in Esd.; had "Esd." followed v. ⁶ he certainly would have written
κατέγραψαν τὴν ἐπιστολήν. This position and the order of the words in
Gk. suggest that they may stand for פרשׁגן אגרתא in v. ¹¹ Ὑπογεγραμμένην
occurs only in the Apocr. On פרשׁגן *v. i.* critical note. Finally, χρόνοις
may represent ימי, but never elsw. stands for מצוות.

The whole section vv. ⁷⁻¹¹ should therefore rd. as follows: **And in
the days of Art., Rehum the reporter and Shimshai the scribe,
and the rest of their companions, wrote a letter against Jerus. to
Art. the king of Pers. And this is a copy of the letter which they
sent to him: To Art. the king our lord. Thy servants Rehum the
commander and Shimshai the scribe and the rest of their companions who dwell in the cities of Sam. and in the remainder of the
province beyond the River. And now—**

It must be noted that this result is not attained by the free play
of a critic's imagination, but it is entirely obtained from a text which as
it stands is utterly unintelligible. A literal translation of MT. will be
the most convincing evidence of its impossibility for the reader not
versed in Aram.: (7) *And in the days of Art. wrote Bishlam, Mithredates,
Tabeel and the rest of their companions unto Art. the king of Pers. and the
writing of the letter was written in Aram. and interpreted in Aram.* (8)
*Rehum the commander and Shimshai the scribe wrote a letter against
Jerus. to Art. the king as follows.* (9) *Then Rehum the reporter and
Shimshai the scribe and the rest of their companions, the Dinaites and the
Apharsathchites, the Tarpelites, the Apharsites, the Archevites, the Babylonians, the Shushanchites, the Dehavites, the Elamites,* (10) *and the
rest of the nations whom the great and noble Asnappar took captive and
caused them to dwell in the cities of Sam. and the rest of the province beyond
the River. And now.—*(11) *This is a copy of the letter which they sent
unto him, unto Art. the king: Thy servants the men of the province beyond
the River. And now—*

We find in the king's reply (v. ¹⁷) the names of the men who sent the
charge. Obviously the same names and titles must have stood in the
accusing letter. It is a justification of the reconstruction that the two
lists of names and titles agree save in the words "cities of," which do
not occur in v. ¹⁷.

7. ביִמי] in v. ⁶ the same idea is expressed by במלכות, showing a different hand.—ארתחששתא] an Aramaised form. In 𝕲 only ᴸ and Esd.

show the regular Gk. form Ἀρταξέρξου; ᴮ has Ασαρδαθα, ᴬ Αρθασασθα. Bab. form is *Ar-tak-šat-su*, Achamenian, *Urtaxšasa*.—כתב] from this sg. and the sg. sf. (*his* companions) Mey. argues that Rehum was the principal instigator of the letter. But a sg. vb. with more than one subj. is a common Semitic usage.—כנותו] does not occur in Heb., but is frequent in the Aram. passages, vv. ⁹· ¹⁷· ²³ 5⁶ 6⁶· ¹³. It is contended by Zimmern that its As. equivalent *kinattu* means only "house servants" (Mar.⁶⁶); but here it means "associates," as in the Eleph. pap. The former sense would be unsuitable unless the antecedent of "his" were "Art.," a possibility in this v., but not in v. ¹⁷.—כתב] may signify "character of writing" in Est. 1²² 3¹² 8⁹, but not in 4⁸; "mode of writing" is a rather forced sense; the natural mng. is the thing written, *cf.* 2⁶². 𝕲 renders as a vb., ἔγραψεν.—הנשתון] also 7¹¹; the Chr. has taken this from Aram. vv. ¹⁸· ²³ 5⁵. Andreas says middle-Iranian ptc. pf. pass. *nibhist = scriptum* (Mar.), Hoffmann (*ZA*. ii,⁵²) and Str. similarly. Mey. holds that it is an error for פתשגן, Pers. *patigama*, "report" or "message." As it is synonymous with כתב, he contends that the latter is an explanatory gl. of the Pers. word. 𝕲 here and v. ¹⁸ ὁ φορολόγος, which in Job 3¹⁸ 39⁷ = נגש, "oppressor," but the mng. here, as appears from Esd. 2²³, is "tax-collector."—כתוב] 𝕲 γραφήν.—ארמית²] lacking in 𝕲, while מתרגם is ἑρμηνευμένην, so agreeing with γραφήν. 𝕲 gives, therefore: "The tax-collector wrote a letter in Aram. and it was translated." We must either change one "Aram." to "Pers.," the reasons urged for which are not very convincing, or else explain, "the letter was written in Aram. and it had been translated into Aram.," implying that it was first composed in some other language. As Aram. was the diplomatic language of Pers., as it had been of the Bab. and Hebrews (2 K. 18²⁶), it is difficult to see why the letter must have been first composed in one language and then translated into another. Mar. after 𝕲 calls ארמית a gl. We might solve the problem by reading פתשגן (v. on v. ¹¹) "copy," and thus have *the letter was written in Aram. and there was an Aram. copy*, the copy being preserved in vv. ¹¹ ᶠᶠ. The most prob. solution is that we have a jargon of copyists' marginal notes or directions, *e. g.*, "write the letter," "write in Aram.," "translated into Aram." The words really stand at the head of the Aram. sections of Ezr., and may have been directions to note the change of language, a change much less obvious in 𝔤 than in MT.—**8.** רחום]. Both this and שמשי are declared to be Syrian names by Mey. (*Ent.*³⁴). Rehum was regarded as Pers. by Rawlinson, while Andreas (Mar.⁸⁶) regards שמשי as a popular etymological adaptation from an Iranian ששמי. Thus is it determined to make foreigners of two good Heb. names.—בעל-טעם] was misunderstood in 𝕲, and transliterated in various ways, βαδαταμὲνᴮ, βααλταμᴬ, βελτεεμᴸ. Esd. Βεέλτεμος, but in v. ¹¹ τὰ προσπίπτοντα, to which Torrey rightly adds from v. ¹⁷ ὁ γράφων. Andreas explains as a translation of an old Pers. title; Mey. says it is applied to the governor of a small Pers. district. It seems to be a compound, "master of commands," a sense suitable in v. ²³. Torrey renders "reporter."—כנמא] from כן and indefinite מא and mng. "as follows" (Str. Mar.⁹⁴). It is lacking in 𝕲, but appears in Esd. apparently as Περσων.—**9.** אדין]. Contrary to the general statement, this is represented in 𝕲 by a doublet, τάδε ἔκρινεν. Str. regards as gl. Berth. explains it as a doublet from דיניא in v. ᵇ. In this corrupt text a word or two more or less makes little difference. Vv. ⁹ ᶠ. are simply a more amplified repetition of v. ⁸ with a vb. lacking. 𝕲 saw the defect and supplied it by taking אדין in two senses (אדין דן). We have in this v. a list of nine words or names which have sorely perplexed all students. It is useless to print all the desperate conjectures which have been offered. Passing by the first four names for the present, we arrive for the rest at pretty definite results.—(א)ארכוי]. Jensen, *Theol. Ltz.* 1895, proposed to identify with Gk. ἄρχοι, an interpretation generally rejected in favour of "people of Erech."—בבליא] is clearly "people of the city of Bab."—שושנכיא]. Zimmern (*KAT.*³· ⁴⁸⁵) suggests that here is preserved an identification of the Susian god *Sušinak* with the name of the city. Andreas, Mar.⁸⁵, (*cf.* De. *Par.*³²⁷) explains *ak* as a sf.; so Str.—שושן] is the place-name.—דהוא] De. (BD.ˣ) suggested *Du-u-a*, found in As. contract tablets. Virtually all scholars now agree with 𝕲ᴮ οἱ εἰσίν = די הוא, "that is," and so explaining the fact that the Susians were Elamites. This explanation is generally regarded as a gl., the Elamites being much better known than the Susians (Mey. Mar. *et al.*). We have then peoples named from three well-known cities, Erech, Bab., and Susa. To revert to the first four names, we have an unsolved problem and must rest content with conjecture.—דיניא] Schrader proposed *Da-ja-e-ni* (*KAT.*³· ²⁴⁶). De. *Din-šarru*, a city near Susa (BD.ˣ). 𝕲ᴸ οἱ κριταί, and so virtually all scholars rd. דָּיָנֵא, "the judges," regarded by Andreas as an Aram. translation of the Pers. *dātabhar.*—טרפליא] made a Latin name by Jensen, *tabellarii*, rejected by Andreas, Mar. *et al.* Pers. is diligently sought in this document, and its presence would be natural enough, but Latin is scarcely admissible. Andreas is quite sure that we should point טרפלָיֵא and find in the word some unknown official title (so Mey.⁴⁰). Hoffmann explains from Pers. *taraparda*, "the provinces beyond the River."—אפרסתכיא, אפרסיא; and אפרסכיא] 5⁶ are much alike, and may justly be regarded as variants. De. (DB.ⁱˣ) suggested for the first *Partakka* or *Partukka*, towns in Media mentioned by Esarhaddon; in the second he saw *Parsua*. The desperate state of the case is shown by Mey.; he notes that the root in all three is פרס, "Persia." א, he says, may be prefixed or left off at will in Iranian names; ת in the first is a corruption; in (1) and (3) the adj. sf. *Ka* appeared, so each word is reduced to Pers. (*Ent.*³⁷ ᶠ.); thus he gets out of the passage: "the Pers. judges, the Pers. ———, the Erechites, the Bab., and the Susians." Others have made official titles of all

the words: "the judges, messengers, tablet-writers, scribes." All
these identifications reckon with the single words and forget the
context. The passage shows that names of peoples are required in
each case. The v. begins with names of two persons and their offices:
*Rehum the commander and Shimshai the scribe and the rest of their asso-
ciates:* then in apposition to the last word we have the catalogue of the
races of which the Sam. were composed, which cannot be a mixture of
offices and peoples. As part of the names are peoples, they must all
be. So v. ¹⁰ begins *and the rest of the peoples.* That we cannot identify
them merely proves a corruption of the text, or else the transplanting
to Sam. of peoples from places as yet quite unknown. The ransack-
ing of every language under heaven to make offices out of this jargon
is an unwarranted extravagance of criticism. It is better frankly to
confess our ignorance. The writer, having an animus against the Sam.,
may have sought the most outlandish names he knew.—**10.** אסנפר]
almost unanimously identified with Assurbanipal (668–626), son and
successor of Esarhaddon (v. ²). Schrader identified with Esarhaddon
to agree with v. ² (*KAT.*³, ²⁴⁶). Mey. and others who are searching
diligently for Pers. influences in a document conceived to have been
written by Persians sees a choice bit of evidence in this word; he supplies two missing letters, אסורבוזנפר, and decides that the final ר is due
to the fact that Pers. has no ל (*Ent.*²⁹ ᶠ·). As the adj. רבא (Heb. רב)
is directly applied to this king, it would appear that the writer took out
a part of two syllables from the name and made it into a title. The
resemblance is the only ground for this identification, resting therefore
on a slender basis in spite of its general acceptance. 𝔊ᴸ has Σαλμα-
νασσάρης, this text being credited with correcting the name on the
basis of 2 K. 17, a critical acumen not otherwise apparent. This identification is, however, impossible chronologically; Shalmaneser was too
early. Marquart (*Fund.*⁵⁰) saw the old Heb. אסרגון, Sargon. We
know that Sargon colonised Sam.; acc. to v. ² Esarhaddon did likewise. As generally understood Assurbanipal added to the confusion
of tongues and religions. The name is corrupt and may be Sargon or
Esarhaddon as well as Assurbanipal.—רבא ויקירא]. Sieg. says: "Aram.
translation of the As. royal title *šarru rabbu*," but we lack *šarru*, and have
another adj. which has no parallel in the As. inscriptions.—ויקיר] occurs
elsw. only in Dn. 2¹¹, where it means *difficult.* Here it is equivalent to
Heb. יקר and means *famous.* It is not easy to see why Assurbanipal
should be singled out for praise by those whom he had carried into
exile.—קריה] 𝔊 has pl. πόλεσιν, the most suitable text, for while the
chief complainants might live in the city of Sam., the description of
peoples covers a much wider territory. If MT. is right, it would appear
that all these peoples were not made a party to the complaint. The
difficulty may be avoided by reading וֹ שאר:.

11. פרשגן] V. ²³ 5⁶ and as loan-word in Heb. 7¹¹ †. We may compare

פתשגן having same sense, "copy," Est. 3¹⁴ 4⁸ 8¹³. Mar. says both words come from Pers. In Gk. we find five renderings: (1) ὑπογεγραμμένην, Esd. 2¹⁶. (2) ὑποκείμενον, Esd. 7¹¹. (3) ἀντίγραφον, Esd. 5⁶ 𝕮ᴸ. (4) διαταγή, 𝕮ᴮᴬ. (5) διασάφησις, 𝕮ᴮᴬ in 5⁶ 7¹¹.—עלוהי] lacking in 𝕮ᴸ and in ARV. through misunderstanding the corruption of the text. The letter proper begins with על־ל־ארח'.—אנש] = Heb. אנוש. Esd. has οἱ ἐπίλοιποι τῆς βουλῆς αὐτῶν. This shows a different text.

12–16. The charges against the Jews.—12. In Esd. we have a slightly different and more deferential address than MT.: *be it known to our lord the king,* the same difference recurring in v. ¹³. The next clause is almost always translated wrong; it should run thus: *the Jews, who have come up from thee unto us, have gone to Jerusalem, a rebellious and evil city*]. The last words are in apposition to Jerusalem, and not the object of "build."

> We note that the Jews here denounced are recent arrivals. There must therefore have been an extensive migration in the time of Art., of which we have no other record. From their undertakings the company must have been a large one. This could not refer to Neh.'s company, for he had authority from the king to do the very things which are here prohibited. In 𝕮ᴮ we find "from Cy." instead of "from thee," the editor supposing there was only one migration, *i. e.,* that in the reign of Cy.

Now we come to the heart of the matter, a description of what the returned Jews were doing which aroused the suspicions of the local Persian officials. But unfortunately at this critical point the text is corrupt and obscure. With the help of Esd. it is possible to get a fairly good sense: *They are building it* [the city or some unknown object], *they are repairing the walls, and they have completed a temple.* It is true that the Jews who had come from Artaxerxes had not built a temple, but the fact that a temple was standing would be an incentive for the rebuilding of the city and its walls. The essence of the charge is certainly the statement about the restoring of the walls. All other conditions could be ignored, but once the walls were about the city, Jerusalem could defy all the peoples in the Syrian province. —**13.** *They will not pay tribute, custom or toll*]. It is not pos-

sible to differentiate these words; the meaning of the first is
assured, any kind of tribute or tax.   The meaning of the others
is mostly guesswork.   Esd. yields better sense and says all that
is necessary: *they will not only refuse to pay tribute.—But in the
end it will damage the king*] is a very doubtful rendering of a
very obscure passage.   Mey. gets "the revenue of the king
will suffer," a good enough sense, but a mere repetition.   Esd.
offers the best solution known to me: *but also they will stand out
against even kings*.   What is apprehended is described fully and
clearly in v.[16]; the loss to the Persian empire of the whole Syrian
province, the plaintiffs greatly exaggerating the power of the
Jews and perverting their purpose.—**14.** *Now because we eat
the salt of the palace*], lacking in 𝕲[BA].   𝕲[L] has "temple" instead of "palace," making the Samaritans priests.   On the
Bond of Salt *v.* RS. *Relig. Sem.*[252].   The idea is that the salt
constituted a bond which those who ate were bound to respect.

> We might compare the covenant of salt by which the pr. were bound
> to Yahweh, Nu. 18[19], *cf.* 2 Ch. 13[5], where it is the sign of the divine title
> of the Davidic dynasty.   Here it might therefore be a sign of the agree-
> ment of fidelity of the officers to the Pers. king.   It is possible that the
> mng. here is simpler, the idea being that the officers were in the king's
> pay; see AV. "have maintenance from the king's palace," so Ryle, Sieg.
> The old Jewish interpretation was based upon the sowing with salt
> as a sign of utter destruction (Ju. 9[45]) and was, "because we aforetime
> destroyed the temple," *i. e.*, salted the salt of the temple.   Nestle in-
> terpreted the text a little differently, "because the salt of the palace is
> our salt" (*v.* Sieg.), because we will suffer if the king's tribute falls off—
> not a very high motive for their fidelity.   The mng. must be, because
> we are bound to protect the king's interests, therefore we send this
> despatch.   Esd. offers a radically different text, and a sadly erroneous
> one: *because matters at the temple are pressed forward*, another reflection
> of the temple-building story.

A second reason for their report is: *it is not right for us to witness the king's dishonor*].   The word rendered "dishonor" has
the root meaning *nakedness;* that is the idea here, it is not right
to see the king stripped bare of his lawful tribute and territory.
—**15.** *In the book of thy father's memoirs*].   The words imply
that the kings kept a record of events presumably for reference.

These Sam. knew that the records desired could be found only in the archives of the kings of As. and Bab.; "fathers" therefore is used in the sense of *predecessors*. Any story of Judean revolts since the time of Cy. would not be adequate, esp. as it is added that the revolts were in the olden days. The reference is to the revolts of Judah in the century preceding the collapse of 587: note *therefore this city was destroyed, i. e.*, by Nebuchadrezzar: from the Bab. point of view the destruction of Jerus. was a punishment for rebellion. In fact, Judah had been a vassal long before 587, but was ever ready to seize a promising moment for rebellion. The Sam. knew the history of Jerus., and knew it correctly. Curiously Art. and his officers were entirely ignorant of the past history of this province.

16. This verse is a summarising of the whole matter: *we make known to the king* [Esd. "to thee, O lord king"] *that if this city is built and its walls finished, then thou wilt have no portion beyond the River*] that is, the whole Syrian province will be lost to Persia. In other words, the complainants assume that if the Jews complete their project, they will proceed to reduce their neighbours to subjection by restoring the old empire of David. There could hardly be plainer evidence of the correct date, for such a result could never ensue from the building of a temple, but only from the repairing of the walls and the restoration of the houses in the city. Esd. has a different reading for the latter part of the verse: *there will no longer be an outlet for thee to the province beyond the River*. The meaning is not essentially different.

12. להוא] Esd. τῷ κυρίῳ reading יהוה. Mar. explains preformative ל as a change due to the similarity of the form with יהוה (§ ^{65a}); Str. otherwise (§ ^{23k}); *v. AJSL.* xiii.—מן־לותך].† There is difference of opinion about the composition, *v.* Mar. § ^{95d}, Kautzsch,$^{128.1}$. There is prob. a n. which has lost its force in the prep.; the mng. is like Heb. מעם, and so "from thee" or "from thy presence." 𝕲 has ἀπὸ κύρου^B, ἀπο σοῦ^A, παρ' ὑμῶν^L and Esd.—עלינא]. The Massoretic pointing separates this from preceding word, giving, therefore, the impression that the complainants were at Jerus. The pause should be on this word, separating it from what follows.—קריתא] lacking in 𝕲^B, but by an obvious error.—מרדתא] Vv. $^{15-19}$; on the form *v.* Mar. § ^{84}, Kautzsch, § ^{59d} (*ḳaṭṭal*). It is equivalent to Heb. מרד. From Esd. we infer some further n. than *city*. The passage would then run *to Jerus. the rebellious city, and they are building its* ——.—Mar. *et al.*, adopt Qr. ושוריא שכללו]

but this cannot mean *they have finished the walls,* otherwise the complaint would have been too late. V. [13] indicates that the walls are not finished. The Vrss. offer some variety: 𝔊 καὶ τὰ τείχη αὐτῆς κατηρτισμένοι εἰσίν, *they are repairing* (or *finishing*) *the walls,* using the same word for כלל in vv. [13. 16] 5[3. 9. 11] 6[14] (but in v. [13] L has ἐτοιμασθῇ). Esd. has καὶ τὰ τείχη θεραπεύουσι, but συντελεσθῇ in v. [13], showing a different Aram. vb. here. 3 Esd. *et statuunt muros.* Θερ. may have the mng. *repair,* and that is the sense required here.—[ואשיא יחיטו] offers serious difficulty. 𝔊 has καὶ θεμελίους αὐτῆς ἀνύψωσαν, 𝔙 *et parietes componentes.* Esd. καὶ ναὸν ὑποβάλλονται[BA], κ. ν. ὑπερβάλλοντα θεμελιοῦσιν[L]. 3 Esd. *et templum suscitant.* Esd. is clear in one respect, the reference being to the temple. The usual rendering "they have repaired the foundations," is impossible after the statement about the walls. Many conjectures have been made (*v.* BDB. *s. v.* חוש and the comm.). Str. reads יהיבו, as 5[16], "laid the foundations." Jensen derives from As. *ḫaṭu,* "examine," an unsuitable sense here. Haupt calls it Afil of חטש, "excavate the rubbish" (Guthe,[62]), likewise impossible here. "They are repairing the gates" would be the best sense, but there is no basis for this reading. It is more natural to follow Esd. and place ובאישתא . . . קריאתא in apposition with ירושלם. The separation of the obj. from its vb. by these adjectives, as is usually done, is very awkward.—[בנין] is left without an obj., but the text is wrong in any event; the ptc. would not be used with the verbs following in the impf. 𝔊[L] has καὶ οἰκοδομοῦσιν αὐτήν. Esd. has οἰκοῦσιν [οἰκοδομοῦσι[AL]] τάς τε ἀγορὰς αὐτῆς. 3 Esd. *ædificant furnos ejus.* Ἀγορά is used in Eccl. 12[4. 5] Ct. 3[2] for שוק, "a street," which is really an Aram. word, and which may have been confused with שור though שור is represented. In the case of a modern city, laying out its streets would be a first step, but that would hardly be the case in an ancient Oriental town. Yet from v. [13] *if this city be built,* and v. [21] *this city shall not be built,* we might infer that *city* was meant here; but there are three counts in v. [12], reduced to two in v. [13] and to one in v. [21], so that the phrases are not repeated. Indeed, we should expect a generalisation in the latter passage. Some form of בנה is well attested, and some obj. is required. Now ובאישתא does not recur with קריאה in v. [15], and is an anticlimax. The crux of the charge is that Jerus. had been a rebellious city. That it was "bad" would have had no significance. It may be that the obj. of "build" is concealed in this word, though it is not easy to conjecture its nature.

13. Esd. lacks למלכא . . . כען. The words may be an accidental repetition from v. [12].—[מנדה בלו והלך] v. [20] 7[24], 𝔊 φόροι οὐκ ἔσονται[BA], φόρων πρᾶξιν καὶ συντέλεσμα[L], Esd. φορολογίαν οὐ μὴ ὑπομείνωσιν δοῦναι. L as often shows correction from MT. 𝔊 has had our text, but in בלו has seen a negative (לא) and in הלך a vb. (יהלך). מנדה, or, better, מדה, so Heb. Ne. 5[4] (*cf.* מדת 6[8]) is derived from As. *mandatu (nadanu,* "give"

= Heb. נתן). בלו is explained from As. *biltu*, "tax," or, better, from Iranian *bali*, "tribute." Mey. explains as tax in kind. הלך from vb. "go," is explained as money paid for going, "toll" (Mar. Glossary, Str. *et al.*); but such a derivation is not convincing though generally accepted. Another explanation is found in As. *ilku*, "tax" (Ges.ᴮ, Winckler, *Alt. Forsch.* xv,⁴⁶³ ᶠ·). Winckler supposes בלו to be a corruption of יכלו of the original text, and renders the passage: "they will withhold tribute and pay no taxes" (*op. cit.*). He is close to the truth, but it is better to follow Esd. (*v. s.*). Mey. regards 𝕲 as evidence that the translators were no longer able to distinguish the three kinds of tribute.—אפרס] † mng. dub.; Andreas emends אפסס, Pers. *afsos*, "injury"; usually explained as mng. "in the end"; Scheft. (BDB.) "treasuries," from Zend *pathwa*. Mey. gets mng. "income."—מלכים] "an unsupportable Hebraism" (Mey. *Ent.*²⁴); he would rd. מלכא, so "the revenues of the king."—תהנזק] vv. ¹⁵· ²² Dn. 6³ †; on the form *v.* Kautzsch, § ³³· ²ᵇ, third p. f. used in neuter sense, "it will injure," or it may go back at least in sense to קרית (Berth.). 𝕲 κακοποιεῖᴮᴬ, ὀχλήσουσινᴸ, Esd. ἀντιστήσονται. The last word in 2 Ch. 13⁷ ᶠ· represents חזק in Hithp., but sense prob. "rebel against" as 3 Esd. *resistent.* —**14.** ערות] 𝕲 with great literalness, ἀσχημοσύνη, the rendering in many places of Heb. ערוה, which is apparently the same word used here.— **15.** דכרניא] Heb. זכרון, *cf.* Mal. 3¹⁶, "memorandum-book"; here the royal annals. The phrase is wanting in 𝕲ᴮᴬ in the second place; Esd. ἐν τοῖς ἀπὸ τῶν πατέρων σου βιβλίοις.—מדנן] Heb. מדינה, *cf.* 2¹, Esd. πόλεις. —אשתדור] v. ¹⁹ † from שרר, Dn. 6¹⁵, Mar. § ⁸², 𝕲 φυγαδεία.—עבדין] 𝕲 δούλων, by an easy misunderstanding. Esd. πολιορκίας συνεσταμένοι, may represent this text, giving to אשתדר a mng. somewhat different from the received one, "enduring sieges."—**16ᵇ.** 𝕲ᴮᴬ has only οὐκ ἔστιν σοι εἰρήνη. Esd., ἔξοδος, has rd. חלק as הלך (*cf.* v. ¹³). 𝕲 is certainly not based on our text exc. for לא לך.

17–24ᵃ. The edict of Artaxerxes and its execution.

The king sent a reply to Rehum, Shimshai, and their associates saying that the annals had been searched and their charges against Jerus. sustained. Therefore he directs his officers to stop the building of the city until authorisation is given by him. The officers proceed to Jerus. with a body of troops and stop the operations.

17. As the text stands we naturally take the whole verse, except the last two words, as introductory to the letter, *the king sent a decree to Rehum*]. The passage is so read in the Vrss. The Greek has *and the king sent back to Rehum . . . peace and command.* Esd., *then the king wrote back to Rehum . . . the*

subjoined letter, as in v. ¹¹. The names of the persons addressed
are, however, an essential part of the letter itself, and we have
a good beginning of the letter with those names: *to Rehum.* . . .
Peace to you. And now]. The first clause is then all that we have
by way of introduction, *the king sent a decree*. We note, however, that the name of the king is not found in the reply at all.
It is therefore quite likely that the text is corrupt and that the
verse originally read: *Artaxerxes the king to Rehum et al.*, that is,
there was no introduction at all, but only the letter itself.—
18. *The letter which you sent unto us has been read before me in
translation*]. As the singular is used elsewhere, "unto us" must
be a mistake for "unto me." "Plainly read," as usually rendered, is found also in Ne. 8⁸; ARV.ᵐ has "or translated." That
is the correct sense. The king probably did not understand
Aramaic, and his scribes therefore would translate the letter.
The word occurs in the Eleph. pap. v,³ where "explained" seems
to be the meaning. Esd. has a simpler text: *I have read the letter which you sent to me*, obtained by omitting two of the Aramaic
words.—**19.** *I issued an order and they searched and found*].
The search was made in the annals suggested in v. ¹⁵. The dis-
coveries amply justified the charges of the accusers; for the
king's secretaries unearthed these facts concerning Jerusalem:
*this city from olden time has risen against kings, and rebellion and
insurrection have been made in it*]. This verse indorses the complaint of v. ¹⁵, which should apparently be reproduced. The
words all recur, but in a different connection.—**20.** The search
uncovered more than the accusers had charged; for three new
points are made: (1) *Mighty kings were over Jerusalem*], showing that only the Judean kingdom was involved. (2) *And they
ruled over all the province beyond the River*], all the Persian dominions west of the Euphrates. (3) *And tribute, custom and toll
(v. on v. ¹³) were paid to them*]. The last two clauses are combined
in Esd., *ruling and taxing the province beyond the River*. The
conditions described in (2) and (3) were never true except in
the time of David and Solomon, and Ryle supposes that those
kings are meant here. But Sieg. rightly questions whether the
archives found in Persia would preserve records of the Judean

history of that period. In the time of David, moreover, Jerusalem could hardly be described as a rebellious city, at least so
far as foreign kings were concerned. If the king had a copy of
the inscriptions of Sennacherib, there would be adequate data
for his purpose. There is really no need of assuming the presence of a Jewish hand here. It is assumed that should Jerusalem
be rebuilt and its walls restored, it would regain the power it
had had in the pre-exilic days. This expectation was far from
realisation in the period before Nehemiah; but it was sufficient
to arouse the apprehensions of a king who was always fearing
rebellion in the subject provinces.—**21.** *Make now a decree*] is
surely not what we look for, since the officers could scarcely
expect to stop the building by a decree. It is better to read as
in v. ¹⁹, *now a decree is made, i. e.*, by this letter; or as Esd., *now
therefore I command to stop these men, i. e.*, the Jewish builders.
—*And that city shall not be built*]. Nothing is said about walls,
but the word "city" is used comprehensively, so that the injunction stops every kind of building operations. Esd. combines the
clauses, *to prevent those men from building the city.—Until a decree
is issued from me*]. A clause lacking in Esd. The injunction
could only be dissolved by the one who made it. This condition was necessary, as without it the decree might be regarded
as binding even though the king had changed his mind, and
such a change was surely possible.

22. *Be warned against doing remissly in this matter*]. The
king did not appreciate the hostile purpose of the complainants;
he did not realise how eager they would be to execute his orders;
and he was aware that royal decrees were not always taken very
seriously in remote provinces.—*Lest injury should increase to
royal loss*]. The interrogative sentence of EV^s. shows a strange
misunderstanding of the text.—**23.** *Then after the copy of the
letter*]. "Copy" creates the same difficulty here as in v. ¹¹
and as "plainly" in v. ¹⁸, which is from the same root. "Translation of the letter" would be better.—*Was read in the presence
of Rehum*]. The royal messenger who brought the edict probably read or translated it to the officers and their council. Here
only Rehum's official title is lacking, probably due to an error

of a copyist. Esd. has here a preferable text: *then the writing of King Artaxerxes being read, Rehum et al. proceeded,* etc.—*They proceeded in haste to Jerusalem against the Jews*]. A considerable time must have elapsed between the sending of the despatch and the receipt of the reply, especially as an investigation of the archives in Persia was necessary. The building meanwhile had continued, all the more vigorously if the Jews suspected the effort to stop their work. The moment the injunction comes to hand the zealous officials hasten to put it in force.—*And stopped them with force and power*]. Esd. has a better reading in two points. It says *marching to Jerusalem at speed with cavalry and a multitude in battle array, they began to restrain the builders.* The clauses are in better order, the "armed force" being connected with "march." Then it brings out the fact that the officers required armed men to enforce obedience to the royal decree, showing that Jerusalem had a considerable power at the time. —**24ª.** *Then the work stopped*]. This is the concluding portion of the "correspondence." The rest of the verse is connected with c. 5, the Aramaic account of the building of the temple. The narrative of Nehemiah shows graphically how utterly the attempt to restore Jerusalem had failed. We may safely infer that the builders scattered to the various towns of Judah, that the enemy destroyed the work that had been accomplished, so that Jerusalem was left as desolate as in 587; for again "its walls were broken down, and its gates burnt with fire."

17. פתגמא] 5⁷· ¹¹ 6¹¹ Dn. 3¹⁶ 4¹⁴ † Bib. Heb. Eccl. 8¹¹ Est. 1²⁰ †. From Old Pers. *patigama* (Andreas, Mey. *Ent.*²² ᶠ·). 𝕲ᴮᴬ lacks the word, possibly because its mng. was unknown; 𝕲ᴸ has a feeble rendering, τὸν λόγον. Esd. combines with שלח, if that represents same text, τότε ἀντέγραψεν. —ושלם (וכעה)] 𝕲ᴮᴬ εἰρήνην καὶ φάσιν, both being apparently obj. of ἀπέσ-τειλεν. 𝕲ᴸ εἰρήνη ὑμῖν. καὶ νῦν. This represents a good text reading לכין for וכעת. שלם is not "prosperity," as BDB., but "peace to you," a common greeting. The greeting is lacking in Esd.; in place of last two words there is τὰ ὑπογεγραμμένα as in v. ¹¹. 3 Esd. *ea quæ subjecta sunt.*—**18.** מפרש] † lacking in 𝕲ᴮᴬ and Esd.; 𝕲ᴸ σάφως. It is a good Heb. word, *v.* Ne. 8⁸, and has the same sense. It is here used adverbially.—קרי] as in Heb. means *call* or *read.* 𝕲ᴮᴬ ἐκλήθη, a rendering necessitated by translating נשתונא, φορόλογος. 𝕲ᴸ follows closely MT. Esd. has a simpler text for the whole v.: 'Ανέγνων [*legi* 3 Esd.]

τὴν ἐπιστολὴν ἣν πεπόμφατε πρὸς μέ, lacking therefore מפרש and קרמי.
—**19.** טעם]. Here and in v. ²¹ *bis* 𝕲 was forced to translate and uses
γνώμη; but 𝕲ᴸ in ²¹ᵇ δόγμα.—מתעבר] 𝕲 γίνονταιᴮᴸ, γίγνονταιᴬ. Esd.
has οἱ ἄνθρωποι as subj.—**20.** תקיפין] see Mar. § ⁸². Esd. ἰσχυροὶ καὶ
σκληροί.—שליטין] 𝕲 ἐπικρατοῦντες, Esd. κυριεύοντες, both texts reading
as a ptc. The rest of v. appears in Esd. thus: καὶ φορολογοῦντες κοίλην
Συρίαν καὶ Φοινίκην; whether this is a free rendering or represents a
simpler text, it is hard to say.—**21.** שימו] rd. as in v. ¹⁹, שים שים or שְׂמֵת, *I
make a decree; cf.* Esd. ἐπέταξα.—ער-מני טעמא יתשם]. 𝕲ᴮᴬ was apparently
puzzled by this passage; we find ἔτι [ὅπως^A] ἀπὸ τῆς γνώμης = ער מן
טעמא. 𝕲ᴸ shows our text, though disarranged in Lagarde. Esd. lacks
the passage altogether; but in v. ²²ᵃ it has a rendering which covers the
ground, *and to take heed that nothing be against this*, reading על, *against*,
and getting a negative in שלו.—**22.** זהירין] † Pe. pass. ptc.; it is the
same as Heb. זהר, which may be of Aram. origin. 𝕲 πεφυλαγμένοιᴮᴬ, προ-
σέχετεᴸ, Esd. προνοηθῆναι.—שלו] 𝕲 ἄνεσινᴮᴬ παρὰ λόγονᴸ.—למה] 𝕲 μή
ποτε, Esd. μη, *i. e.,* לא. The force is that of Heb. פֶּן, *cf.* Kautzsch, § ⁶⁹· ¹⁰.
—ישנא] appears in Esd., προβῇ ἐπὶ πλεῖον, evidence of the free rendering which often characterises this text. 𝕲ᴸ πληθυνθῇ σφόδρα.—חבלא] 𝕲
ἀφανισμός, apparently interpreting like Heb. חבל "destruction," Esd.
τῆς κακίας.—**23.** מן-רי פרשגן] lacking in 𝕲ᴮᴬ, τὸ αντίγραφονᴸ=נשתונא, τοῦ
δόγματοςᴸ. The title of Rehum is missing here; it is found only in 𝕲ᴸ
(βέλτεεμ). In spite of the strong support of MT., the title must have
been in the original.—אזלו] Esd. graphically brings out the true conception in ἀναζεύξαντες, a common word in Mac. representing Heb.
נסע in Ex. and Nu. (*v.* Hatch and Redpath, *Concord.*).—על-יהודיא]
lacking in Esd.; 𝕲 καὶ ἐν Ἰούδαᴮᴬ, ἐπὶ τοὺς Ἰουδαίουςᴸ correctly.—
באארע] 𝕲 ἐν ἵπποις, Esd. μετ᾽ ἵππουᴮᴬ, μετ᾽ ἵππωνᴸ. The word means
arm literally as Heb. אזרוע. The Gk. rendering is hard to explain,
but as רֶכֶב is thus translated in Ex. 14⁷ Jos. 17¹⁶· ¹⁸ 1 K. 16⁹ 2 Ch. 21⁹
Is. 38⁹, that may be what was seen or imagined here.—חיל] 𝕲 δυνάμει,
Esd. ὄχλου παρατάξεως (ταχέωςᴸ).—**24ᵃ.** באדין 𝕲 τότε. This form with
prep. occurs 26 t. in Dn., but in Ezr. only here and 5² 6². The mng. is
the same as אדין.

I formerly thought that v. ²⁴ was from the Chr.'s hand, and written
to connect the correspondence of Art. with the building of the temple
in c. 5. The text of Esd. forbids that commonly received interpretation. In Esd. 2³¹ we have the v. in its entirety: *and the building of the
temple which is in Jerus. ceased until the 2d year of the reign of Dar.
the king of Pers.* This differs from Aram. in having "temple" instead
of "house of God," and in the omission of the meaningless "and it
was ceasing" (והות בטלא). But we find a part of this repeated in Esd.
5⁷⁰, "and they prevented the building two years until the reign of
Dar.; and in the 2d year of the reign of Dar. Hg. and Zc. prophe-

sied" (6¹). **24ᵇ** of Aram. text is plainly discerned here. The clause
"until the reign of Dar." is from 4⁵, where we have added "king of
Pers." as in Esd. 2³¹. Now 5¹ in MT. lacks a necessary date, and the
defect is supplied in Esd. correctly. It appears, therefore, that the Art.
correspondence originally ended with the words, "and the work ceased,"
while the Aram. temple-building narrative began "in the 2d year of
the reign of Dar." When these two narratives were joined as in MT.
there was added in 4²⁴ "the house of God which is in Jerus." The
meaningless words "and it was ceasing" first appeared in the Esd. text
to connect 5¹ with 4⁵ (of MT.).

NE. I, 2. NEHEMIAH BECOMES GOVERNOR OF JUDAH.

**1ᴵ⁻ᴵᴵᵃ. Pilgrims from Judah bring tidings of the sad plight
of Jerusalem.**—**1.** *The words of Nehemiah the son of Hachaliah*].
This is a heading, like a title-page prefixed to any other book.
This was probably added by an editor when our books were
compiled.—*And it was in the month Kislev, twentieth year*].
Kislev is the 9th month in the Hebrew calendar (*cf.* Ezr.
10⁹) = November–December (Zc. 7¹ 1 Mac. 1⁵⁴). "Twentieth
year" is defective, as there is no further definition; it is an
interpolation by the Chronicler. This date as well as that in
2¹ were taken from 5¹⁴. The date in 2¹ is the 1st month of the
20th year, therefore this must be the 19th year of Artaxerxes,
unless, as Wellhausen suggests, the year is reckoned after the
Syrian fashion as beginning in the autumn (*Is.-Jud. Gesch.*¹⁷³).
Susa or Shushan (Dn. 8² Est. 1². ⁵) was the winter residence of the
Persian kings. We find a correct geographical note in a Greek
text, "Susa the metropolis of the Persians." This story opens,
therefore, like Ezra's, on foreign soil. The *palace* or royal castle
is added to define more closely the abode of Nehemiah. He was
at the palace in the city of Shusban, because he was a court
official (v. ⁴ᵇ).—**2.** *And Hanani came in to me*] "to me" being
rightly added from 𝕲.—*One of my brethren*] or *one of my brothers.*
"Brother" in OT. may denote one born of the same parents, a
more distant relative, a fellow-countryman, or even one bound
to another by a covenant. From the expression in 7², "Hanani
my brother," it is likely that he was a near relative and may be
a literal brother. He went to Jerusalem with Nehemiah and

was placed in a position of trust by him.—*He and men from Judah*]. Hanani apparently had not been in Judah himself, but he had heard tidings from a company of returning pilgrims, and had brought them to the cup-bearer, because of his high position and commanding influence, as well as his known interest in the welfare of Jerusalem. The visit was scarcely accidental, and so Hanani deserves credit for starting the important mission of Nehemiah.—*And I asked them*], not Hanani, but the men from Judah. They had been introduced to him as returning pilgrims and the question to them was natural.—*Concerning the Judeans, the remnant who have survived from the captivity, and concerning Jerusalem*]. The text is overloaded probably by a gloss (the remnant). The implication is that those who had survived the captivity were few in number. The reference may be either to those who had always remained in Judah, and so support in a way the radical view that there was no return, or to the small number who were left of those who had gone up from Babylonia. It is probably a specific reference to those who had gone up in the time of Artaxerxes (Ezr. 4¹²) and who had made a vain attempt to restore the walls.—**3.** *The survivors who have survived from the exile there in the province*]. For *province* v. on Ezr. 2¹. The particularity of these words supports the view that Nehemiah has in mind those who had gone up to Jerusalem, otherwise "exile" would be strangely used as a note of time.—*Are in great distress and in contempt*]. Nearly a century after the decree of Cyrus, the condition of the people in Judah was almost hopeless. They were few in number, at least in Jerusalem, and were poor and oppressed.—*And the wall of Jerusalem is breached and its gates have been burned with fire*]. This is said not to explain the distress of the people, but to reply to the second part of Nehemiah's question. He had inquired about the people and about the city. Both questions are answered, but with singular brevity. Nehemiah may have only recorded the substance of the report. It suffices, however, to show that some great calamity had befallen the holy city.— *Breached* or perhaps *broken down*] the word is too indefinite to describe accurately the extent of damage to the walls.

To what catastrophe does this report refer? The great majority of scholars have explained it as that of 586 B.C. Then the Bab. army broke down (נתץ) the whole wall of Jerus. and burned (שרף) the temple, the palace, and all the houses of the city (2 K. 25⁹ᵇ Jer. 39⁸ 52¹³ ᶠ. 2 Ch. 36¹⁹. The last clause Torrey regards as a gl. (ES.³⁰⁰), but it is immaterial, for the city was pretty effectually destroyed, but there is nothing said about the gates, though they must also have been burnt, as that was the usual course in the destruction of a city. Yet a very plausible description is found in Lam. 2⁹, "her gates are sunk into the ground," implying that being made useless by the breaking of the walls they were left to rot. These accounts are all manifestly dependent upon a single source, for they all use the same words for "break down" and "burn." Now in our text with "walls" we have the pred. מפרצת, the only occurrence of the Pu., and strictly speaking the word means *breached*. Little stress can be laid on that (against Sieg.), for in Is. 5⁵ and other places the same word seems to refer to complete destruction. For the burning we have יצת here and in 2¹⁷ and אכל in 2³· ¹³ instead of שרף in 2 K. That this story is not dependent, therefore, upon the historical sources cited above is shown by the employment of different words for the same act and by the silence in regard to the gates; and it is to be noted that the burning of the gates is a prominent feature of this narrative.

Neh. is deeply affected by the tidings about Jerus. He makes no reference to what was said about the people, but the destruction of Jerus. depresses him deeply. He weeps, fasts, and prays for days and nights, and even after three months is unable to control his distress when in the presence of the king and when his depression is perilous to himself. The query insistently arises whether he would have been so distressed by hearing of a calamity which had occurred one hundred and fifty years before. Kost. explains his distress as due to the continued dispersion of Israel (*Wied.*⁶⁰ ᶠ·), but this scholar lays too much stress upon the prayer, which is not authentic, and too little upon undisputed facts. Neh.'s work was the rebuilding of the city, not the gathering of the scattered exiles. Furthermore, when he asked the pilgrims about the condition of Jerus. it is most unnatural that their sole report should be a description of a condition which had stood unchanged for a century and a half. That might have been a true account, but it could scarcely be regarded as the latest *news* from the holy city. Suppose Neh. as ignorant of Judean conditions as we may, it is incredible that he should be unaware of Nebuchadrezzar's destruction of the walls.

We might find an explanation by supposing that there was an expectation that the walls and gates had been restored, and the grief of Neh. would then be due to his disappointment that such is not the case. The report would then be tantamount to the statement that nothing had yet been done. But the language used forbids such an interpretation, even if it would meet the case. The report is *the wall of Jerus. is breached and its gates have been burned with fire.* This news is a great surprise to Neh. and is the most significant fact in the affairs of Jerus. The conditions require a recent calamity, not one of one hundred and fifty years' standing.

Therefore we must suppose that since 536 B.C. the walls had been restored in some sort of way and new gates set in place. On *a priori* grounds such a movement is highly prob. For the people had been able to build ceiled houses for themselves (Hg. 1⁴), and had restored the temple. Without walls the city would be at the mercy of any marauding band of hostile neighbours. We are not left to conjecture, however, for we have exact information in Ezr. 4⁷⁻²⁴, where there is a clear account of an attempt to rebuild the walls of Jerus. Neh. knew of that expedition and was anxiously awaiting news of the accomplishment of its supreme purpose. Hanani fell in with some pilgrims who had just come back from Judah, and took them to his influential and patriotic brother. From them Neh. learned of the disastrous failure of the expedition. It was natural that he should be surprised and depressed.

4. *And when I had heard these words I sat down and wept*]. That was the immediate result of the surprise and disappointment in regard to affairs at Jerusalem. As Nehemiah's distress was too great to be relieved by one outburst of tears, we have the description of continued action: *and I mourned for days* [denoting an indefinite period] *and* [during those days] *I was fasting and praying before the God of heaven*]. On the *God of heaven* v. Ezr. 1². ⁵⁻¹¹ᵃ.

Nehemiah's prayer.—**5.** *Yahweh the great and terrible God*], for which 𝕲 reads *the mighty, the great and the terrible,* usual attributes of the God of heaven, v. 4⁸ 9³². Yahweh occurs nowhere in N.—*Keeping the covenant and mercy*] joins incongruous ideas; for the first clause means being faithful to an agreement made with the nation. We should expect a word like "showing" before "mercy." But we find "keep mercy" in Ps. 89²⁹. On the nature of "mercy" v. Bennet, *Post-Ex. Pr.*¹⁵⁶ ᶠ.. The phrase is a hackneyed one and is of Deuteronomic origin (Dt. 7⁹. ¹² 1 K. 8²³ Dn. 9⁴). The whole verse is found in the last-named passage with very slight differences. It appears to be a stereotyped form of prayer.—**6.** *Let now thy ears be attentive*] called by Sieg. "a special Nehemian formula," on the basis of

v. [11]. But we find the expression in Solomon's prayer, 2 Ch. 6[40]
Ps. 130[2] (also a prayer).—*And thine eyes open*] cf. 1 K. 8[29. 52]
2 Ch. 6[20] 7[15]. Here again we have the stock phrases of prayer.
—*Which I am praying before thee to-day, day and night*]. The
participle denotes continuous action in harmony with v. [4] and
with "day and night"; but "to-day" would mean a specific
time. The text seems to be original, but we may suspect the
Chronicler's hand.—*And making confession of the sins of the sons
of Israel which they have sinned against thee*]. The text has
"we" as subject of "have sinned," but with 𝔊 and 𝔙 we must
read "they." Confession was a typical part of the Hebrew
prayers, and indeed is a part of the true prayers of all worshippers.—*And I and the house of my father have sinned*]. From this
statement Nehemiah's Davidic descent has been inferred. Such
a conclusion is not improbable, as the sin of his house is separated from that of the people generally. That relationship
would explain his interest in Judah and his sense of responsibility. The view has other support (*cf.* note on 2[3]). The sin is the
general disregard of the law of God, going back through past
centuries and extending down to the present. To this long-
standing wickedness is ascribed the present unhappy failure to
restore the walls and thus make Jerusalem a city capable of
defence against her neighbours.—**7.** *We have acted very cor-
ruptly against thee*], a general positive statement, followed by
the negative and more specific: *and we have not kept the commandments and the statutes and the judgments* [typical Deuteronomic
words] *which thou didst command Moses thy servant*]. Moses is
very often called the servant of God (Jos. 1 *pass.* 1 K. 8[53. 56] and
cf. further in Ryle).—**8.** *Saying*] would properly introduce a
direct quotation from the words of Moses. The alleged quotation extends through v. [10]. But these words are not found in
the Pentateuch. Nevertheless the phrases are mostly Deuteronomic. The passage from which this is mainly drawn is Dt.
30[1-5], not 29[20 ff.], as Sieg. says. But the passage in Dt. has
nothing in it about transgressing; it presupposes the exile as a
punishment for sin, and deals with the repentance of Israel and
the consequent restoration of the exiles to the land of their

fathers, making them greater than they had ever been before; therefore the passage must be exilic.—*If you transgress, I will scatter you among the nations*]. The threat of dispersion is frequent in the pre-exilic literature: Dt. 4²⁷ (the same words, but in third person with Yahweh as subject) 28⁶⁴ Je. 9¹⁵ Ez. 11¹⁶ *et pass.*—**9.** *If you return unto me and keep my commandments and do them*], the first part of the conditional sentence, containing the protasis. Returning to God and keeping his commandments are not the same thing, as Ryle states; the latter is the result of the former.—*Though your banishment be in the end of heaven*], taken *verbatim* from Dt. 30⁴ except "thy" becomes "your." Some MSS. of 𝕲 have *from the end of heaven to the end of heaven, i. e.*, from one end of heaven to the other, as Dt. 4³² (but not Ju. 7¹¹ which Ryle cites). In Dt. 28⁶⁴ we have the more appropriate idea: "Yahweh will scatter thee among the nations from one end of the earth to the other end of the earth." *Heaven* cannot be right. It is true that it is conceived possible for a man to climb up to heaven (Am. 9²), but that is the bold flight of the prophet, while our passage is intensely literal.—Then comes the apodosis: *From there I will gather you and bring you in*]. We must read "you" instead of "them," as Dt. 30⁴ and some Greek texts and 𝕳.—*Unto the place*], but Dt. 30⁵ has "unto the land." Here the reference is to the city.—*Where I have elected to cause my name to dwell*] is a frequent Deuteronomic description of Jerusalem, Dt. 12¹¹ 14¹² 16⁶· ¹¹ 26² + fifteen times. The phrase is not found elsewhere in the Pentateuch.—**10.** *And these are thy servants and thy people*]. "These" would refer to the Jews struggling in Jerusalem; but the whole verse is a loose quotation from Dt. 9²⁹: "and these are thy people and thy inheritance whom thou broughtest out with thy great power and with thy outstretched arm." The words differ slightly, but the sense is the same.—*Mighty hand*] occurs in Dt. many times; so does *redeem*. 𝕲ᴸ gives a different turn, *we are thy servants and thy people.*—**11ᵃ.** The prayer returns to supplication and repeats in part v. ⁶. 𝕲ᴸ adds a clause: *do not turn away thy face.* —*And unto the prayer of thy servants*] implies that others than Nehemiah joined in his prayers. The following paradoxical

clause *who delight to fear thy name*] requires some such antecedent
as 𝕲 provides. But there is no hint of any other supplicant.—
*And prosper, I pray, thy servant this day, and grant him compas-
sion before this man*]. These words have a genuine ring and,
unlike the rest of the prayer, they have something to do with
the case in hand. But they have no relation to the preceding
passage, which was a lament over Israel's unhappy condition.
The words show that the supplicant has a definite purpose in
hand, and that he was about to make some request from the
king. Artaxerxes is called "this man," a use absolutely inexplicable as the connection stands, for the king has not been
mentioned, and he certainly was not present, as the words imply. But we can easily put this clause in its right place. In
2⁴ we have *I prayed unto the God of heaven*. That was a critical
moment, and the prayer in v. ¹¹ is in part exactly appropriate to
that situation (*v. i.* 2⁴).

> *The authenticity of Neh.'s prayer.*—Neh. was certainly much given to
> prayer. Doubtless he offered many prayers during the three months
> between his receipt of the bad report from Jerus. and his official audi-
> ence with the king. But it is difficult to believe that we have in vv. ⁵⁻¹⁰
> the words he used. There are favourite words of the Chr. like מֵעַל,
> v. ⁸, and the whole prayer is made up of passages and phrases from Dt.
> It is true that in Christian praying there is an unhappy tendency to
> use stock and hackneyed expressions, and so the resemblance of this
> prayer to others in the OT. may not justify suspicion. But Neh. was
> not a common man, and would be unlikely to use such phrases. His
> memoirs show a peculiar, clear, succinct, and business-like style, and
> this prayer has no traces whatever of his hand. We must regard the
> prayer vv. ⁵⁻¹⁰ and part of v. ¹¹ as the compilation of the Chr. It is in-
> deed perfectly possible that the Chr. has worked over a brief prayer
> found in N., since "I and the house of my fathers have sinned" is ap-
> parently genuine. But the Chr. has wrested v. ¹¹ from its true connec-
> tion, and he may have composed the whole passage. It is true that even
> the most radical scholars have not questioned this passage. Torrey, for
> example, says: "C. 1 Ne. [the Chr.] seems to have left untouched"
> (*Comp.*³⁶). Mitchell, by no means radical, does doubt its authenticity
> (JBL. 1903,³⁷). But I cannot believe that the striking similarity in
> ideas and phrases between this prayer on the one hand and Ezra's
> (Ezr. 9⁶ ᶠᶠ·) and Daniel's (Dn. 9⁴ ᶠᶠ·) on the other can be explained on the
> theory of Nehemian authorship. Moreover, ¹¹ᵇ joins very well to v. ⁴.

If Neh. recorded his prayer at all, it has been so elaborately worked over that the original cannot be recovered. Whoever composed the prayer either had Dt. before him, or knew it by heart.

Note. *Esd. fails us for Ne. (exc. 8¹⁻¹²) and consequently our sources for textual criticism are comparatively poor.*—**1.** חכליה] Χελκεία^B, Χελκίου^L (חלקיה), Αχαλία^{NA}.—כסלו] only elsw. Zc. 7¹, Σεχεηλού^B, χασεηλού^A, χασαλευ^L; Bab. loan-word *kislivu* (JBL. 1892,¹⁶⁷, *ZA.* ii,²¹⁰).—הבירה] is applied to the temple (1 Ch. 29¹· ¹⁹, *v. i.* 2⁸). It may come from As. *birtu* or Pers. *bura.* The Greeks did not understand it, and so transliterated ἀβειρά^B, ἀβειρρά^A, τῇ βάρει.^{L}—**2.** ויבא] + πρὸς μέ^L = אלי, a good reading.—מיהודה] 𝕲^{BAN} Ἰούδα, but the prep. is better.—היהודים] lacking in 𝕲^{BAN}. A better text would be obtained by omitting פליטה, which might easily be an explanatory gl.—**3.** אשר נשארו] lacking in 𝕲^A; it is better omitted, as such overloading is more characteristic of the Chr. than of N.—ברעה] 𝕲^{BN} has a blundering dup., ἐν πόλει [בעיר] ἐν πονηρίᾳ; ἐν κακοῖς^L. The use of the ptc. מפרצת followed by pf. נצתו is apparently accidental, as there is no difference in time intended. The only distinction we can make is that the one describes an existent condition: the wall is breached, and the other a past act: the gates have been burned with fire.—**4.** In sense the v. divides at ואבכו; the construction has misled the Massorites.—ימים] ἐφ' ἡμέραις πολλαῖς^L, *diebus multis* 𝕳; this may be a free rendering, as it gives the correct idea (BDB. *s. v.*).—**5.** האל] 𝕲 ὁ ἰσχυρός, 𝕳 *fortis.*—חסר] 𝕲^{BAN} τὸ ἔλεός σου, ε. αὐτοῦ^L. Elsw. we find החסר (Dt. 7⁹ Dn. 9⁴).—**6.** קשבת] occurs elsw. only in v. ¹¹. Rd. קשבות אזניך] (Guthe) so 𝕲^L τὰ ὦτά σου προσέχοντα, 𝕳 *aures tuae auscultantes.*—וחטאנו] 𝕲^L ἥμαρτον, 𝕳 *peccaverunt;* rd. חטאו.—**7.** חבל] inf. cstr.; but used as absolute. 𝕲^{BAN} renders διαλύσει, ματαιώσει^L. Kittel suggests Pi., or עול עולינו.—לך] om. 𝕲^B ἐν σοί^L.—עברך] 𝕲 παιδί, so v. ⁸, but elsw. δοῦλος, 𝕳 *famulo.*—**8.** הדבר] 𝕲^L τὸν λόγον σου.—אתם תמעלו]. 𝕲 has ἐάν, ^{L} adds μοι=לי, which might easily have dropped after לו. Guthe inserts אם after אתם, but a conditional sentence in Heb. may dispense with the part. Ges.$^{§ 159 bc}$—**9.** נדחכם] 𝕲^L διαστροφή, but ^{BAN} διασπορά, which becomes a technical word and is taken over into English, the diaspora = the scattering of the Jews among the nations. It is better with 𝕲 to give the word an abstract sense, "banishment," rather than "banished ones."—השמים] 𝕲^{LN} add ἕως ἄκρου τοῦ οὐρανοῦ = עד קצה השמים. This may be implied also in 𝕲^{BN} which has for בקצה ἀπ' ἄκρου = מקצה.—אקבצם] 𝕲^L συνάξω ὑμᾶς, 𝕳 *congregabo vos;* rd. therefore אקבצכם and on the same grounds: הביאתיכם.—**10.** והם] 𝕲^L καὶ νῦν ἡμεῖς = ועתה נחנו] 𝕲 has here παῖδες.—**11ᵃ.** 𝕲^{LN} has a plus after אדני, μὴ ἐπιστρέψῃς τὸ πρόσωπόν σου.—עבדיך] 𝕲^L τοῦ λαοῦ σου, and so having: *the prayer of thy people and the prayer of thy servants* which corresponds to *we are thy servants and thy people* of v. ¹⁰ and makes Neh. pray in a representative sense.

1^{11b}-2^9. **Nehemiah's depression was observed by the king; its cause is ascertained; and the cup-bearer is granted leave of absence and authority to rebuild Jerusalem.—11^b.** *Now I was one of the king's cupbearers*] two texts of 𝕲 have *eunuchs*. Whatever the text may have been, it is not improbable that Nehemiah was eunuch as well as butler (*v.* Sta. *BT.*[339]). Graetz supposes Ps. 127 to be directed against him, to which Is. 56[36] might be a reply (Berth.). The office of butler was honourable and lucrative at an Oriental court (*DB*. i,[533]). Indeed, in almost any court the most menial duties were performed by the nobility. Piers Gaveston, son of a Gascon knight, was made royal bootjack to Edward I, an office for which men of the highest birth were pining (Andrew Lang, *Century,* Oct. 1907).

> This section begins exactly as the first part of N. (1^1) *now I was*, etc. These words belong to the narrative in c. 2. They explain how Neh. obtained his audience with the king in the regular course of his duties; months of waiting intervened, however; therefore it is unlikely that he was the chief butler. It appears that his personal attendance upon the king was but infrequent. This fact lends support to the notion that he was a eunuch and so a general servant of the court. The words are more closely connected with 2^{1b}, and the intervening date is due to the Chr., who has borrowed it from 5^{14}. Following MT. we must connect thus: "I was one of the royal butlers, and in the month Nisan of King Art.'s 20th year, the wine was given to me, and I took up the wine and gave it to the king."

II. 1. *Nisan*] was the 1st month. Since Artaxerxes reigned 464–424, his 20th year would be 444 B.C.—*Wine was before me*]. So we must read with 𝕲. *Before him* of 𝕳 is contrary to fact, as the following statements show.—*And I took up the wine and gave it to the king*]. The wine was placed in Nehemiah's hands by the chief butler, and he took it up and carried it to the king. If 𝕳 were right the meaning would be that the scene opened in the royal presence.

> The EV[s]. have tried to make black white by rendering the next clause, "now I had not been beforetime sad in his presence." But on what ground can we import "beforetime," and thus make the words imply the exact opposite of what they say? For the text says plainly

I was not sad before him. This statement in turn is contradicted by the king's question in v. ² which shows that Neh. was depressed in spirit and that the depression showed in his face. ⑮ reads *and there was no companion with him;* but that is contrary to v. ⁶ unless we limit "companion" to the sense of court official. There is no difficulty if we interpret the words correctly. In the subsequent narrative the expressions are: *why is thy face sad? why should my face not be sad?* but "face" is lacking here, and the word for "sad" is slightly different. In v.⁵ we have *if thy servant is good before thee, i. e.,* is *in favour.* Here we have the negative antithesis: *I was not evil before him, i. e.,* not out of favour with him, therefore Neh. had good hopes of a successful preferring of his request.

2. *Why is your face sad?*] The same question, in identical words, was asked by Joseph of Pharaoh's eunuchs, the butler and the baker, Gn. 40⁷.—*Now thou art not sick; there is nothing now except sadness of heart*]. The king's diagnosis is accurate and penetrating. The servant shows by his appearance that he has no physical disease, but the months of fasting, praying, and worrying had left their indelible marks upon his face. The trouble was accurately located in the mind, for the heart is thus commonly used in Hebrew. Nehemiah's sufferings were mental.—*And I was very badly frightened*]. Nehemiah had desired an audience with the king, though he had not intended to reveal his depressed spirits. But the consciousness of Jerusalem's woes, his own anxiety to secure favour from his royal master, the natural embarrassment of the long-sought opportunity, made a bigger burden than he could carry in concealment. Now an Oriental monarch did not expect his servants to carry their personal troubles to him or to reveal them in his presence; indeed, very few people desire that of servants. Nehemiah knew that summary action might be taken. He might be punished, or, worse still, he might be banished from the royal presence without an opportunity to prefer his request. There was, therefore, abundant occasion for his fear. The king would scarcely believe that "by sadness of face the heart is made good" (Eccl. 7³). Nevertheless he did not allow his emotions to destroy his privilege, but promptly and frankly stated his case.—**3.** *May the king live forever*]. This form of

greeting is found elsewhere only in Aramaic, Dn. 2⁴ 3⁹, and in
slightly different form in 1 K. 1³¹. The usual greeting is "may
the king live."—*Inasmuch as the city of the house of the graves
of my fathers lies waste and its gates have been consumed with fire*].
"House" is lacking in v. ⁵ and may be dispensed with here also.
Nehemiah's statement is not quite the same in the first part as
that of the pilgrims, 1³. They said "the wall is broken down,"
while Nehemiah says "the city lies waste." He wisely chose
a more general statement, for the mention of defensive walls
would not make a favourable impression upon the king, who a
few years before had ordered their restoration to stop. Nehemiah was patriotic and perhaps of the seed royal; his words here
indicate Davidic descent, for Jerusalem was particularly the
burying-ground of the kings. Therefore he could not be other
than sad in view of the desolation of Jerusalem. It is difficult
to think we must here presuppose a catastrophe 150 years old.
—**4.** *For what now dost thou make request?*] The king's question shows that the great moment had come. Artaxerxes disclosed an opening favourable to the patriot's purpose in that he
invited his servant to make known his plan to right the evil
conditions which lay so heavily upon his spirit. *And I prayed
to the God of heaven*]. Nehemiah was a devoutly religious man.
He believed strongly in the direct help of God at critical mo-
ments. He had now reached the supreme moment of his life.
Coolness and judgment were required on his part and sympathy
and kindness on the king's part. Before making his plea, he
pauses for a moment to invoke the interposition of God. His
prayer must have been very short, as the king would not brook
continued silence. The prayer is not given here, but, as shown
above, we have the very petition required in 1¹¹, *i. e., prosper,
I pray, thy servant this day, and give him pity before this man.*
The use of the term "this man" is clear now, but incomprehensible in connection with c. 1 (*v. s.*).—**5.** *That thou wilt let him
go to Judah, to the city of my fathers' graves that I may rebuild it*].
"Him" with 𝔊 and 1¹¹ is better than "me" of 𝔥 after "thy
servant." The last clause "to the city," etc., is introduced for
more exact definition of his destination. Nehemiah's request is

simply for leave of absence, and the purpose of the leave was
to rebuild the ruined city. He still says nothing about the
walls. The naming of the city as the place of his ancestors'
graves was to make an effective appeal to the king, as there was
then as now great regard for the abode of the dead.—**6.** *Now
the queen was sitting beside him*]. It is pretty certain that
"queen" is not the right rendering; it is equally sure that the
exact meaning is unknown. It is probable that the name was
applied to a favourite member of the harem, denoting the one
who had the most dominating influence. Such situations have
been known at other courts.

𝕲 and 𝔥 were puzzled by the passage and render: *The king and the
queen who was sitting by him said to me.* Some scholars have emended
the text to conform to this idea. But the clause is manifestly parenthetical. This woman is not mentioned elsw. There is no hint that
she did or said anything. Yet the mention of her presence seems to be
genuine. One explanation offers itself readily. Neh. attributes, at
least in part, the gracious attitude of his sovereign to the presence of
this woman. Without her saying a word, the king was moved to show
the generous side of his character. But if Neh. owed anything to her
presence, a more appropriate place to mention her would have been at
the beginning or at the end of his story. Moreover, he would very
prob. have stated more exactly what her good offices were. Therefore
it may be that the suppliant sees in her presence an obstacle to his plans.

The king shows an interest in spite of the presence of this
woman.—*For how long shall thy journey be? and when wilt thou
return?*] RV. Then the king asks only a single question, repeating it in different words. That is improbable on the face
of it, though that rendering is generally accepted. The first
clause should read: *at what time shall be thy departure? i. e.*, when
do you wish to start? Then we have the two salient points for
a leave of absence, the time of departure and the time of return.
—In v.[b] the clauses have become inverted by an error of a copyist. That will be made plain by restoring the right connection
and order thus: *at what time shall be thy departure? and when
wilt thou return? Then I proposed to him a time. And it was
acceptable to the king, and he granted me leave*]. The received

text empties the passage of logical sense and has led to unnecessary emendation. According to 5^{14} it appears that Nehemiah
was appointed governor of Judah and that he was absent twelve
years. Berth. says, "v. ^{6} foresees no twelve years' absence."
That is true, but, on the other hand, as Nehemiah proposed to
rebuild the city he could not have asked for a very short leave.
If 5^{14} is correct it is easy to suppose that Nehemiah secured from
time to time an extension of his leave, a course by no means
uncommon.

> **7–9**^{a} is accepted as genuine by most scholars, but the whole pas-
> sage as it stands has been so changed by the Chr. that one can pick out
> but little of the original. **9**^{b} comes badly after **9**^{a}, which describes the
> arrival in Syria, and puts the cart before the horse. The leave car-
> ried with it ample authority to pass through Syria, esp. to one with
> an armed escort. Torrey rejects the whole (see his arguments from
> the language, *Comp.*^{36}). Winckler regards a part of the passage as
> genuine, but his criticism does not go to the root of the matter. In
> Neh.'s own account there is no reference to this grant exc. in v.^{9},
> where it is unnecessary. There is buried in the passage, however, an
> important bit of information for which *v. i.*

7. *And I said to the king*]. Nehemiah would have deferen-
tially shown that he was making a supplementary request, such
as we find in Gn. 18^{23} $^{ff.}$; the Chronicler was not so tactful.
—*That they will let me pass through until I shall come into Judah*].
The idea of the writer is that the Syrian satraps would have
barred even the king's servant unless he were armed with a
proper passport.—**8.** *Asaph the keeper of the king's park*]. Who
Asaph was we do not know, but *v. i.* The name is Hebrew, but
Nehemiah would not be likely to know the name of such an
official in Syria. The Persian king would scarcely have a park
in Palestine, and if he did, it would scarcely be the scene of
extensive lumbering. Smith is content with saying we do not
know where this park was (*Jer.* i,^{17}). Asaph was to furnish
timber for three purposes: (1) *To make beams for the gates of
the castle of the house*]. The *birah* or castle here, says Torrey,
means "the fortified enclosure of the temple" (*Comp.*^{36}). But
such an enclosure did not exist at this time, and the Chronicler

uses *birah* for the temple itself (1 Ch. 29¹· ¹⁹). Perhaps we
should read *the castle, which is the temple,* or *the gates which
appertain to the temple.* (2) *For the wall of the city*]. The walls
were built of stone, and the idea of beams seems to be due
entirely to the Chronicler. It is unlikely that Nehemiah would
have mentioned the "walls," but the Chronicler liked to see
his characters clothed with ample and specific authority. (3)
And for the house which I shall enter]. As Nehemiah's declared
purpose was to rebuild the city, he is here by the Chronicler's
hand removed rather far from his design.—**9.** The first half
of the verse relates Nehemiah's arrival before the governors
beyond the river and the presentation of his credentials. Then
the memoirs are reached again, but the construction forbids
rendering as a circumstantial clause as EVˢ.; it is a straightforward narrative: *and the king sent with me army officers and
horsemen*]. In the Chronicler's arrangement this follows the
arrival in Syria. Ezra at a later time felt the need of an armed
escort (*v.* 8²²), but he had forestalled such an aid by his religious
protestations. Nehemiah had no such scruples. The mention
of officers and cavalry indicates that the guard was of considerable size. The dangers of the journey were doubtless very
real. We have not a word about the trip. The patriot was
not concerned about a history of his travels, but only about
the work to be done in Jerusalem.

11ᵇ. משקה] εὐνοῦχος^BN, οἰνοχόος^AL, *pincerna* 𝔙. The first is prob.
a confusion within 𝔊, on account of the similarity of words, as we
could hardly explain a change from סרים. On the syntax, *v.* Ges.§ ¹²⁹ᶜ.
מקשה is really a ptc. and means "one who gives drink." In the sense
of "butler" it is used only here and in the story of Joseph (Gn. 40 *f.*).
—**II. 1.** ניסן] Est. 3⁷ †, often in later Heb.; from Bab. *nisânu.* The old
Heb. name is אביב.—ולפניו] 𝔊^BAN ἐνώπιον ἐμοῦ, rd. with Kittel, *et al.*
לפני.—For נתן] in this sense *v.* Gn. 40¹¹.—²לפניו]. To get the accepted
meaning Kittel reads לפנים, so Kent. But we should require היו פני as
vv. ² ᶠ·. The text is good, but it has not been correctly interpreted.
—רע] is antithetic to ייטב in v. ⁵ and means "in disfavour." 𝔊 gets an
entirely different sense: ἦν ἕτερος = היה רע; that is difficult to reconcile
with v. ⁶, and is unnecessary. But see my note in Guthe,⁶⁶. 𝔊^LN adds
καὶ ἤμην σκυθρωπός, *and I was of a sad countenance,* lacking לא, but
this is a dup.—**2.** מדוע] *cf.* Gn. 40⁷ מדוע פניכם רעים, and רע פנים Eccl. 7³,

—חולה] 𝕲ᴮᴬᴺ μετριάζων, α. λ. in 𝕲. This gives a different sense: *why is thy face sad and thou art not composed?* This is an interesting variant, but 𝔐 is prob. correct.—רע לב] in 1 S. 17²⁵ רע לבב means "badness of heart," "evil purpose": "sadness of heart" is עצבת-לב (Prov. 15¹³), מגנת-לב (Lam. 3⁶⁵). 𝕲ᴮᴬᴺ renders רעים and רע colourlessly by πονηρόν and πονηρία; ᴸ with better discrimination by σκυθρωπόν and λύπη. The context fixes the mng. here, and "sadness" is the right idea.— **3.** יחיה] 𝕲 ζήτω. We should rd. יחי as in other cases of this greeting, 1 S. 10²⁴ 1 K. 1²⁵ ᶠᶠ.—יִרְעוּ] Ges.§ 67. 𝕲ᴮᴬᴺ adhere to πονηρόν, 𝕲ᴸ στυγνάσει. בית does not recur in v. ⁵ and is doubtful here, needlessly cumbering the text.—קברות] 𝕲ᴮᴬᴺ μνημείων, so v. ⁵, τάφων ᴸ.—חרבה] corresponds to מפרצת in 1³ as אכלו to נצתו.—**4.** בקש] in the sense of *requesting* is found only in late Heb. (*v.* BDB. for references).—**5.** 𝕲ᴸ has a plus after אצל: ἐπίσταμαι τὸν βασιλέα ἀγαθόν. καὶ.—**6.** שגל] is a difficult word. Haupt says it is identical with As. *šigrâti*, "ladies of the harem" (Guthe,⁶⁶). Lagarde also calls it a loan-word. In Heb. there is a vb., שגל "to ravish," which became so obscene that the Massorites everywhere substituted שכן. On this account a similarity of root is denied. But we have no business to resort to As. loan-words without exhausting the Heb. first. For Neh. uses good Heb. words. He could not have been ignorant of such common terms as מלכה or גבירה. We must remember that words used for delicate purposes tend to take on an indecent character. AV. teems with words which were seemly in 1611, but which cannot properly be rd. now to a mixed congregation. We find the word in Aram., Dn. 5². ³· ²³, followed by "concubines," and therefore "wives" might be the sense intended. Behrmann refers to Ct. 6⁸, where we have "wives, concubines and maidens without number," and so the passage proves too much. In Heb. many scholars following Ew. substitute שגל for שלל in Ju. 5³⁰, in which case it would mean a captive woman added to Sisera's harem. But Nowack objects to the insertion of a late word into one of the oldest Heb. poems. We have then only Ps. 45¹⁰, where unhappily we have a corrupt text and a dub. mng. It is uncertain whether the words are applied to the king or to the bride. See Br.ᴾˢ. It is clear that if שגל means the *bride* the art. is required; if it refers to the bride's maid it is hard to see why she should be arrayed in "gold of Ophir." Perhaps the maid stands at the bride's side "with gold of Ophir" for the queen. Further the address to the bride begins at v. ⁹ not at v. ¹¹. Finally 𝕲 renders παλλήκη here and in Dn. It appears impossible to get the mng. *queen* for this word. It is very likely that it indicates a mere member of the harem. But we cannot define it exactly.—It is unnecessary to prefix art. to יושבת] with Guthe, as that would change the sense. 𝕲 has it, but that is never decisive.—עד מתי] 𝕲ᴺᴸ have one additional question: ἵνα τί κάθησαι παρ' ἐμοί; but it offers no help, and it not very intelligible.—מהלך] means *journey* without doubt, but as הלך means *go* the subst. may

surely mean *going, starting,* and so *departure,* the sense required here.
—זמן] means a fixed or suitable time, or season.   Here it involves a
reply to both of the king's questions, a time to go and a time to come
back.   Winckler emends last clause to ויתן לי זמן (*Alt. Forsch.* xv,⁴⁷²);
but that was due to a misunderstanding of the passage (*v. s.*).—**7.** ויתנו]
ᵫ δότω, ﬡ *det.,* both attest sg. and understand the king as subj.—
8. פרדס]   Ct. 4¹³ Eccl. 2⁵†, a loan-word from Zend and carried over into
English "paradise."   The word does not apply to a forest for lumbering, but to a preserve.   The expression שמר פרדס can no more be due to
the Chr. than to Neh.   There is an important reading in ᵫᴸᴬ which
as so often elsw. has escaped the attention of scholars.   The text runs:
Ασαφατ τὸν φυλάσσοντα τὰς ἡμιόνους τοῦ βασιλέως καὶ τὸν παράδεισον ὅς
ἐστι τῷ βασιλεῖ.   The illumination appears when we put this back
into Heb.: אסף שמר פרדי המלך והפרדס אשר למלך.   It appears that we
have a dup. for פרדס and (פרדיום have evidently been confused.   Now
keeper of the royal mules has a true ring, but this officer would have been
in Pers., not in Syria.   Neh. would have had little use for mules after
reaching his destination.   It is not unlikely that the Chr. has hopelessly obscured a genuine part of N. in which he described his outfit
and to which v. ⁹ᵇ would be an appropriate conclusion.   Out of the
present confusion we may extract the following and pretty confidently
label it N.: ויתן לי המלך כיר-אלהי הטובה עלי (v. ⁸ᵇ) אגרת אל-אסף שמר הפרדים
אשר למלך אשר יתן לי.   Then we can easily conjecture that the actual
grant was mules for the caravan, but, the Chr. has corrupted it to
timber for building.   Directly following the leave of absence, the passage originally continued: *and the king gave to me, according to the good
hand of God upon me, a letter to Asaph the keeper of the king's mules who
gave to me* [*animals for the journey*].   *And the king sent with me army
officers and cavalry.*   Neh. rode a mule on the night journey described
in the section following.—קרות] is regarded by Torrey as a word characteristic of the Chr. (*Comp.*³⁶).—שערי הבירה אשר לבית].   ᵫᴮᴬ has only
τὰς πύλας.   בירה and בית are syn. and we should rd. either אשר הבית, a
note explaining the unusual הבירה, or השערים אשר לבית, to which הבירה
is a gl.   The mng. would then be *the gates which appertain to the temple,* to distinguish them from the city gates.   Torrey implies that ᵫ's
omission was due to the difficulty, and he notes only the omission of
בירה (*op. cit.*).   But he sees in the passage only the Chr.'s hand, and
not the additional corruption of an original text.

10–20. In this section we have two distinct subjects: (1)
The opposition of Sanballat, Tobiah, and Geshem, vv. ¹⁰· ¹⁹ ᶠ·.
(2) Nehemiah's secret inspection of the ruined walls of Jerusalem, vv. ¹¹⁻¹⁸.   There is no need further to confuse this material

by dividing the chapter at the end of v. ⁸, as most scholars still do, following the wrong guidance of 𝕲.

10. *Sanballat the Horonite*]. The name is Babylonian, but it does not follow that the man was of that race, as Sieg. holds. Among the subject peoples we naturally find Babylonian names. Sanballat is named often in Ne. v. ¹⁹ 3³³ 4¹ 6¹· ²· ⁵· ¹²· ¹⁴ 13²⁸, always as an inveterate enemy. The epithet "Horonite" is found in but three of the above-named places; it would naturally mean an inhabitant of Beth-horon, a town or two neighbouring towns of Ephraim. But Winckler holds that since Tobiah was an Ammonite, Sanballat must be located in Horon in Moab (*Alt. Forsch.* xv,²²⁹ ᶠᶠ·). The Elephantine documents, however, show that Sanballat was governor of Samaria, hence the former place is meant.—*Tobiah the slave, the Ammonite*] v. ¹⁹ 3³⁵ 4¹ 6¹· ¹²· ¹⁴· ¹⁷· ¹⁹ 13⁴· ⁷· ⁸ †. This whole expression recurs in v. ¹⁹; in 3³⁵ we have *Tobiah the Ammonite;* elsewhere *Tobiah* alone. He has been identified with Tabeel of Ezr. 4⁷ by Van Hoonacker (*Sac. Lev.*³⁷⁵). The names are similar, one meaning "God is good," the other "Yahweh is good"; but *Tobiah* is Hebrew, while *Tabeel*, as in Is. 7⁶, is Aramaic; but, as Tabeel has been shown to belong to the reign of Xerxes, the identification is difficult, as the letter to Xerxes was written forty years be-before Nehemiah's advent in Jerusalem. *Slave* is added as a term of opprobrium. Tobiah was very probably a slave of the Persian king who had risen to a position of consequence (Kue. *Abh.*²³³). Nöldeke holds that a true Ammonite could not have borne the name Tobiah; but Torrey rightly says that we do not know enough about true Ammonites to draw such conclusions (ES.¹⁶⁸). Delitzsch suggests that the name is evidence of the worship of Yahweh by other peoples (*Wo lag das Paradies,*¹⁶²). —*It was evil to them with a great evil*]. The text may be wrong, but the sense is not affected. The meaning is that it was a very great evil to these enemies of the Jews.—*That a man had come to seek good for the sons of Israel*]. These words make us suspect that the verse is either due to the Chronicler or is misplaced. Nehemiah's arrival at Jerusalem is chronicled in v. ¹¹. It may further be doubted whether Nehemiah would have used the impersonal phrase "a man had come." Further, Nehemiah does not describe his mission in such general terms as we find here. His purpose was very specific. The enemies of Israel, according to this verse, had heard of his arrival before his actual advent, and they knew the object of his mission. But Nehemiah keeps his purpose a secret even from his fellow-Israelites.—**12.** After three days (*cf.* Ezr. 8³³) spent in resting from the journey and in sheltering his companions, Nehemiah starts out on his famous night ride.

> On which *v.* GAS. *Jer.* Sta. *Gesch.* ii,¹⁶⁷, JBL. 1896,¹²⁹, and the map in Kent's *Hist. Biog. Nar.*³⁴⁹, and esp. Mitchell, JBL. 1903,⁹⁹ ᶠᶠ·, who has made the most elaborate attempt to follow the course of Neh.'s wall.

I arose at night, I and a few men with me]. Secrecy was the design, therefore the inspection was made by night (though there is doubt about this term; *v.* v. ¹⁵), and with but a few attendants. These were probably servants who would have no idea of the object in view, or a selected body, including Hanani, who could be trusted.—*And I had not made known to any man what my God was putting in my heart to do for Jerusalem*]. 𝕲 lacks "my" before "God," and that may be right. The participle "was putting" suggests that Nehemiah had reached a definite purpose only since his arrival at Jerusalem. God is conceived as the author of all good thoughts (Sta. *BT.*³²⁵). *For Jerusalem* may be contrasted with *for the sons of Israel* in v. ¹⁰.—*And there was no animal with me except that upon which I was riding*] a further indication that his attendants were servants, perhaps Persians. If all the company had been mounted it would have been more likely to attract attention. The animal was probably one of the mules which Nehemiah had brought from Persia (*v. s.* v. ⁸).—**13.** *And I went out at the valley gate*] to which *by night* is needlessly added from v. ¹². The valley gate (v. ¹⁵ 3¹³ 2 Ch. 26⁹) is the gate leading to the valley of Hinnom (on which *v.* GAS. *Jer.* i,¹⁷¹ ᶠ· ¹⁷⁶ ᶠ·), and on the western wall of Jerusalem. The corresponding modern entrance is the Jaffa gate (*v.* Ryle's note).—*And unto the mouth of the dragon-spring*],

or according to some texts of 𝕲, *the fig-spring*. This spring is
not mentioned elsewhere and cannot be identified. "Towards"
(RV.) is not correct. Nehemiah means that in going from the
valley gate he passed the outlet of this spring. The water,
therefore, must have emerged just outside of the ruined wall.
—*And unto the dung gate*] 3¹³ ᶠ· 12³¹ †, the gate out of which the
refuse of the city was carried and so might better be called the
garbage gate. It was probably the southern outlet.—*And I
was inspecting the wall of Jerusalem which had been pulled down,
and its gates had been burned by fire*]. All or at least a part of
the clause is an addition by R. The repetition interrupts the
succinct story of the ride.

14. *And I passed along unto the fountain gate*] 3¹⁵ 12³⁷. This
gate was probably at the eastern side of the Tyropœon valley.
—*And unto the king's pool*], identified with the pool of Siloam,
perhaps because of Hezekiah's famous tunnel, or, as Ryle says,
"because it adjoined the king's garden."—*And there was no
place for the animal to pass under me*]. This is hard to understand; EV. *the beast that was under me* is based on 𝕳 *cui sede-
bam*, but cannot be fairly taken from the text. Sieg. interprets
"under me" as meaning "so long as I sat thereon," indicating
a "low bridge." However pregnant the sense of תחתי may be,
it is doubtful if that interpretation does not stretch its meaning.
—The narrative makes a break at this place. Nehemiah had
been following the course of the wall and now goes up a valley.
It would be natural to suppose that he reached a point beyond
which exploration was impossible. But as the mule could go
almost any place a pedestrian could, it is far from clear why he
describes the obstacle in this way.—**15.** *And I was going up the
wady by night and I was inspecting the wall*]. The participial
construction does not connect well with the preceding. There
is nothing except the doubtful phrase in v. ¹⁴ to indicate that
his going up the valley was due to the impossibility of continuing his direct course. Some texts of 𝕲 have *I was going
up by the wady wall*, the wall along the valley, and thus suitably introducing the statement about the inspection.—The last
clause is best rendered *and I came in again by the valley gate*],

the same place at which he had started. $\mathfrak{G}^L$ has an interesting variant: *and I was at the wady gate; and I went back and entered through the valley gate.*   It does not, however, clear up the difficulties of Nehemiah's tour of inspection.   This verse is in large part a repetition; "I was inspecting the wall" is needless after v. [13].

> The passage vv. [12-15] is very perplexing.   The taking of the trip by night is explained almost too easily by the necessity of secrecy.   In the first place, Neh. discloses his purpose immediately upon his return from his ride.   At that time there was a large company of nobles, pr. *et al.* gathered.   Was this early in the morning or still at night?   Then if it was dark enough to screen the party from observation, it would surely be too dark to make a satisfactory investigation of the condition of the walls.   The examination might have been made in the daytime without unmasking the object.   He could have determined the condition of the walls sufficiently without actually traversing the course of the wall.   *By night* recurs three times in the passage, and everywhere is loosely thrown in.   It may be that the phrase was added by an editor, who deemed it an essential part of the secret purpose of the trip.

16. *Now the guards did not know where I had gone nor what I was doing*].   Our text has *rulers*, but *guards* as $\mathfrak{G}$ is better. *Rulers* recurs in v.[b] and would not stand in both places.   Nehemiah had kept his course secret from the watchmen, though they must have witnessed his departure and return.   Perhaps we have thus the explanation of his coming back through the same gate by which he had gone out, as that would prevent their suspecting his real itinerary.—*And to the Judeans and to the priests and to the Levites and to the officers and to the rest doing the work I had as yet not made known*] supply *what I was about to do* from v.[a].   "Levites" is substituted for "nobles" on the basis of [L].   Still we cannot lay too much stress on the text, as it plainly betrays retouching by the Chronicler.   Nehemiah often uses the phrase "nobles and deputies" (on these officials *v.* Mey. *Ent.*[132, 184], GAS. *Jer.* i,[382]), but he would not say "and the rest doing the work," as that is anticipating.   This phrase in Ezr. 3[9] is used of the temple-builders; here it refers to the wall-builders and is due to the Chronicler.   Nehemiah's

phrase is "the nobles and deputies and the rest of the people"
(4⁸·¹³). "Judeans" here would include all the other classes.
The fact is again emphasised that Nehemiah had not yet disclosed the object of his mission even to the highest official
classes. Until he was ready for action, the objective point
would not be revealed.—**17.** In some way not explained there
had now gathered about the new envoy a body of officials and
others, and for the first time he makes known the secret of his
coming to Jerusalem. First, he arouses their appreciation of
the unhappy condition of affairs: *you perceive the evil state we
are in, in that Jerusalem lies a waste and its gates are burned with
fire*]. This is the oft-repeated description based on 1³. Then
follows the exhortation to act: *come and let us build the wall of
Jerusalem and we shall be a reproach no longer*]. The returning
pilgrims had told Nehemiah at the beginning that the Jews
were in contempt, 1³. So long as the city was unprotected by
walls they must remain the butt and scorn of their neighbours.
—**18.** The rebuilding of the walls of Jerusalem was a big undertaking. Nehemiah was no near-sighted fanatic going to war
without reckoning the cost. He did not desire to kindle an
enthusiasm quick to begin and soon to end. He proposed to
carry the project to its conclusion. Therefore he now discloses
two facts which were the foundation of his confidence. First,
he tells them how God had at every point opened the way before
him; and second, how he was supported by the authority of the
king. In his record, though, he does not put down what he
said, for that would be a *résumé* of 1¹–2⁹; he gives only the subject of his address: *and I revealed to them the hand of my God, that
it had been favorable towards me, and also the words of the king
which he had spoken to me*]. The sense in which Nehemiah uses
hand of God becomes clear now; it is *guidance* rather than *power*,
as BDB.³⁹⁰ᵃ. God had led him to the king's presence at a favourable moment, had moved the king to note his depression,
had caused him to speak the right words to move the king, and
had induced Artaxerxes to comply with all his requests.—The
rest of the verse is difficult, and we have many readings. MT.
has: *and they said, we will up and build; and they strengthened*

their hands for good], making this the favourable response of the
nobles and people to Nehemiah's plea. In 𝕲 and 𝔅 we find:
*and I said, let us up and build; and their hands were strengthened
for good;* or: *and these said to me, we will up and build, and they
were strengthened, and their hand was for good.* We are in doubt,
therefore, whether this is the final exhortation of Nehemiah, following naturally his recital of the guidance of God and the favour of the king, or the assent of the assembly to his appeal.
It would put us on the right track if we could get at the true
sense of "strengthening the hands." We note that Nehemiah
uses the phrase "for good" in the sense of "auspiciously," 5¹⁹.
It will appear further that these words in all their varied interpretations really make no sense. It is clear that we have
no statement of the actual beginning of the work on the walls;
but vv. ¹⁹ ᶠ· imply that the work has begun. The words before
us may be rendered equally well: *and their hands took hold auspiciously.* Therefore I should follow 𝕲 in part and translate:
*and I said, let us up and build! and their hands took hold [of the
work] auspiciously.*

19. *And Sanballat et al. heard*]. There is no object and we
have to infer what they heard from the preceding and from their
actions. Now their charge and Nehemiah's reply show that it
was the building of the walls which excited their scorn. That
presupposes the interpretation put upon v. ¹⁸. The enemy had
heard, not of a plan, but of an action, the work on the walls.—
A third enemy is named here (*cf.* v. ¹⁰), *Geshem the Arabian*]
v. 6¹· ²· ⁶; in the last place the name is *Gashmu.* The foes are
all foreigners and the gentilic name is added to show that fact.
They were evidently keeping a close and jealous watch on
Jerusalem, especially since the arrival of Nehemiah with a Persian escort. For some time now a large part of Nehemiah's
story concerns his trouble with these enemies. Making a necessary correction from 𝕲, the text continues: *and they held us
in derision; and they came unto us and said*]. MT., lacking
"and they came unto us," implies that these enemies were
already at Jerusalem; but it is much more likely that they had
for years been preying upon the defenceless Jews, and hear-

ing of the rebuilding of the walls came at once to Jerusalem.—
*What is this thing that you are doing? Are you raising a revolt
against the king?*] The first question shows that Sanballat *et al.*
found the Jews at work; the second is asked ironically, for they
had no idea that the Jews could carry the walls and gates very
far before they would be able again to appear on the scene with
battering-rams and torches. It is the same charge made by
Rehum to Artaxerxes in Ezr. 4¹³ ᶠᶠ.—**20.** In his reply Nehemiah first addresses himself to their jesting at the Jews' big
undertaking: *the God of heaven will prosper us*], cf. 1¹¹. Then he
throws off all disguise, which would indeed be vain now: *and
we are his servants; we will up and build*]. But 𝕲 has a tempting
variant: *we are his innocent servants*, that is, innocent of any evil
design against the king. But in that case the antecedent of
"his" should be Artaxerxes rather than "God." Now when
Nehemiah says "we are his servants," in view of the charge
just made we inevitably think of the king, as if Nehemiah had
said, "we are his loyal subjects and as such we are building."
It is at least possible that a clause has dropped out, and that
Nehemiah said that God would further them, the king had approved their work, and they were his loyal subjects. In his
appeal to his followers he had named both the favour of God and
of the king. The mention of the king's authority would be
far more impressive to Sanballat than the grace of God, and
Nehemiah might well not overlook so formidable a weapon.—
Then he proceeds to serve notice upon them that their days of
preying upon the Jews is over: *and for you there is neither portion nor right nor memorial in Jerusalem*]. By *portion* Nehemiah
means property, real or personal. The enemy may have owned
land or houses, or more probably may have exacted tribute,
which would be equivalent to levying blackmail as David did
of Nabal, 1 S. 25. *Right* is not "just claim," Ryle, Sieg. Berth.,
but *authority*. That these enemies claimed a certain authority
over the people of Jerusalem is shown by their subsequent
actions, and may be due to the decree of Artaxerxes (Ezr. 4⁷⁻²³).
Memorial is interpreted as meaning that their descendants
should have no place in the community of God (Berth. Sieg.

B.-Rys.), a proof of their past connection with Jerusalem (Ryle); proof of citizenship (BDB.); it may be used in a general broad sense: there will not be a thing by which even to remember you; you will soon be a thing of the past and completely forgotten. By the restoration of the walls Jerusalem would recover its autonomy and would no longer be open to the raids of roving bands in quest of plunder.

Mitchell infers from Neh.'s words that the Sam. had offered to aid in the building of the wall, and attributes the above passage to the Chr., presumably for this reason (ICC.¹²). There is nothing in the remarks of Sanb. to indicate any such friendly purpose, and Neh. is not declining a neighbourly offer, but serving emphatic notice on the Sam. that, since he is the direct representative of the Pers. king, their interference with the Jewish people will no longer be tolerated.

10. סנבלט] 𝕲 Σαναβαλ(λ)ατ. The name is Bab. *Sin-uballit*, or acc. to Winckler *Sin-muballit*, but Haupt notes that this *m* in Bab. is often silent (Guthe-Batten,⁶⁷). 𝕲 preserves the pronunciation better than MT.—"ה העבר טוביה] is lacking in 𝕲ᴮ, but as we find αὐτοῖς for להם it is evident that the omission is a mistake.—גדלה רעה] sounds more like the Chr. than N. The words are lacking in 𝕲ᴮᴬᴺ, while ᴸ has a vb., καὶ ἐλυπήθησαν = ויחרו (?).—**11** is almost an exact reproduction of Ezr. 8³³ or the converse. There the verbs are pl. and we have נשב instead of אהי.—**12.** לירושלם] μετὰ τοῦ 'Ισραήλᴮᴬᴺ, ᴸ has a dup., prefixing τῇ 'Ιερουσαλημ. 𝕲 was influenced by the Chr.'s "sons of Israel" in v. ¹⁰, perhaps even to a correction of the text.—בה] 𝕲ᴮᴬᴺ ἐπ' αὐτῷ = עליה. ᴸ has the usual dup. ἐν ᾧ . . . ἐπ' αὐτῷ. ב in this sense is so rare and על so common that we must suspect the text.—**13.** הגיא לילה] 𝕲 transliterates γωληλά, to which we find a correction in ᴸᴺ, νυκτός. V. ¹⁵, giving the terminus at the valley gate, shows that the text is sound. לילה is certainly unnecessary after v. ¹², and is a gl.—התנין] 𝕲 συκῶνᴮᴬᴺ = התאנים; δράκοντοςᴸ.—שבר] συντρίβωνᴮᴬᴺ, κατανοῶνᴸ, 𝕳 *considerabam*, so v. ¹⁵. The former stands for שבר and makes no sense. שבר occurs only here and in v. ¹⁵, but *inspect* is the sense required.—חומת] τείχειᴮᴬᴺ, τείχεσινᴸ, *murum* 𝕳: point חומַת.—המפרוצים] or פרוצים הם as Qr.; in 1³ מפרצת; 𝕲 has: ὃ αὐτοὶ καθαιροῦσινᴮᴬᴺ, τοῖς κατεσπασμένοιςᴸ.—באש . . . אשר] has been added from 1³. There is no jugglery by which we can join it to its context. We might retain המפרצה אשר, but that fails in v. ¹⁵. Indeed, the whole of v.ᵇ interrupts the narrative of the itinerary and needlessly anticipates v. ¹⁵. Houtsma reads מפרציב אשריה, comparing Aram. אשרנא, Ezr. 5³· ⁹, and believes the first word has a special architectural mng. like *gate-structure* (*ZAW*. 1907,⁵⁸ ᶠ·).—**14.** העין] 𝕲 τοῦ

Αἰνά^{ΒΝ}, Αιν^Α, τ. πηγῆς^L.—15. [בנחל] 𝕲 ἐν τῷ τείχει χειμάρρους^{ΒΑΝ}, διὰ τοῦ χειμάρρου^L = בהומת הנחל. The former reading is not improb.—[לילה] is a gl. or the corrupted name of the valley.—[ואשוב] lacking in 𝕲. It is better to om. in the second place and interpret the first adverbially. —[ואבוא] 𝕲 καὶ ἤμην = ואהי. 𝕲^L has καὶ ἤμην ἐν τῇ πύλῃ τῆς φάραγγος. καὶ ἀνέστρεψα. καὶ διῆλθον διὰ τῆς πύλης Γαι. It is difficult to say whether this is one of ^L's frequent corrections from MT. by addition or a genuine text.—16. [הסגנים]. Rd. with 𝕲 οἱ φυλάσσοντες = השמרים.—[לחרים] τοῖς ἐντίμοις^{ΒΑΝ}, Λευιταις^L.—[לסגנים] om. ^{ΒΑ}, but the combination חרים וסגנים is common in Ne. (4^{8. 13} 5⁷ 7⁵) v. Dr.^{Intr},⁵⁵³.—[ער-כן] † may be an Aramaism; cf. ער-כען, Ezr. 5¹⁶; the mng. is the same, *up to the present*. It may be a txt. err. for ער-עתה.—17. [נתצו] 𝕲^{ΒΑΝ} ἐδόθησαν = נתנו.—18. [אף] πρὸς^Β (אל) τοῦς^{ΑΝ} (את), περὶ^L (על), את is correct, as it is used with יד, the other obj. of the same vb.—אגיד.—[ויאמרו] καὶ εἶπα^{ΒΑΝ} = ואומר. ^L shows that it is correcting and will leave no doubt about the sense: καὶ αὐτοὶ εἶπόν μοι.—[ידיהם] 𝕲^L makes a separate clause and reads sg. καὶ ἡ χεὶρ αὐτῶν εἰς ἀγαθόν. 𝕲^{ΒΑΝ} makes αἱ χεῖρες subj. not obj. Berth. says: "perhaps the vb. should be pointed as a pass."; but the pass. does not elsw. occur, and we have no warrant here for a new form. I should rd. ואומר with 𝕲 and point וַיְחַזְּקוּ. If ידיהם were the obj. it would certainly have את before it.—19. [ויבזו עלינו]. Nowhere else is בזה followed by על; it usually takes direct obj., though occasionally we find ל. 𝕲^{ΒΑΝ} has καὶ ἦλθον ἐφ' ἡμᾶς, *i. e.*, ויבואו, and that is the correct text (*v. s.*). 𝕲^L has here also the original 𝕲 + a correction from Heb.: κατεφρόνουν ἡμῶν καὶ ἦλθον ἐφ' ἡμᾶς.—20. [נקום] 𝕲^{ΒΑΝ} καθαροὶ = נקים. ^L has the usual dup., καθαροὶ ἀναστησόμεθα.

NE. 3¹⁻³².   THE DISTRIBUTION OF THE WORK ON THE WALL.

In the list of the wall-builders as it stands in the text there are 39 names of men, of whom 6 were apparently Lev. (vv. ¹⁷⁻²¹), and possibly 13 were pr. There were five companies of the builders who are named only by the towns in which they live, Jericho, Hassenaah, Tekoa, Gibeon and Mispah, and Zanoah. The genealogical interest is very marked. In 32 cases the father's name is given, and in 5 instances the name of the grandfather or some earlier ancestor is added. In a number of cases the civil office held by the builder is appended, vv. ^{9. 12. 14-19. 29}. It thus appears that for the most part these officials are grouped together. As in other lists, there is frequent repetition of the same name, vv. ^{4. 21; 4. 6. 30; 4. 29; 11. 14. 31; 11. 23}. Many of the names recur in other lists in our books.

The narrative shows but a poor connection with 2¹⁸. It has all the appearance of an independent piece, as we may note from the beginning "and Eliashib arose." There are many characteristics of the

Chr.: the prominence of pr. and Lev.; the expressions "and his brethren"; the exact genealogical data; the mechanical system; repetition of phrases "and by his hand," "sét up its doors," "repaired," etc.   See further arguments by Mitchell, JBL. 1903,^{88 ff.}

On the other hand, there is not a single trace of N. in the whole passage, though it is assigned tò N. by Berth. Sieg. and many others.   The statement in v.³⁸ connects directly with 2¹⁸, leaving space between for the visit of Sanb. *et al.* (2^{19 f.}).   Neh. was not concerned with the details of the building methods, but with securing suitable protection for the city.

The section is needlessly anticipative, for it is a description of the complete work, whereas v.³⁸ shows that much was yet to be done, and the walls were not finished until some time later.   Acc. to this c. all parts were carried on simultaneously, whereas N. states explicitly that the walls were finished before the gates were touched, 6¹.   The passage is obviously quite out of place, and would come in better after c. 6.

Torrey regards the whole section as due to the Chr. (*Comp.*^{37 f.}). But the evidence of its composite character is convincing to the contrary.   We cannot resist the evidence of the use of "at his, or their, hand" in vv.²⁻¹⁵ and "after him" in vv.¹⁹⁻³².   Other indications are pointed out in the notes.   The Chr.'s hand is indeed evident in the editing, but not in the composition.   We are constrained then to suppose that some one had composed an account of the building of the walls, others had made additions, and the Chr. combines, edits, and as usual, where it is possible, misplaces his material.

The account in general may be quite correct.   The memoirs agree very closely with the method described here.   There were certainly many workers who lived outside of Jerus., 4⁶, and the builders were widely scattered on the walls, 4¹³.   But we have no data to control the details, and some of them excite suspicion.

The gates mentioned in this c. are ten in number, as appears from the following list in which all the other references are cited: (1) the sheep gate, v.¹ 12³⁹ Jn. 5²; (2) the fish gate, v.³ 12³⁹ 2 Ch. 33¹⁴ Zp. 1¹⁰; (3) the old gate, v.⁶ 12³⁹; (4) the dung gate, v.^{13 f.} 2¹³ 12³¹; (5) the valley gate, v.¹³ 2^{13. 15} 2 Ch. 26⁹; (6) the fountain gate, v.¹⁵ 2¹⁴ 12³⁷; (7) the water gate east, v.²⁶ 12³⁷, *cf.* the water gate, 8^{1. 3. 16}; (8) the horse gate, v.²⁸ Je. 31⁴⁰; (9) the east gate, v.²⁹; (10) the gate of the muster, v.³¹.

The catalogue is manifestly incomplete.   Twice a "second portion" is mentioned without an antecedent first portion (vv.^{11. 20}).   Sm. supposes a considerable gap before v.¹¹, basing his conclusion on a comparison with 12^{38 f.} (*Listen,*^{11 f.}).   On the geographical elements in this list *v.* also Mey. *Ent.*^{107 f. 166 ff.}   On the topography *v.* the valuable article by Mitchell, JBL. 1903,^{148 ff.}, and particularly his map, p. 162.

1. *Eliashib the high priest*] mentioned often in our books. Ezr. 10⁶ Ne. 3²⁰· ²¹ 12¹⁰· ²²· ²³ 13⁴· ⁷· ²⁸; in 13⁴ he is called "the priest," but in 13²⁸, as here, "the high priest." His son was a prominent priest in the time of Ezra, Ezr. 10⁶. According to Ne. 12¹⁰ he was a grandson of Jeshua the co-worker of Zerubbabel. In the list of builders the names of the priests with this exception are put last, vv. ²²⁻²⁹; but Eliashib is named first on account of his prominent position.—Associated with him in the work were *his brethren the priests*], meaning apparently those belonging to his own course.—*And they built the sheep gate*]. There are four terms for the building operations, "build," "lay beams," "erect," and "repair," the last occurring thirty-three times. "Build" is found here, in v. ² twice, and in vv. ¹³· ¹⁴· ¹⁵. Except in v. ² it has always "gate" as its object. Therefore we may conclude that the work described in v. ² was a part of the erection of the sheep gate. It is to be noted, however, that "repair" is frequently found with "gate" as object, vv. ⁶· ¹³· ¹⁴· ¹⁵. *The sheep gate* is mentioned only in Ne. v. ³² 12³⁹, but *cf.* Jn. 5². It was on the north of the temple and was so named because it was the entrance for sacrificial animals.—*These consecrated it*], *i. e.*, the gate. Consecrating a gate, especially before "they erected its doors," arouses suspicion. The appeal for support is mainly made to Solomon's consecration of the court before the temple (1 K. 8⁶⁴), but that was done because he was preparing to offer sacrifices there. Doubtless we should read "laid its beams," as in vv. ³· ⁶. The change was due to the fact that consecrating was regarded as more appropriate work for priests than laying beams, showing the trace of an editor with priestly sympathies.—*And they erected its doors, its hinges and its bars*], so we should read as in all other cases where doors are mentioned. For *hinge v.* note to v. ³. In the Chronicler's fashion we have an anticipation, for in 6¹ the doors were not yet built.—*And unto the tower of Hammeah they consecrated it unto the tower of Hananel*]. There could scarcely be a gate of this extent. Moreover, this description does not fit in here, because it refers to a section of the wall, whereas Eliashib and his fellow-priests built the gate. It might be

misplaced from v. ^{2} or some other section. It may have been
inserted here from 12^{39}.—**2.** *And at his hand*] meaning next
to him. We find *at his* (or *their*) *hand* in vv. $^{2-15}$, and "after
him," to express the same idea in vv. $^{16-32}$ (except in vv. $^{17-19}$).
This proves that we have a composite production, as a single
writer would either have used the same term throughout or
mixed the words indiscriminately. In both cases in this verse
we should read *at their hand*, for the antecedent is plural.—*The
men of Jericho*]. In Ezr. 2 before place-names we found both
"men of" and "sons of"; in this list we have further the gentilic *Tekoites*, vv. $^{5.\ 27}$, and "inhabitants of," v. ^{13}. It appears
that companies came from some of the Judean towns to aid in
the wall-building. It is not stated whether they were giving
their service from patriotic motives or whether they were working for wages.—*Zaccur*] recurs in our books, Ezr. 8^{14} Qr. Ne. 10^{13}
12^{35} 13^{13}, but there is no certain identification.—**3.** *The fish
gate*] 12^{39} Zp. 1^{10} 2 Ch. 33^{14}†. It was probably the market-place
where the Tyrians sold their fish, 13^{16}. It lay in the northern
part of the city (*v.* Mar. on Zp. 1^{10}, GAS. *Jer.* i,^{317}).—*The sons
of Hassenaah*] *v.* Ezr. 2^{35}.—**4.** *Meremoth*] is repeated in v. ^{21} and
with the same pedigree. The text is wrong in one case or the
other. The same person is named as a travelling companion of
Ezra, Ezr. 8^{33}.—*And next to them*]. We should expect "him,"
but as we note from v. ^{2} the pronouns frequently do not correspond with the antecedent, an evidence of confusion in the text.
—The second clause, about *Meshullam* is lacking in some texts
of 𝕲. As Meshullam occurs in vv. $^{6.\ 30}$, we can easily dispense
with him here. In v. ^{30} he has the same father, but the grandfather is not given. In v. ^{6} the name of the father may be corrupt, or that may be a different person.—*Zadok*] recurs in v. ^{29},
but the father is different.—**5.** *The Tekoites*]. Tekoa was the
home of Amos the prophet (Am. 1^1). It is on the border of the
Judean wilderness, five miles south of Bethlehem.—*But their
chiefs did not bring their neck into the service of their lords*]. The
natural inference, especially from 𝕲 (*v. i.*), is that the governor
of Tekoa was interested in the work and brought a band of the
humble classes to assist him, but was unable to induce his chiefs

to take part. "Bring the neck unto," with "yoke" understood, is found in Je. 27¹¹ ᶠ·, but there it refers to the submission of a conquered people. "Their lords" is also interpreted to mean Nehemiah and his associates (Berth.). The meaning would then be that while the lower classes of Tekoa responded to Nehemiah's call, the rulers refused to recognise his authority. As but four or five towns are mentioned in the list, it would appear that many other towns had made a similar refusal; for if Nehemiah called upon some of the neighbouring villages for help, he would certainly have called upon all, and of such towns we have a much larger list in Ezr. 2 and Ne. 11²⁵ ᶠᶠ·—**6.** *The old gate*] mentioned also in 12³⁹, is supposed to have been on the northern side of the city and to the west of the fish gate. Mitchell reads "the gate of the old pool" (JBL. 1903,¹³² ᶠᶠ·).—*Repaired Joiada and Meshullam*]. We should expect "built," as in vv. ¹·³, but we find "repaired," with gates as object, in vv. ¹³·¹⁴·¹⁵. It is tempting to suppose that these particular gates had not been entirely destroyed, and so "repaired," rather than "built," is an accurate description of the work done. But as the statement is everywhere that Jerusalem's "gates had been burned with fire," we are warned against assuming that four out of the six were only damaged. It may be that the author, having started with "repaired," repeats it without much consideration for exactness. It is possible that the expression "its gates burned" may be a general rather than an exact description.—**7.** *Meletiah the Gibeonite and Jadon the Meronothite, the men of Gibeon and Mispah*]. Sachau (p.⁸) identifies ידון with the ידניה of *Pap.* i. Here we find men designated by their homes instead of by their fathers. Meronothite, elsewhere only 1 Ch. 27³⁰, is unknown. If "men of Gibeon and Mispah" is an appositive clause, then we should probably read *Mispite,* or with Mey. read *Meronoth* instead of *Mispah (Ent.*¹⁰⁸). But as this is the only place where we find this use of gentilic names, and as the whole verse is lacking in the best texts of 𝔊, we look upon it with suspicion. Mispah is mentioned in vv. ¹⁵·¹⁹.—*Of the jurisdiction of the governor beyond the River*]. This would refer to the satrap of the Syrian province. As Gibeon and Mispah were in Benjamin and close to Jerusalem, it is hard

to see why they were any more under his authority than Jericho.
GAS. argues that the satrap of the province sometimes held
his court at Mispah (*Jer.* ii,³⁵⁴). Further it is very doubtful
whether נסכ means *jurisdiction*. The text of 𝕲 which has this
passage renders: *unto the throne of the governor beyond the Enna.*
I have no idea what Enna stands for, but this rendering makes
the passage descriptive of the part of the wall repaired by these
men. We should then have to suppose that some governor maintained a residence or office in Jerusalem, a supposition by no
means improbable, and such a place would be a well-understood
designation. Mitchell renders "the seat of the governor beyond the River," and holds that the clause defines which of the
numerous Mispahs is meant (JBL. 1903,¹⁴⁸ ᶠᶠ·).—**8.** *Uzziel*] is
a common Hebrew name, but *Harahiah*, his father's name, is
not found elsewhere, and in spite of the divine name, which is a
part of it, its root is unknown. But we should probably read
Barakiah (*v. i.*).—*Hananiah the son of the ointment-makers*], *i. e.*,
one engaged in that craft (*cf.* v. ³¹). Probably the word rendered "ointment-makers" is a disguised form of the name of
Hananiah's father. Mey. argues that these men are denoted by
their trade because they had no connection with a family group
(*Ent.*¹⁵³).—*And they abandoned Jerusalem as far as the broad wall*]
makes no sense; "fortified" of EVˢ. is unwarranted. The modern authorities generally connect with a late Hebrew word and
give the meaning "repair" or "complete." That gives good
sense, at all events. It may be, however, that the reference is
to some part of the old city that was not included in the new,
and "abandoned" would then be right. Mitchell suggests "en-
close" (JBL. 1903,¹³²). Our information is too slight, however,
to determine positively what the words do imply. The broad
wall according to 12³⁸ was that portion lying between the gate of
Ephraim and the tower of the ovens. From its position in this
passage, though, it would appear to be a part of the wall between
the old gate, v. ⁶, and the valley gate, v. ¹³. It is far from certain, however, that we have a systematic description, and our
ignorance of the topography is still very great. Ryle suggests
that it was this part which was destroyed by Amaziah and which

Hezekiah strengthened (2 K. 14¹³ 2 Ch. 32⁵).—**9.** *Rephaiah the son of Hur* [a Calebite according to Mey. *Ent.*¹¹⁹], was *ruler of half the district of Jerusalem*]. Following וֹ *vici* (for half-district) the passage is interpreted to mean that Jerusalem was divided into two districts or wards, of which Rephaiah rules one and Shallum the other, v. ¹². But the meaning of the word is far from certain, and the Greek rendering is "the country around," so that the domain of these men was not the city, but the suburbs (so GAS. *Jer.* i,²⁹²). The latter is the more probable explanation. In this chapter eight such divisions of the Judean province are named: two about the cities of Jerusalem, Mispah, vv. ¹⁵· ¹⁹, Keilah, vv. ¹⁷ ᶠ·, one about Beth-haccerem, v. ¹⁴, and one of the two about Beth-zur, v. ¹⁶. (On these districts *v.* Mey. *Ent.*¹⁶⁶ ᶠᶠ·). It is plain from the mention of these places that so far as possible the people from the whole province of Judah were enlisted in the great undertaking.—**10.** *Jedaiah*] cannot be identified with any other person in our books, though the name may be a shortened form of *Jeda'iah* (Ezr. 2³⁶ Ne. 11¹⁰ 12⁶ ᶠ· ¹⁹· ²¹. Mey. thinks that the name of his father, Harumaph, indicates a non-Jewish clan (*Ent.*¹⁴⁷). Berth. gives the meaning "with a split nose" (*Anhang*,¹⁰⁰), thus making it a Hebrew name, Harum-aph. That could only be a nickname acquired in later life.—*Even before his house*]. The part of the wall repaired by Jedaiah lay in front of his own house, which was probably on or near the wall. Naturally he would be especially interested in the restoration of the part of the wall which would insure him protection. We find the same expression in vv. ²³· ²⁸· ²⁹, *cf.* v. ³⁰. It is likely that every builder who had a residence in Jerusalem was assigned the part of the wall nearest his home.—*Hattush the son of Hashabneiah*] Ezr. 8² Ne. 10⁵ 12².—**11.** *A second portion repaired Malkiiah the son of Harim and Hasshub the son of Pahath-Moab, and unto the tower of the furnaces*] or *ovens*, Mitchell, JBL. 1903,¹²⁸ ᶠᶠ·.

"Second portion" recurs in vv. ¹⁹· ²⁰· ²¹· ²⁴· ²⁷· ³⁰, but in all those cases as obj., the sentence having the regular intr. "after him." In this v. "second portion" stands in place of the usual "and next to him." The more general term used in RV., "another portion," is inadmissible.

The ordinal means *second* and nothing else. We should infer, therefore, that certain large sections of the wall were divided into two parts, and a gang of workmen assigned to each part. But then it seems incredible that the first portion is never mentioned at all, and that "second portion" recurs without any intervening assignment, vv. [19-21]. It is to be noted, however, that in all of the cases, exc. v. [30], where this designation is used, we have a fuller description of the particular section of the wall. The words have also been interpreted to mean that these particular builders were esp. energetic or had a larger force of helpers, and that after completing their first assignment they undertook a second portion. This view is supported by the repetition of the names in vv. [21. 27], *cf.* vv. [4. 5]. But other names recur without any mention of a second portion, and in four of the six cases before us there is no recurrence of the name. About the only certain inference is that the Chr. has after all his labours left us but an imperfectly intelligible description of the building operations.

Pahath-Moab] (*v.* Ezr. 2[6]) is surely a clan-name, suggesting that we may have clan-names all through the chapter. But as most of the heads of the genealogies are not known to us, in spite of our formidable lists, the suggestion is to be taken cautiously.—*The tower of the furnaces*] or *ovens* is mentioned in 12[38] as next to the broad wall (v. [8]), and between the gate of Ephraim and the valley gate. "Unto the tower" is based on 𝕲 and is doubtless correct (Guthe); for the second portion could not be the tower, but the section of wall adjoining.—**12.** *Shallum*] is a common name, but that of his father, *Hallohesh*, is found elsewhere only in 10[25]. It means *charmer* or *magician;* Mey. argues that it is an appellative clan-name, and marks a family which had remained in Judah rather than one coming from the exile (*Ent.*[157]). Shallum was ruler of the other part of the district about Jerusalem (*v. s.* v. [9]).—*He and his daughters*] is regarded by Mey. as a corruption for *and its daughters, i. e., its hamlets* (*Ent.*[107]). But if this is the sense we might render *it* [Jerusalem] *and its hamlets*, making the district over which Shallum ruled include both a part of Jerusalem and of the surrounding country.

"Daughters" is a regular term for the hamlets which grow up about a city and which are dependent upon it, 11[25-31]. Ryle prefers a literal interpretation that Shallum's daughters aided him in the work. But as women in the East were quite sure to have a large share in such work as this, their especial mention here is unnecessary. Against the other view it may be urged that a solitary mention of hamlets is inexplicable. Berth. says it would be easiest to reject the words but that such a course is arbitrary. The meaning is really unknown.

13. *Hanun*] recurs in v. [30] among the priests, but there is no reason for identifying the two. From the fact that *the inhabitants of Zanoah*] collaborated with him, he may have been a resident of that town. Sieg. says he was the principal officer of the town.

> Zanoah is in the list of postex. Jewish towns, 11[30], *cf*. Jos. 15[34], 1 Ch. 4[18]. It is located 13 miles west of Jerus. There was prob. a large company of the Zanoites, in spite of the considerable distance which they came; for they built both the valley gate and the section of the wall between that and the dung gate (*v*. on 2[13]). This section was 1,000 cubits; and roughly speaking that would be a quarter of a mile. Hence some have doubted whether one body would accomplish so large a portion, and have interpreted the words as a parenthetical topographical description, giving the distance between the gates. But the expression is too specific, *and a thousand cubits on the wall*, to admit of such a mng. It may be that some parts of the wall were less damaged than others, and so could be easily and quickly repaired. We note that it is hard to say whether it is meant in 1[3] that the walls were breached or broken down.

14. *The dung gate**] itself was repaired or rebuilt by *Malchijah the son of Rekab ruler of the Beth-hakkarem district*]. Malchijah, with other fathers, is mentioned also in vv. [11. 31]. It is naturally a common name, meaning "Yahweh is my king."
—*Beth-hakkarem*] means *vineyard house*. From Je. 6[1] it must have been south of Jerusalem beyond Tekoa, and so not between the latter place and Bethlehem as Ryle states.—*He built it and set up*]. Making a slight change and a restoration from 𝔊, we get a better text: *he and his sons, and they made its beams and set them up*, *v. i.*—**15.** *The fountain gate*] follows the dung gate in 2[13 f.], *q. v.*—*Shallum the son of Kal-hozeh*]. *Kal-hozeh* means "every seer"; Mey. says it is not a personal name, but

---

*On the prob. location of this gate *v*. GAS. *Jer.* i,[m].

probably the clan designation of a Calebite guild of soothsayers
(*Ent.*[147]). In 11⁵ this name occurs as that of the grandfather
of one of the prominent Jerusalemites, and there it is surely
used as a personal name.—*Ruler of the Mispah district*]. Workers from Mispah have already been mentioned, v. ⁷. In view
of v. ¹⁹ we may read with Mey., *ruler of half the Mispah district*, but as *Ezer* is there called simply *ruler of Mispah*, it may
be that he governed the city and *Shallum* the surrounding
country.—*He built it*]. Perhaps we should emend as in v. ¹⁴:
he and his sons; though we lack here the support of 𝔊, we
have the fact that "set up" is plural in the original text.—
Then we are told that *Shallum* repaired also a section of the
wall, a section very minutely described: *and the wall of* [or *from*]
*the pool of Siloam at the king's garden and unto the stairs descend-
ing from the city of David*]. The pool of Shelah or Sheloah in
Is. 8⁶ is the same as the Siloam of Jn. 9⁷˙ ¹¹. There was also a
town of Siloam, Lu. 13⁴. It was in the conduit of this pool
that the famous Siloam inscription was found. Guthe questions
this identification (*ZDPV.* 1882,³⁷¹ ᶠ˙). The *king's garden* occurs in 2 K. 25⁴ Je. 39⁴ 52⁷, all, however, parallel and describing the route by which Zedekiah fled from the defenceless city.
*Stairs of the city of David** recurs in 12³⁷ as being near the fountain gate. *The city of David* has been regarded as the southern
part of the western hill, as the northern portion, and as the
temple hill, which last Ryle regards as established by this passage. In spite of the exact description of this section of wall,
it is not possible for us to locate it with very great confidence.
—**16.** *Nehemiah the son of Azbuk, the ruler of half the district
of Beth-zur*] is thus carefully differentiated from the hero of
our book. He is not mentioned elsewhere, nor is his father.
Beth-zur is in the list of Judean towns, Jos. 15³⁸, and among
those built by Rehoboam, 2 Ch. 11⁷. Robinson located it in
the modern *Beit-Ṣur*, about twelve miles south of Jerusalem.
So GAS. *Jer.* ii,³⁸¹. See also 1 Mac. 4²⁹ 11⁶⁵ ᶠ˙ 14⁷. The part
of the wall rebuilt by Nehemiah is also elaborately described:
to a point opposite the sepulchre of David, and to the artificial pool

* See Wright's treatise, JBL. 1897,¹⁷¹ ᶠ˙, also GAS. *Jer.* i,¹⁵⁶.

and to the armoury]. We find the unusual expression, literally,
unto before, indicating that there was no good marking-point
at the wall, and implying that the tomb of David was some
distance away. In 2 Ch. 32³³ we find "the sepulchres of the
sons of David" given as the burial-place of Hezekiah. But
see Benzinger *in loc*. This royal cemetery was in the city of
David, v. ¹⁵, where David himself was buried, 1 K. 2¹⁰.—*The
artificial pool*] literally, *the pool that was made*, was still new, according to Sieg. But it is more likely to be the reservoir referred to in Is. 22¹¹: "You made a reservoir between the walls
for the waters of the old pool."—*House of the heroes*]. The
location is unknown, though Guthe proposes a place southwest
of the Virgin spring (*ZDPV*. 1882,³³²). It must have been the
military headquarters, or the armoury. B.-Rys. regards it as the
residence of the gate-watch, in which case it would be witness
of the late date of this passage; but it is very probable that
the watch lived in their homes. As before, we find darkness
rather than light from the details given. As the text stands,
we have three statements about the terminating-point of Nehemiah's work, but none about its beginning. As Shallum's section extended to the city of David, v. ¹⁵, we should probably read
from the sepulchres of David, though such a correction is purely
conjectural.—**17-20** apparently covers the account of the labour
of the Levites who took part in the work, but the text is in poor
shape.—**17**. *After him repaired the Levites: Rehum the son of
Bani*]. Then we expect a further list of Levitical names, but
the narrative goes back to the old formula. Both *Rehum* and
Hashabiah are given in the list of the heads of the people, 10²⁶.
Hashabiah was *ruler of half the district of Keilah*], a place famous
in David's early history, 1 S. 23, a Judean town, near the
Philistine border, and about eight miles northwest of Hebron
(GAS. *Hist. Geog.*²³⁰). Mey. infers that Keilah had been set-
tled by the Levites during and after the exile (*Ent.*¹⁷⁸).—*For
his district*]. AV. *in his part* is unjustifiable.

> Ryle interprets as distinguishing the part he represented from the other
> part named in v. ¹⁸. B.-Rys. goes so far as to argue from this state-
> ment that the two parties from the Keilah district were separated from

each other in their work. This authority also suggests that the word implies that this workman participated, not as a Lev., but as the ruler of a Keilah district. It is doubtful about his being a Lev. at all, and the word is too obscure in this solitary use to serve as a good basis for such large inferences.

18. *Their brethren*] implies a preceding list of Levites, for the antecedent of *their* is *Levites.—Bavvai the son of Henadad*]. Henadad was a Levite chief, v. ²⁴ 10¹⁰ Ezr. 3⁹. As the name means *Hadad favours*, it must be of Aramaic origin. It is a strange title for Levites of the postexilic age, and it may be an old clan-name.—*Binnui*, as v. ²⁴, is the form of the name adopted by Guthe and Berth. But *son of Henadad* is a clan designation. Moreover, Binnui is among the priests. Both priests and Levites might be sons of Henadad, for that name goes back to a time when the two offices were not distinguished; but they would not be confused in this list.—**19.** *Ezer the son of Jeshua*]. The name is not found elsewhere in our books. As he was the ruler of Mispah (*v.* on v. ¹⁵), he was probably not connected with the guild of Jeshua the associate of Zerubbabel. Indeed, it is very improbable that these district rulers were Levites.

We note here a changed order at the beginning: *and then repaired at his hand*]. The variation is prob. a scribal error, but it is old, for it is reproduced in 𝕲. The description of this second section is very obscure: *from opposite the ascent of the arms, the corner*]. *The corner*, vv. ²⁰. ²⁴. ²⁵, 2 Ch. 26⁹, is a local name well known to the author, but not clear to us. 𝕲 offers two readings: *the tower going up at the junction of the corner;* and *the tower of the ascent of the arms joining at the corner behind its hill.* Now it is impossible to make sense out of any of these readings. Partly aided by the latter Greek text, I would correct and render: *from opposite the armoury to the corner of the hill,* and so reaching a definite point, the northwest corner of the wall. Mitchell proposes *past the armour chamber to the corner* (JBL. 1903,¹⁵⁵).

20. *Baruch the son of Zabbai*], or *Zakkai* as Qr. *From the corner*] of the hill, v. ¹⁹ *to the door of the house of Eliashib the high priest*], who was the first builder named, v. ¹. This house was evidently hard by the wall, and near the corner. From the prominence of the occupant, the house would be well known.

The proximity of the high priest's residence indicates that "the hill" of v. [19] is the temple hill. The mention of the door may mean that Eliashib's house was too wide to serve as a defining mark, or that the description has become very exact. —**21.** The same person mentioned in v. [4] is here appropriately described as repairing a second portion, and still further appropriately it was a very small portion, only that fronting on a part of Eliashib's house: *from the door of Eliashib's house to the end of Eliashib's house*]. To be sure, there may have been a bad piece of wall at this point which required much labour. —**22.** *The priests, the men of the plain*]. The *plain* is a technical name for the oval plain of the Jordan. The full designation is *the plain* (or *oval*) *of the Jordan*, Gn. 13[10], but naturally *Jordan* could easily be dispensed with. "The river" or "the town" has a specific sense in every locality. The brief passage implies that this plain was especially the abode of priests. The statement is incomplete, as there is no description of the part of the wall repaired by these priests.—**23.** *Benjamin* and *Hasshub* apparently lived together *opposite their house*] and their house adjoined Azariah's, for the latter also built opposite his house and from that point *Binnui repaired*, v. [24]. If v. [22] is misplaced, as it may well be, then the jointly occupied house would adjoin the residence of the high priest.—**24.** On *Binnui v. s.* v. [18]. The part he repaired is described as extending *from the house of Azariah*, v. [23], *to the corner and to the turn*]. If we have reached a corner or turn in the wall, it must be a different one from that mentioned in vv. [19, 20]. Naturally the wall had more than one corner.—**25.** At the beginning we must supply *after him repaired*. Neither *Palal* nor his father *Uzai* occurs elsewhere in OT. The section is described thus: *from opposite the corner* [*i. e.*, the corner or turn of v. [24]] *and the tower which goes down from the upper palace which is at the court of the guard*]. The text is obviously wrong; for the *tower* is not the same as the *corner;* and there were not two royal palaces in Jerusalem, an upper and a lower. With 𝕲[L] we get intelligibility: *from opposite the corner of the tower which projects from the royal palace above the court of the guard.* The end of the section is

described in v. ²⁶.—*Pedaiah the son of Parosh*], or of the clan of
Parosh, Ezr. 2³, is misplaced. The word "repaired" is lacking
and the names interrupt the description of the section repaired
by Palal.—**26**. *Now the Nethinim were living in Ophel*], a par-
enthetic expression which has strayed from its original place
(*v*. Ezr. 2⁴³, and on *Ophel*, GAS. *Jer*. i,¹⁵²). It would naturally
come in where Ophel has been mentioned. The name occurs
at the end of v. ²⁷, and to that place these words should be transposed. Then we have, not a further description of the abode
of the Nethinim, but the missing *terminus* belonging to v. ²⁵.
As our text stands, we have: *unto opposite the water gate on the
east and the projecting tower*]. As the water gate was in the wall,
"opposite" is out of the question. 𝕲^N offers us quite a different
text: *unto the garden of the gate which is in Ophel on the east.*
The projecting tower is used for both *termini* of Palal's section,
and as it serves as the initial point for the Tekoites' second section, that must be right. Probably it should be connected with
Ophel thus: *on the east of the projecting tower*]. According to the
Talmud, the water gate was so named because water was carried
from the Virgin spring through this gate to the temple at the
Feast of Booths. Before it there was a plaza, 8^{1. 3. 16}, used for
assemblies. From the term in 12³⁷ it was evidently in the east
wall.—**27**. *After him repaired the Tekoites a second portion* (*cf.*
v. ⁵) *from the great projecting tower even to the wall of Ophel*].
This overhanging tower was a prominent spot, and must have
survived the catastrophes which had befallen Jerusalem, as it
would not have been rebuilt by the new community. Restor-
ing the text and transposing in vv. ²⁵⁻²⁷, as shown above to be
necessary, we get the following: (25) *After him repaired Palal the
son of Uzai from opposite the corner of the tower which projects
from the royal palace above the court of the guard,* (26) *unto the
garden of the gate which is in Ophel to the east of the projecting
tower.* (27) *After him repaired the Tekoites a second portion from
opposite the great projecting tower and to the wall of Ophel.* (26^a)
(*Now the Nethinim were living in Ophel.*) (25^b) *After them repaired Pedaiah the son of Parosh.*

28. *Above the horse gate*] cf. Je. 31⁴⁰, from which it appears to

have been near the brook Kidron, *repaired the priests each one
opposite his house*]. Evidently this was a part of the city occupied chiefly by priests. It may be the very section which
Jeremiah said would become holy unto Yahweh (31⁴⁰).—**29.**
Zadok the son of Immer] cf. v. ⁴, must be a priest.—*Shemaiah
the son of Shekaniah was the keeper of the east gate*]. This may be
the gate described in v. ²⁶ as the east water gate. One Greek
MS. reads *the east house*. The name Shemaiah occurs often in
our lists, but we cannot identify this builder with any other.
As the name means *Yahweh has heard* [*my prayer*], it would
naturally be given to children born in answer to a woman's fervent prayers. We may recall the case of Hannah (1 S. 1).—
30. A *Hananiah*] was mentioned in v. ⁸ as one of the ointment-
makers. This would be the same man, if *second portion* (*v. s.*
v. ¹¹) were to be strictly pressed. *Hanun the sixth son of Zalaph*].
Here we have an unparalleled particularity in the genealogy,
and an assurance that Zalaph is not a clan-name, but the name
of the actual father of Hanun. Guthe, however, thinks that
"sixth" is a corruption for the abode of Hanun. A Hanun is
mentioned in v. ¹³ in connection with the inhabitants of Zanoah.
—*Meshullam*] with the same father is named in v. ⁴. Perhaps
it is meant here to describe a second portion built by him *opposite his chamber*]. Meshullam did not have a house, but only
a room. As Meshullam was probably a priest, this room would
be in the temple.—**31.** We should probably read *Malchijah
one of the goldsmiths. Unto the house of the Nethinim and of
the traders*]. The Nethinim dwelt in Ophel, v. ²⁶, and apparently
had a house there in which they lived in common. The addition of *and of the traders* is suspicious. If the text is correct
the reference would be not to the residence, but to the ware-
house of the merchants. *Opposite the gate of the muster*], a
gate not elsewhere mentioned, may be a gate near which military enrolments were made, but the matter is hopelessly obscure, as, for that matter, is all this long description. The text
is probably wrong. *And unto the ascent of the tower*]. Another
bend in the wall on a hill is probably meant, but 𝕲 has *to the
middle of the bend*, which is somewhat clearer.

32. At the beginning of this v. we find the Massoretic note "the middle of the book," showing that Ezr. and Ne. were reckoned as one. By actual space we are quite past the middle, but the Massorites counted by vv.

Then follows a description of a section of the wall repaired by two guilds, without specifying any individuals, *the goldsmiths and the traders between the ascent of the turn and the sheep gate*]. 𝕲 gives a variant *between the ascent of the sheep gate*, but this is defective, as it gives but one *terminus*. This brings us around to the point at which we began, viz., the sheep gate, v. ¹, showing that at least in theory we have been carried around the whole circumference of the wall.

1. קדשׁוהו], acc. to Berth. and Torrey, is without an obj. in 𝕲; but that is only true in v. ⁶, and then only in ᴮᴬᴺ. But with Torrey we should rd. קרוהו as in vv. ³· ⁶. In v. ⁶ it is better with Kent to om. the word altogether. Kittel changes ²קדשׁוהו to קרוהו.—דלתתיו] should be followed by ומנעוליו ובריחיו as in vv. ³· ⁶· ¹³· ¹⁴· ¹⁵.—ומנעוליו] has been corrupted into ועד־מגדל.—**2.** 𝕲ᴮᴬᴺ υἱῶν, shows בני for בנו and בנה, and ידי for ידו. בנו is indeed difficult, for it should have an obj., and if a section of the wall is intended, החזיק would be the proper term. But it is hard to make good sense out of 𝕲.—**3.** קרוהו] 2⁸ v. ⁶ 2 Ch. 34¹¹ Ps. 104³ †. From the infrequent use Torrey's contention that the word is characteristic of the Chr. is not sustained. It is called a denominative from קורה, "rafter," "beam," BDB. Ges.ᴮ, and the mng. given is "lay beams." In Ch. that mng. will not serve, though RV. "make beams" may pass. 𝕲 renders στεγάζειν, once σκεπάζειν, "to cover"; so 𝔘 *texerunt*. If a denominative, it must refer to rafters or roof as Gn. 19⁸. The mng. here is the putting of the roof over the gates.—יעמידו 𝕲ᴮᴺ ἐστέγασαν = קרו, but this is prob. a scribal error for ἐστήσαν.— מנעול] is given the mng. *bolt;* 𝕲 κλεῖθρον, 𝔘 *sera*. The word occurs outside of this c. only in Ct. 5⁵ Dt. 33²⁵, for a different pointing does not make a different word. But *bolts* does not fit the case here, as it could not be differentiated from *bars*, and would be needlessly repetitious, as if the chief concern were the fastenings. The vb. נעל means to *fasten on a sandal*, whence מנעול would be that by which a sandal is fastened, therefore *thong* or *strap*. Now that which binds on a door is not a bolt, but the hinges or straps. Indeed, we have the technical term "strap-hinges." With 𝕲 we should rd. as in v. ⁶ ומנעוליו, so vv. ¹³· ¹⁴· ¹⁵.—**4.** החזק] occurs in this c. 33 t. besides v. ¹⁹, where the wrong pointing gives Pi. In 𝕲ᴮᴬᴺ we have κατέσχεν in vv. ⁴· ⁵ and ἐκράτησαν elsw.; ᴸ has ἐκραταίωσε exc. v. ¹³. 𝕲 may have rd. the vb.

אחז.—𝕲ᴮ lacks the second clause.—**5.** אדיריהם] was transliterated by
𝕲ᴮᴬᴺ ἀδωρηέμ. This shows the same text and the word is common;
the transliteration may be due to the obscurity of the passage.—בעבדת
ארניהם] 𝕲ᴮᴬᴺ εἰς δουλείαν αὐτῶν; ᴸ ἐν τῇ δουλείᾳ τοῦ κυρίου.—**6.** [הישנה].
Kittel suggests המשנה, presumably on the basis of Zp. 1¹⁰ and Ne. 11⁹.
But we could hardly understand a loose term, *the gate of the second half
of the city*, where so many other gates are specifically named. 𝕲 transliterates as n. p. 'Ισανά, thus bearing witness to our text. 𝕳 *veterem*.
—**7.** Mey. puts ו before אנשי (*Ent.* ¹⁰⁵. ¹).—המרנתי] 1 Ch. 27³⁰ † 𝕲ᴸ
Μηρωναθαῖος; but in Ch. ἐκ Μεράθων (Μαράθων^A).—לכסא] 𝕲ᴸ ἕως τ.
θρόνου, *i. e.*, עד כסא.—הנער] 𝕲ᴸ τοῦ Εννα. The v. is wanting in 𝕲ᴮᴬᴺ.
—**8.** חרחיה]. As חרח is unknown, we may have an error of the text.
𝕲ᴮᴬᴺ lacks first clause, and 𝕲ᴸ has Βαραχίου = ברכיה, a good Heb.
name.—צורפים] could not be in app. with "Uzziel," and as this guild
comes in at v. ³¹, the word must be omitted here.—הרקחים] m. only
here; 𝕲ᴮᴺ, 'Ιωακείμ, Ρωκεείμ^A, τῶν μυρεψῶν^L, 𝕳 *pigmentarii*.—ויעזבו]
𝕲ᴸ ἔθηκαν, but that represents thirty-six Heb. words, though usually שים, which would not help us much. In Prov. 8²⁸ this word represents עזז, and so we might rd. ויעזו, *and they strengthened*, implying
that the wall was standing, but in a weakened state. Sieg. suggests
ויאזרו, *i. e.*, *they surrounded Jerus.* [*with a wall*] *as far as the broad wall*.
Most authorities regard עזב as a technical building term, the exact
mng. of which is unknown, but may be "pave," "repair," "complete"
(*cf.* Ges.ᴮ BDB. and *v. s.*). The lexicons separate the word from the
regular עזב. But if the mng. is "repair," we should expect the usual
החזק. If the text is sound, then we have further witness to an older
story underlying the present composition.—**9.** בן־חור] om. ᴮᴬᴺ, while
ᴸ adds a link between Rephaiah and Hur: υἱὸς Σαβανίου υἱοῦ Σουρ
(בן־צור).—פלך] mng. *district* or *portion* is found only in this c., where
it occurs 8 t. 𝕲 renders περιχώρος, *the country around* Jerus., and not
Jerus. itself.—**11.** מרה שנית] καὶ δεύτερος^BAN.—ואת] καὶ ἕως^BAN = ועד.
—התנורים] τῶν ναθουρείμ^BN, τὸν Θαννουρείμ^AL.—**13.** 𝕲ᴸ has a peculiar
text. It transliterates, τὴν πύλην Γαι, and connects that with v. ¹³.—
החזיק] is here rendered ἐνίσχυσαν, and חנון is lacking altogether. This
departure indicates one spot which escaped the eye of the free editor
of Lucian's text. Still the context shows that the people of Zanoah, and
not Shallum, rebuilt the valley gate.—השפות] is regarded by Ges.§ ³⁵ ᵈ.
as a syncopated form; it is more likely a scribal error.—**14.** הוא יבננו]
𝕲ᴮᴬᴺ αὐτὸς καὶ οἱ υἱοὶ αὐτοῦ, and adds καὶ ἐσκέπασαν αὐτήν, and then
consistently uses pl. ἔστησαν. ᴸ has same text exc. ἐστέγασαν for ἐσκέπασαν. 𝕲 had therefore this text: הוא ובניו ויקרוהו ויעמידו. This reading
is preferable to MT.; for we have thus the regular formula for the gate
building, *v.* vv. ³· ⁶. Guthe reads בנהו.—**15.** V.ᵃ is lacking in 𝕲ᴮᴬᴺ.—
שלון †] 𝕲ᴸ Εμμων.—כל־חזה] 𝕲ᴸ Χολοζει.—ויטללנו] 𝕲 ἐστέγασεν, the same
word being used for קרוהו in vv. ³· ⁶.—טללו] is defined as *roof over*, the

same sense required for קרו (*cf.* on v. ³). The Chr. would not use a
α. λ. for one of his so-called characteristic words, nor could we explain
it as a txt. err. It is another link in the chain by which the composite
character of this c. is surely established.—[השלח לנו] 𝕲ᴮᴬ τῶν κωδίων τῇ
κουρᾷ. Underlying this we must presuppose השה לנו.—**16.** [עד־נגר ק׳]
𝕲 ἔως κήπου (κήπων ᴸ) τάφου = עד־גן קבר, making the reference to the
tomb of David rather than the royal cemetery.—עד־נגר implies that
the tombs were not close to the wall, but 𝕲 reads otherwise.—[העשויה]
regarded by Birch as an error for הישנה, Is. 22¹¹ (*PEFQ.* 1890,²⁰⁵).
But the מקרה of Isaiah's time has become the *artificial pool* of Neh.'s.
—**17.** [לפלכו] lacking in 𝕲ᴸ, perhaps because of its obscurity.—**18.** [בוי]
𝕲 Βεδεί ᴮ, Βέξερ ᴺ, Βένετ ᴬ, Βαναι ᴸ. Berth. says: "*nach LXX Textfehler =*
בנוי." The conclusion may be better than the reason. Guthe corrects
accordingly.—**19.** [שר] 𝕲ᴸ has ἄρχων τοῦ ἡμίσους = שר חצי. If this is
right, as Mey. holds, we should have to add פלך, and insert חצי in v. ¹⁵.
But the Heb. is clear enough, *v.* on v. ¹⁵.—[עלת] 𝕲ᴮᴬᴺ ἀναβάσεως τῆς συναπτούσης τῆς γωνίας; but ἀναβάσεως τῶν ὅπλων τῆς
συναπτούσης εἰς τὴν γωνίαν ὀπίσω εἰς τὸ ὄρος αὐτοῦ ᴸ. It is clear that
𝕲 rd. some other word than נשק, perhaps פגע, and 𝕲ᴸ has corrected
as usual by addition. Our text is suspicious on account of the unusual combination: *the arms, the corner.* The plus in ᴸ is found in the
first two words of v. ²⁰, reading אחרי להרה. נשק is usually rendered
armoury, but that is a mng. it does not bear. The text is surely corrupt. For various suggested emendations, *v.* my note in Guthe. None
yet offered is acceptable, for they are all patchwork. In a description
of a section of a wall we require both a *terminus a quo* and a *terminus
ad quem.* Our text gives us the former only. With a hint from 𝕲ᴸ I
would rd.: מנגר בית הנשק עד מקצע ההרה. This is bold, but there is
no use in emending unless in the process we can make sense. מקצע,
being thus defined, is used in vv. ²⁰· ²⁴· ²⁵ as an established point. ההרה
does not appear in v. ²⁰ in 𝕲, but 𝖂 has *in monte.* Mitchell suggests מנגר
עלית הנשק עד המקצע [בית אלישב] (JBL. 1903,¹⁵⁵).—**20.** 𝕲ᴮ Βηθελισουβ,
Βηθαιλισουβ ᴺ, Βηθελει Ασσουβ ᴬ, οἴκου Αλιασουβ ᴸ.—**22.** [הכר] 𝕲 has:
ἀχεχάρ ᴮ, χεχάρ ᴺ, ἀχχεχξάρ ᴬ, τοῦ πρωτοτόκου ᴸ. The last represents a
different text, *i. e.,* הבכר. 𝖂 is sufficiently interpretative: *de campes-
tribus Jordanis.*—**23.** [אצל] is suspicious, for the author shows no fondness for variety in expression and would have said נגר ביתו as v. ᵃ. 𝕲
has ἐχόμενα, 𝖂 *contra* (נגר).—**24.** [המקצוע ועד־הפנה] looks like an explanation of an unusual word. It is prob. that the original text had
simply ועד־הפנה, suggesting another bend in the wall, and some early
scribe wrongly identified this with that of vv. ¹⁹· ²⁰.—**25.** [פלל †] 𝕲 Φα-
λαλβ ᴮ, Φαλακ ᴺ, Φαλαξ ᴬ, Φαλλη ᴸ.—[אוזי †] 𝕲 Ευετ ᴮᴺ, Ευζαι ᴬ, Ουζαι ᴸ.—
[והמגדל] τοῦ πύργου ᴸ. Rd. therefore פנת המגדל [היוצא] 𝕲 ὁ ἐξέχων ᴮᴬᴺ,
τοῦ ἐξέχοντος ᴸ. This is the only case of the mng. "project" for יצא,
so also vv. ²⁶· ²⁷.—[העליון] cannot mean "upper," describing a second

palace. 𝕲ᴸ has ἐπ' ἄνω, which stands for עליון in Gn. 40¹⁷ 2 K. 15³⁵, but usually represents a prep., and we may substitute למעלה, as ᴸ continues τῆς αὐλῆς τῆς φυλακῆς.—26. [ער-נגר] 𝕲 ἕως κήπουᴮᴬᴺ = ער-גן; ᴸ shows both MT. and 𝕲: ἕως ἀπ' ἔναντι κήπου (cf. note on v. ¹⁹).—[המים] 𝕲ᴬ ἐν τῷ Ωφαλ.—29. [איש] 𝕲ᴸ, ἀπὸ Νηρ, which must be a corruption of ἀνήρ.—[שער] 𝕲ᴮ οἴκου.—30. [אחרי] rd. as Qr. אחריו.—[שני] must be a scribal error of שנית, the correct form, and occurring in every other place in this c.—[נשכה] 12⁴⁴ 13⁷ †, usually לשכה, for which this form may be a scribal error.—31. [הצרפי] 𝕲 Σαραφείᴮ, Σεραφειᴺ, Σαρεφιᴬ, Σεραφειᴸ. But a n. p. is scarcely right here. Guthe suggests a gentilic from צרפת. It is simpler to rd. after 𝕲ᴬ הצרפים, one of the goldsmiths.—[בית הנתינים] 𝕲 Βηθαναθείμᴮ, Βηθανναθανιμᴬ.—[והרכלים] 𝕲 καὶ οἱ ῥοβοπῶλαιᴮ, ῥοπο-πῶλαιᴺᴬ, καὶ τῶν μεταβόλωνᴸ. The last elsw. represents הסחרים; the others are both errors for ῥωποπῶλαι.—[המפקד] 𝕲ᴮᴬ τοῦ Μαφεκάδ Μα-φεθάδᴺ, τῆς ἐπισκέψεωςᴸ. As this name does not occur elsw., we should prob. rd. המסרה, as in 12³⁹.—[עד עלית הפנה] 𝕲 ἕως ἀνὰ μέσον [ἀναβά-σεωςᴺᴬᴸ] καμπῆςᴮ [τῆς πύληςᴸ]. We have then בין instead of עלית.—32. We have here the Massoretic note חצי הספר.—[הפנה] and the fol-lowing ל are lacking in 𝕲 and ᴬ lacks also עלית.

NE. 3³³–4¹⁷ (EV. 4¹⁻²³). THE EFFORTS OF THE ENEMY TO STOP THE WORK ON THE WALLS.

Sanb. and his fellows tried first ridicule and then force, but neither was effective against the genius of the great leader. He met sneers by imprecation and a fighting force with a large army, his people being ready to use either the trowel or the sword. Whether the enemy really attacked or not is uncertain, though an actual assault is improb. in view of the silence of the text. But the long continuance of the pre-cautions—and precautions which in a degree checked the progress of the work—indicates that the danger was always real, and we may infer that the enemy hovered in the vicinity of the city for a considerable period (v. Intr. § ⁹).

The text in several places is very corrupt, and sometimes it is im-possible to be sure of the mng. Every effort has been made to clear up the difficulties, though we must frequently be content with various degrees of probability.

In the account of the wall-building the interference of the enemy occupies a very conspicuous place. There is always an independent intr., 2¹⁰· ¹⁹ 3³³ 4¹ 6¹ and between these stories there is in N. some statement about the condition of the work. But between the appearance of the enemy in 2¹⁹ and that in 3³³ there is not a word from N. There never could have been, since 3³⁸ follows 2¹⁸, so we cannot fall back upon the theory of a lost section of N. Then we note that vv. ³³⁻³⁵ are in substance a repetition of 2¹⁹ ᶠ·. The enemy did nothing new here. It is difficult to see why there should be two accounts of their jeering the Judeans. In 2¹⁹ we lack an obj. for *heard*, and yet it must have been the same thing we have here, viz., that "we were building the wall," a clause which really belongs to 2¹⁹. We note here that the enemy "scorned the Judeans," while in 2¹⁹ "they scorned us." Outside of the transposed clause cited above, this passage is in the third p. It does not belong to N., and so is prob. not authentic. It was either added to his section by the author of 3¹⁻³², or was composed by the Chr. when he put the list of wall-builders in the midst of N. The imprecation of v. ³⁶ then really belongs to 2²⁰, which it follows naturally. The gross corruption of vv. ³³⁻³⁵ may suggest another explanation of its appearance here. Originally it was identical with 2¹⁹ ᶠ·, and accidentally appeared both before and after the insertion, vv. ¹⁻³², possibly from uncertainty as to which was the more suitable position. Then by a process of changes it was differentiated from 2¹⁹ and made into a mess from which clear sense can scarcely be extracted.

33–35. The wrath of Sanballat when he heard that the building operations were progressing.—33. *That we were building the wall*]. The wall had not progressed very far before Sanballat, the watchful enemy, heard of it.—*And he was angry and deeply incensed*], because he was jealous and dreaded to see Jerusalem regain its importance.—*And he derided the Judeans*], perhaps sincerely believing that their pretentious efforts would amount to nothing.—**34 f.** As far as we can decipher this very corrupt text, it may be rendered: *And he said before his brethren and the army of Samaria, and he said: what are the feeble Jews doing? will they give up to them? will they sacrifice? will they prevail in the day? will they revive the stones from the earth-heaps? and these are burned. And Tobiah the Ammonite was by him, and he said: Even what these build, if a jackal shall go up, he can tear down the wall of their stones*]. In part that is not very promising or intelligible.

𝕲 has simply: *and he said before his brethren, is this the army of Sam. that these Judeans are building their city? And To. the Ammonite came with him; and he said to them, shall they sacrifice or eat at their place? Will not a jackal go up and tear down the wall of their stones?* The mng. of 𝕲 is this: Sanb. is amazed to think that the Sam. army was

so inactive as to allow the Jews to engage in extensive building operations.   In defence of the army To. asserts that the feeble efforts of the
Jews is a negligible quantity.   In 4²³ we have a record of the interference of a Sam. army in the affairs of Jerus.   𝔊 further makes it clear
that Sanb. and To. had come to Jerus., but there is no record in either
text of anything that they did.   To take what is most prob. out of a
very difficult text we get: *And he* [Sanb.] *said in the presence of his
brethren and the crowd of Sam.*   On the whole, this rendering seems to
me preferable to 𝔊.   The idea is that Sanb. came to the outskirts of
Jerus. with To. Geshem, and a number of Sam.   To. and Geshem are
covered by "his brethren," *i. e.*, his associates.   *Frenquentia Samari-
tanorum* of 𝔙 is preferable to *the army of Sam.*   If an army had been
present, the attempt would have been made at once to stop the work.
The crowd was not a body prepared to fight.   There are two hard
problems about Sanb.'s speech, the length and the contents.   It is
difficult to choose between MT. *what are these feeble Jews doing?* and
𝔊 *that these Jews are building their city.*   𝔙 supports MT.   On the
whole, I incline to the latter, for it is more specific, and the idea of the
weakness of the Jews was introduced by To.   Sanb. seems to have been
seriously alarmed at Neh.'s activity.   In 𝔊 the rest of v. ³⁴ is part of
To.'s speech, but it does not altogether fit his other remarks.   Besides,
it would be strange to introduce Sanb. so elaborately and then have
him make a single self-evident remark.   *Will they abandon to them?* as
MT. reads, is out of the question.   *Will they fortify themselves* as EVˢ.
is scarcely permissible.   Following Sta. many have emended and rendered: *Will they commit themselves unto God?*   So Sieg. Ryle.   The
phrase is lacking in most Gk. texts, but ᴸ renders *shall we let them alone?*
𝔙 has *will they drive out those nations?*   ᴸ gives us the most intelligible
reading and the least amendment to make sense.   The phrase is then
a part of a conditional sentence, *if we let them alone, i. e.*, refrain from
forcible interference.   *Will they sacrifice?* is supported by all Vrss., but
I do not understand its mng.   All attempts to explain it fail.   The
Jews had been sacrificing from their first arrival in the time of Cy.;
they could offer sacrifices equally well whether the walls were built or
not, and sacrificing was considered a perfectly innocent practice.   In
spite of the antiquity of the error, the text seems to be wrong.—*Will
they make an end in a day?*]   Here we have a variety of renderings.
𝔊 offers us *prevail* or *eat.*   EVˢ. follow 𝔙 *complebunt in una die.*
Without changing 𝔥 much, we may rd. in any one of the three ways.—
Can they revive (i. e., restore) the stones from the earth-heaps?]   The stones
were so buried in the mass of débris that it seems impossible that they
should ever be got back into a wall.—*And these are burned*].   This is
not very clear, but prob. refers to the increased difficulty of restoration
from the fire-swept ruins.   To.'s remark is intended to be the final
sarcasm on the Jewish labourers; if a jackal walks along any stone wall

that these people build, it will break down under his tread. The building of a proper wall, adequate for defence, is a difficult and laborious task; the Jews had not shown capability or inclination for such an effort. The enemy has only sneers for the present essay; but they fail to reckon with the new personality back of the efforts.

36 f. Nehemiah's imprecation.—His words imply that Nehemiah had heard the jeering of the enemy. Doubtless Sanballat and Tobiah spoke in the presence of the people in order to weaken their hands, *cf.* 2 K. 18²⁶.—**36.** *In the land of captivity*]. It would be better with some Hebrew MSS. to read *their* captivity. The reference would then be to the fact that many of the enemy were exiles in Samaria, and so were still enduring the shame from which the Jews had been delivered. That reference is not, however, very satisfactory, and it may be that the true reading is found in 𝕲: *give them over to shame and to exile* (*v. i.*).—**37.** *And do not cover their iniquity*], *i. e.*, keep it in sight as a reminder that it is to be avenged. The sin may be the ridiculing of the patriotic efforts of God's people, or that which is common to mankind. As this is a quotation from Je. 18²³, we may doubt its genuineness in N.

> *For they provoke before the builders*] is difficult. The vb. usually has Yahweh as obj., and so Sieg. interprets here: "Yahweh's wrath is aroused as regards the builders." But the clause could then not mean that Yahweh's wrath was stirred up against the builders, but on behalf of the builders. That sense is scarcely extractable from 𝔥, and besides would be a good thing for which Neh. might thank the enemy. We must start with the fact that this clause gives the reasons for Neh.'s imprecation, and that the last clause means *in the presence of the builders;* therefore we should expect *because they jeered in the presence*, trying to discourage their efforts. Perhaps that is the idea of 𝔙 *quia irriserunt ædificantes, because they derided the builders*. It is not a part of the imprecation which is prob. contained wholly in v. ³⁶, and may be a gl. to justify the strong language.

38. The wall is half completed.—*And we built the wall*]. Nehemiah ejaculates his maledictions, but the work goes right on. *And the whole wall was joined unto its half*]. According to c. 3, different gangs of men were engaged on various parts of the work. A memorable point in the progress is now recorded, when the gangs met and so all gaps were stopped. *Unto its half* can therefore only mean with Berth. half the height, not half the circumference, for note the words "the whole wall," *i. e.*, the whole circumference was joined together. This alone is consistent with the stopping of the breaches in 4¹.—The wall was now of considerable significance as a means of defence.— The unexpectedly quick result is explained, *and the heart of the people was in the work*], the condition for all effective effort.

4¹⁻⁵ (EV. = 4⁷⁻¹¹). The enemy comes to Jerusalem to stop the work by force.—1. The enemy is enlarged now by the presence of the *Arabians, Ammonites,* and *Ashdodites,* though the last name may be a gloss. Tobiah was an Ammonite and Geshem an Arabian (2¹⁹). Geshem is not named here, but he was probably in the company. The jeering at the walls had not stopped the work. An early inspection had apparently satisfied the foe that nothing effective would be accomplished by the feeble Jews. Now another story comes to their ears, for they heard *that the restoration of the walls of Jerusalem went on, for the breaches were being stopped*], the condition marked by the statement of 3³⁸; the walls were finished to half the required height.—*And they were exceedingly angry*] for all their projects were going astray. Once the walls were up, the despised and easily harassed Jews would be a thorn in the flesh of their neighbours.—**2.** *And they all conspired together*]. It is simpler with 𝕲 and 𝕳 to read *gathered together*. A conspiracy was hardly necessary after 2¹⁹ ᶠ· 3³³ ᶠᶠ·. The leaders now collected a considerable force with the aggressively hostile purpose *to go fight in Jerusalem*] not "against," for they had no idea that an effort would be required to capture the city, but expected to enter and force the unwarlike builders to stop work.—*And to cause it confusion*]. This is all clear in itself, except the masculine suffix (לו) referring to Jerusalem, which is feminine. Still a Greek text offers a tempting amplification *to wipe it* [*Jerusalem*] *off the face of the earth and to cause me confusion.* This gives us the first person characteristic of N. It also makes clear the purpose of the enemy; they were determined to strike such a blow that Jerusalem would be no further a menace.—**3.** Nehe-

miah, like all true leaders, was kept informed of the movements
of the enemy.   That no surprise should be sprung he stationed
a guard which kept watch both day and night.   Doubtless the
guard was placed as outposts beyond the city walls.   The
community was pious and believed in God's power to help,
and therefore they prayed as well as watched, anticipating our
Lord's "watch and pray" (Mt. 26⁴¹).

4. *And Judah said*].   *Judah* cannot be tribal here, but as
suggested by 3³³ ᶠ· it is the name of the postexilic community.
The latter part of the verse is clear: *and we are not able to build at
the wall*].   This is a serious declaration.   The whole body of
workers announce to Nehemiah that they can go on with the
task no longer.   The reason for this critical situation is given in
the intervening words.   The text runs: *the strength of the burden-
bearers has failed, and the earth is great*].   *Earth* is usually interpreted as *rubbish-heaps*, and that sense fits in with 3³⁴, where
Sanballat jestingly asks if the Jews can restore the stones from
the earth ruins.   But if this is the meaning, then the verse is
misplaced, for we are dealing here with the attack of the enemy,
not with the exhaustion of the labourers.   𝕲 has a very different
text: *for the strength of the enemy is exhausted and the multitude is
large*.   The verb "exhausted" is indeed incongruous, yet 𝕲
follows MT.   The original verb must have said the very opposite: the strength of the enemy is boundless.   That text makes
the passage fit in admirably with the context and is doubtless
right.   The Jews felt that with the large hostile force assembled
against them that they could no longer take the risk, even with
their prayers and the guard.   They were not afraid of the work,
but they were afraid of the warriors.—**5.** The plan of Sanballat
and his company was to take the city by surprise and then to
slay the workmen (in agreement with 𝕲 of v. ²) and thus effec-
tively to bring the wall-building to an end.

**6–8 (EV.¹²⁻¹⁴). Nehemiah sets a large armed guard
against the enemy.—6.** *And it was that when the Judeans who
were living by them* [*i. e., the enemy*, not *the Jerusalemites* as Sieg.
holds] *came in they said to us*].   The enemy had proposed to
surprise the builders.   They were assembling for the attack.

Among the builders, as correctly indicated in c. 3, were many who came from the country. It was evidently their custom to return home at intervals. Some of these lived close by the rendezvous of the Samaritans. They came up to Jerusalem now with an alarming report. But this report is in hopeless confusion in our text, which runs: *ten times from all places when ye return unto us*]. No commentator has yet been able to give a satisfactory interpretation of these words. Naturally, for they are wrong. 𝕲 preserves a simple and intelligible reading: *they are coming up against us from all places*, perhaps adding, *where we live*. We understand now the alarming character of their report and the prompt measures taken for defence.—**7.** Here again we have a hopeless text.—*And I stationed*] cannot be right, for the verb has no object expressed or implied, and that verb belongs to the second part of the verse. We might read *I stood*, but while grammatical, it would not be clear. With 𝕲 read *and they stood*, as most modern interpreters. But the subject, contrary to general opinion, is *the enemy*, not *the builders*. Where they stood is in any case unintelligible from the description: *at the lowest part of the place behind the wall in the open places*]. For the last expression with 𝕲 we might read *in the breaches*, or *in the sheltered places*. The general sense seems to be that the enemy had advanced to the best cover they could find opposite the lowest parts of the rapidly rising wall. They were therefore in the most available place for an attack, sheltered from the sight of the builders and ready to rush to those places in the wall where it could most easily be scaled.—Their plan was thwarted by Nehemiah's action: *And I stationed the people by families* [or *companies*] *with their swords and their spears and their bows*]. This action shows a distinct advance on v. [3], where a guard was set for the purpose of watching; here we have an army equipped and posted for the purpose of fighting.—**8.** Our text runs: *and I looked and I arose and I said*]. This is pretty redundant for the terse Nehemiah. With Guthe we may emend on the basis of 𝕲: *and I adjured them by the Lord, saying*. Berth.'s proposal, "and I saw their fear and arose and said," seems to be less satisfactory. The brief exhortation was addressed to the whole army: *to the nobles, and to the deputies* [⑤ *generals*], *and to the rest of the people*]. The appeal forcibly aims at the sentiments of courage, religion, and patriotism. *Do not fear on their account; remember our God* [so ⑤, *the Lord* 〚〛] *the great, and the one to be feared* [*cf.* 1⁵ Lu. 12⁴ ᶠ· Dt. 20¹ ᶠᶠ·] *and fight on behalf of your brethren, your sons and your daughters, your wives and your homes*].

9-17 (EV.¹⁵⁻²³). The enemy gives up the contemplated attack.—9. This verse is so difficult in the relation of its parts that we may well suspect an omission. The parts are clear in themselves, but are hard to join so as to make sense.—*And it was when our enemies heard that it was known to us*] certainly must originally have been followed by some statement as to what the enemy did under these circumstances; but what course of action they pursued we do not know. We do not hear of them again until c. 6, and that is some time later. It is clear, however, that there was no actual battle. The enemy perhaps stayed in the neighbourhood, watching for an opportunity that never came.—*And God frustrated their plot, and we all returned to the wall, each man to his work*]. This resumption of work naturally follows the unknown action of the enemy, whatever that may have been. As the foe took no aggressive measures, Nehemiah deemed it safe to return to the work. Every day of labour made an effective assault less possible. The people laying stones were doing more for defence than standing under arms.—**10.** The text goes on to describe the conditions under which the work was now carried on. First there is described the arrangement of Nehemiah's own followers: *half of my servants were engaged in the work*]. These men were the governor's personal servants, perhaps a body-guard brought from Persia, *cf.* 5¹⁶: *and half of them held the lances and the shields and the bows and the coats of mail*]. Sieg. regards all after "spears" as a later addition, but the reason he gives is that no one would possess a coat of mail. The Jews certainly would not have such accoutrements, but Nehemiah's body-guard, the ones referred to here, trained and equipped in Persia, would surely possess a complete armament. Reuss, on the contrary, supposed "swords"

to have dropped out of the list, so Berth.; but swords are abundantly provided for below. 𝔥 has undoubtedly got the sense
when it merely summarises: *and half were prepared for war.*
Nehemiah's servants were the best fighters, and so apparently
half of them were working on the wall, while the other half were
kept under arms to be ready to resist an attack at a moment's
notice.—The rest of the verse is unintelligible, for no sense
can be made out of *and the princes were behind the whole house of
Judah*], at least not in this connection. 𝔊 vainly connects with
v. [11] *and the princes of the whole house of Judah building on the
wall.* But v. [11] begins a new passage and is clear enough, while
the above would imply that the princes alone were working now,
contrary to v. [9]. Either "princes" is an accidental repetition
after the similar Hebrew word for coats of mail or it is an error
for some verb like *drawn up.* *Behind the whole house of Judah*
then would indicate the station of the armed guard; they were
divided into squads and were close by the various bodies of
workmen, giving moral as well as material support.—**11.** Now
we come to the warlike preparation of the workers: *those who
were building on the wall and those who were carrying burdens were
working, with one hand he was doing the work, and with the other
he was holding a missile*]. *Working* is a conjecture. The Hebrew word might mean *laden*, but that makes no sense. Most
authorities follow 𝔊 *armed.* It is hard to see how a mason could
lay stones with one hand grasping a weapon. But it may be
that what the statement really means is that the weapon was
close at hand, not necessarily in the hand. Or the last clause
may refer only to the burden-bearers. What the missile was
we do not know. 𝔥 has *sword*, but the swords were girded on
the waist, v. [12]. The Hebrew word means *sent* and implies that
it was a weapon used for hurling like a javelin.—**12ª.** *And the
builders* [in addition to the missile close at hand and distinguished from the burden-bearers] *had each one his sword girded
upon his loins, and were building*], that is, the masons went
right on with the work, but fully prepared to meet an attack.—
12ᵇ. With v. ᵇ we begin a new section in which the governor
describes the measures he took to collect the forces quickly at

any spot where an assault was made or threatened.—*Now the trumpeter was by my side*].   In vv. ¹³ ᶠ· we learn that the blast of the trumpet was to indicate the point to which the whole body of guards and workmen should rush in case of a threatened attack.   Now if there was but one bugler and he always by Nehemiah, there would be much delay in the event of an assault. For Nehemiah would have to be informed, and the trumpeter sent to the threatened point before he blew the alarm.   This would be poor generalship.   The probability is that there were several trumpeters, one with each squad of the armed guard of v. ¹⁰.   The blast would be given without waiting for the governor.   Why then does he say "by my side"?   We have no great confidence in the details of this somewhat corrupt text, but the word may be collective and the trumpeters gathered while Nehemiah gave orders both to them and to the people.   The trumpeter was a city watchman whose business it was to warn the people of impending danger (GAS. *Jer*. i,³⁸⁴).

13. *The work is extensive and wide*].   The builders, as in c. 3, are spread around the whole circuit of the walls, so that at any one point there was but a small body, perhaps the very conditions for which the enemy was watching.—**14.** *Unto us*], for Nehemiah and his servants would repair quickly to any point of danger.—*Our God will fight for us*] *cf*. v. ⁸.   Nehemiah's stirring address would not fail to arouse the people.   Ps. 83 is ascribed to this occasion in *Psalms Chronologically Arranged*, by Four Friends, Macmillan, 1891.—**15.** *And half of them were holding the spears*] is a copyist's repetition from v. ¹⁰.   The words have no meaning here, and they force asunder related clauses.   Omitting this we have an intelligible statement: *Now we were engaged on the work from the rising of the dawn until the appearance of the stars*].   The point brought out is therefore the high pressure under which the work was done.   Since the enemy had approached and was now probably lurking in the neighbourhood, speed was of the utmost importance.   Every stone laid added to the security of the city.   Night-shifts were hardly possible under the limitations of ancient times, but the working hours were prolonged from daylight until the stars

could be seen, when it became too dark to work any longer.
The omitted words spoil this fine sense; as the text stands, we
have the long day, not for working, but for holding weapons,
and the weapons would then be laid aside at night when they
might be most needed.—**16.** *Let each man and his servant lodge
in the midst of Jerusalem*]. As we have seen (*v. v.* [6]), many
of the people (most of them perhaps, since these words are addressed *to the people* and since Jerusalem had few inhabitants,
7[4]) lived outside of the city, and went home at certain times,
those who lived near probably each night.—*And they shall be for
us a guard by night and a working force by day*]. The Hebrew
מלאכה has nowhere else exactly this sense, but the context makes
clear the meaning. It is not "occupation" or "the work,"
but the force doing the work. The antithesis is to "guard,"
which may have an abstract sense like "defence," but English
has no suitable corresponding word for מלאכה.—**17.** Here we
have an impressive statement that shows again the pressure
under which work was done and the criticalness of the situation. *I and my brethren and my servants and the men of the guard
following me, we did not take off our clothes*]. Those who were
especially charged with the defence were ready for action at a
moment's notice, showing that a night attack was feared.

The rest of the passage is obscure. Most scholars correct text and
render: *each one with his missile in his hand.* But to say nothing about
the lack of support, a further statement about arming is not appropriate here. That point has been abundantly covered above. The
text runs literally: *each man his missile the water*, which lacks both construction and sense. In a Gk. text we find the passage amplified: *and
the one whom they sent for water, a man and his missile to the water.* But
this has no connection with the otherwise incomplete statement about
sleeping with the clothes on, and is pretty confused in itself. Moreover, we have שלח translated in two different senses. The water was
within the walls, and the carrying of a weapon esp. then is unintelligible. The Latin seems to mean that *each one stripped for bathing*,
making an exception to v.[a], but it is difficult to get this sense from our
text. As some emendation is essential, we may regard the Latin as
the clearest. EV[s]. "every one went with his weapon to the water" is
highly interpretative, and certainly gives the wrong idea. The words
must in some way have qualified the retention of the clothing. If I
might draw a bow at a venture, I should conjecture *neither by night*

nor by day. This text is not so very different from MT., and some heroic course is required. This proposal has at least the recommendation that it makes good sense, completing the statement about wearing the clothes. In the preceding clause, *we did not take off our clothes,* we miss a confidently expected note of time, and the proposed emendation supplies it. Under any circumstances the passage is too short for a complete independent statement.

33. סנבלט] 𝕲ᴸ adds ὁ Ὡρωνίτης as 2¹⁰.—[ויכעס] 𝕲ᴸ ἐλυπήθη καὶ ὠργίσθη, *cf.* 4¹.—וילעג]. The Hiph. with same sense as Qal is late usage. 𝕲ᴸ ἐμυκτήρισε καὶ ἐξεγέλα. I suspect that in both cases we have a double translation of the same Heb. word rather than a witness to an originally more amplified text.—**34 f.** 𝕲 is shorter than MT., and differs considerably from it. As usual, ᴮᴬᴺ has simplest form. Beginning with וחיל we find: Αὔτη ἡ δύναμις Σομορών, ὅτι οἱ Ἰουδαῖοι οὗτοι οἰκοδομοῦσιν τὴν ἑαυτῶν πόλιν = זה חיל שמרון כי היהודים האלה יבנו את־עירם; ᴸ follows 𝕳 to היעזבו להם, for which it has ὅτι οἰκοδομοῦσι τὴν ἑαυτῶν πόλιν, and thus shows that 𝕲 rd. those words as יבנו עירם. Several of the letters of these words are common with 𝕳, and this variant is eloquent of the occasional troubles of those who tried to decipher ancient mss. Mitchell renders the clause "if they be left to themselves," and for "sacrifice" he suggests יגבהו, "they will build high" (JBL 1903,⁹⁰). A part of the balance of this v. is found in the speech of To.—For גם and what follows 𝕲ᴮ has: μὴ θουσιάσουσιν ἢ φάγονται ἐπὶ τοῦ τόπου αὐτῶν; οὐχὶ ἀναβήσεται ἀλώπηξ καὶ καθελεῖ τὸ τεῖχος λίθων αὐτῶν; 𝕲ᴸ has the customary elaboration and duplication showing the original 𝕲 corrected by addition of the extra matter of MT.—[היכלו] appears as φάγονται, *i. e.,* יאכלו, though ᴸ has as dup. in one place δυνήσονται.—שרופות . . . [ביום found only in ᴸ and then as follows: καὶ εἰ σήμερον ἰάσονται τοὺς λίθους μετὰ τὸ γενέσθαι γῆς χῶμα καυθέντας καὶ τὸ τεῖχος ἐμπεπρησμένον. This text shows ירפאו for יחיו or ארץ or ארצות for ערמות, חומה for המה; and בער or a synonym is added, unless καυθέντας represents מערמות, which then would be understood as a form from בער.—The first problem of textual criticism is to determine where To. begins to speak. 𝕲ᴮᴬᴺ starts him at היזבחו. 𝕲ᴸ introduces him at this point and then reintroduces him at v. ³⁵. 𝕳 agrees with MT. To.'s speech seems to be an answer to the timid note in Sanb.'s. Therefore in this respect MT. is preferable. —The clause ויאמר עשים should be emended in part after 𝕲 (*v. s.*).— עשים] might be an erroneous reading in a bad copy for עירם; then we might conjecture: היעזבו להם.—לאמר למה היהורים האלה בנים את עירם]. These words correspond, apparently, to 𝕲ᴮᴬ καὶ εἶπαν πρὸς ἑαυτούς, εἶπενᴺ. 𝕲ᴸ has this plus Μὴ καταλείψομεν αὐτούς = הנעזב אתם. This reading makes the best sense. 𝕳 *num dimittent eos gentes,* =את ישלחו האלה העמים.—'ב היכלו] 𝕲ᴮᴬᴺ φάγονται [אכל] ἐπὶ τοῦ τόπου αὐτῶν. 𝕲ᴸ has this, but in the dup. ἄρα δυνήσονται [יכל]; 𝕳 *et complebunt* [כלה] *in una* *die*, reading האחר for היחיו.—𝔙 has a plus here: *numquid ædificare poterunt*.—המה] 𝔊ᴸ τεῖχος, 𝔙 *qui* (אשר).—**36.** בחר] 𝔊 has seen לבזה as in v. ᵇ.—בארץ שביה] 19 MSS. שבים (*v.* Kittel); 𝔊ᴸ καὶ εἰς αἰχμαλωσίαν, *i. e.*, ולשיה.—**37.** עונם] 𝔊ᴮᴬᴺ rd. עון and lack the remainder of this v. and v. ³⁸.—כי . . . . בנונים] 𝔙 *quia irreserunt ædificantes*.

4. 1. והאשרודים] lacking in 𝔊ᴮᴬ.—ארוכה] usually *healing*, but here and 2 Ch. 24¹³, *restoration* of walls. 𝔊 φύη.—לחמת] some Gk. MSS. and 𝔙 have sg., which is better.—הפרצים] 𝔊 διασφαγαί, only occurrence of this word in LXX. Kittel suggests פרצים.—**2.** ויקשרו] 𝔊 συνήχθησαν; συνάγω stands for 50 Heb. words (see Hatch and Redpath, *Concord.*), but nowhere else for קשר. We should rd. קבץ, so 𝔙 *congregati sunt.*—ולעשות] lacking in 𝔊ᴮᴬᴺ, 𝔊ᴸ τοῦ ποιῆσαι αὐτὴν ἀφανῆ καὶ ποιῆσαι μοι πλάνησιν. The first clause is lacking in MT., and we have the interesting לי. Kittel suggests לה, which is better if text is otherwise right.—**3.** אלהינו] 𝔊ᴸ κύριον τὸν θεὸν ἡμῶν = יהוה אלהינו.—**4.** הסבל] 𝔊ᴮᴬᴺ τῶν ἐχθρῶν, 𝔊ᴸ τ. ε. ἡμῶν.—העפר] 𝔊ᴮᴬ ὄχλος = המון, 𝔊ᴬᴸ ὁ χοῦς.—**6.** עשר־עלינו] MT. cannot be forced to yield any sense. The simplest text is 𝔊ᴮᴬᴺ ἀναβαίνουσιν [יעלו] ἐκ πάντων τῶν τόπων ἐφ᾽ ἡμᾶς. 𝔊ᴸ inserts ὅτι ἐπιστρέψατε after τόπων, and thus shows תשובו. I would rd.: אשר יעלו מכל־המקמות אשר־ישבו עלינו. This is clear and intelligible and might easily be corrupted into the present hopeless form.—**7.** There is corruption here also, but it is not so deep-seated. With 𝔊ᴺᴸ rd. ויעמרו for ואתמיד.—בצחחים] occurs elsw. only in Ez. 24⁷·⁸ 26⁴·¹⁴, with sense of *smooth* or *bare*, and here the mng. *bare places* is assigned. But such an interpretation is difficult. 𝔊ᴸ comes to the rescue, having a dup., first that of 𝔊ᴮ, then Lucian's own text: καὶ ἔστησαν ὑποκάτωθεν τοῦ τόπου ἐξόπισθεν τοῦ τείχους ἐν τοῖς ἀναπεπταμένοις. The last word occurs in LXX only in Jb. 39²⁶, corresponding to פרש; so here we might infer בפרשים. 𝔊ᴮᴬᴺ has σκεπεινοῖς, "sheltered places." 𝔙 has a text in which v. ᵃ· ᵇ are compressed into a single sentence: *statui in loco post murum per circuitum populum in ordinem cum gladiis suis, et lanceis et arcubus.*—**8.** ואל־הסגנים] lacking in 𝔊ᴮᴬ.—אדני] 𝔊 τοῦ θέου ἡμῶν, *i. e.*, אלהינו. 𝔊ᴸ has an important plus preceding אל־תיראו, καὶ ὤρκισα αὐτοὺς κύριον λέγων = ואשביעם ארני לאמר. Guthe puts this vb. at the beginning of the v. in place of the superfluous וארא ואקום. That certainly improves the text very greatly. Torrey regards the addition as purely arbitrary (ES.¹⁰⁹).

9. וַנֵּשָׁב] is to be rd. with the Vrss. and virtually all commentators. —**10.** נערי עשיה] 𝔊ᴮᴬᴺ τῶν ἐκτετιναγμένων ἐποίουν, 𝔊ᴸ παρατεταγμένων επ. (ערוכים), 𝔙 *juvenum eorum faciebat*. We might infer that 𝔊 and 𝔙 took the י from נער and prefixed to the vb., but 𝔊 generally disregards the participles in this troublesome passage.—מחזיקים] 𝔊 ἀντείχοντο, 𝔙 *parata erat ad bellum.*—והרמחים]. Sieg. follows B.-Rys., reading ברמחים after v. ¹⁵, but in view of מחזקת השלח, v. ¹¹, the emendation is unnecessary.—**11.** הבנים בחומה]. In their despair the Vrss. generally connect with preceding; Guthe and Kittel follow these and change verse-ending

accordingly.—[נסבל] 𝔊 ἐν τοῖς ἀρτῆρσιν.—[עמשים] 𝔊ᴮᴬᴺ ἐν ὅπλοις, 𝔊ᴸ
ἔνοπλοι, 𝔘 et imponentium. There is no root עמש, and the word has
been identified with עמס, but that makes a hopeless redundancy, and
after 𝔊 חמשים is now generally substituted. The word is pred. both to
"builders" and "bearers," but armed is not good, as that is too general
a statement for the workmen. Perhaps עשים is all that is needed.—
12. [והבנים] is a second pred. after אסרים, they were armed and were building, i. e., armed while engaged in building. 𝔘 begins a new sentence and
connects with following: et ædificabant, et clangebant buccina juxta me.
—[אצלי] 𝔊ᴮᴬᴺ ἐχόμενα αὐτοῦ, but MT. is right.—**15.** [וחצים ... ברמחים]
can only be a repetition from v. ¹⁰ and does not belong here. In place
of [אנחנו] 𝔊ᴬ has ἡμίσυ, making more repetition. If the words were retained, this text would be right, as חצים needs a complement.—**16.** איש
[ונערו] om. 𝔊ᴮᴬᴺᴸ.—[וילינו] 𝔊 αὐλίσθητε.—[ירושלם] 𝔊ᴸ πόλεως.—**17.** [ואין] 𝔊
χαὶ ἤμην, i. e., ואהי.—[ואהי ונערי] om. 𝔊ᴮᴬᴺ.—[אנחנו] 𝔊 ἐξ ἡμῶν = מאנחנו.
—[איש ש"] 𝔊ᴮᴬᴺ connects איש with preceding and lacks שלחו המים; 𝔊ᴸ
has χαὶ ἄνδρα ὃν ἀπέστελλον ἐπὶ τὸ ὕδωρ, ἀνὴρ χαὶ ὅπλον αὐτοῦ εἰς τὸ
ὕδωρ. 𝔘 unusquisque tantum nudabatur ad baptismum, apparently
interpreting שלח in the sense of taking off the clothes. Guthe follows
𝔊ᴸ and has ואיש אשר שלחו על־המים איש ושלחו אל המים. Most scholars
rd. בידו for המים. As a bold guess I would propose אין הלילה והיום, neither
by night nor by day.

NE. 5. THE ECONOMIC DIFFICULTIES WHICH CONFRONTED
NEHEMIAH.

The placing of this c. so that it breaks the story of the rebuilding of
the wall indicates that the compiler regarded these hard conditions as
due to the work on the walls. And many authorities have followed this
suggestion. It is true that the forced labour without pay would take
many away from the ordinary means of livelihood. On the other hand,
the work was done in too short a time for a serious economic disturb-
ance, esp. of the kind described here. There is no hint in the text that
the distress was connected with the great work. It is more likely due
to the governor's efforts to secure a population for Jerus. A long
time must have elapsed to bring about the state of affairs described.
Neh. would scarcely have stopped work to hold an assembly, esp. in
view of the pressing danger, which never ceased until the last stone was
laid and the last gate in place. Finally, the date in v. ¹⁴ shows that we
are at the end of twelve years of Neh.'s rule. The passage therefore
belongs to a later period than the building of the walls. It describes
one of the last acts of Neh.'s first administration. The c. falls into two
main parts: vv. ¹⁻¹³, the distress and its relief; vv. ¹⁴⁻¹⁹, the economic
aspects of Neh.'s administration.

**1-5. Three complaints are made against the Judeans by
three different groups of people.**—These complaints were:
(1) There was insufficient food for the large number of
children. (2) Property had been mortgaged to buy food.
(3) Money had been borrowed to pay taxes. The result was
the alienation of property and the slavery of some of the
people.

1. The cry was one of distress on account of dire want. The
complainants were *the people and their wives*], and the defendants
were *their brethren the Judeans*]. The people, therefore, are Hebrews who were not reckoned to the house of Judah, and may
be those who had survived the exile in the surrounding territory, unless the "Judeans" means here the Jews living in Jerusalem, as v. [3] may imply.—**2.** *With our sons and our daughters
we are numerous*]. Such is the apparent meaning, and this
rendering is found in 𝕲. The population had increased faster
than the means of support. Guthe, adopting a slight emendation proposed first in 1753, gets "our sons and our daughters we
give as security." But that would make this complaint virtually identical with that of v. [3] and needlessly anticipatory of
v. [5]. This change does, however, make a connection with v. [b],
while as the text stands the transition is very abrupt: *that we
may get corn and eat and live*]. 𝕲[L] gives a different rendering,
give us therefore corn. But the people do not seem to be begging;
they are complaining of the gradual loss of their property.—
3. The second statement is clear: *our fields and our vineyards
and our houses we are mortgaging*]. The complainants therefore
belonged to a class that had considerable property, and who
lived outside of the city. The situation is like that described
in Is. 5[8]. The gathering of the land into the hands of the rich
was not a new condition. The text gives us a reason for this
alienation of property, *that we may get corn in the famine*].
"Corn," as in v. [2], is used for food generally, like "bread" and
"meat." There is no use in softening "famine" to "dearth,"
as EV[s]. That rendering is based on the false connection with
the wall-building. Famines were plentiful enough in Judah,
owing to the failure of rain, and the situation requires a real

and perhaps long-continued meagreness of crops. It is true
that 𝕲 has "eat," as v. ², instead of "famine," but the Hebrew
text is better here.—**4.** The third trouble is in part plain: *we
have borrowed money for the king's tax*]. This is the only reference to the taxing of the people by the Persian king. Like
all other taxes, this is a preferred claim. As their crops had
failed, and the people had little or nothing to sell, the money
had to be borrowed. In the text we have following only *our
fields and our vineyards*], to which 𝕲 adds *our houses*, as v. ³,
and one text makes sense by a preceding "upon," so EVˢ. According to that reading, the real estate had been pledged both
for food and for taxes. It is not unlikely that the words are
a repetition by accident from v. ³. (So Böhme, see Guthe's
note.) They are unnecessary here. It quite suffices to say
that they had borrowed money, for whatever property they
had would, of course, be security.—**5.** One class of people com-
plained that their families were so large that they could not
supply them with food; another that they had mortgaged
their property because of famine; and a third that they could
only pay their taxes by resort to the money-lenders. Then we
have the plea of the relationship of the oppressor and the oppressed. *And yet as the flesh of our brothers* [the Judeans, v. ¹]
so is our flesh]. "Flesh" is used here in the sense of "blood"
to indicate race identity. These people were not suffering
from the oppression of foreign tyrants, but from the exactions
of those who were Jews like themselves.—*As their sons are our
sons*], not meaning that the poor loved their children as truly as
the rich, and suffered the pangs of separation as they would,
but repeating the idea of the blood relationship. The sons of
the borrowers were children of Abraham as well as those of the
lenders.—The result of the hard condition is now stated: *lo,
we are reducing our sons and our daughters to slavery*]. The people had come back from Babylonian bondage to find a Judean
bondage, and the last state was worse than the first. In Babylon the whole family stood as one, but now children were taken
from their parents to become the slaves of those of their own
blood.

Then follows an unintelligible passage. Rendered as literally as possible, we have: *and there are some of our daughters subjugated, and they are not for the strength of our hand*]. The difficulty was felt by the ancient translators. In one Gk. text we find: *some of our daughters they take by force, and our hand is not strong, i. e.*, enough to make effective resistance. This text is interesting because it discloses measures of oppression that were lawless. In the complaints above there was no hint of violent action; the rich kept well within the law, as they love to do. Here is a stage in which the law was disregarded, and young women were seized and taken from their homes by superior force. 𝔅 renders: *some of our daughters are slaves; and we have no means by which they may be redeemed*, in part showing a different underlying Heb. text. I do not think "reduced to bondage" right, for that would be a repetition of what was just said of both sons and daughters. Either we must om. "and daughters" in the preceding statement or substitute some other vb. in this passage, as in ᴸ (taken by force). The lack of strength in the hand refers to the pecuniary loss. A daughter represented a certain money value as a prospective wife, and the price was presumably high in this period, so that many Jews married cheaper foreign women (Ezr. 9, 10 Ne. 13²⁴ ᶠᶠ·). Leaving out a single Heb. letter in the last word, as in 𝔊, we get the conclusion of the trouble: *our fields and our vineyards belong to the nobles* ("nobles" instead of "others" of MT.). These were naturally the wealthier classes, as always land-hungry, and striving to get together large estates.

6-13. Nehemiah is greatly incensed at the oppression and takes prompt measures to relieve the distress.—6. *And I was very angry*]. Nehemiah was capable of great passion when his sense of right was outraged.—*Their cry and these words*]. The cry was the general wail of the distressed of v.¹; the words were the specific complaints made in vv. ²⁻⁵. 𝔅 interprets differently and happily: *their cry according to these words, i. e.*, their complaint as just specified.—7. Literally, *and my heart counselled upon me*], EVˢ. "then I consulted with myself." This does not make very satisfactory sense, and the word does not occur elsewhere in Hebrew. We might render: *my heart was king* [or *ruler*] *over me*. It would be more natural to find something like "my heart was hot within me," as in Ps. 39⁴.—*And I reproved the nobles and the rulers*], the two dominant classes in this period. The nobles had acquired the property of their brethren (*v. s.* v. ⁵); and the rulers were probably condemned because they had

permitted the oppression. Of course, they may have been a
party to it and shared in the plunder.—*You have exacted interest
each one of his brethren*] is the specific charge against them. This
was a violation of the law which forbade interest from Hebrews,
but allowed it from foreigners, Dt. 23²⁰ ᶠ·, *cf.* Ex. 22²⁵ Lv. 25³⁵ ᶠᶠ·.
The prohibition was not merely against usury as we might infer from EVˢ., *i. e.*, interest above the rate established by law,
but against any compensation whatever for a loan. Now the
charges made against the Judeans in vv. ²⁻⁵ say nothing about
interest, and they do not even imply that interest was charged.
The inability to pay the principal of the loans would account for
the loss of property. Nehemiah may have assumed that interest was exacted in order to bring the oppressors within the
pale of the law.—*And I gave against them a great assembly*] can
scarcely be right, though supported by the Vrss.; for the nobles
and lenders and complainants were already present, and v. ⁸
continues the charge already begun. The true text was probably *I gave a great curse against them, v. i.* Nehemiah was not
averse to such a course (see 13²⁵), where we have a similar
conjunction of expressions: "I reproved them and I cursed
them," and note Guthe's text in 4⁸.—**8.** *And I said to them*],
i. e., to the nobles and rulers of v. ⁷, *we have bought our brethren
the Judeans who had been sold to the nations, according to our
ability*], or better with 𝕲 *of our own free will.* This introduces a
new feature in Nehemiah's administration. He had for twelve
years been wont to purchase such Hebrews as he found who had
been sold as slaves to foreigners, and had set them free. The
text as it stands would imply that he repurchased the slaves as
his means permitted. 𝕲 is stronger, indicating that he bought
these slaves voluntarily that he might give them freedom.
"The nation" means the foreigners in and about Judah, so
Ryle and Kost. There is no reason to suppose that Nehemiah
refers to people he had bought in Persia and brought back with
him, apparently Stade's view (*BT.*³²³). That would weaken
the contrast now plainly stated, *but* YOU *on your part are selling
your brothers; and they are sold back to us*], so that some of the
slaves which he had been buying, as he now discovers, were the

very ones sold by these nobles. No wonder he was exceedingly angry and cursed them roundly. No wonder, in view of this public exposure, that *they were silent and not a word did they find*], *i. e.*, for reply. In Jb. 32³ we have a similar expression, "and they found no answer." The expression is peculiar and happy, implying inability of the accused to find any defence to the charge.

9. Nehemiah now appeals to the nobles both on religious—*should ye not walk in the fear of our God*—and on patriotic grounds—*because of the reproach of the nations our enemies*]. *The fear of God* here, as often in the late literature, is merely synonymous with "religion" or "law." The meaning is not that the people should dread God, for to fear him is to live according to his laws. In the latter clause 𝕲 lacks "the nations." "The enemies" would refer to people like Sanballat and his crew, who had made so much trouble during the building of the wall. "The nations" are the foreigners to whom the slaves had been sold. It is impossible to make these identical, and one term or the other must be dropped. In later times than Nehemiah "foreigner" and "enemy" were synonymous. The appeal to the people and to God to avoid the scorn of their enemies is common in the postexilic literature (see, *e. g.*, Ps. 42⁴· ¹¹ Jo. 2¹⁷). How could these Jews have the face to claim superiority for their God and for their religion if their enemies saw the strong and rich taking advantage of the weak and poor.—**10.** The Hebrew text has: *and now, I, my brethren and my servants, have loaned them money and corn*]. Nehemiah then admits that he has done the same thing for which he curses the nobles (v. ⁷).—The latter part does not help much, *let us therefore remit this interest*]. The ancients were puzzled by the passage. 𝕲 reads: *we have supported them with money and corn.* 𝕳 keeps text in v.ᵃ, but in v.ᵇ has: *we do not ask back what is due to us; we grant that that is another's money for common use.* One Greek text adds to v.ᵇ: *and we will give for them money to put away from you this interest.* The course of least resistance to make sense would be to render: *we have loaned them money and corn and we have remitted this interest*, that is, they also had made loans to the needy, but had scrupulously followed the law, making no interest charges.—**11.** Nehemiah now leaves off the denunciation of the oppressors and the recitation of his own good deeds and makes a definite demand: *restore to them this very day their fields, their vineyards, their oliveyards and their houses*]. "Oliveyards" is not found in vv. [2-5] and is an addition because of its constant use in Dt., which law-book is the basis of the actions described here.—The text continues: *and the hundredth of the money and the corn, the wine and the oil which you loan them*]. "Wine and oil," like "oliveyards" above, are added from Dt. "Hundredth" cannot be right. Such a petty remission would be useless to relieve the distress. 𝕳 saw the difficulty and renders: *rather more than the hundredth*. Most authorities by a slight change of text render: *the interest of the money and corn*. The demand was therefore to restore the real estate so that the people would have the means to subsist and to pay their just debts, and to relinquish the unlawful interest which had been charged. Geike reads, "remit this exaction of a pledge" (*Hours*, vi,[497]).—**12.** The nobles and leaders had been silent in the face of the accusation, v. [8], for they could only plead guilty, and silence sufficed for that. Now they are called upon to speak, for a definite requirement was laid upon them. They accept in full the governor's terms: *we will give back* [the fields, vineyards, and houses being understood as objects], *and we will not exact from them* [the interest of the money and the corn also understood as objects].—*And I summoned the priests*], for either they alone had the right to administer an oath or an oath sworn by them was peculiarly solemn and binding: *and I made them* [the accused] *swear to do according to this word*]. Nehemiah was not satisfied with their bare word. An affidavit is more convincing than a mere personal statement, even after all the centuries since Christ taught the contrary.—**13.** *Further I shook out my arms*]. "Lap" of RV. is quite unjustifiable. In one text we find *hands*. The Hebrew word is usually rendered *bosom*, and after *sinum* of 𝕳, interpreted to mean the *bosom of the garment;* see Ryle's highly imaginative description. The action was symbolical, a common method among the Hebrews of reinforcing an idea. The

point of the action appears in the following: *so may God shake out
every man who does not establish this word from his house and from
his property and so may he be shaken loose and empty*]. The
man is to be separated violently from his property, so that they
part company. To make the symbol effective, therefore, we
should expect that Nehemiah's shaking would result in loosen-
ing something from him. This could not be his arms or his
bosom, but might well be his cloak. If he shook loose his
outer garment, so that it fell from his shoulders, then the point
would be clear. But perhaps it would not be necessary to say
all this, as the people were looking on. What happened may
be put thus: *and I shook my arms* [or *bosom*], and then as the
garment fell from him, he went on: *so may God shake it.—And
all the assembly said, Amen*]. The assembly does not mean a
formally called and authoritative body, but the crowd of people which had gathered. Indeed, Nehemiah's summoning the
priests (v. [12]) shows that there was no formal assembly, otherwise they would have been present. "Amen," which plays such
an important rôle in Christian worship, was much used as a
form of solemn congregational assent in postexilic times.—
And they praised Yahweh]. The subject is "assembly"; naturally those who had been released from their oppressive burdens would have good cause for praise.—*And the people did according to this word*]. The "people," however, had been the
complainants, v. [1]. It would be more natural to find *the nobles
and the rulers*. At all events, they are meant; for the reference
is to the execution of the demand made upon the rich by Nehemiah. The people had nothing to do except to go back to their
houses and fields.

> This passage, vv. [1-13], is from N., but it has been worked over more or
> less by the Chr. 𝕲 shows that in some texts the process had gone
> further than appears in MT. The most liberal expansion is in vv. [9 f.],
> which are probably wholly from Chr. ויאמר can easily be explained
> then. Chr. introduces a speech for Neh. by prefixing the natural
> "and *he* said," forgetting that Neh. always wrote "and *I* said."

14–19. Nehemiah recites the good features of his rule, that he had imposed no exactions upon the people, that he

had supported the poor from his own purse, and that he had contributed to the work on the wall.—**14.** *He commanded me*], *i. e.*, King Artaxerxes. We might transpose "the king" from v.ᵇ to this place as subject.—*To be governor in the land of Judah*]. This is the only reference to the official position of satrap, to which Nehemiah had been duly appointed. The fact is important in view of the question of Ezra's relation to Nehemiah. The latter could scarcely have accomplished such great works in development and administration without the support of official status.—*From the 20th year even to the 32d year of Artaxerxes*]. The 20th year (2¹) was the date of his coming to Jerusalem; from 13⁶ it appears that the 32d year indicates the close of his term. He merely says here that he served for twelve years without pay, but the implication is that his whole period of service is included.—*The bread of the governor I did not eat*]. The satrap was wont to require provisions for his extensive household to be supplied by the people over which he ruled; *cf.* Solomon's method, 1 K 4⁷ ᶠᶠ·. Nehemiah did not exact this customary demand, but lived from his own purse.—**15.** In contrast to his own generous rule, he describes the precedents he had ignored: *now the former governors who had preceded me laid a heavy burden upon the people*]. The implication is clear that there had been Jewish governors before Nehemiah, so Mey. (*Ent.*⁸⁸). The general statement is followed by specifications: *they took from them for bread and wine forty shekels of silver each day*]. 𝔊 furnishes *daily* in place of the meaningless *after*, which would mean that forty shekels (about $25) were required daily from the whole people, a reading followed by Guthe, Ryle, *et al.*, interpreting the words to mean forty shekels of silver each day for the purchase of bread and wine.—Another specification is: *also their servants domineered over the people*]. The meaning must be that the satrap's servants were not only insolent and haughty, but also that they filled their hands at the expense of those who were helpless before them. The person in authority is never wont to lend a very willing ear to complaints against his subordinates.—**16.** *And further the work of this wall I supported*]. *This wall* shows that Nehemiah was in Jerusalem when

he wrote (or spoke) those words. In the Chronicler's report,
c. 3, there is no statement of work done by Nehemiah. The
meaning may be that he contributed of his means toward the
work. "Continued" (for "supported") of EV[s]. is meaningless
and unjustifiable, being due to the misplacing of this chapter.—
And a field I did not acquire]. He may mean that he had not
taken land for debt as the nobles had, or that he had acquired
no landed property in any way during his governorship. He
was not richer, but poorer, as the result of twelve years' rule.—
And all my servants were gathered there at the work]. This would
more naturally follow the first clause describing Nehemiah's
personal efforts toward laying up the walls. The clause about
the field introduces a different subject and breaks the narrative,
and it may be misplaced.—**17.** Now we come to another point
in Nehemiah's generosity. *The Judeans, to the number of a
hundred and fifty, who had come to us from the surrounding nations*
[ate] *at my table*].

> The text adds: *and the rulers.* But it is difficult to see what place
> they have here. Their presence would not be accounted a good deed
> on his part. Feeding the poor is meritorious, but feeding the rich is
> a different matter. We may best follow 𝔊 and om. this word. Fur-
> ther the text inserts *and*, making two classes sitting at the governor's
> table, the Judeans and *those who had come in from the nations.* This
> again obscures the point of merit. After the fall of Jerus. in 586 many
> Jews found homes among the neighbouring peoples, just as a large
> colony went to Egypt and settled there. Neh. was endeavouring to
> build up not only the walls of the city, but a state, and therefore would
> naturally strive for the return of his own people. Some were induced to
> return. They would surely be the poorer classes, and would for a time
> have no means of subsistence. Neh. generously fed them at his own
> expense. This charitable act he might properly ask God to reckon to
> him for righteousness, v. [19].

18. To feed this large body would require liberal provisions,
so we have information from the commissary department: *and
that which was prepared for one day*]. עשה is often used in this
sense of preparing food for the table, *v.* BDB.—*One ox, six
choice sheep and fowl were prepared for me*]. This would provide
meat for one meal for six or eight hundred people, provided

they ate as we do with other varieties of food. With the 150
poor Judeans and Nehemiah's own household, he had to feed
some four or five hundred people.—The next statement is not
so clear; literally, it runs: *and between ten days with all wine
in abundance*]. With the aid of 𝕲 we may get: *and every ten
days wine for the whole multitude.* The "multitude" was probably the large body which fed at the governor's table. While
the select few might have had wine daily, only at intervals of
ten days was this drink served to the whole household.—*And
even with this I did not exact the bread of the governor*]. In spite
of the unusual requirements of his court, he did not collect his
just dues. The reason he gives adds greatly to his credit: *because the service was heavy upon this people*]. The "service"
would naturally suggest the rebuilding of the walls; but such a
restricted sense is not admissible, and the word may properly
refer to the whole labour imposed upon a feeble people by the
effort to build up a respectable state. 𝕴 expresses the true idea
very well: *for the people were enfeebled,* a condition made clear
by the testimony of this whole chapter.—**19.** Nehemiah closes
with a characteristic prayer: *remember to me for good, O my God,
all that I have done for this people*], cf. 6¹⁴ 13²². ²⁹. ³¹.

2. **וב"בנינו**] 𝕲 ἐν υἱοῖς η. καὶ ἐν θυ.; 𝕴 *filii nostri et filiæ nostræ multæ
sunt nimis.*—**רבים**] Guthe follows an old proposal and reads **ערבים**, as
v. ³.—**ונקחה**] 𝕲ᴸ δότε οὖν ἡμῖν = **תנו לכן לנו**; 𝕴 *accipiamus pro pretio
eorum.*—**3.** **ברעב**] 𝕲 καὶ φαγόμεθα, so **ונאכלה** as in v. ².—**4.** 𝕲 adds:
καὶ οἰκίαι ἡμῶν; 𝕲ᴸ puts the nouns in the dative preceded by ἐπι; 𝕴
precedes by *deniusque.*—**5.** 𝕲ᴮ has υἱοὶ ἡμῶν υἱοὶ αὐτῶν by transposition. To this 𝕲ᴸ adds ὅτι σάρξ μία ἐσμέν, an expression not elsw. in
OT., for Gn. 2²⁴ refers to marriage.—**לעבדים**] 𝕲ᴮ εἰς δούλας; 𝕴 *in servi-
tutem.*—**נכבשות**] 𝕲ᴸ βίᾳ ἀφαιροῦνται.—**ואין לאל ידינו**] 𝕴 *nec habemus, unde
possint redimi* (**גאל**); 𝕲ᴮ reads χειρὸς, 𝕲ᴸ καὶ οὐχ ἰσχύει ἡ χεὶρ ἡμῶν.—
לאחרים] 𝕲 τοῖς ἐντίμοις, a word which always stands in Ne. for **חור**
(2¹⁶ 4⁸. ¹³ 5⁷ 6¹⁷ 7⁵), rd. therefore **להורים**.—**6.** **ויעקתם**] 𝕲ᴸ amplifies:
τὴν φωνὴν τῆς κραυγῆς αὐτῶν.—**7.** **וימלך**] † is explained as a loan-word
from the Aram. mng. *counsel;* BDB. explains: "I considered carefully." But from his course there seems to have been no cause for very
deep pondering before the attack on the rich. Ges.ᴮ gives, "I went
to myself for advice"; but Neh. was not wont to go to any one else.
The Vrss. all understand the word in this sense. It might easily be

connected with the common מלך, *my heart was king over me, i. e.*, he
acted according to his feelings.—קהלה] is found in late poetry in but
two places, Dt. 33⁴ Sirach 7⁷. We have קהל in v. ¹³. But the governing vb. would not be נתן, for which 𝕲ᴸ has συνήγογον, 𝕳 *congregavi.*
Moreover, what sort of an assembly would Neh. call against the leaders? There was no democracy in those days. If this were right, להם
in v. ⁸ would refer to the assembly. In spite of the Vrss. I would rd.
קללה, *curse.*—8. אנחנו] 𝕳 adds *ut scitis.*—כדי בנו] 𝕲 ἐν ἑκουσίῳ ἡμῶν; 𝕳
secundum possibilitatem nostram. 𝕲 shows בנדבתנו, a reading generally
ignored, but better than MT. 𝕲ᴸ has a long insertion or plus at this
point: ἡμῖν δὲ δουλεύουσιν οἱ ἀδελφοὶ ἡμῶν οἱ υἱοὶ Ἰσραήλ; ἐπαινέσω ὑμᾶς
οὐκ εὖ πεποιηκότας. καὶ ἡμεῖς γὰρ ἀποδωσόμεθα τοὺς ἀδελφοὺς ἡμῶν τοὺς
Ἰουδαίους τοὺς πραθέντας ἐν τοῖς ἔθνεσιν. ἱκανῶς, τέκνα, ἐποιήσατε. εἰδὲ μή,
κἂν ὑμῖν ἀποδώσεσθε αὐτούς. In part, this is a repetition, and generally
speaking it does not throw any additional light upon the situation.—
ונמכרו לנו] lacking in 𝕲ᴮᴬᴬ.—דבר־] 𝕲ᴸ adds ἀποκρίνασθαι (לענות); 𝕳 *nec
invenerunt quid responderent.* In Jb. 32³ we find מענה מצאו לא.—9.
ויאמר] Qr. ואמר, but we should rd. ואמרה as vv. ⁷ ꜰ.—הלוא] 𝕲 οὐχ οὕτως.
—ביראת־] 𝕲ᴸ οὐδὲ ὡς φοβούμενοι τὸν θεὸν ἀπεστρέψατε τὸν ἀνειδισμόν
κ. τ. λ.—הגים] lacking in 𝕲ᴮᴬᴺ.—10. נערי] 𝕲 οἱ γνωστοί μου = ידעי, but
MT. agrees with 4¹⁷.—נשים] 𝕲 ἐθήκαμεν, i. e., נשׂים, from שים. 𝕲ᴸ adds
to the v. καὶ δώσομεν ὑπὲρ αὐτῶν ἀργύριον ἀποθέσθαι ἀφ᾽ ὑμῶν τὸ βάρος
τοῦτο. 𝕳 has: *non repetamus, in cummune istud æs alienum conce-
damus, quod debetur nobis.*—11. ומאת] 𝕲ᴮᴬᴺ καὶ ἀπὸ, 𝕲ᴸ καὶ ἐκ. Most
authorities rd. משאת, v. Guthe's note.—אשר־] 𝕲ᴮᴬᴺ καὶ, 𝕲ᴸ ὑμεῖς.—
נשים] 𝕲 ἐξενέγκατε (יצא). 𝕳 adds to v., *date pro illis.*—הצני] 𝕲ᴸ τὰς χεῖρας μου, representing חָפְנִי, *hollow of the hand,* as in Ex. 9⁸ Lv. 16¹². חצן
is defined as *bosom,* but in the few places of its occurrence (Ps. 129⁷
Is. 49²²) it might better mean *arms.*

14. גם] lacking in 𝕲ᴮᴬ.—פחם] is, as Guthe says, impossible. Following 𝕲 εἰς ἄρχοντα αὐτῶν, he reads פחהם. But as the sf. has no
antecedent, I should prefer פחה.—המלך] is lacking in 𝕲ᴮᴬ; 𝕳 has *rex*
as subj. of צוה. Such a subj. is required there, and I would transpose
accordingly.—לחם הפחה] 𝕲ᴮᴬᴺ βίαν αὐτῶν. In v. ¹⁵ these texts have
τὰς βίας for הפחות. Hatch and Redpath give no Heb. equivalent in
these places. Βία represents a different Heb. word in almost every
place it is used. It is therefore difficult to ascertain what the Gk.
translators had before them. It is certain, however, that they had
neither לחם nor הפחה. In v. ¹⁸ we have ἄρτους τῆς βίας, so βία represents some word which was rd. in place of פחה in all three places. 𝕲ᴸ
has ἄρτον τῆς ἡγεμονίας μου, 𝕳 *quæ ducibus debebantur.*—15. 𝕲ᴸ lacks
הראשנים and avoids a redundancy which, however, is not uncommon
in Heb. The same text adds κλοιόν as obj. of הכבידו, reading therefore
על־העם.—For על העם] 𝕲ᴮᴬᴺ has ἐπ᾽ αὐτούς = עליהם.—אחר כסף] 𝕲 ἔσ-
χατον ἀργύριον (ουᴸ), 𝕳 *et pecunia quotidie.*—נעריהם] 𝕲ᴮᴬᴺ οἱ ἐκτετιναγ-

μένοι αὐτῶν = נעוריהם.—שלטו] ⑤ᴮᴬᴺ ἐξουσιάζονται, ⑤ᴸ ἐκυρίευσαν.—16. החזקתי] ⑤ᴮᴬᴺ οὐκ ἐκράτησα.—נערי] lacking in ⑤ᴮᴬᴺ. ⑤ᴸ has τὰ παιδάρια μου καὶ πάντες οἱ συναγμένοι.—17. הסגנים] lacking in ⑤ᴮᴬᴺ. והבאים] ו is lacking in ⑤ᴬᴺ.—על-שלחני] ⑤ᴸ ἐπὶ τὴν τράπεζάν μου ἐξενίζοντο; the last word not occurring elsw. in ⑤ and mng. "to wash out" is scarcely appropriate here. Some vb. like "sat" or "ate" might have stood here.—18. שש] lacking in ⑤ᴮ.—צפרים] ⑤ χίμαρος = צפיר; ℿ exceptis volatilibus.—להרבה] ⑤ᴮᴬᴺ τῷ πλήθει; ⑤ᴸ παντὶ τῷ πλήθει, παντὶ τῷ λαῷ, an explanatory dup. ⑤ rd. לרב and that is clearer than MT.—זה] ⑤ τούτοις, referring to the people whom Neh. fed. In v. ᵇ ℿ has in some respects a variant text: et alia multa tribuebam: insuper et annonas ducatus mei non quaesivi, valde enim attenuatus erat populus.

NE. 6. FURTHER EFFORTS OF SANBALLAT AND THE OTHERS TO THWART NEHEMIAH.

This c. is the direct continuation of c. 4. The wall proper is finished on the 25th of Elul. The enemy first tries to tempt Neh. to a conference in the plain of Ono. He puts them off repeatedly with a promise to meet them when his great work is finished. The enemy then tries to frighten him with a rumour that he is planning rebellion and aspiring to royalty. These measures proving futile, the foe tries a new method and hires a prophet to induce him to act as a coward and to commit sacrilege. A secret correspondence was carried on between To., who was related by marriage to prominent Judeans, and certain conspiring nobles, trying to frighten Neh. to some overt and self-condemning action. In this narrative the plots of the enemy are so much in evidence that we hear of the walls only incidentally.

1-4. Sanballat, being thwarted in his efforts to check the work on the walls by force, now falls back on treachery.—1. Here the three leaders of the conspiracy are named, as in 2¹⁹, Sanballat, Tobiah, and Geshem; in v. ² Tobiah is not mentioned. We might suppose that only two were willing to go so far as to indulge in personal violence. It may be that Tobiah had reasons for declining to be a party to the plot, since he was related to some Jewish magnates, but it is more likely that the name has been accidentally dropped in v. ².—*The rest of our enemies*] is explained by the full list in 4¹. We note a change of construction, *when it was reported to Sanballat*, etc., perhaps indicating that the enemy had left the immediate neighbourhood of Jerusalem.—*That I had built the wall, and that there was not left a breach in it*]. The tenses show that the wall proper was now finished, a distinct advance on the last notice in 3³⁸.

> In spite of the trying conditions described in c. 4, the last stone had been laid in the wall. ᵔ, however, offers a tempting substitute for the second clause, *i. e.*, *then there was no spirit left in them*, *cf.* 1 K. 10⁵, where a similar statement is made of the Queen of Sheba. Grammatically this text is better, as the sentence makes a suitable apodosis, thus: *when it was reported to them . . . there was no spirit left in them*. They were dispirited because of their failure to check the upbuilding of the old hostile city. On the other hand, MT. makes a more suitable connection with the following clause, which continues the description of the progress of the work. Neh.'s own account of the work reads very unlike the story told in c. 3.

Up to that time I had not set up doors in the gates]. The expression shows that Nehemiah was writing some time after the event, and that at the time of writing the gates were finished. This is in agreement with 5¹⁴ (*v. s.*). The gate is the open space in the wall, and the "doors" would close that gap. Jerusalem was still vulnerable, but only at a few narrow points, and thus comparatively easily defended.—**2.** Therefore the opportunity for a secret or open attack had gone by. The enemy must adopt a different plan of campaign. It appears that the city with its menacing walls was not so dispiriting as the capable and energetic leader. The purpose of the enemy was now to accomplish his destruction, not openly but by subtlety. If they could get rid of Nehemiah they could easily dispose of the walls he had built. They sent him a message therefore: *come, let us meet together in the hamlets in the plain of Ono*]. ᵔ is more specific, reading: *let us make a treaty*, presumably of peace, and intending to throw Nehemiah off his guard.

> Ono is found only in postex. writings (Ezr. 2³³ Ne. 7³⁷ 11³⁵ 1 Ch. 8¹²), in all these places as the name of a city. The place is located near Lydda, about 12 miles north of Jerus. Stress is laid upon the fact that Neh.'s reply indicates that the rendezvous was some distance away, Berth. Sieg. Ryle; but Neh. might have made the same reply if the appointed place were close by. The conference would interfere with his work without any travelling. The indefiniteness of the proposed

meeting-place is apparent; therefore it has been suggested that under the word for villages is concealed a n. p., perhaps Kephirah. The art., at all events, indicates a definite place.

Now they were devising to do me harm]. This is Nehemiah's own divination of the purpose of the meeting, a conviction amply justified by future events. The character of the harm cannot be determined by the very general Hebrew word; but it is difficult to conceive of any other aim than personal violence, for the mere slackening of the work would be useless to these foes.— **3.** Sanballat must have sent some one to Nehemiah to convey this message, probably his servant, as v. [5]. The governor does not reply by those who had brought the invitation, but sends messengers of his own. Perhaps he could not trust hostile persons to give his exact words. This reply is, as our text runs: *I am engaged on a great work and am not able to go down. Why should the work stop while I forsake it and go down to you?*] The excuse made is not the conviction of a sinister purpose in the invitation. Nehemiah does not see fit to disclose his suspicions, or possibly his knowledge. He lays stress upon his exacting occupation. The interrogative sentence is questionable, as we find some interesting variants in ⅌, viz., *lest the work should stop. When I have finished it, I will go down to you.* This makes an important change in Nehemiah's answer and reveals his shrewd purpose. He is striving to gain time so that the gates may be finished. We see then why he gives no hint of his suspicions, and indulges in no defiance, as he well might as governor of Judah; for he wants to keep his enemies idle and expectant until he is in a sufficiently strong position openly to defy them. The superiority of this text is evident, and the change required in MT. is not very great. It does, however, make Nehemiah indulge in a somewhat vague promise to do what he presumably never expected to do, vague because the clause "when his work was finished" might point to a very indefinite period indeed.— **4.** *And they sent unto me according to this word four times*], that is substantially the same message, possibly with an addition, like "the matter is too important for delay." If MT. is accepted in v. [3], then the "four times" is unintelligible. If ⅌

is received, then the repetition of the request with increased
urgency and Nehemiah's reiterated reply, "I will go down as
soon as I finish the work," are alike clear. But curiously 𝔊,
which requires it, lacks the "four times," and MT., which cannot endure it, contains the words. To find a true original text,
selection is frequently essential.

**5–9. Sanballat sends a letter to Nehemiah trying to alarm
him with a report that he was aiming at royalty.—5.** *According to this word*] is a meaningless repetition from v. [4]. The
phrase could only be retained by a loose interpretation like
"for a similar purpose."—*A fifth time*] referring to the four
times of v. [4]. This time Sanballat, who alone is credited with
action, sends his servant, but the servant is not his spokes-
man, for he carries *an open letter in his hand*]. Why Sanballat
changed from oral messages to a written document is not made
clear—possibly to make the damaging charge more forcible.

> Many efforts have been made to explain the statement that the
> letter was open. In Je. 32[11] we have the statement that the purchaser
> of land was given "a deed [book] of purchase, the sealed and the open."
> This may be explained by comparison with a Bab. contract tablet in
> which the real document was covered with an outer envelope of clay
> upon which a summary of the contents was written. If Sanb. sent a
> tablet, as is surely possible, the mng. is that there was no outer en-
> velope. We are still in the dark, however, as to why attention is
> called to this fact. The common idea that an open letter was insulting
> —as held, *e. g.*, by Thomson, *Land and Book*, iii,[64] is wrong, for it would
> be stupid for Sanb. to insult a man whom he was trying to entice to a
> meeting. It is tempting to change a single Heb. letter and rd. "a *large*
> letter." The letter was short so far as our information goes, but it was
> long relatively to the short oral messages, and we may have only a sum-
> mary. Or "open" may be a technical term no longer understood.

6. The charge now made, Sanballat says, came to him from
reports among the nations, the foreign peoples surrounding
Judah.—*And Gashmu says*] is troublesome. It can hardly mean
that Gashmu—before called Geshem—indorses the report, the
implication of EV[s]. We may omit with 𝔊, or understand *so
Gashmu says*. Sanballat is the author of the letter, but he
makes his co-conspirator the author of the report.—*Thou and*

the Judeans are minding to rebel]. This, of course, is a serious charge: *therefore thou dost build the wall*], not as a defence against such foes as Sanballat, but against a possible Persian army.— *And thou wilt become for them a king*]. The charge is now, indeed, grave. To change from satrap to king would be an open act of rebellion. This is a similar accusation to that by which the Jews finally made Pilate listen to their cries (Jn. 19$^{12 \text{ f.}}$). The charge appears plausible enough in itself in view of the general restlessness of subject peoples, the Jews in particular having a genius for rebellion.—*According to these words*] must either be omitted, for sense cannot be forced into it in this connection, or transferred to the beginning of the verse, thus: *in it was written according to these words*].—**7.** The gravamen of the letter was the suspected aspiration toward royalty. Upon this point the changes are rung: *Even prophets thou hast set up to proclaim concerning thee in Jerusalem*]. In the old kingdom of northern Israel most of the numerous revolutions were instigated by prophets (*v.* my *Hebrew Prophet*, c. 7), but we naturally suppose that men like Ahijah and Elisha acted in accord with the spirit of God which was in them. In the time of Judah's dependency prophets were active in fomenting rebellion (*v.*, *e. g.*, Je. 28). They were the natural media for this purpose because they were patriotic. But unfortunately there is abundant evidence that it was easy to find prophets to proclaim whatever was desired. Balak could not understand a prophet who would not speak as he was paid. Zechariah had pretty nearly said of Zerubbabel that he would be king (Zc. 4$^{6 \text{ ff.}}$). We know that there were hordes of prophets in Jerusalem in the postexilic period (*Hebrew Prophet*, c. 4). It is perfectly possible that some of these had actually said the words charged by Sanballat, but it is certain that Nehemiah had not inspired their utterances, for these prophets were a despised class (Zc. 13$^{3-5}$), and Nehemiah would not be likely to have dealings with them. If we may judge from Zc. the prophets of the period deserved the contempt in which they were held (Sta.^{320}). The prophecy which Nehemiah was accused of instigating consists of two words in Hebrew, but requires more space in English: *there is a king*

in Judah]. The idea is that this terse oracle would be reiterated again and again, until the passions of the people were
aroused for action. Some texts of **G** render quite differently:
thou hast set up prophets for thyself, that thou mayst sit [or *rule*]
in Jerusalem for a king over Judah. There is no advantage in
this reading, but it shows the difficulty in the ancient deciphering
of obscure passages in MSS. The danger of such reports is now
plainly indicated: *and now it will be reported to the king according to these words*] or better with **GH**: *these matters will be reported
to the king, i. e.,* Artaxerxes. Sanballat's letter is very shrewd:
he does not himself make a charge, but pretends to give friendly
information of the dangerous gossip which is so widespread that
the Persian king is sure to hear it. It does not matter whether
it is true or not. If such a report reached the ears of a sovereign,
ever suspicious of disloyalty in subject peoples, the result would
be disastrous, even though the charge were false.—Sanballat
concludes by repeating the substance of his first message, v. [2]:
and now come and let us take counsel together], or possibly *meet together.* The object of the conference is made to appear friendly
that they might counsel as to the best means of extricating
the satrap from a situation full of peril to him.—**8.** *And I
sent unto him*], whether by a written or oral reply we are not
informed.—*It has not been done according to these words which
thou sayest, but thou inventest them from thy heart*]. The reply
is brief and covers two points, a general denial of the accusation,
and the assertion that Sanballat had made it out of whole
cloth. Nehemiah may mean merely to deny that he has any
disloyal aspirations, but he may mean to deny the charge *in
toto*, even that there was any such report among the foreign
neighbours. At last he speaks plainly to the enemy and by accusing him of manufacturing the story in his own mind breaks
off all negotiations. Meanwhile the work on the gates had
reached a point enabling him boldly to scorn his enemies.—
9. This verse cannot be original. It may be wholly an interpolation by the Chronicler or a modification of some comment of
Nehemiah, now no longer recoverable.—*All of them would make
us afraid*], but it was Sanballat alone who wrote the letter.—

Their hands will let go the work and it will not be done]. The work is, as always in N., the wall-building. Sanballat had tried to stop that, but as the wall was already finished, v. ¹, an effort to scare the people from the task is manifestly out of place here.—*And now strengthen my hands*] is a fragment of a prayer which may be genuine. On account of its broken character and to make it fit the context, 𝔊 has rendered, *I strengthened my hands*. In this form the clause might be a part of the section following.

10-14. Shemaiah the prophet is hired by the enemy to persuade Nehemiah to do some act by which he might be discredited.—In large part this narrative is obscure, the text is corrupt in places, and there are transactions indicated which are no longer intelligible.—**10.** *And I went to the house of Shemaiah.*] The name occurs many times in our books, but this person is not mentioned elsewhere. Sachau cites the name of Shemaiah and his father Delaiah in illustration, but the names there are Delaiah and Shelemaiah (*Pap. u. Ost.*²⁰). He is particularised from the others by naming his father and grandfather, whose names are not found otherwise in our sources. He was certainly a prophet, but a corrupt one, and that is all we know about him. For what purpose Nehemiah went to his house is not clear. *I* is emphatic, though that use of the pronoun for emphasis is weakened by repetition in our sources, being especially common in N. It is probable that the governor depended, to a certain extent, upon the prophets for information about the purposes and plans of the enemy. The prophets were often possessed of much political information, and that is the object of his voluntarily seeking out Shemaiah, *v. i.*—*And he was shut up*]. This cannot mean that he was ceremonially unclean, as Robertson Smith suggests, for the prophet straightway proposes that they shall go to the temple. The meaning can hardly be "kept under cover," as in Je. 36⁵, for Shemaiah was in his own house. "Secretly" as 𝔥 has, perhaps by interpretation, is not right, for Nehemiah would scarcely have gone secretly to a paid tool of Sanballat's. Since the following "and he said" lacks an introduction, we may best sup-

pose there was originally in the text something like "now he
had sent for me." Shemaiah was the one desiring the interview,
and Nehemiah came to his house at his request. The plot
which the prophet pretends to reveal would be abundant reason
for his summons. Or it may be that the original read, *now he
was a prophet;* that statement would be helpfully enlightening
here.—Shemaiah's proposal is: *let us meet at the house of God in
the midst of the temple and let us shut the doors of the temple*]. The
verb is very suspicious in the first clause. The two who would
go together could hardly meet by appointment. Shemaiah's
idea is plainly that they should *conceal* themselves and thus
avoid the danger which is impending. "Temple" as distinguished from "house of God" would mean the inner sanctuary,
and that would naturally be the best place of refuge. The holy
of holies in Zerubbabel's temple therefore had doors of its own,
which would be shut for more effective concealment. Shemaiah's
meaning is evidently that assassins would not look for their
victim in such an unwonted place.—The reason for hiding is
given in impressive amplitude in the text, the redundancy, however, not occurring in the best Greek versions: *for they are coming
in to slay thee, yea, at night they are coming in to slay thee*]. The
character of the message implies that Shemaiah had sought the
interview. The assassins are naturally the emissaries of Sanballat, who could get into the city in some disguise. *At night*
is general, but the impression conveyed is *this very night,* and if
that were the correct reading the repetition would be less ob-
jectionable. There would be no use hiding in the sanctuary
against foes coming "some night." The urgency of the situation would explain Shemaiah's sending for the governor at
this particular time.—**11.** Nehemiah's reply, as our text stands,
is in parts sadly lacking in clearness: *should a man like me flee?
And who is there like me that should go into the temple and live?
I will not go in*]. $\mathfrak{G}^B$ has at least a more intelligible text: *who is
the man that would go into the house and live? i. e.,* to save his life.
The air is cleared, perhaps sufficiently, by dropping the second
like me, which is an error by dittography. Then we would have:
should a man like me, holding the highest position in the state,

and so carrying great responsibilities, flee from danger?   And even so, who is the man [so cowardly and base] that would enter the temple, not to pray or offer sacrifice, but to save his life?   The temple is a place for worship, not an asylum in time of danger.

12. *And I discerned, and lo! no God had sent him*], so we may represent the unusual place of the negative in the original. How Nehemiah recognised that Shemaiah spoke without inspiration is a mystery.   Perhaps in a very human way: Nehemiah could not accept the counsel of the prophet; if the word had been of God, he must obey; as he refused to hearken, he could only justify his course by drawing the conclusion, certainly justified, that no God had part in the message.—*For the prophecy he spoke unto me*], after which we should expect a clause like, *came from his own heart*, to make an antithesis to *no God had sent him*.   It may be that we should read: *for the prophetess had spoken to me, v. i.* on v. [14], and thus he had received warning of the plot.—*And Tobiah and Sanballat had hired him*].   This text we may accept as reasonably certain, though Guthe gives some weight to a Greek reading *had hired a multitude*.   But while we might believe that the foe had bribed several people in Jerusalem, the collective term *multitude* or *crowd* could scarcely be applied to Shemaiah.   Further, the statement is necessary to explain Shemaiah's attempt to lead the governor astray; for he would scarcely take such a course of his own accord.   The bribe explains his action.

13. *In order that he be bribed*], the only permissible rendering, shows the impossibility of the text.   The fact seems to be that the words are a dittographic repetition.   It suffices to drop *in order that*, so we should have *he was bribed in order that I might*, etc.   The rest of the verse connects directly with v. [12], explaining why Shemaiah was hired: *in order that I might be afraid and do thus and sin, and it [I] should be to them for an evil name, in order that they might reproach me*].   With 𝕲 we may read *I* instead of *it*, though *it* might be explained with some forcing. *Do thus* can only refer to hiding in the temple.

The sinning must refer to his taking asylum in the temple.   The whole thing then reduces to two points, showing cowardice, and entering the sanctuary. A leader who is a coward can scarcely pilot the ship of state unless the seas are very smooth. Neh. would, indeed, get an evil name if he were known as a coward and as one who misused the temple. We might well ask what harm it would do Neh. if his enemies had grounds to heap reproaches upon him. Neh., indeed, was little concerned with what his enemies outside the city might say; but their effort in this stroke was to weaken his influence in the city among those over whom he ruled. Once get him to show timidity and they would have a story to circulate which would undermine his great influence and power. This section is important because it is the first intimation we have that Neh. had enemies in the city, enemies not due to his acts but to Sanb.'s pay.

14. Another imprecation is poured out against the two bribers (cf. 3³⁶ ᶠ·): *Remember, O my God, against Tobiah and Sanballat according to these their deeds*]. We note the absence of Geshem: cf. absence of Tobiah, v. ². As we have really "*his* deeds" perhaps *Tobiah* is a gloss. The prayer is that God would do to them as they had vowed to do to him. He asks God to remember their evil deeds, as he had asked for the remembrance of his own righteous acts, cf. 5¹⁹. The rest of the verse may be interpreted in two exactly opposite senses, according to the text we accept. MT. makes it a continuation of the imprecation, but directed toward *Noadiah the prophetess and the rest of the prophets who were scaring me*]. This is difficult, for surely Shemaiah would be named and not included in the group of "the rest of the prophets." Again, the meaning would have to be *who tried to scare me;* "would have put me in fear," ARV. The English translators strove for intelligibility, but that rendering is certainly not extractable from the Hebrew. Quite another sense is given by a reading in 𝕲ᴸ, in which the remembrance for evil of v. ª becomes now a remembrance for good toward the prophets, *who were giving me warning*. We thus understand the omission of Shemaiah. Noadiah, a prophetess not otherwise mentioned, was working for Nehemiah as Shemaiah was working against him. She may be the prophetess suggested in v. ¹², who disclosed the source of Shemaiah's cunning advice. While the change from imprecation to supplication is surprising, on the whole the latter interpretation seems preferable.

**15-19. The completion of the walls produces consterna-
tion among the enemy and fear among the nations. Further
plots are revealed in Jerusalem.—15.** *And the wall was completed on the twenty-fifth day of Elul*]. Elul, mentioned only here,
is the 6th month, corresponding to August–September. The
wall was completed therefore about September 10. *Of the
fifty-second day*]. This reckoning, in spite of the reproduced
awkward phrasing, must mean the period within which the
walls were reconstructed. The shortness of the time has
aroused wonder in some quarters and suspicion in others. The
work must have been done with astonishing celerity. The
enemy were constantly surprised at the rapid progress. It
seemed to the nations the work of God, v. [16], because concluded
with miraculous speed. There was every incentive for Nehemiah to rush the defences of the city. There was evidently a
vast force at work, and skilfully distributed so as not to interfere
with each other. Josephus, who followed the Esd. text, gives
two years and four months as the time for the work on the walls
(*Ant.* xi, 5, 8). If the date Elul is correct, it was less than six
months since Nehemiah obtained leave of absence from Artaxerxes, 2[1]. He could therefore scarcely have been in Jerusalem
much more than two months. The whole verse looks like the
work of the Chronicler, and yet some statement about the wall
is natural here.—**16.** That this verse is hopeless as it stands
is shown by a fairly literal rendering: *and it was when all our
enemies heard—and all the nations round about us were afraid,
and they fell greatly in their eyes, and they knew that this work had
been done of God.*

There are two ways in which we can clear up the passage: (1) By assuming an ellipsis which told the effect upon the enemy of hearing about
the completion of the walls. (2) By supposing that "all the nations
round about us" is an interpolation by the Chr. to whom *enemy* and
foreigner were syn. The real sense seems to be: *when our enemies
heard, they fell greatly in their own eyes, and they were exceedingly afraid.*
In the text as it stands, *and they fell greatly in their eyes*, we have
to assume "they" to refer to the *enemy* and "their" to the *nations.*
Such looseness is hardly conceivable in such a writing as we know
these memoirs to be. Neh. is all through describing his struggles with

a particular enemy and "the nations" have no place in the story. The latter part is clear. As explained above, on v. [15], the hand of God alone enabled the Jews to do such a stupendous work in so incredible a time.

17. Now we have further light on the desperate attempts of Tobiah to overthrow the great leader; for Tobiah becomes the leader now in place of the discredited Sanballat. Two slight corrections are necessary to make good grammar: *also in those days*], note the vague reference to the time, an expression generally referring to a period long antecedent, *many letters from the Judean nobles were going to Tobiah, and Tobiah's* [letters] *came in to them*]. A vigorous correspondence was carried on between Tobiah and those high in Judean affairs, the object of which is explained in v. [19b], to frighten the great leader. Naturally this correspondence was carried on secretly. Nehemiah may have learned about it from Noadiah and the other prophets (*v. s.* v. [14]). The governor of ancient times, like the present rulers in despotic governments, must have an extensive secret-service department. Nehemiah naturally regards this correspondence as disloyal to him; the mere mention of it shows his attitude.—**18.** *For many in Judah were conspirators with him*], or were bound to him by an oath, but the sense is best expressed by conspirators (BDB.). These were the Judean nobles of v. [17]. The reason he could inveigle so many Jews is made clear by his connections in marriage: *he himself was son-in-law to Shekaniah*]. Shekaniah is a common name in our sources, but this one cannot be identified unless with one named in 3[29] (*cf.* Che. *A. Jr. Th.* 1901,[441]). It is clear though that Shekaniah must have been one of the nobility or occupied some prominent position in Jerusalem. Then again Tobiah had contrived a marriage between his son Johanan and the daughter of Meshullam. (Sanballat's daughter was the wife of Eliashib the chief priest, 13[28].) The name of the wife's father only is given, because he was a prominent man (*cf.* Ne. 3[4, 30]). It is even contended that he was the contemporary head of the house of David (Herzfeld, *Gesch. Isr.* i,[384].—**19.** The contents of the correspondence are now exposed. *Also his goodness they were reciting before me*].

Most Greek texts have *his words*. If MT. is correct, there is a play on Tobiah's name, which may be translated "goodness of Yahweh." The sarcasm is evident. The purpose would plainly be to make Nehemiah think well of Tobiah. His efforts must therefore have been in line with Shemaiah's, to undo the governor by advice which had a friendly appearance.—*And my words they were carrying to him*]. Perhaps *words* may mean more than *speech* here. Tobiah would be much more concerned to know what Nehemiah did than to hear what he said.—*Tobiah sent letters to frighten me*], that is, by telling Nehemiah of imaginary dangers, *v. s.* on v. [17].

Here we reach the end of the long story of obstacles placed in Neh.'s path by the determined efforts of Sanb. To. and Geshem to prevent his restoration of the defences of Jerus. The section dealing with the walls in N. ($2^{10}-7^4$, omitting c. 3, 5) is really a history of Neh.'s successful thwarting of all their plots. The work on the walls is mentioned only incidentally. We cannot appreciate the stupendous accomplishment of the great leader unless we take into account the fact that the walls were restored in the face of great danger and of constant interference.

1. [בניתי] 𝔊ᴮ ᾠκοδομήθη.—[בה פרץ] 𝔊ᴮᴬᴺ ἐν αὐτοῖς πνοή, *i. e.*, בהם נפץ or possibly רוח, as 1 K. 10⁶. 𝔊ᴸ has a dup. ὑπελείφθη ἐν αὐτῷ διακοπή, καὶ οὐ κατελείφθη ἐν αὐτοῖς πνοή, bearing most convincing testimony to this reading.—**2.** [נועדה] 𝔘 *percutiamus foedus* = נכרתה.—[כפירים]. A definite place is indicated and Sieg. suggests כפירה.—**3.** [למה] 𝔊 μὴ ποτε, prob. למען.—[ארפה] 𝔊 τελειώσω αὐτό, 𝔘 *venero;* 𝔊 shows אמלאה.—**4.** [ארבע פ'] lacking in 𝔊ᴮᴬᴺ.—[כדבר הזה] 𝔊 κατὰ ταῦτα, 𝔘 *juxta sermonem priorem.* 𝔊ᴬ lacks all of v.ᵃ, one of the rare cases in which this cod. has the shortest text.—**5.** [כדבר הזה] lacking in 𝔊ᴮᴬᴺ. It is an erroneous repetition from v. ⁴.—[פעם ה'] lacking in 𝔊ᴮᴬᴺ; 𝔊ᴸ πέμπτον, so lacking פעם.—**6.** [ונשמו אמר] lacking in 𝔊ᴮᴬᴺ, elsw. always גשם, though former is prob. correct.—[כדברים האלה] is meaningless here. 𝔊 and 𝔘 connect with following, καὶ πρὸς τούτοις, reading only והאלה; 𝔘 *propter quam causam.*—**7.** [לקרא] 𝔘 *quæ prædicent.* 𝔊ᴮᴬᴺ ἵνα καθίσῃς (ישב).—[מלך] 𝔊ᴸ ἐβασίλευσας.—[כדברים] 𝔊 οἱ λόγοι = הדברים, so 𝔘 *verba hæc* in acc.—[לכה ... יחדו] differs from the invitation in v. ² by a single letter, א for ר. Surely the vb. must be alike in both cases. It is hard to choose, as either makes good sense.—**8.** [בוראם] elsw. only in 1 K. 12³³; 𝔊 ψεύδη, 𝔘 *componis.*—**9.** [חזק] 𝔊ᴮᴬᴺ ἐκραταίωσα; 𝔊ᴸ ἐκραταιώθησαν (αἱ χεῖρές μου); 𝔘 *confortavi.*—**10.** [והוא עצר] 𝔘 *secreto*, which may be an interpretation or represent הוא סתור. Perhaps we should rd. נביא והוא, *v. s.* —[ההיכל] *bis* lacking in 𝔊, but 𝔊ᴸ has θύρας τ. ναοῦ.—[כי ... להרגך].

𝕲ᴮᴬᴺ ὅτι ἔρχονται νυκτὸς φονεῦσαί σε = כי באים לילה להרגך. Our text shows the repetition of a word by dittog.—**11.** 𝕲ᴮᴬᴺ καὶ εἶπα τίς ἐστιν ὁ ἀνὴρ ὃς εἰσελεύσεται εἰς τὸν οἶκον καὶ ζήσεται = ואמרה מי האיש אשר יבא אל־הבית וחי, an important reading which has not received much notice.—**12 f.** [דבר 𝕲ᴮᴬᴺ λόγος = דָּבָר.—שכרו למען שכור הוא]. Guthe says truly that this passage defies any attempt at interpretation as it stands. There is undoubted evidence of corruption, largely by a copyist's error. 𝕲 offers some help; we find: ἐμισθώσαντο ἐπ᾽ ἐμὲ ὄχλονᴮᴬᴺ, *i. e.,* שכרו עלי המון. But this scarcely represents MT. 𝕲ᴸ has ἐμισθώσαντο αὐτόν; that would be merely שכרוהו, and thus we have intelligibility. שכור למען is explicable as a case of dittog., and הוא is the misplaced obj. of the vb. The least change to make sense is to om. למען.—והיה] after 𝕲 rd. ויהיתי.—**14.** [הנבאים 𝕲ᴮ τῶν ἱερέων.—מיראים] 𝕲ᴸ ἐνουθέτουν = מבנים, giving an entirely different sense.—**16.** [כל lacking in 𝕲ᴮ; the word is unnecessary.—ויפלו . . . . בעיניהם] 𝕲 has φόβος (𝕲ᴬ φ. μέγας) as subj. of יפל. 𝕳 renders *et conciderent intra semetipsos.* Difficult as the text is, these variants offer no help.—**17.** [מרבים]. 𝕲ᴮᴬᴺ ἀπὸ πολλῶν = מֵרַבִּים.—אגרותיהם] sf. lacking in 𝕲ᴮᴬᴺ, so 𝕳, which has *multæ epistolæ.*—**18.** 𝕲 adds to end of v. εἰς γυναῖκα = לאשה, necessary acc. to Heb. usage.—**19.** [טובתיו 𝕲ᴮᴬᴺ τοὺς λόγους αὐτοῦ = דבריו; 𝕲ᴸ τὰ συμφέροντα αὐτῷ.

7¹⁻⁵. The doors are put in place; a guard is stationed to watch the gates. On account of the magnitude of the enclosed city and the paucity of the inhabitants, Nehemiah calls a general assembly.—1. This is the first part of a temporal sentence: *and it was when the wall was built and I had set up the doors, and gatekeepers were appointed*]. To this the Chronicler was irresistibly drawn to add the completion of the trio *and the singers and the Levites*] (so Sm. *Listen,* 26⁴⁶), who had nothing whatever to do with the present situation. The setting up of the gates is mentioned only incidentally, as a second note of time after "the wall was built." We do not know when they were completed, probably not within the fifty-two days of 6¹⁵. We have only negative information in 6¹. The events described certainly took place upon the finishing of the gates, therefore soon after the story of c. 6. The gatekeepers were charged with the custody of the gates, and certainly performed some police duties.—**2.** *Then I commanded Hanani my brother and Hananiah the captain of the fortress in Jerusalem*]. On *Hanani v.* 1². On *fortress v.* 2⁸. The fortress was probably connected with the temple and was doubtless the military head-quarters as well as the seat of government. *Hananiah* is a name recurring frequently, Ezr. 10^{28} Ne. 3$^{8.\ 30}$ 10^{24} 12$^{12.\ 41}$. Whether these are all different persons, it is hard to say. From the particularity of his mention here it is apparent that this one cannot be identified with any other.—Nehemiah had given him a position of trust on account of his character, *for he was like a man of truth*], and so different from the lying prophets and conspiring nobles; and because of his religious zeal, *and he feared God more than many*]. *Fearing God* is here following God's will, not living in dread. Nehemiah does not need to give any reason for the selection of Hanani; it sufficed that he was his own brother.—**3.** To these trustworthy officers Nehemiah's orders are given for the safety of the city, *the gates of Jerusalem shall not be opened until the sun is hot*]. The time is not very specific, but the conditions would be met some time after sunrise.—The next clause is corrupt. From the part which is clear, *let them close the doors and bar them*], we can infer that the corrupt clause must have indicated the time for shutting the gates. But our text has *and until they are standing*], which is meaningless. 𝕲 has as a substitute: *and while they are still watching*. This is clear in itself, but there is no antecedent to the pronoun, for the guard is mentioned later. Without changing the text much, we may get good sense, *while it is still standing*, "it" referring to the sun, and the time indicated is then shortly before sunset. That corresponds suitably with the hour for opening the gates. The doors were to be kept securely fastened except during the hours of broad daylight. Instead of *he stationed*] we must read either *I stationed* or *station ye*, preferably the former.—*Guards of the inhabitants of Jerusalem*]. The great difficulty in this treacherous community was to find men that could be trusted. Those who lived in the city would, at all events, have the strongest motive to fidelity.—*Each one in his watch*] shows that there was a regular military organisation; the guards were divided into watches, being on duty a certain number of hours each day.—*And each one in front of his house*] sounds like the voice of the Chronicler. The guards must have been stationed on the walls and at the gates; for they were not so much po-

licemen as sentries to watch against attack from the enemy
outside. It is doubtful whether as yet there were houses in
which they could live, *v. i.*

4. Here we begin a new section, dealing with the sparseness
of the population. Perhaps songs like Ps. 127, 128, were composed at this period by a poet who was sympathetic with Nehemiah.—*Now the city was wide of hands*]. *Of hands* is omitted
in 𝔊 because not understood. The phrase *wide of hands* is
common, Gn. 34⁴¹ Ju. 18¹⁰ Is. 22¹⁸ 33²¹ 1 Ch. 4⁴⁰ Ps. 104²⁵. This
is predicated of land, of the sea, and of streams. The meaning is given usually as wide in both directions. It really means
wide in all directions and is equivalent to *long and broad*, otherwise *of hands* would add nothing to *wide*.—*And great*] emphasises
the extent of the city, and makes an effective contrast with the
following: *but the people in its midst are few*]. Those who actually lived within the city walls, from whom the guard had to be
enlisted, were few in number, and besides were obliged virtually
to camp out, *for houses had not been built*]. In spite of this the
Chronicler had each sentry stationed in front of his house, v. ³!
This statement is authentic and important. When Nehemiah
came to Jerusalem he found the temple restored, and that was
practically all there was of Jerusalem, so the city was indeed
in ruins, 2³. The houses referred to in Hg. 1⁴ may have been
without the city. The new Judah had been built up on agricultural lines, a necessary condition in a new community, and
was without a headquarters. We can see clearly that Nehemiah's mission was to restore Jerusalem. Now the city had
walls and was safe as a residence, and so the problem confront-
ing Nehemiah was to induce people to live in the city and to
see that they had houses to dwell in. He proceeds to take
measures accordingly.—**5.** *And my God put it into my heart*].
Doubtless he had earnestly pondered the grave problem of this
great empty space enclosed with walls; then the solution comes
to him, as to many earnest souls in ancient times and modern, by
inspiration.—*And I assembled the nobles and the rulers and the
people*], and then the Chronicler, deciding to attach a list of
names at this point, makes Nehemiah say appropriately *for
taking their genealogies*]. Nehemiah had a vastly different pur-

pose, fortunately recorded in most Greek Vrss., *i. e., for a conference*. To provide people and houses in the city the governor needs the co-operation of the people, and therefore he calls a great assembly to consider the problem.—*And I found the genealogical record of those who came up in the former time, and I found written in it*]. This is the Chronicler's note to connect the preceding passage with his list. Here we say farewell to Nehemiah and his work until we reach c. 11, which describes the effort to secure residents for Jerusalem and therefore directly follows.

2. הבירה] ⑤^{BAN} τῆς βείρα, βάρεως^L, 𝔙 *domus.*—עליריד"] ⑤^{BAN} ἐν I. The prep. is lacking in ⑤^L; 𝔙 *de.*—**3.** With Qr. rd. ואמר.—ועד הם עמרים] ⑤ καὶ ἔτι αὐτῶν ἐγρηγορούντων = ועיר הם שקרים; 𝔙 *cumque adhuc assisterent.* I should rd. ועיר היא עמדה.—אחזו] ⑤^{BAN} σφηνούσθωσαν = נעל, ἀσφαλιζέσθωσαν^L = ואחז. 𝔙 *oppitatæ.*—והעמיר] rd. והעמרו or better ואעמיר.—להתיחש]—**4.** רחבת ירים] ⑤ πλατεῖα^{BAN} + χερσί^L.—**5.** אלהי] ⑤ ὁ θεός.—and היחש] εἰς συνοδίας^{BAN} = לעצרות. 𝔙 *ut recenserem eos.*

7^6–8^{1a} is a duplicate of Ezr. 2–3^1. The notes are found on the former passage. For convenience of reference, a table of corresponding vv. is given. In the list of the Neth. (Ezr.$^{43-54}$ Ne.$^{46-56}$) the v. divisions are not the same in the two recensions, and therefore in that part the table is only approximately correct.

EZR.	NE.	EZR.	NE.	EZR.	NE.	EZR.	NE.
1	6	19	22	37	40	55	57
2	7	20	25	38	41	56	58
3	8	21 }	26	39	42	57	59
4	9	22 }		40	43	58	60
5	10	23	27	41	44	59	61
6	11	24	28	42	45	60	62
7	12	25	29	43	46	61	63
8	13	26	30	44	47	62	64
9	14	27	31	45 }	48	63	65
10	15	28	32	46 }		64	66
11	16	29	33	47	49	65	67
12	17	30		48	50	66	68
13	18	31	34	49	51	67	69
14	19	32	35	50	52	68	70
15	20	33	37	51	53	69	71, 72
16	21	34	36	52	54	70	73
17	23	35	38	53	55	(3) 1	(8) 1^a
18	24	36	39	54	56		

NE. II. THE DISTRIBUTION OF THE POPULATION OF JUDAH.

There are three parts to the c.: (1) The drafting of people to live in Jerus., vv. ¹ f.; (2) the list of the residents of the holy city, vv. ³⁻²⁴; (3) the towns of the Judean province, vv. ²⁵⁻³⁶. The list is parall. that in Ezr. 2 = Ne. 7⁶⁻⁷², both lists covering essentially the same classes, laity and temple officers. and both containing geographical as well as genealogical material. The list before us is earlier, for here we find but a handful of people in Jerus. (1,400 laity) and their presence the result of Neh.'s special efforts, while the great majority of the people live in the smaller towns, 33 of which were occupied. And yet it can scarcely be in its original form, since the elaborate genealogy of the few clansmen named would have no place. 𝕲 shows expansion since the list was made (see notes). The text has certainly suffered from corruption, as is evidenced by comparison with the parallel in 1 Ch. 9, and it has also suffered, like many other writings, from the hands of editors. Vv. ¹ f. connect directly with 7⁵ᵃ, not with 7⁷³ᵃ as Sta. (*Gesch.* ii,⁹⁸) and Sm. (*Listen*,²³) hold, and show the measures adopted by the assembly to secure a population for the newly walled city. Ew. has been followed by many scholars in the belief that the reference is to the first settlement in the time of Cy. The passage is not so badly placed as that contention would require. The list which follows, vv. ³⁻²⁴, originally contained the names of those who had taken residence in Jerus. The rest, vv. ²⁵⁻³⁶, is an appendix to show the distribution of the remainder of the people in the province, and so completing the record. On the names see Sm. *Listen*,⁷ ᶠ·, Kost. *Wied.*⁸⁷ ᶠ·, Mey. *Ent.*¹⁰⁵ ᶠ·.

1. *And the chiefs of the people resided in Jerusalem*]. That describes the condition when the assembly of 7⁵ met; the official classes alone resided in Jerusalem. There are indications here and there to support this statement, such as the secret correspondence with Tobiah, the ruling classes being the Jewish party. The wealthier people, being few in numbers, might live in the city, while the working people remained on the soil from which they derived their living.—*And the rest of the people*], in contrast to the preceding, hence the common people, *cast lots to bring one out of ten to dwell in Jerusalem*]. As the lot was always deemed sacred, then the one chosen would feel a strong obligation to move to Jerusalem. It is plain that residence in the holy city was not considered desirable.—*And nine parts* [were left] *in the cities*] is the correct idea. Yet a strict construction would connect with the lots: one part to dwell in Jerusalem and nine parts allotted to the cities, *i. e.*, those named in vv. 25 ff.. We must assume that all the common people had been residing in the cities, such as are enumerated at the close of the chapter, and that now one-tenth of them come to Jerusalem. For *hands* denoting fractional parts see also Gn. 47²⁴ 2 S. 19⁴⁴ 2 K. 11⁷.—**2.** *And the people praised all the men who volunteered to dwell in Jerusalem*]. Some evidently offered themselves as residents for the holy city, and these would be in addition to those drafted by lot. The commendation shows the desperate plight of a city largely devoid of a population.

3-24. The residents are treated as in other lists by classes. We note, as in Ezr. 2, that the laity precede the temple officers.—
3-9. The list of laymen in Jerusalem. This is parallel to 1 Ch. 9²⁻⁹.—**3.** *These are the chief men of the province who dwelt in Jerusalem*]. These are the same as the officers of the people, v. ¹. This is the Chronicler's introduction to the catalogue of names which follows.—The rest of the verse connects more appropriately with vv. 20 ff.; in fact, it is a duplicate of v. 20 and has no place here.—*And in the cities of Judah there dwelt, each man in his possession, in their cities, Israel, the priests and the Levites and the Nethinim and the sons of Solomon's servants*]. The last class is not mentioned subsequently, while we miss from the catalogue "porters," v. ¹⁹, and "judges," v. ²². If *in their cities* is authentic, the meaning is *each one in his own city*. The list of these cities is found in vv. 25 ff.. The implication is that in Jerusalem dwelt only the civil officers and the common people, drafted by lot or volunteering, v. ¹, while the temple officials and laity alike dwelt in the towns. The statement is almost exactly what we have in 7⁷³ = Ezr. 2⁷⁰ and in 1 Ch. 9².—**4.** The original sequence to v. ² runs: *and in Jerusalem there dwelt some*

of the sons of Judah and of the sons of Benjamin] see on Ezr. 1⁵.
The two tribes of the postexilic period, the Jerusalemites coming
from both tribes. 1 Ch. 9³ adds "Ephraim and Manasseh."
Of the sons of Judah would connect very well with v. ³ᵃ. *Judah*
is individual here, not tribal, since the sons are traced back to
him.

Now we have had sufficient intr. to expect a formidable list of names.
As a matter of fact, we have just two, Athaiah, whose ancestry is traced
to the sixth generation, and Maaseiah, traced to the eighth generation.
If these were chief officers, perhaps two Judeans would be all that are
required. The elaborate genealogy marks them as important person-
ages. Athaiah is *of the sons of Peres*]. Peres was a son of Judah and
Tamar, Gn. 38²⁹.—**5.** *Kal-hozeh*] was the father of one of the gate-
builders, the ruler of the district of *Mizpah*, 3¹⁵.—*The son of the Shi-
lonite*] or with most scholars the Shelanite, a descendant of Shelah, another son of Judah from a Canaanite, Gn. 38⁵.—**6.** *All the sons of Peres
who dwelt in Jerusalem were* 468 *men of valour*] cannot be right here, for
we are dealing with two individuals, one of whom was a descendant
of Peres. A Gk. text saw the trouble in part and made Maaseiah a
son of Peres; but that is an attempt to correct one error by creating
another. The v. is either to be regarded as a fragment having reference to the common people drawn by lot to reside in Jerus., or we
should substitute *Judah* for *Peres*, and then we learn that 468 Judeans
were living in the holy city. In 1 Ch. 9⁴⁻⁶ we find three clan-names,
Uthai, Asaiah, and Jeuel, with a total for the three clans of 690. Uthai
is traced to Peres with four intermediate generations as against five
here, and without a single name in common, yet עתיה and עותי are certainly identical. Asaiah has no genealogy assigned save that he is a
descendant of Shelah, therefore מעשיה and עשיה are identical (*v.* Curt.).
—**7.** Of the Benj. we are sure of but one name, Sallu, who is carried
back to the eighth generation to Isaiah, but not the well-known
prophet.—**8.** That this v. is corrupt is clear from a literal rendering—
and no other is possible—*and after him Gabbai Sallai* 928]. A Gk.
text offers *his brothers* in place of *after him*, but then the numeral is
in the air. We should expect after v. ⁶ *all the sons of Sallu were* 928. It
is prob. that the original text named two Judean leaders who had 468
followers, and one Benj. with 928 clansmen. Gabbai Sallai is assumed to be a double name, but that explanation is very unlikely.
Sallai is a priest in 12⁷·²⁰. The alternative is to emend on basis of

𝕭, and rd.: *and his brothers Gabbai and Sallai: all the sons of Benj.*
The Chr.'s corresponding phrase is "and their brethren for their generations."—**9**. *Overseer over them*], *i. e.*, over the 928 Benj. of v. **ˢ**.—*Over
the second city*], *i. e.*, one of the two districts into which the city was
divided for administrative purposes, 3⁹· ¹². Senuah occurring also in 1
Ch. 9⁷ can hardly be a different name from Senaah, Ezr. 2³⁵ Ne. 3³ 7³⁸;
v. s. on Ezr. 2³⁵. For Judah the son of Senuah the Chr. has Hadaniah
the son of Senuah, but in the genealogy of Sallu! In 1 Ch. 9⁷⁻⁹ we find
the list of Benj. with four clan-names, Sallu, Ibniah, Elah, Meshullam,
and the total is 956. There is little else in common. In Ch. Sallu is a
son of Hassenuah, and there is no mention of the officers.

10–14. The list of the priests who dwelt in Jerusalem.—
These are arranged in three groups: (1) 10–12ª, Jedaiah, Jakin,
and Seraiah, and their brethren engaged upon the work of the
temple, numbering 822; (2) 12ᵇ–13ª, Adaiah and his brethren
who were heads of the fathers, numbering 242; (3) 13ᵇ–14ª,
Amashsai and his brethren, men of valour, numbering 128,
making 1,192 in all. The ancestry of the priests is traced back
in various degrees, Adaiah's to the seventh generation. This
is the same list found in 1 Ch. 9¹⁰⁻¹³, though with numerous
variations as noted below.

.**10**. *Jedaiah the son of Jojarib, Jakin*]. 1 Ch. 9¹⁰ has Jedaiah and
Jehojarib (the same name) and Jakin. Our text cannot be right,
for Jakin lacks the conj. As Jedaiah and Jojarib are separate pr. in
12⁶· ¹⁹, Ch. is more likely to be right. Jedaiah was one of four pr. who
came from the captivity in the time of Zer. before the temple was rebuilt, Zc. 6¹⁰· ¹⁴ (*v.* Mar.). This is prob. the same man.—**11**. This v.
is identical with 1 Ch. 9¹¹ exc. that *Azariah* appears in place of *Seraiah*
Both are common priestly names, occurring together in 10³, and it is
impossible to tell which is correct. Acc. to 1 Ch. 5⁴⁰ (*cf.* Ezr. 7²),
Seraiah was the son of Azariah, but Seraiah's son was carried into
captivity by Nebuchadrezzar, so that both Seraiah and Azariah were
pre-ex. pr., another warning as to the dependence to be placed on these
lists. The line in 1 Ch. 5³⁸ ᶠᶠ· and Ezr. 7¹· ² is Ahitub, Zadok, Shallum,
Hilkiah, Azariah, Seraiah, while ours is Ahitub (Merajoth), Zadok,
Meshullam, Hilkiah, Seraiah. Acc. to Ezr. 7² Seraiah was the father
of Ezra.—*Chief officer of the house of God*], *i. e.*, high pr. As our text
stands this chief pr. may be either Seraiah or Ahitub.—**12**. *And their
brethren doing the work for the house*]. Ch. more specifically: "the
work of the service [or worship] of the house of God." The reference is
here prob. to the official ministrations of the pr. in the restored temple,

though it may refer to the work on the building of the temple. Jedaiah was a pr. who returned before the temple was built.

12ᵇ–13ᵃ. *Adaiah*]. His ancestry in 1 Ch. 9¹² is Jeroham, Pashhur, Malchijah, lacking Pelaljah, Amsi, and Zechariah.—**13ᵃ.** *His brethren heads of the fathers*], *v.* Ezr. 1⁵. Ch. has "their brethren heads for the house of their fathers." These pr. had a higher official position than those in the first group, though the title does not suggest what that position was. It is, strictly speaking, a lay title, but is surely applied to pr. here.

13ᵇ–14ᵃ. *Amashsai*] occurs nowhere else, and is a very dub. Heb. name. BDB. suggests *Amasai*, but 1 Ch. 9¹² has *Maasai*, a very common postex. name (Gray,¹⁷³) and differing from *Amasai* only in the order of the first two consonants. The genealogy differs as in the other cases, but the identification of persons is clear. The ancestors in Ch. are Adiel, Jahzerah, Meshullam, Meshillemith, and Immer.—**14.** *And their brethren*]. As our text runs we should rd. *his* brethren as in v. ¹³, since Amashsai is the antecedent; but *men of valour*] standing alone is a military term and hardly applicable to the pr. In 1 Ch. 9¹³ we have a statement grouping Jedaiah, Adaiah, and Maasai, and combining 12ᵃ 13ᵇ and 14ᵃ, thus: "and their brethren, heads for the house of their fathers, 1,760, men of valour for the work of the service of the house of God." The Chr. ignores the three classes of our text, and makes a larger total, 1,760 as against 1,192. The valour is shown in the temple work, and that does not consist in laying stones, but in performing rites and ceremonies. Ch. therefore shows a later hand than our text.—**14ᵇ.** *And the overseer over them was Zabdiel the son of the great ones*]. This name is not elsw. found save as an officer of David, 1 Ch. 27². He must be regarded as overseer of the third group only, since Jedaiah was the chief at the temple. There may be a n. p. concealed under the title "great ones," but it is absurd to regard this as such a name, as even ARV. does. The texts of 𝔊 either lack the title or translate it.

15–18 = 1 Ch. 9¹⁴⁻¹⁶. The Levites.—The two Hebrew texts differ materially, though the agreements are such as to make original identity certain. The chief Greek Vrss. show a shorter text, containing less than half of the material here. The list consists essentially of the genealogy of three Levites, Shemaiah, Mattaniah, and Abdah. Ch. adds a fourth, Berechiah, but his name is lacking here because he dwelt in the villages of the Netophatites, *cf.* 12²⁸.

15. Shemaiah's ancestry is identical in 1 Ch. 9¹⁴ until we come to *the son of Bunni*], for which we find "of the sons of Merari," a son

of Levi.—**16.** This v. is represented in Ch. only by three n. p., of
which Bakbukkai may be the Bakbukiah of v. ¹⁷. The v. is lacking in
the chief Gk. texts; it is a parenthetical note and properly construed
says: *and Shabbethai and Jozabad of the chiefs of the Lev. were over the
outside work of the house of God*]. The Gk. text which has this passage
construes *outside* with *house*, mng., as in Ez. 41¹⁷, *the holy place* in contradistinction to *the holy of holies*. But we find "outside work" in 1
Ch. 26²⁹, which is specified as that of officers and judges, therefore it
is secular. Here the word differentiates the Lev. work from the more
sacred offices of the pr., and perhaps refers to menial tasks.—
Chiefs of the Lev.], similar to "chiefs of the fathers," applied to the
pr. in v. ¹³.—**17.** The best Gk. texts have only *Mattaniah the son of
Macha and Obed [Abdah] the son of Samonei*, showing how these genealogical records have grown even in late times. Mattaniah is here a contemporary of Neh., but in v.²¹ he is three generations earlier. In 1 Ch.
9¹⁵ we find *Zichri* instead of *Zabdi*, names which resemble each other
more closely in Heb. than in English. After Asaph we have four words
not in Ch. EVˢ. make no use of them. The words must give some
further information about Mattaniah, not about Asaph. By emending
the text we get *chief of the praise* [singing], *teacher of the* [liturgical]
prayers]. The Lev. had an important rôle in the public services, and
Mattaniah was the leader in the offices.—*Second of his brethren*] is a
sore puzzle. *Second*, however, is connected with the preceding "chief"
or "first," and the prob. mng. then is that Bakbukiah was next in office
to Mattaniah the chief. "His brethren" would refer to that section
of the Lev. who were trained to lead the chants and prayers.—*Abdah
the son of Shammua*]. 1 Ch. 9¹⁶ has "Obadiah the son of Shemaiah,"
differing chiefly in having *iah* at the end of both names.—**18.** *All the
Lev. in the holy city were two hundred and eighty-four*]. There were
1,192 pr. (*v. s.*), and we see here as elsw. testimony to the comparative
paucity of men belonging to the Levitical order. There are slightly
more than four pr. to each Lev.

19. The Porters.—But two names are given, Akkub and Talmon.
1 Ch. 9¹⁷ adds *Shallum* and *Ahiman*. In Ezr. 2⁴² we find six names of
porters, *Akkub* and *Talmon* being among them. In 12²⁵ six porters
are named, *Mattaniah, Bakbukiah, Obadiah, Meshullam, Talmon*, and
Akkub, the first three of whom are in this list classed as Levitical
singers (v. ¹⁷).—*Who keep watch in the gates*] (lacking in the best Gk.
texts) is the only definition of the function of the porters in these lists.
1 Ch. 9¹⁷⁻³² gives an elaborate statement of their duties, showing that their
office was chiefly connected with the temple gates (*cf.* 1 Ch. 26).—**20.**
This v. is virtually a repetition of v. ³ ᵇ. It may serve as a transition to
mark the fact that the Neth. did not dwell in Jerus. proper. It would
be more appropriate as an intr. to vv. ²⁶ ᶠᶠ.. Vv. ²⁰ ᶠ. are lacking in
the chief Gk. texts.—**21.** *The Neth. were dwelling in Ophel*], so 3²⁶,

q. v. Of the leaders of the Neth., *Ziha* is found in the list, Ezr. 2⁴³ *f.*
Ne. 7⁴⁶ ᶠᶠ., but *Gishpa* is not found elsw. It may be a corruption for
Hasupha, the second name in the list in Ezr. 2.

**22–24. Miscellaneous notes about certain officers and
about the singers.—22ᵃ.** *The chief of the Levites in Jerusalem
was Uzzi*] seems to belong to the list of Levites, vv. ¹⁵⁻¹⁸; 𝕲 lacks
"in Jerusalem," better adapting the clause to its present place.
Uzzi's ancestry is in part common with Shemaiah's and Mattaniah's, vv. ¹⁵⁻¹⁸.—**22ᵇ–23.** *The singers.*—The confusion in the
list is very marked here, but on the whole it is best to follow
MT. and begin a new section with *of the sons of Asaph*], though
Mika is a grandson of *Asaph* according to 4¹⁷.—*The singers were
over the business of the house of God*], so ARV. "Over" is doubtful, as the original means rather *in front of.* It may be that an
attempt was made to say that the quarters of the singers were
in front of the temple.

23. *For the commandment of the king was upon them*], *cf.* 12²⁴, where in
accord with the theory of the Chr. the king who instituted the temple
ritual was David, and David is meant here.—*And a settled provision
for the singers, as every day required*] as ARV. is surely wrong, for we are
not dealing with the support of the singers, but with their duties. It
is difficult to render אמנה in any satisfactory way. Some texts of 𝕲
show another word, "stood over the singers." On the basis of this
hint, we may conjecture: *he imposed upon the singers the duty of a day
in its day.* This resembles closely the confused note in Ch. David
exacted of the singers the strict and punctual performance of their
daily duties.—**24.** *And Pethahiah the son of Meshezabel of the sons of
Zerah the son of Judah was at the king's hand for all business with the
people*]. We are suddenly removed far away from temple officials and
services and plunged into civilian affairs. This v. would fit a record of
the royal officers such as we find in 2 S. 8¹⁵ ᶠᶠ..

**25–36. The Judeans and the Benjamites outside of Jeru-
salem.**—The list is no longer genealogical, but geographical;
we have not a list of the heads of clans, but of the towns inhabited by Jews in the postexilic period. These are in the old
Benjamite and Judean territories. Jerusalem is the centre, but
the holy city was on the ancient borderland between Judah

and Benjamin. The postexilic Judea comprises territory on the north and still more on the south.

The Judean list is contained in vv. ²⁵⁻³⁰ and comprises seventeen towns, located from Beersheba to the environs of Jerus. Of Benj. towns there are sixteen in vv. ³¹⁻³⁶. After some of the names we have "daughters," 6 t., after others "villages" (*bis*), after one (Lachish) "fields," all in connection with the Judean list exc. one (Bethel). Of the seventeen Judean towns, all but two, *Jeshua* (v. ²⁶) and *Meconah* (v. ²⁸), are in the list of towns assigned to Judah in Jos. 15, and the order is the same in both lists. Of the fifteen or sixteen Benj. towns, but three, *Geba*, *Bethel*, and *Ramah*, are among the fourteen assigned to Benj. in Jos. 18. On the other hand, seven are found among the places enumerated in Ezr. 2 = Ne. 7, while not one of the Judean towns finds a place. Possibly the Judeans were reckoned as belonging to the holy city, and the Benj. were the country people so often mentioned *as living in their towns*. Of all these thirty-three towns but one occurs in the list of places from which the wall-builders came, *i. e.*, *Zanoah*, v. ³⁰ (*cf.* Ne. 3¹³). A comparison with the shorter lists of 𝕲 suggests that names have been added in the list at a late period; such additions would be made as the population spread so as to keep the list up to date.

25–30. The Judean towns.—25. *And unto the villages in their fields*] evidently requires something preceding. It would connect very well with 2ᵇ, showing the disposition of the nine parts not allotted to Jerus. We can join to this more immediately the misplaced v. ²⁰; making some necessary corrections by comparison with v. ³ and 1 Ch. 9², we have: *and the rest of Israel were in all their cities, each one in his possession, and* [spread] *unto the villages in their fields.—Some of the sons of Judah dwelt*], the others, of course, being those in Jerus. as described in vv. ⁴ ᶠᶠ·. There follows the list of seventeen towns. *Dibon* is a city of Moab, prob. to be identified with the Judean *Dimonah* (Haupt, in *ZA*, 1887,²⁶⁸). *Yekabseel* appears in Jos. 15²¹ as *Kabseel*, so 2 S. 23³⁰ 1 Ch. 11²²; of course, the same place is meant.—**26.** *In Jeshua*]. This sounds rather strange as a place-name. As no such name is known, and as an unheard-of place is scarcely possible in a list like this, the other names being common, we have to suppose a corruption, as 𝕲ᴸ suggests, or that *in Jeshua* is a marginal note, originally intended to call attention to the fact that these names were to be found in the book of Jos. —**28.** *Meconah*] does not occur elsw. Doubtless it is a corruption for מדמנה, occupying the corresponding place in Jos. 15³¹.—**29.** *En-rimmon*] is incorrectly divided in Jos. 15³², "Ain and Rimmon." On *Zorah* see Moore's *Judges*,³¹⁶.—*Its fields*]. The term originally meant *mountain* or *wild land*, but here the reference is to the cultivated land (GAS. *Jer.* i,²⁹¹).—**30.** *And they encamped from Beersheba to Ge-hinnom*]. The valley of Hinnom ran along the western wall of Jerus., and is given in Jos. 15⁸ as the northern boundary of Judah. Beersheba was the proverbial southern limit of the whole land. The term "encamped," though parall. "dwelt" in v. 2⁵, suggests a temporary condition, and so gives colour to the theory that this c. was originally intended to describe the settlement of a caravan which had recently arrived.

31–36. The Benjamite towns.—The first clause has puzzled interpreters. "The children also of Benj. from Geba dwelt at Michmash" of AV. was revised to "the children of Benj. also dwelt from Geba onward, at Michmash," in ARV. The fact is that we have a slight corruption of a single letter, and the true text reads very simply: *and the sons of Benj. in Geba, Michmash*, etc.—**33.** *Nob*] is doubtless the same as *Nebo*, Ezr. 2²⁹.—*Ananiah*] occurs nowhere else, and is certainly corrupt.—**34** *Hazor*] is doubtless the same as *Baal-hazor*, 2 S. 13²³, as the situation on the border between Ephraim and Benj. favours such identification.—*Gittaim*] elsw. only in 2 S. 4³, where it appears to be a Benj. place.—**35.** *Neballat*] is found nowhere else.—*Ge-haharashim*] means *valley of the craftsmen*, but n. pr. loc. is required here, as in 1 Ch. 4¹⁴. It was prob. a wady near Jerus., known as the residence of a certain class of workmen. Acc. to 1 Ch. 4¹⁴ it was founded by Joab.—**36.** Lit., *and from the Lev. portions of Judah for Benj.*], the mng. of which may be *and some of the Lev. had allotments of Judah and of Benj.*

3. הנתנים] lacking in 𝕲ᴮᴺ.—**4.** עתיה] 𝕲ᴸ Αθαρασθας = התרשתא.—מבני.—] 𝕲 καὶ ἀπὸ υἱῶν.—**5.** השלני]. The pointing should be—הַשֵׁלָנִי, from שֵׁלָה; 𝕲 τοῦ Αηλωνε ᴮᴺ, Ηλωνι ᴬ, Σηλωνει ᴸ; 𝕲 makes מעשיה one of the sons of Peres, having *of the sons of Peres*, corresponding to *of the sons of Judah* in v. ⁴.—**8.** 𝕲ᴸ has καὶ ὀπίσω αὐτοῦ οἱ ἀδελφοὶ αὐτοῦ Γεβουε Σηλεει. οἱ πάντες ἐννακόσιοι εἴκοσι ὀκτὼ τοῦ Βενιαμιν. I suspect a dup. at the beginning rather than a plus, ואחיו being rd. instead of אחריו, the original being, therefore: ואחיו גבי וסלי כל בני בנימין . . . . In that case we should rd. יהודה for פרץ in v. ⁶. The least emendation for v.ᵃ is to rd. וכל בני—**9.** הודויה בן־הסנואה] is to be identified with יהודה בן־הסנואה, 1 Ch. 9⁷.—**10 f.** identical with 1 Ch. 9¹⁰ exc. that בן fails before יויריב and שמנה.—**11.** עזריה = שריה] נגד] 𝕲ᴮᴬᴬ ἀπέναντι (גגר), ἡγούμενος ᴸ.—**12.** . . . . מצי אמצי before בן and lacks first three names 𝕲ᴮ .ᴮᴺ lacking in [ושנים.—**13.** ואחיו] lacking in 𝕲ᴮᴺᴬ.—אמר . . . . אמר lacking in 𝕲ᴮᴺ.—**14.** ופקיר] to end, 𝕲ᴮᴬᴬ καὶ ἐπίσκοπος Βαδιήλ.—בן־הגדלים] 𝕲ᴸ υἱὸς τῶν μεγάλων.—**15 f.** הלוים . . . ועזורסקם] lacking in 𝕲ᴮᴬᴬ.—החיצנה] 𝕲ᴸ ἔργα τοῦ οἴκου τοῦ θεοῦ τοῦ ἐξωτάτου.—**17.** 𝕲ᴮᴺᴬ has only καὶ Μαθανιὰ υἱὸς Μαχὰ καὶ Ὠβήδ υἱὸς Σαμουέι.—יהודה לתפלה] 𝕲ᴸ 'Ασαφ ἄρχων τοῦ αἴνου καὶ 'Ιουδας τῆς προσευχῆς, one of the rare cases where Torrey admits the value of this text (ES.¹¹⁰). In אᵐ· we find, taking in a little of the context to show connection, 'Ασαφ ἀρχηγος τοῦ αἴνου τοῦ 'Ιουδὰ εἰς προσεύχην. To get sense we should rd. התהלה, used in a technical sense for *a psalm;* for יהורה we might rd. יהורע, *teacher.* תפלה has a technical sense as in Ps. 72²⁰ and in psalm titles and means a *liturgical prayer.*—18. הקדיש...כל] lacking in 𝕲ᴮᴷᴬ.—23ᵇ lacking in 𝕲ᴮᴷ. 𝕲ᴸ καὶ διέμενεν ἐν πίστει ἔπὶ τοῖς ᾠδοῖς κ. τ. λ. This is a dup., corrected from MT., but showing originally יעמד for אמנה, since ᴷᵐ· has διέμεινεν ἐπὶ τοῖς ᾠδοῖς. We must rd. וַיַּעֲמֵד, *v. s.*—24. משיזבאל] 𝕲ᴮᴬᴷ Βασηζα.—יהורה...מבני] lacking in 𝕲ᴮᴬᴷ. לויד] 𝕲ᴸ ἐχόμενα.—25. From בע, last syl. of הארבע, to end of v. is lacking in 𝕲ᴮᴬᴷ (save that ᴬ has αρβο).—חצריה] 𝕲ᴸ θυγατράσιν αὐτῆς = בנתיה.—26. 𝕲ᴮᴬᴷ has only καὶ ἐν Ἰησού, 𝕲ᴸ καὶ ἐν Σουα κ. τ. λ.—27. 𝕲ᴮᴬᴷ has only καὶ ἐν Βεηρσάβεε.—28 f. lacking in 𝕲ᴮᴬᴷ. מכנה] 𝕲ᴸ Μαμη, Μαχνα ᴷᵐ·.—30. זנח ערלם] and עזקה וב"] lacking in 𝕲ᴮᴬᴷ.—מבאר] 𝕲ᴮᴬᴸ ἐν Β.—עד גיא הנכ] lacking in 𝕲ᴮᴬᴷ.—31. ועיה] to end of v.³⁵ lacking in 𝕲ᴮᴬᴷ.—36. ...מחלקות] 𝕲ᴸ μερίδες ἐν τῷ Ἰουδὰ καὶ τῷ Βενιαμιν.

NE. 12¹⁻²⁶. A LIST OF PRIESTS AND LEVITES ARRANGED BY PERIODS.

This list was inserted here prob. as a sort of appendix to the preceding lists. It carries us down to a late period, certainly to the Gk. age. The basis of the chron. system is the succession of high pr., v. ¹⁰ ᶠ·, put in by the Chr. as a guide, and covering the whole Pers. period. There are five parts: (1) the names of those belonging to the time of Jes., the associate of Zer., vv. ¹⁻⁹; (2) the succession of high pr.; (3) those of the period of Jojakim, Jes.'s successor, vv. ¹²⁻²¹; (4) Lev. of the time of Eliashib, a generation later, v. ²²; (5) apparently intended to be a list of those of the time of Johanan called here the son (but acc. to v. ¹⁰ ᶠ· the grandson) of Eliashib, vv. ²³⁻²⁵. It appears, therefore, that the passage was originally designed to furnish a list of the pr. and Lev. who were heads of their guilds during the whole of the Pers. period. The passage shows the hand of the Chr. throughout. The big gaps in the best MSS. of 𝕲 show that the list was developed at a late date, and yet it was never completed, unless we suppose that some of the Chr.'s systematic work has been lost. As in c. 11 there is here and there interspersed a phrase defining the functions of certain Lev. On the lists see Mey. *Ent.*¹⁷¹ ᶠ· ¹⁷⁹, Sm. *Listen,*¹⁰.

1-9. A list of priests and Levites who came up with Zerubbabel and Jeshua. The passage purports to be parallel to the list in Ezr. 2³⁶⁻⁴⁰ and Ne. 7³⁹⁻⁴³.

1. *Jes.*]. To make the identification certain 𝕲ᴸ inserts *the son of Josedek.* After this we should expect *the pr.* as we have *the Lev.* in v. ⁸, *cf.* 11⁴. All the names after Shekaniah, *i. e.*, out of the total

22, are lacking in the chief Gk. texts.—**7.** *These were the heads of the pr. and their brethren in the days of Jes.*]. *Brethren* was mechanically inserted after pr., apparently for no other reason than its constant recurrence in the lists of pr. and Lev. It has a technical sense in these lists, like *associates*, those of the same class. The list does not pretend to name all the individual pr., but only the heads of clans.—**8.** The Lev. in two groups; first six names, and then it is said of one of them: *He and his brethren were* [appointed] *over the thanksgivings*]. The antecedent, therefore, must be sg. In view of 11¹⁷ (of which 8ᵇ is a dup.), we should prob. rd.: *and the Lev.; Jes., Binuni, Kadmiel, Sherebiah, Judah, Mattaniah; and Mattaniah was over the thanksgivings, he and his brethren.* Instead of *Jes., Binuni, Kadmiel*, v. ²⁴ has *Jes. the son of Kadmiel.*—**9.** *And Bakbukiah and Unni* [and] *their brethren were opposite them for the functions*]. This may refer to antiphonal singing, or to the changes of orders for different occasions. It is an elaboration of the vague "second" of 11¹⁷, whatever that may mean.—*Unni*] = *Obadiah* in v. ²⁵ and *Abda* in 11¹⁷.

10 f. gives a priestly genealogy from Jeshua, the son of Josedek, to Jaddua. According to Jos. (*Ant.* xi, 8, 5), Jaddua was a contemporary of Alexander the Great. The list therefore extends through two centuries; as there are six generations, the time covered corresponds very closely to that date. Further confirmation comes from the identification of Eliashib with the high priest of Nehemiah's time, 3¹.

12–21. Priests and Levites of a later period.—12. *And in the days of Jojakim*], the father or predecessor of Eliashib, and therefore we are in the period just before Neh.'s advent.—*Priests the heads of guilds were*]. The list in vv. ¹⁻⁶ was of the contemporaries of Zer.; this list gives the heads of those clans a century later. The scheme is to give a clan-name and then the contemporary representative, thus; of the guild or course of Seraiah, Meraiah. The clan-names are those of vv. ¹⁻⁶.—**14.** *Meliki*], but *Malluk* in v. ².—*Hattush* of v. ² fails us here. The omission may be accidental, or, as 𝕲 lacks the name in v. ², it may be an error there.—*Shebaniah*] = *Shekaniah*, v. ³.—**15.** *Harim*] = *Rehum*, v. ³.—*Merajoth*] = *Meremoth*, v. ³.—**16.** *Ginnethon*] = *Ginnetho*, v. ⁴.—**17.** *Minjamin*] = *Mijamin*, v. ⁵. The name of the representative of this clan has fallen out.—*Moadjah*] = *Maadjah*, v. ⁵.—**20.** *Salli*] = *Sallu*, v. ⁶.

22. A list of the Levites of a generation succeeding, i. e., in the days of Eliashib, contemporary with Nehemiah.—All three names recur in the genealogy of high pr., v. ¹¹, being the last three of that list; for Jonathan and Johanan are identical. As Eliashib was the father of Jojada, we might render: *the Lev. in the days of Eliashib, Jojada, Jonathan and Jaddua were recorded as heads of guilds*]. At all events, the three high pr. cannot be classed as Lev.—*And the pr. unto the reign of Dar. the Pers.*] is quite unintelligible here. The idea seems to be that a certain list covered the pr. known as far down the period as the reign of Dar., *cf.* v. ^{23}. It may be misplaced from vv. $^{1-7}$, where the date would be accurate. It is obviously but a fragment. Dar. the Pers. is peculiar, the only case of the gentilic form, and suggests a fragment from an unfamiliar hand.

23–26. Another list of Levites and notes of their duties.—23. Here we find the unusual *sons of Levi* in place of the common *Lev.*, "perhaps to include them with pr.," Berth.—*Written upon the book of the deeds of the days*]. "The deeds of the days" is equiv. to annals or chronicles; it is a technical term used many times, though usually with some further definition, as the annals of the kings of Israel (or Judah). It refers, though, to a historical record, not to a genealogy. But the Chr. wrote history on the theory that genealogies were an important part, and this may pass as his work. In 7^5, however, the correct term, "book of genealogy," occurs.—*And down to the days of Johanan* [or *Jonathan*, v. ^{10}] *the son of Eliashib*], or strictly *the grandson*, vv. $^{10\,f.}$, *cf.* Ezr. 10^6; "son" is not employed very strictly in these records. The words do not fit their present connection, as they require a preceding statement of an earlier date than that of Jonathan. Instead of the inappropriate "book of the chronicles," there may have originally stood "in the days of . . . and down to," etc. Or v. ^{23b} may be connected with v. ^{22a}, the record extending from Eliashib to his grandson. The idea is that there was a record of the Lev. who were heads of guilds down to the time of Johanan, that is, later than Neh.—**24.** The Lev. are divided into two classes by their offices. In the first class we find nearly the same names as in v. ^{8}, Hashahiah, Sherebiah, and Jes. the son of Kadmiel.—*And their brethren in front of them*], 𝔅 *in their courses*, *v.* on v. ^{9}.—The office of this class is *to praise and give thanks*] *cf.* v. ^{8} 11^{17}.—*David*] is here given the prophetic title *the man of God*, to show that his authority in the regulation of the temple service was not royal but prophetic. How different is the David of 2 S. 7, who was enjoined from building the temple by Nathan the prophet!—*Watch next to watch*] ARV., but see v. ^{9} for their watches or functions. 𝔅 renders freely *and they in turn kept watch equally*. It seems more natural to suppose that the reference here is not to standing watches by turn, but to the antiphonal singing, one body of singers opposite another body.—**25.** The second class of Lev. consists of six men, the first three of whom—Mattaniah, Bakbukiah, and Obadiah (=Abda=Unni)—are named in vv. $^{8\,f.}$ 11^{17}, and the last two, Talmon and Akkub, are named as porters in 11^{19}. In 1 Ch. 9^{17} we find also Shallum, corresponding to our Meshullam.—As our text stands their

duties are thus defined: *watchmen, gatekeepers* [their] *office, at the storehouses of the gates*]. Such a description is very prob. wrong. The
Vrss. render variously, 𝕲 having *watchmen, gatekeepers of the watch
when I gathered the gatekeepers.* 𝕳 has: *keepers of the gates and of the
fore-courts before the gates,* a rendering which has the advantage of making sense. All we can say positively is that these men were charged
with the duty prescribed in 7³ of seeing that the gates were watched and
opened and closed at the proper time. This fact, as well as the "I" of
𝕲, suggests a fragment of N. The same function in 11¹⁹ is prescribed
for the gatekeepers. The confusion is surely bewildering. The implication is that the gatekeepers were a branch of the Levitical body.—
26. The text contains two dates, one that of Jojakim the predecessor
of Eliashib, the other that of Neh. and Ezra. But the theory is that
Ezra and Neh. were contemporaries, and it is possibly the intention of
the writer to name three men assumed to be of the same age, and therefore we should expect Eliashib instead of Jojakim. One Gk. cod. connects this date with the following story of the dedication of the walls.
It is suggestive to find Neh. preceding Ezra, contrary to the Chr.'s
arrangement of his material. Strictly speaking, we might interpret
this v. as mng. that the lists enumerated cover the period from Jojakim
to Ezra, a period of considerable length.

2. חטוש] lacking in 𝕲ᴮᴬᴺ.—ישוע] 𝕲ᴸ Ιησου του Ιωσεδεκ.—אמריה] 𝕲ᴸ
Αζαριας.—**3.** From רחם to v.⁷ᵃ, the end of the list, there is a blank
in 𝕲ᴮᴬᴺ.—**4.** עדו] 𝕲ᴸ Αδαιας.—**8.** מתניה] 𝕲ᴮᵀ Μαχανια.—בנוי] 𝕲ᴸ και
οἱ υἱοὶ αὐτοῦ = ובניו.—על-הידות] 𝕲ᴮᴬᴺ ἐπὶ τῶν χειρῶν, 𝕲ᴸ ἐπὶ τῶν ἐξο-
μολογήσεων = על-ההודות as in v.²⁷. And so we should rd. instead of
α. λ., which is a form hard to explain. 𝕲 shows that the error was an
old one.—**9.** 𝕲ᴮᴬᴺ omits all but last word, which is connected with v.⁸.
—After אחיהם] 𝕲ᴸ inserts ἀνεκρούοντο, which in five places represents
four different Heb. words, no one of which can readily be inferred here.—
10. ישוע] 𝕲ᴸ Ἰησους ὁ τοῦ Ἰωσεδεκ.—**12.** היו] 𝕲ᴮᴬᴺ ἀδελφοὶ αὐτοῦ =
אחיו, 𝕲ᴸ has the dup. ἦσαν οἱ ἀδ.—חנניה] lacking in 𝕲ᴮ.—למלוכי] 𝕲 τῷ
Μαλουχ = מלוך, as v.². 𝕲ᴮᴬᴺ omits all the rest of the names down to
the end of v.²¹.—**15.** חרים] 𝕲ᴸ Ρεουμ = רהום, as v.³.—**17.** After למנימים]
𝕲ᴸ has Μασαι. Some name is required. 𝕲ᴺ has Βενιαμειν ἐν καί-
ροις τῷ φελῆτει, reading במועדים.—**24.** חשביה. 𝕲 Αβια Ασαβια(ς)ᴬᴺᴸ.—
בן-קדמיאל] 𝕲ᴮᴬᴺ καὶ οἱ υἱοὶ Καδμιήλ; 𝕲ᴸ καὶ οἱ υἱοὶ αὐτοῦ, Κεδμιήλ; consistently that text reads οἱ ἀδελφοὶ αὐτοῦ, showing אחיו, and having
Kadmiel alone as antecedent.—**25.** משמר ... מתניה] lacking in 𝕲ᴮᴬᴺ.
—שוערים משמר] 𝕲ᴸ πυλωροὶ φυλακῆς.—באספי הש"ר] 𝕲 ἐν τῷ συναγαγεῖν με
τοὺς πυλωρούς. We should rd. בָּאְסֻפִּים, as in 11¹⁹.—... משמר] 𝕳 *custodes
portarum et vestibulorum ante portas.*—**26.** 𝕲ᴮᴬᴺ lacks אלה and הפחה.
—Before וכימי] 𝕲ᴸ has a part of what is also found in v.²⁷, giving this
as the date of the dedication of the walls.

NE. 12²⁷⁻⁴³. THE DEDICATION OF THE WALLS.

The subject shows that we must go back to 7³, for the dedication would be the natural sequence to the completion of the building. It is prob. that the original order was 7³ 12²⁷⁻⁴³ 7⁴⁻⁵ᵃ 11¹ ᶠ·. Editors and compilers have done much more damage, however, than merely to disarrange the chron. connections; for in this part the confusion is prob. unparalleled in the OT. It is beyond the bounds of probability that any ingenuity of criticism will be able to restore the original. At the basis there seems to be a mere unintelligible fragment of N. which has been worked over and over until the passage is hopelessly obscure. We have two recensions of the expanded text, of which the Gk. is by far the simpler.

But the main course of the narrative may be followed. The Lev. were brought from their rural abodes to lead in the joyful songs. The people were drawn up in two companies, each with its leader, and with a company of pr. carrying clarions. One company started from the dung gate eastward, traversing the wall to the east water gate, and halting in the temple area. The second company with Neh. at its head went in the opposite direction, and after going along a portion of the wall halted also in the temple area. The whole body, now reunited, witnessed the offering of splendid sacrifices and participated in the loud rejoicings. On this section see Kost. *Wied.*⁴⁹ ᶠ·, and esp. the excellent article by Mitchell, JBL. 1903,¹²⁰ ᶠᶠ·, in which he has attempted, with the aid of all the modern light, to show the course of march of each company.

Its place here is prob. due to the fact that in its present form it is much more concerned with the pr. and Lev. than with the walls. We might perhaps give it as a title: *The Great Place of the Priests and Levites in the Dedication of the Walls.* Nevertheless there seems to be a fragment of N. discernible here and there, though so worked over by the Chr. as to be barely distinguishable. It is noteworthy that 𝔊ᴮᴬᴺ here generally agree, showing a single prototype and that their version is much shorter than MT. MT. therefore reveals much editing and amplifying. The passage begins with such abruptness that we may assume that some introductory words have been lost.

27. *And at the dedication of the wall of Jerusalem*], a phrase which shows that we are not dealing with N. He would not have named the city.—*They sought the Levites from all their places*]. Here we have an exact statement of fact. In Nehemiah's time the Levites did not live in Jerusalem, but were scattered about the country.—*To make a dedication and rejoicing*]. In joyful singing the Levites are assumed to be leaders, *cf.* v. [24].—*And with thanksgivings*] fits in very poorly, as it interrupts the connection. The dedication and rejoicing were to be made *with song of cymbals and of lutes*], *i. e.*, songs sung to the accompaniment of cymbals and lutes. An editor has added the third common instrument, *and with harps*]; for the construction differs from the preceding and the word fails in 𝕲. Harps would hardly be suitable in a procession.—**28 f.** is parallel with v. [27]. The Levites were gathered from their places to sing joyful songs, and now *the sons of the singers*] are collected from the same places and for the same purpose. "Sons of the singers" means those skilled in song.—*From the plain* around Jerusalem and from the villages and from the fields*] so 𝕲, to which in MT. we find additions thus: *from the villages of the Netophathites and from Beth-haggilgal and from the fields of Geba and Azmaweth*]. *Netophah* is about fifteen miles south-west of Jerusalem, and was in later days the home of Levites. *Beth-haggilgal* is a mystery, but as other names have a noun preceding, this may mean, from the Levite house at Gilgal, a name given to several localities, any one of which may be meant here. *Geba* and *Azmaweth* are north of Jerusalem. The use of hamlets and fields shows that the Levites of Nehemiah's time were earning their living from the soil. The simpler text of 𝕲 is the original, a conclusion borne out by the note following: *for the singers had built their hamlets about Jerusalem*]. The Chronicler was overfond of loading down his narrative with such comments.—**30.** In preparation for a religious office *the priests and Levites purified themselves*], *cf.* Ezr. 6[20]. This would be necessary for the Levites who had been engaged in agriculture; perhaps also for the priests, because they had been labouring on the walls. The singers are not mentioned, because they are the same as the Levites. After purifying themselves, they in turn *purified the people and the gates and the wall*]. 𝕲 saw the incongruity and rendered, as is perfectly possible by change of pointing, "gatekeepers" for

---

* G. A. Smith holds that *plain* or *circuit* here has a political rather than a geographical sense (*Jer.* i,[202]).

"gates," but we still have "wall," and "gatekeepers" is not appropriate here. How this purifying was accomplished we are not informed; Sieg. says by a sacrifice, and by sprinkling with the blood of the victim.—**31.** *And I had the princes of Judah go upon the wall; and I stationed two great processions and they were proceeding to the right at the dung gate*]. The first person shows that we have a trace of N. again. There is a general description of the whole company which took part in the dedication upon the wall, consisting of the princes and the processions of singers or of the people generally. Mitchell, however, proposes "and the one went" for "and they were proceeding" (JBL. 1903,⁹⁷), making the passage refer to one of the two companies. The place where they ascended the wall was at the dung gate in the Tyropœon valley on the south. (But *cf.* note on v. ³².)— **32.** *And there went after them Hoshaiah and half of the princes of Judah*], but corresponding to this in v. ³⁸ we have *half of the people*, and should so read here. It is plain that as we have half of the parade here, and find the other half with Nehemiah, v. ⁴⁰, and as we have the second procession, v. ³⁸, we are dealing now with the first procession only. Further, this division goes to the right, while the second goes to the left, v. ³⁸. Possibly the clauses are transposed in v. ³¹ and that we should read: *and I stationed two great divisions upon the wall; one was at the dung gate; and I caused the princes of Judah* [the first division] *to go to the right.*—**33f.** Some names are inserted here absolutely without connection. Most of them we can identify with Levites. Judah and Benjamin as they stand in the list are persons, not tribes, and yet it is tempting to think that they are really used here to cover the whole community.—**35f.** *And some of the sons of the priests with clarions*], *cf.* "sons of the singers," v. ²⁸. The clarion was a priestly instrument. It was not intended for tunes but for signals, like our bugle. The priests named are Zechariah, whose ancestry is traced to Asaph the singer, and (according to Ⓖ) Shemaiah and Azarel. The other names are partly corrupt forms not found elsewehere.—*With the singing instruments of David the man of God*], *cf.* v. ²⁴ and Am. 6⁵. This can hardly be original; for the priests had clarions and the Levites had the accompanying instruments, v. [27].—*And Ezra the scribe was before them*]. The Chronicler is bound to magnify his favourite and so he does not hesitate here to make him the leader of the band. **37.** The course of this procession is now described: *unto the fountain gate*], "by" of RV., instead of "unto," or literally "upon," is a doubtful rendering forced by the difficulty of the situation: *and straight before them*], RV., rather *and over against them*, but it is impossible to say over against what.—*They went up by the stairs of the city of David*] v. 3[15].—It is generally assumed that the procession leaves the wall and goes straight north, Ryle, Sieg. But from the qualifying clause *by the ascent of the wall above the house of David*], it would appear that the company followed the wall. Our ignorance of the ancient topography makes it impossible to determine the exact force of the words.—*And to the water gate on the east*] of the temple, *cf.* 3[26]. This was the end of the journey of the first company. The march took them around something like one-fourth of the circuit of the walls, from the dung gate to the water gate.—**38.** *And the second procession was going to the left*], *i. e.*, to the west: *to meet them there* in one Greek text.—*And I was following it; and half the people*]. Nehemiah himself was in the rear of this procession, as Hoshaiah followed the other, v. [32]; the Chronicler put Ezra with the former, a high dignitary being with each company.—*Upon the wall above the tower of the ovens as far as the broad wall*] is the description of the course followed by the second division.—**39.** Here we find the course of the march resumed: *beyond the gate of Ephraim and past the old gate* and the fish gate and the tower of Hananel and the tower of Hammeah and to the sheep gate and they stopped at the gate of the guard*]. This procession went out by the gate of Ephraim and marched around the walls to the sheep gate, and then keeping within the walls finished the circuit to the gate of the guard, which was close by the temple. There must have been bad going outside of the walls for the latter part of the march, or else the company came inside because it had nearly reached the meeting-place at the temple area. The distance traversed was thus about

---

* Strictly "gate of the old [pool]," Mitchell, JBL. 1903,[132 ff.].

the same as that of the first procession.—**40.** *And both proces-sions came to a halt at the house of God*]. One had come into the city at the water gate, the other at the sheep gate, both places in the temple precincts. It is assumed that they marched on until they met and stopped at the temple. The story then is resumed in v. ⁴³, for vv. ⁴¹ ᶠ· contain material inappropriate to this place.—*And I and half the nobles with me*] is doubtless a genuine fragment of N., but the predicate is gone beyond re-covery, perhaps buried in the list of priestly names. It may be a duplicate of "I and half of the people," v. ³⁸.—**41.** This con-tains a list of seven priests who had trumpets. It is perhaps in-tended to imply that this is the body of priests in the second company corresponding to those assigned to the first company, v. ³⁵, and so the Chronicler has put his material in at a very bad place, for here we have done with the second procession and are dealing with the whole body at rest before the temple. —**42.** A further list of eight priests is given, but with no in-timation of their office.—*And the singers chanted aloud*] seems to be authentic, as this singing would naturally begin as the two processions halted before the temple.—The following *and Izrahiah was the overseer*] is certainly corrupt or a bald inter-polation by the Chronicler. ⑤ has *and the singers were heard and paid attention*.—**43.** The conclusion of the dedicatory exer-cises consisted of great sacrifices, for which purpose the pro-cessions had halted at the temple, and rejoicing on the part of the whole people, including women and children, who had nat-urally gathered to watch the great proceedings.—*The rejoicing of Jerusalem was heard afar off*], *i. e.*, the joyful shouting was loud and participated in by many people, *cf.* Ezr. 3¹³.

44–47. Provision to secure the collection of the priestly revenues. The connection with the dedication of the walls is purely artificial. "On that day" (*cf.* 13¹) is about as vague as "once upon a time." The passage by subject matter is con-nected with 10²⁸⁻³⁹, and with some parts of c. 13. It is quite im-possible to assign any definite date. It appears to be due to the Chronicler or to some other whose supreme interest was the cult.

44. *Men were appointed over the storerooms*], the rooms in which the sacrificial supplies and the dues of the temple officers were kept. It was the business of these men, not to guard the stuff collected, but rather to see that a good amount was kept on hand.—*For the supplies*], in apposition to which, describing what these supplies were, we read: *for the heave-offerings, for the first-fruits and for the tithes*], the chief offerings that are made by an agricultural people.—*To gather into them*], *i. e.*, the storerooms.—*For the fields of the cities*] makes poor sense. *From the fields*, as we find in 𝕲ᴸ, would do in itself, but why fields of the cities? 𝕲ᴮ, by a difference of a single letter, gives *for the chiefs of the cities*, a better reading, as the meaning is that general officers were delegated to make collections for the whole country instead of intrusting the task to the local officials.—*The legal portions*] or *apportionments;* the amount to be gathered was not left to the discretion or the greed of the temple officers, but was determined strictly by law. The collections described here are exclusively for the support of the priests and Levites. It was possible now to make such collections, for Judah rejoiced in *the priests and Levites who served*] literally, *stood, i. e.*, cared for the interests of the whole people in the temple services.— **45.** As this verse stands, sense cannot be extracted from it save by violence. The subject of *kept* cannot be the "collectors" of v. [44], for we are finished with them; nor "the priests and Levites," for they are objects in this passage, not subjects. There is only one other choice: read therefore *and the singers and the gate-keepers performed the offices of their God and the office of purification according to the command of David and of Solomon his son*]. "Purification" is more than doubtful; possibly we should substitute *the law*, an emendation requiring but a slight change in the original.—**46.** The Chronicler persists in attributing the temple institutions to David and Solomon. *For in the days of David and of Asaph of old*]. We should expect *Solomon* in place of *Asaph*, as v. [45].—*There were chiefs of the singers*], or, as Sulzberger renders: "a guild of singers" (*Am-ha-aretz,*[45]), Asaph himself being the great chief, at least according to the Chronicler. The text should run: *for in the days of David, Asaph* *was of old the chief of the singers, cf.* 1 Ch. 6³¹· ³⁹. We know noth-ing of Asaph from the authentic history of David's time.—*And a song of praise and thanksgiving to God*] is certainly disjointed. The meaning is apparently that temple songs as well as singers go back to the time of David. 𝕳 forces a connection, *leaders of songs were appointed over the songs,* etc.—**47.** *In the days of Zerubbabel and in the days of Nehemiah*], unconscious testimony to the fact that in this period there were but two real civil leaders known. Jeshua and Ezra evidently had no place in the government.—*All Israel paid the portions of the singers and of the porters, the obligation of a day on its day*]; the support of these officials is here separated from that of the priests and Levites, and is described as if the payments were made volun-tarily without the intermediaries named in v. ⁴⁴.—From the fol-lowing we get a different story from that told in v. ⁴⁴: *and they set apart for the Levites and the Levites set apart for the sons of Aaron*]. From this it would appear that the singers and porters received support from the people, and they gave a part of their supplies to the Levites and the latter in turn bestowed a part on the priests. To say nothing of the contradiction, this method of supporting the men higher up is extremely improbable.

27. בתורות] 𝕲 ἐν θωλαθά^BAN, a transliteration, though there is a con-fusion of letters in 𝕲; ℵ adds ἐν ἐξομολογῆσει, showing a dup. ᴸ has καὶ ἀγαλλιάσει = וברננה, 𝕳 *in actione gratiarum.*—שיר] 𝕲 ᾠδαῖς = שירים.—ובכנרות] lacking in 𝕲^BAN.—**28.** בני המשררים] 𝕲ᴸ οἱ υἱοὶ Λευι.—נטפתי] lacking in 𝕲^BAN.—**29.** ומבית הגלגל] lacking in 𝕲^BAN (𝕲ᴸ ἐν Βαιθγαλ), so סביבות].—גבע ועזמות.—**30.** 𝕲^BAN ἐν. [השערים] 𝕲^BAN τοὺς πυλωρούς.—**31.** ואעלה] 𝕲 ἀνήνεγκαν; v. ᵇ lacking in 𝕲^BAN.—ותהלכת] 𝕲ᴸ καὶ διῆλθον, 𝕳 *et ierunt* preceded by the plus *laudantium.* Rd. וההולכת ptc. as in v. ³⁸. Or with Mitchell, JBL. 1903,⁹⁷, והאחת הלכת for ותהלכת.—**33.** עזריה] 𝕲 ᴬᴮ Ζαχαριας = זכריה.—**34.** בנימין] 𝕲ᴸ Μιαμειν = מימין, *cf.* v. ¹⁷.—שמעיה] 𝕲ᴮᴬ Σαραια.—**36.** מללי . . . . שיר] 𝕲^BAN αἰνεῖν ἐν ᾠδαῖς, prob. reading מְהַלְלֵי שירים. 𝕲ᴸ has all the names and then τοῦ αἰνεῖν ἐν σκεύεσι καὶ ᾠδαῖς, showing a dup.—**37.** העין] 𝕲^BAN τοῦ αἰνεῖν. This may be a transliteration which has then crept back to the preceding v.—מזרח] to אפרים, v. ³⁹, lacking in 𝕲^BAN.—**38.** למואל] 𝕲ᴸ συναντῶσα αὐτοῖς, *i. e.,* לקראתם. Many rd. לשמואל, corresponding to לימין, v. ³¹, and this is right.—**39.** ועל שער היש"] lacking in 𝕲^BAN, so ומגדל המאה and עמדו to end of v.—**40-42**ᵃ lacking in 𝕲^BAN.—**42.** ויזרחיה] lacking in 𝕲^BAN.

—הפקיד] 𝕲ᴮᴬᴺ καὶ ἐπεσκέπησαν = ויפקדו.—**44.** לתרומות] lacking in 𝕲.—
לשרי] 𝕲 ἄρχουσιν = שרי. 𝕲ᴸ has a doublet, ἀπὸ τῶν ἀγρῶν κ. τ. πόλεων
τοῖς ἄρχουσι τ. πόλεων.—התורה] lacking in 𝕲ᴮᴬᴺ, 𝕳 *principes civitatis in
decore gratiarum actionis.*—**46.** ואסף], ו lacking in 𝕲.—והורת ... שיר] 𝕲ᴮᴬᴺ
ὕμνον καὶ αἴνεσιν, ᴸ ὕμνος κ. ἐξομολόγησις κ. αἴνεσις.—**47.** ובימי נחמיה]
lacking in 𝕲ᴮᴺ.

NE. 13. NEHEMIAH'S SECOND ADMINISTRATION.

This c. deals wholly with the reforms effected by Neh. during his
second administration. After twelve years had been spent in Jerus.,
his leave having expired, he returned to Pers. We have no information
as to the time of his coming back to Jerus., but since Eliashib was still
high pr., though an old man (*v.* note on v. 28), and To. the Ammonite
was still a troublesome character, the interval between the two administrations could not have been long (*v.* Intr. § 11 (3)).

The reforms remind us of the matter in c. 5, though a number of
evils are dealt with here as against a single one in c. 5; but the description of each is characteristically brief. The affairs receiving attention were: (1) To.'s residence in a chamber of the temple, vv. 1-9;
(2) the securing of the tithes to the Lev. so that they could give their
services to the temple, vv. 10-14; (3) the prevention of traffic on the Sabbath, vv. 15-22; (4) the abolition of marriages with foreign women,
vv. 23-27; and (5) the banishment of a pr., vv. 28-31. Clearly all is from
N. save vv. 1-5. 22. 26 f. 29b-31a. In regard to vv. 1-5 it is hard to reach a
definite conclusion. The material is practically all drawn from vv. 6-9
and from Dt. The passage was prob. composed by the Chr. to connect the work of Neh. with Ezra's reading of the law. W. R. Smith
suspected that vv. 1-3 originally stood after Ezr. 109 (*OTJC.*427), but
Mitchell rightly rejects this (JBL. 1903,97). In this connection the
latter writer sets forth convincing proof of the place of 136 ff. in N.
Obviously the section vv. 6-31 is incomplete, and the conclusion is plain
that the Chr. preserved but a small section of the record of the second
administration, selecting only those parts which dealt with the enforce-
ment of the law.

1-5. Tobiah is installed in one of the chambers of the temple.

The law is found that an Ammonite and a Moabite are excluded from
the congregation, whereupon all of alien blood are excommunicated.
Eliashib, however, being overseer of the temple chambers, had fitted
up a sumptuous room for his friend To. These things took place while
Neh. was away in Pers.

1. *On that day it was read* [or *we read*] *in the book of Moses*].
This reminds us of the public reading of the law as described in
c. 8.   But the story is introduced here to connect the incident
with the admission of Tobiah to the temple and his subsequent
expulsion by Nehemiah.

> The law in Dt. 23⁴ contains a dup.: "An Ammonite and a Moabite
> shall not come into the congregation of Yahweh [even to the tenth
> generation; there shall not come in of them to the congregation of
> Yahweh] forever."   The part in brackets is omitted in our text.   Per-
> haps it is a later addition in Dt., v. Dr.   As provision was made that
> Edomites might be received in the third generation (Dt. 23⁹), the ex-
> clusion to the tenth, acc. to a later writer, would be a sufficient penalty
> for the other peoples.

2. The cause of the exclusion was not hostility to the foreigners
as such, but the failure of these two races to supply the needs of
Israel at the time of their invasion of the east-Jordan country.
—*And he hired*], the change to the singular follows text of Dt.*
and may be due to the unconscious transition to Balak as subject.   Our text omits the details about Balaam as given in Dt.,
because they are not germane here.   Vv.¹ ᶠ· are a reproduction
of Dt. 23⁴⁻⁶ (Eng.³⁻⁵), though somewhat abbreviated.   For the
whole story see Nu. 22–24.—*Turned the curse into a blessing*].
As a matter of fact, all of Balaam's oracles were blessings.   He
tried, however, to earn Balak's tendered prize by pronouncing
a blighting curse on Israel.   But Balaam was a true prophet
of Yahweh and could only utter in the ecstatic state what
Yahweh put into his mouth (Nu. 22¹⁸· ³⁸ 24¹³).   What Balaam
intended to be a curse proved to be a benediction.—**3.** When
the people heard the law, as usual they proceeded to put it
into execution; therefore they *excommunicated from Israel every
one of alien blood*].   The meaning is not that the foreigners were
banished from the land, but merely that they were denied the
privileges of the temple.   It is evident that a liberal construction was put upon the law.   Dt. refers to Ammonites and Moabites, but not to any other peoples whatsoever.   The leaders

* ARV. has rendered erroneously "they hired."

here make the law apply to all foreigners, no matter of what nationality. It is plain that if this event is historical, the work of Ezra must have followed, for the condition described here could not have existed after his complete separation of the Jews from foreigners.—**4.** *Now before this*], earlier than the excommunication of the foreigners, *Eliashib the priest had been appointed in charge of the chambers of the house of our God*]. Eliashib was high priest and is named often in these books.—*And he was near to Tobiah*]. This is Tobiah the Ammonite slave who was one of Nehemiah's chief enemies, 2¹⁰. "Near" is usually interpreted as referring to blood relationship, BDB. Ges.ᴮ, Ryle. There is no evidence of such a connection, and the meaning may well be that the relationship was purely one of friendship, or that Eliashib had attempted to placate an enemy of the people. According to 6¹⁸ he was related by marriage to Shekaniah and to Meshullam. If he had also such a close connection with the high priest, the fact would not have been overlooked there. Moreover, Sanballat was related to Eliashib, v. ²⁸. It is not likely that Tobiah was also.—**5.** *And he assigned to him a great chamber*]. Eliashib, who was overseer, designated one of the finest chambers to Tobiah, and the latter evidently used it as a place of residence, v. ⁸. During Nehemiah's rule he kept up a correspondence with leaders in Jerusalem, but could not get into the city. Now that the governor was away, he not only entered the city, but actually found an abode in the temple. The desecration was the more pronounced as this was the very room which had been set apart for the offerings of the people, both those used for sacrifice and those for the support of the four groups of temple officers.—The description of the offerings is quite different from that in c. 12, and shows another hand, influenced a good deal by Dt.—*The commandment*] makes poor sense and lacks support in the Vrss. Retained we should understand it to mean that the tithe was by the command of the law given to the Levites *et al.* But it is better to follow the Latin and render by a slight emendation "portions." The verse shows amplification by a later hand. Comparing v. ⁹ we note that this room was used for the sacred vessels and for two kinds of offerings, vegetable and incense. But at a later period other things were kept in this room, and an editor adds a list to bring the story down to date.

1. נקרא] may be Niph. or first p. pl. Qal. As we have אלהינו in vv. ². ⁴, this passage may be one of those in first p. pl., though v. ³ is against this conclusion. After ספר] 𝕲ᴸ adds νόμου. From לא יבוא to end of v. ² consists of extracts of Dt. 23⁴⁻⁶, giving the substance of the law.— האלהים] Dt. יהוה, showing plainly the Elohistic bias of our author.— **2.** כי] Dt. אשר על־דבר אשר.—ואשר שכר] Dt. וישכר.—אתחכם] Dt. אתחבני ישראל.—וישכר] Dt. וישכר; אלהינו].—לקללך] Dt.לקלל.—לקללו] Dt. עליו.—עליך] 𝕲 reads pl. ἐμισθώσαντο, so 𝕳.—עליו] Dt. עליו. Dt. לך אלהיך יהוה.—הקללה] 𝕲ᴸ κατάραν αὐτοῦ.—**3.** ערב] is a rare word, but the mng. *mixture* is well established. The word naturally means a people not of pure blood, though it may sometimes be applied to a mass of people made up of various races. In this passage both senses may apply. There may have been some foreigners of different races, but certainly there were many of mixed blood.—מישראל] 𝕲 ἐν I.—**4.** לפני מזה] means before a particular event, while לפנים in v. ⁵ is a general word, "formerly."—נתון] 𝕲 οἴκων, 𝕳 *fuerat præpositus*. 𝕲 has missed the idea, but 𝕳 has rendered correctly. The sense "appoint" is found in 1 S. 12¹³ 1 Ch. 12⁹, v. BDB.—לשכת] must be pointed as a pl. to make the sense required.—**5.** מצות] 𝕲ᴸ ἄζυμα = מצות, *unleavened cakes*, 𝕳 *partes* = מניות, as 12⁴⁷, which gives the best sense.—תרומת] 𝕲 ἀπαρχαί, 𝕳 *primitias*, which represents also ראשית, as in 12⁴⁴.

6–9. Tobiah's belongings are ejected from the temple.

After an absence of uncertain duration Neh. returns to Jerus., and finding To. residing in the temple chamber, he ejects his furnishings, orders the room cleansed, and puts back the vessels and offerings for which the room had formerly been used. We are certainly dealing with N. again. The intr., *in all this*, and the contents show a connection with the preceding. Yet vv. ¹⁻⁵ are not from N.

6. *In all this*] refers only to the events described in vv. ¹⁻⁵, not to the long story of Ezra's promulgation of the law.— *Thirty-second year*] as 5¹⁴, indicating the end of the first administration.—*King of Babylon*] is hardly original. Nehemiah refers to Artaxerxes merely as "the king" (2¹), the natural use for a contemporary. "Babylon" is from a later hand.—The last clause of the verse is usually connected with what follows, thus: *and at the end of a time I* [again] *asked leave* [of absence] *from the* *king and came to Jerusalem*. But in a Greek text preserved only in a duplicate rendering (*v. i.*) we find a better sense. The clause should be closely connected with what precedes, for our verse division is here right, thus: *I came in to the king even at the end of the period for which I had asked leave from the king*. The point that Nehemiah makes is that he had gone back because the period for which he had been appointed governor had expired. He was not driven from Jerusalem by his foes, nor did he break faith with the king. The latter point was important in view of the charges of rebellion that had been made against him. It must be recalled that Artaxerxes exacted a limit of time from Nehemiah before consenting to his departure (2^6), and Nehemiah takes pains to say that he returned at the time agreed upon. The words "at the end of days" are sufficiently definite in this connection, as they refer to the term described earlier in the verse, *i. e.*, the end of days means the 32d year of Artaxerxes, the end of the leave of absence.—**7.** *And I came to Jerusalem*]. This is abrupt, and one might wonder whether the above interpretation does not leave something wanting here. But we note that the clause in v. ⁶ does not make a very happy introduction to the second administration; and while Nehemiah was concerned to explain his absence for a period, he is at no pains to explain how he had come to return. In view of the full report of c. 1 *f.*, perhaps he thought it would be assumed that a second furlough would easily be obtained. Probably Nehemiah was led to return because rumours of what he found at Jerusalem had already reached him in Persia.— The words are closely connected with what follows: *and understood the evil*] of EV^s. is not happy; *observed* is better. The evil from the narrow Jewish point of view would consist in the profanation of the temple because Tobiah was an Ammonite. Nehemiah may have made use of this sentiment in view of the purifying which followed (v. ⁹); but one may wonder whether Nehemiah was not largely moved by his remembrance of Tobiah's striving to thwart him in his efforts to rebuild the wall.— The room in which Tobiah had taken abode is further described as in *the courts of the house of God*]. The "courts" were strictly the open spaces in the temple area, and doubtless the room opened upon these courts.—**8.** Nehemiah acted with his customary promptness and decision; every article in the sumptuous chamber was thrown out. The word implies more than "set outside"; "thrown out" is none too strong. As there is no mention of Tobiah himself, the ejecting was probably done in his absence. With Nehemiah on the ground Tobiah would very likely prefer to live elsewhere for a time.—*House of Tobiah*] implies that he had set up a regular housekeeping establishment and that his family lived with him, thus explaining the large room assigned him, v. ⁵.—**9.** *And I spoke*], equivalent to commanded; *and they purified the chamber*]. Nearly all texts have *chambers*. Of itself there is nothing improbable in the notion that a series of rooms should have been occupied (so Ryle); but as the singular is used everywhere else, it must be restored here. The purifying was limited to the room occupied as shown from its restoration to its original use. Ceremonial cleansing was common even in early times, and was performed in various ways, usually by the symbolic use of blood or water. The list of articles returned to this room is shorter than in v. ⁵, in which there is doubtless an editorial addition.

6. ולקץ ... המלך] 𝕲ᴸ εἰς τὸν καιρὸν τῶν ἡμερῶν ὧν ἠτησάμην παρὰ τοῦ βασιλέως, καὶ μετὰ τὸ τέλος τῶν ἡμερῶν ὧν ἠτησάμην παρὰ τοῦ βασιλέως. This represents two interpretations rather than two texts.—ימים] has the specific sense of a year (BDB.) in numerous passages, and should be so understood here if we retain the usual interpretation, referring to the time when Neh. started for his second visit to Jerus. But Neh. is usually very exact in his dates, and presumably would have specified the time accurately if that had been his mng.—**7.** נשכה] is found elsw. only in Ne. 3³⁰ 12⁴⁴, and the mng. is exactly the same as the common לשכה, for which it is prob. an error. Neh. would hardly use a strange word alongside of a familiar one.—**8.** וירע לי מאד] 𝕲ᴸ has a dup., καὶ πονηρόν μοι ἐφάνη, καὶ ἐλυπήθην σφόδρα, cf. ויחר לי מאד, 5⁶.—**9.** הלשכות] 𝕲ᴸ has sg. which the sense requires.

10-14. Tithes are paid to the Levites.

Neh., finding that the Lev. had received no portions and were driven to their fields to make a living, rebukes the people, and all Judah pays

the tithes.   Officers are appointed to supervise the distribution of the
offerings.   Neh. prays that he may be remembered for his good offices
on behalf of the temple.

10. *And I learned that the portions of the Levites had not been
paid*].   This condition had arisen during Nehemiah's absence
in Persia.   In the twelve years of his former governorship
such neglect would not have been tolerated.   In the whole
Persian period the people seem to have been slow to discharge
the lawful obligations to the temple, *cf.* Mal. $3^{8\ \text{ff.}}$.—*And the
Levites had fled each one to his land*].   The Levites may have
owned land, or they may have hired themselves out to other
landowners to make the living which the temple offices no
longer furnished them.—*And the singers doing the work*] is apparently a gloss.   Nehemiah seems to be concerned only with the
Levites.—**11.** *And I contended with the rulers*], *v.* 5^7, where we
have "with the nobles and rulers."   *With the rulers* is lacking
in the best Greek texts.   The fault lay with the whole people,
not with limited classes as in c. 5.   If the text is right, the rulers
were reproved because they had not enforced the law.—*Why
is the house of God neglected?*]   The implication is that the sacred
offices were not conducted at all in the house of God, and that
situation in turn implies that the Levites were those who executed the priestly offices, that is, that the Deuteronomic condition in which priests and Levites were identical still pre-
vails.—*And I gathered them, i. e.,* the Levites, from the fields
where they had been employed in secular work; *and I placed
them at their station*] in the temple, so that they could fulfil their
holy offices.   *Station* implies not only place in the sense of
locality, but also covers the particular office in which the Levites
were employed.—**12.** *And all Judah brought in*].   The response
to Nehemiah's demand was general; for he would brook no
further neglect and ruled always with a strong hand.   Benjamin
is not mentioned, but obviously "Judah" covers the whole
people.—*The tithe of the corn and of the wine and of the oil*].   In
Dt. the tithe of the corn, etc., was paid every 3d year, and
was to be eaten at the sanctuary.   The Levites and the poor
were to share in these feasts, $12^{6.\ 11.\ 17}$ $14^{23.\ 28}$ 26^{12}.   In the

later law of Holiness the tithe became the absolute property of the Levites (Lv. 18²¹⁻³²).—**13.** This verse is sadly confused in our text; by eliminating some unnecessary lumber and correcting from 𝔊, we get the true sense: *and I committed to the hands of Shelemiah the priest and of Zadok the scribe, and of Pedaiah of the Levites and of Hanan the son of Zakkur the son of Mattaniah, because they were accounted trustworthy, to them* [I committed] *to distribute to their brethren*]. The tithes were paid into the treasury by the whole people, and they were for the common support of the Levites. But these were human, like many other ecclesiastical officials, and the problem which confronted Nehemiah was to make sure of an equitable distribution so that every one should have a just share and none be neglected (*cf.* Acts 6, a similar condition which led to the appointment of the seven deacons). *Shelemiah* we know nothing more about, as he cannot be identified with the men of that name in Ezr. 9³⁴ 10³⁹· ⁴¹ Ne. 3³⁰. Two *Zadoks* worked on the wall, 3⁴· ²⁹, but the scribe may be a different one still. *Pedaiah* cannot be the one who stood with Ezra, Ne. 8⁴, and is hardly the wall-builder of 3²⁵. In spite of the elaborate genealogy of Hanan and the frequent recurrence of the name, we cannot identify this man either. The treasurers are therefore unknown to us save in this enumeration, but were appointed because they were deemed honest so as to insure a just apportionment of the Levitical dues. —*To their brethren*] would imply that all the officers were Levites; but the expressions, *the priest*, *the scribe*, and especially *of the Levites*, would suggest that only Pedaiah belonged to that order. *Of the Levites* may, however, be a predicate of Shelemiah and Zadok as well as of Pedaiah, since the priest was also a Levite and the scribe may have well been. On the other hand, "brethren" is used pretty broadly, and the Levites might be regarded as the brethren of any of the people.—**14.** See similar ejaculatory petitions, 2⁴ 3³⁶ 5¹⁹.—*My kindness*], *i. e.*, in restoring the support of the Levites and so the re-establishment of the sacred offices.—*In the house of my God and in its observances*], the last clause is lacking in 𝔊 and may be a gloss added by the Chronicler.

10. עשי] 𝕲ᴸ καὶ οἱ ποιοῦντες, similarly 𝔘.—**11.** ואריבה] 𝔅ᴸ καὶ ἐκρίθην. —את־הסגנים] lacking in 𝕲ᴮᴬᴺ.—**13.** ואוצרה על־האוצרות] 𝕲ᴮᴬᴺ ἐπὶ χεῖρα(ς), 𝕲ᴸ καὶ ἐνετειλάμην ἐπὶ χεῖρας = ואצוה על־ידי. This is the only occurrence of the Hiph., and it is used in a peculiar sense, not "I caused to store," but "appointed treasurer." It is difficult to extract this sense by the usual devices of calling it a denominative (BDB.). 𝕲 offers a better text and one that should be adopted here, for the point is not the naming of a number of treasurers, but the assignment to certain officers of the delicate task of distributing the tithes.—על־ידם] could only be retained by rendering *and with them*. But it stands here for על־ידי as 𝕲, being misplaced in the confusion of the text.—ועליהם] 𝕲ᴮᴬᴺ ἐπ' αὐτούς.—**14.** אלהי וכ׳] 𝕲ᴮᴬᴺ κυρίου τοῦ θεοῦ.

15–22. The enforcement of the Sabbath law.

Finding the people working in the fields and trading with the Phœnicians on the Sabbath, Neh. rebuked the nobles and ordered the gates of the city closed during the holy day. He threatened the merchants who lodged by the wall over the Sabbath waiting for the first day of the week. Note the similar conditions described in 10³².

15. *In those days*] *cf.* v. ¹, another indefinite note of time. Nehemiah evidently made a tour of the country on the Sabbath, possibly for the purpose of noting the way in which the day was kept.—The points of violation may easily be obscured in translation. These are only two, as I understand the text: (1) [people] *were treading wine-presses on the sabbath*]. This is the only case in OT. where we find the literal use of this expression. But the figurative use shows that the wine-press was always trodden, for another verb in Jos. 4¹³ is suspicious. (2) *And* [people] *were gathering in the harvests and loading asses with grape-wine and figs and all sorts of produce and bringing them to Jerusalem on the sabbath day*]. All the deeds enumerated were contributing to the one point of importance, the carrying produce to Jerusalem on the Sabbath, and naturally selling it on that day. The recurrent use of *sabbath day* justifies this connection. —*And I testified on the day they sold provisions*].

Ryle says this could not have taken place on the Sabbath, but on a subsequent day when the food gathered on the Sabbath was sold. There was objection then apparently because the food had been gathered on the Sabbath and so was tainted. Easy-going criticism surely!

The Vrss. offer a suggestive hint.   One Gk. text has: *in the day of their traffic because they sold provisions;* and 𝕭: *I protested that they should sell on a day when it was lawful to sell.*   On this basis we can easily reconstruct the text and get: *I protested because they sold provisions on the sabbath day.*   The food was manifestly sold on the Sabbath as it was borne to Jerus. on that day; and the offence was the selling as much as the gathering.   Neh. does not seem to have raised his voice against the work that was done in the fields, but only against the traffic, which disturbed the peace of Jerus.   While he notices the work done, v. 15, at least nothing more is said about that phase of the trouble.   This brings us into exact agreement with the conditions in Am. 8⁵, where barter alone was suspended on the Sabbath.   Evidently the amplification of the Sabbath law was later than Neh.

16. *Now the Tyrians dwelt in it*]; "it" could only be Jerusalem, but the use of that name in v. 15 can hardly serve as an antecedent here.

Tyrians is lacking in 𝕲, and prob. should be omitted, for they are not named again in the long passage.   Neh. blames the nobles of Judah and calls them the profaners of the Sabbath.   It is true that their guilt might consist in buying what was offered for sale, *cf.* 10³².   But it is difficult to think of Phœnician merchants as residents of Jerus. at this period.   On the other hand, c. 5 shows that the nobles were greedy of money, and would not be likely to stickle at profitable traffic even on the Sabbath.   The passage seems to me so corrupt that understanding is not possible.   Perhaps the best we can do is to follow 𝕲 and render: *and there resided therein those who brought in fish and other merchandise and sold them on the sabbath to the people of Judah in Jerus.*   "People of Judah" admittedly suggests that the traders were foreigners; but, on the other hand, in a passage so full of difficulties we cannot press details.   Moreover, the purchasers could hardly be described in any other way.   To try to get sense I propose: *and the provision bearers returned therein, bringing fish*, etc.   Neh. had warned them on their first offence, v. 15, protesting against the desecration, and supposing that the matter was ended.   On the next Sabbath the dealers returned bringing other wares.   Neh. had objected to their traffic, possibly mentioning the wine and figs which they offered for sale.   The dealers may have supposed that he could not object to fish, but the reading may be "corn."—Neh. is, at all events, aroused now, and his usual vigour and resource show themselves.

17. *And I contended with the nobles of Judah*], *cf.* v. 11, either because they made no attempt to stop this barter, or because they were engaged in it. It is possible that *sons* should be read for *nobles* (*v. i.*), and in that case the reproof is administered to those who had purchased supplies on the Sabbath.— *Profaning the sabbath day*] is late, found only in Ex. 31¹⁴ (P), Is. 56². ⁶ Ez. *pass.*—**18.** The implication is that the woes of Israel were due to the desecration of the Sabbath. In the scant testimony we have from the earlier days (Am. 8⁵), the Sabbath was kept in letter but not in spirit. Ez. makes the profanation of the Sabbath one of the serious offences, 20¹³ 22⁸ 23³⁸. But our passage more likely refers to the general disobedience to the law which was supposed to be the cause of Israel's downfall, from which Jerusalem was still suffering.—*And ye would add wrath upon Israel by profaning the sabbath*]. Another violation of law would lead to further manifestations of divine wrath, of which Israel would be the victim. This sort of speech is couched in the hackneyed terms of which N. is free, and doubtless what Nehemiah actually said has been replaced with the conventional prophetic utterance.—**19.** Nehemiah now takes measures to enforce the law against barter on the Sabbath.—*When the gates of Jerusalem grew dark before the sabbath*] is an impossible way of saying "when evening came on." The text must be changed and we may best render with 𝕲: *when the gates were put in place*. The reference plainly is to the closing of the gates, and only indirectly the approach of evening. The time is sufficiently indicated by the phrase *before the sabbath*. Nehemiah had previously directed the closing of the gates at night (7³), and it is to that customary act to which reference is made here.—*And I spoke*] is an accidental repetition from its use further on in the verse. The doors in the gates were naturally closed when the gates were shut.—*And I said*] = *commanded*, as in v. ⁹, because now a new regulation is issued (to the porters) *that they should not open them until after the sabbath*]. It now became impossible for a person to go in or out of Jerusalem on the Sabbath.—*And I stationed some of my servants at the gates*]; a superfluous precaution, says Winckler, *Alt. Forsch.* ii,⁴⁸⁷, since no one could pass through the closed gates. Not if they were kept closed, but Nehemiah puts his trusty servants by the gates to see that no porter is induced to reopen the gates by bribery, persuasion, or threats.—*That no produce should come in on the sabbath day*], showing plainly the purpose of Nehemiah's elaborate precautions. Perhaps the words may imply that a person might find passage through the gates if he carried no merchandise.—**20.** *And the traders and the dealers in all kinds of wares lodged without Jerusalem*]. The usual explanation is that the merchants, finding the gates shut, lodged outside of the city until the Sabbath was over. But it is difficult to see why Nehemiah should so seriously object to that. Indeed, their camping outside was no violation of the law from any point of view. The text is doubtful. In 𝕲 we find a striking reading: *and they all lodged and engaged in traffic outside of Jerusalem*]. There is abundant cause for the wrath of the governor. He had stopped the trading in Jerusalem and had kept the gates closed, only to find the traffic resumed outside of the walls. The purchasers may have been those who resided outside the city, or Jerusalemites may have been allowed to pass through the gates.— *Once or twice*], *i. e.*, for one or two Sabbaths. This traffic went on for a few weeks before Nehemiah took notice of it. When he did act, he went at the task with his usual thoroughness.— **21.** *And I protested to them and said unto them*]. "Testified," of EV³., hardly gives the sense. The word serves to introduce the threat.—*Why are you lodging before the wall?*] There is no word of trading; but 𝕲 may be right in v. ²⁰ none the less. The only way to break up the trading would be to keep the merchants away altogether.—*If you do it a second time*]. According to v. ²⁰ they may have done it a second time already. If that is correct, we must render more generally: "if you do it again," a sense the words easily bear.—*I will put a hand on you*], *i. e.*, inflict punishment, though the same expression is used elsewhere in a good sense. The threat of punishment served its purpose, for the traders *did not come* [to Jerusalem any more] *on the sabbath.*—**22.** *And I said to the Levites that they should purify themselves and come in to watch the gates to sanctify the sabbath day*]. The passage plainly shows a later hand. Nehemiah had already brought the Levites to Jerusalem, v. ¹¹. If they were the porters, they were not trusted, as Nehemiah set his own servants over them, v. [19]. The passage naturally ends with v. [22], but the Chronicler was not satisfied to have the Levites ignored. —On the closing prayer, *cf.* v. [14].—*According to God's good deeds*] now, not his own as in v. [14].

15. נחות] = גִּנְתוֹת, from יגן, which does not occur in Heb., pl. only here. The wine-press was usually hewn from the rock (*DB.* Benz.[212 f.], *v.* also Haupt, *SBOT.* on 1 K. 1[15]). On this account it was generally in a hillside, in an out-of-the-way place, and so the wine-press served Gideon as a secret threshing-floor (Ju. 6[11]). The word is found also in Is. 63[2] Lam. 1[15] Jo. 4[13]. The passage last cited rd. דרכו, as ררו is never found with גת and is inappropriate, *v.* Mar. *Dodekapr.*— הערמות] does not mean "sheaves," as Wetzstein contends (*Zeit. f. Eth.* 1873, art. "Dreschtafel"), though it might mean "shocks of grain." But in Ru. 3[7] Ct. 7[3] Hg. 2[16] it refers to the heap of threshed grain. That cannot be its mng. here, for the grain season (3d month) was long past when grapes and figs were ripe (7th month), and Ryle is reduced to the desperate expedient of supposing the people were bringing in the straw! The word means piles of any sort as we use "pile" in "wood pile," "potato pile," etc. In 2 Ch. 31[6-9] it refers to droves of oxen and sheep as well as to other dedicated offerings, perhaps of grain and fruits. I have rendered by the general word *harvests*, for it refers to the wine in skins, figs, and whatever else was carried to market.—ואף־] is rightly ignored in 𝔊 𝔙. Even if original it has no translatable force. It may be an error for את.—In late Heb. we may find ו before a direct obj., for יין *et sq.* is obj. of עמסים.—יין ענבים] might be wine and grapes as Vrss. and all authorities render; but the absence of a conj. suggests st. cstr., and it is better to translate "grape-wine."—כל־משא] is easy to understand, but hard to render tersely. It means all the other marketable stuff.—ביום . . . ציר] 𝔊[BAN] ἐν ἡμέρᾳ πράσεως αὐτῶν, lacking ציר; 𝔊[L] adds ὅτε ἐπώλουν ἐπισιτισμὸν, showing one of the usual duplicates. 𝔙 has an interesting reading, or possibly interpretation: *ut in die qua vendere liceret venderent.* The original text must have been ביום השבת במכרם ציד.—**16.** והצדים] lacking in 𝔊[BAN]. The clause is quite unintelligible, and some conjectural emendation is essential. I venture to suggest והצדים ישובו בה. The changes are very slight, and good sense is secured. This text has the further advantage of being a suitable sequel to v. [15], for we can hardly be dealing with a new situation entirely. Neh. was not fighting Phœnicians, but Sabbath-trading among the Jews. Tyrians may have been substituted by a later hand on the basis of 10[32].—ראני] is wrong, and we may substitute דגן as easily as דג.—**17.** חרי] 𝔊[BAN] τοῖς υἱοῖς τοῖς ἐλευθέροις, showing an original text, בני, and a later correction, fortunately not by substitution.—**18.** אלהינו] 𝕲ᴮᴬᴺᴸ has ἐπ᾽ αὐτοὺς ὁ θεὸς ἡμῶν, a dup. showing אליהם and אלהינו.—**19.** צללו] is impossible. To describe the coming of evening by saying "the gates grew dark" is too far-fetched. Indeed, this vb. must be ejected from the Heb. lexicon. It occurs elsw. only in Ez. 31³, but is corrected by most recent writers. 𝕲 has κατέστησαν, prob. עמד. As this may be rendered "put in place," the sense is good. 𝕲ᴸ precedes by ἡσύχασα = שקט. Similarly 𝔅 cum quievissent portæ. Winckler (Alt. Forsch. ii,⁴⁸⁷) follows 𝔐 and renders from As. salalu, "drop," "the merchants deposited their fish at the gates" (reading בשערי). Why that should be done he does not say and I cannot guess. —ויאמרה] lacking in 𝕲ᴮ.—ומענרי] lacking in 𝕲ᴮᴬᴺא.—**20.** ילינו] does not necessarily imply that they spent the night, but means rather "went into camp," perhaps setting up a sort of temporary market.—הרכלים] 𝕲ᴮᴬᴺ πάντες, 𝕲ᴸ πάντες οἱ μετάβολοι.—ומכרי כל ממכר] 𝕲ᴮᴬᴺ καὶ ἐποίησαν πρᾶσιν. At end 𝕲ᴸ reads καὶ ἐκωλύθησαν ἅπαξ καὶ δίς, adding ויכלאו.— **22.** מטהרים . . . השערים] 𝕲ᴸ ἵνα ἐρχόμενοι ἁγνίζωνται καὶ φυλάσσωσι τὰς πύλας, showing no difference of text but only an interpretation.

23-31. Mixed marriages.

Neh. finds Judeans married to Philistine women and the children were unable to speak Jewish. He punished the offenders severely and exacted an oath against the repetition of the offence. The case of Solomon's downfall is cited. The son-in-law of Sanb., a grandson of Eliashib, was banished from Jerus. The book closes with general statements about the temple ritual. Not more than vv. ²³⁻²⁵. ²⁸. ²⁹ᵃ. ³¹ᵇ are from N. This is the kind of story which the Chr. would delight in elaborating.

23. *In those days [cf. v. ¹⁵] I saw the Judeans who had married women that were Ashdodites]. Ammonites, Moabites,* seems to me a later addition. These were the people toward whom there was the greatest animosity, *cf.* v. ¹, and therefore these names are added here. There may have been marriages with these peoples, but Ashdodite in *cf.* v. ²⁴ shows that Nehemiah is dealing with a single class.—**24.** We may render: *and their sons were speaking half Ashdodite],* a corruption of speech producing a patois, half foreign and half Jewish; or *and half their sons spoke Ashdodite**]. The latter is more probable, in spite of the balance of opinion in favour of the former. A patois can only be developed in the course of several generations. The children would

---

* Really Nabatæan, Neubauer, *Studia Biblica*,²³⁰.

be pretty certain to use the speech of the mother. And the
clause *and they were not able to speak Jewish*] supports this
view, for it is in contrast with the statement that some of the
sons spoke another tongue. From the free intercourse between
Israelites and Philistines in the early days we would infer that
their languages were mutually intelligible.

יהודית] is used of the Jewish speech in 2 K. 18²⁶· ²⁸, to which we
have the parallels in Is. 36¹¹· ¹³ and 2 Ch. 32¹⁸, the only occurrences.
The word in those passages certainly means *Hebrew;* indeed, Hezekiah's officers asked the Assyrians not to speak Heb. as they were
doing, but Aram. The word prob. means the same thing here, and not
Aram. (Smith, *Jer.* ii,¹⁶⁵). Neh. wrote good Heb., and that was doubtless still the language of the people. The construction indicates an
incomplete clause. The rendering strictly correct is: *and their sons, half
of them spoke Ashdodite;* we expect a corresponding clause, "and half
of them spoke ————." The resumption of the pl. shows that we go
back to "sons" and that it is predicated of the whole body that "they
were unable to speak Jewish," that is, half of them spoke one language
and half another, but none of them could speak Heb.—*But according to
the tongue of people and people*] is a gl. intended to define more accurately
the foregoing, but the definition is quite as obscure as the text.—לשׁון]
is used often in the sense of language, but mostly in late passages.

25. The violence of the punishment shows how greatly Nehemiah was incensed: *I cursed them and I smote certain of them*],
perhaps some chief offenders, *and I pulled out their hair*], usually
from the beard, *cf.* Is. 50⁶, but in Ezr. 9³ both hair of head and
beard as a sign of distress; "my cheeks to them that pulled out
the hair," Is. 50⁶, would indicate that this was a regular form of
punishment, as we might say he gave his neck to the hangman.
The hair was all pulled out, as the word means to be smooth.
The loss of the beard was in itself a disgrace, 2 S. 10⁴.—*And I
made them swear by* [the name of] *God*]. The oath is put in the
second person, either to conform to Dt. 7³, though there we find
the singular and a different word for "take," or to reproduce
the exact form of the oath, though according to our usage that
would be in the first person. Nehemiah had found Jewish men
married to Philistine women, not the reverse. Still the general
oath would be natural in view of the Deuteronomic law.—*And*

for yourselves] is not in Dt. nor in the oldest Greek MSS. Yet it is the most appropriate part of the oath, as Nehemiah is dealing with men who had themselves married foreign women. —**26.** Solomon is now quoted as a horrible example of a great man led astray by foreign wives. This is not due to Nehemiah, as he appears to have been disturbed purely by the corruption of the language, and feared the Jewish people were in danger of losing their identity.—*Did not Solomon the king of Israel sin in regard to these* [foreign wives]. *And among many nations there was not a king like him*] is based upon the promise in I K. 3^{13}. *And he was beloved of his God*], cf. 2 S. 12$^{24\,f.}$. *Even him*], in spite of his greatness and the blessings showered upon him from on high, *the foreign wives made to sin*] or turned aside as in I K. 11^3 "turned aside his heart."—**27.** The conclusion of Nehemiah's assumed address. As it stands the verse is barely translatable. 𝔊 has often a happy disposition to insist on sense and gives us: *and shall we by disobedience do all this great evil that we should act insolently toward our God and marry foreign women.* To make a bold try at the text, we might extract: *and as for you shall we listen to* [tolerate] *the doing of this great evil, the acting violently against our God, the marrying of foreign women?*—**28.** We find now a specific instance of a foreign alliance which naturally aroused the governor.—*And one of the sons of Jehoiada, the son of Eliashib the high priest, was son-in-law to Sanballat the Horonite*]. The offender could hardly be Jonathan the successor of Jehoiada, 12$^{10\,f.}$, but must have been another son, since his name is not given. As Eliashib was contemporary with Nehemiah (cf. v. ^{4}), he must have been an old man at this time to have a grandson old enough to marry. It is strange to find a person so vaguely introduced; as v. ^{28} introduces a new section, I suspect that the original text read: "and in those days Jehoiada the son of Eliashib." That would agree better with the chronology. Sanballat was one of the most troublesome of Nehemiah's enemies, 2^{10} 3^{33} 4^1 6^1. It was by such alliances that the enemy was kept posted in regard to Nehemiah's doings, cf. 6^{18}.—*And I drove him from me*]. *Drove away* is used of putting enemies to flight, I Ch. 8^{13} 12^{15}, of driving a mother

(from her house), Prov. 19²⁶. Doubtless the offender was banished from Jerusalem. His punishment was different from that
inflicted upon the others, v. ²⁵, because of the hostility toward
Sanballat and his house.—**29.** Instead of supplication we find
now imprecation as in 6¹⁴. *Remember against them, O my God,
for they are corrupters of the priesthood*]. But there was only
one priestly offender mentioned, and Nehemiah was not concerned about the purity of the priesthood. Jehoiada's son was
not a grave offender because he was a priest, but because he
had married Sanballat's daughter. **גאלי** has another sense,
which appears in 𝕲, and Nehemiah may have said: *because they
have sought kinship with the priesthood*. The imprecation would
then be against the house of Sanballat; perhaps with a recol-
lection of Tobiah, vv. ⁴ ᶠᶠ·.—*The covenant of the priesthood and of
the Levites*]. For which we find in the Greek text: *of the priests
and of the Levites*, and in 𝕳: *the priestly and the Levitical right*.
As the passage stands it is part of the object of "corrupters,"
cf. Dt. 33⁸⁻¹¹ Mal. 2¹⁻⁸.—**30.** *And I purified them from everything
foreign*]. This expression is more comprehensive than "mixed
marriages." But it is probably a late addition.—*And I appointed the charges for the priests and for the Levites each one for
his task*]. For the Levites this had already been done, v. ¹¹.—
31. *And for the offering of wood in its appointed seasons*], *cf.* 10³⁵;
and for the first-fruits], *cf.* 10³⁶ ᶠᶠ·.—*Remember me, O my God, for
good*], breaking off the supplication abruptly, *cf.* vv. ¹⁴· ¹⁹· ²².

23. השיבו] is impossible after an acc. subj.; 𝕲 οἱ ἐκάθισαν, 𝕳 *ducentes*.
We may rd. המשיבים or substitute אשר for את before היהודים. On ישב,
mng. *to marry*, found only in Ezr.-Ne., *v.* Ezr. 10².—**24.** [וכלישון עם ועם
lacking in 𝕲ᴮᴬᴺ. It has the appearance of a crude explanatory gl.
—**25.** ואמרטם] lacking in 𝕲ᴮᴬᴺ.—ולכס] lacking in 𝕲ᴮᴬᴺ.—**26.** [על-אלה
𝕲ᴮᴬᴺ οὕτως, 𝕲ᴸ περ' τούτων.—After [כמהו 𝕲ᴸ has μέγας.—[החטיאו 𝕲
ἐξέκλινον = הטו, the word used in 1 K. 11³.—**28.** החרני] lacking in 𝕲ᴮᴬᴺ.
—**29.** גאלי] 𝕲ᴮᴬᴺ ἀγχιστείᾳ, *i. e.*, understanding גאל, *to act as kinsman;*
𝕲ᴸ ἀλίσγοντας.—[והכהנה 𝕲ᴸ τῶν ἱερέων.—[ברית" 𝕳 *jusque sacerdotale et
Leviticum*.

EZR. 7–10. THE HISTORY OF EZRA.

The priest-scribe receives a liberal firman from Artaxerxes, gathers a company, and goes to Jerusalem. There he learns of the mixed marriages, and after prayer and fasting measures are taken for their dissolution. Ezra's career is continued in Ne. 8 and in Esd. a part of that chapter follows Ezr. 10 directly, an order adopted here. It has been shown in the Intr. § 10 that Ezra is later than Nehemiah, belonging to the period of Artaxerxes II.

The basis of this section is, I believe, the memoirs of Ezra (*v.* Intr. § 8(2)). This source is used with few exceptions in c. 8 *f.* In c. 10 there are but two buried indications of the original E., *v.* on vv. 15. 19. Who revised the text of c. 10 and how radical the revision was it is hard to say. It seems plain that there is more than one hand visible in the editing. Vv. 1-8 do not seem to come from the same source as vv. 9-17. It appears that there was a gradual transforming of the memoirs into the third p., for various Gk. texts show more of it than MT. In the main the story seems to be entirely worthy of confidence.

7^{1-10} = Esd. 8^{1-7}. **The introduction to the story of Ezra.**— The narrative consists chiefly of the priest's genealogy and office and of the dates of his departure from Babylon and arrival at Jerusalem.—**1.** *And after these things*], a general statement meant to connect this passage with Ezr. 6 which precedes in MT., a favourite phrase of the Chronicler.—*In the reign of Artaxerxes the king of Persia*]. The reference is to Artaxerxes II (404–358).

Ezra's genealogy is traced through seventeen generations back to Aaron. The genealogy is wrong in several respects, *v. i.* Were we to allow three generations to a century, this would carry us back 567 years, that is, about to the period of Solomon. *Seraiah* is the same pr. named in Ne. 11¹¹. *Azariah* is lacking in the priestly genealogy, Ne. 11¹¹, but recurs 3 t. in that of 1 Ch. 5²⁹ ff. (EV. 6³ ff.). The name, which means *Yahweh hath helped*, was borne by many persons. *Hilkiah* was a high pr. of Josiah's time, 2 K. 22⁴, the one who found the book of Dt., and from the table in 1 Ch. 5 this might be the same one.—**2.** *Shallum* is found as Meshullam in Ne. 11¹¹ 1 Ch. 9¹¹. Like others in the list, it was a common name.—*Zadok* occurs twice in 1 Ch. 5³⁴. ³⁸. The best-known pr. of this name was the one whom Solomon exalted over the

deposed Abiathar, 1 K. 2³⁵. *Ahitub* is named as father of Zadok in
2 S. 8¹⁷, but the text is rejected by We. (*Bücher Sam.*).—**3.** *Amariah*.
This name is also repeated in 1 Ch. 5³³· ³⁷. *Azariah* in the Chr.'s table
is wanting at this place, though found 3 t. elsw., Amariah being the son
of Meraioth. The name fails also in Esd.ᴮᴸ. *Meraioth* occurs in Ne.
11¹¹ 1 Ch. 9¹¹ between *Zadok* and *Ahitub*, evidence of the imperfection
of these genealogies.—**4.** *Zerahiah*, outside of the lists in Ch., occurs
only in 8⁴. *Bukki* is the name of a chief in Dan, Nu. 34²².—**5.** *Abishua*
is named among the sons of Bela, 1 Ch. 8⁴, Bela being a son of Benj.
Phinehas, Eleazer, and Aaron are well known.—*The first pr.*] applies
to Aaron and should not be rendered "the chief pr." as in EVˢ.
𝔊 gives it correctly.

6. *This Ezra*] is not right. The words can only be explained
as a resumption, the subject in v. ¹ being too far separated from
the verb, and we should render: *he* [Ezra] *went up from Babylon*].
But the text is made to fit the later introduction of the genealogy.—*He was a ready scribe in the law of Moses*]. Ezra would
not have applied this term to himself. The word rendered
scribe is used often in the pre-exilic writings of a royal official,
a secretary; so in Persia, Est. 3¹² 8⁹; it is given to Baruch,
Jeremiah's private secretary, who wrote his prophecies at his
dictation, Je. 36³². The royal scribe's business was to write a
report of the historic events as they occurred and to inscribe
the king's edicts. The idea of the word became then essentially "a writer." The term applied to Ezra does not imply
primarily that he was learned in the law (Str. *Neuheb. Spr.*³),
but that he was an expert with the pen, writing or copying
the law. Inevitably the scribes became learned in the law;
see the fine passage in Sirach 38²⁴–39¹¹. The adjective "ready"
or "quick" shows the true idea. In papyrus 49 there is the
term "a wise and ready scribe" (Sachau,¹⁴⁸). The law of
Moses is either the completed Pentateuch or the priestly portion thereof. Ezra is supposed to have brought this law-book
with him.—*Which Yahweh the God of Israel had given*], the antecedent being *the law*, which is everywhere assigned to a divine
origin, Moses having received it from God. V.ᵇ is very obscure.
The best we can make out of MT. is: *and the king gave to him all
that he sought according to the hand of Yahweh upon him*]; or

with 𝕲: *because the hand of Yahweh was upon him.* Esd. reads: *and the king gave him honor, for he found favor with him for all his undertakings.*—**7.** The classes that went up with Ezra are the same as those in c. 2. In his own account priests, Levites, and Nethinim are mentioned, but not singers or porters, $8^{15\,\text{ff.}}$.— *In the seventh year of Artaxerxes the king*]. On this date, *v. i.*, Intr. § 10, Kost. *Wied.*[115].—**8.** Esd. omits *and he came to Jerusalem*] and has in one text (^{B}) "second" year instead of "seventh." Wellhausen proposed twenty-seventh, but that does not help much.—**9.** *For on the first day of the first month*]. This date is found in nearly all the Vrss., and is emphasised because it was the beginning of the year.—*That was the beginning of the going up from Babylon*]. This as well as the date preceding is lacking in two Greek texts, but that makes the repetition more meaningless than it is even in MT.

Esd. reads: *he went out from Bab.* The text is not very certain. But the statement shows that the journey from Bab. to Jerus. lasted exactly four months. The time is meant to include the encampment at Ahava, 8^{15}, from which place a final start was made on the 12th day of the 1st month. The obscure statement above may be due to the distinction between the original start from Bab. and the later one from Ahava. As the distance was about 900 miles (Ryle), and the journey lasted more than 100 days, the caravan moved slowly.

10. This verse states the object of Ezra and explains his solicitude to have Levites as well as priests: *to seek the law of Yahweh and to do it, and to teach in Israel statute and judgment*], or with 𝕲 *statutes and judgments,* both being familiar synonyms for the law. Esd. has a different idea: *for Ezra possessed much knowledge, not to omit anything of the law of the Lord and of his commands to all Israel, statutes and judgments,* the last two words being a corrective gloss.

As the passage vv. [1-10] runs, it is not surprising that it is labelled Chr. and passed by as unimportant; for it is overloaded with genealogy, with specific and repeated dates, and other details. But a close examination reveals the fact that a single statement runs through the mass, thus: (1) *In the reign of Art. the king of Pers.* Ezra (6) *went up from Bab. Now he was an accomplished scribe in the law of Moses which Yahweh the*

God of Israel had given. *And the king granted all his requests, acc. to the* [good] *hand of God upon him.* (10) *For Ezra had set his heart upon following and executing the law of Yahweh, and to teach his statutes and judgments in Israel.* (8) *And he came to Jerus. in the 5th month of the 7th year of the king;* (9ᵃ) *for he had departed from Bab. on the 1st day of the 1st month.*

To this v. ⁷ is surely an addition, for the verbs before and after are all in the sg. It is true that we find the pl. in some Vrss., but they are obvious corrections. The material is easily gathered from the body of the narrative, and an intr. which named only Ezra did not suit an editor who kept ever in mind a return from captivity. The genealogy has been added apparently by stages, Esd. having a briefer one than MT., and the latter even being less full than Ch. The insertion of this genealogy made necessary the repetition of הוא עזר in v. ⁶. Esd. has gone further and added a vb. in v. ¹. A comparison with Esd. shows that there has been tampering with the dates in v. ⁸ ᶠ·. It is difficult to determine whether "acc. to the good hand," etc., in v. ⁹, is an accidental repetition, a good text, or, as Esd. suggests, wrong in both cases.

It is apparent that to the story of Ezra there was an original and simple note of intr. In this all emph. was laid upon Ezra's mission and upon his fitness for its accomplishment. The material, it is true, is drawn from the body of the narrative, but that is generally the case with introductions. In my opinion, this original intr. long preceded the editing of the Chr. We note that the writer has chiefly in mind the intr. of the law.

That the genealogy has been shoved in is disclosed most plainly in 𝕲ᴸ, where we have: *and after these things in the reign of Art. the king of Bab., Ezra went up from Bab. Ezra the son of Seraiah. . . . That Ezra went up from Bab.* All the texts show efforts to piece the narrative here. The genealogy may have been a marginal note, and then the clause following would be repeated after it had got into the text. The addition may well be the work of the Chr., but in his genealogical table some names have dropped from our text. The reason for most of the added material is fairly obvious. The passage is much later than E., however, as the stress is laid on the law.

1. עזרא] Εσραςᴮ, Εζραςᴬᴸ. Esd. has προσέβη Εσρας, 𝕲ᴸ ἀνέβη Εζρας, 3 Esd. *accesit Esdras.*—**5.** הכהן הראש] 𝕲ᴸ Esd.ᴸ τοῦ ἱερέως τοῦ πρώτου, Esd.ᴮ τοῦ πρώτου ἱερέως, 𝕲ᴮᴬ τοῦ πατρῴου, an adj. in Prov. 27¹⁰ and representing אב: otherwise it is found only in Apocr. 𝔚 *sacerdotes ab initio,* 3 Esd. *primi sacerdotes.* The words bring out the idea very well that Aaron was the father of the priestly order.—**6.** הוא עזרא] om. 𝕲ᴮ. ᴸ adds to this ἐκ Βαβυλωνος and then repeats Εζρας υἱός κ. τ. λ. מהיר—] seems sufficiently explained from מהר, "to hasten," and to have the mng. *quick*, a sense applicable in the only other occurrences of the word, Ps. 45² Prov. 22²⁹ Is. 16⁵. Müller (*As. u. Eu.*¹⁷³) compares Egyptian *mahira*, "capable." 𝕲 gives a variety of renderings: ταχύς^B, ὀξύς^L, Esd. εὐφυής; 𝔙 *velox*, 3 Esd. *ingeniosus*.—כיד] 𝕲 ὅτι χείρ, *i. e.*, כי יד, so v. ⁹. Esd. has in v.ᵇ: καὶ ἔδωκεν αὐτῷ ὁ βασιλεὺς δόξαν, εὑρόντος χάριν ἐναντίον αὐτοῦ ἐπὶ πάντα τὰ ἀξιώματα αὐτοῦ, thus reading כיד as לבוד, עליו as על, אלהיו as אליו, and יהוה as חן.—מצא 7. הלוים] 𝕲 prefixes ἀπό correctly, since the partitive should be used with each n.; its absence before the last three nouns in all texts suggests either carelessness of the Chr. or more prob. a later addition.—8. ויבא] 𝕲 𝔙 Esd rd. יבאו here and v. ⁹.—השביעית] Esd.ᴮ δεύτερος, but this offers very little help, unless for We.'s conjecture that we should rd. 27th year.—9ᵃ is lacking in 𝕲ᴮᴬ.—הוא יסר המעלה] is difficult; 𝕲ᴸ runs: αὐτὸς ἐθεμελίωσε τὴν ἀνάβασιν ἀπό, *i. e.*, יְסַר, a reading generally accepted, and interpreted "he began the journey from Bab." BDB. gives sense "appoint" here. Esd. has ἐξελθόντος γὰρ ἐκᴮ, lacking יסר.—. . . כיד] Esd. κατὰ τὴν δοθεῖσαν αὐτοῖς εὐοδίαν παρὰ τοῦ κυρίου ἐπ᾽ αὐτῷ: *acc. to the good journey given to them from the Lord to him*, the last two words being added as a correction from MT., and lacking in ᴬ.—10. הכין] 𝕲 ἔδωκενᴮᴬ, ἡτοίμαζεᴸ. Esd. reads: ὁ γὰρ Ἔζρας [Ἀφαρας^B] πολλὴν ἐπιστήμην περιεῖχεν εἰς τὸ μηδὲν παραλείπειν τῶν ἐκ τοῦ νόμου κυρίου καὶ ἐκ τῶν ἐντολῶν [πρὸςᴸ] πάντα τὸν Ἰσραὴλ διακώματα κὰι κρίματα. In part this is traceable, reading הבינה הרבה for הכין לבבו. 3 Esd. shows further correction from MT., reading at end: *et docendo universam Israel omnem justitiam et judicium.*

7¹¹⁻²⁶ = Esd. 8⁸⁻²⁴. The edict of Artaxerxes.

Of all the official documents in our books this one arouses the greatest suspicion. It is difficult to believe that the Pers. king would bestow such immense grants upon Ezra, including *c.* $140,000 in cash; indeed, it is impossible that Ezra, whose purpose was the proper institution of the temple ritual, should need any such sum. It is absolutely out of the question that such enormous powers were conferred upon a Jewish pr., making him really the supreme authority in the whole Syrian province, with power to impose even the death penalty. The decree is even inconsistent with itself in this respect, for a part of it authorises the Pers. officers to pay Ezra money, and then he is clothed with a power that would have enabled him to displace them if he saw fit. Moreover, a large part of the decree is flatly at variance with the work of Ezra, which is described with more fulness than any other event in this period. There is not a hint in the whole story that this pr. ever received as much as a kid from any foreigner whatever. He says himself that he would not ask even a guard from the Pers. king. There is no hint of any tremendous sacrifices such as we should have heard of if the leader had received such liberal donations.

Ezra is here clothed with all of the power of the Pers. king in the whole of Syria, yet he was unable to effect a single divorce except by a pathetic appeal to the people. The official titles which he bears are humble enough, pr. and reader of the law, nothing more. And those titles cover everything that he actually did at Jerus. No great movements of any kind can be traced to him exc. in connection with the cult and with the law. Even Sta. seems to accept the idea that Ezra's law became the law of the king (*BT*.³³⁵). There were two things for which Ezra needed the authorisation of Art., and two only: the permit to take a caravan to Jerus., and to make the *Torah* the law for the Jewish people. Now these two points are explicitly covered in the edict, and if there were nothing else, no one would ever have questioned the authenticity of this decree.

On account of his work in connection with the temple and the law, Ezra is exalted above every other character in this period. In the portion of Esd. which has come down to us, Neh. is not mentioned. To make him as conspicuous as later ages supposed him to be, the historic sources available to the Chr. have been freely worked over. Evidence of this contention abounds everywhere. In this initial c. of his story we have abundant instances. The havoc which has been made of his memoirs offers further proof. To dispose of this edict as a whole by calling it the invention of the Chr., as Torrey among others does, is quite unnecessary. It is hard to see why the Chr. should have written in Aram. Torrey's argument that he does it to give colour to the genuineness of the document breaks down in view of the fact that he is supposed to have written the edict of Cy. in c. 1 in Heb., and that even Torrey admits that the other Aram. sections antedate the Chr.

Now if we dissect this decree, as Torrey dissects that of Dar, we may find perfectly good authority for Ezra's course. There is, indeed, a greater elaboration than in other sections, but Ezra was the hero of the age, and greater glorification was demanded. To find the original we have first the easy task of eliminating vv. ²¹⁻²⁴. In this part there is so unusually close an agreement between MT. and Esd. as alone to offer good ground for suspicion. This agreement is best explained as due to the fact that the passage is later than the rest of the section. The passage in form consists of a decree to the Syrian treasurers, and yet it runs into the decree of Ezra. Vv. ²⁵ ᶠ· may be original, but the officers whom Ezra was authorised to appoint were not civil rulers. The texts show uncertainty, 𝕲 having "scribes" in place of "judges." These officers were mere assistants to be appointed to aid Ezra in his religious duties, and such as we find working with him in large numbers, Ne. 8. The punishments named in v. ²⁶ were not to be imposed by Ezra or his assistants, but by the properly constituted civil officers in the satrapy.

The condition described there had always held good in every part of the Pers. empire, so far as the law of the king is concerned. The new feature is the obligation to obey the law of Yahweh. This law Ezra seems authorised to impose on the Jews.

With the rest of the decree there is little occasion to quarrel. Fischer accepts as genuine vv. [13-16]. [23]. [25]. [26], but this presupposes too much amplification. There may have been a little retouching here and there to enlarge the conception of Ezra's mission, but what it really amounts to is that Ezra had a free hand to beg all the money he could for sacred purposes, and that is assuredly not extravagant in its claims. V. [20] is not quite so natural, and yet Oriental kings were often not averse to doing liberal things on paper. Witness the gold bricks so freely interchanged between the courts of Egypt and Bab. on the unimpeachable evidence of the Tell-Amarna letters. Yet the Esd. texts say that Ezra may take from the royal treasury, presumably in Bab., the vessels for the house of God; quite a different proposition. The version of Esd. differs so much from the Aram. that a translation of the former is appended, for while the detailed variants are cited in the notes, the matter will be grasped better by comparing the Vrss. as a whole. Among the differing texts of Esd. I have chosen that which in each instance seems to be best: (11) *But the person approaching who did the writing of King Art., he delivered the writing, which had come from King Art. to Ezra the pr. and reader of the law of the Lord, of which the subjoined is a copy:* (12) *King Art. to Ezra the pr. and reader of the law of the Lord, greeting.* (13) *And I having a preference for benevolent acts have ordered that those who desire of the nation of the Jews, of their own election, and of the pr. and Lev. who are in our kingdom, may proceed with thee to Jerus. As many therefore as are eager, let them set forth together,* (14) *as seems good to me and to the seven friends counselling with me, that they look after the welfare of Judah and Jerus. in accordance with the law of the Lord;* (15) *and to carry to Jerus. gifts which I and my friends have vowed to the Lord.* (16) *And all the gold and silver which shall be found in the province of Bab., for the Lord at Jerus., with that which is given by the nations for the temple of the Lord which is in Jerus.,* (17) *shall be collected, and the gold and silver for bulls and rams and lambs and the things which go with them, in order that they may offer sacrifices on the altar of the Lord which is in Jerus.* (18) *And all that seems right to thy brethren to do with the gold and silver let it be done, acc. to the will of thy God.* (19) *And the sacred vessels which are given thee for the service of the temple of thy God which is in Jerus.,* (20) *and the rest whatever shall come to thee for the service of the temple of thy God, thou shalt take from the royal treasury.*

(21) *And I, Art. the king, give orders to the treasurers of Syria and Phœnicia, that whatever Ezra the pr. and reader of the law of the most high God demands, shall be scrupulously given to him,* (22) *up to a hundred talents of silver, likewise up to a hundred cor of wheat and a hundred*

bottles of wine. (23) *And acc. to the law of God, let everything be completed for the most high God that there be no wrath against the realm of
the king and of his sons.* (24) *And to you it is said that to all the pr. and
Lev. and singers and porters and Neth. and scribes of the temple, there
shall be no tribute nor other imposition, and no one shall have authority
to lay anything upon them.* (25) *And thou, Ezra, according to the wisdom
of God, appoint judges and magistrates of those who know the law that they
may judge in all Syria and Phœnicia; and all who do not know the law
of thy God do thou teach.* (26) *And all as many as shall trangress the law*
[of thy God and of the king] *shall be strictly punished, whether it be by
death, or by torture, or by fines, or by banishment.*

11. This verse is Hebrew and is the Chronicler's introduction
to the letter which is in Aramaic.—*Copy of the letter*], *cf.* 4¹¹
5⁶. The writer claims to have an authentic document before
him.—*The scribe, the scribe of the words of Yahweh's commandments*]. In place of "scribe," Esd. in one place, by pointing
differently, reads "book."

In this v. 3 Esd. has an interesting plus: *but those approaching who
did the writing of King Art., they delivered the writing which had come from
King Art. to Ezra, the pr. and reader of the law of the Lord, of which the
subjoined is a copy.* It is impossible to think this text an invention of
translators, and yet it is rather startling in its implications; for it reveals plainly a beginning *in medias res.* In other words, this passage
was preceded by an account of the way in which Ezra obtained his
favour from the king, a natural part of the story; *cf.* the story of the
Three Youths, Esd. 3, 4 and Ne. 1, 2. It appears that Ezra was not
at the Pers. court when the decree was issued, but that it was brought
to him at the river Ahava in Bab.

12–26. The letter.—12. *God of heaven*], *v.* 1 ²; Esd. reads
the Lord.—Perfect and so forth] as ARV. is nonsense. By a
slight emendation we get the true sense, *perfect peace. And
now,* coming to the real business.—**13.** *In my empire*]. Ezra is
free to gather his caravan from any part of the vast Persian
kingdom.—**14.** The purpose of Ezra's mission, a mission supported by the king and his seven counsellors (*cf.* the seven
princes, Est. 1¹⁴), was to investigate the condition of Judah,
but from the point of view of the law of God which he carried
with him; that is, to see whether the law was enforced or not.

—15. *Silver and gold*], Esd. *gifts for the Lord which I and my friends have vowed for Jerusalem*]. This implies that Ezra's mission was in some part due to a vow taken by the king, the conditions of which had been fulfilled. We may compare the appeal to the vow of Darius, Esd. 4⁴³ ᶠᶠ·. The expression "vow" is stronger than the Aramaic "offered."—*The God of Israel whose dwelling-place is in Jerusalem*]. The dwelling-place is strictly the temple; but the meaning is more comprehensive than that: Jerusalem was the place Yahweh had selected as his abode. The statement therefore shows a distinct Jewish colouring.— **16.** *All the silver and gold which thou shalt find in the whole province of Babylon*]. This is not qualified by the following words, since the voluntary gifts of the people and priests are quite distinct. Ezra has a roving commission so far as raising money is concerned.

> Ryle explains by saying that the neighbours of the Jews would gladly assist their undertaking. Sieg. supposes it to be a compulsory tax which Ezra had the right to levy upon Jewish property in Bab. Seis. contends that this money came from Jews, since 8²⁵ names only king, counsellors, princes, and all Israel as contributors. Berth. thinks this gift came from foreigners, and if exactness is insisted upon, we might identify this "find" with the gift of the princes, though they are not mentioned here. In spite of his antipathy to aliens in Judah, Ezra might be willing to receive money from them. But all suggestions to explain the money overlook the troublesome word "find," which recurs, by the way, in 8²⁵, and is supported by all texts and Vrss. In Esd. we might render: *all the gold and silver belonging to the Lord of Jerus. which can be found in the province of Bab.* From this we get an entirely new idea. The temple had been repeatedly plundered by As. and Bab. kings, and the booty carried ultimately to temples and palaces in Bab. Now Ezra is authorised to take back all of that spoil which he can find. This makes the passage intelligible, at all events, and makes good sense. If that is the right conception it speaks for the authenticity of the decree.

For the house of God who [or *which*] *is in Jerusalem*]. In Aramaic it is not possible to tell whether the relative stands for "house" or "God"; 𝕲ᴮᴬ 𝔥 have former, ᴸ latter, for in Greek and Latin the distinction must be made, *cf.* 1⁴.—**17.** *That thou mayst faith-*

fully buy with the money], showing that the purpose for which it was collected was the proper institution of the cultus.—*Bullocks, rams, lambs*], the same animals (lacking the goats) named as offered at the dedication of the temple, 6¹⁷.—*And their meat offerings and their drink offerings*], that is, those which properly accompanied the animal sacrifices, *v.* Nu. 15¹⁻¹⁰. Esd. has merely: *and those things which accompany them.*—**18.** But all the money would not be required for sacrifices, therefore the general statement is made that Ezra and his brethren (the priests) may use the balance of the money as may seem to them good; but that it was only to be used for sacred purposes is shown by the limitation, *according to the pleasure of your God*].—**19.** *And the vessels which are given thee for the service of the house of thy God*]. These are doubtless the same as those enumerated in 8²⁵⁻²⁷, and are gifts of the king, members of his court, and Israelites. They are not vessels that had previously been in the temple and which had been already returned, *cf.* 1⁷ ᶠᶠ. 5¹⁴ 6⁵. The direction about these vessels is that they shall be placed in the temple as votive memorials.—**20.** Provision is now made to cover any expenditure not provided in the above grant by allowing the priest to draw upon the royal treasury to meet any requirement for the temple which might fall upon him.—**21.** The king then limits this permission by decreeing that all the treasurers in the Syrian province shall honour the requisitions of Ezra, **22**, up to a hundred talents of silver, a hundred cor of wheat, a hundred bottles of wine and of oil, and an unlimited supply of salt: *salt which is not written*, or restricted. The cor is the same as homer = 393.9 litres. The oil and salt are not mentioned in Esd. According to Meyer's computation the silver would be worth about $140,000, a much larger sum than we should expect. Meyer adds, "but the amount appears to me unsuspicious in view of the rich gifts of the king and his magnates which Ezra brought with him." It is difficult to share this view; *v.* on 8²⁶.—**23.** *Everything which is by the command of the God of heaven shall be correctly executed for the house of the God of heaven*]. This is the most sweeping of all the provisions. Ezra is assumed to have the law as the basis

of his plea for assistance. That law showed in detail what
God demanded in the service at his temple in Jerusalem. That
service was not yet rendered according to this law, and with
such a condition God was not well pleased.—Ezra had shrewdly
appealed to the king's fears and so the decree continues: *why
should there be wrath upon the empire of the king and his sons?*]
The displeasure of God, which might fall upon the Persian empire, may be averted by establishing the rightful cult at Jerusalem. That kind of an appeal would be the most effective and
adds probability to the liberal terms of the edict, *cf.* 6¹⁰ᵇ.—**24.**
To you it is directed]. The antecedent can only be the treasurers named in v. ²¹.

> As the decree was issued to Ezra (v. ¹²) and in view of the material
> intervening between v. ²¹ and v. ²⁴, the construction makes the passage
> suspicious, esp. the use of the second p., as if the decree were directed
> to the treasurers named in v. ²¹. We find here a supposedly exhaustive
> list of the temple officials: pr. Lev. singers, porters, Neth. and ser-
> vants of the house of God. This agrees with the lists of c. 2 exc. for
> the last-named, corresponding to which we find "servants of Solomon."
> These may be identical, but "servants" in our passage has a more
> technical mng. than Berth. gives: *whoever besides has to oversee the ser-
> vice at the temple.* Our text simply asserts that it shall be unlawful
> to impose any kind of tax upon the temple officers; but 𝕲 adds to this
> a provision that no kind of [public] service may be exacted of them.

25. *And thou, Ezra*]. The name recurs because a passage,
vv. ²¹ ᶠᶠ·, had been addressed to others.—*According to the wisdom
of thy God which is in thy hand*], does not mean, according to
the priests' inspired discretion, as Esd. implies, but according
to the written law-book which he carries and to which he must
conform, *cf.* v. ¹⁴; "wisdom" is often in late literature used as a
synonym for "law." The government established by Ezra was
therefore to be hierarchical.—*Appoint judges and magistrates*].
𝕲 better *scribes and judges,* as they were the administrators of
the religious law.—*To all the people who are beyond the River*] is
qualified by the following: *i. e., to all who observe the law of thy
God*], so that Ezra's jurisdiction is confined to Jews in the Syrian
province.—*And whoever does not observe* [the law] *you shall in-*

struct]. This does not open the way to a propaganda among the non-Jewish residents, but means that Ezra and others shall teach the law to those Jews who now do not know or follow it. —**26.** *And every one who does not obey the law of thy God and the law of the king*]. Here is the beginning of the double law under which the Jews have lived to this day, and which causes so much confusion and perplexity (*cf*. Jn. 19⁷). The officers appointed by Ezra were authorised to administer both the religious and the civil law. The various punishments permitted are death, banishment, imposition of fines, and imprisonment. These are comprehensive enough for all purposes.—This brings us to the end of the decree and of the Aramaic sections of the book of Ezra.

11. The Heb. is clear and in good order. Esd. has a different text; it runs: προσπεσόντος [δὲ τοῦ γραφέντος]ᵒᵐ· ᴸ προστάγματοςᵒᵐ· ᴮ παρὰ Ἀρταξέρξου τοῦ βασιλέως πρὸς Ἔσραν τὸν ἱερέα καὶ ἀναγνώστην τοῦ νόμου κυρίου οὗ ἐστιν ἀντίγραφον τὸ ὑποκείμενον. This is nonsense as it stands, because a clause has dropped out after προστάγματος. The deficit is found in 3 Esd.: *accidentes autem, qui scribebant scripta Artaxerxis regis, tradiderunt scriptum, quod obvenerat ab Artaxerxe rege ad Esdram sacerdotem et lectorem legis Domini, cujus exemplum subjectum est.* Doubtless 𝕲 is right in the use of the sg.—המלך] om. 𝕲ᴮᴬ.—ספר] 𝕲 βιβλίου = סֵפֶר, Esd. ἀναγνώστην = קְרָא. The title "scribe" is never found in Esd. (save for the gl. in 9⁵⁵ ᴸ). "Reader" is doubtless the earlier term. For ישראל . . דברי] Esd. shows only תורת יהוה, agreeing essentially with title in v. ¹².—**12.** כהנא om. 𝕲ᴮᴬ.—דתא] is Pers. *dadh* (Andreas, in Mar.⁵⁹).—וכענת] גמיר is a much-disputed phrase. In 𝕲 we find: τετέλεστο λόγος καὶ ἡ ἀπόκρισιςᴮᴬ, *let the word and the answer be performed;* in ᴸ to the above is added: καὶ νῦν = וכענת; Esd. χαίρειν; 3 Esd. *salutem;* Esd. begins v. ¹³: καὶ τὰ φιλάνθρωπα ἐγὼ κρίνας, which is not represented in the Aram. גמיר would correspond to τετέλεστο, though Berth. says Gk. did not understand this word; but the rest, at all events, is not discoverable. Torrey thinks שלם has fallen out after שמיא (*Comp.*⁵⁸), a correction supported by Esd. and now frequently adopted. But if we rely on the Vrss. we must suppose more lost than a single word.—כענת] *v.* 4¹¹.—**13.** במלכותי] Esd.ᴮ καὶ τῶνδε ἐν τῇ ἡμετέρᾳ βασιλείᾳ.—ישראל] Esd. τῶν Ἰουδαίων, a reading overlooked by Kost.— **14.** כל־קבל די] wanting in 𝕲ᴮᴬ, καθ' ὅτιᴸ.—ויעטוהי] *cf*. יעט, Sachau,⁴⁰; it corresponds to Heb. יעץ and has the same mng.—**15.** להיבלה] 𝕲ᴮᴬ εἰς οἶκον κυρίου, *i. e.*, היכל. ᴸ has a dup.: ἀπενεγκεῖν εἰς κ. τ. λ.—החנרו] Esd. ηὐξάμην = Heb. נדר not found in B. Aram.—**16.** תהשכח] Esd. ὃ

ἐὰν εὑρεθῇ (השתכח *cf.* 6²) ἐν τῇ χώρᾳ τῆς B. τῷ κυρίῳ Ιερ. Κυρίῳ is best interpreted as a dative of possession, *i. e.*, *belonging to the Lord of Jerus.*—**16.** וכהניא] lacking in Esd., which knows of no contribution from the pr.; this agrees with 8²⁵ and is prob. right.—מתנרבין .... עם] Esd. σὺν τῷ δεδωρημένῳ ὑπὸ τοῦ ἔθνους, referring to Bab.—**17.** כל .... רנה²] 𝕲ᴮᴬ καὶ πᾶν προσπορευόμενον, τοῦτον ἑτοίμως ἔνταξον ἐν βιβλίῳ τούτῳ; ᴸ adds to this a lit. rendering of the Aram.; 𝔙 *libere accipe et studiose eme de hac pecunia;* Esd. συνηχθῆναι τό τε χρυσίον καὶ ἀργύριον; so 3 Esd. *ut colligatur hoc aurum et argentum.* 𝕲 looks like a bad corruption: πᾶν = כל, προσπ. = קרב (קבל), τοῦτον = רנה, ἑτοίμως = אספרנא, ἔνταξον = תקנא (קרא), βιβλίῳ = כספא (ספר). MT. is poorly supported, but the words are not of great moment.—**19.** פלחן] only here as subst., but *cf.* v.²⁴. 𝕲 λειτουργίαν. Esd. uses a less technical word, χρείαν, in Heb. עבורה.—השלם] 𝕲 παράδος. The word is lacking in Esd.ᴮᴬ, as well as the preceding and following, so that we have merely *the temple of thy God which is in Jerus.* Sieg. Berth. BDB. render "deliver in full number." That implies a certain distrust of Ezra, and would be superfluous in any case. Ges.ᴮ renders "restore," implying, wrongly I think, that these vessels had previously been taken from the temple. Torrey renders "deliver in the presence of." We should prob. assign a weakened sense, "lay up," as Esd.ᴸ θήσεις.—אלה ירושלם] 𝕲 ἐν 'Ιερ. Guthe emends אלה ישראל די ביר" to correspond to v.¹⁵. The most elaborate text is Esd.ᴸ: εἰς τὴν χρείαν τοῦ ἱεροῦ τοῦ θεοῦ σου τοῦ ἐν 'Ιερ. θήσεις ἐναντίον τοῦ θεοῦ 'Ισραήλ.—**20.** חשבות] † All Gk. texts have χρείαν = פלחן, v.¹⁹.—**22.** בתין משה] lacking in 𝕲ᴮ and Esd.: ᴬ ἐλαίου βαδῶν ἑκατόν; ᴸ ἐλαίου ἕως βατῶν ἑκατόν. The unusual order and the witness of 𝕲 make the mention of the oil suspicious.—די־לא כתב] means *without prescription, i. e.,* acc. to requirement.—**23.** מן־טעם] 𝕲 ἐν γνώμῃ; but MT. shows no need of correction.—**24.** לכם] is a manifest Hebraism; Mar. corrects to לכן; similarly we should have עליהן at end of v.—מהורעין] 𝕲 ἐγνώρισταιᴮᴬ, γνωρίζομενᴸ, λέγεταιᴱˢᵈ. The idiom is explained in Kautzsch, § ⁷⁶. The Gk. variants prob. represent only different attempts to make intelligible a circumlocutory expression.—זמריא] Heb. המשררים, 2⁴¹, *v.* Kautzsch, § ⁵⁹. Zimmern connects with Bab. *zammarê* (*v.* Haupt's note in Guthe,⁶⁴).—פלחי] (*v.* פלחן, v.¹ᵃ) 𝕲 λειτουργοῖς = Heb. שרת; Esd. πραγματικοῖςᴮᴬ, γραμματικοῖςᴸ. The word must have some technical sense, but just what it is impossible to say. 𝕲 offers a variety of renderings of v.ᵇ. ᴸ alone agrees with MT. ᴮᴬ has: φόρος μὴ ἔστω σοι οὐκ ἐξουσιάσεις καταδουλοῦσθαι αὐτούς. The first part is easily derivable from MT. בלו = ουκ, והלך = εστω σοι, *i. e.,* הוה. With this reading Esd. in part agrees: μηδεμία φορολογία μηδὲ ἄλλη ἐπιβουλὴ γίνηται, μηδένα ἔχειν ἐξουσίαν ἐπιβαλεῖν τούτοις.— **25.** ואנת] *Masora magna in* B *disertis verbis ait. In libris Danielis et Esdræ ubique* אנתה *scriptum est, uno loco* אנת *excepto* (Str.). Doubtless the text preserves a mere scribal error.—די בידך] lacking in Esd.—

שפטין] γραμματεῖς[BAL] (ספרין), κριτάς[Esd.]. It is hard to say whether 𝕲 is right or merely trying to avoid a tautology, since the two Aram. words both mean *judges* and cannot be distinguished. In Dt. 16¹⁸ we find שפטים ושטרים, 𝕲 κριτὰς κ. γραμματοεισαγωγεῖς. The officers were ecclesiastical, not civil.—דתי] 𝕲 νόμον[BA Esd.], [L] νόμιμα; with Torrey rd. דת.—תהורעון] Guthe corrects to תהו ענה, 𝕲[L] γνωριεῖτε αὐτά. Guthe appears not to have noted this reading, but his emendation has little support.—**26.** שרש] 𝕲 παιδείαν[BA], ἐκιζῶσαι αὐτὸν ἢ παιδεῦσαι[L]; Esd. ἀτιμίᾳ[L], *disfranchisement*, τιμωρίᾳ[BA], *torture*, so 3 Esd. *cruciatu*. שרש means *root*, so the lexicographers argue *uprooting*, *banishment*, ignoring the big gaps in the chain of reasoning. Sieg., perhaps taking a hint from Ges.[B], refers to Ps. 52⁷, where Pi. is rendered "uproot," but we should rd. with 𝕲, שָׁרְשְׁךָ, "thy root." The Gk. translators did not know what the word meant, and we are no better off to-day; "excommunication" would be the most natural mng.—ענש נכסין] 𝕲 ζημίαν βίου[BA], "loss of life"; ζημιῶσαι τὰ ὑπάρχοντα[L], Esd. ἀργυρίῳζη. The punishment is the imposition of fines.—אסורין] 𝕲 παράδοσιν[B], δέσμα[A], φυλακὴν ἐγκλεῖσαι[L]; Esd. ἀπαγωγῇ[BA], δεσμεῦσαι[L].

7²⁷ ᶠ· = Esd. 8²⁵⁻²⁷. Ezra's thanksgiving.

As usually interpreted the leader gives thanks for the decree of Art., but it is really much more than that. The true connection has been destroyed by the editorial work of the Chr. Doubtless this was originally not an appendix to a royal decree, but the conclusion of Ezra's own story of his successful plea to the king. The brief passage expresses thanksgiving in a few words and then proceeds to action, describing how the pr. began to collect leaders to take part in his expedition. The passage is directly continued in 8¹⁵, the Chr. having interjected one of the lists in which he so much delighted. This is the beginning of the fragments of E.

27. One Greek ms. in Esd. begins: *And Ezra the scribe said.* MT. begins: *who has thus put it into the heart of the king*], or better *into my heart.* This refers not to the decree, which was no part of E., but, if MT. is right, to the favourable disposition already described by Ezra in a lost section of his story. The good office of Artaxerxes is due to the moving of God's spirit in his heart. But Esd.[B] has *my heart*, doubtless the original reading. *Of the king* was added to make a closer connection with the decree. Ezra expresses gratitude first that he was moved to do something for the temple, and then that he had received

favour·from the king.—*To glorify the house of Yahweh*] by establishing the full system of sacrifices. "Glorify" is a favourite
word of Is.² 44²³ 49³ 55⁵ 60⁷· ⁹· ¹³· ²¹ 61³. These words express
the great purpose of Ezra's mission, which was concerned with
the temple rather than the law.—**28**. The second ground for
praising God is: *he extended mercy to me before the king and his
counsellors and his officers*] as we should probably read like 8²⁵.
All the mighty officers of the king is in MT., but as the last named
were the least important, *mighty* is out of place, and the repetition of *king* is awkward.—*As the good hand of Yahweh my God
was upon me*]. "Good" is inserted from 𝕲. Esd. reads: *according to the support of Yahweh my God*. The substance is the
same. All of his success is ascribed to the loving kindness of
God.—*And I gathered leaders* [*i. e.*, heads of fathers, Esd. *men*]
from Israel], that is, of course, from the race, not the land. Each
leader would have a number of his clan associated with him.
Having obtained a grant from the king, Ezra proceeds at once
to gather a company from the exiles who are ready to take part
in his expedition. His narrative is now interrupted by a list
of the names of those who went up with him. On these vv. *v.*
also Intr. § ¹¹ ⁽⁴⁾.

27. Esd.ᴬ begins: καὶ εἶπεν Ἔζρας ὁ γραμματεύς (so 3 Esd.). Very
little attention has been paid to this reading. Guthe, Sieg. B.-Rys.
Seis. do not refer to it. Berth. quotes it without a word of comment,
but does not note that it is found only in ᴬ and 3 Esd. Were we to
hold that this is the true beginning of E., we should surely regard this
as an authentic note by the compiler, for Ezra's name is not mentioned
in the genuine memoirs. The abruptness is explained by comparing
6⁶, but it is really due to the Chr.'s omission of the introductory part of
E. The passage serves its purpose here, but is poorly supported, and
shows only a marginal note which was found in some texts, but not in
all. It did not come from the Chr., but was a later editor's note and
so did not find a place in all texts.—אבותינו] lacking in Esd.ᴮᴸ; πατέρων
μουᴬ = אבותי, a better reading.—כזאת] Esd. ταῦτα, prob. a free rendering.—כלב המלך] Esd. εἰς τὴν καρδίαν μου τοῦ βασιλέως. The last two
words are a corrective addition.—ויהוה] om. 𝕲ᴮᴸ, while Esd. curiously
reads αὐτοῦ.—**28.** הטה חסר] is a peculiar combination, but recurs in 9⁹;
Esd. ἐτίμησεν, prob. הרר for הסר.—לפני] 𝕲 ἐν ὀφθαλμοῖς = בעיני. Esd.
ἔναντι. Prob. a case of an obscure word rd. in two different ways.—
ואלכל . . . הגבר]. The change of construction and its peculiar character

raise suspicions. 𝕲 reads: πάντων τ. ἀρχόντων τ. β. τ. ἐπηρμένων^{BA}
[δυνατῶν^L]. Esd. has a different text for the whole: βασιλέως καὶ πάντων
τῶν φίλων αὐτοῦ καὶ τῶν μεγιστάνων αὐτοῦ. It is likely that the original
was the same as 8²⁵, and is here awkwardly amplified.—אלהי] on basis
of 𝕲 Guthe adds הטובה, cf. 7⁹. Esd. has a simpler text: εὐθαρσὴς ἐγε-
νόμην κατὰ τὴν ἀντίληψιν κυρίου θεοῦ μου.—ראשים] Esd. ἄνδρας = אישים;
𝕲 ἄρχοντας = שרים in v. ª. This is another case of an obscure word;
ראשים may be a correction from 8¹.

8¹⁻¹⁴ = Esd. 8²⁸⁻⁴⁰. The list of the leaders of Ezra's company.—1. *Heads of the fathers*] v. s. on 1⁵.—*And their genealogy*], read with Esd. *companies.—In the reign of Artaxerxes the king*]. These words show that this list was not originally composed for this place, or the date would be quite superfluous after c. 7; still less would it be necessary in E. The separation of "with me" from "from Babylonia" indicates that the date was not originally in the text. The Chronicler evidently found the list ready to his hand. "With me" is an editorial note to lend plausibility to the insertion in the body of the memoirs.

2. Phineas, a grandson of Aaron, and Ithamar, a son, are named as heads of priestly clans (*v.* Kue. *Abh.*⁴⁹⁰). Daniel and Hattush are mentioned among the pr. in Ne. 10²⁶ ᶠ·. It is very doubtful whether David here means the famous son of Jesse, though Hattush is given as of Davidic descent in 1 Ch. 3²².—3. Here begins a list of twelve names of heads of houses all originally with a formula: *of the sons of* ——, —— *the son of* ——, *and with him were* —— *males*. There are some places in which the text has been corrupted and thus the formula is marred. Of these names eight recur among "the heads of the people" in Ne. 10¹⁵ ᶠᶠ·, identifying Adonikam and Adoniah, *i. e.*, all except Shekaniah, Shephatiah, Joab, and Shelomith. In the list of Ezr. 2 we find ten of these names, *i. e.*, all exc. Shekaniah and Shelomith. The text is therefore very doubtful and the name Shekaniah is certainly wrong. Shekaniah is a priestly name in our books, Ne. 3²⁹ 10⁵ 12³· ¹⁴. 𝕲 has Zattu, a name found in both Ne. 10 and Ezr. 2, and that is prob. right. *Shelomith* is a Levitical name found often in Ch., and does not belong here as head of a clan. Esd. supplies the true text: *of the sons of Bani, Shelomith the son of Josephiah*. Bani is found in both parallel lists. It is not without interest to note that the first ten names in Ne. agree with ten in our list, and that with two exceptions (Arach, v. ⁵, Zaccai, v. ⁹) they agree with the first twelve in Ezr. 2. B.-Rys. argues that the twelve heads of fathers are due to the theory that the restored Israel was to be made up from the twelve tribes.—13. *And of the sons of Adonikam the last*]. What *the last* means is quite un-

known. Something is apparently lacking. As we rd. *of the sons of
Adonikam . . . and these are their names*, it is clear that there must have
been some statement about these sons, for the last clause would not
be required otherwise. Something like "there were three brothers"
would properly fill up the gap. It may be that we should render:
"and of the sons of Adonikam there were others, and these are their
names." It is noteworthy that here alone we find three names instead
of one, and that here alone the names of the fathers are lacking. The
Vrss. do not agree with our text, Esd.ᴮ and 𝔘 having: *Eliphalet the son
of Jeuel and Shemaiah.*—**14.** Instead of Uthai and Zabbud we should
rd. *Uthai* the son of Zabbud, or Zacchur, as some texts have. The
numbers vary somewhat in the different texts.

1. ראשי] 𝔊ᴸ adds οἴκων as Ex. 6¹⁴ *et pass.*, but *cf.* 1⁵.—[והתיחשם
Hithp. inf. with sf. Ges.⸿⁶⁴. The word is hard to render here. Esd. has
καὶ τὰς μεριδαρχίας (+ αὐτοῦᴸ); 𝔊ᴮᴬ οἱ ὁδηγοί connected with העלים,
the guides going up with me; μεριδαρχίας recurs in 1⁵ = 2 Ch. 35⁵ for
פלגות, in 1¹¹ = 2 Ch. 35¹², מפלגות; we should rd. here ומפלגותם = *and
their divisions* [or *companies*].—מבבל] 𝔊ᴮᴬ lack מ and rd. *king of Bab.*
The date is a late insertion. Esd. transposes: *went up with me from Bab.*,
though this does not presuppose a different text.—עמי] is found in all
the texts. It was doubtless added by the Chr. to make the list fit into
its context.—מבני שכניה]. The expected name following does not appear. In v. ⁵ this name is repeated, but still with a name lacking. Esd.
omits the name in v. ³, and 𝔊ᴮ omits v. ⁵ altogether. We should om.
the name here and supply a name in v. ⁵. Since in 1 Ch. 3²² Hattush
is the grandson of Shekaniah, we might rd. חטוש בן שכניה.—**5.** After
𝔊ᴬ Esd. ἐκ τῶν υἱῶν Ζαθοῆς Εἰεχονίας 'Ιεθήλου (so 3 Esd.), rd. מבני זתוא
שכניה בן־יחזיאל.—התיחש לזכרים] puzzled the ancients, but the real mng.
is *counting only the males;* further on it is deemed sufficient to repeat
only "males," which in Esd. is always ἄνδρες.—**6.** עבר] should certainly be a n. p., but it is peculiar certainly. 𝔊 offers Ωβηθᴮ, Ωβηᴬ,
Αμιναδαβᴸ (= עדין עבר); Esd. Ουβηνᴮ, Ωβηθᴬ, Αμινδαβᴸ. On the whole,
עובֵר is best supported and may be an abbreviated form, as there are
numerous n. p. with עבד as the initial element.—**10.** A name is evidently lacking, as Esd. offers ἐκ τῶν υἱῶν Βανιάς Σαλειμώθ Ιωσαφιουᴮᴬ.
𝔊ᴬ has a similar text. In Esd.ᴸ the first two names are transposed.
Rd. . . . ומבני בני. In 1 Ch. 26²⁵ ישעיהו is the great-grandfather of a Shelomith. There is a suspicious phonic resemblance to יוספיהו, here named
as father of Shelomith.—**11.** In 𝔊ᴸ Esd. the names are differentiated;
correct with Guthe to . . . מבני בקי, *v.* on 10²⁸.—𝔊ᴮᴬ has 78, MT. 28,
i. e., שבעים for עשרים.—**12.** הקטן] *the little one, cf.* "James the less,"
Mk. 15⁴⁰; the name is attested by 𝔊 𝔘 Esd.—𝔊ᴸ has 120 for 110.—**13.**
אחרנים "unintelligible" (Berth.); Seis. says it has a distinguishing significance in view of "the sons of Adonikam," 2¹³, but other names are

repeated without marks of distinction. The "other" of 2³¹ is supposed to distinguish names in the same list. 𝔊 renders ἔσχατοι, 𝕳 qui erant novissimi, 3 Esd. ipsis postremis. The text is well supported; but, if correct, is a mystery.—**14.** וזבוד] om. 𝔊ᴮ; text is wrong, as עמו, the best reading, indicates but one name. Esd. has: Οὐτοῦ Ἰσταχάλχουᴮ, Οὐθὶ ὁ τοῦ Ἰσταλχούρουᴬ; ᴸ agrees with MT. Guthe suggests איש as the first part of this name, after which we should expect the name of a place. But elsw. in this list we have the name of the father, not of the place of residence, and following the easiest way we may rd. עיתי בן-זבור. But Ἰσταχάλχου may be אשמח אליך, "I have spread out unto thee." Qr. substitutes זכור and the Vrss. vary greatly: Ζαβουδᴬ, Ζαχχουρᴸ, Zachur 𝕳. The whole v. is lacking in 3 Esd.

8¹⁵⁻³⁰ = Esd. 8⁴¹⁻⁵⁹. The assembly at the river Ahava.

Here Ezra collects his company. During a three days' encampment it is discovered that no Lev. have joined the expedition. Ezra despatches messengers who return with a suitable supply of temple servants. The company fasts and prays for a safe journey, Ezra being ashamed to ask a guard because he has assured the king that Yahweh would adequately protect those who sought him. This section is from E. and has suffered chiefly by addition of vv. ²⁷ ᶠ. ³⁰.

15. *And I assembled them*]. The antecedent is *heads* or *chiefs*, 7²⁸, not those named in the list (vv. ¹⁻¹⁴) interpolated by the Chronicler. In 7²⁸ the reference is to collecting the people to form a caravan; here it is to the assembling of the company at a particular place in preparation for departure.—*The river which comes into Ahava*]. With Esd. we must read: *the river which is called Ahava;* for in vv. ²¹· ³¹ we find "the river Ahava," this being the name of a river not of a place (so Ewald, *Hist.* v,¹³⁷⁴); Winckler identifies it with *Hables-suk,* which enters the Tigris near Seleucia. But he considers it not a canal of water, but a trade route (*Alt. Forsch.* iii,⁵¹⁸ ᶠ·).—*And I viewed the people and the priests, but I did not find any of the sons of Levi there*]. This explains the purpose of the three days' encampment. Ezra made a scrutiny of the caravan, which had collected voluntarily, his object being to note its composition. Now it would be strange for him to say that he looked among the laity and priests and found no Levites there, as if one were to say "I searched among the privates and found no officers there." Esd. offers a more intelligible text: *I carefully observed them* [the assembled

caravan], *and of the priests and of the Levites I found none there,*
i. e., priests as well as Levites were wanting. It will appear
below that Ezra secured others than Levites when he sent to
Casiphia.—**16.** Making a necessary correction of the text, to secure the lacking temple servants, it appears that an embassy
was sent out comprising two classes of men: one called "heads,"
consisting of nine men whose names are given; the other called
"intelligent," and consisting of two men. But we find *Elna-*
than three times, and the very similar *Nathan* once. *Jarib*
and *Jojarib* are repetitions, and thus a noun, "leaders," and
its adjective, "intelligent," have been separated. We should
therefore read: *I sent Eliezer, et al., intelligent leaders,* men competent for the task in hand. Of these leaders but two, Zechariah
and Shemaiah, are mentioned in the Chronicler's list, vv. [1-14],
an evidence of the character of that list. It is impossible to
tell just how many Ezra sent. The shortest and critically best
list is found in Esd.[L]: *Eliezer, Ariel, Shemaia, Elnathan, Nathan,*
Zecheriah, Meshullam, seven in all.—**17.** *And I sent them*], not
"I commanded them," which we find as an alternative reading.
—*Unto Iddo the chief in Casiphia the place*]. We must omit *the*
place to make good sense. The text shows a Babylonian idiom.
Iddo, otherwise unknown, was the head of a Jewish colony
in Casiphia, which Winckler locates on the Tigris, opposite
Seleucia, and so not far from Ahava (*Alt. Forsch.* iii,[509 ff.]).—
I put words into their mouth]. In spite of his care to choose
intelligent chiefs for his embassy, Ezra framed carefully the
message they were to carry to Iddo.—*Unto Iddo his brethren*
the Nethinim] cannot be right. We should read *unto Iddo and*
his brethren the Nethinim, or possibly *Iddo and his brethren*
dwelling in. Unless Levites and Nethinim are synonymous, it
was evidently not merely Levites which Ezra sought to add to
his company. On the Nethinim, *v. s.* 2[43]. It is evident that
Ezra was quite ignorant of the list in c. 2, or he would not
have been at such pains to secure the attendance of classes
already supposed to be largely represented at Jerusalem.—*To*
bring to us ministers for the house of our God]. Esd. has *send,*
a better reading, since the message was to Iddo, who could

send but not bring. Though some Vrss. read "singers" for "ministers," the more general word, which includes all classes of temple officers, is preferable. Certainly this term would not be used if Levites alone were desired.—**18.** *And they brought to us*]. Another, but erroneous, text, though found in 𝕲, is: *and there came to us*. The meaning is that the intelligent leaders were successful in their quest, for "the good hand of God was over" the whole enterprise, and they brought back from Casiphia to the caravan at Ahava those enumerated in the list following. —The rest of the verse is confusing: *a man of prudence, of the sons of Mahli a son of Levi a son of Israel, and Sherebiah and his sons and his brethren eighteen*]. With Guthe on basis of Esd. we may omit "and," and thus make Sherebiah the man of prudence; for he was a prominent Levite in Ezra's administration, v. [24] Ne. 8[7] 9[4 f.]. "Son of Levi" is here not genealogical, but official, being equivalent to Levite. "Son of Israel" is a corruption. *Mahli* was a son or grandson of Merari, v. [19], and Merari was a son of Levi. There were eighteen Levites of the kin of the prudent Sherebiah who joined him to go up for the temple service. The true reading is: *a prudent man of the sons of Mahli a Levite as the chief, Sherebiah*, etc.—**19.** *And with him Isaiah of the sons of Merari, his brethren and their sons twenty*]. The text is obviously impossible. 𝕲 Esd. omit "with him," thus coupling the two names as co-ordinate; but as this Isaiah is not named elsewhere he could not have been so important a personage. The Vrss. vary, but 𝔘 gives good sense: *Hashabiah, and with him Isaiah of the sons of Merari, and his brethren and his sons twenty.* —**20.** *And of the Nethinim*], following which we have the only historical account of this order, from which it appears that the order was established by David and his ministers for the service of the Levites

The Chr. traces all the temple institutions to David, and the interpolation from his hand is easily recognised here. It is prob. that kings had been wont to present slaves to the temple (*v.* Smith, *OT. Hist.*[222]). The statement is amplified in 3 Esd.: *and they themselves were the chiefs for the work of the Lev. who served in the temple.* It is barely possible that with 𝕲 we should understand two classes here: (1) *of the*

Neth. whom David established, (2) *and the chiefs for the Levitical service,
the Neth.* 220.—*All of them were mentioned by name*], or designated by
name, is a phrase of the Chr. and shows another interpolation. It
appears that the embassy secured 38 Lev. belonging to two families
and 220 Neth. The caravan is now prepared to start on its great
journey, but first the favour of Yahweh must be secured.

21. Ezra proclaims a fast that the people might humble
themselves before God in order to secure an auspicious road.—
22. The reason for the fast is now stated in other terms. *Ezra
was ashamed to ask the king for a guard to protect them from the
enemy on the road*], because he had assured the king that the
hand of God was adequate both to *protect those who sought him*
(Sta.³²⁵), *and his wrath was against those who abandoned him*].
The closing threat is wanting in Esd., which runs: *the power of
the Lord is with those who seek him for every reparation.* It is
rather strange for Ezra to say that God's *power* and *wrath* are
against those who forsake him.—**23.** *And we fasted and sought
from our God touching this, and he was entreated of us*]. Esd.
reads: *and we again sought from our Lord all these things and we
found him favorable.* The beneficent disposition was not determinable at the time, but was shown by the ultimate success of
the enterprise.—**24.** The first person singular is resumed: *and
I selected* [literally, *separated*] *twelve of the leaders of the priests*],
but two are mentioned by name, Sherebiah and Hashabiah, the
very ones who were called Levites in vv. ¹⁸ ᶠ·. 3 Esd. has: *from
the leaders of the people and the priests of the temple*, making a lay
representation in this important body. It looks as if there
were a gap here and that originally the text ran: *and I set apart
from the leaders of the people twelve, and from the priests of the
temple Sherebiah and Hashabiah and with them ten of their brethren.* The whole committee comprised 24, half laymen and half
priests.—**25.** The purpose of their selection is now given: *and
I weighed out to them the silver and the gold and the vessels, the
offering for the house of our God*], the gifts to which reference
is made, at least according to the Chronicler, in the king's decree, 7¹⁵ ᶠᶠ·. It appears that the property, which was sacred
on account of its destination, was carefully weighed and then

committed to hands deemed peculiarly trustworthy.—*And all Israel that were found*]. So is designated one of the sources of the gifts. The qualifying clause is not found in Esd., but is attested by 𝕲. It is not the kind of expression that would be added as a gloss. The explanation may be in 7¹⁶: "all the silver and the gold that thou shalt find in the province of Babylonia." The search was for Israelites from whom contributions could be asked. All that could be found were solicited. There may be an intimation that some of the exiles were not conspicuous when subscriptions for the temple were collected.

26 f. The total amount is given as 650 talents of silver, 100 talents of gold, 100 silver vessels, 20 bowls of gold, and 2 vessels of brass. The silver talents would be about a million dollars, the gold more than three millions. There is, indeed, some uncertainty in the values, but make it as low as possible and still the figures are impossibly big. We realise the Chr.'s fondness for large sums, and his imagination may have led to raising the figures in Ezra's chronicle. *As I weighed to them* or *to their hand* is repeated from v. ²⁵, and as v. ²⁸ connects closely with v. ²⁵, vv. ²⁷ ᶠ· are almost certainly a gl., an opinion supported by the closer agreement of Esd. and the unnatural description of the words in what is supposed to be a mere list. We have no idea of the value of the silver vessels, because the number of talents is wanting, but the worth of the 20 golden bowls is given as 1,000 darics, acc. to Mey. about $5,000. On the daric, a Pers. coin, *v.* 2⁶⁹.—*And two vessels of . . . brass, desirable as gold*]. The character of the brass is usually given as "finely polished," but the construction is ungrammatical and the mng. obscure. Esd. reads: *brass vessels of the best brass, ten* [or *twelve*] *polished vessels*.

28. *You are holy to Yahweh*] by virtue of your sacred office, *and the vessels are holy*], because they were to be placed in the temple, 7¹⁹, *and the silver and the gold is a free-will offering to Yahweh*], and therefore that also is a sacred trust. With 𝕲 and Esd. we should read *God of our fathers*, since Ezra would not say *your* fathers.—29. *Be watchful and vigilant until you weigh it again in the presence of the leaders of the priests and Levites and leaders* of the fathers of Israel in Jerusalem*]. Whatever may

---

* Guthe makes a slight change and reads "heads," the more common expression for the laity; but "heads" is characteristic of the Chr., not of E. There is no need to emend where the Chr. has let the text alone.

have been the amount of the sacred property, Ezra carefully impresses upon its guardians their great responsibility.—*The chambers of the house of Yahweh*] designates more particularly the place where the gifts were to be put. With 𝕲 we should prefix "for" or "in."

30. This v. is an addition by the Chr., for the third p. is used at the beginning and the first at the end; pr. and Lev. are here the custodians of the valuables, whereas above twelve chief pr. were the treasurers; the statement gets ahead of Ezra's narrative in v. ³¹, and it adds nothing whatever to the story. Esd. has a radically different text: *and the pr. and Lev., receiving the silver and the gold and the vessels which were in Jerus., brought them to the house of the Lord.* It becomes thus an exact dup. of v. ³³.

15. הבא אל־אהוא] Esd.ᴸ τὸν ποταμὸν τὸν λεγόμενον Εεια; so rd. הקרא. This important reading seems to have escaped all the commentators. The text is at variance with vv. ²¹·³¹. The Vrss. give several forms of the name: Ευειμᴮ, Ευειᴬ ᴸ (vv. ²¹·³¹), Θουιᴮ, Λουεᴬ, Δαουαθᴸ. Esd. Θεραν; 𝕳 *Ahava*, Esd. *Thia*. Winckler reads: אובה or אבה.—אבינה] 𝕲 συνῆκαᴮ, κατενόησαᴸ, 𝕳 *quæsivi*, Esd. κατέμαθον, 3 Esd. *recognovi*. These all support the text.—For what follows Esd. has a better text: κατέμαθον αὐτοὺς καὶ ἐκ τῶν ἱερέων καὶ ἐκ τῶν Λευιτῶν οὐχ εὑρὼν ἐκεῖ. Therefore rd. ...ואבינם ומכהנים. The Chr. having put pr. in the list (vv. ² ff.) must, of course, have them here.—**16.** We must either drop the prep. ל before each name, as 𝕲ᴸ 𝕳 and Esd.ᴸ, or interpret שלח ל as mng. "summon" or "sent for." V. ¹⁷ shows that the men named were Ezra's messengers. The Vrss. show much discrepancy in the list of names: 𝕲ᴮ has Αρεβ for יריב and ויריב; the names are certainly duplications; 𝕲ᴸ omits from ראשים to end of v.; Esd. lacks the last two names altogether, and so recognises no classes. The evidence shows that ויריב ואלנתן are accidental repetitions. Then ראשים and מבינים should be joined together as in Esd.: ἡγουμένους καὶ ἐπιστήμοναςᴮᴬ, ἄρχοντας συνετούςᴸ.—**17.** אוצאה] so 𝕲ᴮᴬ ἐξήνεγκα. Qr. אצוה, so 𝕲ᴸ ἐνετειλάμην. The former is the better reading. Esd.ᴮᴬ καὶ εἶπα αὐτοῖς ἐλθεῖν = ואמרם לאתות.—...ארו]. For this very difficult text 𝕲ᴮ has: ἐπὶ ἄρχοντος ἐν ἀργυρίῳ τοῦ τόπου, *i. e.*, על ראש בכספי המקום. This makes no sense and this version is still more hopeless in v. ᵇ. Esd. πρὸς Λααδαῖον [Αδδαιᴸ, Δολδαιονᴬ], τὸν ἡγούμενον τὸν ἐν τῷ τόπῳ γαζοφυλακίου, *i. e.*, אל־אדי הראש במקום הגזבר. In spite of the antiquity of the corruption, it is best to regard the ungrammatical המקום as a marginal note to show that the unknown Casiphia was a place; it is employed like the Bab. determinative. We might easily imagine that this passage was originally written in Bab.—ארי אחיו] 𝕲ᴮᴬ πρὸς τοὺς ἀδελφοὺς

αὐτῶν τῶν Ἀθανείμ; ᴸ καὶ πρὸς τ. α. α. τοὺς Ναθιναίους. It suffices to
rd. with Esd. וְאָחָיו. Esd. lacks הַנְּתִנִים, and this may be an error for
הַיּשְׁבִים.—לְהָבִיא] Esd. ἀποστέλαι = שְׁלֹחַ.—מְשָׁרְתִים] ᴳ ἄδοντας^{BA} (מְשֹׁרֲרִים);
ᴸ has dup., λειτουργοὺς καὶ ἄδοντας, Esd. ἱερατεύσαντος, in agreement with
its reading in v. ¹⁵; so 3 Esd. eos qui sacerdotio fungerentur = מְכַהֲנִים.—
18. וַיְבִיאוּ] so Esd.ᴸ ἤγαγον, 𝔙 and 3 Esd. adduxerunt; Qr. וַיָּבִיאוּ, so ᴳ
ἤλθοσαν^{BA}, ἦλθον^{L}. The first clause is lacking in Esd.ᴮ. Kt. is prefer-
erable, as the Hiph. corresponds to לְהָבִיא, v. ¹⁷.—הַשּׂוּכֵב] Esd.^{AL} κρατιάν
= הַחֲזָקָה.—אִישׁ שֶׂכֶל] puzzled the translators; ᴳ has ἀνὴρ σαχιώ(χ)^{BA}, α.
συνετός^{L}, doctissimum 𝔙, Esd. ἄνδρα ἐπιστήμονα^{BL}, ἄνδρας ἐπιστήμονας^{A},
viros peritos 3 Esd. There is no good reason for a pl., as the words
apply only to Sherebiah.—וְשֵׁרֵבְיָה] ᴳ καὶ ἀρχὴν ἤλθοσαν^{BA}, ἐν ἀρχῇ Σα-
ρουια^{L}, so Esd.^{L}; ἄρχη is used to translate twenty-four different Heb.
words (Hatch and Redpath, Concord.), but the text was apparently
בְרֹאשׁוֹן, "at the head," and that has been corrupted to בֶן־יִשְׂרָאֵל. That
designation would agree with the statement that Sherebiah was a
prudent man.—בֶן לֵוִי] is wanting in ᴳᴸ.—19. The text is corrupt. 𝔙
requires the slightest change to make sense: et Hasabiam, et cum eo
Isaiam de filiis Merari, fratresque ejus, et filios ejus viginti. ᴳ and Esd.
rd. את for אִתּוֹ. ᴳᴮᴬ have υἱοὶ αὐτῶν, ᴸ τῶν υἱῶν αὐτοῦ καὶ τῶν ἀδελφῶν
αὐτοῦ, transposing in agreement with v. ¹⁸. But in Esd. ᴸ has αὐτῶν
in both cases, while ᴮ has for the whole v.: οἱ ἐκ τῶν υἱῶν χανουνάιου
καὶ οἱ υἱοὶ αὐτῶν εἴκοσι ἄνδρες; 3 Esd. Asbiam et Amin ex filiis filiorum
Chananæi, et filii eorum viri viginti. Two names are pretty well attested, but there is doubt between Merari and חֲנֻנִיָה. On the whole,
the reading of the Latin is the simplest, requiring but a single change,
i. e., וּבָנָיו.—20. נָתַן] = "appoint," cf. BDB.—הַשֹּׁעֲרִים] ᴳ οἱ ἄρχοντες, Esd.
οἱ ἡγούμενοι, 3 Esd. principes. Therefore there is no support for
Winckler's emendation, מְשָׁרְתִים.—נְתִינִים .... שֵׁנָתוּ] is inserted by the Chr.
as an explanatory note. The rel. שׁ never occurs elsw. in Ezr.-Ne.,
but twice in Ch. (Dr.^{Intr. 549 f.}). Sieg. regards whole v. as a gl.—
נִקְּבוּ] ᴳ συνήχθησαν^{BA}, ὠνομάσθησαν^{L}, 𝔙 vocabantur, Esd. πάντων ἐσ-
ημάνθη [ὀνομασθη^{A}] ὀνοματογραφία^{B}; οὗτοι ἐσημάνθησαν ἐν ὀνοματογραφίᾳ^{L};
3 Esd. omnia nomina significata sunt in scripturis. It is a favourite
phrase of the Chr. (Dr.^{Intr. 536}).—22. לְעֶזְרֵנוּ] ᴳ σῶσαι, Esd. ἀσφαλείας.
There is much variety in the rendering of the last clause: ᴳ renders
lit., but Esd. has: ἰσχὺς [עֹז for יַד] τοῦ κυρίου ἡμῶν ἔσται μετὰ τῶν
ἐπιζητούντων αὐτὸν εἰς πᾶσαν ἐπανόρθωσιν; 3 Esd. virtus Domini erit cum
eis qui inquirunt eum in omni affectu. This lacks the last clause entirely,
i. e., the threat to those who abandon God.—23. נָצוּמוּ] Esd. πάλιν =
נָשׁוּבָה.—24. מִשָּׂרֵי הַכֹּהֲנִים] 3 Esd. ex plebis præpositis et sacerdotibus tem-
pli = מִשָּׂרֵי הָעָם וּכֹהֲנֵי הַהֵיכָל.—לְשֵׁרֵבְיָה]. The prep. is supported by ᴳᴮᴬ,
but not by ᴳᴸ Esd. It is an error, but not, I think, accidental. It
was prob. put in to avoid the statement that Sherebiah and Hashabiah
were pr.—25. אֶשְׁקֳלָה] ᴳ ἔστησα, so vv. ²⁶. ²⁹. ³³, Esd. as ᴳ, but in vv.

26. 29 παρέδωκεν. In my addenda to Guthe (*SBOT*.⁵⁷) I stated that in Ezr. 8²⁶·³³ παρέδωκεν stands for שקל. Torrey denies this and insists that שקל is represented by στήσας and σταθέν (ES.¹²³). It is true that ἱστάναι stands for שקל, though very rarely, but in Esd. 8⁵⁸ (= Ezr. 8²⁹), παραδοῦναι does represent שקל. In 8⁵⁶·⁶¹ (= Ezr. 8²⁶·³³) we have both Gk. words, παρέδωκεν στήσας, σταθὲν παρεδόθη; στήσας and σταθέν may therefore be complementary vbs.—**26. לככרים**] cannot be connected with any word as it stands; מאה gives the number of the vessels, not of talents as RV. The word is lacking in 𝔊 𝔙. Mey. suggests that a number has fallen out, but says that it may be that each vessel averaged a talent (*Ent*.⁶⁹). Guthe omits the word as a gl. On the analogy of לאררכנים אלף, v. ²⁷, the most natural supposition is that a number followed, so that the text originally rd.: 100 *silver vessels* [weighing] . . . *talents*.—**27. לאררכנים**] 𝔊 εἰς τὴν ὁδὸν χαμανείμ (δράχμωνᴬ, δράχμαςᴸ). This is a dup. reading, first לדרך and then correcting by adding a weight. Esd. lacks the word and the numeral following as well.— **כלי נחשת**]. Here we have a mpl. followed by a f. adj. The Vrss. vary: 𝔊 σκεύη χαλκοῦ στίλβοντος ἀγαθοῦ διάφορα ἐπιθυμητὰ ἐν [ὡςᴸ] χρυσίῳ, Esd. σκεύη χαλκᾶ ἀπὸ χαλκοῦ χρηστοῦ στίλβοντα σκεύη δέκα [χρυσοειδοῦς δέκα δύο]ᴸ, showing a correction from MT. This would be: כלי נחשת מנחשת טובה כלים מצהבים עשר. Sieg. emends מצהב טובה to מזהב טוב, "better than gold," and then disposes of המורות as a later gl. In spite of lack of textual support this is ingenious. Some emendation is necessary, but it is dub. if brass would be considered as desirable as gold, unless it were of an unusual kind.—**29. תשקלו**] Esd. παραδοῦναι αὐτὰ ὑμᾶς.—**לישראל**] lacking in 𝔊ᴮᴬ, but it is used in place of a genitive and denotes the lay order that had a part in the government as well as the pr. and Lev.—**הלשכות**] 𝔊 εἰς σκηνάςᴮᴬ, εἰς τὰ παστοφόριαᴸ, 𝔙 *in thesaurum*, 3 Esd. *in pastoporio*. Doubtless we should rd. ב or ל for ה; the art. could not be used with st. cstr.—**30. משקל** lacking in Esd.; it is certainly unnecessary.

As our text stands, Ezra discovered that there were no Lev. in his caravan, and therefore he sent a large embassy, seven or possibly eleven men, to Iddo to make good the deficiency, or, as he says, "to bring us ministers for the house of God." Sherebiah with 18 brethren, Hashabiah with 20, and 220 Neth. were brought back. But these two men are called "leaders of the pr." in v. ²⁴, and rightly, for the precious money and vessels would have been committed to the highest class of sacred officials. בן-לוי in v. ¹⁸ is lacking in 𝔊ᴸ and may be a gl. to harmonise with v. ¹⁵. Esd., indeed, says that both pr. and Lev. were lacking, and that agrees with the mission to bring ministers for the temple. But it is strange that in the assembly called by the great pr. Ezra, there was neither pr. nor Lev. Nevertheless it is possible that these officers were wedded to the old ways and were not in sympathy with the new order which Ezra proposed to institute, and only joined the caravan after much persuasion and perhaps with liberal promises. Then we should explain the large number of Neth. as being a subordinate order of Lev. In regard to the descent of Sherebiah from Mahli and Hashabiah from Merari, it suffices to say that every pr. was of Levitical descent.

8^{31-36} = Esd. 8^{60-64}. The caravan goes to Jerusalem.

Upon the arrival of the company the money and vessels were counted and placed in the temple, sacrifices were offered, and the royal edict was delivered to the officers of the Syrian province. Only vv. $^{31\ f.}$ are from E.; the rest is the Chr.'s.

31. *On the twelfth day of the first month*]. On the date, *v.* $7^{7\ ff.}$. According to that passage the journey lasted about four months, Jerusalem being reached in the 5th month of the 7th year of Artaxerxes.—*And the hand of our God was upon us*]. We miss the usual adjective qualifying "hand," but in Esd. we find *mighty hand.*—*And he delivered us from the hand of the enemy and lier-in-wait on the way*], or better with Esd.: *from every foe on the way.* So they knew that God had heeded their petition, v. ^{23}. Emphasis is laid upon the safety of their journey, because such caravans were always exposed to the attacks of plundering Bedouin; though the caravan comprised upward of 2,000 people their defensive power was little, v. ^{22}; the large amount of treasure carried, the possession of which could scarcely be kept a secret, made an attack especially inviting.—**32 f.** *And we remained there three days, and on the fourth day*]. This statement is scarcely natural, as we should expect to continue by saying "they went to some other place." If we could render "rested," that would make good sense, but ‏ישב‎ does not mean that. Therefore we had better follow Esd.: *on the third day of our being there, we weighed,* etc., or better with 𝕲 *placed,* since *in the house of God* shows the ultimate destination of the treasure, not the mere place of reweighing.—The final custodians are now named; there were two priests: *Meremoth*] 10^{36} Ne. $3^{4.\ 21}$ 10^6 $12^{3.\ 15}$, not the same person, though, in every case, and *Eliezer*], who had been one of those deputed to fetch temple servants, v. ^{16}. Besides there were two Levites, *Jozabad*] ($10^{22\ f.}$ Ne. 8^7 11^{16}) and *Noadiah*], a name elsewhere only of a prophetess, Ne. 6¹⁴. In spite of the lower office of the Levites they were associated with the priests in the care of the temple treasures. The peculiar expression *Meremoth . . . and with him Eliezer . . . and with them*], supported by all the Vrss., means that Meremoth was chief, his first associate being a fellow-priest, and their associates being two Levites.—**34.** The awkward expression *by number and by weight for everything*] shows the hand of the Chronicler, who dearly loved amplification. It is quite superfluous in view of the following: *and the whole weight was recorded*], to tally with the list made at Ahava, and to show for what amount Meremoth and his associates were responsible. The care of the treasure reveals at every point a commendable business sagacity. The writer may have recalled such stories as that in 2 K. 12, where the priests purloined money given for the repair of the temple. —*At that time*] is better connected with v. ³⁵, as in some Greek texts.—**35.** *The sons of the captivity who had come from the exile*] is intended to emphasise the statement that the great sacrifices were made wholly by Ezra's company and were not participated in by those already in Jerusalem.—*Twelve bullocks for all Israel*], *i. e.*, one for each tribe, showing the persistent theory that the new Israel comprised the whole nation. The specific number of rams, 96, it is to be noted is a multiple of 12. Note also 12 he-goats, and according to Esd. there were 72 lambs (instead of 77). Our text has *he-goats of a sin offering*] (*v.* on 6¹⁷), but Esd. reads 12 *he-goats for deliverance*, making this sacrifice a thank-offering for the safe journey, or it may be a peace-offering.—**36.** *And they delivered the king's decree*] not *decrees*, presumably meaning the edict in 7¹² ᶠᶠ·], to *the king's satraps, the governors beyond the River*]. There should be no "and unto" before "governors," though the last clause is a gloss. These were, of course, the Persian officers in the province.—*And they supported the people and the house of God*] is difficult. We may take recourse in one Greek text: *and they supported the people and honored the house of God*, or emend the text slightly, reading: *the people honored the house of God*, thus explaining the large offerings. The subject of "supported" is usually held to be

the Persian officials, and that is presumably what the Chronicler
meant, but grammatically it is the same as that of "delivered."

Vv. ³⁵ ᶠ· are surely by the Chr. The use of the third p. as well as the
character of the passage shows that (so Fischer, *Chr. Fr.*⁷). In the
rest we have the first p. pl. throughout, but it is consistent in vv. ³¹ ᶠ·
with Ezra's usage to employ the pl. to describe a corporate act. In
v. ³⁶ we should surely have ואתן, though MT. is supported by all texts.
In v. ³¹ᵇ Esd.ᴮ has third p. throughout; and other MSS. of Esd. and ᕮ
have it in places. Yet something is required between v. ²⁹ and 9¹. The
only part of our text which inspires confidence is vv. ³¹ ᶠ·. The rest is
written by the Chr. or edited by him beyond recognition of the original. It is plain that, omitting the Chr.'s "after these things," v. ³² connects well with 9¹.

31. נהר אהוא] Esd. τόπου Θεράᴮ, ποταμοῦᴬᴸ.—וייד] Esd. κατὰ κραταιὰν
χεῖρα. We should restore חזקה for the superfluous היתה.—מכף אויב ואורב]
ᕮ ἀπὸ χειρὸς ἐχθροῦ καὶ πολεμίουᴮᴬ + ἐνεδρεύοντοςᴸ, showing a double
rendering of אורב; Esd. has only ἀπὸ πάντος ἐχθροῦ (מכל־אויב). 3 Esd.
lacks v. ᵇ. It is prob. that כל was corrupted to כף and that אורב is an
amplification by the Chr. or an accidental repetition of a similar word.
—**32 f.** . . . ונשב]. The unrevised Esd. gives merely: γενομένης (ἡμῖν)
αὐτόθι ἡμέρας τρίτηςᴮ, to which τῇ ἡμέρᾳ τῇ τετάρτῃ has been added
in ᴬᴸ from MT., but without changing the construction, and so making no
sense. 3 Esd. *et cum factus fuisset tertius dies, quarta autem die.*—נשקל]
ἐστήσαμεν of ᕮ goes better with כבית.—**34.** . . . במספר] Esd. πρὸς ἀριθ-
μὸν καὶ ὁλκὴν πάντα.—**35.** שבעים ושבעה] Esd.ᴬᴸ ἑβδομήκοντα δύο, rightly,
since every offering is twelve or a multiple of twelve.—צפירי חטאת] *cf.*
צפירי לחטיא, 6¹⁷; ᕮ χιμάρους περὶ ἁμαρτίας; Esd.ᴮᴬ τράγους ὑπὲρ σωτηρίου,
i. e., צפרים לשלה, or השועה לשלה ⁴⁊.—**36.** דתי] *cf.* 7¹²; in spite of ᕮ we must rd.
sg. דת.—אחשדרכני] Pers. *Khshaltapavan*, used also in Est. 3¹¹ 8⁹ 9³. ᕮᴮᴬ
τοῖς διοικηταῖς. Esd. τοῖς οἰκονόμοις, 3 Esd. *dispensatoribus*. ᕮᴸ has a
wholly different text: *the governors of the king and the officers beyond
the River gave the burnt-offerings of the king.*—. . . פחוות] is an explanatory
gl.—נשאו] ᕮᴮᴬ Esd. ἐδόξασαν, ᴸ ἐπῆραν τὸν λαὸν καὶ ἐδόξασαν τὸν οἶκον τ. θ.

EZR. 9, 10.   THE MIXED MARRIAGES AND THEIR DISSOLUTION.

In this section we find Ezra dealing with the Jews already in Judah.
This is the only event of his administration recorded in the book called
by his name. The rest of his mission is described in Ne. 8.

**9¹⁻⁵ = Esd. 8⁶⁸⁻⁷⁰. The officers report to Ezra that the
Jews had been marrying women of alien races.—1.** *Now
when these things were completed*]. As our text stands the ref-

erence is to the depositing of the treasure in the temple, the
sacrifices, and the delivery of the edict. But it is far from certain that we have the whole of the memoirs, and there may be
a gap between 8³² and 9¹, poorly filled by the Chronicler's notes.
These words are certainly a connecting link due to the Chronicler. So far as we can see, though, this passage directly follows
v. ³², and the connection is passable.—*We dwelt there three days,*
[when] *there drew near unto me the leaders reporting*]. "Leaders"
is characteristic of E.; the Chronicler uses "heads." They
cannot be the same as those named in v. ² ᵇ as chief trespassers.
After this the text is bad, but probably ran somewhat as follows: *the magistrates and the priests and the Levites have not
separated themselves from the peoples of the lands*]. On peoples
of the lands, *v.* on 4⁴. The rest of the verse is a gloss, added to
increase the stigma. *According to their abominations*] has no
place here; for that word refers to the religious practices, while
here the only fault is the mixed marriages. Ewald's proposal
to emend and read "from their abominations" (*Hist.* v. ¹³⁹)
improves the grammatical construction, and should be adopted
if the phrase is accepted.—The list of foreigners is based on
Dt. 7¹, where we find Girgashite and Hivite, but not Ammonite,
Moabite, or Egyptian; in 𝔊ᴸ these three are at the end of the
list, suggesting a gloss. Esd. omits *Ammonite*, and reads *Edomite* for *Amorite*, a reading accepted by Smend (*Listen*,²⁴), thus
having seven nations (*cf.* Acts 13¹⁹). Nehemiah found marriages only with the Ashdodites (*v.* 13²⁷).—**2.** The specific
charge is now made to explain the general accusation in v. ¹:
they have taken wives of their [peoples of the lands'] *daughters for
themselves and for their sons*]. There is no hint that Jewish
women had married foreign men. The condition is attributable
to the scarcity of women in the new community.—The result
is that *the holy seed is amalgamated with the peoples of the lands*].
Israel is called a "holy seed" in Is. 6¹³, *cf.* 62¹² Mal. 2¹⁵.—
Now the hand of the leaders and nobles was chief in this wrong] is
usually regarded as the conclusion of the accusation; but from
the structure it could only be a note by Ezra or the Chronicler.
3 Esd. preserves what I deem the original text: *the officer of*

lawlessness has been a participant [in the wrong] *from the beginning of his rule.* Here is a specific charge of dereliction on the part of one of the high Jewish officials. The words then give the climax of the accusation.—**3.** Upon hearing this Ezra exhibited the outward acts of mourning, tearing his clothes, and pulling his hair from his head and beard, *and sat down appalled*]. Esd. forcefully renders *anxious and very sad,* 𝕲ᴸ *silent and wondering.* It appears that the mourner showed his distress by his actions, but that all the day he was silent, uttering no cry until the evening oblation.—**4.** *And there gathered unto me all that trembled at the word* [not *words*] *of the God of Israel*], all that showed any purpose to keep the law. 𝕲 has *all that followed the word,* a rather better sense, though we have a parallel to the text in Is. 66⁵.—*Because of the wrong of the captivity*] is difficult here. Esd. has a better sense: *while I was mourning because of the lawlessness.*—**5.** *And at the evening oblation*] used as a mark of time (*cf.* 1 K. 18²⁹) and to indicate the appropriate moment for prayer.—*I rose from my humiliation*], a doubtful sense; the word is only used here. Esd. renders *fasting.*—*Even with my garment and my robe rent*] RV., which Ryle prefers to AV. "having rent my garment and my mantle."

> The latter is an accurate rendering; indeed, the text will not allow RV., which is made to harmonise with the statement of v. ³ that Ezra had already rent his garments. Moreover, some such action is required to explain his getting up and then kneeling down. It may be that he rent his garments again, though the act would scarcely be appropriate at the beginning of his prayer. The attitude of prayer is bowing the knees and spreading forth the hands. So Solomon knelt upon his knees with his hands spread forth toward heaven, 1 K. 8⁵⁴. The hands were extended upward (Ex. 17¹²), so the supplicant could not have bowed his face to the ground.

9⁶⁻¹⁵ = Esd. 8⁷¹⁻⁸⁷. Ezra's prayer.

> The history of Israel is reviewed, showing that the sufferings of the people were due to their sins. Just now God had shown a gracious purpose which was in danger of being thwarted by the violation of the prophetic word forbidding mingling with aliens. The prayer closes with a despondent cry that the people cannot stand before an offended God.

6. *And I said*]. In some MSS. of Esd. we read: *and Ezra said.*
—I am ashamed and confounded before thee], as Esd. lacking *to
lift up my face*, is better language than MT. If we retain *to
lift up my face unto thee* we should expect but one preceding
verb.—*For our iniquities are many above head*] is what MT. has,
but this is unintelligible. The idea cannot be "higher than our
head" in parallelism with *our guilt is great unto the heavens*];
for the verb רבה means "to be many" not "to be high." EVˢ.
"our iniquities are increased over our head" is obscure, as
above the head is a strange place for the increase of wrongs.
On the basis of Esd. we may read: *our iniquities are more numerous than the hairs of our head, cf.* Ps. 40¹³ 69⁵.—*Unto the heavens*]
so as to reach the heavens, viewed as a definite place above the
earth.—**7.** *From the days of our fathers*], as shown by *unto this
day*, means from the beginning of history.—*Because of our iniquities we, our kings, our priests, have been delivered*]. It is
hard to see why kings and priests should be specified as the
victims of *the sword, captivity, plundering and shame of face*].
The Vrss. vary greatly, but I have ventured to restore *we all
with our brethren and our sons*, and thus we get a characteristic
general description so frequent in these books. Esd. has a plus:
our iniquities and those of our fathers, showing the idea that the
past suffering could not be due to present sins.—*Into the hands
of the kings of the lands*], "lands" as often meaning foreign countries; so 𝕲 plainly, *kings of the gentiles.*—**8.** *And now* [to come to
the heart of the matter] *as for a moment, there was mercy from
Yahweh our God* [for which 𝕲 has only *and now our God has restored us*] *to leave us a root and a name in his holy place*], emending
on the basis of Esd. MT. has *to give us a tent-pin in his holy
place*, interpreted to mean a secure position. Why a tent-pin
should have such a significance is not clear, and besides Ezra
regards the position of the people as very insecure. The holy
place covers more than the temple, including the sacred city.
—*To lighten our eyes, O our God*] occurs in Prov. 29¹³ Ps. 13⁴
19⁹, but fits poorly here. The real meaning is to give understanding or to restore health or to refresh, *cf.* 1 S. 14²⁷. Esd.
has a suggestive text: *to uncover our light in the house of God.*

The idea then would be that God had enabled his people once more to worship him in his holy temple; they were no longer constrained to sing Yahweh's songs in a strange land (Ps. 137⁴). —*Give us a little reviving in our bondage*], ARV., is scarcely to be extracted from MT. Making a slight correction from Esd. and translating correctly we have: *to give us sustenance in the time of our bondage*. That may seem to refer to the past rather than the present; but the condition of bondage in a way persists, v. ⁹, and the meaning is that God was supporting them in their servitude.—**9.** The benefits conferred by their God through the agency of the Persian kings, the plural (kings) showing that Ezra is not dealing with a single incident, are: (1) *to give us sustenance*]; but this is a repetition of the statement in v. ⁸; therefore with Esd.ᴸ read *to show us mercy, i. e.*, by the release from captivity; (2) *to erect the house of our God*], referring to the rebuilding by Zerubbabel and Joshua; (3) *to raise up its ruins*], so amplifying the preceding; but this is a needless repetition, therefore read with Esd. *to raise up the desolation of Zion*, and so we have a more comprehensive statement than building the temple and referring to the new houses which had certainly been erected in the city by Nehemiah; (4) *to give us a wall in Judah and Jerusalem*]. "Wall" is occasionally used in a figurative sense, for the divine protection, and Mey. so interprets here (*Ent.*⁹⁰); but the preceding statements are literal, and the natural reference is to the wall built by Nehemiah. As Ezra would scarcely say *a wall in Judah and Jerusalem*, we may best omit *in Judah* or read *around Jerusalem*, as due to the Chronicler's idea that Ezra preceded Nehemiah. The reference to the building of the wall is strong support for the true date of Ezra.—**10.** *And now what further shall we say?* What follows is best taken as the answer to this question. All that we can say is that *we have forsaken thy commandments*].—**11.** These were given by *thy servants the prophets*]. The quotations are all from Dt., and *the prophets* therefore means *Moses*. On this conception of the prophetic origin of the law, *v. OTJC.*³⁰⁴·³¹³.

What follows is the commandment said to be given by the prophets; I translate it all, putting in quotation-marks that which is traceable:

"*The land which you go in to possess it*" (Dt. 7¹) *is a polluted land,
by the pollution of the peoples of the lands, by their abominations in that
they have filled it from end to end with their uncleanness.* (12) "*And
now you shall not give your daughters to their sons nor shall you take their
daughters for your sons*" (Dt. 7³). "*And you shall not seek their peace
and their good forever*" (Dt. 23⁷) *in order that you may be strong and eat
the good of the land and possess it for your sons forever.* All direct quotations are from Dt. We may note the change to the pl. in Ezr., but
that does not tell the whole story, for otherwise the passage abounds
in Deut. phrases. The word rendered "abominations" occurs in Dt.
13 t., and indicates practices of aliens which are forbidden to Israel.
"Be strong" and "possess it" are frequent in Dt. "The good of the
land" in the sense of its best products occurs in Gn. 45¹⁸· ²⁰ Is. 1¹⁹.
But nowhere in the Pentateuch is Palestine called a polluted land; on
the contrary, it is called "a land flowing with milk and honey" (Nu.
13²⁸ *et pass.*), "a good land, a land of brooks of water," etc. (Dt. 8⁷ ᶠ·).
Nevertheless the idea is found in Lv. 18²⁴⁻³⁰, where the land is called
unclean by reason of the abominations practised by the peoples who
preceded Israel in its occupation. The expression *from end to end*,
lit., *from mouth to mouth*, is found in 2 K. 10²¹ 21¹⁶. On the other
hand, *peoples of the lands, i. e., foreigners,* is characteristic of the Chr.
The citation is made up of Deut. phrases patched together loosely and
with the insertion of a free adaptation of a passage from Lv. But it
is cited as a divine command given by the prophets. Ezra is thought
to have carried the law-book in his hand and should have been able
to quote literally; and the particular precept which was so flagrantly
disobeyed is quoted lit. enough (against intermarriage), and the statement about the land is made to reinforce the danger of marital alliance.
By marrying foreign women the abominations which have made the
land unclean will adhere to Israel. The whole passage (from *saying*)
seems to show the Chr.'s hand.

13. *And after all that has befallen us because of our evil deeds
and our great guilt*]. The sentence is left in the air; the connection with what follows is only made by violence. The
reference is to the exile which resulted from the evil deeds of
pre-exilic Israel. We must go back to v. ¹⁰ᵇ to get sense: *we have
transgressed thy commandments which thou didst command by thy
servants, the prophets, and all that has come upon us* [has come]
because of our evil deeds and our great guilt, i. e., in the transgres-
sion stated in v. ¹⁰ᵇ.—*For thou, O our God, reckonest our sins down-
wards*]. Determined to extract sense, this is usually interpreted
"punished less than our iniquities deserve." Esd. reads: *for*

thou, O Lord, art he who lightenest our sins; this makes sense, but requires some correction of the text. 𝕲 has a much longer passage: *for thou, O our God, hast taken away our sceptre because of our sins, and it is not like thee; for thou lightenest our sins.* This would connect fairly well with v. ª, and with the following, *and givest us a remnant,* or with 𝕲 *deliverance.* Good sense is obtained by two slight emendations: *and now thou hast withheld the rod from our sins, and hast given us deliverance.—14. Yet we have again broken thy commandments and intermarried with the peoples of these lands].* *Yet* as 𝕲 is better than the interrogative of 𝕳; for the intermarriage was an accomplished fact.—*Wilt thou not be angry with us to a finish, without residue or remnant?*] This very awkward passage is much smoother in Esd.: *Wilt thou not be angry* [enough] *to destroy us until there is left neither root nor seed nor name.—15. Thou art righteous]* or *innocent,* or *truthful* (Esd.). The punishment which Israel had endured was not due to the injustice of God; for the people had richly deserved their woes. Then the supplicant reverts to the present condition: *we are left* [but] *a remnant this day].*—The future can be read from the past which has been in review, and the outlook is gloomy: *behold we are before thee in our guilt].* The same conditions which destroyed early Israel are prevalent now; therefore the conclusion is inevitable: *it is not possible to stand before thee in this matter].* If the guilt of Israel persists, their life will be short. The future depends upon strict obedience to the law.

This prayer was evidently intended to produce an effect upon the audience rather than upon God, perhaps like many other public prayers. Ezra waited until a considerable congregation had assembled before he began to pray. The whole tenor of the prayer shows the desire to touch the heart of the guilty and to impel them to abandon the course of life which seemed so evil. Sieg. regards the prayer as "a verbal extract from Ezra's memoirs." Torrey ascribes the whole to the Chr. There are some words characteristic of the Chr. even if we cannot accept all of Torrey's list (*Comp.*[19 f.]). Further, there are several awkward phrases and constructions more like the Chr. than E. It is quite prob. that the passage has suffered in part from doubt about obscure words and in part from the Chr.'s retouching. Nevertheless, the substance of the prayer is so appropriate to a pr. zealous for the law, profoundly believing that the fate of the new Israel depended upon its observance, and shrewd in his devices for securing adherence to it, that we must admit the great cleverness of the Chr., or hold that we have substantially the genuine prayer of Ezra. The latter is surely the simpler alternative. We must, however, excise vv. 11b. 12, which are due to the Chr.

1-5 in Esd.ᴸ is in the third p. throughout, having τῷ Ἐζδρα for אלי. Other texts of Esd. lack all sf. of the first p.—**1.** העם ישראל] is, of course, not original. We might explain ישראל as an explanatory gl., or drop the art.—כעבותיהם] is without construction. 𝕲ᴮᴬ has ἐν μακρύμμασιν, a word used only here and v. ¹¹ in 𝕲. Esd. renders prep. ἀπό; the latter offers a variant: οὐκ ἐχώρισαν καὶ οἱ ἄρχοντες καὶ οἱ ἱερεῖς καὶ οἱ Λευεῖται καὶ ἀλλογενῆ ἔθνη τῆς γῆς (ἀπὸ) ἀκαθαρσίας αὐτῶν. ᴬᴸ show a correction from 𝔐, inserting τὸ ἔθνος τοῦ Ἰσραήλ after καὶ². ᴸ has ἀπὸ τῶν αλλογενῶν ἐθνῶν, while ᴬ has ἀπὸ τῶν ἐθνῶν in place of αὐτῶν. 3 Esd. has a still further amplification: *non segregaverunt genus Israel et principes et sacerdotes et Levitæ et alienigenæ gentes et nationes terræ immunditias suas a Chananæis*, etc. The evidence is very strong in favour of reading הראשים or some word of similar mng. instead of העם יש".—האמרי] Esd. Ιδουμαιων.—**2.** התערבו] 𝕲ᴮᴬ παρήχθη = עבר; συνεμίγηᴸ, ἐπεμίγη Esd. All Vrss. have a sg. vb. with "seed" as subj. BDB. gives six roots, but wrongly translates here "have fellowship with"; Ges.ᴮ is correct, *i. e.*, "mix."—ויד] om. Esd. The circumstantial clause of MT. suggests a note by the writer rather than a part of the charge. V. ᵇ in Esd. runs: καὶ μετεῖχον [μετέσχονᴸ] οἱ προηγούμενοι καὶ οἱ μεγιστᾶνες τῆς ἀνομίας ταύτης ἀπὸ τῆς ἀρχῆς τοῦ πράγματος. 3 Esd. has a startling text: *et participes erant et magistratus iniquitatus ejus ab initio ipsius regni*. The peculiar construction in these texts shows that we should rd. סגן החטאת, corrupted into הסגנים היתן, and mng. "the officer of lawlessness," the one whose duty was to restrain all kinds of wrong-doing. Then Esd. shows מראשון מלכותו, the last word a corruption of מעל הזה. How יד השרים became *participes erant*, originally *particips erat*, is not clear. סגן is from As. *šaknu*. The word occurs in the Eleph. pap. in connection with "judges," *i. e.*, סגן ודין (*Pap.* ²⁹,ˡ. ¹³, v. Sachau,ˣᵛⁱ).—**3.** ומעילי] ἐπαλλόμην 𝕲ᴮᴬ, leap, a word only here in 𝕲, but in Gn. 31¹⁰. ¹² we have העלים, mng. *leaped*. Esd. τὴν ἱερὰν ἐσθῆτα, so v. ⁵.—משומם] 𝕲 ἠρεμάζωνᴮ, ἐρεμάζωνᴬ, ἠρεμῶν καὶ θαυμάζωνᴸ, Esd. σύννους καὶ περίλυπος.—**4.** חרד] 𝕲 διωκώνᴮᴬ, ἔντρομος καὶ ἐπιδιώκωνᴸ, showing originally 𝕲 and a correction from MT. Esd. ἐπεκενοῦντοᴮᴸ (α. λ. in LXX), to which ᴬ prefixes ζηλῶται καί.—דברי] λόγον 𝕲, ῥήματιᴱˢᵈ., so rd. דבר.—על מעל הגולה] Esd. ἐμοῦ [αὐτοῦᴸ] πενθοῦντος ἐπὶ τῇ ἀνομίᾳ, so ואני מתאבל על מעל (Guthe).—**5.** . . . ובקרעי] Esd. διερρηγμένα ἔχων τὰ ἱμάτια καὶ τὴν ἱερὰν ἐσθῆτα.—ובמנחה הערב] om. Esd.—מתעניתי] Esd. ἐκ τῆς νηστείας = מצום.—ואכרעה על־ברכי] Esd. κάμψας τὰ γόνατα.—אלהי] om. Esd.

6. אמרה] εἶπον 𝕲L, Esd. εἴπενL, ἔλεγονBA, but 3 Esd. *dicebam.*—אלהי]
om. 𝕲B, so Esd. κύριεAL.—להרים] om. Esd.—אלהי²] om. B Esd.—פני אליך]
Esd. κατὰ πρόσωπόν σου = על־פניך = למעלה ראש] an expression occurring nowhere else. 𝕲 ὑπὲρ κεφαλῆς ἡμῶνBA, ὑπὲρ ἄνωL, Esd. κεφαλὰςBA,
ὑπὲρ τὰς τρίχας τῆς κεφαλῆς ἡμῶνL. The evidence is convincing for
ראשנו. The presence of τρίχας = שער in L is interesting; by modify-
ing a little more we get good sense, *i. e.,* משערות ראשנו, *cf.* Ps. 69⁵,
רבו משערות ראשי. No one seems to have noticed the important text of
L, though every one sees the difficulty. Torrey rendered למעלה, "exceedingly" (*cf.* 1 Ch. 23¹⁷) and explains ראש as due to dittog. (*Comp.*¹⁹,
ES.¹⁷¹).—**7.** כהנינו] 𝕲 οἱ υἱοὶ ἡμῶνBA, οἱ ἱερεῖς ἡμῶν καὶ οἱ πάντες ἡμῶνL;
Esd. σὺν τοῖς ἀδελφοῖς ἡμῶν, σὺν τοῖς βασιλεῦσιν ἡμῶν, καὶ σὺν τοῖς ἱερεῦ-
σιν ἡμῶν. אנחנו] is here rd. as אחינו, 3 Esd. *cum fratribus nostris, et
sum sacerdotibus nostris.* By an eclectic process I would restore the
text thus: נתנו כלינו ואחינו ובנינו. כלינו became מלכינו, אחינו became אנחנו,
and בנינו became כהנינו.—ביד] lacking in Esd.; 𝕲L ἐν χερσί (בידי).—
הארצות] τῶν ἐθνῶν, Esd. τῆς γῆς.—פנים] lacking in Esd., 𝕲 προσώπου
ἡμῶν = פנינו.—כהיום הזה] Esd. μέχρι τῆς σήμερον ἡμέρας, a better sense
and prob. from בהיום.—**8.** 𝕲 offers variant for the awkward beginning of MT.: καὶ νῦν ἐπεσκευάσατο ἡμῖν ὁ θεὸς ἡμῶν, *i. e.,* ועתה חזק לנו
אלהינו. L adds ὡς βραχύ. 𝔥 reads: *et nunc quasi parum et ad momen-
tum facta est deprecatio nostra apud Dominum Deum nostrum;* 3 Esd. *et
nunc quantum est hoc, quod contigit nobis misericordia abs te Domine
Deus.*—קדשו . . . להשאיר]. Esd. καταλειφθῆναι ἡμῖν ῥίζαν καὶ ὄνομα ἐν τῷ
τόπῳ τοῦ [τούτῳB] ἁγιάσματος [+ αὐτουL]. 𝔥 *relinque nobis radicum et
nomen in locum sanctificationis tuæ.* We must, at all events, get rid
of the inappropriate יתר. 𝕲 has στήριγ[σ]μα, which elsw. stands for
מטה. Esd. may have rd. נכד "posterity."—לחת לנו] would scarcely be
used here in view of לחתנו, v. ᵇ אלהינו . . . [להאיר 𝕲 lacks אלהינו, the
least possible emendation. Esd. has: τοῦ ἀνακαλύψαι φωστῆρα ἡμῶν ἐν
τῷ οἴκῳ τοῦ κυρίου ἡμῶν = לגלות מאורנו בבית אלהינו.—מחיה מעט] 𝕲 ζωο-
ποίησιν μικράνB, περιποίησινL, Esd. τροφὴν ἐν τῷ καιρῷ τῆς δουλείας
ἡμῶν; 𝔥 *cibum in omni tempore servitentis nostræ.*—מעט] cannot be an
adj. as 𝕲 and EVˢ. render; "a little sustenance" would be מעט מחיה.
Therefore substitute with Esd. בעת.—מחיה] can scarcely mean *reviving,* RV. BDB. It indicates that which supports life, so *food,* as Ju.
6⁴ 17¹⁰.—**9.** 𝕲L ἐν τῇ παραβάσει ἡμῶν ἐν ᾗ παρέβημεν ἡμεῖς, connecting
אנחנו כי עברים with בעברתנו of v. ⁸. This reading avoids the monotonous
repetition of "in our servitude." Esd. has ἐν τῷ δουλεύειν ἡμᾶς, reading בעברנו, and lacking ובעברתנו.—עברנו] is rd. as Pu. in Esd. ἐγκατε-
λείφθημεν.—אלהינו] preceded in 𝕲 by κύριος, Esd κυρίου ἡμῶν; Gk.
and 𝔥 often disagree in the use of the divine names; Esd. is the work
of a pretty consistent Yahwist.—ויט . . .] Esd. ἐποίησεν ἡμᾶς ἐν χάριτι =
ויעשינו בחן.—לחת לנו מחיה] Esd.L δοῦναι ἡμῖν ἔλεον (חסר).—לרומם] 𝕲 τοῦ
ὑψῶσαι αὐτούς, mistaking Polel for Qal with sf.; Esd. καὶ δοξάσαι ἱερὸν

ημῶν.—חרבחיו], Esd. τὴν ἔρημον Σίων, 3 Esd. *ædificare deserta Sion* =
חרבת ציון—גדר.] ⑤ φραγμόν^BAN, τεῖχος^L, στερέωμα^Esd. (רקיע), 3 Esd. *sta-
bilitatem.—*ביהורה וב'] is supported by all Vrss., yet we might better
rd. ל" בסביב, *v. s.*—**10.** ועתה] lacking in ⑤^BAN.—אחרי זאת] Esd. ἔχοντες
ταῦτα, ⑤ μετὰ τοῦτο.—עזבנו] Esd. παρέβησαν^B, παρέβημεν^AL, *i. e.,* עברנו.
—**11.** צויתה] ἔδωκας ⑤ and Esd.—עבריך] om. ⑤^L.—. . . מפה] to end of
v. is lacking in Esd.—**13.** אחרי] om. Esd.—עלינו] ⑤ ἐφ' ὑμᾶς^B, and consistently second p. in v.^a. V.^b is amplified in ⑤^L: ὅτι σὺ ὁ θεὸς ἡμῶν,
κατέπαυσας τὸ σκῆπτρον ἡμῶν διὰ τὰς ἁμαρτίας ἡμῶν, καὶ οὐκ ἔστιν ὡς σὺ,
ὅτι ἐκούφισας τὰς ἀνομίας ἡμῶν, καὶ ἔδωκας ἡμῖν ὑπόλειμμα. Esd. has:
σὺ γάρ, κύριε, ὁ κουφίσας τὰς ἁμαρτίας ἡμῶν ἔδωκας ἡμῖν τοιαύτην ῥίζαν.
⑤ has rd. הִשְׁבַּתָּ מַטֶּה for חשכת למטה, a very slight change. Esd. shows
חשרת, but not למטה. ⑤ therefore shows a dup., but ⑤^BA represents an
approximation to Esd.: οὐκ ἔστιν ὡς ὁ θεὸς ἡμῶν, ὅτι ἐκούφισας ἡμῶν τὰς
ἀνομίας καὶ ἔδωκας ἡμῖν σωτηρίαν (*i. e.,* ישועה). It is possible that one
of two similar passages has been lost. This text is entirely ignored
by Guthe.—**14.** הנשוב] better with ⑤ כי for ה interrogative.—בעמי ח"]
⑤ τοῖς λαοῖς^BN + τῶν γαιῶν^A + τούτων^L, Esd. τῇ ἀκαθαρσίᾳ τῶν ἐθνῶν
τῆς γῆς, *i. e.,* בתעבת עמי הארצות האלה.]. For consistency we find ἐπι-
μιγῆναι = (התערב) in Esd., where ⑤ has γαμβρεῦσαι (= התחתו).—ער-
כלה] . . . Esd. ἀπολέσαι ἡμᾶς ἕως τοῦ μὴ καταλιπεῖν ῥίζαν καὶ σπέρμα καὶ
ὄνομα ἡμῶν = כלותנו עד לאין השאר.—**15.** הננו] om. ⑤^B.—צדיק] Esd. ἀλη-
θινός.—כהיום] Esd. ἐν τῇ σήμερον = בהיום.—פליטה] may be construed as
an acc. or as appos. with the subj. of the vb. (Ges.§ 118).

10^1-8 = Esd. 8^8b-9^4. The people agree to divorce the foreign wives.

Ezra's praying and loud weeping attracts a very large crowd. Shekaniah admits that Israel has done wrong and proposes that the offenders shall be put under oath to cast out their foreign wives and the children born from them. Ezra accepts the plan and a decree is issued
ordering all Israel to convene within three days under penalty of con-
fiscation and excommunication. The narrative is now in the third p.
as in 7^1-26. This form continues in the rest of the Ezra story.

1. *And while Ezra was praying and while he was making confession, weeping and prostrating himself before the house of God*].
The language is exhausted to show Ezra's deep distress. Here
for the first time a place is indicated; the priest offered his public
prayer in the open space before the temple.—*From Israel*] or
more appropriately with Esd., *from Jerusalem*, since the crowd
could hardly come from all Judah.—*Men and women and chil-*

dren], or *boys and girls*, or *children and slaves*, as some Greek
texts have in place of *children*. (On the place of the assembly in
postexilic Israel *v.* Smith, *Jer.* i, c. x.).—*For the people wept with a
great weeping*] is scarcely intelligible as a reason for the vast assembly. We have heard only of Ezra's weeping heretofore. It
is a loose construction: the writer apparently meant that Ezra's
tears were contagious, and that the multitude began to weep as
it gathered. This verse quite ignores the assembly already collected, 9⁴; the terms are different here, the crowd being of a more
general composition.—**2.** *Then answered Shekaniah*]. "Answer"
is used idiomatically in Hebrew to introduce a statement made,
not as a reply to a spoken word, but with reference to an act
upon which the answer is a comment. *Shekaniah* is classed here
among the sons of Elam, and there was such a clan in Ezra's
company, 8⁷. This may be a man of royal descent, a son of Jehoiakim, I Ch. 3²¹ ⁱ·.—*There is hope for Israel in regard to this*],
i. e., something can be done to rectify the wrong.—*By the
counsel of the Lord*]. The plan is Shekaniah's, for there was no
law ordering a divorce in such cases. The Vrss. vary greatly;
Esd. has: *as it seemeth good to thee*, making far better sense.—
And they who tremble at the command of our God] is quite without connection.

> The ordinary rendering is secured by changing "the Lord" to "my
> lord," and thus getting: *at the counsel of my lord [i. e.*, Ezra] *and of those
> who tremble at the command of God*. In 9⁴ there gathered about Ezra
> at the beginning "all who trembled at the words of the God of Israel."
> The rendering cited would make them a party to the pr.' plan, and
> would put the proposal for divorce in his mouth. In his prayer he had
> suggested no drastic remedy; in fact, it seems that he left it entirely
> to others to advise the heroic course to be followed. If this reading
> were accepted, two slight changes should be made so as to get: *acc.
> to the counsel of my lord . . . and acc. to the law of Moses*, reading משה
> for יעשה. There are several variants for "those who tremble," etc.;
> 𝕲 reads: *stand up and make them tremble at the command of our God;*
> Esd.ᴸ: *and as many as obeyed the law of the Lord, standing up, said to
> Ezra, rise, act*. Though this breaks off Shekaniah's speech suddenly,
> it is prob. the best text we have. *Let it be done according to the law*], but
> while the law forbade the mixed marriages, it did not, unless by in-
> ference, provide for their dissolution.

4. *The matter is upon thee*] or belongs to thee, a recognition of Ezra's leadership in the matter.—*And we are with thee*] a pledge of the speaker's support in the righting of the wrong. —*Take courage and act*] an appeal to Ezra as if he needed urging.—**5.** *And Ezra rose and adjured*] but whom? The text has *the leaders of the priests, Levites and of all Israel*, making the Levites equivalent to priests. ᵍ has: *the leaders, the Levites and all Israel*ᴮ*; the leaders of the Judean priests and of the Levites and all Israel*ᴸ. By a single change we get the best text: *the leaders of the priests and of the Levites and of all Israel*. The leaders alone were required to take the oath to carry out Shekaniah's plan.— *And they took the oath*], *i. e.*, the leaders just named, thus becoming a party to the solemn covenant with God, v. ¹.—**6.** *And Ezra arose from before the house of God*] where he had been prostrating himself, v. ¹, and where this verse presupposes that he is still, ignoring v. ⁵ altogether, evidence of disorder in the text.—*And he went to the room of Jehohanan*], one of the quarters in the temple cloisters in which the temple officers lived. For Jehohanan *v.* Ne. 12¹⁰ ᶠ·. Our text gives no hint as to the reason for Ezra's going to those quarters. In Esd. we find the right reading; instead of the repeated *and he went there*, we have: *and he spent the night there*. Ezra's prayer had been offered at the time of the evening oblation, 9⁵. The events which had taken place meanwhile carry us down to nightfall, and next we are told of Ezra's temporary lodging-place. The business was urgent and he remained upon the ground until its completion.—*Bread he did not eat and water he did not drink, i. e.*, overnight; fasting enters largely into the religious life of the people of this period (Sta.³²⁴), and becomes more prominent later (*cf.* Est.).—*For he was mourning for the sins of the captivity*] *cf.* Dt. 9¹⁸; in place of "the sins of the captivity," *cf.* 9⁴, Esd. has *the great sins of the exalted ones*, or *of the multitude*. Sieg. by a slight change reads: "for the great sin." If MT. is right, "captivity" designates the new community, conceived as wholly composed of returned exiles. The phrase betrays the Chronicler, to whom the Judeans and the *golah* are one.—**7.** *And they* [the leaders and elders of v. ⁸] *issued a proclamation in Judah and*

Jerusalem to all the sons of the captivity to gather at Jerusalem].
The assembly was to be general and was to carry out the agreement subscribed by the oath of the leaders.—**8**. *And all who did not arrive within three days*]. The short time allowed shows the narrow bounds of the new community (Berth.).—*According to the command of the leaders and elders*]. This supplies the missing subject in v. [7]. Ezra himself was much in the background. He was impelling the rulers to act.—A severe penalty was to be imposed upon those who did not comply with the edict; the punishment would be twofold: *all his property should be confiscated and he should be separated from the assembly of the captivity*], *i. e.*, excommunicated. The word rendered "confiscated" means *put under a religious ban, devote*, and property so devoted was to be destroyed, Jos. 6²¹ Dt. 20¹⁶. But the word here probably means *confiscated to sacred uses*, as for the support of the temple.

The authority for the edict, and which undertook to punish heavily those who disobeyed it, was not that of Ezra, but of the oligarchy, "the leaders and elders," v. ⁸. Indeed, in the whole passage, barring the single expression "the matter is upon thee," there is no hint of any authority vested in Ezra. He does not even evolve a plan to right the wrong which distresses him, and he administers an oath to bind the leaders to execute the plan proposed by Shekaniah. Ezra shows fervent zeal, a passion for the law, an eloquence in prayer, but not a shred of authority to enforce his ideas.

1. [ומתנפל] 𝕲 προσευχόμενος^Bᴬ, thus repeating מתפלל.—[בית־האלהים] Esd. here as often elsw. τοῦ ἱεροῦ.—[מישראל] Esd. ἀπὸ Ἰερουσαλήμ.—[קהל] 𝕲 ἐκκλησία, Esd. ὄχλος, v. on v. ⁸.—[ילדים] 𝕲ᴸ and Esd.ᴸ νεανίαι καὶ παιδάρια = ילדים ונערים.—בכה ....[כי] 𝕲 ὅτι ἔκλαυσεν ὁ λαὸς καὶ ὕψωσεν κλαίων^Bᴬᴺ, ὅτι κλαυθμῷ μεγάλῳ ἔκλαυσεν ὁ λαός^ᴸ, Esd. κλαυθμὸς γὰρ ἦν μέγας ἐν τῷ πλήθει, 3 Esd. *fletus enim erat magnus in ipsa multitudine*.—**2**. [עולם] Esd. Ἰσραήλ.—[נשב] 𝕲 ἐκαθίσαμεν^Bᴬ (= ישב, "to dwell"), ἐλάβομεν^ᴺᴸ, Esd. κατῴκησαν^B, συνῳκίσαμεν^ᴬ, κατῳκίσαμεν^ᴸ. The mng. *marry* is peculiar to Ezr.–Ne., but the usage is so frequent (7 t.) that the text can scarcely be distrusted. This mng. is derived from the idea of giving a house in connection with marriage. But in Esd. 9⁷ (= Ezr. 10¹⁰) we have συνοικήσατε γυναξίν. The idea, therefore, may be "cohabit," the prep. which would naturally follow being dropped idiomatically.—[מקוה] 𝕲 ὑπομονή^Bᴬᴺ, ἐλπίς^ᴸ, Esd. ἐπάνω πᾶς Ἰσ.^Bᴬ = מעלה.—[כרית] 3, Esd. ὁρκωμοσία.—[נשים] γυναῖκας τὰς ἀλλοτρίας 𝕲ᴸ, "כל־יש

Esd. γυναῖκας ἡμῶν τὰς ἐκ τῶν ἀλλογενῶν ἐθνῶν, a necessary qualifica-
tion.—[והנלך מהם] Esd. σὺν τεκνοῖς αὐτῶν = [בעצה . . . .—.—.בילריהן] 𝔊 ὡς ἂν
βούλῃ ἀνάστηθι καὶ φοβέρισον αὐτούς^BA, Esd. ὡς ἐκρίθη σοι καὶ ὅσοι πει-
θαρχήσουσιν. 𝔊 shows החרדם, Esd. שמעו; Esd.^L has a noteworthy variant: καὶ ὅσοι πειθαρχοῦσι τῷ νόμῳ κυρίου ἀναστάντες εἶπον πρὸς Ἔζραν
Ἀνάστα, ἐπιτέλει. This reading is accepted by Guthe; v. his text.—
[מצוה] 𝔊 ἐντολαῖς, Esd. νόμου, cf. 9^10.—[כתורה יעשה] 𝔊 ὁ νόμος γενη-
θήτω^BA, om. Esd.^BA.—4. [דבר] 𝔊^BA ῥῆμα, so v. ^5; λόγος^L, but ῥῆμα,
v. ^5; Esd. πρᾶγμα, om. v. ^5. In v. ^4 the mng. is general, e. g., matter,
but specific in v. ^5, plan.—[חזק] 𝔊^L, ἀνδρίζου, act like a man.—6. וילך
שם] is an impossible redundancy. 𝔊^L omits perhaps from a critical
motive. Esd. has the true text: αὐλισθεὶς ἐκεῖ = וילן שם, so most modern scholars.—[מעל הגולה] Esd. τ. ἀνομιῶν τ. μεγάλων τοῦ πλήθους =
מעלי הרב הגדלים. Sieg. translates wegen des grossen Vergebens = המעל
הגדלה.—7. 𝔊^BA om. לכל to end of v.—8. [השרים והזקנים] Esd. τ. προ-
καθημένων [a word peculiar to Esd.] πρεσβυτέρων; 3 Esd. assidentium
seniorum.

10^9-17 = Esd. 9^5-17. The putting away of the foreign wives and of their children.

Agreeably to the call, the people of Judah and Benj. assembled on
the 20th day of the 9th month in the open space before the temple.
Ezra would proceed at once in spite of the magnitude of the task and
the storm that was raging. The people, however, asked that officers
be appointed from each city to whom the execution of the plan should
be committed. Ezra acceded to this plea, the business was taken in
hand, and completed at the end of the year. The source is different
from vv. ^1-8, as other terms are used for the same ideas.

9. *And all the men of Judah and Benjamin assembled*]. The
proclamation was issued in Judah and Jerusalem according to
v. ^7. The difference of terms is one of the numerous signs of a
different source in this section. It appears that the threat in
v. ^8 was effective, as the response is declared to be general, the
whole people gathering without exception.—*On the 20th day of the
9th month*], *i. e.*, Kislev, so in the early part of December. Ezra
had been in Jerusalem, therefore, more than four months; but,
as the material has come down to us, there was nothing done in
this time.—*And all the people sat in the plaza of the house of God*].
The plaza of the temple, badly rendered "street" in AV., was

the open space before the water gate, Ne. 3^{26} 8^{1}, a favourite place for assemblies. The number of people was not as great as v.^{a} would imply, for there could not have been a large space there.—*Trembling for the matter and because of the rain*] is a dubious conjunction of ideas. The Vrss. show enough discrepancy to make the text questionable. Esd. reads: *shivering on account of the persistent storm*. That may be modified slightly so as to get *shivering because of standing in the rain.*—**10**. *Ezra the priest*] previously called the priest the scribe, $7^{11 \text{ f. } 21}$, *cf.* Ne. 12^{26}; but the duties he is now performing are not scribal, and so that title does not appear; "priest" is wanting in Esd., and it may be a gloss.—*To add to the guilt of Israel*]. Esd. *to add guilt to Israel*. By the violation of the law the present generation was increasing the already large record of national sin. —**11**. *Give praise to Yahweh the God of our fathers*], not "your" fathers as MT. "Our" is found in 𝕲 and Esd. The ground for praise is not very apparent, at least from the people's standpoint. The rendering of EV^{s}., based on 𝕳, "make confession" is impossible. The same appeal is made to Achan, Jos. 7^{18}, where as a parallel we have "give glory." The author of this passage seems to have drawn from that story. The idea may be that praise was due to God because the culprits were brought to a state of amendment.—The double demand is made: *separate yourselves from the nations of the land and from the foreign women*]. This is in agreement with $9^{1 \text{ f.}}$, *cf.* Dt. $7^{3 \text{ f.}}$. The clauses are practically synonymous, the former being somewhat broader. The Israelites were called upon to cut off all association with the aliens.—**12**. Why should the assembly answer in a *loud voice?* and why should that be emphasised? It may be explained as a Hebrew usage to express earnestness, *cf.* 3^{12} 2 S. 15^{23} I K. 8^{55} 2 Ch. 15^{14} 20^{19} Ez. 8^{18} Lv. 17^{15}. But 𝕲 preserves an interesting variant: *and all the assembly answered and said, great is thy demand for us to do*, *i. e.*, you have laid a heavy burden upon us.—**13**. But *the people are many and the season is stormy*]. The assembly was ready to meet the leaders' demands, but the conditions made it impossible; there were too many cases and the weather was too bad. "A time of much rain" (EV.) is based on 𝔐 and gives a wrong idea, viz., that the day was too wet. The people say rather, "it is the rainy season," and the rains therefore will persist. It was the period of the winter rains, called "the former rain" in Dt. 11¹⁴, see Nowack, *Arch.* i,⁴⁹ ᶠ˙.—*We are not able to stand without*] is based on the rendering of the ancient Vrss., especially Esd. But "we" does not appear in 𝔐, and the idea is: *it is not fit to stand outside*, on account of the rain. Ezra's zeal was not dependent upon the weather.—*For we have transgressed very much in this respect*], corresponding to "the people are many"; the number who had married foreigners was relatively very large.

14. This v. contains the counter-proposal of the people, but the text is very troublesome; we may render: *Let now our leaders stand for the whole assembly, and let all who are in our cities that have married foreign women come at appointed times; and with them elders of each city and its judges, unto the averting from us of the fury of the wrath of our God in regard to this matter*]. In the latter part esp. we find obscurity and bad constructions, greater in the original than in this translation. 𝕲 varies considerably in detail. Esd. runs: *and let the leaders of the assembly stand, and let all from our homes who have foreign wives be at hand when opportunity serves; and the elders and judges of each place until,* etc. 3 Esd. gives a connection for the last clause: *and let the elders and judges from each place assist,* but it lacks a pred. for *all who have foreign wives·* We get little help from these sources; the ancients were puzzled by the passage, and their difficulties appear in their translation. The mng. apparently is that (1) leaders should take charge of the business for the whole assembly; (2) to this tribunal all transgressors should come at appointed times (*cf.* Ne. 10³⁵); (3) with the guilty should appear the local elders and judges. The function of the local officers is left to conjecture; it is natural to suppose, however, that their office was to see that the decrees of the tribunal were carried out. From the emph. laid on these officers Sm. argues that most of the offenders were inhabitants of the country districts (*Listen,*²²). It appears that the divorce court sat in Jerus. and that all proceedings took place there. For "until," etc., we should rd.: *in order to turn away from us the fury of the wrath of our God.*—15. This v. contains a sore puzzle. But by an emendation of the text on the basis of 𝕲 we discover a fragment of E. and evidence of decided opposition to the divorce. As it stands in MT. two opposing constructions have been put upon the v.: (1) We may translate: *But Jonathan the son of Asahel and Johaziah the son of Tikvah stood over this, and Meshullam and Shabbethai*

the Lev. aided them, so AV. Esd. Michaelis, Kue. and many of the older interpreters. The mng. would then be that the four men named constituted the divorce tribunal. But that rendering must be pronounced impossible. For (*a*) v. [16] connects directly with v. [14]; (*b*) the appointment of the court is described in v. [16]; (*c*) the introductory אך has a restrictive not a continuative sense; (*d*) the circumstantial clause shows that this v. cannot describe the execution of the plan previously proposed, but must be an attendant circumstance. (2) Instead of "stood over" we may render עמד *stood against,* a late usage found in Lv. 19[16] 1 Ch. 21[1] 2 Ch. 20[23] Dn. 8[25] 11[14] (see Moore's *Judges,*[195]). The mng. then is that these four men stood in opposition to the ruthless proceedings. This idea we find in RV. Lightfoot, B.-Rys. Ryle, Sieg. Berth. Ges.[B], BDB. The construction fits in finely with this idea; but we find עמד used in opposite senses in two successive vv. It is plain, therefore, that if this is the right mng. the two vv. are not from the same hand. To express his mng. the author would have used a common and unmistakable word, קום. The authorities have quite disregarded the reading of 𝕲: *only Jonathan et al. were with me in this matter.* This text requires but an infinitesimal change in 𝔥. But can we get any sense out of that? *With me* would, of course, mean *with Ezra.*

Now it is a commonly accepted theory that c. 10 is the Chr.'s revision of E. In most places the original has been revised beyond recognition. But here we may have a scrap which escaped the blue pencil, a genuine fragment of E. The brief passage then becomes of great significance. The question naturally arises why E. was so thoroughly revised here. It is surprising that the whole community submitted like tame sheep to the breaking up of their homes. Now the Chr. was pretty certain to make the path of the enforcer of law easy; but apparently historic facts were of a different mind. At some stage of the story of his efforts Ezra cries out pathetically: "only Jonathan and Johaziah were with me in this matter and Meshullam and Shabbethai the Lev. aided them." Perhaps the actual divorce was not such a sweeping success as the Chr. makes out; or it may be that with the aid of the four original supporters the great zealot did succeed in bearing down all opposition.

16. *And the sons of the captivity did so*] naturally would refer to the carrying out of the plan for divorce. But the sons of the captivity had proposed the plan; what we should expect is a statement that Ezra accepted the proposal, *e. g., and Ezra did so.* The text is apparently disarranged by the Chronicler and the true connection is obscured.—*And Ezra the priest selected*

for him men], so we must read after Esd. supported in part by 𝔊.
The rendering of RV. disregards the text and makes Ezra the
head of the divorce tribunal. Torrey renders: "Ezra the priest
and certain chief men . . . were set apart" (ES.[273 f.]).—*The
heads of the fathers for the house of their fathers and all of them
with names*] is not a very satisfactory description. "The heads
of the fathers" are the clan leaders called "our leaders" by the
people, v. [14]. The Vrss. show that the text is overloaded; Esd.
has: *heads of their fathers all of them according to names*, and
that is quite sufficient.—*And they sat on the 1st day of the 10th
month to investigate the matter*]. One text of Esd. has *and they
were convened*, which is a better expression. The 10th month
corresponds to December–January. Some Vrss. have "12th
month"; but that would make the session of the court one
month instead of three; and it would convene two and one-third
months after the assembly, v. [9], instead of ten days. Esd. offers
for the last clause *to transact the business*, and the greater defi-
niteness commends this reading, for investigation was not required. The tribunal was charged with executive rather than
judicial functions. 𝔊[L] has a somewhat different reading of a
part of this verse: *Ezra the priest set apart the leaders of their
fathers' houses; and all being called together by name on the 1st
day of the 12th month they sat down to investigate the matter.* This
reading is certainly less awkward than MT.

9. Berth. thinks כסלו] has dropped out before הוא, so Guthe before
him, but בחרש כסלו would be required, and then the correction is more
prob. I suspect that the date is a note by the Chr. After 𝔊 Esd. τοῦ
μηνός, we should rd. לחרש for בחרש.—. . . מרעירים] 𝔊 ἀπὸ θορύβου αὐτῶν
περὶ τοῦ ῥήματος καὶ ἀπὸ τοῦ χειμῶνος[BA𝔑], ἐν τρόμῳ ἀπὸ τ. ῥήματος κ.
ἀπὸ τ. χειμῶνος[L]; Esd. τρέμοντες [διὰ[L]] τὸν ἐνεστῶτα χειμῶνα. The first
reading is interesting, explaining the assembly in the open as due to
the large number and to the storm; but the two ideas harmonise no
better than in MT. The important reading in Esd., the only one that
makes good sense, has escaped the attention of the commentators.
Instead of the meaningless על-הרבר, it had, perhaps, העמרים. עמר means
persist in Eccl. 8[3] (BDB.), and is represented by ἐνιστᾶναι in 2 K. 13[6];
"persistent rains" would do well here. This, however, requires a transposition of words, and I hazard a conjecture, מהעמרים ב", *shivering
because of standing in the rain.*—**11.** תורה] 𝔊 αἴνεσιν καὶ ἐξομολόγησιν[L],

Esd. ἐξομολόγησιν καὶ δόξαν^L, ὁμολ. δόξαν^{BA}. Prob. we should add כבוד, cf. 7^{19}.—אבותיכם] with 𝕲 and Esd. rd. אבותינו.—רצונו] 𝕲 τὸ ἀρεστὸν ἐνώπιον αὐτοῦ, which may be paraphrastic as in Ne. 9^{24}. Esd. τὸ θέλημα αὐτοῦ.—12. ויענו] Esd.^{BA} καὶ ἐφώνησαν, a rendering found in v. ^{2} = ויקראו.—... קול] 𝕲 μέγα τοῦτο τὸ ῥῆμά σου^{BA}; 𝕲^L has φωνῇ μεγάλῃ with "answered" and continues: μέγα τοῦτο τὸ ῥῆμα ἐφ' ἡμᾶς, καὶ κατὰ τοὺς λόγους σου οὓς ἔφης, οὕτως ποιήσομεν, a double reading with variations; Esd. οὕτως ὡς εἴρηκας ποιήσομεν; 𝕳 juxta verbum tuum ad nos sic fiat, 3 Esd. sicut dixisti faciemus. Certainly we must rd. כדברך (v. Moore's Judges,^{322}), inf. and prob. נעשה, though 𝕲 may be a free rendering; it is incumbent upon us to do is not, however, as strong as we will do.—13. אבל] in late Heb. is strongly adversative.—העת] 𝕲^B ὁ τόπος καιρός^{ANL}, ὥρα$^{Esd.}$. The mng. is season, not day.—גשמים] has an adjectival force corresponding to רב, so 𝕲 and Esd., but 𝕳 tempus pluviæ, 3 Esd. tempus hybernum, is perpetuated in EV^s. The lexicons ignore this use. It is impossible to render "a time of rain" without unnecessarily emending the text.—ואין ... בחוץ] Esd. καὶ οὐκ ἰσχύ[σ]ομεν στῆναι αἴθριοι [καὶ οὐχ εὕρομεν], bracketed parts in ^{B} only. Αἴθριος elsw. stands for מפתן, "threshold," or פנים, but it would serve as well for בחוץ. We note here a neat idiomatic rendering instead of the slavish literalism of 𝕲. ^{B}'s plus is difficult to understand unless we get מצא out of מלאכה, though the latter is represented by ἔργον, followed, it may be noted, by ἡμῶν^L ἡμῖν^{BA}.—14. עמד] is here given the mng. among rare uses, "be appointed," BDB. This would require על־הקהל, and the subj. would be שׁרים; שׂרינו shows that existing officials are meant. Ges.^{B} proposes die Gemeinde vertreten. The idea seems to be: let our officers stand for [or represent] the whole assembly.—לכל קהל] om. 𝕲^B, ἐν πάσῃ^L, Esd. οἱ προηγούμενοι τοῦ πλήθους = שׂרי הקהל.—בערינו] Esd. ἐκ τῶν κατοικιῶν ἡμῶν = ממושבינו, 3 Esd. qui vobiscum inhabitant. —לעתים מזמנים] Ne. 10^{35} 13^{31}, 𝕲 εἰς καίρους ἀπὸ συναγωγῶν^B [συνταγῶν^{AN}] ἀπὸ καιρῶν^L; Esd. λαβόντες χρόνον; 3 Esd. accepto tempore. ^{B} has rd. מעדות, ממועדים ^{AL}, and Esd. perhaps מועדים.—עת] עת מועדים is of obscure origin, but in early use is construed as f. Later, as in this passage, it is treated as m. in accordance with the rule that expressions of time are m. (ZAW. 1896,^{44}).—ועיר] om. 𝕲^L. Esd. lacks this and also עמהם.—חרון אף] ὀργὴ 𝕲^A Esd.—עד לדבר הזה] 𝕳 super peccato hoc. For ל' rd. על as Sieg. —15. אך] 𝕲 πλήν, om. Esd.^{BA}, 𝕳 igitur, 3 Esd. autem. The mng. is important; it never represents a continuation like "and so," but has a restrictive or adversative sense. The construction, vb. following subj., indicates a circumstantial clause, another fact having significance for the exegesis.—עמדו] μετ' ἐμοῦ = עמדי, Esd. ἐπεδέξαντο, 𝕳 steterunt susceperunt.—עזרם] 𝕲 βοηθῶν αὐτοῖς^{BAN}, ἀντελαμβάνον τὸ αὐτῶν^L, Esd. συνεβράβευσαν αὐτοῖς.—16. כן] more emph. in Esd.: κατὰ πάντα ταῦτα. —יבדלו] is grammatically impossible. 𝕲^{BA} διεστάλησαν, thus making all the nouns the subj.; 𝕲^{LN} διέστειλεν, having the nouns in acc.; Esd.

ἐπελέξατο αὐτῷ . . . ἄνδρας κ. τ. λ. = ‏וַיַּבְדֵּל לֹו‎ acc. to Guthe, Berth. *et al.*
But ‏בדל‎ is used always with a bad association, as in "separate yourself
from people of land"; ἐπελέγειν never stands for ‏בדל‎, but for ‏בחר‎ or, by
confusion of gutturals, ‏בער‎. Therefore rd. ‏יבחר לו.—אנשים בשמות‎]. 𝕲ᴮᴬᴺ
om.—‏אבותם‎]. Esd. ἄνδρας ἡγουμένους τῶν πατριῶν αὐτῶν πάντας κατ'
ὄνομα, so lacking ‏לביתו‎.—האבות בשמות‎] *cf.* 8²¹, where ‏נקבו‎ intervenes.
𝕲ᴸ puts this after ‏ישבו‎ and renders: πάντες οἱ κληθέντες ἐν ὀνόμασιν =
‏כל הנקרא ב"‎. It is tempting to see a confusion of ‏נקבו‎ and ‏נקרא‎, and we
may have the true text in a reading ignored by all scholars so far as
I know.—‏וישבו‎] is not easy. 𝕲 has ὅτι ἐπέστραψανᴮᴬᴺ, καὶ ἐκάθισαν +
πάντες οἱ κληθέντεςᴸ, Esd. καὶ συνεκλείσθησανᴮ, συνεκάθισανᴬᴸ, 3 Esd.
considerunt. Esd.ᴮ must be an error for συνεκλήθησαν, *cf.* 𝕲ᴸ, and then
we have the best sense: *they were convened for business*, etc.—‏העשירי‎]
δωδεκάτου 𝕲ᴺᴸ, Esd.ᴸ.—‏לדריוש‎] must be pointed ‏לְדָרִיֹשׁ‎, but the word
is inappropriate; we should expect a word like "begin" or as Esd.
ἐτάσαι, *to transact* (the business).—**17.** ‏ויכלו בכל אנשים‎] 𝔙 *et consummati
sunt omnes viri,* Esd. καὶ ἤχθη ἐπὶ πέρας τὰ κατὰ τοὺς ἄνδρας = ‏ויכל על-‎
‏האנשים‎; ‏כל‎ is explained by dittog.—‏עד‎] is well supported, and has here
the unusual sense *at*, or *on;* but we should expect ‏ביום‎.

10¹⁸⁻⁴⁴ = Esd. 9¹⁸⁻³⁶. The list of the divorced.—The names
are arranged in two classes, clerical and lay; in the clerical section we find four orders, priests, Levites, singers, and porters.
The laity are grouped under clan-names. The scheme is the
same as in c. 2 and other lists.

18–22. The pr. are grouped by clans, of which there were four,
the sons of Jes. Immer, Harim, and Pashhur. These are the same
priestly clans found in 2³⁶⁻³⁹, but the order in the latter passage is
Jes., Immer, Pashhur, Harim.—**18.** *Jes. the son of Jozadak*] a full notice
so as to identify this person with the associate of Zer.—*And his
brethren*] implies that the descendants of Jes.'s brothers were classed
under the more celebrated name. The Chr., however, thrusts in
"sons" and "brothers" rather recklessly when writing about pr. or
Lev.—**19.** *And they gave their hand to put away their wives*]. "Give
the hand" as a symbol of swearing is old usage, 2 K. 10¹⁵.—*And guilty,
a ram of the flock for their guilt*] requires some editing. RV. inserts
"they offered"; Kue. emends to read: "and their guilt-offering was a
ram of the flock for their guilt." Torrey renders: "they were fined a
ram of the flock." A slight change yields: *and I appointed a ram of the
flock for their guilt*, with the startling result that we have another fragment of E., which the Chr. disguised but imperfectly. It is difficult
to see why this is said of the clan of Jes. and not of the other pr.
Ryle supposes this requirement to be imposed upon all the offenders,

but the position of the clause forbids such a wide application. Other scholars are discreetly silent. The natural explanation lies in the greater prominence of the Jes. guild. They were of the chief pr., and so were required to take an oath and pay a penalty. It is not unlikely that the whole v. is out of place. It might belong after v. ²², or better after v. ¹⁸ᵃ, which connects poorly with v. ¹⁸ᵇ, but very well with v. ¹⁹. The passage would then rd.: *and there were found some of the pr. who had married foreign wives, and they gave their hand to put away their wives; and I appointed a ram of the flock for their guilt. Of the sons of Jes.*, etc. This is a great improvement on MT.—**23.** *And of the Lev.*] of whom six are named as offenders.—**24.** We find but one singer and three porters, but Esd. has two in each class. In contrast with the 17 pr. and 6 Lev., we note the absence of the Neth.; it appears that the humbler officials were the stricter observers of the law, but perhaps they were foreigners and their marriage with foreign women was permitted.

25-43. The laity are grouped under the clans of Parosh, Elam, Zattu, Bebai, Bani, Pahath-Moab, Harim, Hashum, Bani, and Nebo. These are all found in c. 2, exc. one of the Banis, but in quite a different order. Four of the names are included in the list of Ezra's company: Parosh, Elam, Bebai, and Pahath-Moab.—**30.** Esd. lacks Pahath-Moab, making Addin (=Adnah) the clan-name. There was such a clan which was represented in Ezra's caravan, 8⁶, but not found in c. 2.—**34.** For Bani, which is already found in v. ²⁹, we may possibly rd. Binoui.—**38.** Instead of Bani and Binnui on basis of 𝕲 we should introduce another clan: *and of the sons of Bigvai* or some other name. The text in this part is so corrupt that the original names can no longer be determined. **44.** *All these had taken foreign wives, and they had wives of them, and they —sons*]. The omitted vb. of last clause means *to place*, but it cannot be translated so as to make sense. The text is doubtless corrupt. 𝕲 offers: *all these had taken foreign wives and had begotten sons of them.* This would mean either that all who had foreign wives had children also, or that only those who had children were required to put away their wives. This reminds us of the ground of Neh.'s divorce proceedings, Ne. 13²⁴. Esd. reads still differently: *all these had married foreign wives and they put them away with their children.* A pretty radical emendation is necessary, and I would rd.: *all these put away foreign wives, and some of them had children, and they restored the children* (to their mothers). The children in divorce proceedings are always the bone of contention. In a sparsely settled Jewish community the children would be esp. prized. The mng. is that the reform was radical and the children were sent with their mothers to their old homes among their own people. Being of mixed blood, they would be deemed undesirable in a community seeking to eliminate all foreign influences.

18. וַיִּמָּצְאוּ] so we should rd. with 𝕲ᴬᴺᴸ Esd. instead of sg. of MT. —**19.** וַיִּתְּנוּ] Esd. ἐπέβαλον.—ידם] 𝕲 χεῖρας αὐτῶν, Esd. τὰς χεῖρας.—

אשמים] 𝕲ᴸ περὶ πλημμελείας, Esd. εἰς ἐξιλασμόν, 𝕳 *pro delicto suo*, 3 Esd. *ad litandum in exorationem*. Kue. proposes אשמם, "their guilt-offering" (*Abh.*²⁴⁵). It is natural, though, to expect a vb. here, and I suggest וָאָשִׂים, "and I appointed."—אשמתם] Esd. ἀγνοίας αὐτῶν, 3 Esd. *ignorantia sua*.—**23.** הלוים] τῶν υἰῶν τῶν Λευιτων 𝕲ᴸ Esd.ᴸ.—. . . קליה] 𝕲 Κωλειὰ αὐτὸς Κωλιεύ, Esd. οὖτος.—הוא] is to identify this Lev. with קליטה of Ne. 8⁷ 10¹¹ (*JBL.* 1898,¹⁹⁹).—**24.** אלשיב] Esd. Ελιασεβος, Βαχχουρος (Σαχχουρᴸ).—אורי] lacking in Esd.ᴮᴬ, 𝕲 Ωδουθᴮ, Ωδουεᴬ, Ουριαςᴸ. —**37.** ויעשו] 𝕲ᴮᴬᴺ καὶ ἐποίησαν. It is lacking in Esd. and 𝕲ᴸ; 𝕳 *Jasi*. Qr. reads יעשו, to which we may add ה.—**38.** . . . . ובני] 𝕲ᴮᴬᴺ οἱ υἱοὶ Βανουὶ καὶ υἱοὶ Σεμεί, 𝕲ᴸ Βοννὰι καὶ υἱοὶ Βοννέι. We might rd. as Guthe, ומבני בנוי. But we have already had two Bani clans, and Banui (the name is really identical) is embarrassing. It is little more than guessing, but we might rd. בנוי in v. ³⁴ as above and substitute בנוי or some other clan in this passage.—**44.** Nearly every scholar has tried his hand at this impossible text, but there is no agreement about results. Curiously the first part of the v. is passed without notice. But why should we have here the statement that these men had taken foreign wives, a fact already sufficiently emphasised? Moreover, we find here נשא for *marry*, while in the body of this story ישב is always used, vv. ². ¹⁰. ¹⁴. ¹⁷. ¹⁸. We do find נשא in 9², but it is followed by מן. The point here is the putting away, and that is expressed in this story by יצא (vv. ³. ¹⁹), not שלח, as Guthe has it. Rd. therefore היציאו for נשאי: *all these put away foreign wives*. To clear up the rest of the v., substitute בנים for נשים (repeated from v. ᵃ), thus: *and some of them* [the men] *had children*. What must have been done with these children appears from v. ³. We may rd. וישיבו in place of the impossible וישימו: *and they restored the children* (to their mothers).

The ethics of the great divorce.—Sta. has pointed out the evil consequences of the mixed marriages, in that they tended to threaten the imperfectly established solidarity of the community and the development of the religious life (*BT.* 3³⁰ ᶠ·). But actions cannot always be judged from a consideration of their consequences. Moreover, it must be noted that the record is that of mixed marriages in one direction only. There is nothing here of the marriage of Jewish women to foreign men, but only of Jewish men to foreign women. Incidentally, this would suggest that the offenders belonged chiefly to the *golah*. A large number of unmarried men might well have come back from exile, and the provision of wives for them may have been as serious a problem as that of the Benj. centuries before (Ju. 19–21). In spite of the classic story of Solomon's downfall (1 K. 11 Ne. 13²⁶), the position of a Jewish wife was not such as to make her a very influential factor in the religious life of the nation. The number of offenders looks pretty big, but after all there are only 103 names in the list, an inconsiderable number for the whole Judean province.

Ezra's act must not be judged from the highest standards of our day, but from the ethical conceptions of his own time and people. Divorce was a very simple process in Israel, and there was no stigma attached to it. A public hearing was not necessary, and no official sanction was required. A man who wanted to get rid of a wife for any cause whatever had only to give her a bill of divorce of his own making and send her away. Neh. had made short work of several such alliances a generation earlier, and no one opposed him then or criticised him since. The possible hardships to the women are easily exaggerated from sentimental considerations, but such an idea would hardly enter the mind of Ezra or his contemporaries. The law had long forbidden such marriages, and the law was meant to be obeyed.

One may well doubt, though, whether any great good resulted from such a drastic course, and rejoice in the development of more humane methods of dealing with social problems, even if these reforms came slowly.

NE. 8–10. THE READING OF THE LAW. THE LEVITES' PRAYER.
THE SUPPORT OF THE TEMPLE.

It is usual to group c. 8–10 together as a description of the closing part of Ezra's administration. It is shown in the intr. to c. 10 that that c. really belongs to Neh.'s second administration. C. 9 also contains no evidence of Ezra's presence. This name in v. 6 in 𝕲 is a late interpolation, and contradicts vv. 1-5. As certain Lev. are the only officials who have any part in the proceedings, Ezra is really excluded, for he was not likely ever to be an idle spectator. The c. really describes the wailing and praying on a great fast day, such as is described in Jo., and the statement about the reading of the law, v. 3, is the only connection with c. 8, as if there never had been a public reading of the law in postex. Israel exc. under the guidance of Ezra. Indeed, v. 3 is so disjointed that it may well be an addition by the Chr. to make an artificial connection between two unrelated passages.

We have left then only c. 8 as a part of Ezra's story. In regard to vv. 1-12 there is no room for doubt, but the case is not quite so clear for vv. 13-18. In the first place, the passage contains a detailed description of the keeping of the Feast of Booths, which is not particularly happy in an account of the promulgation of the law. Again, we note that Esd. ends with v. 12, for the one word of v. 13, which is found in Esd., being the same word essentially as found in 𝕲, is decidedly suspicious. It is true that in v. 13 we are told that "the heads of the fathers the pr. and the Lev. were gathered unto Ezra the scribe." But as they assembled "to give attention to the words of the law," and as the assembly then directed the keeping of the Feast of Booths, it is certainly prob. that "unto Ezra the scribe" is another of the Chr.'s ingenious connecting links. The v. loses nothing, but rather gains, by the omission of these words, and without them there is no hint of Ezra's presence. Still the reinstitution of an ancient feast is more in harmony with Ezra's chief purpose "to glorify the house of God," Ezr. 7^{27}, than the reading of the law.

It is impossible to trace c. 9 to its origin. It may be from the pen of the Chr., but such narratives as this might be written by almost anybody. The Chr. may have had scores of documents that we know nothing about. Surely writings of various sorts were numerous enough in this period without ascribing everything to the Chr., unless we know positively to the contrary. It is very likely that the Chr. found this story of the keeping of a fast, and incorporated it in his book, adding some of his characteristic editorial annotations. In its original form the story certainly had nothing to do with Ezra's mission.

8. The promulgation of the law, and the Feast of Booths.

The story properly begins as in Esd. with 7^{72}, for notes on which *v.* Ezr. 2^{70}. Connecting the text of MT. after Esd. we find this preliminary notice: *and the pr. and the Lev. and some of the people dwelt in Jerus., and all Israel in their cities. And the 7th month approached, and all the people with one accord assembled in the plaza at the east gate of the temple.* This is part of the long deuterograph (Ezr. 2^1–3^1 = Ne. 7^6–8^{1a}); the section is used in Ezr. as the intr. to the building of the altar, in Ne. as the intr. to the issue of the law. Mey. dates this c. in the 1st year of Neh., but that is much too early, *v.* Intr. § 10.

1^b–12 = Esd. 9^{38-55}. The public reading of the law.—All the people being gathered, Ezra reads the law of Moses.—1^b. *And they said to Ezra*]. It is assumed that the people knew that Ezra had the law and had gathered for the purpose of hearing it. As in Ezr. $10^{2 f.}$, the leader does not act on his own initiative, but in response to the suggestions of others.—*Which Yahweh commanded Israel*] is preserved better in Esd. : *which was given by Yahweh the God of Israel.*—**2.** *Before the congregation*]. Esd. uses the less technical term *multitude.* The assembly was composed of men, women, and children, a condition emphasised in this section because it was unusual in Jewish practice.—*And all understanding to hear*] is a literal rendering of an obscure phrase. Esd. has *all the priests to hear the law*. This is clear, but does not suit the context. The words really mean children old enough to understand what was read.

> This is clear from a comparative study. In v. ³ there are three constituents in the assembly, men, women, and all able to hear understandingly. In 10²⁹ besides the men in the assembly there are "their wives, their sons and their daughters, all knowing how to understand." The last clause qualifies "sons and daughters." The mng. is then that all the children old enough to comprehend the business were a part of the gathering, and that is the sense here, the children being a third element in the congregation.

On the 1st day of the 7th month] in the early autumn. This date is probably original in the body of the story, and may be the ground of the connection with c. 7. That passage leads up to an assembly in the 7th month, and here we have an assembly of the 7th month, and on that slender basis some rather obtuse editor has made the two assemblies identical.—**3.** *And he read in it . . . from daylight until the middle of the day*]. 𝕲 is more specific: *from the hour the sun gives light.* 𝕳 was not satisfied with a half-day's reading of the law, and so has *until evening* instead of *until noon*. In Esd.ᴸ we have *and I read*, suggesting a trace of E.—*Before the men and the women and the children*]. The same components of the assembly are named in v. ², but the last word is lacking in Esd.—*And the ears of all the people were towards the book of the law*]. Esd. has a reading here which is clearer than MT.: *and they gave their whole attention to the law.* The people not only remained during this long reading, but were attentive to what they heard. The fact is noteworthy because of the length of the session.—**4.** The narrative comes back now to describe with minuteness the conditions under which Ezra was reading. Evidently the author considered this an important occasion.—*And Ezra the scribe stood upon a wooden platform*]. The word properly means *tower;* it is very common, and nowhere else has any other sense. But a tower here indicates a high platform, large enough for Ezra and his companions to stand upon, so that the reader could be heard by the large audience.—*Which they had made for the purpose*], indicating that the platform was newly erected in view of this anticipated reading of the law. "Purpose" is not too broad a meaning for the comprehensive דבר, though the strict meaning is *word*. It is tempting with some ancient texts to read *for speaking*. In that case Ezra uses a platform which had already been long in use by those like Nehemiah (*cf.*, *e. g.*, Ne. 5) who addressed the assembled people. Esd., however, has merely: *upon the wooden platform which had been made.—And there stood by his side*], and then follows a list of six men *on his right* and seven *on his left*.

> The list of names is regarded by Mey. as quite worthless (*Ent.* 179[4]). Torrey regards these men as laymen (ES.[268]). There must originally have been but twelve, six on each side. *Meshullam* is lacking in 𝕲 and Esd., and, as Torrey suggests, may be a variant of משמאל, *on the left*. Sm. thinks with much plausibility that the readers of the law were Lev. (*Listen,*[26]).

8[5–9]. **Another story of the reading of the law.**—As the text stands, we make little, if any, advance over vv. [1–4]. The only thing new is the effect upon the people.—5. *And Ezra opened the book in the sight of all the people*]. As he had already been reading the law for a half-day, v. [3], this must be a duplicate. 𝕲 has *before the people*, but our text is better, for it means that Ezra stood so that all the people saw him.—*For he was above all the people*], certainly unnecessary after v. [4], and another evidence of a duplicate account. Esd. gives a less physical sense, reading: *for he sat in glory in the sight of all.—And as he opened it all the people stood up*]. The standing was a mark of recognition of the divine source of the law; so King Eglon rose from his seat when Ehud told him he had a message from God (Ju. 3[20]).—6. *And Ezra blessed Yahweh the great God*]. Before beginning to read, Ezra, holding the open roll in his hands, blessed or praised God, probably for giving the people the law, v. [1].—*With a raising of their hands*] in token of adoration, the attitude of prayer. So Moses held up his hands in prayer while Joshua fought with Amalek (Ex. 17[11]). BDB. interprets this passage as equivalent to taking an oath, but it is not easy to see what place an oath has here.—*And they bowed down and prostrated themselves to Yahweh with the face to the ground*], an Oriental posture of homage, universal to-day among the Mohammedans, and supporting the interpretation given to the preceding clause.

7. In this list of 13 names, not one is found among those of the men who stood on the platform with Ezra. With Esd. we must om. "and" before "the Lev.," which stands in app. with the names. Then, unfortunately, we reach obscurity abundantly witnessed in the Vrss. The furthest removal from our text, and yet the best sense is found in 𝔥: *caused silence among the people for the hearing of the law*, a function of the Lev. acc. to v. [11]. The people had been crying "amen," and were prostrating themselves, perhaps with loud cries. While this commotion lasted, the reading of the law was out of the question. The usual rendering, *caused the people to understand the law*, is impossible, for that puts the cart before the horse with a vengeance, as it makes the interpretation of the law precede its reading, which in this section first comes in v. [8]. The last clause is lit. *and the people upon their standing*], which is rendered in EV[s]. after 𝔥 "the people stood in their place." The words are best connected with v. [8], and out of the corruption we may extract *and when the people rose again*, from the prostration described in v. [6], for the reading would not begin until the people stood up.

8. *They read in the book of the law of God*]. The plural verb is evidently a mistake, for Ezra alone was the lector.—The rest is so obscure that we cannot be sure what word stood here. The ordinary rendering is: *distinctly, and they gave the sense, and the people understood the reading*], but this is a doubtful translation of a loosely constructed passage. The first clause is lacking in Esd. 𝔊 renders: *and he taught and instructed them in the knowledge of Yahweh, and the people understood at the reading.* 3 Esd. has: *and individually they singled out those who understood the reading.*

On the basis of Ezr. 4[18] the word for "distinctly" may be rendered *in translation*. The last clause is clear, *and they understood what was read*. מפרש must define the means by which the people understood. The obscure clause may mean: *and the translator set forth the meaning.* The office of translating is given to the Lev. who were teachers, and who certainly stood by Ezra while he rd. The law was in Heb., and

this interpretation assumes that most of the people no longer understood that tongue. Ne. 13²⁴ shows the beginning of the decadence of
Heb. as a living tongue. This event was surely later and may have
been very much later.

The alternative is to suppose the word really to mean *with a loud
voice*. The point then would be that Ezra reads a sentence, which is
repeated by the Lev., famous for their high, far-carrying tones, so that
it could be heard by all the assembly.

8⁹⁻¹². The keeping of a feast.—The effect of hearing the
law was to produce mourning and weeping among the people. They are cheered with the assurance that the day is holy
and are bade to keep a joyful feast.—**9.** The speakers named in
our text are *Nehemiah, that is the governor, and Ezra, the priest,
the scribe, and the Levites who taught the people*]. *Nehemiah the
governor* has been interpolated into the text by the Chronicler
to justify his wrong chronology, making Ezra and Nehemiah
contemporaries (so Mey.¹⁹⁴). Torrey considers only "Nehemiah" as the interpolation (ES.²⁶⁹). Esd. has an interesting
text: *the governor said to Ezra and to the Levites*. It would have
been unseemly to the Chronicler that a civil governor should
inform the priest about holy days.—*To-day is holy to Yahweh
our God*]. *Our* of 𝕲 is preferable to *your* of 𝕳. The 1st day
of the 7th month (Tisri, v. ²) was set apart for the Feast of
Trumpets, Lv. 23²³⁻²⁵ Nu. 29¹⁻⁶. But the observance of the day
as described here does not conform to the law. Ryle thinks
the day became holy because the law was read, since the people would not yet know anything about this festival. The
people did not know that it was a holy day until they were told,
and certainly Ezra could not have been ignorant about the requirements for the Feast of Trumpets.—*Do not mourn and do
not weep, for all the people were weeping as they heard the words
of the law*]. The law produced an undesired effect, for the people broke out into weeping. Why did they shed tears? We
have at least a striking parallel, for King Josiah rent his clothes
when the new law of Dt. was read to him (2 K. 22¹¹). We
know further that the cause of his distress was the expected
execution of the threats in a law which had never been obeyed

(*ib.* v. [13]).   The same reasons might explain the mourning of the people now, *cf.* Ezr. 10[1].—**10.** Directions are given by Ezra for the people's observance of the holy day: *come, eat the fat pieces and drink sweet drinks*].   The fat pieces, from the Oriental point of view, are the most dainty morsels of the meat.   The sweet drink is presumably the new sweet wine.—*And send portions to those for whom nothing is prepared*], or better with 𝕲 *who have nothing, i. e.*, the poor.   There is no law enjoining this distribution except the general law of charity.

The words taken altogether imply that a feast was held and sacrifices made, from which the people were to eat as in the early times. The words sound like an invitation to a meal.   The reading had proceeded from dawn till noon.   The people were hungry.   Animals may already have been slain and now the invitation is given to feast.   The last sentence is obscure on account of corruption; the text may be rendered: *and do not grieve, for the joy of Yahweh is your stronghold*]. This word for "joy" is found elsw. only 1 Ch. 16[27]; "stronghold" as a place of shelter is often found as a pred. of God, *e. g.*, Ps. 27[1] 31[5] Is. 25[4].   But how could the joy of Yahweh be a shelter?   We might possibly suppose a very refined sense: you will find your refuge from the dire threats of the law by filling yourselves now with a divine joy. The Vrss. show that the text was hard to rd. or to understand, Esd., *e. g.*, reading *for Yahweh will give you glory*.   𝕲 has merely: *for he is our strength*.   The trouble is not so much the words themselves as their unsuitableness to the context.   The sentence is designed to give reason why the people should cease to mourn.

11. This verse is in a way parenthetical, describing more particularly the method by which the people were quieted.—*And the Levites were quieting all the people saying, Be still, for to-day is holy, and do not grieve*.   This repeats what has been already said in preceding places.—**12.** The people did as enjoined in v. [10], the writer adding *and to make a great rejoicing*].   The reason for the joyful feasting is then given in words hard to comprehend: *for they understood the words which had been taught them*].   Here again the statement is clear in itself, but it serves poorly as a ground for the feasting.

We would naturally refer the statement to their comprehension of the law, but that had produced mourning and lamentation and woe.

The only other possible reference is to the words of vv. ¹⁰ ᶠ·, about the
holy day and the feast. But it would seem superfluous to explain
that the people understood such simple directions as to eat and drink.
It may be that the meaning is: *they perceived the duty to feast in the words
of the law which had been taught them.* As we cannot find a hint of such
a duty in the passage, the understanding of the people was noteworthy.
3 Esd. shows an alternative, though not a very hopeful one: *they were
greatly exalted by the words which they had been taught.*

1. כל העם] Esd. πᾶν τὸ πλῆθος = קהל as v. ².—אחד] 𝕲ᴸ adds εἰς Ἰερουσαλήμ, thus completing the sentence as Ezr. 3¹.—המים . . . אשר]
Esd. τοῦ πρὸς ἀνατολὰς ἱεροῦ πυλῶνος.—הספר] Esd. τῷ ἱερεῖ καὶ ἀναγ-
νώστῃ = הכהן וקרא.—. . . את יהוה] om. 𝕲ᴮ; Esd.ᴬᴸ ὑπὸ κυρίου θεοῦ Ἰσραήλ, ᴮ om. κυρίου.—**2.** הכהן] 𝕲ᴸ adds ὁ γραμματεύς, Esd.ᴮᴬ ὁ ἀρχιερεύς,
which ᴬ has in v. ¹ also.—וכל־מבין] 𝕲ᴸ καὶ παντὸς ἀκούοντος συνιέναι, Esd.
καὶ πᾶσιν τοῖς ἱερεῦσιᴮᴬ, showing כהן for מבין, eloquent witness of the il-
legibility of mss. ᴸ adds καὶ παντὶ ἀκούοντι τοῦ συνιέναι, showing the
common correcting dup.—לשמע] Esd.ᴮᴬ, ἀκοῦσαι τὸν νόμον.—**3.** ויקרא]
Esd.ᴸ ἀνέγνω.—לפני המים] lacking in 𝕲ᴮᴬᴺ, Esd. ἐν τῷ πρὸ τοῦ ἱεροῦ
πυλῶνος εὐρυχώρουᴮᴬ, ἐν τῷ εὐροχώρῳ τοῦ πρώτου ἱεροῦ πωλῶνοςᴸ.—מן־
האור] Esd. ἀπὸ ὄρθρου, 𝕲 ἀπὸ τῆς ὥρας διαφωτίσαι τὸν ἥλιον = מעת הָאיר
השמש.—התורה . . . ומבינים] Esd. καὶ ἐπέδωκαν πάντα [πᾶν τὸ πλῆθοςᴬᴸ] τὸν
νοῦν εἰς τὸν νόμον. This text lacks ואזני and ספר and construes מבינים
as pred. of העם or הקהל.—**4.** הספר] Esd. ὁ ἱερεὺς καὶ ἀναγνώστης τοῦ
νόμου.—אשר . . . לדבר] om. 𝕲ᴮᴬᴺ, ᴸ has ὁ ἐποίησεν εἰς τὸ δημηγορῆσαι =
אשר עשה לדָבָר; Esd. τοῦ κατασκευασθέντος.—על־ימינו] 𝕲 Esd. ἐκ. Of
the last four names 𝕲ᴮ has only *Zechariah*.—**5.** ויפתח] Esd. καὶ ἀνα-
λαβὼν, ἀνέλαβενᴸ = ונשא or ולקח.—הספר] Esd.ᴬ τὸ βιβλίον τοῦ νόμου.—
לעיני] 𝕲 and Esd. ἐνώπιον = לפני.—כל העם] Esd. τοῦ πλήθους.—כי . . . היה]
Esd. προεκάθητο γὰρ ἐπιδόξως ἐνώπιον πάντων. 3 Esd. *praesidebat enim
in gloria in conspectu omnium,* showing לעיני here.—**6.** עזרא] lacking
in 𝕲ᴮ, Esd.ᴮ has Ἀζαριας, one of those on Ezra's right hand in v. ⁴.
—יהוה . . .] Esd. κυρίῳ θεῷ τῷ ὑψίστῳ θεῷ σαβαὼθ Παντοκράτορᴵᴬᴸ.—
וענו] Esd. ἐφώνησενᴮᴬ, ἐξεφώνησεᴸ.—אמן²] 𝕲 καὶ εἶπαν = ואמן.ויאמרו—[ואמרו]
om. Esd.ᴬᴸ. Esd. lacks אפים and puts ארצה directly after ויקדו, thus
προσπεσόντες ἐπὶ τὴν γῆν προσεκύνησαν τῷ θεῷ.—**7.** ובני] 𝕲ᴸ and Esd.ᴸ
καὶ οἱ υἱοὶ αὐτοῦ καὶ Βαναιας.—ימיו . . . והלוים] lacking in 𝕲ᴮᴬᴺ, perhaps
accidentally skipping a line.—והלוים]. The conj. is lacking in Esd.—
מבינים . . . לתורה] 𝔅 *silentium faciebant in populo ad audiendam legem,*
showing מחשים for מבנים. Esd. has ἐδίδασκονᴮ, but "teaching" anticipates v. ⁸, and teaching could not precede reading. For the whole
clause 3 Esd. has: *et praeferebant singuli eos qui intelligebant lectionem,
and they each one chose those who understood the reading.*—והעם על־עמדם]
Esd. καὶ πρὸς τὸ πλῆθος (connecting with ויקרא v. ⁸) = על־העם. MT.
may be due to careless dittog.—**8.** ויקראו] 𝕲ᴸ καὶ ἀνέγνω Ἔζδρας.—

שכל . . . מפרש‎] 𝕲 καὶ ἐδίδασκεν [Ἔσρας^{om. L}] καὶ διέστελλεν ἐν ἐπιστήμῃ Κυρίου; the words are lacking in Esd., rd. ומפרש שום שכל‎, *and the translator gave the mng.*—ויבינו במקרא‎] 𝕲 καὶ συνῆκεν ὁ λαὸς ἐν τῇ ἀναγνώσει; Esd. ἐμφυσιοῦντες ἅμα τὴν ἀνάγνωσιν; 𝕳 *et intellexerunt, cum legeretur.*—**9.** החת״ הוא נחמיה‎] 𝕲^{BAℵ} Νεεμίας. Esd. has καὶ εἶπεν Ἀτταρατή Ἔσρα τῷ κ. τ. λ. One Gk. version lacks "Neh.," the other the title. Esd. did not understand this title and transliterates it. It appears that this title was put into the text first, and that "Neh." was added in a new recension in which Ne. 1–7 was placed in the midst of the Ezra narrative. The title may in the original have been applied to Ezra, though it is given to him nowhere else.—אלהיכם‎] lacking in Esd. 𝕲^{BAℵ} τῷ θεῷ ἡμῶν correctly.—אל . . . תבכו‎] lacking in Esd.—דברי‎] lacking in Esd.—**10.** ויאמר להם‎] lacking in Esd.^{BA}, 3 Esd. *et dixit Esdras.*—ושתו ממתקים‎] lacking in Esd.^{B}.—מנות‎] Esd. ἀποστολάς = שלוחים.—לאין נכון לו‎] 𝕲 and Esd. τοῖς μὴ ἔχουσιν.—כי . . . . מעזכם‎] 𝕲 ὅτι ἐστὶν ἰσχὺς ἡμῶν^{Bℵ} (ὑμῶν^{A}); Esd. ὁ γὰρ κύριος δοξάσει ὑμᾶς.—**11.** מחשים‎] *v.* on v. ⁷; Esd. ἐκέλευον, only used in Apocr., but mng. "make an announcement"; so 3 Esd. *denuntiebant.*—הסו‎] lacking in Esd.^{BA}; transposed and placed after קרש in ᴸ, *i. e.,* σιγᾶτε καὶ μὴ λυπεῖσθε.—כי הבינו‎] Esd. ὅτι καὶ ἐνεφυσιώθησαν; 3 Esd. *magnifice enim sunt exaltati*, where we may note גדולה lacking in its proper place, and רום has been rd. for בין.

8¹³⁻¹⁸. The Feast of Booths.

—Continuing the reading of the law, the command to keep the Feast of Booths, or Tabernacles, as it is wrongly called, is found and the people go to the mountain for branches to build booths. The reading of the law is continued daily for the seven days.—**13.** *On the 2d day* of the 7th month, and so directly after the events described in vv. ¹⁻¹², all of which are assumed to have taken place in one day, *cf.* v. ². The assembly is now described as composed of *the heads of the fathers of all the people*, a favourite term of the Chronicler, *the priests and the Levites*]. The mass of the people, who had participated in the first day's proceedings, are not mentioned, and were probably not present. *Unto Ezra the scribe*] is probably a gloss, *v. s.*—The object of this assembly was not the reading of the law, but its study, *to get an insight into* [or *give heed to*] *the words of the law*]. The clan leaders and the ecclesiastics were gathered now to put the law into effect.—**14.** *And they found written in the law which Yahweh commanded by the hand of Moses that the sons of Israel should dwell in booths on the feast of the 7th month.* RV. "how that Yahweh had commanded"

is wrong.   The first אשר is a relative and the second a conjunction.

The law referred to is found in Dt. 16¹³⁻¹⁵ Lv. 23³³ ᶠᶠ.. The time
prescribed in Dt. is after the gathering of the harvest, and the festival
corresponds with the ingathering of the earlier code (Ex. 23¹⁶ ᵇ 34²² ᵇ).
The Levitical code gives the 15th of the 7th month as the appointed
time, but connects the feast with the gathering of the harvest. Acc.
to our dates the feast was kept on the 2d day of the month. This
story is based on the Lev. code, where alone a specific date is prescribed,
and where the making of booths is ordered. It is inconceivable that
Ezra should have held the feast on the wrong day. We may suppose
that either the 1st day of v. ² is an error, "2d" in v. ¹³ mng. the next
day, or, more prob., 13 days had elapsed between the assembly of students in v. ¹³ and the actual keeping of the festival. In 9¹ we are
transported to the 24th day, just right if the seven-day feast began
on the 15th. We must remember, though, that the two sections are
loosely joined and may have no original connection at all.

15. *And they commanded and issued a proclamation*]. So we
must read by a slight correction, for here we have the orders
given to the people, and not a continuation of the law. On
"issuing a proclamation" *v.* on Ezr. 1¹.—*In all their cities and
in Jerusalem*. As the message convening all the people to the
feast was sent all over Judah, a period of seven days would be
required before the orders could be complied with, and so we
can account for the 13 days between v. ¹³ and v. ¹⁷.—*Go to the
mountain*], referring probably to the hill country of Judah generally and not to any one mountain.—*And bring in leaves*],
here meaning the leaves attached to the twigs and so used for
branches. There follows the catalogue of trees, the most extensive in the Bible, except Is. 41¹⁹: *olive, oil-tree (oleaster), myrtle,**
palm, and thick trees (with heavy foliage, perhaps *evergreens*).
In Lv. 23⁴⁰ we find "palm, thick trees and willows," only two
trees common in the two passages. Perhaps the Chronicler has
amplified the passage according to the usage in his own day, or
the leaders may have named all the trees which might easily
be found, thinking rightly that it was not material what kind
of trees the branches were from.—**16.** The people obeyed the

---

*Once common in Palestine, and still found, though rarely (GAS. *Twelve Prophets*, ii,²³³).

proclamation and built the booths *each one upon his roof,** and
in their courts*], for those who had residences in Jerusalem, *and
in the courts of the house of God*], for the priests, Levites, and
other temple officials, *and in the open place of the water gate*],
where the first assembly had been held, v. ¹, and therefore presumably the largest open space in the city, *and in the open place
of the gate of Ephraim*], for those who lived outside of Jerusalem.
The gate of Ephraim is named in 2 K. 14^{13} = 2 Ch. 25^{23} Ne.
12^{39}. See Guthe, *ZDPV*. viii,²⁸⁰ ᶠᶠ·. It was presumably the
main outlet to the north country.

17. *And all the congregation who had returned from the captivity*] shows a note of the Chronicler, who assumed that all the
people who were in Judah in Ezra's time were returned exiles.
—*For the sons of Israel had not done so from the days of Joshua
the son of Nun until that day*]. The reference is not to some
keeping of this feast by Joshua, for we know of no other celebration, but the meaning is that in all Hebrew history the festival had not been kept. Ryle argues that the meaning is not
that no feast was kept, but that it had not been kept in the
strict way required by Ezra, and this big conclusion is based
on the words "done so." "So" or "thus" is indeed an indefinite word, but here it can only refer to the particular festival described. The feast had been kept by Solomon, 2 Ch.
7^8 8^{13}, by Zerubbabel and Jeshua, Ezr. 3^4, *cf.* Zc. 14^{16-18}. Hos.
12^9 shows that the feast was generally kept in his time. But
the author ignores this evidence. The law was new, and every
institution appears to be new.—*And there was a very great
rejoicing*]. This was but complying with the law for the feast
according to Dt. 16^{15} Lv. 23^{40}.—**18.** With a Greek text we
must read: *and Ezra read in the book of the law of God daily from
the 1st day* [*of the Feast of Booths*, as we find in a Greek MS.]
until the last day], *i. e.*, the 7th day of the feast.—*And on the
8th day there was an assembly according to the ordinance*]. This
word for "assembly" is found in Lv. 23^{36} to define *holy convoca-
tion*. The law forbade any work on that day; perhaps thus we
may explain the abrupt stop of the narrative at this point.

* Simple tents were often set up on the roofs for transient guests (Kittel, *Könige*,¹⁹⁸).

The narrative assumes that the people were absolutely ignorant of the law prescribing the Feast of Booths. As it had been celebrated already in the postex. period, this section cannot have originated with the Chr. He would not have been guilty of such a stupid blunder as to contradict Ezr. 3⁴. Some other writer might easily have displayed such ignorance, for many Jews may have been uneducated in the history of Israel.

13-18. At this point the book of Esd. ends, though we find in ᴮᴬ καὶ ἐπισυνήχθησαν corresponding to נאספו in v. ¹³. In ᴸ we have the whole of v. ¹³, but it agrees so exactly with 𝔊ᴸ that the broken sentence of Esd. must have been completed from 𝔊, perhaps by Lucian himself. Material for textual criticism, therefore, is sadly deficient for the rest of the book.—**14.** ביד] lacking in 𝔊.—**15.** ויעבירו קול] 𝔊 σάλπιγξιν = הצוצרה, "clarion," a word found often in P (v. BDB. and Benz. *Arch.*²⁷⁷).— לאמר] 𝔊 καὶ εἶπεν Ἔσρας. This is prob. an original reading, as may be determined by the disinclination of the Gk. translators to depart from the text in the interest of intelligibility, but the Heb. has the better text nevertheless.—**16.** שער המים וברחוב] 𝔊ᴮᴬᴺ τῆς πόλεως καὶ ἕως = העיר ועד. ᴸ has this and then adds full text of MT., showing the frequent correction by addition.—**17.** מאד] lacking in 𝔊ᴮᴬᴺ.—**18.** וייקרא] + Ἔζδρας ᴸ.—הראשון] + τῶν σκηνῶν ᴸ.—כמשפט] lacking in 𝔊ᴮ.

9. The great confession.

—A great fast is kept and on the day of its observance a long confession is said. The two things are but loosely connected, and the confession reveals clearly conditions later than the Persian period.

1-5. The fast.—1. *And on the 24th day of this month*]. The day but one after the completion of the Feast of Booths by all the people of Judah, 8¹⁸. For so the Chronicler connects the events.—Our text has: *and earth was upon them*]. This is not found in the best Greek texts, and where it does occur it is correctly specified *upon their head*. This was a common sign of deep distress (v., e. g., 1 S. 4¹² 2 S. 1² 15³² Jb. 2¹²).—**2.** *And the seed of Israel separated themselves from all the sons of foreigners*. This shows the priestly spirit. The pure-blooded son of Abraham was alone a fit subject for Yahweh's favour. The presence of an alien was a disturbing influence. Just how the separation was made it is hard to say. Perhaps foreigners were not hard to exclude from a service characterised by fasting, sackcloth, and earth. Sta. says we do not know who these

foreigners were nor their relation to the Jewish community
(*BT*.[329]). They must include all that could not prove their
Israelite blood (Ezr. 2[5-9]; see further Mey. *Ent*.[228]). This
statement is inconceivable after Ezr. 9 *f*. The separation had
already taken place according to that story.—*And they stood and
made confession of their sins and of the iniquity of their fathers*].
The sin of themselves and of their fathers was the failure to
observe the law.—**3**. *And they stood upon their place and read*].
The subject strictly is the *seed of Israel*, v. [2]. Probably the
Levites of v. [4] are really meant.—*The fourth of the day and a
fourth they made confession and prostrated themselves to Yahweh
their God*]. The assembly was apparently held only in the morning, as that was the duration of Ezra's reading, 8[3]. Half of the
morning was spent in reading the law and the other half in
bemoaning its long neglect.—**4**. *And there stood upon the stairs
of the Levites*] cannot be right; for we know of no such stairs,
though of course ignorance is not equivalent to knowledge.
But the place of the assembly is the same as in c. 8, and *Levites*
is the body whose names are recited. We may easily translate:
and there stood upon the elevation, the wooden platform already
described, 8[4]. Eight Levites are named, three common with
8[7], Jeshua, Bani, and Sherebiah; two Banis and a Buni (for
all of which 𝕲 has *son* or *sons*) make the list suspicious.—*And
they cried with a loud voice unto Yahweh their God*]. The Levites
were characterised by their loud voices, doubtless the result of
cultivation. They wanted to be heard by the whole assembly.
So they had silenced the crowd by their high voices penetrating
even through the loud wailing of the people, 8[11]. It looks as
if we should have "unto the people" instead of "unto Yahweh,"
for in v. [5] the Levites address the assembly. It may be that
the Levites led the people in chanting some psalm.—**5**. *And the
Levites said*], this time to the assembled people. There follows
a list of eight names of Levites, the same number as in v. [4],
and surely we should expect the same names. Our text, however, has but five in common. This is an unmistakable sign of
corruption.—The direction to the people is *rise, bless Yahweh
OUR* [as 𝕲] *God from everlasting to everlasting*]. The call is for

the people to rise from their prostration, v. ³, in order to praise Yahweh and to be ready to listen.—The people obeyed, doubt-less following the Levites in some ritual, *and they blessed the name of thy glory and exalted above all blessing and praise*]. For this jumble 𝕲ᴸ has tried to make sense by rendering: *bless the name of the glory exalted above all with joy and with praise*. 𝔙 makes "exalted" a predicate of "name" and thus helps to determine the true meaning: *and they blessed his glorious name exalting it above all blessing and praise*. A slight change in the text is re-quired, but some correction is essential.

9⁶⁻³⁹. The confession.

This is much like many other prayers, exhortations, and addresses found in the Bible, the NT. parallel being the speech of Stephen (Acts 7). It is quite unlike the confession of Ezra (Ezr. 9), and if that be genuine, as I doubt not, this one is a production from another source incorporated by the Chr. The state of the Gk. text shows a passage so well preserved that it may be well regarded as a late insertion. It is in substance a review of Israel's history, dealing with events well known to us. The purpose is to show God's goodness to Israel and Israel's failure to respond. The spirit of the passage is prophetic rather than priestly. It clearly belongs to the Gk. age, *v. i.*, vv. ³⁶ ᶠ. On the character of the prayer, *v.* further Kost.⁸² ᶠᶠ·, Sta.³⁴¹.

In MT. the confession is anonymous, and it is natural to assume that it is a continuation of the Lev. call to prayer preceding. The prayer must come from an individual, and 𝕲 has a prefatory note, *and Ezra said*. From this note the c. has been associated wrongly with Ezra.

6. *Thou alone art Yahweh*] is obviously not original, God being the proper word. The change was presumably due to an illogical Yahwist.—As usual, the history goes back to the creation as told in Gn. Yahweh had created not only the heavens, but also *the heaven of heavens*], an expression found in Dt. 10¹⁴ and elsewhere. It would naturally be the heavens *par excellence*, somewhat as we say the seventh heaven.—**7.** The history jumps to Abraham as the real father of the Hebrew people. The historical points are the migration from Ur-Kasdim and the change of name, both events from P.—**8.** *Thou didst find his heart faithful before thee*] might be a reference to Abraham's whole life of fidelity, but the author had especially in mind the great act of obedience (Gn. 22).—*The land of the Canaanite*]. In the E. story of this covenant ten nations are mentioned (Gn. 15¹⁹⁻²¹), of which we find but six here. This same list is found in Ex. 23³³ Jos. 24¹¹.—*And thou didst establish thy words, for thou art righteous*]. God, though foreseeing the poor use which would be made of his boon, nevertheless from his own righteousness, which includes truthfulness, must make good his promise.—**9.** We plunge into the midst of the Egyptian bondage, for the author is reciting the most conspicuous of God's gracious acts toward his people.—*Thou didst hear their cry at the Red Sea*]. This refers to the cry when the pursuing Egyptians overtook the fleeing Israelites (Ex. 14¹⁰). —**10.** *And thou didst give signs and wonders*]. We naturally think of the plagues, but these long preceded the wonders at the Red Sea, which in themselves would be sufficient. The author does not keep strictly to chronological order, and the plagues were doubtless in his mind.—The reason for intervention is now given: *for thou* [Yahweh] *knowest that they* [the Egyptians] *acted presumptuously against them*]. The same expression occurs in a speech of Jethro's reviewing this deliverance, Ex. 18¹¹. The presumption consisted in the pursuit of a people to whom liberty had been accorded.—*And thou didst make for thyself a name as this day*]. *Name* is here and frequently in the OT. nearly equivalent to *reputation*.—**11.** *Into the depths like a stone*] is a quotation from the Song of the Sea, Ex. 15⁵; *thou didst cast* replaces "they sank" in Ex., showing the speaker's conception of God's intervention.—**12.** The pillar of cloud by day and pillar of fire by night are described in Ex. 13²¹, where it is said that Yahweh himself was in the pillars or columns. Our passage refines the earlier theology of J. Yahweh leads the people by the pillars, but is not himself in them.—**13.** Here, too, the later ideas are revealed; though Yahweh is said to descend upon Mt. Sinai, he spoke with the people *from heaven*]. In Ex. 19²⁰ Yahweh actually descended to the top of the mountain and spoke to Moses face to face (Dt. 5⁴ 34¹⁰).—**14.** One part of the law is emphasised: *thy holy sabbath thou didst make* *known to them*], indicating a supremacy for this law such as we find in NT. times (Mk. 2²⁷ ᶠᶠ· Lu. 13¹⁰ ᶠᶠ· Ju. 5¹⁸).—**15.** *Bread from heaven thou gavest them for their hunger*]. The story of the giving of the manna is found in Ex. 16⁴ ᶠᶠ· The supposed miraculous character of this bread makes its gift one of the great acts of God.—*And water from the rock thou broughtest out to them for their thirst*], v. Ex. 17⁶, and a longer account in Nu. 20⁷⁻¹³.—*To go in to take possession of the land*] as we find commanded in Dt. 1⁸; *which I raised my hand to give them*]. We find Yahweh *swore* to give Israel the land of Canaan (v. Gn. 26³ Ex. 33¹ Nu. 14²³ 32¹¹). Raising the hand is the gesture accompanying the oath and is here its equivalent, so Ex. 6⁸ Nu. 14³⁰ Ez. 20²⁸· ⁴² 47¹⁴ Ps. 106²⁶, v. on 8⁶.—**16.** The list of Yahweh's gracious acts ends and the speaker turns to the attitude of the people toward God. *They and our fathers acted presumptuously*]. *They* are the people of Moses' time; *our fathers* the later generations. Yahweh kept his compact, but the people did not.—*Hardened their neck*] is quoted from Dt. 10¹⁶, and v. Je. 7²⁶ 17²³ 19¹⁵ and vv. ¹⁷· ²⁹. The repetition in v. ¹⁷ is probably a copyist's error.—**17.** The rebellious spirit of Israel is elaborated after the manner of some of the prophets to impress the hearers: *and they refused to listen* [obey], *nor did they remember thy wonders which thou didst with them*]. Then we come again to a specific act of insubordination: *and they appointed a leader to return to their servitude in Egypt*]. By the accidental dropping of a letter, MT. has *in their rebellion*, v. Nu. 14.—But the salvation of Israel was assured from the character of God. Our text runs: *thou art a God of forgiveness, gracious and merciful, slow to anger and abundant in loving kindness*]. With the exception of *of forgiveness* these are conventional attributes of God and are found verbatim in Ex. 34⁶ Jon. 4².—**18.** *Nevertheless* [with reference to the preceding] *thou didst not abandon them*]. In spite of God's overlooking their wrong in resolving to choose a leader of their own in place of the one appointed by him, they proceed to a further act of gross apostasy. EVˢ· render *yea, when* (so BDB.) and connect with v. ¹⁹, but the above-named connection is better.—

And they committed great blasphemies]. This may refer to the idolatry just described, but it is more natural to refer it to the general faithless attitude of early Israel toward God.—**19.** *And thou by reason of thy abundant compassion didst not abandon them in the desert*], evidence of the long suffering of God as described in v. [17].—**20.** *Thy good spirit thou gavest to make them wise*]. A Greek text has the more common *holy spirit*. There is no reference to this gift in the Pentateuch, for Nu. [11][17] deals with quite another matter, but it is in harmony with the later conception, as we find the same idea in Is. 63[11].—**21.** This verse is a free quotation of passages in Dt. 8[4. 9], *v.* Dr. *Dt.* The common rendering "swell" is not so good as "blister" as a description of the trouble caused to the feet by long marches. The actual hunger, thirst, and other privations of the desert were decidedly minimised by those who looked back to them from a later period of time.—**22.** The narrative jumps now to the time when Israel emerged from the desert and began the permanent conquest of the land. The kingdoms and peoples are explained to be the two districts conquered on the east of the Jordan, while still under Moses' leadership. *Thou didst allot them* [the kingdoms and peoples] *to a corner*] is interpreted to mean "into every corner" (BDB), *i. e.*, the land was divided to its utmost extent. The rendering of EV[s]. "after their portion" is unjustifiable. But the sense is vague at best, and the phrase needless; therefore it is better to read with 𝕲 *allot to them.*—The text is badly confused in the following: *and they took possession of the land of Sihon [and the land of] the king of Heshbon*]. The bracketed words are an accidental repetition. For the history *v.* Nu. 21.—**23.** *And their sons thou didst multiply like the stars of heaven*] is a reference to the promise to Abraham, Gn. 15[5] 22[17] 26[4]. But this passage may come from Dt. 1[10]. With v. [b] we are brought to the conquest of Canaan and so to the period after Moses.—**24.** *Their kings and the peoples of the lands to do with them according to their [Israel's] pleasure*]. The theory that Joshua exterminated the whole body of Canaanites (Jos. 1–12) finds no reflection here.—**25.** The expressions are for the most part taken from Dt.: *fortified cities, 3[5], houses* *full of everything good, cisterns* [already] *hewn, vineyards and olive-yards,* is condensed from 6[11]; *fat land* occurs in Nu. 13[20] with a different word for "land."—**26.** *And have cast thy law behind their back*]. We find references to disobedient persons casting God behind the back, 1 K. 14[9] Ez. 23[35]. The phrase is equivalent to turning the back to the law (*cf.* Je. 2[27]), and so disregarding it. It is interesting to note the late conception which puts the law where earlier writers put God.—*Thy proph-ets* [standing first for emphasis] *who testified against them to turn them back to thee, they have slain*]. Elsewhere in OT. this crime is cited only by Elijah, 1 K. 19[10]; it is an offence emphasised in NT., Mt. 5[12] 23[31. 37] Lu. 11[50] 13[33] Acts 7[52] Rom. 11[3] Rev. 16[6] 18[24]. The slaying of the prophets was a peculiarly obnoxious crime, because they were executing the will of Yahweh (Je. 26[15]).—**27.** God's efforts being thwarted, punishment was inflicted: *thou didst give them into the hand* [power] *of their tormentors, and they tormented them, and in the time of their torment they cried unto thee*], so we may reproduce the word-play of the original. The reference is not to any specific invasion, but is a general survey of the early period as portrayed in Ju. The moralising here is very like that of the editor of Ju. 2[11 ff.], *et pass.—And thou didst hear from heaven*]. Emphasis is laid upon the fact, as the speaker reads the history, that whenever Israel cried in distress God gave relief.—*And according to thy abundant com-passions* as [v. [19]] *thou didst give saviours*]. The *saviours* are called "judges" (Ju. 2[16. 39]); they were the warlike heroes Ehud, Jerubbaal, *et al.*—**28.** *But when they had a respite*], as soon as the punishment was withdrawn and conditions were fa-vourable, *they again did evil before thee, and thou didst abandon them in the hand of their enemies*]. The idea is that Israel was held up by God's hand, and as soon as he let go, setting the enemy free to act, then Israel was no match for the foe. There follows a repetition of the story of the people's distressful cry and Yahweh's resumed intervention.—*Thou didst deliver them according to thy compassions many times*]. "Many times," as EV[s]., is impossible on any just principles of Hebrew syntax. "Many" or "abundant" must qualify "compassions" as in

vv. ¹⁹· ²⁷. "Times" is lacking in most Greek texts, and where
it occurs it introduces v. ²⁹. "Many times" does not fit in with
the idea. The point is that each time when the people cried Yahweh delivered them. What we should rather expect is *from their
enemies.*—**29.** And *thou didst testify against them*] by the mouth
of the prophets, as v. ²⁶. Here the object is *to bring them back
to thy law*], but in v. ²⁶ *to thee.* God and the law are practically
identified in respect to Israel's obedience.—*Which a man shall
do and live by them*] is a quotation from Lv. 18⁵ with the usual
slight inaccuracies.—**30.** The first clause is difficult; EVˢ. have:
"Many years thou didst bear with them" as in 𝕲ᴸ. The other
Vrss. render literally. Ryle supposes an object, "mercy," to
be omitted, "prolong" being equivalent to "prolong mercy."
But in Ps. 36¹⁰ 101¹² the object is found. Such a sense is suitable. The passage may be rendered: *thou didst draw many years
unto them, i. e.,* a long-suffering God gave them many years of
grace.—*And thou didst give them into the hand of the peoples of
the lands*] refers to the final catastrophes resulting from long-
continued infidelity, therefore the peoples are the Babylonians.

32. *And now*]. The speaker leaps from historic retrospect
to the present consequences of the facts stated above.—*Our
God, the great, the mighty and the terrible God, keeping covenant
and mercy*]. A good instance of the late usage showing a fondness for a long list of divine attributes.—*Let not all the hardship
which has found* [befallen] *us seem little before thee*]. The word
hardship is almost technical like "the exile," referring especially to the bondage in Egypt, Nu. 20¹⁴. The plea is that God
would not minimise the humiliation which his people endured.
These hardships had befallen *us, our kings, our princes, and our
priests, and our prophets, and our fathers, and all thy people*].
The long catalogue is made to emphasise the extent of the hardships which God is asked not to underestimate.—**33.** *But thou
art innocent* [literally, *righteous*] *in regard to all that has come upon
us*]. Great as the degradation of Israel, this prophet does not
charge God with injustice. Indeed, the whole passage is meant
to show the singular forbearance of God.—**34.** This wickedness
is described now as disobedience of the laws, commandments,

and testimonies, in which wrong the higher classes, kings, princes, priests, and fathers, were involved as well as the lowly. —**35**. *And they in their kingdom and in thy great good which thou gavest to them and in the wide and fat land which thou gavest before them have not served thee*]. This literal rendering brings out the extreme awkwardness of an accumulation of phrases such as some of these late writers loved.—*And have not turned from their evil deeds*]. The purpose of God in bestowing his gifts was to make the people righteous as well as prosperous. —**36**. The writer now comes to the clearest description of the present plight, a description which points insistently to the miseries of the Greek period. *And behold, we are to-day bondmen; and the land, which thou gavest to our fathers to eat its fruit and its good, behold we are bondmen upon it*]. The *good* refers to the general abundant products of the land "flowing with milk and honey." Israel was familiar with bondage from the experience in Egypt and in Babylon. Now they are suffering bondage in the holy land itself. The condition is different from that of the Persian period, which was regarded as a relief from the bondage in Babylon.—**37**. *And its abundant yield goes to the kings whom thou hast placed over us on account of our sins*]. The land is still fruitful, but its wealth enriches only the foreign kings.—*And over our bodies they rule*]. Words could scarcely be found which would make Israel's humiliation deeper. The word for *bodies* also means *corpse*. The bodies of these bondmen are virtually dead bodies, for the people are the mere tools of foreign tyrants.—*And with our cattle they do according to their pleasure*]. That is, the foreign rulers take what they want and the nominal owners get what is left. A man might have great herds, but he could never tell how much benefit would accrue to him.—*And we are in great distress*]. Since the oppressors took Israel's property at will, the yield both of the soil and of the herd, we may regard the distress as including dire poverty, though the term also includes the anguish of soul endured by a liberty-loving people, bearing a galling servitude on the land which was theirs by divine gift. Yet there is no murmur against the ways of a mysterious Providence. In all their bitterness there is only self-reproach. God's hand is plain in the people's degradation, but his course is abundantly justified by Israel's sins.

1. ואדמה עליהם] lacking in 𝕲ᴮᴬᴺ; 𝕲ᴸ has καὶ κόνις ἐπὶ τῆς κεφαλῆς αὐτῶν = על־ראשיכם א׳.—**2.** זרע] 𝕲 οἱ υἱοί.—בני] 𝕲 υἱοῦ.—**3.** יהוה] lacking in 𝕲ᴮᴬᴺ.—רביעית היום ורביעית] lacking in 𝕲ᴮᴬᴺ. 𝕲ᴸ has τὸ τέταρτον τῆς ἡμέρας in both clauses.—מחודים] 𝕲 adds τῷ κυρίῳ.—ליהוה] lacking in 𝕲ᴮ.—**4.** ובני קדמיאל] 𝕲 καὶ υἱοὶ Καδμιηλ.—בני כנני] lacking in 𝕲ᴮ, υἱοὶ Χαναντᴬᴺ, Χωνενιαςᴸ = כנניה.—**5.** Of the names 𝕲ᴮᴬᴺ has only Ἰησοῦς καὶ Καδμιήλ. ᴸ has all the names exc. the two *Banis*.—אלהיכם] 𝕲 τὸν θεὸν ἡμῶν.—כרבר ומרומם] 𝕲ᴸ τῆς δόξης τοῦ ὑπερυψουμένου; rd. כברו.—מרומם] is a Polal ptc., the only case of its use. מרמו, *exalting it*, would be better.—ברכה] 𝕲 ἀγαλλιάσει = רננה.—**6.** 𝕲 prefaces to MT. καὶ εἶπεν Ἔσρας = ויאמר עזרא.—והשמים] lacking in 𝕲ᴮᴬ.—צבאם] 𝕲ᴮᴬᴺ τὴν στάσιν αὐτῶν = עמדם.—**7.** יהוה] lacking in 𝕲ᴮ.—אברם] 𝕲ᴺᴸ Αβρααμ as in v. ᵇ.—אור] 𝕲 χώρας = ארץ.—**8.** ולתת] 𝕲 adds αὐτῷ; 𝕲ᴸ adds Ευαιων to the list of peoples.—ולתת] lacking in 𝕲ᴮᴬᴺ.—For לתת לזרעו ולו] rd. לזרעו.—**9.** סוף] ἐρυθράν, as always exc. Is. 63², when it stands for אדם.—**10.** ומפתים] 𝕲 adds ἐν Αἰγύπτῳ.—**15.** אשר] 𝕲 ἐφ᾽ ἤν.—**17.** לא חסרו] במצרים] 𝕲ᴮ ἐν Αἰγύπτῳ = במצרים.—**20.** הטובה] 𝕲ᴸ ἅγιον.—**21.** לא חסרו] 𝕲ᴸ καὶ οὐκ ἐπεδεήθησαν ῥήματος, reading במדבר דבר.—**22.** לפאה] 𝕲ᴮᴬᴺ αὐτοῖς = להם, 𝕲ᴸ εἰς πρόσωπον = לפנים.—**23 f.** לבוא . . . הארץ] 𝕲ᴮᴬᴺ has only καὶ ἐκληρονόμησαν αὐτήν.—**25.** הארץ הכ״] 𝕲 γῆν τῶν Χαναναίων.—**25.** ואדמה שמנה] lacking in 𝕲ᴮᴬᴺ.—**25.** חצובים] 𝕲ᴸ adds οὓς οὐκ ἐξελατόμησαν = אשר לא חצבו as Dt. 6¹¹.—**28.** עתים] lacking in 𝕲ᴮᴬᴺ. 𝕲ᴸ has καὶ ἐν καιροῖς as beginning of v. ²⁹. For רבות] we should rd. הרבים, as vv. ¹⁹· ²⁷· ³¹.—עתים] may be a corruption of מצריהם. There is no possible legitimate construction of the text as it stands.—**29.** והמה הזידו] lacking in 𝕲ᴮᴬᴺ.—**31.** אל] 𝕲 ἰσχυρός, so האל in v. ³².—**35.** ממלכותם] 𝕲 βασιλείᾳ σου.—**36 f.** ואת־טובה . . . מרבה] lacking in 𝕲ᴮᴬᴺ.

10 (EV. 9³⁸–10³⁹). A list of names on a sealed tablet and an agreement to provide supplies for the temple-worship.

The c. is written in the first p. pl. The expression "our princes, our Lev., our pr." is striking, and the ending is in perfect accord: "we did not neglect the house of our God." This construction is lost occasionally. V. ²⁸ begins with third p., but the text shades off into the first p. again in v. ²⁹ ᵇ; so again in v. ⁴⁰, the original form being resumed at the end. The passage is therefore neither from N. nor the Chr. To any one carefully studying the characteristics of N. no argument is needed to show that the governor had no part in this composition. We miss altogether his sharp, brief, and clear expressions. I am per-

suaded that the Chr. never used the first p. exc. occasionally in the
expansion of N. or E., and very little then. Neither is the c. from E.,
for it was not written by a pr. This may be made clear from a single
expression: "We brought the best of our coarse meal . . . to the pr.
. . . and the tithe of our land to the Lev.," v. ³⁸. The conclusion is
therefore apparent that the c. is from the pen of a layman of the period,
possibly a prophet, who was a most zealous supporter of the temple-
worship.

The passage has nothing to do with the time of Ezra. In words
there is, indeed, much about the law; but the inevitable result of a careful study shows that the measures taken for the support of the temple
were not the consequence of legal enactment, but of mutual agreement.
It is prob., therefore, that the phrases referring to the law are interpolated or to be interpreted in a general sense.

The measures agreed upon are: (1) not to intermarry with foreigners;
(2) not to purchase from those who sold merchandise on the Sabbath
day; (3) to keep the seventh year; (4) to impose a cash tax upon themselves for the support of the temple; (5) to provide wood for burning
upon the altar; (6) to offer the first fruits; and (7) to pay the tithes.
Now four of these matters (1, 2, 5, 7) are identical with the reforms
of Neh.'s second administration, c. 13. Indeed, all exc. (3) are practically covered by those reforms. The most fitting place for this c.,
therefore, is found by placing it as a sequel to c. 13. Neh.'s habit
was to put the people under a solemn pledge to continue the right
course instituted by him, 5¹² 13²⁵. We have here a story, by one of
the participants, of the measures taken by the people to perpetuate
Neh.'s reforms. The lists of names in their present forms are all suspicious.

It is easy to see how the c. came to be misplaced. By its structure,
being in first p. pl., it has an external association with the long prayer
in c. 9. By its devotion to the cult, and by the measures taken to
maintain it, which could easily be connected with the keeping of the
law, it afforded an easy sequel to the story of Ezra's promulgation of
the law. In the original form this c. follows the Deut. law, which was,
of course, well known before Ezra; indeed, it is the basis of Neh.'s
reforms. The law-book of Ezra was not Dt.. but either the priestly
law or the whole Pentateuch.

On the character of these regulations, esp. in relation to the Priest
Code, v. Kost.⁷⁹ ᶠᶠ·, GAS. *Jer.* i,³⁵⁷ ᶠ·, Schürer, *Jewish People*, div. ii,
vol. i,²³⁹ ᶠᶠ·.

10¹⁻²⁸. A list of priests, Levites, and chiefs upon a sealed record.—1. *And in all this*] is inserted by the Chronicler to make a connection with the preceding, *cf.* 13⁶, "and in all this

time"; but the connection will scarcely hold here. The usual conception is that the phrase means *in view of this, i. e.*, the condition described in 9^6-37.

> *We make a sure covenant*] RV. The phrase is difficult, but it is hard to get this meaning, as "covenant" is lacking in 𝕳. The words literally mean *we are cutting support*, and "cut" is not equivalent to "make a covenant"; אמנה occurs elsw. only in 11^23, where it is a txt. err. By changing the pointing the word would mean *truly* or *accurately*. But a conception like "pledging faith" (BDB.) does not fit in here at all. We should render, *we are engraving correctly*, referring to the list of names, and thus the word אֲמָנָה is removed from the Heb. lexicon. Thus understood, the phrase prepares the way for what follows, *and writing upon the sealed* (record)]. This is very different from the usual translation. "Seal unto it," RV., or "are at the sealing," RV.^m in v.^2, cannot be wrung from the text. The idea of attesting an agreement to obey the law which had been rd. is as early as 𝕲, but it comes from wresting an impossible mng. from misunderstood words. Indeed, this conception may be as old as the Chr.'s editing. The conj. "and" must be omitted before "upon." As in Je. 32^14 חתום is the part of a clay cylinder or tablet which is sealed up or covered with an outer envelope. The writer gives the list of names which they wrote upon the inner part of the cylinder. For what purpose the record was made we are not informed, but the character and size of the list forbid our thinking of a catalogue of people who were inspired by Ezra to subscribe to an agreement to obey the law.

Our princes, our Levites, our priests] is made the subject of a non-existent verb in the Vrss., ancient and modern. The words may possibly be interpreted as appositives to "me," but are more likely mere headings to the list of names which follows. The words describe the composition of that list, though in reverse order.

> **2–9. The list of priests.**—At the head stands in our text *Neh. the governor the son of Hachaliah.* The doubled specification identifies him with the wall-builder, but his name does not fit in a catalogue of pr., and may be an interpolation here. The official title is not found in the best Gk. Vrss., evidence of a growth. There is a list of 22 priestly names, many of which are common to other catalogues. The absence of Eliashib's name has caused much discussion (Ryle, *Canon*,^33). It is either an accidental omission or the event belongs to the high priest-

hood of his successor. **10-14. The list of Levites.**—There are 17
names, but there are grave uncertainties about the text.—**10.** *Jes. the
son of Azaniah*] is thus differentiated from the contemporary of Zer., but
it is the same Jes. as in other groups of Lev.—*Of the sons of Henadad*],
v. Ezr. 3⁹.—**11.** *And their brethren*] often recurs in Levitical lists, and
generally is interjected awkwardly as here. The implication seems to
be that the names which follow are the brethren of Jes. Binuni, and
Kadmiel. It is not clear whether the relationship is of blood or of
office. **15-28. The list of princes.**—They are called here *heads of the
people*, a title equivalent to the more common heads of the fathers,
Ezr. 1⁵. Many of these names recur in the list, Ezr. 2. On the names
v. Gray, *Heb. Pr. N.*¹⁸⁴ ᶠᶠ·, Sm. *Listen*,¹³.

1. זות] ⅏ τούτοις.—על-החתום] ⅏ ἐπισφραγίζουσιν = ויחתמו. But as this
is the only occurrence of this compound in ⅏ (save that ⅏ᴸ has it in
v. ²), and as we find in v. ² ἐπὶ τῶν σφραγιζόντων, it is easy to find in the
prefix ἐπί an attestation of the על of MT. That is the correct reading.
חתם might mean "to attest by seal," as given in BDB., but how that
can be worked into a pass. with a prep. is incomprehensible, *v. s.* ⅏
does, however, attest the pl. in both cases (חתומים as v. ²). The same
form must belong to both places, and the sg. is preferable.—**2.** התרשתא]
lacking in ⅏ᴮᴬᴺ. In ᴸ it is an obvious insertion, as we find a conj.
ὁ καὶ ʼΑθαρσασθάς.—**11.** אחיהם] ⅏ οἱ ἀδελφοὶ αὐτοῦ.—קליטא] ⅏ᴮ Καντα.
The five names following this are wanting in ⅏ᴮ.—**14.** בני בנינ] ⅏ᴮᴬ
υἱοὶ Βενιαμειν (Βανουαιαιᴬ, Βανουιαᴸ).—**15 f.** בני בני] ⅏ᴮ υἱοὶ Βανι. ᴸ
has only υἱοί. Here the names in ⅏ are confused in division as in
v. ⁴. ᴮ has Βανι ας Γαδ βηδαι ε Δανια.—**20.** נובי] Qr. נבי, ⅏ᴮᴺ Βωναι
(בוני), Νωβαιᴬᴸ.—**22.** ידוע] lacking in ⅏ᴮ, Ιεδδουχᴬ.—**25 f.** As in vv. ⁴ ᶠ·
¹⁵ ᶠ· there is confusion here. ⅏ᴮ has Φαδα εις σω Βηχ ραουμε σα Βανα
μα Ασαια.

29 f. *The compact to obey certain requirements of the law.* The
whole of v. ²⁹ is the subject of the verb in v. ³⁰. To get the
sense the whole must be taken together: *the rest of the people,
the priests, the Levites, the porters, the singers, the Nethinim and
every one who had separated himself from the peoples of the lands
unto the law of God, their wives, their sons and their daughters,
every one knowing how to understand (30) adhering to their brethren, their chiefs, and coming under a curse and an oath to walk in
the law of God, which was given by the hand of Moses the servant
of God, and to observe and do all the commandments of Yahweh
our God and his judgments and his statutes*]. This long state-

ment in 𝔊 lacks a finite verb, and can therefore hardly be in
its original form, unless it was a part of a still longer sentence
the rest of which does not appear here.   It is like much other
work from the pen of the Chronicler.   Kost. notes that the
people accept not a new law, but an old one (*Wied.*[82]).—*Every
one knowing how to understand*] is an appositive to *sons and
daughters* (*v.* 8²).—**30**. *Adhering unto their brethren*] implies that
this large group were following the lead of others in taking
an oath to obey the law.   But it is singular to find the whole
body of temple officers among the last ones to subscribe to the
law.   The words may equally well be rendered *prevailing upon
their brethren*, and thus the situation would be reversed and
this list would give the leaders in the oath of subscription a
more natural situation.—*Their chiefs*] stands in opposition to
their brethren and limits the meaning too closely, especially if
the sense above given is correct.—*Yahweh our Lord*] is an error.
The passage is Elohistic, *God* occurring three times; it is written
in the third person throughout, and we should have here simply
God.   *Yahweh* is wanting in two Greek MSS.

10³¹⁻⁴⁰. The regulations agreed upon.—This is in the
first person and represents the people's point of view, as the
priests and Levites are spoken of in the third person.   It is a
different source from vv. ²⁹ ᶠ·.—**31**. *And that we will not give
our daughters*].   This shows that we are dealing with the specific
forms of an agreement, and that the proper introduction has
been lost in the Chronicler's arrangement.—**32**. *And the peoples
of the land who are bringing wares and all grains on the sabbath
day to sell, we will not take from them on the sabbath nor on a
holy day*].   This also connects with 13¹⁵ ᶠ·.   Here only foreigners are violating the Sabbath, while in 13¹⁵ ᶠ· Judeans are
guilty, though only Tyrians are named as selling wares in
Jerusalem on the Sabbath.   But the point here is the agreement
not to buy on the Sabbath.—*And we will forego the 7th year and
every debt*].   The law that no harvest should be gathered in the
7th year is found in the earliest code, Ex. 23¹⁰ ᶠ·, a law greatly
elaborated in the later codes, Dt. 15¹⁻¹¹ Lv. 25¹⁻⁷.   The remission of the debts is the one obligation of the 7th year in Dt.,

hence the remission of the 7th year may here refer to debts and not to land.—In the passage following we come into a different atmosphere.—**33**. *And we established over us commandments*]. The plain inference is rather startling that the people themselves made ordinances to do the things prescribed in the law. It seems a necessary implication that we are here dealing with the origin of these laws.—*To place upon ourselves the third of a shekel yearly for the service of the house of our God*]. The temple tax according to the law was a half-shekel, Ex. 30¹³ 36²⁶ Mt. 17²⁴ Jos. *BJ.* vii, 6, 6. The provision made at this time by the people was afterward apparently raised, a further evidence that we are here dealing with origins.—**34** is a statement of the purposes for which the temple tax was to be employed. It looks like an elaboration by the Chronicler.—*For the show-bread*], literally, *the bread of the row*, because this bread was arranged in two rows of six cakes each, Lv. 24⁵ ᶠ·. The keeping of bread at the sanctuary is at least as old as David, 1 S. 21²⁻⁷. The term *show-bread* is due to Tindale's rendering לחם פנים, Ex. 25³⁰, "bread of presence," "bread to show Yahweh," *v. DB. s. v.* —*For the continual meal-offering*], a vegetable offering in contradistinction to the common animal sacrifices. The reference must be to the morning and evening sacrifices of a lamb, a meal-offering accompanying it, Ex. 29³⁸ ᶠᶠ· Nu. 28³ ᶠᶠ·.—*And all the work of the house of our God*]. This use of the temple tax has already been specified in v. ³³, but with *service* in place of *work*. The latter term in our books usually refers to the building, the term *service* to the ritual. The phrase scarcely belongs here. In 2 Ch. 24⁶· ⁹ we have a reference to this tax as collected for the restoration of the temple under King Joash. Is it possible that we have here a fragment of the temple-building story which has been misplaced?—**35**. *And we cast the lots with respect to the wood-offering*]. The purpose of the lots must have been to determine the order in which certain ones should supply the wood required to burn upon the altar of Yahweh. Those who joined in the lot were *the priests, the Levites and the people*]. The order of the words makes the text suspicious, and the classing of the priests as wood-carriers is a further indication that these words do not belong to the text. But the Chronicler cannot be credited with this phrase, for he certainly would not have assigned such work to priests.—*At appointed times yearly*]. From this it would appear that the lots determined who were to perform the duty for a year, bringing the wood at such times as it was needed.—*As it is written in the law*]. The only place in the law to which this can refer is Lv. 6¹¹, providing that the priest shall burn wood on the fire every morning and never let the fire go out. The wood was brought to the temple *to burn upon the altar of Yahweh our God as it is written in the law.*— **36 f.** *And to bring in*]. The infinitive requires us to connect this with the casting of lots, v. ³⁵. But manifestly the people could not cast lots to determine who was to do what the law required every man to do. A better connection would be with v. ³⁰, where the people took an oath to obey the law. The connection is broken by the insertion of alien fragments. The specification covers *the first fruits of the land, of the fruit of every tree* [as v. ³⁸, *q. v.*], *of the sons and of the cattle, of the herds and of the flocks*]. The fruits of the ground and of the trees were to be brought in yearly, the others, of course, whenever a first birth occurred. The vegetable offerings were to be brought in for *the house of Yahweh*] the only place where Yahweh occurs in this passage—presumably for the meal or vegetable offering. The animal offerings were to be brought *to the house of our God to the priests who minister in the house of our God*]. The law of the first fruits of the ground is old, Ex. 22¹⁹, *cf*. Dt. 26² ᶠᶠ·. For the fruits of the tree Ryle refers to Nu. 18¹² ᶠ·, but that passage deals with the products of the land, which there belong to the priest.—*As it is written in the law*] is out of place as the passage stands. But the words which follow, "herds and flocks," are included in cattle and are doubtless a marginal gloss which has crept into the text. The law then embraces all the offerings of the first-born.—**38.** *And the best* [or *first fruits*] *of our coarse meal, and our offerings, and the fruit of every tree, wine and oil, we brought in for the priests to the chambers of the house of our God*]. These offerings are not different in kind from those enumerated above, vv. ³⁶ ᶠ·. The

first fruits are enumerated there as well as here, but in this
case the offerings are for the use of the priests, and so were
brought to the store chambers of the temple, whereas those
above were brought to the temple, presumably for sacrificial
purposes. In the oldest times there was a somewhat vague
line dividing what the priest might have for his own use from
what belonged to the temple, v. 1 S. 2¹³ ff.. The coarse meal is
prescribed in Nu. 15²⁰ in the same words as here, but it was to
be lifted up (as a so-called heave-offering) to Yahweh.—*And
the tithe of our land* [we brought] *to the Levites*]. The tithe both
of the land and tree is declared to be Yahweh's in Lv. 27³⁰.—*And
they are the Levites who are collecting the tithes in all the cities of
our labour*]. "Cities of our tillage," RV., is not very happy.
The city is scarcely the place for collecting the tithes of the
land. The meaning may be the hamlets in the midst of the
agricultural districts.—**39.** *The priest the son of Aaron*] is a
definition which sharply marks the division of priests and
Levites as belonging to separate classes.—*Was with the Levites,
when the Levites collected* [or *levied*] *the tithes*]. If the Levites
went about the country collecting tithes, as we may infer from
v. ³⁵, a priest went with them, not for the purpose of seeing
that the full collections were made, but to make sure that a
tenth of the tithe was brought to the temple and placed at the
disposal of the priests. This part of the tithes was brought
to the chambers of the house of the treasury], according to MT.
But it is better to follow a Greek text and read *house of God*.
The chambers were the store-rooms at the temple. There was
no separate building used as a sacred treasury; the rooms all
around the holy edifice sufficed for that purpose.—**40.** *The
offering of the corn, the wine and the oil*], which here is brought
to the temple by both Levites and laymen, is the tithe described
in the preceding verses.—*There were the vessels of the sanctuary*],
the receptacles used for the storage of the contributions brought
in for sacred use.—*The priests who minister*], or the officiating
priests who resided in the temple chambers during their term
of service, or, in military parlance, tour of duty.—*And we did
not neglect the house of our God*] is the ending of the original

document which described the plans adopted by the people to furnish the temple with supplies needed for the sacrifices.

29. [מבין] 𝕲 καὶ συνίων.—**30.** [אדיריהם] 𝕲 κατηράσαντο αὐτούς = ארדום. On the basis of this text Houtsma proposes במארה and renders the passage: "they bound themselves for their brethren through a curse" (*ZAW.* 1907,⁵⁹).—[מצות יהוה] 𝕲ᴮ ἐντολὰς ἡμῶν. This must be an accidental abr. of κυρίου τοῦ θεοῦ ἡμῶν as found in 𝕲ᴸ.—[וחקיו] lacking in 𝕲ᴮ.—**31.** [ואשר לא נתן] 𝕲 καὶ τοῦ μὴ δοῦναι and so making this a part of the subscription beginning, acc. to 𝕲, with ללכת. The rendering is interpretative rather than a witness of a txt. err.—**32.** [משא] 𝕲ᴸ has a dup.: καὶ χρέος [משה] Dt. 15²·¹·] καὶ ἀπαίτησιν. משא occurs only 5⁷·¹⁰, where it has the mng. of *usury* or *interest.* "Usury of every hand" is improbable unless יד means *kind.* In Dt. 15² we have ידו משה בעל כל, "every possessor of a loan of his hand," *i. e.,* "creditor." The law required not merely the remission of interest but of the debt, and perhaps משא is everywhere to be interpreted as the equivalent of משה, so here "loan of every hand" would be naturally borrowed from Dt.—**33.** [והעמדנו] 𝕲ᴮ, καὶ ποιήσομεν, στήσομενᴺᴬ.—**34.** [מלאכת] 𝕲 ἔργα, but עברת, v.³³, δουλείανᴮᴬᴺ, λατρείανᴸ.—**35.** [על־קרבן העצים] 𝕲 περὶ κλήρου ξυλοφορίας.—[בתורה] 𝕲ᴮ ἐν βιβλίῳ.—[קרבן] 13³¹ elsw. always קרבן. The pointing here must be an error. Two words are not required for the same thing.—**36.** [כל פרי]. כל is lacking in 𝕲ᴮᴬᴺ, as MT. in v.³⁸.—[יהוה] lacking in 𝕲ᴮᴺ.—**38.** [עריסתינו] 𝕲 σίτων ἡμῶν always = דגן in Ne.—[ותרומתינו] lacking in 𝕲ᴮᴬᴺ, ἀπαρχὰς ἡμῶνᴸ.—**39.** Point [בעשר] BDB. or after v.ᵃ האוצר.—𝕲ᴮ τοῦ θεοῦ.

INDEXES.

INDEXES.

I. ENGLISH.

II. HEBREW AND ARAMAIC.

The International Critical Commentary

ARRANGEMENT OF VOLUMES AND AUTHORS

THE OLD TESTAMENT

GENESIS. The Rev. JOHN SKINNER, D.D., Principal and Professor of Old Testament Language and Literature, College of Presbyterian Church of England, Cambridge, England. [*Now Ready.*

EXODUS. The Rev. A. R. S. KENNEDY, D.D., Professor of Hebrew, University of Edinburgh.

LEVITICUS. J. F. STENNING, M.A., Fellow of Wadham College, Oxford.

NUMBERS. The Rev. G. BUCHANAN GRAY, D.D., Professor of Hebrew, Mansfield College, Oxford. [*Now Ready.*

DEUTERONOMY. The Rev. S. R. DRIVER, D.D., D.Litt., Regius Professor of Hebrew, Oxford. [*Now Ready.*

JOSHUA. The Rev. GEORGE ADAM SMITH, D.D., LL.D., Principal of the University of Aberdeen.

JUDGES. The Rev. GEORGE MOORE, D.D., LL.D., Professor of Theology, Harvard University, Cambridge, Mass. [*Now Ready.*

SAMUEL. The Rev. H. P. SMITH, D.D., Professor of Old Testament Literature and History of Religion, Meadville, Pa. [*Now Ready.*

KINGS. The Rev. FRANCIS BROWN, D.D., D.Litt., LL.D., President and Professor of Hebrew and Cognate Languages, Union Theological Seminary, New York City.

CHRONICLES. The Rev. EDWARD L. CURTIS, D.D., Professor of Hebrew, Yale University, New Haven, Conn. [*Now Ready.*

EZRA AND NEHEMIAH. The Rev. L. W. BATTEN, Ph.D., D.D., Professor of Old Testament Literature, General Theological Seminary, New York City. [*Now Ready.*

PSALMS. The Rev. CHAS. A. BRIGGS, D.D., D.Litt., sometime Graduate Professor of Theological Encyclopædia and Symbolics, Union Theological Seminary, New York. [*2 vols. Now Ready.*

PROVERBS. The Rev. C. H. TOY, D.D., LL.D., Professor of Hebrew, Harvard University, Cambridge, Mass. [*Now Ready.*

JOB. The Rev. S. R. DRIVER, D.D., D.Litt., Regius Professor of Hebrew, Oxford.

ISAIAH. Chaps. I–XXVII. The Rev. G. BUCHANAN GRAY, D.D., Professor of Hebrew, Mansfield College, Oxford. *[Now Ready.*

ISAIAH. Chaps. XXVIII–XXXIX. The Rev. G. BUCHANAN GRAY, D.D. Chaps. LX–LXVI. The Rev. A. S. PEAKE, M.A., D.D., Dean of the Theological Faculty of the Victoria University and Professor of Biblical Exegesis in the University of Manchester, England.

JEREMIAH. The Rev. A. F. KIRKPATRICK, D.D., Dean of Ely, sometime Regius Professor of Hebrew, Cambridge, England.

EZEKIEL. The Rev. G. A. COOKE, M.A., Oriel Professor of the Interpretation of Holy Scripture, University of Oxford, and the Rev. CHARLES F. BURNEY, D.Litt., Fellow and Lecturer in Hebrew, St. John's College, Oxford.

DANIEL. The Rev. JOHN P. PETERS, Ph.D., D.D., sometime Professor of Hebrew, P. E. Divinity School, Philadelphia, now Rector of St. Michael's Church, New York City.

AMOS AND HOSEA. W. R. HARPER, Ph.D., LL.D., sometime President of the University of Chicago, Illinois. *[Now Ready.*

MICAH, ZEPHANIAH, NAHUM, HABAKKUK, OBADIAH AND JOEL. Prof. JOHN M. P. SMITH, University of Chicago; W. HAYES WARD, D.D., LL.D., Editor of *The Independent*, New York; Prof. JULIUS A. BEWER, Union Theological Seminary, New York. *[Now Ready.*

HAGGAI, ZECHARIAH, MALACHI AND JONAH. Prof. H. G. MITCHELL, D.D.; Prof. JOHN M. P. SMITH, Ph.D., and Prof. J. A. BEWER, Ph.D. *[Now Ready.*

ESTHER. The Rev. L. B. PATON, Ph.D., Professor of Hebrew, Hartford Theological Seminary. *[Now Ready.*

ECCLESIASTES. Prof. GEORGE A. BARTON, Ph.D., Professor of Biblical Literature, Bryn Mawr College, Pa. *[Now Ready.*

RUTH, SONG OF SONGS AND LAMENTATIONS. Rev. CHARLES A. BRIGGS, D.D., D.Litt., sometime Graduate Professor of Theological Encyclopædia and Symbolics, Union Theological Seminary, New York.

THE NEW TESTAMENT

ST. MATTHEW. The Rev. WILLOUGHBY C. ALLEN, M.A., Fellow and Lecturer in Theology and Hebrew, Exeter College, Oxford. *[Now Ready.*

ST. MARK. Rev. E. P. GOULD, D.D., sometime Professor of New Testament Literature, P. E. Divinity School, Philadelphia. *[Now Ready.*

ST. LUKE. The Rev. ALFRED PLUMMER, D.D., sometime Master of University College, Durham. *[Now Ready.*

ST. JOHN. The Right Rev. JOHN HENRY BERNARD, D.D., Bishop of Ossory, Ireland.

HARMONY OF THE GOSPELS. The Rev. WILLIAM SANDAY, D.D., LL.D., Lady Margaret Professor of Divinity, Oxford, and the Rev. WILLOUGHBY C. ALLEN, M.A., Fellow and Lecturer in Divinity and Hebrew, Exeter College, Oxford.

ACTS. The Rev. C. H. TURNER, D.D., Fellow of Magdalen College, Oxford, and the Rev. H. N. BATE, M.A., Examining Chaplain to the Bishop of London.

ROMANS. The Rev. WILLIAM SANDAY, D.D., LL.D., Lady Margaret Professor of Divinity and Canon of Christ Church, Oxford, and the Rev. A. C. HEADLAM, M.A., D.D., Principal of King's College, London.
[Now Ready.

I. CORINTHIANS. The Right Rev. ARCH ROBERTSON, D.D., LL.D., Lord Bishop of Exeter, and Rev. ALFRED PLUMMER, D.D., late Master of University College, Durham. *[Now Ready.*

II. CORINTHIANS. The Rev. DAWSON WALKER, D.D., Theological Tutor in the University of Durham.

GALATIANS. The Rev. ERNEST D. BURTON, D.D., Professor of New Testament Literature, University of Chicago.

EPHESIANS AND COLOSSIANS. The Rev. T. K. ABBOTT, B.D., D.Litt., sometime Professor of Biblical Greek, Trinity College, Dublin, now Librarian of the same. *[Now Ready.*

PHILIPPIANS AND PHILEMON. The Rev. MARVIN R. VINCENT, D.D., Professor of Biblical Literature, Union Theological Seminary, New York City. *[Now Ready.*

THESSALONIANS. The Rev. JAMES E. FRAME, M.A., Professor of Biblical Theology, Union Theological Seminary, New York City.
[Now Ready.
THE PASTORAL EPISTLES. The Rev. WALTER LOCK, D.D., Warden of Keble College and Professor of Exegesis, Oxford.

HEBREWS. The Rev. JAMES MOFFATT, D.D., Minister United Free Church, Broughty Ferry, Scotland.

ST. JAMES. The Rev. JAMES H. ROPES, D.D., Bussey Professor of New Testament Criticism in Harvard University.

PETER AND JUDE. The Rev. CHARLES BIGG, D.D., sometime Regius Professor of Ecclesiastical History and Canon of Christ Church, Oxford.
[Now Ready.
THE JOHANNINE EPISTLES. The Rev. E. A. BROOKE, B.D., Fellow and Divinity Lecturer in King's College, Cambridge. *[Now Ready.*

REVELATION. The Rev. ROBERT H. CHARLES, M.A., D.D., sometime Professor of Biblical Greek in the University of Dublin.

The International Theological Library

ARRANGEMENT OF VOLUMES AND AUTHORS

THEOLOGICAL ENCYCLOPÆDIA. By CHARLES A. BRIGGS, D.D., D.Litt., sometime Professor of Theological Encyclopædia and Symbolics, Union Theological Seminary, New York.

AN INTRODUCTION TO THE LITERATURE OF THE OLD TESTAMENT. By S. R. DRIVER, D.D., D.Litt., Regius Professor of Hebrew and Canon of Christ Church, Oxford. *[Revised and Enlarged Edition.*

CANON AND TEXT OF THE OLD TESTAMENT. By the Rev. JOHN SKINNER, D.D., Principal and Professor of Old Testament Language and Literature, College of the Presbyterian Church of England, Cambridge, England, and the Rev. OWEN WHITEHOUSE, B.A., Principal and Professor of Hebrew, Chestnut College, Cambridge, England.

OLD TESTAMENT HISTORY. By HENRY PRESERVED SMITH, D.D., Professor of Old Testament Literature, Meadville, Pa. *[Now Ready.*

CONTEMPORARY HISTORY OF THE OLD TESTAMENT. By FRANCIS BROWN, D.D., LL.D., D.Litt., President and Professor of Hebrew, Union Theological Seminary, New York.

THEOLOGY OF THE OLD TESTAMENT. By A. B. DAVIDSON, D.D., LL.D., sometime Professor of Hebrew, New College, Edinburgh.
[Now Ready.

AN INTRODUCTION TO THE LITERATURE OF THE NEW TESTAMENT. By Rev. JAMES MOFFATT, B.D., Minister United Free Church, Broughty Ferry, Scotland. *[Now Ready.*

CANON AND TEXT OF THE NEW TESTAMENT. By CASPAR RENÉ GREGORY, D.D., LL.D., Professor of New Testament Exegesis in the University of Leipzig. *[Now Ready.*

THE LIFE OF CHRIST. By WILLIAM SANDAY, D.D., LL.D., Lady Margaret Professor of Divinity and Canon of Christ Church, Oxford.

A HISTORY OF CHRISTIANITY IN THE APOSTOLIC AGE. By ARTHUR C. McGIFFERT, D.D., Professor of Church History, Union Theological Seminary, New York. [*Now Ready.*

CONTEMPORARY HISTORY OF THE NEW TESTAMENT. By FRANK C. PORTER, D.D., Professor of Biblical Theology, Yale University, New Haven, Conn.

THEOLOGY OF THE NEW TESTAMENT. By GEORGE B. STEVENS, D.D., sometime Professor of Systematic Theology, Yale University, New Haven, Conn. [*Now Ready.*

BIBLICAL ARCHÆOLOGY. By G. BUCHANAN GRAY, D.D., Professor of Hebrew, Mansfield College, Oxford.

THE ANCIENT CATHOLIC CHURCH. By ROBERT RAINEY, D.D., LL.D., sometime Principal of New College, Edinburgh. [*Now Ready.*

THE LATIN CHURCH FROM GREGORY THE GREAT TO THE COUNCIL OF TRENT. [*Author to be announced later.*

THE GREEK AND EASTERN CHURCHES. By W. F. ADENEY, D.D., Principal of Independent College, Manchester. [*Now Ready.*

THE REFORMATION. By T. M. LINDSAY, D.D., Principal of the United Free College, Glasgow. [*2 vols. Now Ready.*

CHRISTIANITY IN LATIN COUNTRIES SINCE THE COUNCIL OF TRENT. By PAUL SABATIER, D.Litt., Drome, France.

SYMBOLICS. By CHARLES A. BRIGGS, D.D., D.Litt., sometime Professor of Theological Encyclopædia and Symbolics, Union Theological Seminary, New York.

HISTORY OF CHRISTIAN DOCTRINE. By G. P. FISHER, D.D., LL.D., sometime Professor of Ecclesiastical History, Yale University, New Haven, Conn. [*Revised and Enlarged Edition.*

CHRISTIAN INSTITUTIONS. By A. V. G. ALLEN, D.D., sometime Professor of Ecclesiastical History, Protestant Episcopal Divinity School, Cambridge, Mass. [*Now Ready.*

PHILOSOPHY OF RELIGION. By GEORGE GALLAWAY, D.D., Minister of United Free Church, Castle Douglas, Scotland.

THE HISTORY OF RELIGIONS. By GEORGE F. MOORE, D.D., LL.D., Professor in Harvard University. [*In Press.*

APOLOGETICS. By A. B. BRUCE, D.D., sometime Professor of New Testament Exegesis, Free Church College, Glasgow.
[*Revised and Enlarged Edition.*

THE CHRISTIAN DOCTRINE OF GOD. By WILLIAM N. CLARKE, D.D., Professor of Systematic Theology, Hamilton Theological Seminary.
[*Now Ready.*

THE DOCTRINE OF MAN. By William P. Paterson, D.D., Professor of Divinity, University of Edinburgh.

THE DOCTRINE OF THE PERSON OF JESUS CHRIST. By H. R. Mackintosh, Ph.D., D.D., Professor of Theology, New College, Edinburgh.
[Now Ready.

THE CHRISTIAN DOCTRINE OF SALVATION. By George B. Stevens, D.D., sometime Professor of Systematic Theology, Yale University.
[Now Ready.

THE DOCTRINE OF THE CHRISTIAN LIFE. By William Adams Brown, D.D., Professor of Systematic Theology, Union Theological Seminary, New York.

CHRISTIAN ETHICS. By Newman Smyth, D.D., Pastor of Congregational Church, New Haven. *[Revised and Enlarged Edition.*

THE CHRISTIAN PASTOR AND THE WORKING CHURCH. By Washington Gladden, D.D., Pastor of Congregational Church, Columbus, Ohio. *[Now Ready.*

THE CHRISTIAN PREACHER. By A. E. Garvie, D.D., Principal of New College, London, England.